WORKS ISSUED BY
THE HAKLUYT SOCIETY

———

ENGLISH AND IRISH SETTLEMENT
ON THE RIVER AMAZON
1550–1646

SECOND SERIES
NO. 171

HAKLUYT SOCIETY

COUNCIL AND OFFICERS, 1988–89

English and Irish Settlement
on the River Amazon
1550–1646

★

Edited by
JOYCE LORIMER

THE HAKLUYT SOCIETY
LONDON
1989

ISBN 0 904180 27 1
ISSN 0072–9396

Printed in Great Britain at
the University Press, Cambridge

Published by the Hakluyt Society
c/o The Map Library
British Library, Great Russell Street
London WC1B 3DG

For my mother

Edith Anne Pikett

and in memory of my-father

George Charles Pikett

CONTENTS

TEXTS

MAPS

OUTLINE MAPS

CONTEMPORARY MAPS

PREFACE

The survival of the wilderness of Amazonia and its remaining aboriginal inhabitants hangs in the balance. The last Indian tribes in the interior are facing extinction and a great part of the rich plant and animal resources of the region are threatened with obliteration by the demands of material progress. As concerned people in Brazil and throughout the world struggle to avert this human and environmental tragedy it is instructive to be reminded that the river Amazon was, even during the century after Orellana first explored it, a focus of strong economic interest and fierce colonial rivalry. I have attempted here to document the part played by English and Irish settlers and projectors in the struggle to control and exploit the resources of the Lower Amazon.

The record of their activities is not contained in any one coherent body of material, but rather has to be pieced together from miscellaneous manuscript and printed references preserved in Dutch, English, Irish, Portuguese and Spanish archives. In editing these sources I have followed the editorial practices established by the Hakluyt Society. In the case of the English materials the spelling, punctuation, capitalization and italicization of the originals has been retained with the following exceptions. Contractions have been expanded with the interpolated letters printed in italics. Y^e and y^t have been silently changed to *the* and *that*. The modern usage of u and v and i and j has been adopted. Italicized proper names have been converted to roman. Where the Julian calendar was used both Old and New Style dates have been supplied. In the case of the translations, modern punctuation has been inserted where necessary in order to make the sense clear. The spelling of proper names has been preserved, with the one exception of the numerous versions of the name of the Amazon, all of which have been translated as *the river Amazon*. I have attempted in all the translations to achieve clarity while at the same time respecting sixteenth and seventeenth century usage and the varying literary styles of the documents in question. Marginal notations, whether in the English or foreign materials, have been placed in square brackets and inserted into the text at the place where they occur, as indicated by a footnote. Blanks, doubtful transcriptions and words or figures supplied editorially are also marked by square brackets.

In the course of preparing this volume I have received help from a great many institutions and individuals. Financial assistance from the Trustees of the Twenty-Seven Foundation and from Wilfrid Laurier University made it possible for me to undertake research trips to England and Portugal. During the course of my research I have received expert guidance and assistance from many archivists and librarians. I am particularly indebted to those working in the Institute of Historical Research, the British Library Manuscript and Map departments and the Public Record Office in London. The staffs of the Bodleian, Oxford, the Archivo General de Indias, Seville, the Archivo General de Simancas, and the Biblioteca Nacional, Madrid, and of the Arquivo Histórico Ultramarino, the Arquivo Nacional da Torre do Tombo, the Biblioteca de Ajuda and the Biblioteca Nacional in Lisbon, were also very helpful and cooperative. The Duke of Northumberland has graciously furnished me with a copy of the Gabriel Tatton chart of 1615 and allowed me to print it here. The copy of the Thomas King chart appears by the kind permission of the Bibliothèque Nationale, Paris. I would like to thank the Biblioteca Nacional, Rio de Janeiro for allowing me to reprint the third map of the *Anonymous atlas of Maranhão* and António Vicente Cochado's *Descrição dos Rios Pará Corupá e Amazonas, Parte Primeira*, reproduced in A. Cortesão and A. Teixeira da Mota, eds, *Portugalia Monumenta Cartographica* (Lisbon, 1960), V, plates 600A and 599A respectively.

My debts to individuals are enormous. Dr Marjorie Ratcliffe of the Department of Modern Languages and Literatures at Wilfrid Laurier University translated several of the Spanish and Portuguese documents. Pamela Carnochan and Pamela Schaus of the Geography Department at Wilfrid Laurier University drew the maps. Dr David Souden very generously alerted me to the existence of the 'pedigree' of the Ley family and provided me with a transcript of the material relating to John Ley. Dr David Hebb allowed me to use his copies of the diplomatic reports of António de Sousa Macedo and has given me valuable advice on matters relating to the diplomatic and nautical history of early Stuart England. Dr

Nicholas Tyacke gave me the references for the documents relating to Roger Fry preserved in Trinity College, Dublin. Drs Linda Clark, Carole Rawcliffe and Paula Watson of the History of Parliament were unfailingly helpful on matters relating to biographical research. I am particularly indebted to Mrs Sarah Tyacke of the British Library. Her own researches into early seventeenth century English charting of the river Amazon afforded invaluable information, all of which she very generously shared with me. I would also like to express my gratitude to Mrs Tyacke and to Dr Terence Armstrong as Honorary Secretaries of the Hakluyt Society for helping me to prepare this manuscript for publication.

My husband and fellow historian Dr Douglas Lorimer has supported and advised me throughout this project. Equally importantly, my son Andrew has patiently tolerated my departures on extended trips to the archives. Both know how much I owe to them.

I first began to study the history of the river Amazon as part of my researches for a doctorate under the supervision of Professor David B. Quinn, at the University of Liverpool. Like everyone, whether student or colleague, who has been privileged to work with him, I have been overwhelmed both by his unequalled knowledge of his field and the liberality with which he imparts it to others. From my student days Mrs Alison Quinn has given me personal support and the benefit of her own very considerable expertise in the early history of the New World. The help and constant friendship which I have received from both of them, over many years, has meant more to me than I can possibly express here. This book was inspired by their scholarship, but it can never hope to emulate it.

Waterloo   JOYCE LORIMER
Ontario

INTRODUCTION

ENGLISH AND IRISH SETTLEMENT ON THE RIVER AMAZON, 1550–1646

From as early as the middle of the sixteenth century Englishmen were interested in the possibility of exploring the fabled resources of the great river of the Amazons. During the first half of the seventeenth century English and Irish projectors made persistent efforts to maintain trading factories and plantations there. From at least 1612 to 1632 they inhabited settlements along the north channel of the estuary from Cabo do Norte to the Equator, making very considerable profits from tobacco, dyes and hardwoods. Indeed the profitability of their holdings was such that, when reprisals by the Portuguese made the river too risky for foreign interlopers after 1630, former English and Irish planters sought to be allowed to return to the river under the licence of first the Spanish and then the Portuguese crown. The Irish may actually have been permitted to do so in the mid-1640s.

Almost half a century has elapsed since J. A. Williamson and Aubrey Gwynn published their studies of these colonizing and trading activities.[1] In the intervening period the English, Portuguese and Spanish archives have yielded up considerably more material on the subject and made it possible both to revise the narrative that they established and to re-evaluate their perception of its significance. What were for Williamson, 'dimly-known' undertakings, prove to have been part of a coherent and determined English effort to settle Guiana. It was, in many ways, more hopeful than contemporaneous enterprises in North America, and it failed because its interests were sacrificed, at crucial junctures, to

---

[1] J. A. Williamson, *English colonies in Guiana and the Amazon, 1604–1668* (Oxford, 1923); A. Gwynn, 'An Irish settlement on the Amazon 1612–29', *Proceedings of the Royal Irish Academy*, Section C 41 (1932), 1–54; 'Documents relating to the Irish in the West Indies', *Analecta Hibernica*, IV (1932), 139–286.

the foreign policy priorities of the crown. The Irish ventures in the Amazon, although begun in partnership with the English, can now be seen to have developed into a quite distinct initiative. Some twelve years before the transport of indentured servants to the Leeward Islands began, Irish merchants and gentlemen had established small colonies of their compatriots on the Amazon. By the early 1620s their experience of the river and their expertise in the Indian languages was well known. They were eagerly sought after by the English and Dutch to direct their enterprises. The ventures in the Amazon are probably the earliest example of independent Irish colonial projects in the New World. The tenacity with which both groups, the English and the Irish, pursued their goal of settlement in the Amazon forces us to re-assess assumptions about the seemingly 'inevitable' priority of North America for such activity at this period. The Amazon was not a 'white man's grave' in the early seventeenth century. On the contrary it was the focus of fierce colonial rivalry. The failure of the English and the Irish to hold on to it reflects more about European international relations than it does about the suitability of the environment of Amazonia for northern Europeans.

THE LOWER AMAZON
AND THE RIVER PARÁ

10 0   20   40   60miles

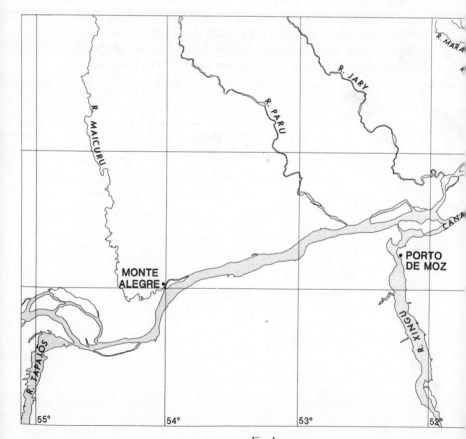

Fig. I

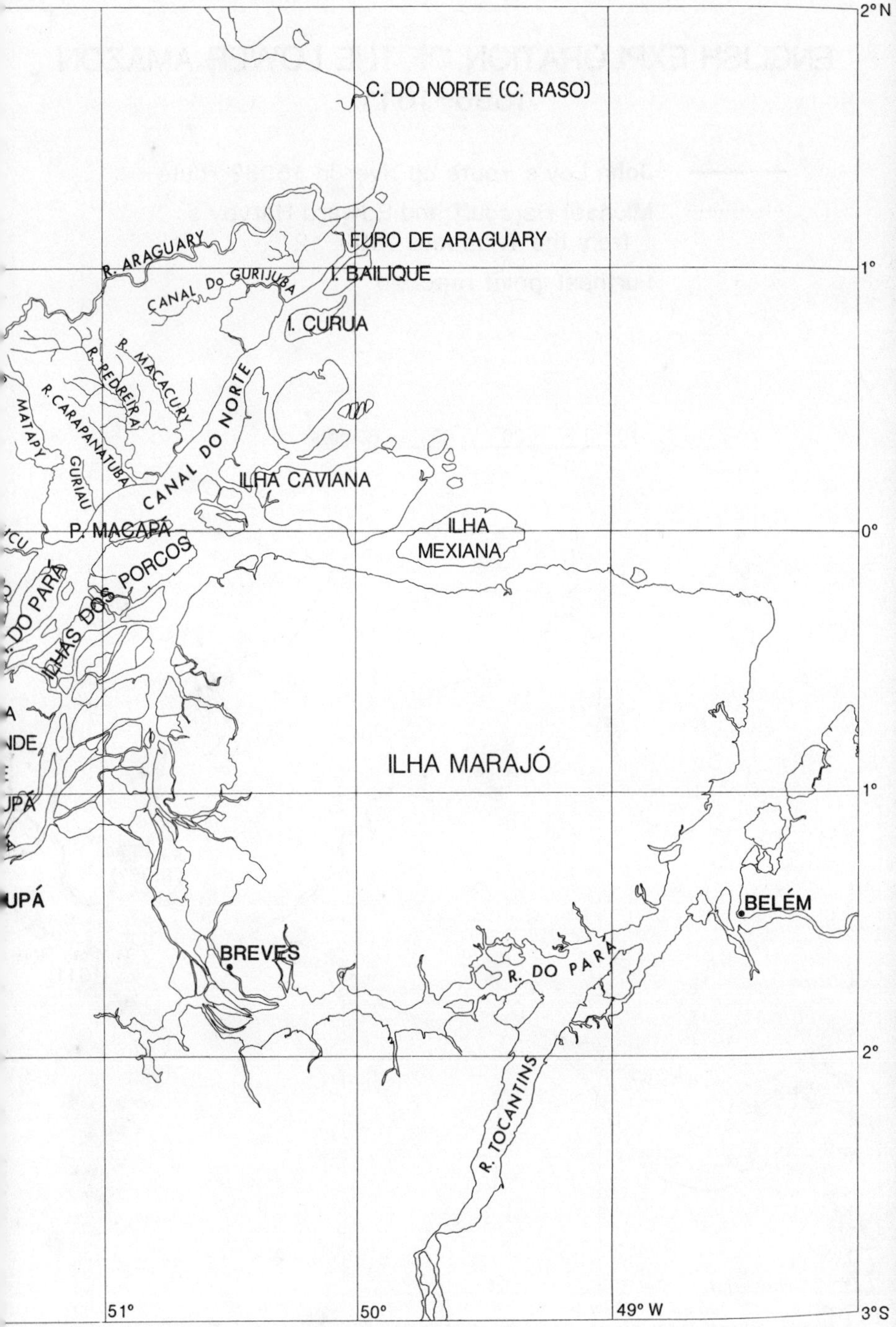
2° N
C. DO NORTE (C. RASO)
FURO DE ARAGUARY
R. ARAGUARY
I. BAILIQUE
1°
CANAL Do GURIJUBA
I. CURUA
R. MACACURY
R. PEDREIRA
R. CARAPANATUBA
MATAPY
GURIAU
CANAL DO NORTE
ILHA CAVIANA
P. MACAPÁ
ILHA
MEXIANA
0°
ILHAS DOS PORCOS
DO PARÁ
NDE
UPÁ
ILHA MARAJÓ
1°
UPÁ
BELÉM
BREVES
R. DO PARÁ
2°
R. TOCANTINS
51°
50°
49° W
3°S

Fig. I

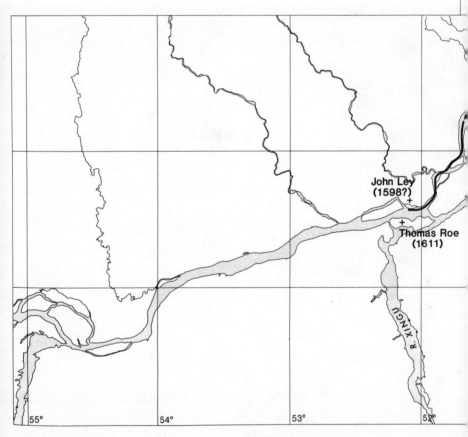

ENGLISH EXPLORATION OF THE LOWER AMAZON
1596-1611

——————— John Ley's route up river in 1598? route

.... Michael Harcourt and Edward Harvey's
from the Wiapoco, 1609-12

+ Furthest point reached

10 0   20   40   60miles

John Ley
(1598?)
+

+
Thomas Roe
(1611)

R. XINGU

55°   54°   53°   52°

Fig. II

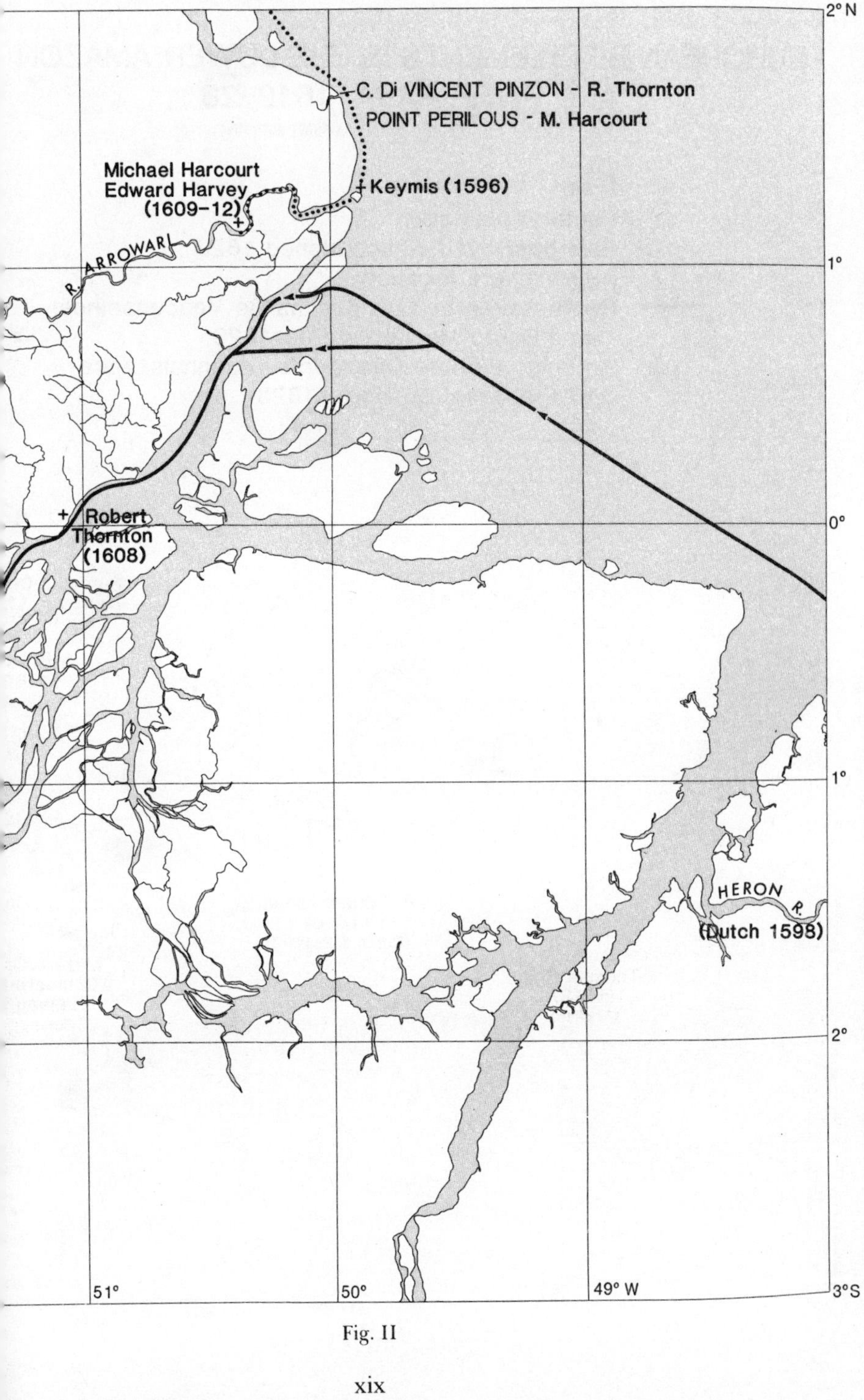

2° N
C. Di VINCENT PINZON - R. Thornton
POINT PERILOUS - M. Harcourt
Michael Harcourt
Edward Harvey
(1609–12)
Keymis (1596)
R. ARROWARI
1°
Robert
Thornton
(1608)
0°
1°
HERON R.
(Dutch 1598)
2°
51°
50°
49° W
3°S

Fig. II

EUROPEAN SETTLEMENTS IN THE LOWER AMAZON AND RIVER PARÁ, 1612-23

with date of foundation when known

- ■ Fort
- ○ Factory/ plantation
- □ Fort destroyed or abandoned 1623
- ○ Approximate location
- —— Route taken by Luis Aranha De Vasconselhos and Bento Maciel Parente 1623
- ········· António Vicente Cochado's reconnaissance of the Canal Do Norte 1623

10 0   20   40   60 miles

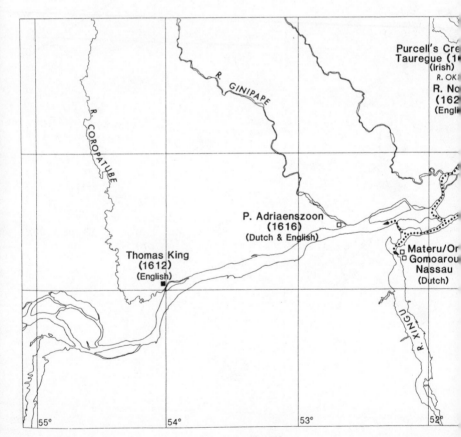

Fig. III

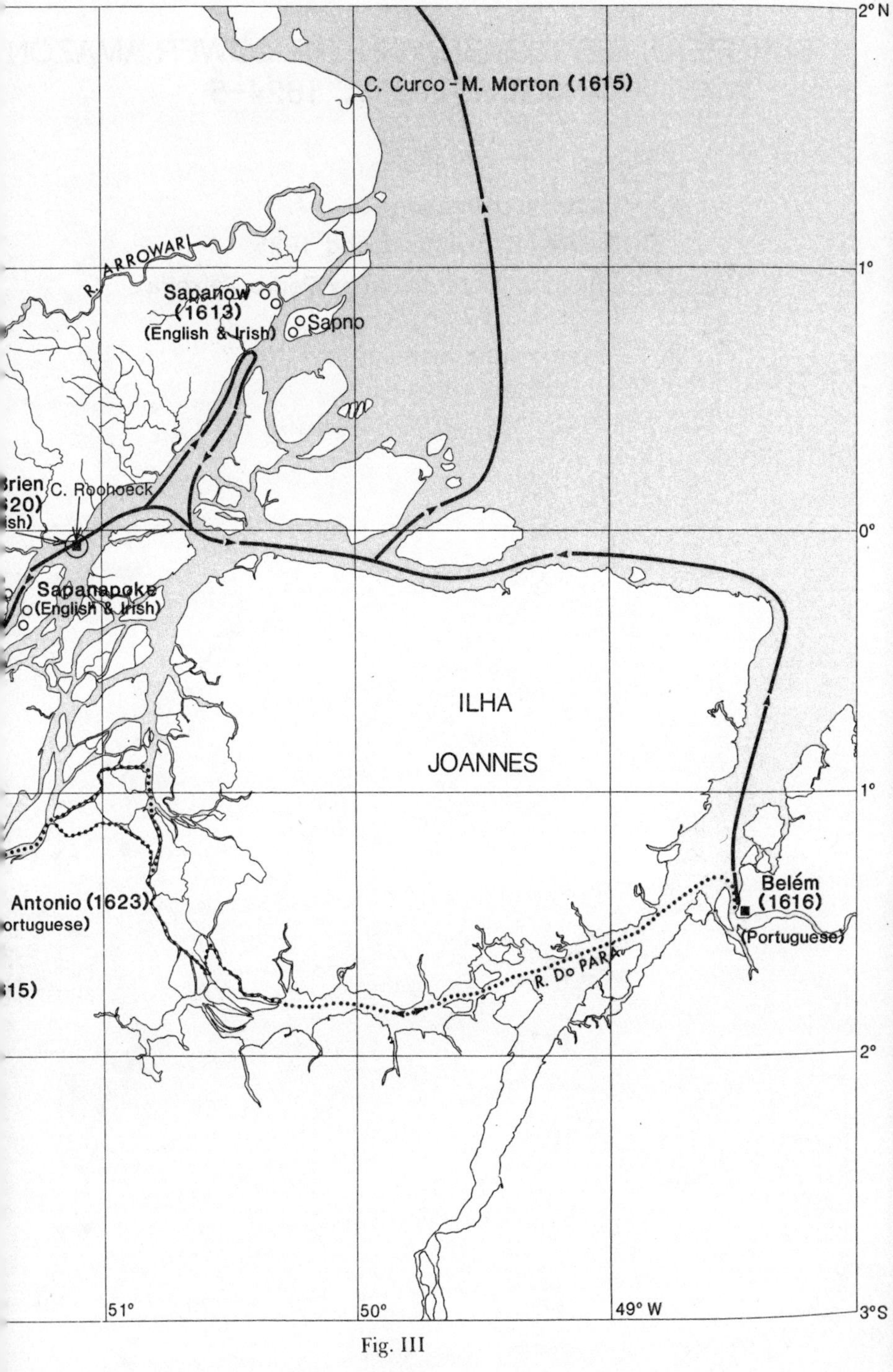
2° N
C. Curco - M. Morton (1615)
R. ARROWARI
1°
Sapanow
(1613)
(English & Irish)
Sapno
C. Roohoeck
0°
Sapanapoke
(English & Irish)
ILHA
JOANNES
1°
Antonio (1623)
ortuguese)
Belém
(1616)
(Portuguese)
R. Do PARA
2°
51°
50°
49° W
3°S

Fig. III

EUROPEAN SETTLEMENTS IN THE LOWER AMAZON AND RIVER PARÁ, 1624–5

■   Fort

○   Factory/plantation

□ ⊠   Destroyed or abandoned 1625

··········   Outward route taken by Pedro Teixeira's forces 1625

◯   Approximate location

10 0   20   40   60miles

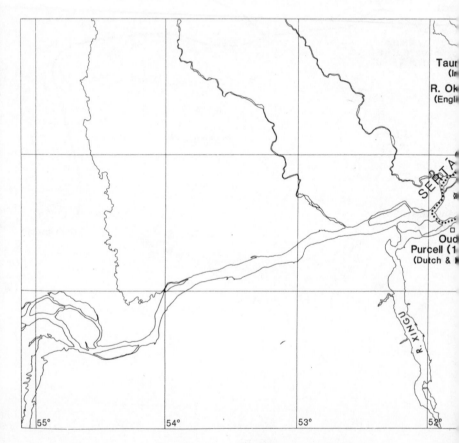

Fig. IV

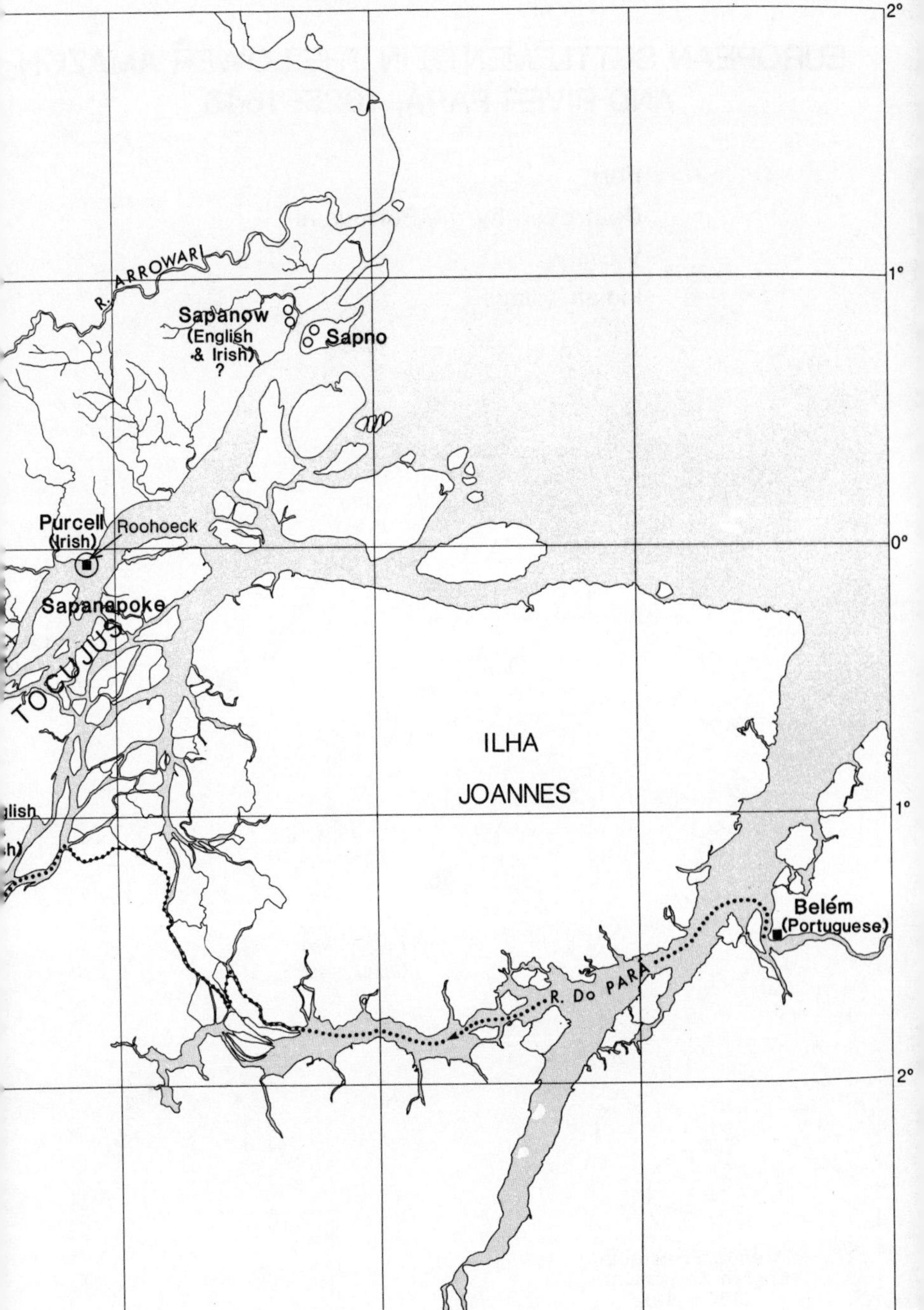
R. ARROWARI
Sapanow
(English
& Irish)
?
Sapno
Purcell
(Irish)
Roohoeck
Sapanapoke
TOCUJUS
ILHA
JOANNES
Belém
(Portuguese)
R. Do PARÁ
2°
1°
0°
1°
2°
3°
51°
50°
49° W

Fig. IV

EUROPEAN SETTLEMENTS IN THE LOWER AMAZON AND RIVER PARÁ, 1625–1646

■   Fort

□   Destroyed by the Portugese

○   Vicinity

▲   Indian village

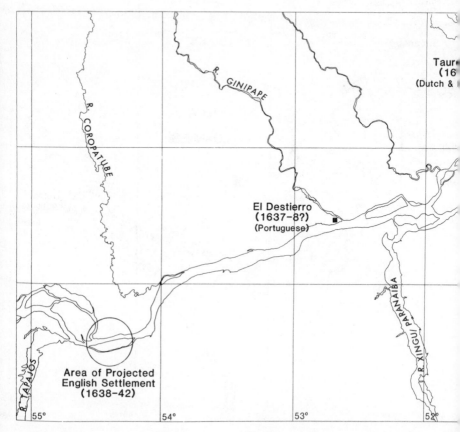

10 0   20   40   60miles

R. GINIPAPE

R. COROPATUBE

Taur●
(16
(Dutch &

El Destierro
(1637–8?)
(Portuguese)

R. XINGU/ PARANAIBA

R. TAPAJOS

Area of Projected
English Settlement
(1638–42)

55°   54°   53°   52°

Fig. V

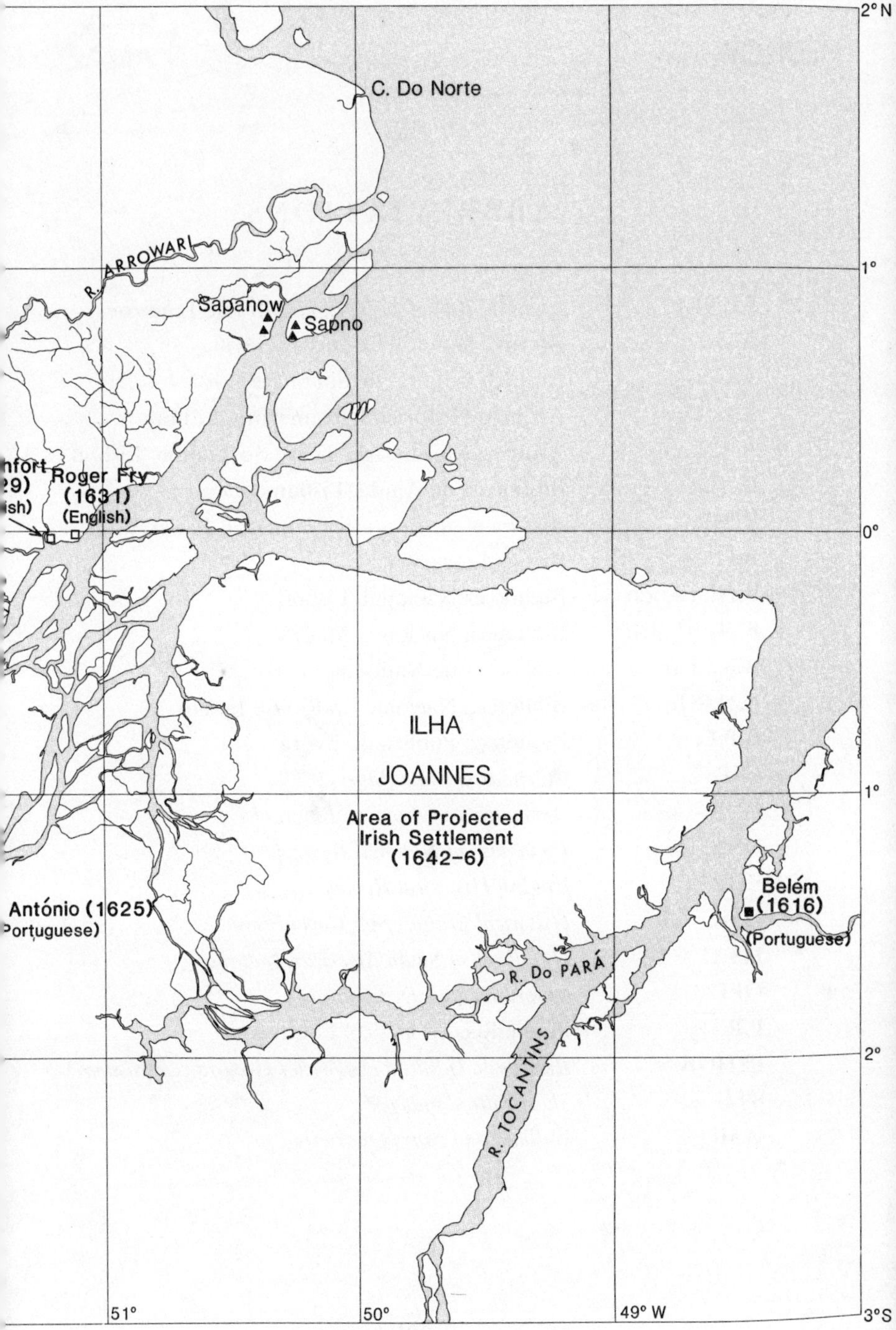

2° N
C. Do Norte
R. ARROWARI
1°
Sapanow
Sapno
nfort
29)
ish)
Roger Fry
(1631)
(English)
0°
ILHA
JOANNES
Area of Projected
Irish Settlement
(1642-6)
1°
Belém
(1616)
(Portuguese)
António (1625)
Portuguese)
R. Do PARÁ
R. TOCANTINS
2°
51°
50°
49° W
3°S

Fig. V

ABBREVIATIONS

ABNRJ	*Anais da Biblioteca Nacional*, Rio de Janeiro
A.G.I.	Archivo General de Indias, Sevilla
A.G.S.	Archivo General de Simancas
A.H.U.	Arquivo Histórico Ultramarino, Lisbon
A.T.T.	Arquivo Nacional da Torre do Tombo, Lisbon
B.A.	Biblioteca de Ajuda, Lisbon
BIHR	*Bulletin of the Institute of Historical Research*
B.L.	British Library
B.N., Lisbon	Biblioteca Nacional, Lisbon
B.N., Madrid	Biblioteca Nacional, Madrid
B.N., Paris	Bibliothèque Nationale, Paris
B.N.R.J.	Biblioteca Nacional do Rio de Janeiro
B.P.É.	Biblioteca Publica de Évora
CSP	*Calendar of State Papers*
DCB	*Dictionary of Canadian Biography*
DNB	*Dictionary of National Biography*
EHR	*English Historical Review*
HMC	*Historical Manuscripts Commission*
HSAI	*Handbook of South American Indians*
OED	*Oxford English Dictionary*
P.R.O.	Public Record Office, London
RIHGB	*Revista do Instituto Histórico e Geografico Brasileiro*
STC	*Short Title Catalogue*
WMQ	*William and Mary Quarterly*

EARLIEST ENGLISH EXPLORATIONS OF
THE AMAZON 1553–1608

On 15th November 1553 Sebastian Cabot sent a letter from England to his former patron, Charles V.[1] He warned the emperor that plans were afoot for an Anglo-French expedition which would fortify the mouth of the Amazon and dispatch forces upriver to attack Peru from the rear. The authors of this project, he claimed, had been the late Duke of Northumberland and the Seigneur de Boisdauphin, the former French ambassador to Edward VI's court. On his return to France, Cabot reported, Boisdauphin had carried with him a considerable sum of money contributed by Northumberland towards the venture. Although the Duke had since been executed Cabot was of the opinion that the expedition might still go ahead.[2]

Sebastian Cabot's letter constitutes the most direct reference to what appears to be the earliest evidence of active English interest in the Amazon. Cabot had returned to England in late 1547 after some thirty-six years in Spain. During the last decade of his life, he is known to have been involved with English voyages to Barbary and Guinea, and in promoting the possibility of trade to the Far East by the northern passages.[3] At the same time, he 'tried to make his own profit

[1] See below, pp. 127–8.
[2] For the career of John Dudley, Viscount Lisle, earl of Warwick and duke of Northumberland, see B. L. Beer, *Northumberland, The political career of John Dudley, earl of Warwick and duke of Northumberland* (Kent, Ohio, 1973), and D. Hoak, 'Rehabilitating the duke of Northumberland: politics and political control, 1549–53', in *The mid-Tudor polity, c. 1540–1560* (Totowa, New Jersey, 1980), eds R. Tittler and J. Loach. Northumberland was executed 22nd August 1553. René de Montmorency-Laval, seigneur de Boisdauphin, began his English embassy in July 1551 departing in late May 1553. For his relationship with Northumberland, see also E. H. Harbison, *Rival ambassadors at the court of Queen Mary* (Oxford, 1940), *passim*.
[3] D. B. Quinn, 'Sebastian Cabot and English exploration', in his *England and the discovery of America, 1481–1620* (London, 1974), ch. 5, provides a comprehensive account of Cabot's career together with an informative bibliography of earlier writings. Cabot died sometime in late 1557.

out of both sides', maintaining regular contact with successive imperial ambassadors between 1549 and 1554. He hinted that he had 'secret information' which would be to Charles V's advantage, and protested a desire to return to his service, always conveniently thwarted by the English Privy Council or his own ill-health. Cabot's concern to protect his remaining property in Seville was a major factor behind these approaches.[1] In late 1553, with Mary Tudor on the throne and negotiations for her marriage to Charles V's son already underway, his instinct for self-preservation may have loomed even larger. Was the alleged Amazon project a mere invention designed to curry favour with the new queen and Charles V? Was it a reality still under active consideration? Was Cabot sending stale news about an enterprise that had not developed beyond the initial phase of consultation? What, if either of the last two hypotheses is correct, had been Cabot's part in it, interested observer, adviser, active promoter?[2] Fragmentary and inconclusive as the corroborative evidence is, it seems most likely that an Amazon expedition had been contemplated, that it had been abandoned some two years before Cabot reported it to Spain, and that he, despite his efforts to disassociate himself, had been closely involved.

We know, at least, that Cabot was interested in the Spanish efforts to explore the Amazon in the 1540s. He was in Seville in 1543, serving as *pilot-major* of the *Casa de Contratación*, when Francisco de Orellana returned to Spain after his epic voyage down the river. He was certainly aware, as would have been any other resident in

[1] The correspondence of the Imperial ambassadors François Van der Delft (resident in England 1544 to May 1550), Jehann Scheyfve (resident May 1550 to October 1553) and Simon Renard (appointed July 1553), detailing their negotiations with Sebastian Cabot, is to be found in *CSP Spanish, 1544–9* (1912), *1550–2* (1914), *1553* (1916). Van der Delft reported his 'suspicion that Cabot has tried to make his own profit out of both sides' in a letter to Charles V, 22nd April 1550 (*CSP Span., 1550–2*, p. 67).
[2] R. Beazley, *John and Sebastian Cabot* (London, 1898), p. 200, argues Cabot's news of the planned Amazon expedition 'was a fabrication for his own safety against another change of fortune'. H. Harrisse, *John Cabot, the discoverer of North America, and Sebastian Cabot his son* (London, 1896), pp. 365–6; J. A. Williamson, *The voyages of the Cabots* (London, 1929), p. 281; R. A. Skelton in his article on Sebastian Cabot in *DCB* (Ottawa, 1965), I, 158; and Quinn in 'Sebastian Cabot and English exploration', 1974, pp. 152–3, accepted Cabot's word that such an expedition had been considered, and that Northumberland had sponsored it. Quinn suggests that the project had probably been abandoned some two years before Cabot revealed it to Charles V.

Seville up to May 1545, of all the vexations which beset Orellana as he struggled to prepare for a return to the Amazon.[1] Cabot, in fact, appears to have published the earliest surviving cartographic record of Orellana's reconnaissance. In 1541 he had contracted with printers in Seville to create a world map of the latest discoveries. The result survives in a unique copy, now in the Bibliothèque Nationale, Paris, engraved, according to the 17th of the 22 legends which accompany it, in 1544. Expert opinion has declared the chart to be derived from a proto-type of the Dieppe school, to which Cabot appended instructions on navigation and references to his own and his father's voyages.[2] But Cabot also appears to have added to the configuration of the map his conception of the results of Orellana's discoveries. The Amazon is depicted following a meandering course from mountains in the west to the Atlantic. The region to the north of its source is entitled, '*Tito Prouincia*', that to the south, '*Peru Prouincia*'. Four cities are marked on its margins, three on the left, about mid-course, and one on the right nearer the estuary.[3] Near the latter, in the Atlantic, is the legend '*Rio de las amazonas q descubrio Francisco de Orillana*'. Cabot's map is now known to pre-date by seventeen years the supposed '1541' world chart of the Dieppe cartographer, Nicholas Desliens, previously thought to be the earliest to register information about Orellana's exploits.[4] Having, himself, spent four years

[1] For Spanish accounts of Orellana's efforts to raise an expedition in Seville to return to the Amazon, see J. Toribio Medina, *The discovery of the Amazon according to the account of Friar Gaspar de Carvajal and other documents*, trans. from the Spanish by B. T. Lee, ed. H. C. Heaton (New York, 1934), pp. 320–61 (referred to henceforth as Toribio Medina, *Carvajal*).

[2] For the history of Cabot's 1544 World chart, see R. Almagia, 'Sull'opera cartografica di Sebastiano Caboto', in *Commemorazione di Sebastiano Caboto nel IV centenario della morte* (Venice, 1958), App. IV, 53–63; Skelton, 'The cartography of the Cabot voyages', in *Cabot voyages* (1962), ed. J. A. Williamson, pp. 322–4, and *DCB*, I (1965), pp. 157–9.

[3] Presumably Cabot's 'Tito provincia' is a mistaken reference to Quito, the power base of the northern provinces of the Inca empire, as opposed to Cuzco, the political and religious heart of Inca Peru in the south. Orellana saw extensive Indian settlements during his journey to the Atlantic, near the Putumayo, the Trombetas and Tapajós.

[4] The earliest surviving copy of the so-called '1541' World chart of Nicolas Desliens is a 1903 facsimile in the Königliche Offentliche Bibliothek, Dresden. The original was destroyed during World War II. Earlier studies of the map have argued, because of its annotations on tribes contacted by Orellana, that it was completed sometime in 1543 to 1544, after Orellana's return to Europe. Dr

exploring the River Plate for a water passage to the Pacific, it is not surprising that Cabot should have been anxious to record the possibilities of the Amazon as an inland waterway to Peru.

After Cabot reached England he set himself to produce a second edition of his world-chart. It was engraved by Clement Adams in 1549 and appears to have been widely circulated. Richard Hakluyt the younger claimed, in 1589, that a copy of it was 'to be seene in her Majesties Priuie Gallerie at Westminster, and in many other auncient merchant's houses'.[1] The primary objective of producing the revised version was undoubtedly to illustrate and win support for Cabot's views about the Northwest Passage.[2] Nevertheless the Amazon material may also have been intended to satisfy or encourage the interest of the small segment of the English maritime community already familiar with South American waters.

English merchants from Plymouth and Southampton had begun to trade on the Brazil coast before 1530, following in the wake and often using the expertise of Norman seamen who had trafficked there since the beginning of the century.[3] Jean Rotz, the Dieppe

---

Helen Wallis's recent study of the facsimile has shown that the date on the original had been altered from '1561' to '1541'. The delineation of the East Indies on the chart clearly indicates that it dates from the early 1560s. H. Wallis, 'The boke in the context of the Dieppe School of Hydrography', and 'Dating and Sources', in *The maps and text of the boke of Idrography presented by Jean Rotz to Henry VIII now in the British Library* (Oxford, 1981), Roxburghe Club, ed. H. Wallis, pt. II, chs. 7, 8.

[1] Richard Hakluyt, *Principall navigations* (1589), pt. III, p. 511. A German scholar, at Oxford in 1569, saw a copy of the 1549 edition there, see N. Chytraeus, *Variorum in Europa itinerum deliciae* (Herborni in Nassau, 1594), pp. 773–94. Richard Willes, *The history of travayle in the West and East Indies* (1577), f. 232, states that the earl of Bedford also had a copy.

[2] Contemporary descriptions of the 1549 engraving indicate that Cabot revised his original to add a claim that he had discovered a Northwest Passage between 61° and 64° N. See Skelton, 'The cartography of the Cabot voyages', 1962, pp. 322–4, and *DCB*, 1965, I, p. 158; and Quinn, 'Sebastian Cabot and English exploration', 1974, p. 155.

[3] For English voyages to Brazil in the first half of the sixteenth century, see R. G. Marsden, 'The voyage of the *Barbara* of London to Brazil in 1540', *EHR*, XXIV (1909), 96–100; J. A. Williamson, *Sir John Hawkins, the time and the man* (Oxford, 1927), pp. 7–19, and *Hawkins and Plymouth* (London, 1949), pp. 24–31. On the French Brazil trade during the same period, see P. Gaffarel, *Histoire du Bresil Français au seizième siècle* (Paris, 1878); C. & P. Breard, *Documents rélatifs a la marine normande et a ses armements au XVIe et XVIIe siècles* (Rouen, 1889), pp. 201–2; E. H. Gosselin, *Documents authentiques et inédits pour servir a l'histoire de la marine Normande et du commerce Rouennais pendant les XVIe et XVIIe siècles* (Rouen, 1876); C. A. Julien, *Les Français en Amerique pendant la premiere moitié du XVIe siècle* (Paris,

hydrographer, who had sailed to Pernambuco in 1539, made his detailed cartographical knowledge of that particular area of the coast available for English use during the period he was in Henry VIII's service, 1542–7.[1] While there is no concrete evidence for English voyages to Brazil in the two decades after 1542, there is every likelihood that some continued to be made. News of Orellana's discoveries on the Amazon, and of his preparations to return to the river, was almost certainly carried back to England by seamen who had been at Seville and San Lucar between 1543 and 1545. Royal inspectors in Seville in 1545, fearing for the security of the discoveries, had actually been obliged to discharge some English sailors who had signed on with Orellana.[2] Other Englishmen trading at Lisbon during these years could have heard details of Portuguese efforts to forestall the Spaniards with a rival expedition to the Amazon.[3] When Cabot arrived in England he would have found some overseas investors interested in Brazil, already in the habit of collaborating with the French in Brazil ventures, and almost certainly aware of Spanish and Portuguese designs for the Amazon. His map, with the most up-to-date configuration of that river, would have clarified for them its geographical relationship with Peru. Whether it was Cabot himself who raised the possibility of using it to attack the heart of the Indies, or whether he merely offered his advice to already interested parties is another question.

Cabot alleged that the duke of Northumberland and ambassador Boisdauphin had concocted the scheme. It is certain that if such an

1946), and *Les voyages de découverte et les premiers établissements* (Paris, 1948); M. Mollat, 'As premeiras relações entre a Franca é o Brasil: dos Verrazani a Villegagnon', *Revista de Historia*, XXXIV (1967), 343–58; J. Hemming, *Red gold, The conquest of the Brazilian Indians* (London, 1978), chs. 1–5.

[1] See Quinn, 'Depictions of America', in *The boke of Idrography*, 1981, pp. 53–6. Rotz's chart of Brazil and the southern reaches of South America (B.L., Royal MS 20 E IX, ff. 27v–8) indicates a considerable familiarity with the Brazilian coast in about 10° S. In his 'Traicte des differences du compas aymenté' presented to Henry VIII in 1542 he stated that he had gone to Brazil in 1539.

[2] Report from officials in Seville on Orellana's preparations, 4th April 1545 (A[rchivo] G[eneral de] I[ndias], Indiferente General, case 143, shelf 3, bundle 12) in Toribio Medina, *Carvajal*, 1934, pp. 352–4.

[3] On the plans for a Portuguese Amazon expedition, see, 'The petition which Orellana presented, together with the opinions of the Council', 1543 (A.G.I., Estado, bundle 61, f. 19), and Fr Pablo de Torres to Charles V, 23rd October and 20th November 1544 (A.G.I., Indiferente General, case 143, shelf 3, bundle 12) in Toribio Medina, *Carvajal* (1934), pp. 323, 349–52.

audacious design was under consideration it would need the blessing of the highest levels of the English and French governments. It is also true that the duke of Northumberland had a strong interest in overseas discoveries. As Lord High Admiral during the last four years of Henry VIII's reign he had established close contact with the French maritime community. Jacques Ribault and the cosmographer, Nicholas de Nicholai, became part of his household during this period.[1] Boisdauphin was in England from July 1551 to late May 1553. During his embassy he worked closely with Northumberland. On his departure he was reported to have been presented with '1,000l and gold plate to a higher value' as a parting gift.[2] This is very probably the basis of Cabot's claim that Northumberland had furnished £2,000 towards the Amazon expedition.

Yet the timing of Cabot's revelations about the venture lead one to question whether either Northumberland or Boisdauphin were really its progenitors. It was in April 1553 that Cabot began to approach the imperial resident, Scheyfve, giving news of English plans to reach China by the northern route, and offering to 'unfold other great secrets to ... [Charles V] concerning navigation, in which many millions were at stake'.[3] In September he pressed to be allowed to go to the emperor to reveal a 'very important' matter.[4] In October, probably much to his dismay, he was given permission to travel.[5] On 15th November, 'too ill to go over', Cabot sent the letter which 'contained the information he wished to impart', ... the plans for the Peru raid. By April 1553, the beginning of this sequence of exchanges, Edward VI was known to be dying. It was in Cabot's best interests to renew his contacts with his former patron. The need to stand well with the emperor became even more imperative after Mary Tudor's accession. The new, catholic queen was closely attached to her cousin, Charles V. Information about English and French plans to attack his Indies was nicely calculated

---

[1] See E. G. R. Taylor, *Tudor geography* (London, 1930), pp. 59–94; Beer, *Northumberland*, 1973, pp. 192–4.

[2] Jehan Scheyfve to Charles V, 30th May 1553, *CSP Span., 1553*, pp. 45–7. See above, p. 1, n. 2.

[3] Scheyfve to Antoine Perrenot de Granvelle, bishop of Arras, 10th April 1553, *CSP Span., 1553*, p. 31.

[4] Advices from the Imperial ambassadors in England to Charles V, 4th September 1553, *CSP Span., 1553*, p. 204.

[5] Simon Renard to Charles V, 19th October 1553, *CSP Span., 1553*, p. 308.

to interest the Emperor without offending the English monarch. This was especially true if the project could be passed off as the brainchild of the late Protector and the former French ambassador. Northumberland was alleged to have used Boisdauphin as an intermediary to Henry II in an attempt to gain French aid to bar Mary from the succession. Other rumours, fostered by the queen's council, suggested that Boisdauphin had poisoned Edward VI.[1] If Cabot wanted to ensure the favour of both Charles V and Mary Tudor, he could not have done better than attribute responsibility for a scheme to conquer Peru to two men of such evil reputation at the Spanish and English courts. As late as 1556, Boisdauphin was still referred to in England as 'the gret and thick embasitor that wase here in King Edwardes time'.[2]

Other independent evidence suggests that it may well have been Cabot who conceived of the Amazon enterprise and approached the English and French governments for support, the reverse of what he claimed in his letter. Andre Thevet, the French cosmographer, in his *Les singularitez de la France antarctique*, published 1558, referred to 'Sebastian Babate, an Englishman, who persuaded Henry the seventh, King of England, that he would go easily by that way, towards the north, to the country of Cathay, and that by these means he would find spices and other things, just as the King of Portugal did in the Indies; in addition to which he proposed to go to Peru and America to people those countries with new inhabitants and establish there a new England. Which project he did not execute: . . .'[3] Although Thevet has to be used with caution as a source,[4] nevertheless this does appear to be a direct allusion to the scheme to raid Peru. Thevet's informant seems to have been Cabot himself. In a later work Thevet commented, 'when I was at St. Malo, in the Isle, lodged in the house of Jacques Cartier, there came the Captain Gabotte, son of the great Gabot, worthy old man, with

---

[1] On Northumberland's efforts to alter the succession, see above p. 1, n. 2, and S. T. Bindoff, 'A kingdom at stake', *History Today*, III (1953), 642–8. Harbison, 1940, p. 51 states that Mary's Council spread rumours that Northumberland had offered Ireland, Calais, Guines and Hammes to Henry II in return for support to establish Lady Jane Grey.

[2] P.R.O., SP 11/17, no. 49.

[3] A. Thevet, *Les singularitez de la France antarctique* (Paris, 1558), f. 148v. Thomas Hackett's translation *The newe founde worlde or Antarctike* (London, 1568), f. 122 reads, 'Nevethelesse his mynd was to go to *Perou*, & *America*, for to people that cuntrie with English*men*, but his purpose toke no effect.'

[4] See below, p. 8, n. 1.

whom I talked for nine whole days, and, being a person of good understanding in marine affairs, lacking nothing of the merits of his father, familiarly discussed with me about the whole coast from Canada to Florida'.[1] Professor Quinn suggests that these conversations may have taken place when Cabot went over to France to consult with Jacques Cartier about the Amazon project.[2] The advice of the French pilots who frequented Brazil would have been even more valuable. Cabot, prone in his old age to puff up his own consequence, could have exaggerated his significance in the affair to Thevet. On the other hand, during his last years in England Cabot established a considerable reputation for himself amongst the merchant community as an authority on overseas navigation.[3] It is possible that his visit to St Malo was part of an effort to stir up support for an improbable enterprise, which was his own idea however much he might want to disclaim it later.

If Cabot was responsible for it, he does not seem to have been able to carry it beyond the preliminary discussion phase. His contention that the Amazon plan was still under consideration in late 1553 has to be questioned. Professor Quinn is of the opinion that Cabot was in St Malo sometime in late 1550 or early 1551, and that the design for an expedition to Peru was abandoned as impracticable shortly thereafter.[4] When one looks at the pattern of Cabot's communications with different imperial ambassadors this does seem probable. In January 1550 he tried to persuade Van der Delft 'that a million in gold is at stake on his being able to give . . . some secret information'.[5] During the next six months the resident relayed to his master confused rumours that the English intended to use their idle shipping 'to look for gold and silver, as they hear that your majesty's vessels return home laden with it',[6] or planned 'to send a few ships towards Iceland by the northern route, to

---

[1] A. Thevet, 'Grande Insulaire', c. 1584–90 (B[ibliothèque] N[ationale], Paris, Fonds Français 15452, f. 176). Translation in Quinn, 'Sebastian Cabot and English exploration', 1974, p. 152.

[2] Quinn, ibid., pp. 152–3. In their recent work, *André Thevet's America* (McGill, 1986), R. Schlesinger and A. P. Sattler question whether this meeting ever took place. Thevet may have been in the Levant at this time.

[3] Ibid., pp. 155–6.

[4] Ibid., pp. 151–2.

[5] François Van der Delft to Charles V, 31st January 1550, *CSP Span., 1550–2*, pp. 17–21.

[6] Van der Delft to Charles V, 12th April 1550, *CSP Span., 1550–2*, p. 63.

discover some island which is rich in gold'.[1] In January 1551, Scheyfve reported that Cabot and Jean Ribault were cooperating on preparations 'to discover some islands or seek a road to the Indies, taking the way of the Arctic Pole'.[2] He had nothing else to dispatch about Cabot until April 1553, when the sequence of approaches which led to the revelation of the plot against Peru began.[3] It is noteworthy that when Cabot began to talk to Scheyfve again he promised that he could unfold 'other great secrets . . . concerning navigation, in which many millions were at stake', in addition to English plans for a northern voyage to China.[4] This is the same claim that he had made in January 1550, suggesting that he was harking back to projects that had been under consideration at that time as he sought for a means to mend his fences with Charles V. In all likelihood, then, the dream of attacking Peru via the Amazon originated in the fertile imagination of Sebastian Cabot. It is unlikely that it was ever taken very seriously and, by the time he reported to Spain, what support there had been for it had long since dwindled.

Almost half a century elapsed before the English took any further interest in the river. Their activities in South America in the intervening period concentrated in two distinct thrusts into the South Atlantic and the Caribbean, leaving the equatorial regions of the Atlantic coastline in limbo. In the 1570s efforts were made to revive the Brazil trade, while other projectors scouted the prospects for English settlement near São Vincente, the River Plate and Magellan's Strait. Determined Portuguese resistance put an end to such schemes by 1583 and for the remainder of the century the pickings of the South Atlantic were left to privateers.[5] The latter had begun a sustained invasion of the Caribbean in the 1560s once more following the French. By the 1580s the number of English intruders had reached epidemic proportions.[6] Some of them, in the

---

[1] Jehann Scheyfve to the Queen Dowager, 24th June 1550, *CSP Span.*, *1550–2*, p. 115.

[2] Advices from Scheyfve, January 1551, *CSP Span.*, *1550–2*, p. 217.

[3] See above, p. 6.

[4] Scheyfve to the bishop of Arras, 10th April 1553, *CSP Span.*, *1553*, p. 31.

[5] On English projects in sub-equatorial South America in the last thirty years of the sixteenth century, see K. R. Andrews, 'Beyond the equinoctial: England and South America in the sixteenth century', *The Journal of Imperial and Commonwealth History*, X (1981), 4–24.

[6] For the most comprehensive study of the development of English and French privateering interest in the Caribbean, see K. R. Andrews, *The Spanish Caribbean: trade and plunder, 1530–1630* (London, 1978), chs. 3–6.

course of bartering with natives of Trinidad and the ill-supplied Spanish settlers of the eastern Main and the Antilles, picked up intelligences about an as yet undiscovered aboriginal empire worth potentially far more than their actual return cargoes. Paradoxically it was rumours that the kingdom of 'El Dorado'[1] lay near to the south margin of the lower Orinoco which helped to refocus English attention on the Amazon. English interest in the river, stirred at the mid-century by its potential as an invasion route to Peru, was revived thirty years later by the possibility that it might provide access to another 'peru', as yet undiscovered, east of the Andes.

Sustained by the stubborn belief that a civilization like that of the Incas could not be unique, Spanish explorers had by the 1580s shifted their searches to the Orinoco basin after repeated failure to find anything in Amazonia. In 1583 the conquistador Antonio de Berrio set out from New Granada in the first of three expeditions in search of El Dorado. By 1591 he had traced the Orinoco to its delta and had become convinced that his objective lay somewhere to the south near the headwaters of the tributary Caroni.[2] The protean myth had coalesced around one indisputable fact long known to Spaniards living in the nearby pearl fisheries, that the Guayana Caribs of the Caroni had gold to trade.[3]

[1] Literally the 'golden' or 'gilded one'. The term 'el indio dorado' appears first as a reference to an envoy of the ruler of Cundinamarca captured in 1534 by a lieutenant of Sebastian Benalcazar, the conqueror of Quito. The official report on the envoy's capture alludes to him as the 'indio dorado' because of his tales about the riches of his native land. By 1541, as the chronicler Gonzalo Fernandez de Oviedo y Valdes reported in bk. 49 of his *Historia general y natural de las Indias, islas y Tierra Firme del Mar Oceano* (bk. 49 not published until 1855), residents in Quito had begun to talk of a 'Golden chief or king' who adorned his body with resin and powdered gold dust. For the best analysis of the evolution of the El Dorado legend from a basis of exaggerated accounts of the wealth and religious ceremonies of the Colombian Muisca, see D. Ramos Perez, *El mito del Dorado. Su genesis y proceso* (Caracas, 1973); and J. Hemming, *The search for El Dorado* (London, 1978).

[2] For the history of the El Dorado expeditions of Antonio de Berrio and others who preceded him, see Ramos Perez, 1973; Hemming, *The search*, 1978; W. Chapman, *The golden dream* (Indianapolis, 1967); V. W. von Hagen, *The gold of El Dorado: The quest for the golden man* (London, 1978); R. Levillier, *El Paititi, El Dorado y las Amazonas* (Buenos Aires, 1976).

[3] Spanish traders from Española, Puerto Rico and the pearl fisheries of Cubagua, Cumaná and Margarita bartered for slaves, gold trinkets and foodstuffs at the Arawak villages on Trinidad and the mainland coast between the Orinoco and the Courantyne from the beginnings of settlement. The earliest recorded contact with the Guayana Caribs inhabiting the gold-bearing region of the upper Caroni was made by members of Diego de Ordaz's expedition in 1531.

It was undoubtedly privateers who first carried tales back to England in the early 1580s about the wealth of the Guayana Caribs and about Berrio's expeditions into the interior.[1] Their news fired the volatile imagination of Sir Walter Ralegh. His interest was confirmed, in 1586, when two of his privateers took a vessel carrying the great Spanish navigator, Pedro Sarmiento de Gamboa. The latter was an expert on the Incas and imparted his knowledge freely in the short time that he remained as Ralegh's honoured guest.[2] Before he himself sailed for the Orinoco in 1595 Ralegh consulted various published sources on the history of exploration of the South American continent. Arriving at Trinidad in 1595, he was lucky enough to capture Antonio de Berrio, and to learn first-hand his opinions on the nature of the hidden empire. Subsequent interviews with Indian chiefs on the Orinoco added further detail to Berrio's account.[3]

In subsequent decades Spaniards from the eastern Main trafficked with the Guayana on the lower Caroni, accumulating gold trinkets and rumours about the power and wealth of the peoples near the source of the tributary. See P. Ojer, S.J., *La formación del oriente Venezolano* (Caracas, 1966), pp. 162–76, 331–8.

[1] On English and French trade with the Arawaks and Caribs of Trinidad and the Orinoco delta in the late 1560s, see Ojer, 1966, pp. 268, 355–6; J. Lorimer, 'English trade and exploration in Trinidad and Guiana, 1569–1648' (unpub. Liverpool Ph.D., 1973), pp. 53–61. Sir John Hawkins told Ralegh that he had met Lope de Aguirre and mutineers from Pedro de Ursua's expedition on the Spanish Main in 1567. William Parker, Ralegh's 'sometime ... servant', picked up rumours about El Dorado sometime during his annual voyages to the Caribbean 1592–5. See Sir W. Ralegh, *The discoverie of the large and bewtifull empyre of Guiana* (London, 1596), ed. V. T. Harlow (London, 1928), pp. 4, 23 (henceforth referred to as *The discoverie*, 1928); K. R. Andrews, *English privateering voyages to the West Indies 1588–95* (Cambridge, 1959), chs. 9. 14.

[2] An account of the voyage of the *Serpent* and the *Mary Sparke*, sent out to the Azores by Ralegh in 1586, was published by Hakluyt in *Principal navigations* (1599), II, ii, 120. Pedro Sarmiento de Gamboa's *History of the Incas*, dedicated to Philip II in 1572 but not published in his lifetime, was translated and edited by Sir C. R. Markham (Cambridge, 1907). Markham's edition also includes the 'Concise narrative by Pedro Sarmiento de Gamboa, Governor and Captain-General of the Strait of the Mother of God, formerly called the Strait of Magellan ...', pp. 339–43, in which he described his dealings with Ralegh, Elizabeth I, Burghley, and the Lord High Admiral, Charles Howard during his brief sojourn in England.

[3] Ralegh appears to have consulted various Spanish and French published sources in preparation for his Guiana expedition, several of which contained significant information on Spanish exploration of the Amazon. In *The discoverie*, 1928, pp. 17–19, he refers to 'Pedro de Cieza' Leon, author of the *Chronica del Peru* (Seville, 1553); 'Francisco López' de Gómara, author of *Historia general de las Indias* (Zaragossa, 1552); and 'Andrew Thevet', whose *Les singularitez de la France*

The composite which Ralegh put together from all these sources was clearly set out in his *Discoverie of the large, rich and bewtifull empyre of Guiana*, and graphically illustrated on a chart. Both, produced in late 1595 shortly after his return from the Orinoco, depicted the domains of El Dorado, with the lake–city of Manoa at their heart, lying between the Orinoco and the Amazon, and walled off from both rivers and the Atlantic coastline, 'with impassable mountaynes on euerie side. ...'[1] While Ralegh had no doubt that the Caroni offered the most direct route through this barrier, he knew that his former prisoner, Antonio de Berrio, 'expected daily a supply out of Spayne, and looked also howerly for his sonne to come downe from *Nueuo reyno de Granada*, with many horse and foote, and had also in *Valentia* in the *Caracas*, 200 horse readie to march. ...'[2] Anticipating

---

Antarctique, and *La cosmographie universelle* appeared in Paris in 1558 and 1575 respectively. The works of López de Gómara and Cieza de León both contain accounts of Orellana's discoveries. Ralegh appears to have got his confused notion of the course of the Amazon from Thevet, see below p. 15. Richard Hakluyt, who assisted Ralegh in his studies, acquired from Lopez Vaz, a Portuguese captured in the earl of Cumberland's fleet in 1587, a 'discourse of the West Indies and the South Sea', extracted in *Principall navigations* (1589), pp. 594–6, 673–4, and printed in full, *Principal navigations* (1600), III, 778–802, Hakluyt soc. extra ser., I–XII (Glasgow, 1903–5), XI, 227–90. Lopez Vaz's 'discourse' contained valuable material on the expeditions of Orellana and Pedro de Ursua to the Amazon. The description of Lope de Aguirre's mutiny against Ursua in *The discoverie*, 1928, pp. 22–3, reads as if summarized from this source. Another account of Orellana's descent of the Amazon was available in the partial translation of Augustin de Zarate's *A history of the discovery and conquest of Peru* (Anvers, 1555), by Thomas Nichols published in London 1581. A. F. Allison, *English translations from the Spanish and Portuguese to the year 1700* (London, 1974) is a useful reference.

[1] *The discoverie*, 1928, pp. 73–4. Ralegh's account was completed by November of 1595, see Sir Walter Ralegh to Sir Robert Cecil, 13/23rd November 1595 in E. Edwards, ed. *The life of Sir Walter Ralegh* (London, 1868). It was entered in the Stationers' Register on the 15/25th March 1596 and went through three editions in that year, see E. Arber, ed. *A transcript of the registers of the Company of Stationers of London, 1554–1640* (London, 1875–94), III, 9. In his letter to Cecil Ralegh also indicated that a 'plott' or map was finished. This would appear to be the chart preserved in the British Library (B.L. Add. MS 17940A). The place names are in Ralegh's hand with the exception of some pencilled notations on the west coast of South America. R. A. Skelton, 'Ralegh as a geographer', *The Virginia Magazine of History and Biography*, LXXII (1963), 140–1, suggested that the British Library chart was most likely that produced by Thomas Harriot in the summer of 1596 incorporating the material from Laurence Keymis's survey of the Guiana coast between January and June of that year, see Thomas Harriot to Sir Robert Cecil, 11/21st July 1596 (Edwards, 1868, II, 420–2). This seems unlikely since the chart incorporates nothing of Keymis's discoveries.

[2] *The discoverie*, 1928, p. 61

that the Spaniards would try to blockade the Orinoco route, Ralegh turned to consider alternative river passages to the south. One possibility was the Amazon. 'Undoubtedly those that trade Amazones returne much gold, which ... commeth by trade from Guiana, by some branch of a river that falleth from that countrey into Amazones. ...'[1]

It was logical that Ralegh should consider the Amazon since the river and the rich tribes said to inhabit its margins were a subsidiary but integral part of the fantasy of El Dorado. The Spanish expeditions which had followed Orellana into Amazonia had first believed that the fabulous kingdom lay in the territories of the Omagua peoples, north of the mainstream.[2] The name of the inner lake–city, Manoa, may have been adopted from Indian references to the Manau of the middle Rio Negro who traded gold to the Omagua.[3] Although searches had now shifted to the Orinoco, the notion that El Dorado might still be reached via one of the northern tributaries of the Amazon had not been abandoned.

The wonders of Mexico and Peru had given licence to fertile european imaginations already disposed to transplant the myths of the Old World into the unexplored terrain of the New. Before Orellana left the Amazon he had endowed the long-haired warriors he had seen there with all the characteristics of the inhabitants of the Isle of Lesbos of classical mythology.[4] Orellana was more

---

[1] Ibid., p. 26.

[2] For the history of the Amazon expeditions to find the El Dorado of the Omagua, see the works quoted above p. 10, n. 2. The Omagua, probably of Tupi-Guarani stock, were a powerful warrior people who appear to have migrated to the banks of the upper Amazon in the pre-Columbian era. Their war parties scoured the vast river basin and settled colonies far up the Napo, Aguarico and Quebeno territories. Orellana passed Omagua villages on the south bank of the mainstream opposite the tributary Putumayo. In 1543 Philip von Hutten contacted Omagua on the eastern slopes of the Andes near the headwaters of the Putumayo.

[3] Hemming, The search, 1978, pp. 153 and 210 argues that the name of the lake-city is more likely to have derived from the Achagua word 'Manoa', for lake, than from allusions to the Manau of the Rio Negro.

[4] Columbus recorded the existence of female warrior societies in the New World, on his first voyage. He claimed to have heard of Amazon women who only cohabited with men once a year living on the island of Matinino or Martinique. He believed that the armed Carib women he encountered on Guadeloupe in 1496 were Amazons. The myth circulated with Spanish explorers in the New World until it found a permanent home on the Amazon after Orellana's expedition. See S. E. Morison, ed. and trans., Journals and other documents on the life and voyages of Christopher Columbus (New York, 1963). Peter

justified in his delusion than others before him who claimed to have sighted Amazons in the Indies. An Indian captive had, it was claimed, informed him that in the Amazon kingdom,

> 'houses were of stone and with regular doors and that from one village to another went roads ... with guards stationed at intervals along them so that no one might enter without paying duty ... there was in their possession a very great wealth of gold and silver, and that in the case of all women of rank and distinction their eating utensils were nothing but gold and silver ... in the capital and principal city in which the ruling mistress presided, there were five very large buildings, which were places of worship, and houses dedicated to the Sun....'[1]

These accounts most likely stemmed from confused tales about the Inca 'Sun Maidens' or 'Chosen Women', current among the rain forest tribes, and judiciously fleshed out by their Spanish auditors who had been in Peru.[2] Although some dismissed Orellana's 'extravagant statements ... that there were Amazons along this river',[3] others were ready to believe them. Ralegh, always sensitive to ridicule, 'bicause of some it is beleeved, of others not', was prepared to assert that such a 'Dominion and Empire' did exist on the 'south border of Guiana', and offer its wealth as an added incentive to those who sought to reach Guiana by the Amazon route.[4]

To counter the arguments of those disposed to dismiss his entire enterprise as the product of an over-active imagination, Ralegh pointed out the growing level of French interest in the Amazon in

---

Martyr d'Anghiera's elaboration of Columbus's account of Amazons passed into English in Richard Eden's translation of *The decades of the newe worlde or West India* (1555). For an account of the transfer of the Amazonian myth to the New World during the first half of the sixteenth century, see A. Wettan Kleinbaum, *The war against the Amazons* (New York, 1983), pp. 71–137.

[1] From the account of Friar Gaspar de Carvajal in Toribio Medina, *Carvajal*, 1934, pp. 221–2.

[2] Hagen, 1978, pp. 266–7 suggests that information about the Inca 'Sun Maidens' or 'Nustas' of the sun temples was infused into the Amazon myth here.

[3] Francisco López de Gómara, *Historia general*, 1552, in *Biblioteca de autores Españoles* (Madrid, 1946), ed. M. Menendez-Pelayo, XXII, 210, trans. in Toribio Medina, *Carvajal*, 1934, p. 26; *The discoverie*, 1928, p. 76. Lopez Vaz also dismissed Orellana's claim that the female warriors he had seen were Amazons, see *Principal navigations*, 1903–5, XI, 246–7.

[4] See below, pp. 130–1.

the past twelve years. Current plans to colonize the river, he argued, reflected the fact that the French had 'made divers voiages, and returned much gold and other rarities'. Ralegh appears to have misinterpreted his information on the French expeditions here. The projected settlement he alluded to was, almost certainly, that established in the Maranhão by Jacques Riffault in 1594. The French ship which had entered Helford in 1595 after '14 moneths at ancor in Amazones', had in all probability been in the Maranhão.[1] Ralegh's mistake stemmed from his own confusion about the geography of the lower reaches of the Amazon. Following late sixteenth-century Spanish usage he used the names '*Maragnon or Amazones*' interchangeably through the *Discoverie*, but ranged himself alongside those who, like the late André Thevet, believed 'that between *Maragnon* and *Amazones* there are 120 leagues: but sure it is that those riuers haue one head and beginning, and that *Maragnon* which *Theuet* describeth is but a braunch of *Amazones* or *Oreliano*....'[2] On Ralegh's chart the mainstream of the Amazon bifurcates before it enters the Atlantic with the incomplete southern fork bearing the title 'Maranion', as depicted in the New World chart engraved for Thevet's *Cosmographie Universelle*.[3] Thevet's 'Marannon', here, was very probably the river Pará. French pilots, with far greater experience of the Brazil coast than Thevet, had, by the mid-century, begun to distinguish the Marañón or Maranhão, from the Amazon.[4] Their understanding of the geography of the

---

[1] See below, p. 129. For the history of the beginnings of French settlement on the Maranhão in 1594, see Claude D'Abbeville, *Histoire de la mission des Pères Capucins en l'isle de Maragnan et terres circonvoisins* (Paris, 1614), ed. A. Métraux and J. Lafaye (Graz, 1963); S. Lussagnet, ed., *Le Brésil et les Brésiliens par Andre Thevet* (Paris, 1953), p. 218, n. 2; Hemming, *Red gold*, 1978, ch. 10. News of French plans to support the Portuguese Pretender, Dom António Prior of Crato, with an expedition to Brazil was sent to Philip II in October 1581. The informant suggested that the French intended to make for 'o en el Rio de los Amazones *que* esta a tres quartos de la equinoçial o otro *que* se llama Maraño distante del primero 50 leguas hazia oriente. ... Tambien dize de otro que se llama San francisco que esta a 50 grados y medio'. Juan Baptista de Tassis to Philip II, 7th October 1581 (A[rchivo] G[eneral de] S[imancas] Estado, K1559/59). Subsequent despatches from Tassis to the King dated 13th, 25th October; 6th, 20th, 22nd November; 11th, 15th, 28th December 1581 (A.G.S. Estado, K1559/61, 63, 67, 71, 72, 79, 83, 86) indicate that the French had dropped these more ambitious plans to concentrate on preparations for the attack on the Azores, mounted 1582.

[2] See *The discoverie*, 1928, pp. 17, 19, 32, 29.

[3] For a copy of Ralegh's chart see ibid., 1928.

[4] See above p. 4, n. 3.

northerly reaches of the Brazil coast deepened over the next four decades as fierce Portuguese counter-attacks made the littoral south of the Rio Grande inhospitable for trade. The bay of Maranhão offered a secure alternative site for barter with the Tupinamba. The men left there by Jacques Riffault in 1594 were the pioneers in what was to be a twenty-year effort by the French to colonize the Maranhão and hold it against the Portuguese.[1] When Ralegh's French informants spoke of voyages to the 'Maranon' it was almost certainly the Maranhão that they meant, not, as he had assumed Orellana's 'Maragnon or Amazones'.

Interested as he was in French activities in the 'Maragnon', nevertheless Ralegh's objective in writing the *Discoverie* was to raise support for the conquest of El Dorado by the Orinoco and Caroni route. The venture would, he hoped, be adopted as an official state project, financed by royal and private capital. Much to his chagrin, neither Elizabeth I nor those of her subjects normally active in overseas enterprise shared his enthusiasm for the scheme. Frustrated by the 'blockishe and slothfull' dullards who ridiculed his dreams of empire, Ralegh managed, with the aid of a few influential supporters, to send out a small interim expedition in January 1596. Two vessels, the *Darling* and the *Discoverer*, under the overall command of Laurence Keymis, were dispatched to the coast. Keymis's instructions were to survey the imperfectly known littoral between the Amazon and the Orinoco, to reassure Ralegh's Indian allies on the Orinoco of his intention to return, and to discover whether the Spaniards had managed to establish any significant forces there.[2] His voyage set what was to become the standard route for navigation along the Guiana coast, ensuring that the north cape and north channel of the Amazon estuary would become a familiar resort for European shipping. At the same time his findings deflected the main thrust of English colonizing efforts in Guiana away from the Amazon for over a decade.

[1] For the history of French activities on the Brazil coast after 1550, see Hemming, *Red gold*, 1978, chs. 6–9, and the works cited above, p. 4, n. 3.

[2] For Ralegh's vision of a tropical empire, his problems with detractors and the history of Laurence Keymis's expedition, see Ralegh to Cecil, 13/23rd November 1595 (Edwards, *The life*, 1868, II; Harriot to Cecil, 11/21st July 1596 (ibid., pp. 420–2); *The discoverie*, 1928, pp. 3–10; 'Of the voyage for Guiana' (B.L., MS Sloane 1133, ff. 45 et seq.), ed. Harlow, *The discoverie*, 1928, pp. 138–49; L. Keymis, *A relation of the second voyage to Guiana* (1596), reprinted in *Principal navigations* (1600), III, 667–92, (1903–5), X, 441–501.

Keymis set his outward course via the Canaries and the Cape Verdes falling away thence to the south-west. Sailing routes along the Guiana coastline were pre-determined by the prevailing north-east trades and the powerful northerly component of the great southern equatorial drift current which sweeps up from the vicinity of Cape São Roque through the Gulf of Paria and into the Caribbean. Shipmasters who failed to lay away sufficiently to the south-west from the Canaries, Barbary coast or Cape Verdes found themselves carried to the northern part of the littoral with no possibility of making their way back southwards. To ensure a southerly landfall it was important to make for the equator and the mouth of the Amazon. The approach of the latter was heralded well out from the shoreline by the discoloration of the ocean from the sediment discharged into it by the huge river.[1]

Keymis's first landfall on the coast narrowly missed the Amazon proper. On the 14th of March the *Darling*, having lost company with its pinnace, anchored 'in the mouth of the Arrowari, a faire and great river'. Keymis, with reasonable accuracy, estimated the Arrowari to lie 1°40' N. From thence he coasted north-westwards to a prominent headland which he named after Sir Robert Cecil, noting the estuaries of 'several great rivers' en route. He gained the erroneous impression that all these rivers, including the Arcooa west of Cape Cecil, 'were branches of the great river of Amazones', and heard from Indians encountered later that he had only been one day's journey from the latter at the river 'Arrowari'. Information from an Indian pilot picked up at the river Cawo, however, rapidly eclipsed the attractions of the Amazon. The man spoke of a great inland 'lake, which the Iaos call Roponowini, the Charibes, Parime: which is of such bignesse, that they know no difference betweene it & the maine sea'. Keymis immediately assumed that 'it is

---

[1] *The West Indies pilot* (London, 1955) and the *South American pilot* (London, 1945) issued by the British Admiralty provide detailed navigational surveys for the Amazon and the entire Guiana coast. The Amazon discharges over 1⅓ million tons of particulate matter into the sea daily causing a characteristic reddish to whiteish chocolate brown discoloration. The heavily sedimented water flows out into the Atlantic for some 32 kilometres. See R. E. Oltman, *Reconnaissance investigations of the discharge and water quality of the Amazon river* (Washington, 1968), U.S. Geological survey, Circular 552; H. O'Reilly Sternberg, *The Amazon river of Brazil* (Weisbaden, 1975), pp. 1–5. John Stoneman's account of Captain John Legat's disastrous second voyage, printed below, illustrates the difficulties encountered when shipmasters made their first landfall to the leeward of their intended destination.

no other then that, wheron Manoa standeth'. Lake Parime lay only twenty-one days' journey from the mouth of the Essequibo. Subsequent inquiries elicited the news that the Wiapoco and Courantyne also offered alternative river routes to El Dorado well south of the Orinoco. This was a matter of considerable importance since Keymis's reconnaissance made a far more unwelcome discovery. The Spaniards had now fortified the mouth of the Caroni and rebuilt their earlier settlement on Trinidad. Since the most direct route to El Dorado could now only be taken by force, the Wiapoco, Courantyne and Essequibo should be explored as alternatives. The Amazon, Keymis felt, offered no such possibility. 'From the mouth of Orellana to seeke entrance with any number of men, & to bore a hole through the mountaines is all one. Neither finde wee, that any seeking it that way, have at any time boasted of their gaines or pleasurable journeys.'[1]

On 15th October 1596, some three months after his return, Keymis registered his *Relation of the second voyage to Guiana* at the Stationers' Company. His publication, supplementing Ralegh's *Discoverie* which went through three editions in 1596,[2] provided possible investors with an update of the progress of the quest for El Dorado as well as an analysis of the commercial potential of the newly explored Guiana coastline.

The sum of the published information did little to convince either Ralegh's detractors or his supporters that the realm of El Dorado was anything more than a myth. In some it only bred confusion. Sir Robert Cecil, up to that point a staunch ally, had set himself, during Keymis's absence in Guiana, to study the sections 'concerning Dorado' in Acosta's *Natural and moral history*. It would appear that Cecil had turned to Richard Hakluyt to select and translate the relevant chapters on the Amazon, the Orinoco and the 'Countrey of Paytity and Dorado'. Acosta's statements seemed, to Cecil, to imply that the Orinoco and the Amazon were one and the same and that El Dorado lay nearer the Amazon. Was Ralegh looking in the wrong direction for the lost empire? When Cecil communicated his reservations to Thomas Harriot he can hardly have been reassured by the latter's rather muddled asseveration that the 'Eldorado which hath been shewed your Honour out of the Spanish booke of Acosta

[1] Keymis, *Of the second voyage*. Quotations from *Principal navigations* (1903–5), X, 500.
[2] Arber, *Transcript of registers*, 1875–94, III, 14b.

... is not ours ... that we meane ... there being three. Nether (sic) doth he say, or meane, that Amazones river and Orinoco is all one, ... as some, I feare, do averre to your Honour. ...'[1]

In an effort to prove to backers like Cecil that his Guiana project was not an unsound investment, Ralegh sent out a pinnace to the coast in late December under the command of Leonard Berry.[2] His instructions were to explore the newly discovered passages to Lake Parime. If the smallness of the survey indicates that support for Ralegh's dream of empire was rapidly dwindling, nevertheless the publicity surrounding the first two expeditions had not been without result. Guiana, 'an untraded place', represented an attractive option for English seamen who were finding their usual Caribbean hunting grounds more risky and less profitable by the late 1590s. When Berry reached the Courantyne in April 1597 he encountered 'a Bark called the *John* of London captaine Leigh being in her'.[3] John Ley, one of several lone traders who began to frequent Guiana during the last years of Elizabeth's reign concentrating on the areas pinpointed by Keymis, has the distinction of being the first Englishman known to have entered the lower Amazon.

Until recently very little was known about the extent of John Ley's activities in Guiana beyond the fact that Ralegh's men encountered him there in 1597, that he returned to the coast in the following year,[4]

---

[1] The Spanish edition of José de Acosta's *Historia natural y moral de las Indias* was published in Seville 1590. Richard Hakluyt's translation of the chapters on the Amazon and the Orinoco, 'Notes concerning Dorado and the discovery of Sir Walter Ralegh translated out of Spanish by Richard Hakluyt', c. 1596 (P.R.O., SP 12/235, f. 43) was subsequently printed as 'Certaine Briefe Testimonies Concerning the mightie river of Amazones ... together with some mention of the rich and stately empire of Dorado, called by Sir Walter Ralegh and the natural inhabitants Guiana ...' in *Principal navigations* (1600), III, 698–9 (1903–5), XI, 16–22. According to Harriot's letter to Cecil, 11/21st July 1596 (Edwards, *The life*, 1868, II, 420–2), Cecil acquired Acosta's work from one 'Wright', probably Edward Wright the navigator.

[2] Thomas Masham, 'The 3. voyage set forth by sir Walter Ralegh to Guiana with a pinnesse called The Wat, begun in the yere 1596 ...' in *Principal navigations* (1600), III, 692–8 (1903–5), XI, 1–15.

[3] Ibid., *Principal navigations* (1903–5), XI, 10.

[4] For references to Ley's second voyage to Guiana in 1598, see John Layfield, 'A large Relation of the Porto Ricco Voyage' in Samuel Purchas, *Hakluytus posthumus or Purchas his pilgrimes* (1625), IV, bk. 6, 1155–76 (Glasgow, 1905–7), XVI, 44–106. Layfield, however, confuses John Ley with 'Captain Charles Leigh', ibid., p. 49; Richard Robinson et al., 'A Journall of the Eleaventh and later Voyage to the West India 1597 ... Porto Rico 1598' in G. C. Williamson, *George, third earl of Cumberland* (Cambridge, 1920), p. 178.

and at some point left a factor in the Wiapoco. Charles Leigh, no relation, heard that the factor had died sometime before he himself arrived at the river with English colonists in 1604.[1] This very spare outline can now be fleshed out as a result of a discovery of a 'pedigree' of the Ley family.[2] The record was compiled sometime about 1608 by James Ley, a younger brother. Sir James Ley, the sixth and youngest son of Henry Ley of the manor of Teffont Evias, Wilts, had a distinguished career on the bench and in government office, culminating in his appointment as Lord High Treasurer and member of the Privy Council in 1624. He was honoured with the title of Earl of Marlborough in 1625. As one of the early members of the Elizabethan Society of Antiquaries, it was his interest in the historical record as much as his pride which prompted him to set down the history of his family.[3] He was particularly anxious to document the exploits of his sea-going brother John and 'often importuned [him] to give some remembrance of ...former tra-veiles. ...' John Ley 'in part and brieflie satisfied his request' in December 1601 during his third voyage out to Guiana.[4] During five days spent at Maio, in the Cape Verdes, Ley put together 'a breef abstract of th[ese] my jornyes for haste beinge unperfect And also I was forced to use memorie, being but little holpen by blurd and torne papers, Omytting manie thinges, which if time would have

[1] 'Captaine Charles Leigh's Letter to Sir Olave Leigh his Brother', 2nd July 1604 in *Purchas his pilgrimes* (1625), IV, bk. 6, 1255 (1905–7), XVI, 323.

[2] 'Ley his pedigree' (Wilts Record Office, 366/1). The manuscript volume was discovered by David Souden, Emmanuel College, Cambridge who very generously passed on the reference and a transcript of the Guiana material to me.

[3] The manuscript volume contains genealogical records of Sir James Ley's own family, a family history of the Ley's from the time of Edward I, biographies of his father and his brothers, details of his own life up to his appointment as attorney of the Court of Wards and Liveries in November 1608, and finally the records of his brother John's Guiana voyages. For the life of Sir James Ley (1550–1629), see T. Hearne, *A collection of curious discourses written by eminent antiquaries upon several heads in our English antiquities* (London, 1775), II, 437–8; R. Harris and Sir R. C. St Hoare, Bart, *The history of modern Wiltshire-Hundred of Westbury* (London, 1830), III, 35–6; *Burkes Extinct peerages* (London, 1866), Div. 2-Fit-Par, p. 321; W. P. S. Bingham, 'James Ley, earl of Marlborough', *The Wiltshire Archaeological and Natural History Magazine*, XXV, no. lxxiii (1891), pp. 86–99; G. D. Squibb, ed., *Wiltshire visitation pedigrees, 1623* (London, 1954), Harleian soc. CVI, 113–5; *DNB*, 1908, 1084–5. The *DNB* entry for James Ley makes no mention of his brother John.

[4] John Ley 'To his loveinge brethren WL, ML and JL or either of them delivered, Maio, 21/31st December 1601 in 'Ley his pedigree', f. 15r.

suffered, I ment not: I desiered the wrightinge soe longe That I protest I had noe time to read it over, after my man had copyed it out. ...'[1] The account of Ley's two earlier voyages, together with lists of the coastal rivers, the tribes inhabiting them and comments on 'Strange shapes and manners of men', were forwarded in a letter to his brothers from Maio. It was probably carried by one of the English ships which Ley had encountered there loading salt. As James Ley records, 'The reporte of the third voyage was not put in writinge but after his Retorne haveinge referred the setting downe thereof he was prevented by death.'[2] Ley died on the 7th of June 1604, at the age of fifty-four. His remembrances of his voyages to Guiana were included in the Ley 'pedigree' as they stood, preceded by his biography and those of his three surviving brothers, William, Matthew and James.[3]

John Ley, as the admirably succinct account in the 'pedigree' states[4]

was first a Child of the college of Winchester and afterwardes mainetained at oxford for a season, And from thence Removed to Clements Inne London, but beinge nothinge affected to studie the lawe he betooke himselfe to marshiall Courses:[5] first sailed twice with martyn Furboiser to the North partes of America,[6] Then served in the Lowe Countries, longe tyme, and became a Captaine there,[7] went into Ireland with Sir William Russell,[8] went divers times to the sea uppon Reprisals at his owne charge served at Sea with Sir martin

---

[1] 'The manners and Customes of the people', in 'Ley his pedigree', f. 19.

[2] John Ley was buried in the chancel of the church of St Andrew in the Wardrobe, London. Stow's *Survey of London* (1633 edn.), f. 407 notes in that church a 'plated stone underneath the Commuuion (sic) with the inscription "Hic jacet Ioannes Ley, Armig. de Comitatu Wiltz Qui obiit 7 die Junii, An. Dom. 1604. Ætat. suae 54" '.

[3] For the parliamentary careers of James and Matthew Ley in Elizabeth I's reign, see P. W. Hasler, ed., *History of parliament. The house of commons, 1558–1603* (London, 1981), II, 476–7.

[4] 'Ley his pedigree', f. 8v.

[5] A military career.

[6] Dionyse Settle, *A true reporte of the last voyage into the west and north-west regions* (1577) refers to a John 'Lee' in the company of the *Ayde* on Frobisher's second voyage.

[7] Elizabeth I maintained an expeditionary force in the Netherlands from 1585, but her subjects had been allowed to volunteer for the services of the Protestant rebels from the late 1560s.

[8] Sir William Russell arrived in Dublin as Lord Deputy in August 1594. He was replaced in the spring of 1597 by Thomas, Lord Burgh. See R. Dudley Edwards, *Ireland in the age of the Tudors* (London, 1977), pp. 159–63.

furboiser and the Earle of Cumberland in the Queenes Shipps, went to the Iles with the Earle, And was Captaine of the Alcedo[1] and sailed to the west Indies thrice at his owne charges sawe manie Countries and Straunge thinges as by his *lette*res, conteyeinge (sic) the discripcon of his voyages may appeare.'

Ley's three West Indies voyages were a natural evolution of a long involvement in land and sea warfare and discovery. While he would appear to have been in Ireland with Sir William Russell in the late summer of 1594, he clearly returned to England in sufficient time to study the results of the voyages of Ralegh and Keymis and to prepare his own small venture for departure by Shrove Tuesday of 1597.[2]

Following Keymis's example, Ley set a south-westerly course across the Atlantic sighting what he called the 'western cape of the River of Amazon' on the 23rd of March [O.S.].[3] In default of any latitude it is impossible to state with any precision which cape he was referring to here. In all likelihood it was the present Cabo do Norte or Raso at 1°40′ N. Although this cape is not significantly elevated from the low swampy littoral, for pilots coming out from the Amazon estuary to pursue a course north-west to the Caribbean it does represent a significant navigational hazard, an eastward bulge in the coastline extended even farther by dangerous shoals which have to be circumnavigated.[4] Ley was describing his first landfall in Guiana some years after the fact, and after a second voyage in which he had entered the Amazon and left it by rounding the treacherous 'Westerlie Cape'. In the 1630 edition of his *New world* Johannes de Laet commented that while the coast near the Amazon was low, tree-covered and devoid of any distinguishing landmarks, nevertheless 'the continent which borders this river towards the west, advances into the sea a vast cape at 2° N. of the line, which is named Cape Race by some, Cape North by others, and by our countrymen Noord Caep. From it a great shoal extends some miles

[1] John 'Leye' commanded the *John Young* of Southampton on reprisals in 1590 (P.R.O., HCA 24/59, no. 191) and John Watt's *Alcedo* in Martin Frobisher's squadron in the Azores in 1592 (*The naval tracts of Sir William Monson*, ed. M. Oppenheim (London, 1902–14), Navy Records soc., I, 281). For Ley's part in Cumberland's 1598 Puerto Rico expedition see below.

[2] The material on Amazons and other fabulous denizens of the empire of Guiana indicates that Ley was familiar with both accounts.

[3] 'The first voyage to the West Indies', in 'Ley his pedigree', f. 15v.

[4] *South American pilot*, 1945, p. 75.

into the sea; the sea breaks furiously upon it and the Cape itself, so that those who are forced to anchor there need a good cable and a good anchor.'[1]

On this occasion Ley made no attempt to enter the Amazon, running instead up the coast to the Wiapoco. There he assembled a shallop and commenced with admirable efficiency to search the lower reaches of every river up to and including the Courantyne. His exploration of the latter was made in consortship with Ralegh's men, who had preceded him up the coast from a first landfall about 2°30' N. in late February. The Courantyne proved impassable beyond the Falls, 'without exceeding Labour', and the news that there was a Spanish trading party somewhere in the vicinity made it seem prudent to leave the coast immediately. The two expeditions made directly for the Windwards and then parted company. Berry sailed for England while Ley 'went downe into the Indies' on reprisals. He returned to England on 24th August with a Spanish frigate taken off Cumaná.[2]

The return of Ralegh's men before him had passed virtually unnoticed. Their expedition had nothing to show for its efforts but more unsubstantiated tales about the river passages to Manoa. Ley, on the other hand, had made some profit. While the inadequate returns of Berry's voyage seem to have deterred Ralegh from any further investment in Guiana for the time being, Ley considered a second voyage there to be a more attractive proposition than participation in the armada being prepared by the earl of Cumberland against Puerto Rico. When the fleet sailed in March 1598 Ley accompanied it only as far as Lanzarote. There he transferred into his prize frigate, now called the *Black Ley*, and made off alone for the Cape Verdes and Guiana.[3] He reached the Amazon delta in June 1598.

It is frustrating that the first Englishman known to have entered the Amazon left so few clues as to exactly where he went. According

[1] Johannes de Laet, *Nieuwe wereldt* (Leyden, 1630), bk. 15, 561, (Latin edn., 1633), bk. 17, 631, (French edn., 1640), bk. 17, 570. The first Dutch edn., 1625, bk. 14, 462, merely describes the extent of the cape and the offshore shoal.

[2] This account of Ley's first Guiana voyage is pieced together from his record of 'The first voyage to the West Indies', in 'Ley his pedigree', ff. 15v–16r; Masham, 'The 3. voyage', *Principal navigations* (1600), III, 692–8 (1903–5), XI, 1–15; the examination of Christopher Adams of London, 2/12th September 1597 (P.R.O., HCA 1/44, f. 223).

[3] See above, p. 19, n. 4.

to his account, Ley sighted the 'Easterlie Cape' first but, finding himself amongst dangerous shoals, made out to sea again and bore west to find 'the best of the Channell'. He provided no further information to help identify his first landfall.[1] Joannes de Laet, over three decades later, applied the title, East Cape, to a promontory lying at 50'S. on the shoaled and indented coastline at the right-hand of the estuary of the Pará. If Ley did make his first sighting south of the line a west-north-westerly run could have carried him to the islands in the Canal do Norte off the west bank of the Amazon estuary. De Laet was told by 'those of our countrymen who have frequented this river to trade there for many years ... that one cannot enter it more easily and with less danger than by passing the coast of N. Brazil and Marannon and from there finding the latitude of one and one half degrees north then running west, in order to avoid more easily the great current of the river'.[2] Ley had with him an expert Indian pilot from the river Cawo, whose navigational skills amazed him. 'My Indian after such time the starrs appeare in the night can point directlie to anie countrie that ever he hath travelled be yt maine or Iland with such assurance that he hath caused us to admire oftentimes And were yt not that nowe of late I made experience thereof I would hardlie believe yt.'[3] Under his guidance Ley very probably found his way into the Canal do Norte. The likelihood of this is strengthened by his references to the 'Arowa who dwell uppon both sides of the great River of Amasono and in a greate Iland and two little Ilandes. ... In the Ilands of Crowacurri, warracayew, and Attowa they also dwell in a river called Wayapowpa which falleth into Amazona. ...'[4] English and Dutch records, dating from 1613 on, agree in placing the island settlement of the 'Auroras', 'Arrowas' or 'Arouen' S.S.W. of the mouth of what is now the Canal do Gurijuba and the island of Curua, its north-western tip estimated to lie between 40' and 28' N.[5] It seems reasonable to assume that the

[1] See below, p. 132.

[2] Laet (1633), bk. 17, 630, (1640), bk. 17, 569–70. See below, p. 27, n. 1.

[3] 'The Indians observacon of the stars' in 'Ley his pedigree', f. 18v.

[4] See below, p. 136.

[5] See the Guiana chart drawn by Gabriel Tatton, 1615, fig. 1; 'Journal of the voyage made by the heads of families sent by the Honorable the Directors of the West India Company to visit the coast of Guiana' (B.L., MS Sloane 179B), extracted below, pp. 258–63; Laet (1625), bk. 14, 462, (1630), bk. 15, 561, (1633), bk. 17, 631, (1640), bk. 17, 570, and the chart of the lower Amazon by Hessel Gerritsz included in Laet's work.

present island of Caviana is meant here. The Arua appear to have occupied the islands of Mexiana, Caviana and Marajó at the turn of the seventeenth century.[1] If Ley did sail upriver by the north channel for more than eighty leagues or two hundred and eighty statute miles he may have reached the confluence of the Xingu and the Canal do Gurupá.

Ley spent about a month in the river, setting off upstream sometime in the first week of June and returning to his first anchorage near Fishers island on the 4th of July. The Indians he encountered were far less welcoming than those contacted on the coast a year earlier. While some were quite willing to trade, others were ready to set upon the English if they could catch them unawares, separated from their fellows and the terrifying guns of the ship. The 'Taparawarur' Ley mentions were clearly Tupinamba, recognizable by the green jadeite lip plugs customarily worn by the warriors.[2] Although it is difficult to distinguish the tribes Ley personally encountered on the detailed descriptive lists supplied by his Iao guide and others, he does appear to have had direct contact with the Tupinamba, trading for victuals and the 'green stones which we call spleene stones' with them before he began his run upriver.[3] Amongst the Arua, and elsewhere, Ley saw long-house dwellings elevated on piles above the periodically inundated varzea. Ley could add little to Ralegh's original account of the Amazons, but his inquiries about them, as well as his visits to Indian settlements in the river, show him to have been an indefatigable explorer with an energy which Keymis and Berry would have done well to emulate.

After leaving the Amazon, Ley directed his course to Caux and the rivers visited 'the yere before'. From thence he made his way to England via the West Indies. There is no evidence to indicate whether he returned to the Amazon in 1602. The fact that he left a servant on the Wiapoco on that voyage would suggest that the latter river, well to the south of the Spanish settlements, in the territory of

---

[1] See C. Nimuendaju, 'The Arua', in *Handbook of South American Indians* (1948), ed. J. H. Steward, III, 195–8 (henceforth referred to as *HSAI*); B. J. Meggers and C. Evans, *Archaeological investigations at the mouth of the Amazon* (Washington, 1957), Bureau of American Ethnology, Bull. 167; Meggers and Evans, 'An interpretation of the cultures of Marajó island', in *Peoples and cultures of native South America* (New York, 1973), ed. D. R. Gross, pp. 39–47.

[2] See below, p. 135, n. 2.

[3] See below, p. 133, n. 3.

friendly Indians and offering a passage to El Dorado, had become the major focus of his interest.

English Guiana projectors in the next decade shared Ley's assessment of the superior attractions of the Wiapoco. The first efforts to settle the coast in the early 1600s were directed to that river. Charles Leigh's colony, established there in May 1604, lasted for two years. Nevertheless the surveys of Keymis, Berry and Ley had established Cabo do Norte and the west bank and islands of the north channel as the first and regular port of call for traders on the coast. Charles Leigh on his voyage out in 1604, possibly following the route set on his first visit to the coast two years earlier, made for the Amazon from the Cape Verdes.[1] It is clear from Leigh's account that the Indians inhabiting the islands near the mouth of the river were becoming used to regular barter with Europeans although understandably loth to be carried off as guides. Leigh was either preceded or followed into the river in 1604 by Captain John Leggat of Plymouth. Another Plymouth man, one Johnston, may have called there in 1605, before going on to the Wiapoco and Cayenne. In 1606 Legatt tried to return to the Amazon, but fell to the windward of the estuary either because of the incompetence or deliberate duplicity of his master.[2] The growing familiarity of English seamen with the rivers of the littoral made their expertise valuable to foreign merchants infected by their interest in the region.

The seafaring community of the United Provinces had taken a strong interest in Ralegh's Guiana ventures since his voyage to the Orinoco in 1595. Although the Dutch version of *The discoverie* did not appear until 1598 Hollanders and Zeelanders had followed Ralegh into the Orinoco at least two years earlier.[3] They entered the Amazon for the first time in 1598. According to Laet, an Amsterdam merchant ran up the coast from Northern Brazil to 'the cape of the great river in that year' with the intention of surveying it. Suddenly finding his vessel amongst dangerous shoals and

[1] See below, p. 137. On Leigh's earlier voyage, see also John Nicholl, *An houre glasse of Indian newes* (1607).

[2] See below, pp. 138–9.

[3] Five Flemings were captured in the Orinoco delta in the summer of 1596, crew members of a ship sent out to traffick at Trinidad and the pearl fisheries. This is the earliest extant reference to Dutch presence in the river. Domingo de Vera Ybarguen to Philip II, 27th October 1597 (B.L., Add. MS 36317, ff. 135 et seqq.).

sandbanks, he sent off a pinnace to explore the mainland and the mouth of a large river. The company of the pinnace reconnoitred a low cape, finding all the land to the rear of it flat, impenetrable mangrove swamp. Sailing further on they discovered another river descending into the main river from the east. Entering the tributary they found themselves amongst a maze of backwaters, few of which were navigable. They named the tributary after the remarkable number of herons which they saw there and went on to visit one or two of the islands to the west of it 'which divided the wide estuary of the great river of Amazones into several branches'. Indians informed them that the part of the continent they had visited was named Marapam. De Laet was convinced that Heron river was 'the same on which the Portuguese built the fort of Para some years afterwards'.[1] At least six Dutch ships reconnoitred the Guiana coast in 1598, certainly from as far south as the Cayenne but possibly from the mouth of the Amazon.[2] Although there is no evidence to support the contention that Zeelanders built two forts on the Xingu before 1600,[3] the Indian settlements in the lower reaches of the Canal do Norte quickly became the first link in the Dutch trading network along the 'Wild Coast'. When Leigh arrived at the Wiapoco in 1604 he found the company of the *Hope* of Amsterdam, with an Englishman John Sims serving as master's mate, trading with the Indians for flax. Another Dutch ship entered shortly afterwards. In all likelihood both had previously been in the Amazon. Certainly Sims entered the Amazon when he returned to the coast as master of the *Hope* late in 1605. Leigh's dwindling colonists were mystified

[1] Laet (1625), bk. 14, 460–1, (1630), bk. 15, 460–1, (1633), bk. 17, 634, (1640), bk. 17, 574.

[2] 'Account of a Journey to Guiana and the Island of Trinidad, performed in the years 1597 and 1598 submitted to the States-General by . . . Adrian Cabeliau, 3 Feb. 1599', printed in *British Guiana boundary arbitration with the United States of Venezuela. The case on behalf of . . . Her Britannic Majesty* (London, 1898), App. I, no. 8, 18–22.

[3] G. Edmundson, 'The Dutch on the Amazon and Negro in the seventeenth century', *EHR*, XVIII (1903), 642–3, appears to have been the first to assert that Dutch forts were established on the Xingu *c.* 1598. His contention was based on too literal a reading of Laet (1633), bk. 17, 634. Laet's comments on the Xingu forts directly followed his account of Dutch exploration of the lower Pará in 1598. Edmundson therefore assumed that Laet meant that the Xingu forts were set up about the same time. In fact Laet prefaces his references to them by the statement 'others in succeeding years have undertaken to examine this mighty river . . .', clearly intended to be a general introduction to Dutch efforts in the next two decades.

by the Indian communication system which enabled the Iaos and Sapayos of the Wiapoco to inform them in early November 'of three ships which were in the River of Amasons, and that one of them would come unto us . . . some two moneths after'. Sims duly arrived on 20th December 1605.[1]

English pilots also entered the service of the French. The settlers left behind by Riffault on the Maranhão survived for fifteen years before receiving any official support from the French crown.[2] In all likelihood small trading parties from the colony, as well as French merchant vessels, explored the Amazon estuary in the early 1600s. Le Père Georges Fournier, S.J., in his *Hydrographie*, published in Paris in 1643, maintained that the Dieppois 'depuis 50 ans vont aussi fort souvent au Cap du Nord de l'Amérique, & autres lieux circonvoisins, scauoir depuis la ligne iusques a 5 ou 6 dégrez de latitude Septentrionale'.[3] In an attempt to assert French primacy in the area Henry IV, in 1602, appointed 'Reney Marée, Lo: of Montbarrott, . . .Lieftenant generall representing our persone in the countries & kingdomes of the Guiana . . .' extending from 'the river of the Amazones untill the Ilande of the Trinitie'. Daniel de la Touche, Sieur de la Ravardière, Montbarrott's associate, made a survey of the coast in that year or earlier.[4] A return expedition there, in 1604, took him via the Canaries, West Africa and the Cape Verdes to the mouth of the Amazon. Arriving on Palm Sunday, just as the Amazon was building towards its crest at the end of the rainy season, they were debarred from entry by the 'great streams there about the sea-side, which run with strange swiftness and horrible noise, carrying along with them Trees and Plants, which they pluck up by the Roots along the Coast'. An Indian war party encountered off the estuary provided guides to the Wiapoco. Ravardière already had in his company, however, an English pilot, five or six English

---

[1] Charles Leigh to Olave Leigh, 2nd July 1604 in *Purchas his pilgrimes* (1625), IV, bk. 6, 1254, (1905–7), XVI, 320; 'The Relation of Master John Wilson of Wansteed in Essex, one of the last ten that returned into England from Wiapoco in Guiana 1606', in ibid., (1625), IV, bk. 6, 1260–5, (1905–7), XVI, 338–51.

[2] See above, p. 15, n. 1.

[3] P. Georges Fournier, S.J., *Hydrographie contenant la theorie et la practique de toutes les parties de la navigation* (Paris, 1643), bk. 4, 221.

[4] 'The Coppie of a letters patents given by king Henrie the 4th of France, for the planting of Guiana, in ano 1602' (B.L., MS Sloane 173, ff. 2–3); Letters Patent granted to Daniel de La Touche, Sieur de la Ravardière by Henri IV, 3rd July 1605 (ibid., f. 4).

crewmen and an Indian, a native of Trinidad, who had been taken to England by Ralegh.[1]

The passing interest of the Grand Duke of Tuscany in the Amazon was also stimulated by English adventurers. The involvement of John Dudley, duke of Northumberland, in the earliest English project to explore the river may be questionable. Some sixty years later, however, his grandson, Robert Dudley, promoted an expedition there on behalf of the Medici of Florence. In September 1608 Ferdinand I despatched three ships to reconnoitre the Amazon and the Guiana coast. The commander of this small fleet was one Robert Thornton in association with an unnamed Dutchman.[2] A good proportion of the mariners were also English, men who had either entered the duke's service voluntarily or been captured by his warfleet and enslaved in the gallies. For William Davies of London, the barber–surgeon who published the fullest account of the venture in 1614, the prospect of a voyage to the New World was better than continued labour as a galley slave.[3] The inspiration, the charts and the detailed instructions for the enterprise came from Robert Dudley.[4] The information brought back by Thornton was recorded by Dudley on a manuscript map. A brief account of Thornton's voyage serves as an explanatory note for the engraved version of this manuscript chart, printed in vol. III of Dudley's great work the *Arcano del Mare*, published in 1647.[5]

Dudley, the illegitimate son of the earl of Leicester by Douglas Sheffield, had, in his own words, 'since I could conceive of anything

---

[1] Nathaniel Pullen, *Travels and voyages into Africa, Asia, and America. ... Performed by Mr John Mocquet keeper of the cabinet of rarities, to the king of France, in the Thuileries* (London, 1696), trans. from French edn. 1616, pp. 48–9, 68, 80, 124.

[2] See below, pp. 140–1, and Stephen Le Sieur to Robert Cecil, earl of Salisbury, 16/26th August 1608 (P.R.O., SP 98/2, pt. II, f. 207).

[3] See below, pp. 140–1.

[4] See below, p. 147.

[5] See fig. X. The manuscript chart is included amongst a series illustrating the Guiana coastline and the estuary of the Amazon now in the Bayerische Staatsbibliothek, Munich, Icon. 139, f. 52v. A manuscript note indicates that it was drawn after Thornton's return. The Guiana charts amongst which it is found were compiled by Dudley *c*. 1636 in preparation for his sea atlas *Dell'Arcano del Mare* (Florence, 1646–7), 3 vols. The engraved version of the 'Thornton' chart constitutes no. XIV in the America series in vol. III, published in 1647. See S. Tyacke, 'English charting of the river Amazon c. 1595–c. 1630', *Imago Mundi*, XXXII (1980), 75, 78, n. 24.

bene delighted with the discoveries of navigation'.[1] The passion had been fostered by his tutor, Thomas Chaloner, and his uncle the Lord High Admiral, Charles Howard, baron of Effingham and earl of Nottingham. Dudley's first marriage to Margaret Cavendish took him further into maritime circles linking him both to Thomas Cavendish and Richard Hakluyt. In the 1590s Dudley invested in voyages to the Far East, thwarted by the queen from going there himself, and, led an expedition to Trinidad and the Orinoco delta in early 1595. He pursued studies in shipbuilding and the art of navigation, writing a volume on the latter subject in 1598. Although he himself never returned to Guiana, he doubtless kept close contact with those who had followed him to the coast, like Keymis, Berry and Ley. The contents of the *Arcano* are a witness to his habit of collecting charts and portolanos and other tidbits of information among the seafaring community.[2]

Dudley left England for the Continent in 1605, enraged and humiliated by the failure of his attempt to prove his legitimacy and title to the earldom of Leicester. He deserted his second wife and five daughters, absconding with his half-cousin, Elizabeth Southwell. Once in France Dudley turned catholic and secured a papal dispensation to set aside his second marriage. In 1606 the couple sought the protection of the Grand Duke of Tuscany. Ferdinand I, engaged in war against the Turks and Barbary corsairs and concerned to build up his navy, was predisposed to receive anyone with expertise in shipbuilding and navigation. Dudley arrived at court in early 1607 and quickly established himself in the shipyards of Leghorn. His new patron encouraged him to retain his contacts with the English seafaring community and to invite them to enter the service of Tuscany to build and man the Duke's new warships. Sir Henry Wotton complained, 'The Grand Duke continues to entice English mariners and shipwrights into his service, has brought ordnance from English ships, and taken English Pirates under his protection. The Tuscan fleet consists principally of

---

[1] 'The voyage of sir Robert Duddely to the yle of Trinidad and the coast of Paria ... Anno 1594, & 1595', in *Principal navigations* (1600), III, 574, (1903–5), X, 203–12.

[2] The above and following biographical details are based on the most recent biography by A. G. Lee, *The son of Leicester: The story of Sir Robert Dudley* (London, 1964). Dudley's first wife, Margaret Cavendish, was a cousin of Thomas Cavendish the circumnavigator and sister of Douglas Cavendish, the wife of Richard Hakluyt.

English sailors. There are two English slaves serving in the Tuscan galleys whom the Duke refuses to release. Also he protects Sir Robert Dudley and captain Eliot and other English exiles and traitors.'[1] Robert Thornton fell into the latter category. The London merchant, Richard Cockayne, swore before the High Court of Admiralty in 1605 and 1606 that he had sent Thornton to the Mediterranean in late 1604 as master of his ship the *Royall Merchant*. The vessel had been leased for the use of one Sebastian Nicholano Demense of Ragusa. Thornton and Demense had fallen out. The master had absconded with the ship and entered Ferdinand de Medici's service.[2]

The expedition to Guiana seems to have been Dudley's idea. An English envoy at Florence informed the Earl of Salisbury in August 1608 that the Grand Duke had been 'first theirunto incouraged by Sir Robert Dudley, who hoped to have ben an aduenturer in it (not with his owne person) with a Pinace of his owne, named the Beare & ragged staffe . . .'. The objective, he reported, corroborated by William Davies' account, was 'to seeke gold', the chief focus, the 'River of the Amazones'.[3] Dudley's own commentary on Thornton's activities indicates that the latter's mandate was to discover the mines of El Dorado or at least a sure route thereto, and to prospect a site for a defensive garrison to hold off interlopers. The special directive to the river Amazon suggests that Dudley had particularly hoped that its north channel, now a frequent resort of European shipping, would provide a passage to either Manoa or the kingdom of the Amazons.[4]

When Thornton set sail for the Amazon in September 1608 he took with him charts and instructions prepared by Dudley. One chart in particular included a depiction of the north channel of the Amazon with warnings about the dangers of the spring tides. The original map for the Amazon and the Guiana coast which Dudley

[1] Quoted in Lee, 1964, p. 136. See also 'The names of such english ships as the Duke of Florence hath presente for his service with a note of others that hee hath dispoyled this Realme of', *c*. 1608 (P.R.O., SP 98/2, pt. I, f. 122).
[2] Protestatio Cokan, 8/18th April 1605, 13/23rd February 1606 (P.R.O., HCA 30/857). A Robert Thornton sailed with Cumberland's Puerto Rico expedition in 1598, but there is no evidence that this was the same man, see G. C. Williamson, *Cumberland*, 1920, pp. 174, 175, 178.
[3] Le Sieur to Salisbury, 16/26th August, 20/30th August 1608 (P.R.O., SP 98/2, pt. II, ff. 207, 211-2).
[4] See below, p. 147.

supplied does not appear to have survived. The surviving manuscript chart, drawn up on the basis of Thornton's survey, constitutes
a revised version of the original map Dudley had provided. This
assumption is strengthened by an analysis of the map itself. It
depicts the Guiana coast from the Maroni or Marrawini to the west
bank of the Amazon, tracing the north channel of the latter as far as
the Equator. A close study of the order and nomenclature of the
rivers on the Atlantic coast and of the names of the tribes or nations
said to reside on or near them indicates that the map was originally
based on the 'Table of the names of the Rivers, Nations, Townes,
and Casiques or Captaines' compiled by Laurence Keymis in 1596.
Keymis's most southerly landfall on the coast had been 'the mouth
of the Arrowari, a faire and great river. It standeth in one degree
and fourtie minutes. . . . The barre without hath at the least three
fathome. . . .' The *R. Arrowari* is drawn at exactly 1°40' N. on
Dudley's map with a sounding of three fathom at its entrance. The
northernmost cape of the estuary, at 2°5' N. is named *C. di Vincent
Pincon* on Dudley's map. Once again he appears to have adopted
this from Keymis, who had noted in his 'Table', 'Here it was it
seemeth, that Vincent Pinzon the Spaniard had his Emeralds.' The
west bank of the Amazon is shown trending due south to a *C. de R.
Amazones* at 1° N. This distinction between *C. di Vincent Pincon*,
which appears to be Cabo do Norte, and *C. de R. Amazones*, may
again reflect Dudley's original cartographical interpretation of
Keymis's note that 'When wee first fell with land, wee were, by the
Indians report, but 1. dayes journey from the greatest river, that is
on that coast'.[1]

---

[1] See 'A table of the names of the Rivers, Nations, Townes, and Caciques or
Captaines, which were discovered in the voyage of M. Laurence Keymis before
mentioned', in *Principal navigations* (1600), III, 687, (1903–5), X, 203–12. The
following comparative lists of the rivers between the Arowari and the Cayenne
and the 'nations' inhabiting on or near them demonstrates the dependance of
Dudley's map on Keymis's table.

KEYMIS'S TABLE		DUDLEY'S MAP	
R. Arowari	Arwaos	Arrowari	Arwaos
	Pararweas	to	
	Charibes		Iaos
Iwaripoco	Mapurwanas	Iwaripoca	Mapurwanas
	Iaos		
Maipuri	Arricari	Maipari	Arricarri
		to	
		Connawini	Arricurri
		to	Marowpans
			Caribes

Keymis, however, had not entered the Amazon. If the original chart given to Thornton contained a warning about the tidal bore which occurs at the spring tides,[1] this information could only have been obtained from some of the other northern Europeans who had entered the river in the decade after 1596. The representation of the north channel on Dudley's surviving manuscript chart is at the best crude. Clearly Thornton neither took out nor brought back a detailed survey. The west bank of the river is shown trending due south to the *C. de R. Amazones* at 1° N. and then S.S.W. to the Equator. No tributaries are indicated. The shoreline north of *C. de R. Amazones* is marked as *Terra Bassa*.[2] Notations about the danger of the tide are appended at 1°30′ N. and 10′ N. Soundings for the channel are given to approximately 10′ N. also. What appear to be circular stockades, probably intended to indicate Indian settlements, are clustered between *C. di Vincent Pincon* and the *Arrowari*, with two others further upstream at 1°15′ N. and 50′ N. respectively. The east cape of the Amazon, named *C. Bianca*, is drawn at approximately 20° N. and 344°10′ of longitude, occupying the extreme right-hand bottom corner of the map. Three islands lie between the west bank and the eastern cape, drawn in parallel sequence N.N.E./S.S.W. across the Equator. The centre one of the three is marked by a circular stockade and the words *Isola dell Amazonas*.[3] Just how much of this information was provided by Thornton, as opposed to those who preceded him into the river, is not ascertainable. Assuming that the area of the west bank shown

Caipurogh	Arricurri	Caipurogh	Coonorachi
Arcooa	Marowanas	Arcooa	Waecacoi
	Caribes	to	Wariseachi
Waipoco	Coonoracki	Wyapogo	Caribes
	Wacacoia		
	Wariseaco	to	
Wanari	Charibes	Wanari	Iaos
		to	Mauori
Capurwacka	Charibes	Capurwaca	Caribes
Cawo	Iaos	Cawo	
Wia	Maworia		
	Charib	to	Wyachs
	Wiaco Ch.		Mavoria
Caiane	Wiaco Ch.	Chiana	

[1] See below, p. 148.
[2] See William Davies' comment below, p. 142.
[3] See below, p. 145, n. 6.

was coterminous with his explorations, then he would appear to have penetrated upriver as far as the maze of islands off Macapá.

Thornton was directed to look for gold, a mandate which, given the terrain, could more easily be fulfilled by inquiry among the Indians than actual prospecting. The expedition clearly spent the ten weeks coasting the west bank bartering at the Indian villages and fishing camps. It was the sight of Indian women fishing on one of the islands which convinced Davies and others that they had seen some of the Amazons. That glimpse kept alive a flicker of hope that the river might yet give access to a rich civilization, although barter had brought 'neither Gold nor Silver Oare, but great store of Hennes'.[1] Like Keymis, Berry and Ley before him, Thornton found more promising signs of mineral wealth further up the Guiana coast. In Cayenne the Caribs, now perfectly familiar with the interests of European visitors, obligingly repeated the old tales about the proximity of Manoa. These, together with their claims to know the whereabouts of a rich silver mine in the hills near the river mouth, established the river as an eminently suitable site for a colony.

However optimistic his projections for the future, Thornton returned to Leghorn in June 1609 with 'little gaine, or benefit for the Duke, for there was nothing to be gained'.[2] Ferdinand I had died in the previous February. The lack of profit, as well as the preoccupations of his own succession probably deterred Duke Cosimo from any further involvement in Guiana schemes. Although RobertDudley remained in high favour at the Medici court he does not seem to have used his influence to promote any more such expeditions from Tuscany. It is possible, however, that he played some part in stimulating a resurgence of English interest in Guiana from which was to come the first settlements in the lower Amazon.

[1] See below, p. 144. [2] See below, p. 142.

THE FIRST ENGLISH AND IRISH SETTLEMENTS ON THE AMAZON, 1611–20

Although he had found both employment and honour in Tuscany, Dudley had not yet abandoned hopes of re-establishing himself in England. The news that his estate of Kenilworth was about to be disposed of prompted him to seek what appeared to be the surest route to a royal pardon, the patronage of Prince Henry. The presence of his former tutor, Sir Thomas Chaloner, in the latter's household gave him access. In the next two and half years, through Chaloner's good offices, Dudley secured the prince's interest and support, working discreetly behind the scenes to persuade him of the advantages of a marriage alliance with Tuscany, and selling him Kenilworth at a unconscionably low price.[1] There is little doubt that it was Dudley's expertise in navigation and shipbuilding and his interest in the New World which most recommended him to the prince. Reports of his planned Guiana voyage had reached England before Thornton ever set sail.[2] It is just as likely that Dudley passed on to Prince Henry an account of Thornton's achievements after his return. This would certainly explain why an extensive survey of the lower Amazon was included in a new Guiana expedition being promoted by the prince and Sir Walter Ralegh. Although Ralegh had always maintained that the Amazon might provide an alternative route to Manoa, subsequent explorations had concentrated on the Wiapoco and the rivers to the north as offering easier entry.

[1] See above p. 30. Chaloner had a strong interest in mathematics, natural science and maritime affairs. He had travelled widely in Europe, particularly in Italy. His influence with Prince Henry increased after the latter was invested as Prince of Wales in May 1610, when he was appointed as Lord Chamberlain of the household. See Lee, 1964, pp. 143–59; R. Strong, 'England and Italy; the marriage of Henry Prince of Wales', in *For Veronica Wedgwood These* (London, 1986), ed. R. Ollard and P. Tudor-Craig, pp. 59–87.

[2] See above p. 33, n. 3.

Dudley's men had similarly been more impressed with the prospects of the Cayenne. They did, nevertheless, believe that they had sighted Amazon women. This would have been enough to have reminded Ralegh that the riches of the reputed empire of warrior women were yet to be found somewhere near the mouth of the Amazon.

For Ralegh, his friendship with Prince Henry offered not only a possibility of winning release from the Tower, but also the opportunity to instruct the future king on the need for war with Spain. As the years of his imprisonment lengthened, Guiana seemed to be the key to both his own and his country's fortunes. Its wealth, either from El Dorado or the gold mines he had discovered on the lower Orinoco, could fund the destruction of Spanish power both in the New World and the Old. Although James I was outwardly opposed to all such anti-Spanish schemes, the prospect of Guiana gold to cure his chronic insolvency would surely tempt him to approve efforts to discover it. The Privy Council seriously considered Ralegh's plans to reconnoitre the Orinoco mines in 1607, but dropped the matter when Newport returned with ore samples from Virginia. Despite his disappointment, Ralegh despatched the company of the *Primrose* of London to Guiana in 1608 to renew his contacts with the Indians along the coast and to join the other English merchants trafficking for tobacco at the Spanish settlements on the lower Orinoco and Trinidad. Ralegh was clearly still hovering between the alternatives of a search for El Dorado by the rivers to the south and an attempt to locate and open the mines on the Orinoco. Sir Thomas Roe's expedition to Guiana, 1610–11, was intended to test both these options.[1]

---

[1] J. W. Williamson, *The myth of the conqueror. Prince Henry Stuart: A study of 17th century personation* (New York, 1978) is the best study of Prince Henry's growing significance as a focus for those who opposed his father's policy towards Spain, of his friendship with Ralegh and their shared interest in New World ventures; see also Strong, 'England and Italy', 1986, pp. 59–87. For Ralegh's negotiations about his Orinoco gold mine, 1607–12, see J. Lorimer, 'The location of Ralegh's Guiana gold mine', *Terrae Incognitae*, XIV (1982), 77–95. The Spanish ambassador, Pedro de Zuñiga, reported to Philip III on the impending departure of two small vessels for Guiana in letters of 3rd December 1609 and 28th January 1610. They were, he wrote, interested in the 'Gold and Silver ... found there' and 'it is thought that they will take Watawales [Walter Ralegh] out of the Tower that he may go there'; John Chamberlain informed Dudley Carleton that Roe was off to Guiana 'to seeke his fortune' in a letter of 30th December 1609/9th January 1610 (P.R.O., SP 14/50, no. 92).

Roe's willingness to undertake the task came partly from his 'desire to serve the Prince'.[1] He, unlike Ralegh, had passed unscathed from the household of Elizabeth I into the court of her successor and had cemented his connection to the royal family by establishing a close friendship with the Princess Elizabeth and Prince Henry. He had, like all the prince's confidantes, a genuine interest in overseas enterprises, and was already involved in Virginia and New England ventures. Roe's personal abilities were to be proven by a long and distinguished diplomatic career.[2] His commitment to the Guiana survey would have been a reassurance to the earl of Salisbury who had been induced to give a cautious approval to the project. Irked by the increasingly aggressive posture of Spain, Salisbury had begun to consider a closer alliance with France in 1609 and wished to know whether Guiana was rich enough to warrant and finance armed intervention in the Spanish Indies. But the gains had to be guaranteed if James I was to be persuaded to abandon his overtly pacifist stance. Roe's men would have to find gold before the king would excuse any conflict with the Spaniards. Otherwise they ran a very real risk of being prosecuted for piracy on their return.[3]

Hedged about by Salisbury's warnings Roe sailed for Guiana in

---

[1] See below p. 155.

[2] For details of Roe's life and career, see the relevant entry in *DNB* (1909), pp. 89–93; A. P. Wire, 'An Essex worthy: Sir Thomas Roe', *Essex Review*, XX (1911); M. J. Brown, *The life of Sir Thomas Roe: 1580–1644* (Ann Arbor, Michigan, 1964); W. Foster, ed., *The embassy of Sir Thomas Roe to the court of the great Mogul, 1615–19* (London, 1899); J. MacLean, ed., *Letters from George Lord Carew to Sir Thomas Roe, ambassador to the court of the great Mogul, 1615–17* (London, 1860); S. R. Gardiner, ed., *Letters relating to the mission of Sir Thomas Roe to Gustavus Adolphus, 1629–30* (Westminster, 1875); R. B. Mowat, 'The mission of Sir Thomas Roe to Vienna, 1641–2', *EHR*, XXV (1910), 642–63. Roe was included with Sir Thomas Chaloner in the extended Council of the Virginia Company in 1607 and invested in New England ventures in 1609.

[3] For the impact of James I's peace with Spain and his pursuit of an Anglo-Spanish marriage alliance upon English ventures in the Spanish Indies and Guiana in particular, see K. R. Andrews, 'Caribbean rivalry and the Anglo-Spanish peace of 1604', *History*, LIX (1974), 1–17; J. Lorimer, 'English trade and exploration', 1973, pp. 337–89; D. B. Quinn, 'James I and the beginnings of empire in America', *Journal of Imperial and Commonwealth History*, II (1974), 135–52. On the diplomatic relations between England and Spain 1604–10, see J. R. Jones, *Britain and Europe in the seventeenth century* (London, 1966), pp. 14–20; C. H. Carter, *The secret diplomacy of the Habsburgs, 1598–1625* (New York, 1964), pp. 47–60; G. D. Howat, *Stuart and Cromwellian foreign policy* (London, 1974), pp. 13–24.

late February 1610. Ralegh, the earl of Southampton, Sir Stephen Powle and 'Sir Thomas Roe himsealfe with his parteners' subsidized the voyage.¹ While there is no record of who Roe's partners were, in all probability Sir Thomas Chalonor had some capital invested, and Roe is likely to have solicited funds from his influential Berkeley relations in Gloucestershire, and from his wealthy kinsmen in the London merchant community.² It is possible that one of the two ships which Roe took out to the coast was the same *Lyons Clawe* of London which carried Matthew Morton to the Amazon for him in 1614, and that the London grocers who refitted her in 1609 to set her forth 'on a merchants voyage to the West Indies' did so in association with Roe.³

Edmund Howes' chronicle tells us little of Roe's activities on the

---

¹ See below p. 152, n. 1.

² Roe's father, Robert Roe of Low Leyton, Essex, was the fourth son of Sir Thomas Roe, Merchant Taylor, elected Lord Mayor of London 1568. Through his grandmother, Roe was connected to the descendants of Sir John Gresham. Roe's paternal uncles, William and Henry, served as Lord Mayor of London in 1590 and 1607 respectively. After the death of his father Roe's mother, Elinor, married a Berkeley of Rendcomb, Gloucs, kin to Lord Berkeley. Michael Strachan, C.B.E., F.R.S.E., currently completing a new biography of Roe informs me that his researches in the Close Rolls indicate that Roe was selling off land 1609–10, probably to raise funds for the Guiana expedition.

³ The *Lyons Clawe* was refitted before June 1609 and subsequently set forth 'on a merchants voyage to the West Indies', returning to the Thames by August 1611. Roe returned to the Isle of Wight in the previous month. The members of her charter party, Emanuell Exall, John Rizelye, William Stannarde, John Wightman, Peter Sohier and Robert Smith disputed with Thomas Knight, Oliver Havers and Francis Brace the 'jointe adventurers and principall dealers' over the disposition of '4000 wt of tobaccoe'. The size of the cargo indicates that it had almost certainly been acquired from the Spanish settlements on the Orinoco and Trinidad during the previous October to March trading season. Francis Brace had ventured to Guiana before, a survivor of the disastrous voyage of the *Oliph Blossom*, bound out for Leigh's Wiapoco colony in 1605. He was still in the *Lyons Clawe* in 1612 and 1613 and was one of those sued by the Spanish ambassador in the High Court of Admiralty for taking a Portuguese prize en route from Brazil. The goods were arrested when the ship's company brought them into Portsmouth in January 1614. The vessel had been set to sea by John Davis who had dispatched the *Archangell* to the Wiapoco in 1613. There is no proof that Brace remained in the *Lyons Clawe* when she set out from Portsmouth for the Amazon in late June 1614, but the evidence does suggest that he and those with whom he associated had a sustained interest in tobacco and the possibilities of trade on the Guiana coast. For the series of cases concerning the *Lyons Clawe* 1609–14, see P.R.O., HCA 13/41, ff. 240, 255–6, 267; 24/73 Pt. II, nos. 69, 312A; 24/74, no. 35; 24/75, nos. 70A, 187; 24/76, nos. 46, 112, 114. On Francis Brace's 1605 voyage to Guiana, see Nicholl, *An houre glasse*, 1607. For the voyage of the *Archangell*, P.R.O., HCA 24/76, nos. 30, 42, 45, 101.

Amazon beyond the fact that he penetrated some three hundred miles upriver, making contact with the Indians and investigating the terrain along its margins.[1] It is not unreasonable to assume that he made for Cabo do Norte and sailed through the narrow shoaled passage between the north bank and the islands of Bailique, Jaburú and Curuá into the north channel. Certainly this was the route used by the men whom he sent out to the river subsequently.[2] On leaving the Amazon he 'thence came along the coast into divers Rivers, and entred the Country by Indian Boates and went over the Chatoracts and hills passed over thirty two falles in the River of Wia Poco'.[3]

In the Wiapoco Roe would have encountered the English settlers carried out by Robert Harcourt in May 1609. Harcourt, a catholic gentleman from Oxfordshire, seems to have financed his colony largely from family resources, drawing upon his brother Michael, his cousins Thomas Harcourt, Edward and Unton Fisher and two friends Edward Gifford and Edward Harvey. His venture had the patronage of Prince Henry and some grudging assistance from Ralegh. In 1610 Roe would have found some twenty men there under the charge of Michael Harcourt and his assistants, Edward Harvey and Edward Gifford. The settlers were busily engaged in developing plantations and exploring the interior and coastal rivers.[4] Sometime before they returned to England in 1612, Michael Harcourt and Edward Harvey coasted southwards, rounded Cabo do Norte and travelled some one hundred and fifty miles up the Arrowari.[5] Whether they did so on their own initiative or in response to conversations with Sir Thomas Roe is not clear. Although Robert Harcourt was to declare in 1613 that he had from the first intended 'to make a perfect discovery of the famous river of *Amazones*, and of her severall branches', he made the claim at a time when he was seeking a monopoly of development of the Guiana coast against growing competition.[6]

[1] See below p. 152.
[2] As demonstrated by the Guiana and Amazon charts drawn by Gabriell Tatton, c. 1613 and 1615, see fig. VI. This is also the route described by Manoel de Sousa d'Eça in 1615, see below pp. 165–7.
[3] See below p. 152.
[4] For the history of the first four years of Harcourt's colony, see Robert Harcourt, *A relation of a voyage to Guiana* (1613), ed. C. A. Harris (London, 1928). [Henceforth distinguished as Harcourt, *Relation*, 1613, and Harris, *Relation*, 1928.]
[5] See below pp. 160–2.
[6] Harcourt, *Relation*, 1613, p. 5; Harris, *Relation*, 1928, p. 70.

Roe found 'nothing new nor strange' in any of the rivers south of the Orinoco to warrant any continued belief in El Dorado. Dissident Spaniards contacted at Port of Spain did confirm the existence of gold mines on the Orinoco.[1] The intelligences Roe brought back were sufficient to keep Ralegh's mine project alive even after the death of Prince Henry in November 1612.[2] The other information Roe picked up at Trinidad was disquieting for those with more mundane trading interests in the Gulf of Paria. The Spanish crown had at last initiated measures to root out the contraband trade in tobacco which had made it such a haven for foreign interlopers. The nervous settlers of S. Tome and Port of Spain were, by early 1611, in hourly expectation of a judge to investigate their misdemeanours. Their unease had provoked them to unwarranted attacks on those on whom they depended for a living; the tobacco traders. For the subjects of James I, the conflict signalled an effective end to their involvement in the traffick. The king was hardly likely to countenance the need to acquire tobacco as a good reason for engaging in hostilities with Spaniards. The hazards of purchasing the commodity at the Spanish settlements were now becoming greater than the profits. For some, however, the discoveries of Sir Thomas Roe opened up new opportunities. Roe had clearly been greatly impressed by the lushness of the land bordering the north channel of the Amazon. The tobacco formerly acquired in the risky commerce on the fringes of the Main, could be cultivated instead on plantations in the safer, unguarded confines of the Amazon. Roe had explored the river in the hopes of finding mineral wealth to justify war with Spain. When those hopes faded, the river became a magnet for those who wanted to continue trading in Guiana without risking James I's wrath.[3]

Between 1611 and 1620 English and Irish projectors initiated several factories and plantations along the north bank of the Amazon between Cabo do Norte and the confluence of the Maicuru. The evidence for their activities is at best patchy and it is not easy to establish their interrelationships. Sir Thomas Roe

---

[1] See below pp. 153–5.
[2] V. T. Harlow, ed., *Ralegh's Last Voyage* (London, 1932); Lorimer, 'Ralegh's Guiana gold mine', 1982.
[3] J. Lorimer, 'The English contraband tobacco trade in Trinidad and Guiana, 1590–1617', in K. R. Andrews, N. P. Canny and P. E. H. Hair, eds., *The westward enterprise* (Liverpool, 1978), pp. 124–50; Andrews, *Spanish Caribbean*, ch. 9.

continued to take a strong interest in the river and most of the English and Irish settlement seems to have begun under his aegis before his departure for India in 1615.

Roe's chief agent for his subsequent activities on the Amazon appears to have been Matthew Morton. Kin to the Moretons of Moreton Hall in Cheshire, 'an expert Sea-man', he had sailed with Newport for Virginia in 1607, and may have gone out with Roe in 1610.[1] Sir Julius Caesar's comment, made in 1618, that 'Matthewe Moreton planted people in June an*no 1611* in the River of the Amazones at S*ir* [Thomas] Roes charge about 6. yeres since' is confusing. Roe did not return to England until July 1611. Caesar's '6 yeres since', which would be 1612, would provide a more reasonable period for the preparation of a colony. Morton may have gone out in the interval to reconnoitre a likely site. He certainly returned to the Amazon in 1614 and had the results of his surveys drafted into a chart by Gabriel Tatton in 1615.[2]

Tatton's latter chart and another general map of Guiana which he produced *circa* 1613, demonstrate the range of Morton's exploratons in the Amazon in the previous four or five years.[3] The 1613 chart appears to have been made to elucidate Robert Harcourt's request for an exclusive Guiana patent. Its association with Harcourt is indicated by the notation on it of the discoveries made by his Wiapoco colonists. Crosses accompanied variously by the initials C:M:H., C:R:H., C:E:F. and C:E:H. clearly refer to the expeditions conducted by the captains Michael and Robert Harcourt, Edward Fisher and Edward Harvey. Tatton uses Michael Harcourt's designation, Point Perilous, for Cabo do Norte and marks the extent of his journey up the Arrowari. Although

---

[1] See below p, 149; P. Barbour, ed., *The Jamestown voyages under the first charter* (Cambridge, 1969), I, 134, 170, II, 379. The Moreton family had held the estate of Little Moreton, Cheshire, since the thirteenth century. William Moreton (1577–1654), head of the family from 1598, spent most of his time attending to the estate but occasionally served as an intermediary between Sir Isaac Wake, ambassador in Turin, and the earl of Conway and duke of Buckingham.

[2] See below pp. 150–1, 155–6.

[3] See fig. VI. A copy of the earlier chart can be found in Harris, *Relation*, 1928. Sarah Tyacke's detailed analysis of the two Tatton charts and the 'Thomas King' in 'English charting', 1980, has provided an invaluable amount of new information on what were the otherwise obscure and minimally documented activities of Roe's men. The analysis of the next few pages is greatly indebted to her work.

Harcourt did not go any further into the Amazon, Tatton's chart provides a rudimentary outline of the north channel as far as 0°40′ S. A cross on the east bank at a place named *Manheno* shows the furthest point of discovery.[1] On the opposite bank, slightly to the north, an unnamed tributary is traced trending S.S.W. into the main. Tatton's informant had as yet no clear understanding of the configuration of the islands bordering the channel to the east, and could only name two Indian villages on them, *Auroras* at 0°15′ N. and *Matianos* close to the Equator.[2] On the other hand the hinterland behind the village of *Sapanow* on the north bank at 0°35′ N. had clearly been extensively surveyed. The region near the mouth of the Canal do Gurijuba is depicted as waterlogged *varzea* intersected by creeks bordered by gallery forest. The same feature appears on Tatton's 1615 Amazon chart based on Matthew Morton's surveys. This would suggest, as Sarah Tyacke points out, a common source. While the information could have come from Roe's voyage, the depiction of the north channel in the 1613 chart more likely reflects the results of Morton's subsequent visits, 1611–13. The 1615 map indicates why the area behind *Sapanow* was of interest to him. A track is shown leading beyond the swampy area past two settlements to a 'Steel Mine' by the side of an unnamed river or creek. If Morton's company had been loading what they believed to be samples of ore for smelting steel, this could explain why the Portuguese reported in 1615 that foreigners were carrying away 'much earth in casks' from the mouth of the Amazon.[3]

By 1615, as Tyacke's careful analysis of Tatton's second chart demonstrates, Matthew Morton had surveyed the north channel to the confluence of the Xingu. The navigational hazards and landmarks for the passage upriver were known, Indian settlements marked, and some thirty-seven river and place names recorded. From the construction of the chart it would appear that he had not yet discovered the main channel of the Amazon beyond this point.[4] He had, however, extensively explored the tributary drawn opposite

---

[1] Harris, *Relation*, 1928, pp. 10, 36, 51–64, 137–40; S. Tyacke, 1980, pp. 78–9.

[2] See above p. 24, n. 5, p. 25, n. 1.

[3] See below p. 166 and fig. VI; S. Tyacke, 1980, pp. 79, 81. Laet, although apparently familiar with Tatton's 1615 chart, see below pp. 51–2, did not mention a 'Steel Mine' on the river in any edition of the *Nieuwe wereldt*, suggesting that by the time the first Dutch edn. was completed in 1625 it had proved to be insignificant.

[4] S. Tyacke, 1980, pp. 80–2.

Manheno on the earlier map. By 1615 it was known as the river *Wocapoco*.[1] Morton, or some of his acquaintance, had followed it south-westward into the interior passing through what appears to be a swampy lake area and turning west and north into another lake set in surrounding sierra. Morton could name five Indian villages on its inner reaches.[2] Clearly the river was of some importance. Probably because some of the colonists whom he had carried to the Amazon for Sir Thomas Roe had settled there.

Philip Purcell, an Irish trader operating out of Dartmouth, alleged that he had first heard about the Amazon while trading for tobacco on Trinidad in 1609.[3] He was to devote much of the next twenty years to trading in the river. Nothing else is known for sure about his background beyond the fact that a James Purcell, possibly a brother, associated with him in his Amazon projects. Their surname would indicate that they were of Anglo-Irish or Anglo-Norman stock, hailing from Munster. A 'Michael Pursell', merchant of Waterford was trading to Chester in 1592. On the other hand a 'William Pursell', merchant of Dublin, had goods going into the same port in 1565. 'Thomas Purcell' of Dublin was trading in Bristol in 1602. Various Purcells, amongst them the Thomas referred to above, served as councillors, aldermen, auditors and sheriff of Dublin between 1600 and 1610. I have no evidence to prove links to Philip and James Purcell. Two other Irishmen involved in Amazon projects had kin or business associates in Dublin. The Purcell brothers were clearly involved in trade to Dartmouth and the ports of the English south-west but whether they operated out of Dublin or the Irish south coast ports remains to be discovered.[4]

---

[1] Allowing for the 25 minute discrepancy in the latitudes of Tatton's 1615 chart (S. Tyacke, 1980, p. 81) the mouth of the unnamed tributary on the earlier chart seems to correspond with that of the river *Wocapoco* on the Amazon chart, both entering the north bank just short of 0°40' S. In both charts the tributary is drawn falling away south-west from the main river.

[2] Fig. VI.

[3] See below p. 157.

[4] See below p. 156. Philip and James Purcell may have been connected to the William Pursell of Dublin, merchant, trading to Chester in 1565 (P.R.O., E190 Chester 1323/1, f. 2) and to the Thomas Purcell trading from Dublin to Bristol in 1602 (P.R.O., E190 Chester 1133/3, f.9v). A Michael Pursell, merchant, of Waterford had commercial dealings in Chester in 1592 (P.R.O., E190 Chester 1326/5, f.5v). Various Purcells or Pursells held significant offices in the city of Dublin in the early 17th century. The Assembly Rolls list one Edmond 'Purssell' as a council member 1600, alderman and former sheriff 1601, and as fined for refusing the election to the mayoralty in 1607. Nicholas 'Purssell', a tanner, was

It seems fairly certain that Philip Purcell first visited the Amazon under Roe's auspices, although he did not acknowledge it to Gondomar. When he spoke to the Spanish ambassador in 1621 he had apparently just returned from the river with Captain Roger North, who had carried out a new English colony. North brought back several Irish passengers as well as a quantity of their tobacco. Sir Thomas Roe informed the House of Commons at that time that the tobacco belonged to his men, long settled on the river and not part of North's endeavours.[1] There is no evidence, however, of how the association with Roe was made. Purcell claimed that he had sailed to Trinidad in 1609 some two years before Roe visited Port of Spain. In 1609 the English contraband tobacco trade to Trinidad and the Orinoco was at its peak. The vessels engaged in it commonly used Dartmouth and the more secluded ports of the South-West in the hopes that the tobacco and the occasional Spanish prizes which they brought back would elude the vigilance of the officers of the Customs and the Admiralty. A. P. Newton asserted that many of the tobacco traders preferred to use the Irish ports for this risky commerce. Robert Harcourt who had called at Trinidad in September 1609, homeward bound from his new colony on the Wiapoco, was driven off course to Ireland and visited 'friends and acquaintance' in Youghal before he returned to England. It is not beyond the bounds of possibility that Philip Purcell had encountered Harcourt on Trinidad and heard of the possibilities of settlement on the Amazon and Wiapoco. Harcourt could have introduced him to the circle of Guiana adventurers surrounding Prince Henry, involved in the preparations for Roe's venture. On the other hand, if Purcell had trading connections in Dartmouth and was already involved in the contraband tobacco trade, then he would have been fully aware of the preparations for Roe's expedition which sailed from that port in February 1610.

---

appointed auditor 1604 and 1608 and elected sheriff and one of the masters of the city works in 1607. A Patrick 'Pursel' was listed as one of the Council in 1600 and another of the same name, a cooper, was enfranchised after serving his apprenticeship in 1611. A Thomas 'Purcell', merchant, possibly the man trading to Bristol in 1602, was listed for 1610. A 'James Purcell sherman' was admitted to the franchise of the city on payment of a fine in the Summer of 1615. J. T. Gilbert, *Calendar of ancient records of Dublin in the possession of the municipal corporation of that city* (Dublin, 1891), II, 343, 352, 354–5, 369, 385, 426, 476, 477–8, 483–6, 491, 503, 533, III, 11, 59.
[1] See below p. 220.

While he may indeed have sailed with Roe, it is more likely that he went out to Trinidad again during the tobacco season of October–March 1610–11 and encountered Sir Thomas Roe at Port of Spain.[1]

Purcell probably first sailed to the Amazon with Matthew Morton, Roe's agent. Investigating the history of the Amazon colonies in 1618, Sir Julius Caesar noted that 'Matthewe Moreton planted people in June an*no 1611* in the River of the Amazones at S*ir* Roes charge about 6. yeres since'. Caesar's mathematics were at fault here since '6. yeres since' would be 1612.[2] Roe did not return to England before July 1611, and it is hardly likely that he dispatched a colony to the Amazon that same year. Morton may however have gone out in the interval to reconnoitre a likely site and taken Purcell with him. Purcell's assertion that he went out in a chartered Dutch vessel does not invalidate the connection with Morton and Roe, since there is reasonable evidence that Roe's subsequent Amazon ventures were launched with the support of associates from the Zeeland port of Flushing. Nothing survives on how Purcell recruited the fourteen Irishmen whom he settled on the Amazon on his second voyage there. While there may have been English and possibly Dutch men amongst them, theirs was essentially an Irish colony and always referred to as such in contemporary accounts.[3]

An indication of its location is provided by the chart of the surveys made by another of Roe's men, Thomas King. According to King 'Porsalls Creek' entered the north bank downstream from the confluence of the Xingu.[4] Sarah Tyacke has tentatively identified 'Porsall's Creek' with Morton's river *Wocapoco*.[5] Visitors to the Amazon in 1623 referred to 'Tauregue River' as the place, 'where the Irish live'. By then Tauregue seems also to have been the name

---

[1] See below p. 153. Apart from Purcell's account of his voyage to Trinidad there is no other evidence of how the association with Roe was begun. A Thomas 'Rowe' had '16 small parcells of wares' in the *Amity* of London outward bound 18/28th August 1609. The same ship had come in from Ireland on the 24th July/3rd August, and was probably returning there in August. If this was the same Thomas Roe then clearly he had some trading interests in Ireland. He was to develop other connections there. In 1613 he married Eleanor, daughter of Sir Thomas Cave of Stamford, niece of Oliver St John, Master of the Ordnance in Ireland and shortly thereafter appointed Lord Deputy and Viscount Grandison.

[2] Roger North agreed with Sir Julius Caesar's estimate that James I's subjects began to settle on the Amazon about 1612. See below, p. 202.

[3] See below, pp. 193, 199, 258–61.   [4] Fig. VII.

[5] S. Tyacke, 1980, p. 83.

of their fort or stockade.[1] The river on which it lay was said to enter
the north bank between the Equator and 0°40' S., surely King's
'Porsalls Creek' or Morton's *Wocapoco*.[2] Laet described the mouth of
the Tauregue as a torrent or rapid, with the village of Tauregue
further inland. It lay slightly upstream from an island and tributary
called Brest. Brest, Caetano da Silva argued, was the English name
for a magnificent natural harbour, some eight miles wide and twenty-
six miles long, guarded from the main channel by the ilha de Pará
and other lesser islands.[3] The Tauregue, either the present Preto or
Maracapuru, which enters the southern limits of the bay, would have
been an obvious place for settlement.

The small party of Irishmen co-existed amicably on the river with
King's men and possibly one or two other English factory settle-
ments. The fort commanded by Thomas King, another of Roe's
associates, was clearly totally separate from Purcell's tobacco
plantation. Sir Julius Caesar's note suggests that he went out to the
Amazon about the same time, 1612.[4] He may have been the same
'Captain Thomas King who, with Mr Pett "the ship wright' and Mr
John Reynolds 'the master-gunner to his Highness', waited upon
Prince Henry at Richmond in August 1612.[5] By the time the
Flushingers, Pieter Lodewycx and his son Jan Pietersz, entered the
Amazon in 1614 King had a 'notable fort . . . from whence he makes
great and profitable returns'.[6] Once again it is the later chart
extrapolated from his surveys which casts the most light upon his
otherwise obscure endeavours. The Lodewycx assigned King's fort
somewhat vaguely to 'the mouth' of the Amazon. According to the
chart, King had settled much further upriver than Purcell and the
Irish. It is a reasonable assumption that the habitation simply
identified as 'the fort' on the north bank beyond the Xingu was
Thomas King's. Sarah Tyacke places this somewhere near present
Monte Alegre, near the mouth of the Maicuru. The content of the

---

[1] See below p. 261.   [2] S. Tyacke, 1980, p. 83.

[3] Laet (1633), bk. 17, 632, (1640), bk. 17, 571; J. Caetano da Silva, *L'Oyapoc et
l'Amazone* (Paris, 1861), I, 490–5.

[4] See below p. 151.

[5] T. Birch, *The life of Henry, Prince of Wales* (London, 1760), p. 294. Sarah Tyacke
discovered the will of one Thomas King, shipowner and mariner of Uphill
Somerset, who died in 1628 and may be the man in question, op. cit., p. 82. The
'Mr Pett' was most probably Phineas Pett the master shipwright who had enjoyed
the Prince's patronage since 1604, see W. G. Perrin, ed., *The autobiography of
Phineas Pett* (London, 1918), p. 51.

[6] See below p. 159.

map indicates that King had penetrated the Tapajós as far as 3° S., and gone some distance farther westward up the main stream.[1] The implication of Caesar's note is that King was no longer on the river by 1618. That does not necessarily mean that his fort had been abandoned, nor does it exclude the possibility that he returned subsequently.

George Percy, the younger brother of the earl of Northumberland, also contemplated going out to the Amazon for two years in 1615 hoping to make enough money to settle his debts. He had the chance of a passage with a 'Captain Bud' who had maintained men on the river since 1612. They had provided him with lucrative cargoes in both intervening years.[2] Budd may, of course, have been dealing with the company of King's fort or the Irish on 'Porsalls Creek'. He may have been supplying another, totally separate English enclave on the river. Clearly somebody was working the supposed 'Steel Mine' in the region behind Sapanow in 1615. Tatton's 1615 chart also delineates the river *Woakathy*, possibly the Mazagdo, in some detail and another tributary which appears to be the present river Anauíra-pucu is traced some distance inland.[3] Morton's interest in them again suggests that they may have been the site of a factory or plantation. A 'W. Budd' brought in tobacco from Virginia in the *Flying Horse* of Flushing in 1615, possibly the same man as the William Budd who associated with Sir Thomas Roe in an application for a monopoly of the import of tobacco in 1620.[4] If the latter was George Percy's 'Captain Bud', then his activities on the Amazon may reflect an even earlier association with Roe. There is no evidence whether George Percy actually went out with him or not. Tatton's chart of the Amazon, now in the collection of the duke of Northumberland at Alnwick, may well have come into the family in the year that it was made, acquired to illustrate the location of the English and Irish settlements there.[5]

---

[1] Fig. VII; S. Tyacke, 1980, pp. 82–6.

[2] See below p. 160 and J. W. Shirley, 'George Percy at Jamestown, 1607–12', *The Virginia Magazine of History and Biography*, LVII (1949), 227–43. Percy sailed with Christopher Newport for Jamestown in December 1606 and would, therefore, have been acquainted with Matthew Morton who served under Newport.

[3] Fig. VI; S. Tyacke, 1980, p. 82.

[4] *HMC, Fourth report*, app., 469; S. M. Kingsbury, ed., *The records of the Virginia Company of London* (Washington, 1933), III, 365.

[5] Shirley, 1949, p. 243 states that the detailed accounts of the expenditures of the Percy household for 1614 and 1615 are missing and thus it is not possible to tell whether George Percy drew a pension from his brother during these years. He did draw one in 1616 and 1617, indicating that he was in England then.

Fig. VI. Gabriel Tatton's chart of the Amazon and Xingu, 1615
(In the collection of the duke of Northumberland.)

Fig. VI. Gabriel Tatton's chart of the Amazon and Xingu, 1615
(In the collection of the duke of Northumberland.)

For Purcell and his Irishmen and indeed for the English, one of the great attractions of the Amazon was their ability to develop their plantations and factories without undue interference from proprietors or chartered companies. Sir Thomas Roe sailed for India in 1615. Theoretically all of these holdings were, after the 28th August 1613, subject to the authority of Robert Harcourt. The patent awarded to him on that date gave him an exclusive administrative and commercial monopoly of the region 'betweene the Ryver of Amazones and the Ryver of Dessequebe ... and all Singular Islands lands and terrytories beinge within twentie leagues thereunto adjacente', which clearly took in the north channel of the former river.[1] Fortunately perhaps for the peace of the early English and Irish ventures, Harcourt was too preoccupied with his Wiapoco colony to interfere seriously with the Amazon planters. He may have made one initial effort to enforce his prerogatives. Daniel Elfrye, who brought a Spanish prize into Bermuda in early 1614, reported that she had been taken while he had been 'servinge under one Fisher, that was sent out upon a discovery into the river of the Amazones'.[2] Fisher may have been the Edward Fisher who lived on the Wiapoco from 1609–12. If so, Robert Harcourt could well have sent him out to inform the English and Irish on the Amazon of his proprietorial rights. If he did so nothing seems to have come of it. As John Smith noted, Harcourt was barely able to keep contact with the residue of the Wiapoco colonists, leaving them to depend on the Zeelanders who began to settle the river in 1612.[3]

The English and Irish on the Amazon were similarly obligated to the Dutch. Purcell, King and the others on the river were free to take their profit where they could find it. After Roe departed for India, if not before, the Irish and English seem to have done the greater part of their trade with Zeeland merchants. A vessel from Dartmouth made two voyages to the Amazon in 1618.[4] Purcell may have maintained regular contacts with his associates there, but no reference to it survives in the Port Books. I have yet to uncover any

[1] For the patent granted to Robert Harcourt Esq. of Stanton Harcourt, Oxon, together with John Robenson Esq. and Sir Thomas Chaloner 28th August 1613, see P.R.O., C66/1986 and PC 2/27, 15th July 1613.
[2] See below p. 163.
[3] See below p. 150 and Lorimer 'English trade and exploration', 1973, pp. 360–2.
[4] See above p. 45, n. 3 and below pp. 187–9.

evidence of direct trade between the Irish ports and the Amazon. Although that is not to say that it did not exist, the greater part of the produce of the Irish plantation likely came first into the port of Flushing.

While the Dutch may have left men on the Amazon before 1610 there is only slender evidence that they did so.[1] Their effort to colonize the rivers of the 'Wild Coast' after that date seems to have been prompted by considerations exactly contrary to those which moved the English and the Irish traders. While the latter migrated southwards down the Guiana coast to avoid the domestic consequences of confrontation with Spaniards, the Dutch projectors deliberately planted their posts in Guiana as a symbol of their opposition to Oldenbarnevelt's truce with Spain. Although some of the investment came from Amsterdam, most of the 'Wild Coast' ventures were generated in Zeeland at Middelburg and Flushing. Flushing, as one of the cautionary towns ceded to Elizabeth I, was virtually an English colony.[2]

At least one and probably most of the Flushinger plantations on the Amazon had English personnel. Sir Thomas Roe may well have drawn backers from the Zeeland port into his enterprises. Such an arrangement would have had many advantages. The Flushingers had capital, equal experience of the Amazon and the Guiana coast and, should problems with Spain arise, could provide a front to obscure the liability of Roe and his English and Irish partners. The evidence is suggestive although certainly not in any way conclusive. Roe visited Flushing in July and December 1613, reported in the latter month as 'going for Captane Floods Companye, who died lately in Frislande. ... He may have been seeking to hire a ship's company with experience of the Guiana rivers.[3] Philip Purcell claimed that his first reconnaissance of the Amazon had been made in a chartered Dutch ship.[4] Laet, who was certainly acquainted with Roe in the 1640s, had access to Matthew Morton's surveys at the very least fifteen if not twenty-five years earlier. He may also have known of the explorations of Thomas King. He remembered, as he

[1] See below p. 253.

[2] For the history of Dutch colonization of the Guiana coast, see G. Edmundson, 'The Dutch on the Amazon and Negro', 1903, and 'The Dutch in Western Guiana', EHR, XVI (1901), 640–9; Ch. C. Ghoslinga, The Dutch in the Caribbean and on the Wild Coast (Assen, 1971).

[3] DNB (1909), pp. 89–93.   [4] See below p. 157.

wrote in 1633, 'having heard some years ago, from a very trustworthy Englishman, that he had ascended the main channel of the river towards the west for three hundred miles, and that he had entered into a great lake, the waters of which were perfectly green, and not fit to drink, and that he had seen an Indian village on the way with two or three hundred houses and about a thousand people in it'.[1] A Dutch commentator observed in 1638 that most of the English and Irish ventures to the Amazon had been 'financed and fitted out' in Flushing.[2] This was certainly true of the enterprises of the 1620s, and may have been equally applicable to those of the previous decade. After Roe departed for India, if not before, the English and Irish in the Amazon outposts were largely dependent on Dutch shipping for the transport of goods and personnel back and forwards across the Atlantic.[3]

Laet did not specify when the Zeelanders built their two forts on the Amazon, 'one which they called Nassau in Coyminne, which resembles an island separated by a straight branch of the river from the rest of the continent for nearly twenty miles; this fort was, moreover, nearly eighty miles/leagues from the mouth of the Amazon. The other which they named Orange about seven miles downstream from the former.'[4] The two stockades, also known by the Indian names of *Gormoarou* and *Materu* respectively, lay on the right bank of the Xingu close to its confluence.[5] Tatton's 1615 chart

---

[1] Laet, (1633), bk. 17, 632, (1640), bk. 17, 571. The description of the Amazon which Laet published in the first Dutch edition of the *Nieuwe wereldt* (1625), bk. 14, 462 was based on 'the most pertinent chart or description of this river which we have yet seen'. Tyacke's comparison of the place-names on Tatton's 1615 Amazon chart with those cited by Laet suggests that he had access to that chart 'or one very much like it', op. cit., p. 81. Laet and Roe corresponded with one another in 1641, see J. A. F. Bekkers, *Correspondence of John Morris with Johannes de Laet, 1634–49* (Assen, 1970), p. 63. It is of course possible that Laet's account of an extended English exploration upstream referred to the reconnaissance conducted by William White, see below pp. 238–9.

[2] Report of Jacob Van Reese, 31st January 1638, cited S. Tyacke, 1980, n. 45.

[3] See below p. 187.

[4] Laet (1633), bk. 17, 634, (1640), bk. 17, 574. See above p. 27. Laet's estimates of the distance here are rather confusing. The Latin (1633) edition uses *millaria*, meaning miles, but clearly Nassau, the fort furthest up the Xingu was 80 leagues rather than 80 miles from the mouth of the Amazon. The French (1640) edition uses *'lieuwes'* for leagues. Cochado, see below p. 250 estimated that Orange or Materu was 12 leagues downstream from Nassau.

[5] See below pp. 249–51. The map prepared by Hessel Gerritsz for the first edition of Laet's *Nieuwe wereldt* (1625), shows *Materoo* and *Gormoarou* on the east

gives no indication that the posts were in existence when Morton made his surveys, although Morton did note the villages of *Matorion* and *Comaranowa* which seem to have been their future sites.[1] The forts were most likely established on the river by Pieter Lodewycx and his associates sometime in 1615, as outposts of the developing plantation in the Wiapoco.[2] When the Portuguese entered the Pará in 1616 they heard that the Dutch and Flemings had 'some 250–300 men split between two wooden forts' in 'Cabo do Norte'. These were most probably the two Xingu settlements.[3] The Portuguese generally used the term 'Cabo do Norte' at this time to refer to the entire area of the north channel frequented by foreign interlopers.

They also heard in 1616 of a much more ambitious development one hundred and fifty leagues upriver from the mouth of the river Pará. These venturers had brought out women and children with them, a sure indication that they planned permanent occupation. There can be little doubt that the Portuguese intelligences referred to the Anglo-Dutch colony carried out from Flushing by Pieter Adriaenszoon Ita in 1616. The redemption of the cautionary towns in June of that year put the English garrisons at Flushing and Rammekins out of work and prompted some to try their luck in the expanding Dutch colonies in Guiana. Scott's account states that Adriaenszoon Ita took his company far up river, presumably to the tortuous 'strait' or Óbidos narrows above the mouth of the Tapajós, before turning back to settle on a point of land between the *Coropatube* and the *Ginipape*. The fort was, according to his reckoning, exactly fifty-four leagues below the

---

bank of the Xingu just above the confluence, as does the unfinished Dutch chart of c. 1620; see A. Cortesão and A. Teixeira da Mota, ed., *Portugalia monumenta cartographica* (Lisbon, 1960), V, pl. 601A; S. Tyacke, 1980, pp. 78, 82. Robert Dudley's 'Carta particolare dell Rio d'Amazone con la costa sin al fiume Maranham', based on Hessel Gerritsz's map and engraved as chart XV of the America series in *Dell'Arcano del Mare* (1647), 3, shows *Materou* and *Gormourou* on the east bank of the Xingu yet places the *Forteza de Nassau* and *Forteza de Orange* on the west bank. Dudley also reversed the position of the forts, placing Orange upriver of Nassau.

[1] Fig. VI.
[2] See below pp. 158–9. For the history of the development of Dutch settlement on the Wiapoco after 1612, see Edmundson, 'The Dutch on the Amazon', 1903, and 'The Dutch in Western Guiana', 1901; Ghoslinga, 1971, ch. 4.
[3] See below p. 171.

Fig. VII. The 'Thomas King' Chart (B.N., Paris pf. 166. Div. I. p. 4)
(By kind permission of the Bibliothèque Nationale, Paris)

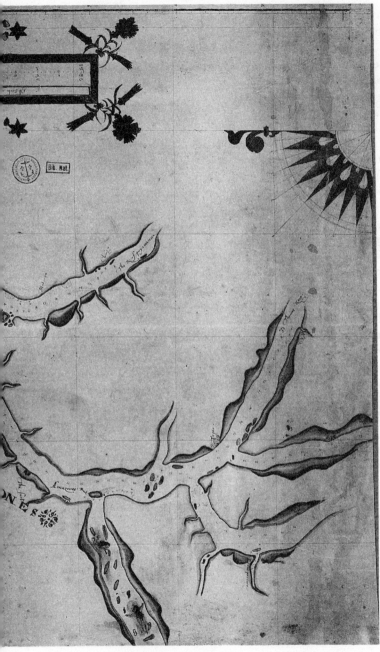

Fig. VII. The 'Thomas King' Chart (B.N., Paris pf. 166. Div. I. p. 4)
(By kind permission of the Bibliothèque Nationale, Paris)

mouth of the *Coropatube*, identifiable as the Maicuru,[1] and six leagues above the *Ginipape* or Paru.

The sudden flurry of foreign settlement on the Amazon caused the Spanish Crown considerable anxiety. Not that it had any economic interest in the vast waterway, but its great fear was that enemies would emulate Orellana's achievements in reverse and use it as a corridor to Peru. On the other hand, if the river was safely garrisoned, it might be possible to transport bullion downstream from Peru to the Atlantic coast.[2] Scarcely able to maintain settlement on Trinidad and the Orinoco the Spanish government could do nothing to defend the rest of the Guiana. It had no option but to turn to its Portuguese subjects in Brazil for help.

After 1600 Portuguese holdings in Brazil advanced steadily up the littoral from Pernambuco. The authorities were particularly concerned to drive out the French traders who treated the north as their own preserve and built up powerful Indian alliances. By 1611 they had news that the Sieur de la Ravardière planned to develop the French trading post at the mouth of the Maranhão into a fully fledged colony. For once the response of both the metropolitan and colonial governments was swift and effective. By November 1615 combined forces from Pernambuco and Lisbon compelled the French to surrender their forts and founded the garrison of São Luis on the site. The French were able to provide the Portuguese with useful information about the Amazon posts. One of their number went as Indian interpreter with the expedition which set out for the Amazon delta in late 1615. A detachment led by Francisco Caldeira de Castelbranco rounded the southern cape in early January 1616 and built the fort of Nossa Senhora de Belém on the right bank of the river Pará, thirty-five leagues from the sea.[3]

---

[1] See below p. 163; Edmundson 'The Dutch on the Amazon', 1903; J. A. Williamson, *English colonies*, 1923, pp. 66–71; Ghoslinga, 1971, ch. 4; S. Tyacke, 1980, pp. 84–5; Hemming, *Red gold*, 1978, pp. 580–1.

[2] See pp. 166–7.

[3] See below pp. 170–1. For the history of Portuguese expansion up the north coast of Brazil, the formation and collapse of the French colony in the Maranhão, and the establishment of the garrisons of São Luis and Belém, see M. de Mello Cardoso Barata, *A jornada de Francisco Caldeira de Castello Branco. Fundação da cidade de Belém* (Belém, 1916); M. J. Guedes, *Brasil-costa norte, cartografía Portuguesa vetustissima* (Rio de Janeiro, 1968), and 'Acçoes navaís contra os estrangeiros na Amazonia, 1616–33', *Historia naval Brasileira*, I pt. 11 (Rio de Janeiro, 1975); Hemming, *Red gold* (1978), chs. 6–10; M. C. Kiemen, *The Indian policy of Portugal in the Amazon region, 1614–93* (New York, 1973), chs. 1–2;

For the first seven years of its existence the garrison at Belém constituted no threat to the English, Irish and Dutch settlers on the Xingu and the north channel. Although it was relatively well supplied and within contact of the two forts in the Maranhão, its commanders were preoccupied by Indian wars and the unruliness of their own men. The Tupinamba of the Maranhão region had been close allies of the French and the limited missions of the Jesuits and Franciscans in the early years of Portuguese occupation could do little to break that allegiance. The efficient brutality of the parties sent out into the hinterland from São Luis, the extortions and abuses committed by the residents of Belém quickly stirred the neighbouring tribes to rebellion. The Nheenghaíbas of the ilha de Marajó were already at war with the Pará garrison in 1617 when the Tupinamba of the Maranhão rose up against São Luis. The revolt quickly spread to the Pará. The Indians in the latter region suffered the most savage Portuguese reprisals. Between 1619 and 1621 Bento Maciel Parente wiped out some thirty thousand Indians in the surrounding territory, according to one contemporary estimate. These punitive measures established a fearsome reputation for the Portuguese of Pará and broke the back of Indian resistance in the vicinity. Their success was to have serious consequences for the other European colonists in the lower Amazon after 1623.[1]

For the time being, however, the English, Irish and Zeelanders prospered. Some of Roe's men, possibly the Irish planters, shipped back £2,300 worth of tobacco to England and the Low Countries in 1617. Adriaenszoon Ita's colonists were returning cargoes valued at £60,000.[2] Most of this profit came from tobacco, dyes and hardwoods. Tobacco from the Spanish Indies, rolled, fermented and cured in the 'Spanish' method which traders like Purcell had learned from the Spanish colonists on Trinidad and the Orinoco, was in great demand on European markets. The best could fetch 30/– to 40/– per lb in England, compared to 1/– to 2/– for that from Virginia.[3] The orange-red dye of the berry Annotto was the second most merchandizable commodity for the Amazon planters. In a

---

Abbeville, *Histoire de la mission des Pères Capucins*, 1963; J. J. Viveiros, *Historia de comercio do Maranhão, 1612–1895* (São Luis, Maranhão, 1954); F. Vasques, *Conquista e colonização do Pará* (Lisbon, 1941).
[1] See below pp. 80–1, 91–2, 100–1, 105–6; Kiemen, 1973, chs. 1–2.
[2] See below p. 164.
[3] Lorimer, 'The English contraband tobacco trade', 1978, pp. 136–7.

period when dyes of all types were much sought after for use in cloth production, Annotto sold for as much as 12/– per lb in Holland and was valued at between 12 and 20 pence in England in 1618.[1] Red dyes obtained from 'Brazil', 'Fernambuck', 'Log'. 'Campeachy' and 'India', and the yellow procured from 'Fustick' wood were not so readily accepted by the clothing interest which felt that the colours were unreliable and hard to fix. Continued experiments did resolve these problems. 'Fustick' was officially rated for subsidy purposes in England in 1608 at 10/– per cwt and 'Farnando-buck wood or Brasill' at 40/–.[2] Even more valuable was the speckled wood brought back by William White for his Dartmouth partners in 1618. One of the many magnificent species of hard wood to be found in the Amazonian rainforest, Harcourt estimated it to be worth '30 or 40 pounds a tunne' in 1613.[3]

What made all these commodities so attractive to the Amazon settlers was the fact that they could be acquired with relatively little labour. Purcell's Irishmen quickly encouraged their Indian allies to expand their tobacco cultivation and showed them how to 'juce their tobacco like the Spaniards'.[4] First return cargoes of Annotto could be gathered from the wild shrubs, and it took little effort to adapt that grown in the village clearings to plantation production. Indian labourers could locate, cut and transport dye and hard-woods to the anchorages used by visiting supply ships. The complaisance of the local Tupi, Carib and Arawak tribes in this arrangement reflected their very real desire for European allies to

[1] See below pp. 136, n. 3, 188–9; *Relation*, 1613, p. 32, Harris, *Relation*, 1928, p. 100.

[2] Records of the deliberations of the House of Lords on dye-woods in 1662 indicate that the use of 'logwood' for dyeing cloth had been prohibited in the 23rd and 39th year of Elizabeth's reign on the grounds that the colours that it produced were 'false and deceitful'. Patents had been issued subsequently for the importation of limited quantities. Experiments in the past half century had been successful in fixing the colours to make them more lasting. House of Lords Journal, 18th April 1662, *HMC, Seventh report*, App., p. 165. For the official value of 'logwood' in 1608, see *The rates of marchandizes, 1608* (Amsterdam, 1969).

[3] See below p. 279; Harcourt, *Relation*, 1613, p. 36, Harris, *Relation*, 1928, p. 104. In May 1619 the *Elizabeth Angell* of London returned from 'the parts of the West Indies' with a cargo of speckled wood, annotto and gum elemi (a white or greenish resin), which may well have been acquired on the Amazon (P.R.O., HCA 24/78, ff. 67, 73–4).

[4] For an account of the curative methods used by the Spaniards of the Orinoco and Trinidad settlements, see Lorimer, 'English trade and exploration', 1973, pp. 265–6.

defend them against the Portuguese driving steadily northwards up the Brazilian coast. None of these activities, however profoundly disruptive of the native subsistence cycle, raised the problems suffered by the Indians neighbouring the European settlements on the Atlantic coast of North America. In the extended growing season at the Equator Indian plots could be expanded with little difficulty to meet the demands of incoming colonists. Bitter and sweet manioc, cara, tara, arrowroot, sweet potatoes, peanuts, maize, lima and kidney beans, the diverse game of the forests and streams provided an adequate and varied diet. There was no 'starving time' on the lower Amazon.[1] The factories and plantations begun there after 1610 proved immediately profitable, and encouraged plans to establish an Amazon Company a decade later.

[1] C. Lévi-Strauss, 'The use of wild plants in tropical South America', in *HSAI*, 1963, VI, 479–82; C. O. Sauer, 'Cultivated plants of South and Central America', ibid., pp. 487–545.

THE FORMATION AND COLLAPSE OF THE AMAZON COMPANY, 1619–21

William White's two voyages to the Amazon in 1618[1] were possibly part of the exploratory moves for the creation of the chartered, joint stock company for trade and settlement in the Amazon which was founded in 1619. Interest in such a company had been aroused by reports of the great commercial potential of the river from those 'who have in theire owne persons visited those partes, and are from thence lately retourned; As also by Letteres from some Englishe, and other his Majesties subjectes who have for theis sixe, or seaven yeares inhabited and continewed resident there. . . .'[2] White, who went out with the settlers sent by the new company in 1620,[3] may well have been despatched two years earlier to make contact with Purcell's Irishmen and the English outposts and to reconnoitre the possibilities of the river. Certainly his second voyage in December 1618 coincided with the beginning of negotiations for the new enterprise.

The prime mover behind the projected company was Captain Roger North, the youngest brother of Dudley, third baron North. Roger North had served with Ralegh on his last Orinoco expedition in 1617. He had heard glowing reports of the Amazon before joining the latter venture, and had been greatly attracted by what he had seen of the Guiana coastline as Ralegh's fleet straggled northwards from its first landfall off the Wiapoco.[4] His moves to

---

[1] See below pp. 188–9.   [2] See below, p. 193.   [3] See below, p. 238.
[4] See below, p. 236. Roger North (1588–1652), was the grandson of Roger, second Baron North, and younger brother of Dudley, third Baron North (1582–1666). The latter married Frances Brockett, a connection of Lawrence Keymis, see above, pp. 16–18. For Roger North's participation in Ralegh's last expedition, see Harlow, *Ralegh's last voyage*, 1932, pp. 25, 36, 56, 72, 76, 84, 86, 97, 238, 247, 257–9, 323.

find undertakers for a colony in the Amazon found influential supporters. The original subscribers to the scheme included, beside his eldest brother, the duke of Lennox, and the earls of Arundel, Warwick, Dorset and Clanricard.[1] The Spanish ambassador, Gondomar, also listed the Archbishop of Canterbury, the Lord Chancellor, the earls of Pembroke and Southampton, the marquises of Buckingham and Hamilton, 'the foremost personages' of the realm, 'the greater part of the Council', as participants. James I remarked to him that 'he had never seen an enterprise so supported'.[2]

The Amazon projectors immediately ran foul of Robert Harcourt's patent.[3] The earliest evidence of North's scheme is to be found in his complaint to the Privy Council, on the 7th/17th March 1619, that Harcourt had refused to come to any accommodation with him, even though the latter had made no plantation in the river Amazon himself. At the direction of the Council, Sir Julius Caesar and Sir Edward Coke weighed the claims of Harcourt and North, noting that Harcourt's ventures had centred on the Wiapoco and that Sir Thomas Roe had opened up the Amazon. The Council decided, on the 16th/26th of March, to cancel Harcourt's patent and to grant separate commissions of discovery to him and to North, as should be appropriate.[4] On the 18th/28th April the Solicitor General was ordered to draw up a bill incorporating North and his associates as a company to develop the area 'from the River of Wyapoco to five degrees of Southerly Latitude, from any parte or Brannch of the River of . . . Amazons . . . and for Longitude into the Lande to be lymitted from Sea to Sea. . . .',[5] again an ambiguous wording which almost certainly intended to leave the Wiapoco to Harcourt.[6]

The charter of the 'Governor and Companie of Noblemen and Gentlemen of the Cittie of London: Adventurers in and about the

---

[1] See below, p. 194.   [2] See below, pp. 204, 208.   [3] See above, p. 50 n. 1.
[4] See below, pp. 150–1, 190–1.   [5] See below, p. 196.
[6] Although the wording of the instructions to Sir Thomas Coventry does not clearly specify that the Wiapoco was excluded from the Amazon Co. patent, that does appear to be the case. The Privy Council intended to confer separate 'commissions of discovery' on Harcourt and North (see below, p. 191). When the Guiana Co. was incorporated in 1627 Harcourt's rights to the coastline from the Essequibo to the Wiapoco were combined with the old Amazon Co. territories stretching thence to 5° S. of any part or branch of the river Amazon (see below, p. 278).

River of the Amazons' was issued on the 10th September 1619.[1]
Although no copy of it survives, the instructions of the Privy
Council to the Solicitor General about its drafting indicate that the
undertakers were to have the usual privileges and immunities.[2]
North and his associates drew up for publication the Preamble for
Subscription on the 6th/16th April 1619, setting £50 as the lowest
sum by which admission might be had into the company. The
investors agreed to pay one-third of their promised subscription for
the first voyage, and were given between the 18th/28th April and
the 6th/16th May to make the requisite payments.[3] The original
group of thirteen had swelled to fifty members by the time the
company was officially incorporated in September. Under the
presidency of the earl of Warwick, regular Thursday afternoon
meetings were held at Arundel House in the Strand to organize the
first plantation.[4]

North's plans for the latter were ambitious, although his capital
was limited. Gondomar's estimate that some 80,000 ducats, approximately £26,000, had been contributed by April 1620 is
undoubtedly an exaggeration.[5] North started with a promised
capital of £2,400[6] and it is unlikely that the final subscription
amounted to more than £5,000. Sir Thomas Roe estimated that the
outfitting of the first voyage cost £3,000, and North asserted that
this outlay had nearly exhausted the resources of the company.[7]
The expenditure covered the carrying out of about one hundred
men with the necessary supplies and munitions. In assembling his
first colonists North was particularly keen to recruit merchants,
dyers, druggists and carpenters from men who had experience of
the region and could rapidly exploit its merchandizable plants and
woods. He intended that his settlers should occupy themselves with
something other than the usual tobacco, annotto and cotton
plantations. Mathew Morton attested to his plan to 'plant sugar
canes & to ereckt ingenies for makinge suger', a scheme involving

---

[1] The title of the company and the date of its incorporation is recorded in the
introduction to the patent of the Guiana Co., issued 19/29th May 1627 (see
below, p. 289).

[2] See below, p. 195. [3] See below, pp. 193–4. [4] See below, p. 194.
[5] See below, p. 205. [6] See below, pp. 194–5.

[7] Roe's figure is recorded in E. Nicholas's notes of his speech to the Grand
Committee, 13/23rd April 1621, in *Proceedings and debates of the House of Commons
in 1620 and 1621* (Oxford, 1766), I, 249. For North's comment, see below, p.
202.

heavy fixed capital investment in skilled labour and machinery. A blacksmith's forge was to be transported out, and the search for mines, of which rumours had persisted since Morton's earlier exploration of the river for Roe, was to be continued. Mathew Morton was to accompany North with a pinnace, to continue his discovery of the Amazon. Morton expected to be away on this business for some three years, although every planter was at liberty to come home with the first supply.[1]

Although Sir Thomas Roe returned from India in 1619, none of the surviving sources for the Amazon Company list him as an undertaker in it. The patent of the company, however, brought the men he had already established in the river under its jurisdiction. Roe appears, at least, to have acted as an intermediary between the Amazon Company and the Irish settlers, arranging for the passage of a second group of them out to the river, and for the transport of tobacco from Purcell's plantation on the return voyage.[2]

When writing to his kinsman of his plans to return to the Amazon, Mathew Morton stated that he hoped to set sail by May or June of 1619. In November of that year, when the company decided to hold back the departure of the first expedition until the spring, he was obliged to abandon the project and sign on for the East Indies instead.[3] The delay, undoubtedly caused by the difficulty of raising the finances to equip the first voyage, was also due to the confusion and uncertainty generated by the growing protests of the Spanish agent against the venture.

There is no doubt that membership in the Amazon Company, for many noblemen and gentlemen of James I's court, was a sign of their adherence to the increasingly outspoken anti-Spanish faction,

---

[1] See below, pp. 196–7, 202–3.

[2] The suggestion that Roe acted as an intermediary for the Irish already on the river and for the new group going out in 1620 is based on the following evidence: both Bernard O'Brien and Jaspar Chillan alleged that a 'Sir Henrique Ro', 'Sir Thomas Rodriguez', or 'Sir Thomas Ro', had been instrumental in shipping the Irish out to the river in 1620; Sir Thomas Roe played a leading role in the debates in the Grand Committee of the House of Commons 1621 on the fate of the Amazon Co. and the disposition of the cargo brought back by North and the Irish planters, claiming the Irish as his 'men' and explaining that North was, by prior arrangement, to have one-fifth of the value of what he transported for them. (See below, pp. 220, 263, 406–7.)

[3] See below, p. 196. Morton's decision to go for the East Indies instead is recorded in his letter to William Moreton of Little Moreton Hall, Cheshire, 19/29th November 1619 (B.L., Add. MS 33,935, f. 32).

in which men like the Archbishop of Canterbury and the earl of Southampton were leading figures. Ventures in Guiana, such as the Amazon Company, were all part of the concerted effort to weaken James I's attachment to catholic Spain. By 1619, the king's virtual bankruptcy and his inability to obtain subsidies from Parliament had made the dowry from a Spanish marriage a necessity, whilst the election of his son-in-law to the Bohemian throne seemed to offer security against involvement in a European war he could not afford. At the same time, growing demands at home for more outright support of co-religionists in Europe made it necessary for him to pursue an ambiguous course, hoping that some concessions to anti-Spanish sentiment might drive the Spanish government to conclude the agreement he desired. The Spaniards, for their part, cynically exploited James I's aims, holding out the lure of a marriage as a means of getting him to limit English incursions into the New World, and to maintain his distance from other enemy powers.[1]

North's plans for an Amazon plantation aroused protests from Spain's representatives in England deliberately calculated to awaken James I's memory of how the violent sequel to Ralegh's last expedition had contradicted his claims before his departure. The agent, Julian Sanchez de Ulloa, contended throughout 1619 that not only was the Amazon Spanish territory, but that the amount of men that North was taking out, four hundred by his information, indicated that he intended to commit some warlike act against Philip III's dominions.[2] He stressed that such an enterprise threatened the present harmony of Anglo-Spanish relations, pointing out that 'at a time in which it is so much labored to dominish the foresayd frendshipp it is needfull to exchew all that which may anie way tende to the breach'. He hoped that the return of the ambassador, the count of Gondomar would put an end to the affair.[3] Similar hopes expressed by Lord Digby led to angry words with Lord North at the Court.[4] Ulloa's representations brought an evasive reaction from James I. While countering

---

[1] For a discussion of James I's foreign policy, his financial problems and his relationship with Parliament by 1620, see Howat, 1974, pp. 13–34; Jones, 1966, pp. 14–26; S. L. Adams, 'Foreign policy and the Parliaments of 1621 and 1624', in *Faction and Parliament* (London, 1978), ed. K. Sharpe, ch. 5.

[2] See below, pp. 198–9.

[3] Julian Sanchez de Ulloa to George, marquis of Buckingham, 29th February 1620 (P.R.O., SP 94/23, f. 311).

[4] See below, p. 198.

that North, unlike Ralegh, was totally trustworthy, and that the Amazon was already inhabited by English and Irishmen, he did agree to forbid his departure until his intentions could be investigated further.[1] The duke of Lennox passed North's written statement of his plans to the king, who instructed Secretary Calvert to have it translated and forwarded to the Spanish Agent.[2]

Any hope that James I's avowal that North had 'good and honourable' purposes might lead him to permit him to sail were dashed in March 1620 by the arrival of Gondomar. The latter immediately secured another twenty days delay to allow him time to put his case to the Privy Council. The packed antechambers and crowded Council, when he arrived to do this on the 14th April, bear testimony to the strength of support for the Amazon Company and the depth of the resentment of Spanish interference with it. To English claims of a long-established presence in the river, Gondomar asserted Spain's prior right 'by a discovery, demarcation and possession', and threatened a breach of the amity between his master and James I. The Council, divided amongst itself and uncertain of the king's position, restrained North again, much to the frustration of his supporters. While Gondomar informed his king that James I had assured him of his intention to put an end to the scheme, he himself, as he informed Buckingham, feared that the Amazon undertakers might take the law into their own hands. His premonitions were justified when North sailed from Plymouth with a ship and a pinnace, without permission, about the first week of May.[3]

What precisely James I had intended to do before North's disobedience let him off the hook, cannot be known. North, who had had the *William and Thomas* under hire from November of the previous year, and who was, by March, complaining that the capital of the company was being consumed in expenses by the delay,[4] was

---

[1] See below, pp. 199–200.

[2] See below, pp. 276–7. Ludovic Stuart (1574–1624), second duke of Lennox, was created earl of Richmond 1613 and duke of Richmond in 1623. North referred to him by his latter title in 1625.

[3] See below, pp. 203–8. For the history of D. Diego Sarmiento de Acuña, the conde de Gondomar's embassies to James I's court, see A. Ballesteros y Beretta, ed., *Documentos inéditos para la historia de España* (Madrid, 1936–45), I–IV, *passim*; Harlow, *Last voyage*, 1932, *passim*; S. L. Adams, 'Captain Thomas Gainsford, the "Vox Spiritus" and the *Vox Populi*', *BIHR*, XLIX (1976), 143.

[4] See below, pp. 202, 224.

to argue later that he had departed on the assumption that it was
what the king expected of him. After Gondomar's appearance
before the Privy Council, North had been allowed to send his two
ships down to Plymouth. He himself had stayed in London to fulfil
his arrangements with his backers and to petition the king to lift the
embargo. Hearing that his ship's companies were beginning to
disperse, he had gone down to Devon. After three weeks of aimless
waiting, he had heard from friends at Court that he was generally
expected to leave without formal licence, and had acted on this.[1] A
report from the French ambassador that Buckingham had admitted
to James I, in Gondomar's presence, to have sold North a passport,
is not substantiated by the Spaniard's accounts.[2]

North's defection gave James I the opportunity to denounce him,
wash his hands of the project and call in the patent of the company
on the 23rd May/2nd June, without having to confront the issue of
English right to settle on the Amazon.[3] The earl of Kelly reflected,
with some shrewdness, that the king's anger over the affair lay in
that he thought 'his reputations tuiched ather that he intendit not to
staye him, or then that he had not the meanes to staye him'.[4] Just
how genuine were the king's protestations to Gondomar, of his
shame and the evil machinations of his ministers, is debateable. It is
to be noted that, whilst Buckingham did, as Gondomar requested,
put in writing all the measures that the monarch had promised to
take against North and the Amazon Company, he did not set on
record James I's alleged commitment that 'during his lifetime he
would never give a commission nor assistance for trade, conquest or
settlement in the West Indies'.[5]

North was arrested after his return in the first week of January
1621 and committed to the Tower. The tobacco and other

---

[1] See below, p. 277.
[2] Report of the French ambassador Tillières, 5th June 1620, translated and
extracted in F. von Raumer, *History of the sixteenth and seventeenth centuries*
(London 1835), II, 244–50.
[3] See below, pp. 208–16.
[4] Thomas, earl of Kellie to John, earl of Mar, 9/19th May 1620, *HMC,
Supplementary report on the manuscripts of the earl of Mar and Kellie* (London, 1930),
p. 100.
[5] See below, p. 212. Buckingham's letter to Gondomar of the 15/25th May
1620 is to be found in A.G.S., Estado 2601, ff. 16–20. James I's commitment on
this matter was restricted to a vague promise to 'so provide that the King of
Spayne shall not need to doubt any further trouble by coulor of the said Patent
or any other hereafter'.

commodities which he brought back were attached as belonging to the king of Spain, and his attempt to counter-sue in the Admiralty disallowed.[1] Yet Gondomar was still not convinced that James I intended to ban further contacts with the Amazon. Pleas from North's supporters to Gondomar, that he should not stand out against a pardon, were seconded by James I, who had no wish to offend the influential Amazon lobby. Gondomar was of the opinion that a pardon might serve Spanish interests better, if it was accompanied by a promise not to revive the enterprise. It was in this atmosphere of mutual accommodation that North was released from the Tower on the 28th February/10th March 1621. The attitude of James I and Gondomar to the former Amazon undertakers soured in early April, when North petitioned the Grand Committee of the House of Commons, during the recess, that he might be allowed either to relieve his settlers or fetch them away. He complained that the dissolution of the company, and the seizure of his cargo had robbed him of the means to take appropriate action. The discussion by Sir Thomas Roe and others, of the English title to the Amazon and of whether the king had the power to disclaim it, their questioning of the legality of the surrender of the Amazon Company patent by only one-fifth of its members, their assertion of North's right to sue the Spanish ambassador for his tobacco, aroused James I to a furious defence of his prerogative. The incident is indicative of the degree to which relations between the king and the House of Commons had deteriorated. North was re-arrested as a result. Gondomar's decision, however, that it was as well to press for his execution or prolonged imprisonment, bore no fruit. North was set free on the 18th/28th July 1621, on the condition that he made no further attempt to make contact with his Amazon plantation.[2]

By the time of his final release, any hope that the defunct Amazon company might show some profit from its first voyage had decayed with the tobacco and other goods that North and some of Purcell's Irish planters had brought back from the river. While Gondomar's arrest of the cargo[3] had been lifted at some point, probably after the discussion in parliament, North's share of it had then been attached in the Admiralty court by the crew of the

---

[1] See below, pp. 216–18, 221.   [2] See below, pp. 217–24.
[3] See below, pp. 217–20.

William and Thomas in lieu of their wages.[1] A subsequent dispute with the farmers of Customs and Impositions on tobacco over the amount owing, delayed the release of the Irishmen's tobacco until at least late July, and of North's until the end of October. By this time North's share of the cargo was virtually worthless.[2] The date of North's release from the Tower coincides with that of the Privy Council's first attempt to settle the problem of the tobacco.[3] The sympathetic tone of the Council's further efforts to alleviate North's difficulties, their report that the king thought 'it fitt both in honour and Justice' to forgo his part of the dues owing, their decision that the former company should be allowed the benefits of its cancelled patent for at least that year,[4] indicates that the influence of North's supporters in the Court and Parliament remained strong. Despite the dissolution of the company and James I's strictures, North and his associates maintained contact with their settlers and received goods from them in the next few years.

[1] See below, pp. 227–9.
[3] See below, p. 223.
[2] See below, pp. 230–2.
[4] See below, p. 232.

THE ABANDONED ENGLISH AND IRISH COLONISTS, 1620–5: FIRST STRUGGLES WITH THE PORTUGUESE

Gondomar's sabotage of the Amazon company occurred at a critical juncture in the history of English and Irish settlement on the lower Amazon. Although the colonies there remained the focus of strong domestic interest throughout the next two decades, the developments on the river between 1620 and 1625 set the pattern for their ultimate failure. Northern European plantations in the river reached their peak during these five years. Portuguese observers estimated that there were anything from two hundred and fifty to four hundred English, Irish and Dutch[1] in the posts scattered along both sides of the north channel from Cabo do Norte to the Equator, and concentrating particularly in what they called the 'Sertão de Tocujúz', the maze of islands and tributaries between the line and the river Paru. The efforts of North to bring the various English and Irish ventures under the wing of an organized trading company occurred simultaneously with the restructuring of Dutch commerce with the Wild Coast. The formation of the West India Company in 1621 was marked initially by tension between the Amsterdam and Zeeland chambers, as the Zeelanders struggled to maintain their control of the trade of the Guiana rivers.[2] For both established and new English and Irish colonists on the Amazon, the period 1620–5 was one of very real prosperity and yet considerable uncertainty, as the rival trading interests competed for their produce. Gondomar's efforts had removed the Amazon Company as a real contender, although some of its servants continued to uphold its claims. The quarrels between the English and Irish planters about their obligations to the defunct company caused

[1] See below, pp. 246, 257.   [2] Ghoslinga, 1971, ch. 5.

them to divide their numbers, creating small holdings which were vulnerable to attack from the now well-organized forces from the garrison at Belém.

North had taken approximately one hundred men out to the river in 1620, leaving them under the command of Thomas Painton. The enthusiasm that the Amazon Company had aroused amongst the English courtiers and gentry was reflected in the number of gentlemen settlers that North carried out with him. John Smith noted at least thirty in the company. Among them was Charles Parker, the brother of William, Lord Mounteagle and Morley, Thomas and William Hixon, John Christmas, and Thomas Warner. Parker was to take over leadership after Painton's death.[1] The new arrivals are reported to have established themselves one hundred leagues upriver, an estimate which, if accurate, would put them upstream of the confluence of the Xingu. John Scott stated that there was 'a plantation of English, AD: 1622' on the river Ginipape who were subsequently 'drove out by the Porteguyz'. It is more likely, however, that North's men first settled themselves on the river Okiari, where Walloon visitors found two English plantations in 1623. The river lay just 0°40' S. of the longer established Irish plantation on the Tauregue, and would be an obvious site for the newcomers.[2] North had hopes of beginning sugar manufacture, but the costly delays to which he had been subjected and the subsequent collapse of the company robbed him of the necessary capital. The planters which Forrest encountered on the Okiari in 1623 had turned their time to good account in concentrating on tobacco cultivation.[3] William White conducted a survey upriver for some two hundred leagues. Such an extensive journey would have taken him past Manaos to the neighbourhood of the confluence of the Negro, where the main river does appear 'to divide it selfe in two parts'.[4]

[1] See above, pp. 60–1 and below, pp. 236–8.
[2] For possible identification of the Okiari see below, p. 158, n. 1. For the location of North's colony, see below, pp. 237, 261; Scott, 'Historical and Geographical Description of the great river of the Amazones', Bodleian, Rawlinson MS, A 175, f. 358v. Hemming, *Red gold*, 1978, p. 580, notes that Charles de la Condamine, the French scientist and explorer, found the ruins of what he believed to be a Dutch fort at the mouth of the Paru in 1743.
[3] See below, p. 261.
[4] See below, pp. 238–40. The confluence of the Tapajós might be similarly described. If, as Harcourt said, they felt the influence of the tide at the farthest point of their journey then they cannot have gone much past Óbidos. Laet's

When he arrived in the river North had immediately informed the 'old' English and Irish planters that they were now subject to the monopoly of the Amazon Company. Smith's statement that he managed to reduce them 'to his company and to leave the *Dutch*' is probably over-optimistic.[1] They had established commitments to the Zeeland merchants who had a proven record of reliability. Those who went out to the river with North knew that the Amazon Company was in a parlous position when they left England and they are hardly likely to have kept that information to themselves. The situation was further complicated in 1621 when, as Harcourt says, the news of the cancellation of the company's patent was sent out to the river 'by *Proclamations* delivered unto them'.[2] The settlers had now no clear lines of authority. Thomas Painton and Charles Parker may have tried to maintain the structures originally laid down by the Amazon projectors, but they had no basis on which to do so. Malcontents might well assert that any agreement made with the company was now null and void. The result seems to have been a division of North's settlers into separate plantations, probably accounting for the two existing on the Okiari in 1623, and possibly the one recorded by Scott on the Ginipape or Paru. Others may have taken themselves off to join the already established English plantations. The men left by Budd and King may have still been on the river. Some may have gone to join the Irish. Some, like Thomas Warner, John Rhodes and Robert Bims, left the Amazon for England about 1622, 'to be free from the disorders that did grow . . . for want of Government amongst their Countrey-men. . . .'[3]

The Irish planters on the Tauregue, understandably, seem to have been determined from the first to retain their independence and their relations with the Zeeland traders. They compounded

---

account of an Englishman who travelled three hundred miles upriver until he entered a great stagnant lake may refer to William White's explorations, although neither Smith nor Harcourt were informed that White encountered such a phenomenon on his voyage; see above, p. 52, n. 1.

[1] See below, p. 237.

[2] See below, p. 240. Roger North, supported by Sir Thomas Roe, had petitioned the Grand Committee of the House of Commons in April 1621 that his colonists should either be relieved or fetched home. There is no evidence as to whether the news of the fate of the Amazon Company was carried out by an English or a Dutch ship, although one would assume the latter.

[3] See below, pp. 238, 240 for the disorders that developed as a result of the collapse of the Amazon Company.

with North for the transport of a cargo of tobacco from Tauregue, allowing for a due percentage to the Amazon Company, and some, Philip Purcell among them, took passage back to England in the *William and Thomas*.[1] James Purcell may well have been left behind to command the plantation.[2] The numbers of the Irish on the Amazon were not thus diminished, since a new party of Irish settlers had sailed for the river with North, possibly under the command of a young gentleman called Bernard O'Brien.[3]

The evidence for this second migration of Irish to the Amazon in 1620 comes mainly from two sets of documents preserved in the Archivo de Indias in Seville. One of them, the collection of memorials addressed to Philip IV of Spain by an Irish merchant, Jaspar Chillan, between 1631–2, was published by Aubrey Gwynn.[4] Gwynn did not know of the existence of a further extensive memorial presented to the Spanish crown about 1636 by a gentleman named Bernard O'Brien.[5] Neither source is easy to use. Jaspar Chillan described himself as a merchant who had resided in Spain since about 1625. He had, he declared, come 'from his country to Bilbao following up some important pleas concerning himself and some eminent citizens of London, pending in the Royal Chancellery of Valladolid'. Nothing much is known about his background. The port books of London record that he was exporting goods to Dublin in September 1618, in the *John* of that city. In the course of his sojourn in Spain Chillan helped plead the cause of fellow Irish men captured by the Portuguese in the Amazon in 1625 and 1629. He had no first hand knowledge of the history of their activities there and his accounts tend to confuse and condense events which occurred over the course of a decade.[6] O'Brien's memorial is a long and detailed account of adventures which might well seem apocryphal were it not for the fact that much of what he had to say is borne out by the Portuguese, Dutch and

[1] See below, pp. 156–8, 217, 230, 230–1. None of the Amazon material lists Roe as an undertaker. Philip Purcell made contact with Gondomar in June 1621. It is most likely that he had returned from the Amazon with North and was one of the Irishmen petitioning for the release of their tobacco. Gondomar undoubtedly sought him out and made it worth his while to provide some information on his former activities, although Purcell seems to have been remarkably careful and very sparing in what he did divulge.

[2] He was certainly there in 1625, see below, p. 306.

[3] See below, pp. 263–4. [4] See below, pp. 398–414.

[5] See below, pp. 263–8, 300–4, 414–41.

[6] See below, p. 398, and P.R.O., E190 London, 22/5.

English sources. His wanderings between 1620 and 1636 were sufficient to merit him the title of the Irish 'Cabeza de Vaca'. O'Brien was, however, anxious to present himself to the Spanish government in the best light and he may well have exaggerated his role in the Irish endeavours on the Amazon in the 1620s. It is hard to assess the nature of his relationship to the Purcell brothers.

O'Brien recalled that 'this supplicant, being 17 years of age, was in England, in London, where he was also with an English gentleman called Sir Henrique Ro, ... To whom certain nobles and commoners of England, with a commission from King James, ... make a foothold and settlement in the great river of the Amazon. ... Sir Henrique Ro departed in this vessel in the aforementioned year of 1621 with 124 persons and the supplicant went amongst them. ...' Chillan informed Philip IV that 'Sir Thomas Rodriguez, an English pirate', had gone out to the Amazon with five ships in 1622, and had abandoned his Irish passengers in the river after one of his vessels was shipwrecked.[1]

The probable truth of the matter is that Roe negotiated with North and the Amazon company to carry a small party of new Irish settlers to the Amazon in 1620.[2] The earl of Clanricard was one of the Amazon projectors and may have associated with Roe in the business. O'Brien identified himself as the son of 'Cornelio Obrien being, in Ireland, a noble gentleman of the house of the Earl of Thomond ... and lord of three estates in which he used to hold three castles, ... taken by the English in 1621 and accused of following the Catholic party in the wars of that kingdom ... and they confiscated his inheritance and goods.' He was clearly not the 'Barnabas O'Brien, 2nd son of Donat, Earl of Thomond in the Kingdom of Ireland', who was admitted to Lincoln's Inn in 1613. A Jerome Brien attended Eton in 1619. None of the O'Brien pedigrees listed by O'Hart provide any suitable candidates, although it is obviously possible that an adventurous younger son

---

[1] See below, pp. 263–4, 406.
[2] Chillan says that the Irish went out under 'Sir Thomas Rodriguez', or 'Sir Thomas Ro'. Williamson, *English colonies*, 1923, pp. 96–8, felt that this could not be a reference to Roe. Williamson was writing without knowing of the existence of the O'Brien memorial and interpreted the allusion to the involvement of Roe too literally, assuming that Chillan meant that Roe had gone out to the Amazon in 1622.

who spent much of his life overseas might well have disappeared from family records.[1]

O'Brien says that the newcomers did not settle near the English. The twelve of them, with four English servants, sited themselves some sixty leagues from Cabo do Norte 'at a place formerly the natives called Pataví, and ever since *Cocodivae*'.[2] They were obviously some distance down river from Tauregue. 'Pataví' means 'coconut grove'. It is possible that O'Brien's settlement was on Laet's 'coci insulam' or 'Cocos Eyland', Forrest's 'Cocq's Eyland' off Roohoeck, modern Point Macapá.[3] When Jesse des Forrest entered the Amazon in 1623, he encountered Irishmen at the islands of Sapno and Sapanapoko which appear to have been assembly points for trade with incoming vessels. He reported that the Irish lived at Tauregue. Wherever O'Brien's company settled, presumably they cooperated with the Irish on the Tauregue. In addition to the two Purcells and O'Brien, 'Estavão Corse', 'Joan Joanssen', 'Ricardo Molram', 'Juan Alein' and possibly William Gayner, all Irishmen, were on the Amazon between 1620 and 1625 but it is impossible to say at which settlement.[4]

O'Brien claims that he built a good stockade and won the friendship of the local Indians by supporting them in raiding parties against their enemies. They reciprocated by providing labour for his tobacco and cotton plantations. The most fascinating part of his entire narrative is his account of a long trip upriver in the course of which he encountered an Amazon queen who was captivated by his charm. One is tempted to dismiss this entire episode as apocryphal. The Portuguese at Belém seem to have been

[1] *Admissions from A.D. 1420–A.D. 1893. The records of the Honorable Society of Lincoln's Inn* (London, 1896), I, 163. For references to Cornelius or Connor McDonogh O'Brien of Lemeaneagh, see J. Ainsworth, ed., *The Inchiquin Mss* (Dublin, 1961), pp. 287, 294–7, 299–301, 312–13, 317, 319, 329, 332–3, 337; J. Morrin, ed., *Cal. of the Patent and Close rolls of Chancery in Ireland, Charles I, 1–8* (Dublin, 1863), p. 427. Connor O'Brien is said to have died 2/12th January 1604. Bernard O'Brien said that he was seventeen when he went out to the Amazon, which would put his birth about 1603. The Earl of Thomond received the castles of Dromoland and Ballyconnell, County Clare, properties of Connor O'Brien of Lemeaneagh, from the Crown by January 1600. Hemming, *Red gold*, 1978, pp. 581–2, suggests that Teige, the middle brother of the Earl of Thomond, may have been Bernard O'Brien's father.

[2] See below, p. 264.

[3] See below, p. 260; Laet (1633) bk. 17, 632, (1640) bk. 17, 571.

[4] See below, pp. 394–7, 409, 412. Chillan states that 'Joanssen', 'Molran', and 'Alein' had gone 'with Sir Thomas Ro' to the Amazon in '1622'.

amused by O'Brien's large claims about his prowess in 1629.[1] It is difficult to establish the route of his expedition as stated. The odyssey which brought him out by the estuary of the Surinam seems incredible, although O'Brien repeated his claim that he had made such a journey. John Hemming argues that it is conceivable that 'O'Brien travelled up the Jari, Paru or even Trombetas rather than the main Amazon. This would explain his meeting Amazons in the area where both Carvajal and Acuña located them. He would then have crossed the watershed to Courantyne or the Surinam river.'[2] While this is feasible, an overland journey to the Wiapoco seems more within the bounds of possibility.

In 1623 the directors of the Dutch West India Company sent out Pieter Fredericz of Haarlem to the Amazon in the *Pigeon*, to reconnoitre the situation in the river. He carried with him Jesse des Forrest and ten other men, representatives of a group of Walloon families who were considering making a settlement somewhere on the Wild Coast.[3] Forrest's journal of the voyage gives a clear account of the whereabouts of many of the European posts on the north channel as far inland as the Okiari. The first port of call in the delta was the village of Sapno, on the island of that name off the present Canal do Gurijuba. The village belonged to the 'Maroans' Indians,[4] but there were clearly English and Irish in the vicinity who came out to meet the ship. They were possibly living on the mainland in the area which Matthew Morton had surveyed in such detail between 1611 and 1615.[5] The Irish may have come down from Cocodivae. Sapno was noted on the map which the Portuguese pilot, António Vicente Cochado, made of his survey of the Amazon delta in 1623 as 'the port where all the ships which traffick with the Indians drop anchor'.[6] It was obviously the first trading station on the river. The next objective, for the company of the *Pigeon*, was the island and village of 'Sapanapoke'. The island lay, according to Laet, on the Equator and is identifiable with the Ilha do Pará opposite the river Anauíra-pucu.[7] This again was clearly an assembly point for the

[1] See below, p. 302.
[2] See below, pp. 265–6, 418; Hemming, *Red gold*, 1978, p. 582.
[3] B.L., MS Sloane 179B.
[4] The Arua, see above, p. 25, n. 1.
[5] See above, p. 42.   [6] Fig. 3.
[7] Laet (1625), bk. 14, 462, (1630), bk. 15, 462, (1633), bk. 17, 632, (1640), bk. 17, 571; S. Tyacke, 1980, p. 82.

English and Irish in the vicinity. Some of the 'old' English planters may still have been on the Anauíra-pucu or the Mazagão.[1] Tauregue and the Okiari were within easy reach. Fredericz took the Walloon passengers to see the settlements on the latter rivers before turning back downstream. The two Dutch forts on the Xingu had by that time been destroyed, and Adriaenszoon Ita's settlers upstream from the Paru were preparing to abandon their plantation.[2] The English on the Paru may also by then have been 'drove out by the Porteguyz'.[3] There is no evidence as to whether Thomas King's fort was still in existence.

Forrest reported that the English on the Okiari had prosperous tobacco plantations. Both the English and the Irish did a vigorous trade with Fredericz as well as with their old acquaintance Pieter Jansz of Flushing.[4] The latter had arrived in the river at the same time and irritated the company of the *Pigeon* by his attempts to pre-empt their traffic with his long-established customers. The Portuguese learned that the northern European holdings in the Amazon returned some 800,000 lbs of tobacco per annum by 1623, and could provide cargo for some twelve to fifteen ships. Some vessels, presumably Dutch, which had been trading on the coasts of Mina, Cabo Verde and Brazil, were beginning to use Sapno as a way-station on their homeward voyage. The Portuguese found black slaves from Angola in the Dutch forts on the Xingu.[5]

Fredericz and Jansz entered the Amazon in October 1623, just over a month after a skirmish between the colonists in the north channel and the Portuguese garrison at Belém. Gondomar's despatches about the Amazon Company had greatly disturbed Philip IV's ministers. In 1621 São Luis, Belém and the holdings in Ceará had been incorporated into the 'Estado do Maranhão e Grão Pará'. The new state was autonomous, responsible only to Lisbon. Consultations with the former governor of Brazil demonstrated the need to reconnoitre the lower Amazon, to discover the true state of affairs there and to dislodge the enemy if possible. The task was

---

[1] See above, p. 47.   [2] See below, pp. 164–5, 244–53.
[3] See above, p. 70, n. 2.
[4] Jansz obviously had well established contacts with the Amazon planters.
[5] See below, pp. 245, 250–1. Bernard O'Brien sold his tobacco and cotton for a considerable sum in Zeeland in 1624/5. Richard Jones heard that North's planters were owed £1,000 for a cargo of goods carried back by Flushing traders. Thomas Fanning estimated that the plantations were returning £40,000 on an initial £300 investment.

conferred upon Luis Aranha de Vasconselhos in May of 1622. The need for action was confirmed by the receipt of a report from Bento Maciel Parente, *capitão-mor* of Belém, in 1623. He had captured two Flemings who had informed him about the dispositions of the intruders on the north shore of the river.[1] Aranha de Vasconselhos arrived on the 20th May 1623, probably shortly after Parente had sent his despatch to Portugal. He had with him the pilot António Vicente Cochado, picked up in Pernambuco.[2] His ship, a caravel of sixty tons, was capable of negotiating the shallow channels of the lower Amazon. The authorities at São Luis had reluctantly provided some men and munitions to supplement the complement of twelve soldiers he had carried out with him.[3] While Parente at Belém was no better supplied, order had been restored to the garrison and brutal punitive expeditions against the surrounding Indians had established the domination of the Portuguese over the southern fringes of the delta.[4]

Luis Aranha de Vasconselhos set out from Belém on the 11th of June. Cochado, who accompanied him, said that his expedition consisted of a caravel, a launch and forty canoes. While Robert Harcourt was to report that some three hundred Portuguese were involved in the expedition, it is unlikely that there were more than seventy, if that many. The strength of the party came from the four hundred or so Indians who were induced to join the Portuguese by realistic assessment of their best interests and the persuasions of the Capuchin missionary, Cristóvão de São José.[5] Vasconselhos took the southern route into the mainstream, passing through the 'fouros de Breves' and 'Aturia'[6] into the Canal do Gurupá, and thence to the

---

[1] See below, p. 256.   [2] See below, pp. 170, 248, n. 1.

[3] António Moniz Barreiros, *capitão-mor* of São Luis do Maranhão fired off a volley of complaints to the king about the undisciplined behaviour of Luis Aranha de Vasconselhos' company, February 1624, A[rquivo] H[istorico] U[ltramarinho], Lisbon, Maranhão 828, caixa 1, no. 60.

[4] On Bento Maciel Parente's activities in Pará, 1619–23, see above, p. 57, and below, p. 187, n. 1; Guedes, *Brasil-costa norte*, 1968, pp. 31–51.

[5] See below, pp. 244, 248.

[6] The name for two of the maze of channels between the Pará and the Amazon. The *Fouro dos Breves*, carrying 5½–20 fathoms of water, runs 24 miles N.W. from Marajó island to a wider stretch of water named the *Poco*. From thence the *Fouro Aturía*, with a mean breadth of 55 yards and carrying 4⅓–11 fathoms, runs N.W. for 55 miles to San Salvador island. From the west end of the *Fouro Aturía* another channel leads 40 miles S.W. to the mouth of the Xingu; *South American Pilot* (London, 1864), pt. I, 278.

mouth of the Xingu, which they reached on the 16th of June. The defenders of the forts Orange and Nassau surrendered with little opposition, recognizing that they were critically outnumbered. Some one hundred and thirty prisoners, thirty-six of them Dutch, the rest Angolan Blacks and Indians, were loaded for transport back to Belém. Vasconselhos had decided that it was better to withdraw than to risk isolating himself from his base.

Twenty leagues from Belém the party encountered Bento Maciel Parente who had set out to relieve them. It was agreed that Parente should continue by the southern route back into the Gurupá. Vasconselhos was to deliver his captives to the garrison and then take the caravel across the outer fringe of the delta into the north channel to rendezvous at Gurupá. Parente probably rounded the southern end of the Ihla de Gurupá and turned against the cluster of foreign settlements in the vicinity. By the time Vasconselhos's forces caught up with him, on the 22nd of August, he had already 'attacked the English ... and captured two in one of the outposts. The rest had fled to where the Irish were.'[1] Parente may have tried to assault Adriaenszoon Ita's settlement and driven out the English on the Paru. The two Portuguese companies appear to have met at Sapanapoco. The Dutch, English and Irish recruited their forces in opposition. Pieter Adriaenszoon Ita was in the river and his vessel was pressed into service, with Charles Parker and others of the English and Irish crammed aboard. After a fierce battle with the Portuguese, Adriaenszoon Ita found himself in danger of being forced aground on the sandbars off the Okiari and was obliged to set fire to his ship. The Portuguese accounts make exaggerated claims that the defenders suffered great losses, but neither Charles Parker nor Pieter Adriaenszoon Ita were among the casualties.[2] The encounter was sufficient to induce Parente to withdraw back into the Gurupá, where he built the fort of São António at Mariocay leaving behind a garrison of fifty men when he returned to Belém. Vasconselhos made off down river for Portugal.

The raid deterred Fredericz's Walloon passengers from settling on the Amazon. It does not seem to have shaken the confidence of the planters of Okiari and Tauregue who drew up a contract for supplies with the West India Company through their agent Fredericz. In fact, shortly after the latter left the Amazon, Pieter

---

[1] See below, pp. 251–2.   [2] See below, pp. 237, n. 3, 245, 253, 257, 261.

Jansz carried a party into the Gurupá to drive out the new fort, destroying the Portuguese foothold in the area. The only definite casualties of the encounter were the two Dutch forts on the Xingu and the Anglo-Dutch colony settled upriver from the Paru since 1616. The loss of Adriaenszoon Ita's vessel unnerved the planters and prompted them to return to Zeeland. They departed in two Dutch ships which had come into the river.[1]

According to Scott, some of the English among them no sooner reached Flushing than they regretted their decision. Nine of them shipped themselves to London, where they apparently made contact with some of the former Amazon Company projectors.[2] By 1624 James I's foreign policy was in ruins and the climate was now favourable for the resurrection of Guiana ventures. It is unlikely, however, that a two hundred ton ship with as many as ninety-six men and fifty women and children was sent out to the Amazon in 1624 or 1625. English settlers did go out to the river in those years, making contact with North's planters. Richard Jones, a gentleman of London, did so, as did Thomas Fanning the factor of George Eveling.[3] Eveling had been stimulated by the news of the great profits made by the English planters and sent out his servant to assess the possibilities. In all probability, both Fanning and Jones sailed out in West India Company vessels. The Guiana lobby in England was preparing but it was not yet ready to mount a new Amazon initiative. Eveling claimed that he could get no support for his plans to launch a new plantation in England in 1625, and that he was thus forced to turn to the Dutch. His complaints should be taken with a pinch of salt. The interest existed by 1625 but not the organization. Eveling impatient of delay had turned to the Dutch and had to defend himself two years later from charges that he had infringed the monopoly of the new Guiana Company.[4]

The West India Company had moved quickly to rebuild Dutch holdings in the Amazon. Late in 1624 or early 1625 a squadron led by Admiral Lucifer carried out Nicolaes Oudaen at the head of a

---

[1] See above, pp. 53, 56, and below, pp. 164–5, 242, 259, 261.
[2] See above, p. 165.
[3] See below, pp. 268, 271, 395–6. Purchas noted in 1624 'There is report also of an English colony left by C. North in Guiana still continuing' (*Purchas his pilgrimes* (1625), IV, bk. 10, 1973, (1905–7), XX, 134), indicating the sudden resurgence of interest in the English Amazon plantations about that time.
[4] See below, pp. 271–3.

large number of colonists.[1] Eighteenth-century Brazilian sources claim that Philip Purcell was part of this company together with a new group of Irish planters.[2] Although both the O'Brien and Chillan memorials mention the arrival of the Dutch in the river in 1624/5, neither admit the presence of any Irish in their company. On the contrary both accounts assert that the Irish already there refused to let the Dutch settle near them. Since both men were engaged in trying to persuade the Spanish Crown that Irish catholics were suitable for admission as colonists within the bounds of the Spanish Indies it would have been extremely foolish of them to admit any connection with the Dutch. It appears that Purcell settled his new men neither at Cocodivae nor Tauregue but went up the Canal do Gurupá with the Dutch to build a new fort near the mouth of the Xingu. Their relations with their fellow countrymen were clearly amiable. O'Brien relates that when he decided to return to Europe in a Dutch vessel in 1625, he left the command of his stockade and plantation to Philip Purcell. This is the first reference to Purcell since he returned to England with North in 1621.[3] While he may have been out to the river in the intervening period, if he did go out with Oudaen in 1624/5 he does not immediately appear to have thrown in his lot with the Irish in the established settlements. The eighteenth-century sources, mentioned above, state that he went upriver with Oudaen and assisted him to build a new fort at Mandiutuba on the Canal do Gurupá, close to the mouth of the Xingu and not far from the river Maxipana.[4]

The timing of O'Brien's decision to return to Europe was impeccable. Shortly after he had departed the Portuguese of Belém struck upriver for the second time. The new fort, obviously

[1] Oudaen and his settlers were taken out by Admiral Lucifer in the *Black Eagle* and Geleyn van Stapels in the *Flying Dragon*. Van Stapels arrived in the Wiapoco on 23rd May 1625 after depositing the colonists on the Amazon. The new colony was estimated to contain about eighty to one hundred soldiers (B.L., MS Sloane 179B, f. 10). Bernardo Pereira de Berredo, *Annaes históricos do estado do Maranhão* (1749), p. 227 put their numbers at two hundred men.
[2] Pereira de Berredo, 1749, p. 227; 'Memória dos Capitães e governadores do Maranhão e Pará', B[iblioteca de] A[juda], Lisbon, 54/XI/27, no. 17, f. 4v.
[3] See below, p. 267.
[4] Pereira de Berredo, 1749, p. 227; 'Memória dos capitáes', B.A., 54/XI/27, no. 17, f. 4v. See also Guedes, *Brasil-costa norte*, 1968, pp. 49–51; 'Accois navais', 1975.

intended to defend the southern route into the main stream from Belém, alarmed Bento Maciel Parente.[1] In May 1625 he launched a pre-emptive strike against the intruders. The force of fifty Portuguese, supported by three hundred Indians, was led by Pedro Teixeira, a brilliant commander with a long experience of Indian wars.[2] Teixeira hit Mandiutuba on the 23rd May. Its defenders resisted the fierce onslaught for a day and a night, before embarking themselves in a large launch for the safety of the north channel. As they fled they alerted the English and Irish scattered about the Ihla de Gurupá. All retreated upon, what the eighteenth-century sources call the Rio Felippe, possibly the Okiari. Survivors of Oudaen's party merely said that they had gone to 'the creek' where the English were settled. Undeterred Teixeira's men pursued them to the river. Some of the fugitives were ashore with the English. Others of the Dutch remained in the launch. The Portuguese moved first against two stronghouses at the river mouth. The defenders of these soon fled inland. In hot pursuit Teixeira came up against a contingent of some eighty English, Irish and Dutch. In the protracted battle that followed approximately sixty of them were killed, including Oudaen and Philip Purcell. The rest threw down their arms and attempted to escape. The men who had remained in the launch, hearing of the disaster, sailed for refuge to the Wiapoco. Teixeira rounded off his striking victories by moving against another small fort with twenty men in it, some fifteen leagues off. Its defenders surrendered in return for the promise that their lives would be spared.[3]

If the company of Mandiutuba did retreat to the Okiari, then the smaller settlement fifteen leagues away may have been the Irish settlement on the Tauregue. Any such identification is at the best tentative. Jaspar Chillan complained to Philip IV that some seventy

---

[1] See below, p. 256, n. 1.

[2] For the career of Pedro Teixeira, see Barata, 'A jornada', 1916, pp. 21–3; P. Calmon, *História do Brasil. A formação, 1600–1700* (São Paulo, 1941), II, 105; Kiemen, 1973, p. 24.

[3] Most secondary accounts of Teixeira's expedition are based on that in Pereira de Berredo, 1749, pp. 227–31 and in the 'Memória dos capitães', B.A., 54/XI/27, no. 17, f. 4v. The existing material in the primary sources is printed below pp. 256–7, 269–72, 406–10. Pereira de Berredo is the only source to state positively that Philip Purcell was killed in 1624. His name does not appear in connection with any further ventures to the Amazon in this period. A Philip Purcell was listed, however, as commanding a company in the Irish regiments in Flanders in 1635, P.R.O., SP 94/37, f. 83.

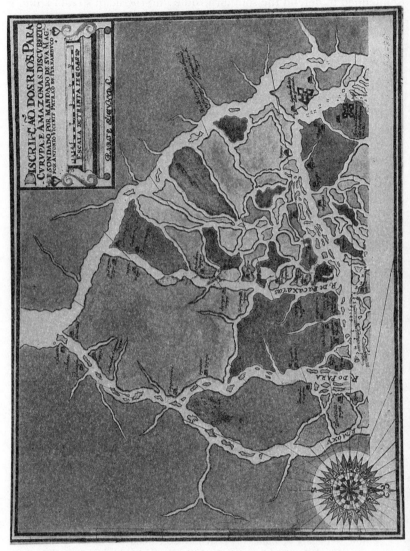

Fig. VIII. António Vicente Cochado 'descrição dos Rios do Pará,
Corupá e Amazonas, Parte Primeira', 1625
(By kind permission of Biblioteca Nacional, Rio de Janeiro)

Fig. VIII. António Vicente Cochado 'descrição dos Rios do Pará,
Corupá e Amazonas, Parte Primeira', 1625
(By kind permission of Biblioteca Nacional, Rio de Janeiro)

Irish had surrendered to Teixeira who had rewarded their trust by immediately massacring fifty-four of them. His claim about the massacre, if not the actual number killed, was supported by documents provided by Friar António de Merciana who deplored Teixeira's action.[1] James Purcell and the other surviving Irish were taken captive, as was the Englishman Richard Jones.[2] There is no mention of what happened to O'Brien's post at Cocodivae. Presumably many of the English and Irish survived the Portuguese onslaught by retiring into the interior among their Indian allies. The Dutch who fled to the Wiapoco squabbled among themselves and fell prey to hostile Caribs who killed most of them.[3]

[1] See below, pp. 306, n. 1, 407, 409–10. Merceana accompanied Teixeira on the expedition.
[2] See below, pp. 306, 396, 407, 409, 412. If Chillan's figure for the number of Irish captives was accurate it probably included those who had recently come to the Amazon with Oudaen as well as the Tauregue settlers.
[3] See below, pp. 270–1.

INTRODUCTION V

THE CREATION OF THE GUIANA COMPANY,
1626–7

Unaware of these disasters, members of the former Amazon
Company took advantage of the breakdown in Anglo-Spanish
relations and the death of James I to press for the reconstitution of
their charter. Sometime in 1625 Roger North presented Charles I's
councillors with a review of the events which had brought his earlier
venture to grief.[1] He also sought the cooperation and support of
Robert Harcourt.[2] Assisted by the duke of Buckingham, both
initiatives rapidly produced favourable results.[3] Harcourt showed
himself willing to surrender his separate patent in return for
incorporation with North and his associates in a new company.
Sometime in the first two months of 1626 Charles I ordered the
Attorney General to draft the requisite charter.[4] The territory to be
granted within it was extensive. Harcourt's rights to the coastline
between the Essequibo and the Wiapoco were now combined with
the monopoly of the former Amazon Company, stretching from the
Wiapoco to five degrees southward of 'any parte or brannch of the
said River of Amazons'. The new company's writ was conceived to
run through the continent from the Atlantic to the Pacific.[5]

North and Harcourt's efforts to launch the venture were
attended by a flurry of publications. Secure in the king's warrant to
the Attorney-General, Robert Harcourt made moves to publish a

---

[1] See below, pp. 276–7.   [2] See below, pp. 275, 277–8.

[3] George Villiers, created duke of Buckingham in 1623, became the first
honorary governor of the Guiana Co. North sent him a handwritten preliminary
draft of his prospectus for the new venture on the 16/26th March 1626 (P.R.O.,
CO 1/4, ff. 9–10). The final published version is printed below, pp. 282–5.

[4] See below, pp. 277–8. Charles I's warrant clearly predates both Robert
Harcourt's moves to issue a revised edition of his *Relation* in February 1626 and
Roger North's publication of his prospectus and preamble for subscription in
March.   [5] See above, p. 61, and below, pp. 190, 196, 278, 294–5.

revised edition of his *Relation* in February 1626.[1] In the next month
Roger North had printed both a prospectus for potential investors,
and a *Preamble for the subscriptions, intimating the conditions of
Adventure* by which they might be included in the expected patent.[2]
The latter did not pass the great seal until the 19th/29th May 1627
formally incorporating the 'Governor and Company of Noblemen
and gentlemen of England for the plantacion of Guyana'.[3]

The official title of the corporate body gives an indication of what
was to be its major weakness. By the early summer of 1627 North
and Harcourt had managed to draw in an impressive list of
associates. Under the patronage of the duke of Buckingham, the
most influential man at court, seventeen other peers and thirty-
seven gentlemen of varying rank and income had been induced to
subscribe, but no significant merchants were to be found among
their numbers. Twenty-four of the patentees had promised £100
each, others £150, none less than £50. The original stock probably
amounted to something over £4,000.[4] The publication of the *breefe
Relation of the present state of the busines*, in June was intended to
encourage further investment, but it already hints at a pressing
shortage of funds. Some of those who had hoped to join in the
charter of incorporation had been unable to raise the minimum
£50. The members felt it prudent to remit any late entry fine which
might deter others from joining.[5] Although the patentees were now
called upon to underwrite the first third of their ventures it is clear
that many could not do so. In 1634, thirty-one of the charter
members still owed on their subscriptions. Sixteen, seven of them
peers, had paid nothing at all.[6]

While some may have defaulted for lack of liquid capital, others
may have had second thoughts about the security of their
investment by the autumn of 1627. The new colonies in the
Leeward islands, that on St Christophers founded by Thomas

---

[1] The copyright for the *Relation* was transferred to W. Stansby, 23rd February
1626, see *STC*, revised edition (London, 1986), I, 559.

[2] See below, pp. 282–7. Neither the prospectus, *Breefe notes*, nor *The coppie of
the preamble*, both printed by T. Purfoot in 1626, were entered in the Stationers'
Register.

[3] See below, p. 294.

[4] See below, p. 298. Adding up Sir Henry Spelman's tally of arrearages due
from thirty-one of the original patentees gives a figure of £2,617 (see below, pp.
390–1). There were twenty-four other subscribers by June 1627.

[5] See below, p. 299.　　　　　　　　　[6] See below, pp. 390–1.

Warner who had left the Amazon in 1622,[1] appeared to offer a safer, alternative source of commodities like tobacco. North had published his prospectus for the new colony in early 1626 in the belief that his 'old' English and Irish planters were still on the river, and that they now had the support of the settlers taken out by Oudaen and Philip Purcell in 1624. Both Harcourt and North based their arguments for the prospect of profitable returns from the first voyage on this assumption. They dismissed fears of the proximity of the Portuguese by pointing to the ability of the English and Irish colonists to resist them in 1623.[2] They can hardly be accused of misrepresentation, since it is unlikely that news of Maciel Parente's ruthlessly effective assault of 1625 had yet reached England. According to George Eveling rumours of it reached the Dutch West India Company in autumn 1626.[3] The Zeelanders who picked up the Dutch survivors in the Wiapoco did not return to the Republic until early September 1627.[4] As word of the loss of the English, Dutch and Irish plantations filtered through the seafaring community, it is not surprising that the Guiana Company was unable to raise sufficient funds to send a ship out to the Amazon before November 1628. The Dutch West India Company had also decided not to send any further settlers to the Amazon until it was certain of the fate of the Dutch and Irish already there.[5]

The discovery of additional material in the English, Portuguese and Spanish archives makes it possible to build a more detailed and accurate picture of the Company's efforts at colonization between 1628 and 1631 than has been previously possible.[6] Hampered from the beginning by underfunding, any real hope of success was further undermined by disagreement among its leaders about the location of its settlements and the unwillingness of the 'old' Irish planters to work with the new English company.

John Smith's statement that the latter despatched its first ship

---

[1] See below, p. 238, n. 2. [2] See below, pp. 281-2, 284.
[3] See below, p. 272. [4] See below, pp. 269-71.
[5] See below, p. 272.
[6] J. A. Williamson's pioneering reconstruction of the Guiana ventures during this period, *English colonies*, 1923, pp. 113-32, can now be re-written. Williamson did not have access to O'Brien's 'Memorial' or much of the Portuguese source material and was forced to rely heavily on Bernardo Pereira de Berredo's *Annaes históricos*, 1749. His account of the activities of James Purcell and the other Irish colonists is now largely inaccurate.

carrying 112 men in 1628[1] is substantiated by depositions made in the High Court of Admiralty two years later. In November 1628 the *Little Hopewell* left Gravesend for the Amazon, carrying out Robert Harcourt as governor of the first colony with Sir Oliver Cheyney as his deputy and other gentlemen such as Robert Hayman, former governor of the Newfoundland settlement of Bristol's Hope, in his company.[2] Harcourt, however, ignored his directives, returning instead to his former haunts on the Wiapoco. Arriving in the latter river in February 1629, he immediately began to undertake fortifications and parcel out land for plantation with a view to sugar production.[3] His actions seem to indicate that the Guiana Company had already split into two factions, centring round the old rivals North and Harcourt. As Richard Thornton shrewdly commented, while North's associates may have wished to attribute Harcourt's defection solely to the latter's stubborn determination to push the Company in the direction of his interests, he could hardly have shanghaied over one hundred colonists to the Wiapoco.[4] Their decision to by-pass the Amazon was probably prompted by distrust of the Portuguese forces in Pará.

---

[1] See below, p. 275.

[2] See below, pp. 318–21. For his activities in Newfoundland, see G. T. Cell, *Newfoundland discovered, English attempts at colonization, 1610–30* (London, 1982), pp. 17–20, 25, 44, 46. Robert Hayman's will is to be found in P.R.O., PCC1, Russell. Made on 17/27th November 1628, before his departure 'by Gods leave to Guiane', it indicates that he had entered into a charter party with 'Frances Gore, Mathew Brett, Robert Hunt, and divers for continuing a plantacon in Guiana'. The profits thereof were to be divided into twenty-six parts of which Hayman was to have twelve. Edward Ellman was also of this group as is indicated by the documents cited below.

[3] See below, p. 349.   [4] See below, pp. 350–1.

THE 'OLD' IRISH PLANTERS GO OUT TO THE AMAZON FOR THE DUTCH WEST INDIA COMPANY, 1629

Believing that Harcourt had sailed for the Amazon, the investors of the Guiana Company appear to have despatched a second vessel to the river in January.[1] Their action may have been prompted by the need to warn him that former Irish planters were returning to the river in the service of the Dutch West India Company. It is ironic that while the English newcomers, under a leader with no practical experience of the Amazon, apparently feared to settle there, the Irish, who had actually suffered at the hands of the Portuguese, were anxious to return.

The incorporation of the Guiana Company, in the eyes of its members, brought any existing or future Irish settlements on the Amazon under its jurisdiction. The presence of Daniel Gookin among the original patentees and the entry of Edward Blennerhasset into the company by 1629 supports other evidence that the company planned to carry out more Irish emigrants to the Amazon. Gookin had shipped men from his Munster estate to Virginia in 1621 and may have purposed to raise more for the Amazon. Blennerhasset may have had similar intentions from his property in Ulster.[2] Even more valuable to the new English venture would be the experience of veteran Irish colonists like James Purcell who had managed to escape captivity in Pará to return to England by 1628.

If the Irish at Tauregue in 1625 had erred in their assumption that their religion would entitle them to different treatment by the

---

[1] See below, p. 275.

[2] See below, pp. 294, n. 9, 340, 391. I am indebted for my information on Edward Blennerhasset's activities in the Ulster plantation to Professor R. J. Hunter of the University of Ulster.

Portuguese, it did help to shorten the captivity of some of their number. The Capuchins in Maranhão and Grão Pará felt them to be the victims of an injustice and secured permission for James Purcell, Stephen 'Corse' and Mathew More to sail for Spain in 1627. They managed, despite the efforts of the governor of the Maranhão to recapture them in the Antilles, to reach the Spanish court. Their case was brought to the attention of Jaspar Chillan. The combined efforts of Chillan and Friar António de Merciana achieved their release and a licence to return to their own country.[1]

Their actions on leaving Spain justified the worst fears of the governor of the Maranhão and indicate the strength of their interest in the Amazon. Making their way to England in 1628 James Purcell and Mathew More contacted the undertakers of the Guiana Company who welcomed their arrival. They soon learned, however, that the Dutch West India Company had similar plans to re-establish an Amazon colony. Preferring to cast in their lot with the more reliable Dutch, Purcell and More secured passports to journey into Holland in September. They probably assured the Guiana venturers that they intended to seek out some of the 'old' planters and bring them into its service. To the anger of North and his associates, they signed on instead with the rival Dutch enterprise.[2]

Both the Portuguese and English sources state that James Purcell was appointed commander of the mixed force of Irish, Dutch, English and French which left the United Provinces for the Amazon in January 1629.[3] Bernard O'Brien claimed, however, that the Dutch made him 'captain-general, merchant, pilot, and interpreter' of the colony. O'Brien had returned to Europe in 1625 to find his father imprisoned for treason. He reports that he was able to secure his release upon securities, 'but they did not return his castles nor more than a sixth of his lands'. Evading the importunities of the reactivated Amazon projectors he embarked on a tour of Europe which appears as incredible as his wanderings in Guiana. When he arrived in Zeeland in 1628 he was, he says 'approached by the Council of Zeeland and they brought to him two Irishmen who had come from the river Amazon', James Purcell and Matthew O'Malley.[4] William Gayner, another Irish man married to a Dutch woman, may well have gone out to the Amazon with this

---

[1] See below, pp. 398–414.
[2] See below, pp. 300–7.
[3] See below, pp. 306–7, 339.
[4] See below, pp. 300–1.

expedition.[1] Sir Thomas Roe arrived at the Hague in December 1628, homeward bound from his mission in Turkey. There is no evidence as to whether he took any interest in the activities of his former Irish associates.[2]

Given full freedom of religion and promised yearly reinforcements of their compatriots, Purcell, O'Brien and others of the 'old' planters returned to the Amazon about April 1629, thus preempting the English Guiana Company. Making their way upstream they rebuilt a substantial stockade on the Tauregue.[3] O'Brien states that he then left Purcell and O'Malley in charge of the garrison and went with a body of soldiers into the interior to renew his alliances with the Indians. While he was there news came to him that the Portuguese were attacking the fort.

In 1629 the balance of forces in the Amazon had shifted against the northern European intruders. The Portuguese had maintained a second fort in the Canal do Gurupá since 1625 and had reconnoitred the mainstream as far as the confluence of the Tapajós. To the distress of the Capuchins, who had insufficient men to carry out their missionary labours, the surrounding tribes had been cowed into obedience by brute force. The arrival of foreign interlopers then did not go unnoticed. The *capitão-mor* of Belém responded quickly sending Pedro da Costa with some forty Portuguese and eight hundred Indians to drive them out. The Tauregue fort was strong enough to beat off the first attack in May, largely, O'Brien says, because he came to its relief. Retreating to the Gurupá Pedro da Costa sent word to the governor in São Luis. Reinforced with men from the Maranhão and under the command of Pedro de Teixeira, the Portuguese launched a more formidable assault in September.[4]

---

[1] See below, p. 394, n. 3.

[2] Brown, *Life*, 1964, pp. 228–30.

[3] See below, pp. 301, 307. The governor of Maranhão and Grão Pará, Francisco Coelho de Carvalho, called the area where the Tauregue lay 'Tuquyn', 'Consulta do Conselho sobre informaçoes prestadas por Francisco Coelho de Carvalho', printed in G. Barão de Studart, *Documentos para a história do Brasil, e espeçialmente a do Ceará* (Fortaleza, 1904–21), IV, 37. He probably meant *Tucujós*, the Portuguese name for both the general region of the mainland and islands bordering the north channel of the lower Amazon, and also the particular territory of the Ilha Grande de Gurupá, neighbouring islands and the area of the north bank immediately opposite.

[4] See below, pp. 301–2, 307–9, and Kiemen, 1973, pp. 32–44; Guedes, 'Acçois navaís', 1975.

The response of the Irish leaders to the new peril reflects both their shrewd assessment of the new strategic reality on the river, as well as their determination to maintain a foothold there. The renewed Portuguese attack coincided with the arrival in early October of both a Dutch supply ship and vessels carrying English colonists sent out under the licence of the Guiana Company. The commanders of the English bore directives from the Company ordering the Irish to submit their jurisdiction. O'Brien's account states that finding himself besieged by the Portuguese, he called the Irish in Tauregue 'to a council, it seeming to him that if they joined with the 400 English and the reinforcements from Zeeland, the Irish and Catholics would lose command to the heretics and the Indians would be heretics not Catholics. He sent three Irishmen and a mulatto to communicate to Pedro Teixeira that he would prefer to serve the King of Spain'.[1] The Jesuit Figueira's account does not cast the actions of the Irish in quite such a heroically religious light. Outnumbered by the Portuguese attackers the Irish leaders clearly tried to play for time, seeking terms from the Portuguese as fellow catholics, yet trying to delay the actual handover of the fort knowing that the English and Dutch vessels had arrived in the river. Purcell had no choice but to surrender when the Portuguese intercepted communications with the incoming ships and threatened reprisals.[2] The newly arrived English colonists regarded this as a great act of treachery.[3]

[1] See below, p. 303.   [2] See below, pp. 309–11.   [3] See below, p. 339.

THE DIFFICULTIES OF THE GUIANA COMPANY'S NEW COLONY, 1628–31

In a sense the English were justified in their accusations. The collapse of the Irish on top of Harcourt's previous defection to the Wiapoco, largely condemned their new colony in the Amazon to failure before it broke its first ground.

Strictly speaking the settlers who arrived in the Amazon in October 1629 had not been sent out by the Guiana Company but by Sir John North, Sir Christopher Neville, Sir Henry Mildmay and others, a syndicate of some of the membership and their associates acting privately under its licence.[1] The meagre joint-stock of the Guiana Company appears to have been exhausted by the heavy expenditure involved in fitting out Harcourt's colony.

Neville and his partners appear to have sent out in the neighbourhood of one hundred colonists to the river, although O'Brien and some of the Portuguese accounts give considerably higher estimates. William Clovell, who had gone to the Amazon in North's company in 1620, went as governor with Thomas Hixon as his deputy.[2] Jácome Raymundo de Noronha subsequently reported that they established their company on the 'Rio Philippe',[3] a

---

[1] See below, p. 321. The associates are listed as Sir John North, Sir Christopher Neville, Sir Henry Mildmay, John Lucas and company, see below, pp. 292, n. 8, 293, ns. 2, 5.

[2] Williamson, *English colonies*, 1923, p. 126, assumed that William Clovell and Thomas Hixon had first sailed to the Wiapoco with Robert Harcourt and then moved down the coast to take charge of the incoming English colonists in the Amazon in the summer of 1629. Hemming, *Red gold*, 1978, p. 586 follows Williamson here. The letter written by Clovell and the members of the Council at North fort in the Amazon, November 1629, indicates that they had come out from England in the two ships which arrived just as James Purcell surrendered the Tauregue; see below, pp. 339–40.

[3] See below, p. 383.

name which Pereira de Berredo, the eighteenth-century historian of the Maranhão, also applied to the river on which the English plantations wiped out in 1625 had been located.[1] It is of course possible that Clovell chose to return to the Okiari, just upriver from Tauregue. It is equally likely, however, that Berredo merely assumed that they had done so. Figueira said that the English turned back downstream from Tauregue. The letter sent back by Clovell and the Council of the plantation in late 1629 implied that the Portuguese expeditions had ravaged the area upriver from their holdings.[2] Johannes Vingboon's chart of the mouth of the Amazon, *c.* 1665, indicates that Clovell and Hixon built their stockade, North fort or Pattacue, down river of Okiari and 'fort op d Torego' further inland on the tributary where the village of 'Callepoke' was situated, just above the Equator.[3]

Begun in an atmosphere of insecurity, misfortune after misfortune fell upon the colony and the Guiana Company in the next two years. The tragi-comic events of the voyage of the *Amazon* and the *Sea-Nymph* leave one feeling profoundly sorry for Sir Christopher Neville, Roger North, and their partners in the syndicate, whose profit and well-being was dependent on the vagaries of shipmasters like Michael Taylor and John Ellinger. It would appear, that had not contrary winds and the truculence and drunkenness of Taylor, the master of the *Amazon*, delayed their departure from England the two ships should have sailed in consort with the vessels which carried out the colonists.[4] Arriving off Cabo do Norte a few weeks after them, Taylor and Ellinger were so crassly stupid as to attempt to pass through the dangerous offshore shoals into the river at night. The risks of this undertaking were increased by the incompetence of the quartermaster on the *Amazon* detailed to take soundings, and by the failure of the company of the latter vessel to give sufficient warning to those of the *Sea-Nymph* when they came aground. As a result the *Sea-Nymph* was cast away, although her company and some of her cargo were rescued. After reaching the

---

[1] Pereira de Berredo, 1749, pp. 230–1, 262.

[2] See below, pp. 311, 339.

[3] See below, p. 261, n. 3. A facsimile of Johannes Vingboon's chart of the mouth of the Amazon from his MS atlas of *c.* 1665 is to be found in T. Wieder, *Monumenta cartographica* (The Hague, 1932), IV, 83.

[4] They arrived within a few weeks of Clovell and Hixon's party, too close to be a distinct supply voyage; see below, pp. 338–90.

the fort, Taylor, in a consummate act of folly, committed two pieces of ordnance to the river bed because of his refusal to stow them properly in the boat taking them ashore. Clovell and Hixon must have been highly relieved to receive from John Ellinger what trade goods, provisions and ordnance had been salvaged from the *Sea-Nymph* as well as the twenty-eight passengers she had conveyed to the river.[1]

Fortunately Ellinger had made use of his letters of marque, granted March 1629, to seize a pinnace on the outward voyage. The shipwrecked company refitted it as the *Guiana* and sailed for Harcourt's plantation on the Wiapoco. The English there were short of supplies and harassed by hostile Caribs. Robert Harcourt was grateful for the meagre assistance and provisions which Ellinger was able to afford him and gave him testimonials to this effect, and five Indian captives to dispose of as he wished. Ellinger navigated the increasingly unseaworthy *Guiana* as far as St Christophers where, apparently at the insistence of her crew, he sold her and one of the Indians for tobacco and annotto. Using part of the proceeds to satisfy his company's demands for wages, he then took passage for England with the residue.[2]

Neville's syndicate can have made very little in the way of profit from the voyage. The colonists in the Amazon and Wiapoco had nothing to return. The *Sea-Nymph* had been lost. Both Taylor and Ellinger were, with good reason, accused of negligence and misappropriation and sued in the High Court of Admiralty after they returned to England in the early summer of 1630.[3] The complement of the *Sea-Nymph* countersued for their wages.[4] These losses may have been sufficient to dissuade Neville and his partners from financing any further ventures to the river. There is no other direct evidence that they had any subsequent interest in Amazon ventures.[5]

Meanwhile, with two colonies to be relieved, the Guiana Company was facing internal dissension. By the autumn of 1629 the company's officers were fully informed of Harcourt's diversion of the first batch of colonists to the Wiapoco. They were not certain

---

[1] See below, pp. 321–9, 338–9.
[2] See below, pp. 329–32, 334–6, 340–1, 344–50.
[3] See below, pp. 321–5, 341–4. [4] See below, pp. 336–8.
[5] Neville and his associates may have been involved in the outfitting of the *Exchange*, but there is no evidence of this or of investment in any further ventures to the Amazon.

Fig. IX. Anonymous map of 'Maranhão Tabõa Tercera', *c.* 1629
(Printed by kind permission of Biblioteca Nacional, Rio de Janeiro)

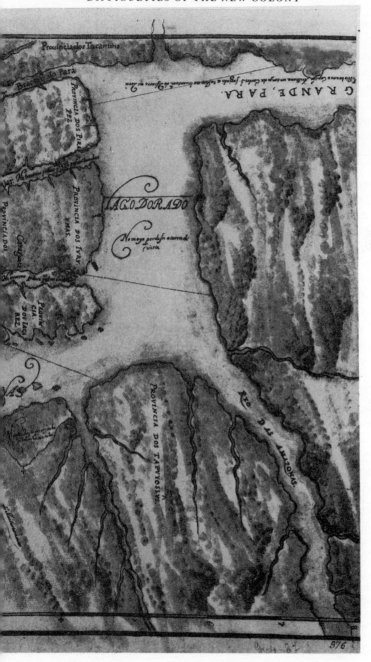

Fig. IX. Anonymous map of 'Maranhão Tabōa Tercera', c. 1629
(Printed by kind permission of Biblioteca Nacional, Rio de Janeiro)

whether Clovell and Hixon's second party would stay in the Amazon once they also discovered this, and feared that they too would choose to remove to the Wiapoco. Roger North was prepared to insist that the priority of the Amazon for settlement be maintained even if it meant uprooting both groups of planters and transporting them down the coast to the river. North's supporters seem to have carried their point in the company's Council, despite the opposition of the Treasurer, Sir Henry Spelman.

Without referring so grave a matter to full discussion in a General Court, they passed several sweeping resolutions in October 1629. One Captain William Bampfield was appointed governor of the colony, superseding the authority of both Harcourt, Clovell and their deputies. Bampfield was to take new colonists out to the Amazon in the *Exchange* of London under one Captain Smith. After delivering the new governor to the Amazon, Smith was to carry directives to the Wiapoco, informing Harcourt that his commission had been revoked and ordering any English planters there to transfer themselves to the Amazon. A small number might be allowed to remain on the Wiapoco at Bampfield's discretion. The *Exchange* was not to stay for more than ten days in the latter river. The errant colonists were to receive no supplies. They would have to go to the Amazon to fetch them.

The record of the Council's high handed measures is preserved in Richard Thornton's 'A happie Shipwrack'.[1] Thornton, a cleric, went aboard the *Exchange* in November 1629 hoping to mend his lack of preferment at home by settling in the new colony. The ship had been outfitted by Captain James Duppa, a professional seaman whose career embraced both naval service, privateering and investment in overseas trade.[2] He also appears to have acted with Roger North and Sir Christopher Neville in the hiring of the crew

[1] See below, pp. 345–55.

[2] See below, pp. 440–5. An account of Duppa's costs for the freight of the *Seahorse*, of which he was part owner between 1626 and 1631, for use in reprisals, the king's service, voyages to Guinea, the Straights, San Lucar and Venice, was submitted to the High Court of Admiralty in 1633 by his partner Adrian Hendrix. Hendrix claimed Duppa owed him one sixteenth part of the freight charges for the various ventures (P.R.O., HCA 13/107, loose sheet; 24/88, nos. 186, 345; 24/89, no. 209). Duppa was also a part owner of the *James*, captured in Barbary by Frenchmen in 1629 (P.R.O., HCA 3/34, ff. 250, 255, 265v, 273v, 290, 299v, 307, 313, 338v, 364, 391v, 419v, 460v; SP 16/229, no. 49).

of the ill-fated *Sea-Nymph*.[1] The conditions aboard the *Exchange*, however, deteriorated as she was held off the Downs for weeks by contrary winds. Before the end of December her crew had mutinied refusing to sail if the apparently authoritarian Bampfield took passage in her. Neither Captain Smith nor members of the Guiana Company could allay their distrust of him. In the face of such determined hostility Bampfield abandoned his commission on the 26th December.

Thornton, a member of the Guiana Company, was now asked to take charge of its written directives. Reading through the documents left by Bampfield, Thornton became aware of the enormity of the Council's measures. The problems and dangers of uprooting the Wiapoco colony were immediately apparent to him. The cavalier treatment of Harcourt would only confirm his supporters in their opposition to the schemes of Roger North. Bampfield had resigned. Thornton had no assurance that Clovell had reached the Amazon. To carry out the company's instructions to remove Harcourt from office would be a recipe for anarchy. Convinced that Bampfield's departure had given the company's officers a much needed opportunity to reconsider, Thornton communicated his concerns to Sir Henry Spelman by letter on the 21st January 1630. The Council gave him short shrift in their written response. If neither Sir Oliver Cheyney, nor William Clovell nor Thomas Hixon were to be found in the Amazon then the designated members of the colony's council were to elect themselves a president and manage affairs until any of the three men 'or some other formerly appointed by us for governement'[2] should arrive. Harcourt was specifically excluded. Thornton, who appears to have had an overdeveloped sense of what was due to him by virtue of his calling, felt himself to have been slighted by the company. Receiving no answers to his further requests for special status and treatment, perturbed by the dwindling of the ship's stores, he took himself ashore at the beginning of February and made for London to present various motions to the Council and the General Court. The *Exchange* set sail without him, doubtless much to his relief. Thornton contented himself with addressing a tedious account of

[1] Testimony of Edmund Parsons before the High Court of Admiralty, 11th June 1631 (P.R.O., HCA 13/49, f. 420).
[2] See below, pp. 353–4.

these events to William earl of Pembroke, the Governor of the Guiana Company.

By 1630 Clovell's settlers at North fort had similarly divided into discontented factions. Even though the *Exchange* brought out new planters their news of the affairs of the company could only have been unsettling, putting established lines of authority in question. It cannot have been clear whether Clovell was to remain in command of the fort or whether the colony's councillors were to elect themselves a president. In September 1630 the *Hopewell* of London was cast away off Sapno with the loss of its cargo and all but eleven of its complement. The survivors who made it up to North fort found that William Clovell was sick and that Thomas Hixon had set himself up as governor and had 'injuriously chosen a Counsell for himselfe'.[1]

The outpost presented an easy prey when the Portuguese attacked in February 1631. Their garrison at Belém was not much larger than that of North fort, but their recent string of victories had, according to Jácome Raymundo de Noronha, left the Indians on the north bank of the Amazon 'so terrified that they will never make alliances with foreigners again'.[2] Noronha left Pará in late January with only thirteen canoes full of soldiers. The Indian villages in Cametá provided another twenty-three boat loads of warriors. The strike force quickly overran North fort killing eighty-six and capturing thirteen of the defenders. Thomas Hixon, a veteran of the Flanders wars, tried to escape by boat under cover of darkness. The Jesuit Luis Figueira was later to describe graphically for Philip IV how Noronha's Indian allies pursued the English 'and splashed them with their paddles, sending so much water into their boat that they soaked everything. They could no longer use their firearms, so our Indians entered and slaughtered them all.'[3] Only seven of the English escaped the onslaught. Two of them were later picked up by a Zeelander and carried back to Flushing. The others lived among the Indians in the forest for five or six months, before being rescued by John Barker in the *Marmaduke* of London, who arrived to trade at the now non-existent settlement in July.[4]

---

[1] See below, pp. 357–8.   [2] See below, p. 380.

[3] From a *consulta* of 1638, 'Sobre hu memorial que fis Luiz figueira Religioso da Companhia de Jesus sobre as cousas tocantes a conquista do maranhão', in Studart, 1904–21, III, p. 28. The passage is translated and quoted in Hemming, *Red gold*, 1978, p. 28.

[4] See below, pp. 355–61.

The *Marmaduke*, the *Amity* of London which was brought into the
Amazon by its master Thomas Harman in December 1631, and the
Hopewell lost the previous year, were probably privately ventured
under the Guiana Company's licence. Roger Glover, a London
merchant who went out in the *Marmaduke* had a brother at North
fort.[1] Captain James Duppa, one Peter Jones and others freighted
the ill-fated *Hopewell* and the *Amity*, which took on tobacco in St
Christophers after leaving the Guiana coast. Duppa himself went on
the latter voyage. Some of the tobacco laded on the *Amity* belonged
to Roger Glover and to 'Master Clovell' who also took passage in the
ship from St Christophers.[2] This was doubtless Henry Clovell, a
survivor of the loss of North fort, who had been carried from the
Amazon to St Christophers in the *Marmaduke* and left there to find
another passage home. Duppa, Glover and Jones may also have
been part of a syndicate which freighted the *Marmaduke*. Duppa had
interest in another ship which reached St Christophers in 1631.[3]
Dutch war fleets were steadily destroying Spanish naval power in
the Caribbean between 1629 and 1633 making the Lesser Antilles a
more secure site for northern European settlement. As the English
plantations in the Leeward and Windward Islands developed, lesser
merchants were more willing to risk trading to outposts on the
Amazon and the Guiana coast, knowing they could make their
voyage in the Caribbean as they returned.

---

[1] See below, pp. 359–61..

[2] See below, pp. 357, 359. Details of the voyage of the *Amity* are to be found in
a long suit brought before the High Court of Admiralty in 1632–4 over tobacco
loaded at St Christophers (P.R.O., HCA 3/34, ff. 162, 167v, 173v, 178, 185, 351,
357, 361, 364, 385v, 392v, 396, 397v, 405, 414v, 434, 454, 460, 463v, 482v, 485,
503v, 512v; 3/35, ff. 3, 7, 39, 62, 97v, 122v, 136; 24/88, nos. 126, 167, 253.

[3] The *Little Exchange*, Captain Gabriel Puckle (P.R.O., HCA 13/50, ff. 174,
200v–201).

THE LAST ENGLISH SETTLEMENTS ON
THE AMAZON, 1630–3

It is not clear why a reconnaissance of the Amazon should have been part of the itinerary of the expedition of Captain Richard Quayle which left England in 1630. On the 29th March in that year Charles I issued Quayle with two copies of a commission. One specified that he was employed 'in our good shippe called the seahorse to range the River of the Amazones and all other the Coasts and Rivers of aMerica soe farre forth as God shall protecte him, and his direccion shall guide him. . . .'[1] The other merely stated that he was 'to range the seas all the world over according to his desire, and request and for private reasons best knowne to us. . . .'[2] He was also granted a commission of martial law on the same day.

Quayle was a naval officer and had been issued with letters of marque against French shipping in 1627.[3] He was the 'favourite' of Richard Weston, the earl of Portland.[4] The latter, appointed Lord High Treasurer in 1629, had considerable influence with the king and probably used it to secure Quayle a loan of a royal ship and his commission.[5] Quayle's instructions for his voyage directed him to shape his course for the Red Sea 'or other eastern ports, and to make prize of all treasure, merchandize and commodities of the King of Spain'.[6] The *Great Seahorse* reached Surat, but Quayle and many of his company were subsequently wiped out by 'a contagion that happened amongst them from which only eight escaped'.[7] When the vessel reached Barbados, in early 1633, her cargo was

[1] See below, p. 362.   [2] P.R.O., SP 12/237, f. 97.
[3] P.R.O., SP 16/157, f. 44.   [4] See below, p. 387.
[5] *DNB*, 1909, pp. 1275–8; M. V. Alexander, *Charles I's Lord Treasurer: Sir Richard Weston, earl of Portland (1577–1635)* (London, 1975).
[6] P.R.O., SP 16/163, ff. 19v–20.
[7] *CSP Domestic, 1634–5* (1864), p. 73.

said to be 'infinite rich', but her complement in 'great distress, most of the company being dead and the others utterly disabled to bring her home'.[1] Crewed by planters from Nevis, the ship limped home to England. She was sold and the proceeds shared out among the surviving crew and the representatives of the deceased.[2] There is no record as to whether the *Great Seahorse* actually entered the Amazon on her return voyage from the East Indies. She may have been the English ship which, according to Cristoval de Acuña, tried to establish an English factory at the confluence of the Tapajós before 1639, only to be driven off by the Indians.[3] On the whole I think this is very unlikely. The promoters of a further English colony on the Amazon founded in early 1632, however, were certainly acquainted with Quayle's mission.

In the summer of 1631, in ignorance of the fate of the inhabitants of North Fort,[4] Thomas Howard, earl of Berkshire,[5] prepared to swell their numbers by sending out a body of settlers to the Amazon. Berkshire appears to have headed up a syndicate formed for the enterprise. John Day,[6] a gentleman of Windsor, was one of his partners. The relationship of his venture to the Guiana Company is nowhere stated. It might be assumed that, since the members of the latter were anxious to strengthen the English hold on the Amazon and unable to act themselves, they were willing to licence Berkshire to develop a private plantation within their proprietary patent. On the other hand, Berkshire may have considered that the patent issued to the old corporation was to all intents and purposes null and void. He attempted to launch his own joint-stock company in 1632

[1] See below, p. 387, and *CSP Colonial, 1574–1660* (1860), p. 171.

[2] For references to the preparations for Quayle's voyages, events during his sojourn in the East Indies and the sale of his ship and her contents after her return in 1634, see *CSP Dom. 1629–31* (1860), pp. 214, 215, 231, 242, 284, 468; *1633–4* (1863), pp. 13, 141, 142, 155, 160, 173, 205, 226, 242, 257, 272, 416, 480, 512, 521; *1634–5*, (1864), pp. 1, 15, 20, 73, 139, 146, 171, 185; P.R.O., HCA 24/90, nos, 38, 74, 134; 3/34, ff. 519v–22; 3/35, ff. 2v, 8, 11, 14v, 15, 22, 26v, 31v–32, 40, 50v, 51v, 58, 65v, 79, 82v, 86. Quayle's ship was not the same as that of which James Duppa was part owner. Adrian Hendrix's account states that his *Sea-horse* was sent on a Guinea voyage in 1629 and freighted for San Lucar in 1631. Duppa sold his interest in her on the 13/23rd January 1632 (P.R.O., HCA 24/88, no. 186).

[3] See below, p. 437.

[4] The *Marmaduke* did not arrive in the Amazon until July 1631. The two survivors brought back by a Dutch ship reached Zeeland sometime in the late summer of that year, see above, p. 101, and below, p. 357.

[5] Sir Thomas Howard (1590–1669), first Baron Howard of Charleton, son of Thomas, first earl of Suffolk, created Viscount Andover 1614, earl of Berkshire 1622; L. Stone, *The crisis of the aristocracy* (Oxford, 1965), p. 817.

[6] See below, pp. 363, 366, n. 1.

without any reference to the prior monopoly granted to the Guiana Company.[1] The fact that Roger North had to apply to the Committee for Foreign Plantations to 'have his Patent againe' in March 1635 suggests that his company had been virtually defunct since 1630.[2]

The leader of the outgoing colonists was a professional seaman from Somerset, Captain Roger Fry. In May 1631, advised by the mariners Samuel Lockram and William Smallbone who were both familiar with the problems of navigating the shoals of the north channel, Fry purchased a 160 tonner in Dunkirk. He renamed her the *Barcke Andevor*.[3] Berkshire clearly had large plans for his colony intending to establish a permanent English settlement, rather than the Indian-worked factory/plantations which seem to have predominated in the earlier English and Irish ventures. In July the Privy Council licenced him to purchase up to fifty pieces of ordnance to protect it 'against the invasion of an Enimy'. He sent out livestock in the first voyage. It is not clear whether any families sailed with Fry but there were plans to send out women and children later.[4]

More interesting are Fry's preparations to do scientific work while he was on the Amazon. Fry is not recorded as ever having attended Oxford as an undergraduate, but he had worked with John Bainbridge, the Professor of Astronomy. In December of 1626 and 1627, they had measured star altitudes together. Fry's plans to go to the Amazon opened up to Bainbridge the prospect of collecting astronomical data from a point under the Equator. The scientist hoped, as Nicholas Tyacke points out, to obtain simultaneous observations of the expected eclipse of 1633, as well as sightings which would elucidate many uncertain areas in astronomy and greatly advance its practical use to seamen and cartographers. More significantly, Bainbridge encouraged Fry to seek financial backing from the earliest promoter of settlement on the Amazon, Sir

---

[1] See below, pp. 366–79. Williamson, *English colonies*, 1923, p. 137, was of the opinion that Berkshire's enterprise was an independent undertaking rival to the Guiana Co.

[2] See below, p. 392.

[3] See below, p. 363. Samuel Lockram had sailed as master's mate of the *Amazon*, and William Smallbone in the crew of the *Sea-Nymph* in 1629, see above, pp. 94–5, and below, pp. 322–4, 337.

[4] See below, pp. 364, 374–6.

Thomas Roe.[1] Back in England by the summer of 1630 after prolonged diplomatic activities in Europe, Roe was in constant correspondence with the courtiers most involved in the Guiana Company and Amazon projects.[2] I have not yet uncovered any evidence as to whether he was persuaded by Fry to invest in Berkshire's venture.

Fry was to observe the 1633 eclipse, but from the Maranhão not the Amazon. The history of his colony can now be clearly established. J. A. Williamson, misreading Jácome Raymundo de Noronha's admittedly terse account, confused the fate of Clovell's planters with that of those taken to the river by Fry. Berkshire's first group sailed for the Amazon in the *Barcke Andevor* and two pataches late in 1631. On arrival at Christmas Fry heard that North Fort had been destroyed almost a year earlier. Disheartened by this discovery Fry sent his ship and one patache back to England. Forty men remained behind with him to hold a fort at a site named Cumahu near Point Macapá. The new garrison found it difficult to survive. The surrounding Indians feared the Portuguese too much to provide necessary supplies. Noronha says that many of the newcomers died of hunger. They had no hope of resisting the Portuguese forces led by Feliciano Coelho de Carvalho which reached the stockade on the 9th July 1632, and surrendered quickly. Fry had gone down river in the patache to look for a supply ship. He was captured on his return to Cumahu on the 14th of the same month.[3] Carried off to São Luis

---

[1] See below, pp. 365–6. Fry's letter to John Bainbridge, 10th May 1633, indicates that he came from Somerset. His work with John Bainbridge, first incumbent of the chair of Astronomy endowed at Oxford by Sir Henry Savile in 1619, is discussed by N. Tyacke in 'Science and religion at Oxford before the Civil War', in *Puritans and revolutionaries* (Oxford, 1978), eds. D. Pennington and K. Thomas, pp. 73–93. Bainbridge and his associates were interested in finding a means to determine longitude by means of simultaneous observations of lunar and solar eclipses. Fry was to observe the expected solar eclipse of 29th March 1633 from the Amazon. Bainbridge was to make a simultaneous observation from Cambridge. I am indebted to Dr N. Tyacke for first bringing to my attention the existence of Fry's letters and notebook in Trinity College, Dublin.

[2] Brown, *Life*, 1964, ch. 6.

[3] See below, p. 384. Williamson, *English colonies*, 1923, pp. 138–40, mistakenly assumed that the eighty-six foreigners massacred by Jácome Raymundo de Noronha at the 'river Phillipe' in 1631 were Fry's men and that Fry himself died in the attack. He, therefore, further assumed that the forty men, said by Noronha to have been left behind at Cumahu in 1632 even after hearing of the loss of the fort on the 'river Phillipe', were part of a second, larger group of settlers sent out by Berkshire in that year. In fact Pereira de Berredo's *Annaes históricos*, 1749, pp. 267–70, which Williamson misread, makes it quite clear that

in the Maranhão, Fry seems to have settled down to a relatively comfortable captivity. His captors doubtless found him a very talented and useful addition to their community. He made his observations of the April 1633 eclipse and sent them off to Bainbridge.[1] The Dutchman, Gedeon Morris de Jonghe, who had been taken at Tauregue in 1629 and lived in the Maranhão for about seven years, knew Fry and recorded that he had also carried out experiments with indigo dye. According to Morris de Jonghe, Fry had been released from his imprisonment by October 1637.[2]

Some six weeks before the garrison at Cumahu surrendered to the Portuguese, the earl of Berkshire published his prospectus for a joint-stock company to raise funds for his plantation.[3] The pamphlet was drafted by John Day, who himself intended to settle on the Amazon with his family and friends.[4] The prospects of the Amazon were described in glowing terms. Drawing heavily on Robert Harcourt's *Relation* and the Guiana material in Purchas, Day stressed the abundance of foodstuffs and merchantable commodities. The Amazon, unlike 'most former plantations except new England ... adventured onely upon hope of one commoditie (as

---

Fry's party at Cumahu was attacked on 9th July 1632 and that Fry, who was downriver at the time, was captured five days later. The 'Mémoria dos Capitães', B.A., 54/XI/27, no. 17, ff. 5v, 11v states that the fort of 'Camau' was demolished on 9th July 1632 and that Feliciano Coelho de Carvalho retreated to Pará burdened with much plunder and an enemy ship. According to Pereira de Berredo, p. 270, another large ship arrived in the river in 1633 to visit Fry's colony. Four of the crew were captured by the Portuguese. This was the supply vessel sent out by Lord Goring in 1633. Hemming, *Red gold*, 1978, relying on Williamson, similarly confuses these ventures.

[1] See below, pp. 385–6.

[2] Gedeon Morris de Jonghe referred to Fry's activities in his 'Brief description presented to the lords directors of the official Company of the West Indies, delegated by the Heeren 19 for the places situated in northern Brazil, named Maranhão, Ceará, Cametá, Grão Pará and other rivers comprised in the basin of the famous river Amazon, where the Portuguese are settled, with all the dispositions and respective circumstances when he departed at the end of November 1637', submitted in Middelburg 22nd October 1637, transcribed, translated and printed by J. Hygino Duarte, 'Relatórios e cartas de Gedeon Morris de Jonge no tempo do dominio Holandez no Brazil', *Revista do Instituto Histórico e Geográfico Brasileiro*, LVIII (1895), pp. 238–50. [Henceforth referred to as *RIHGB*.]

[3] See below, pp. 366–79. *A PUBLICATION OF GUIANA'S PLANTATION*, was entered into the Stationers' Register 24th May/3rd June 1632, See Arber, *A transcript*, 1877, IV, p. 278.

[4] See below, p. 375.

namely Tobacco)', would yield more than one cash crop.[1] He noted, and this had certainly been true before 1629, that most of these things could be acquired by Indian labour with very little effort on the part of the white settlers.[2] Berkshire now intended to send out 'this summer' a new supply of men and women. He hoped particularly to attract skilled craftsmen, who could not only supply the everyday needs of the colonists' households but also run the sugar mills and mines, undertake shipbuilding, and produce the timber, dyes and drugs which would bring lucrative returns.[3]

As he set out the terms by which venturers might enter the company, Day could not ignore the question of the proximity of the Portuguese which would certainly discourage some potential participants. Influenced by the arguments in Robert Harcourt's *Relation*,[4] Day offered two responses to those who might raise this problem. Firstly, the Amazon was big enough for the English to settle out of the way of the Portuguese. Secondly, the Portuguese presented no serious threat as long as the English colonists were well supplied with provisions, arms and ammunition. The news of the loss of North Fort must have reached England by May 1632.[5] Day's references to those who were so foolish as to raise 'a fort for the reliefe of a Colony, and not to victuall it, (as some have carelesly neglected through indiscretion)' would seem to be a dig at the Guiana Company. He reminded his readers that the Irish and English on the Tauregue and Okiari had 'by meanes of the natives' managed to drive off Portuguese attackers in 1623.[6]

---

[1] See below, p. 374.   [2] Ibid.
[3] See below, pp. 375, 378–9.
[4] Day paraphrased the greater part of his material on Guiana from the 1626 edition of Robert Harcourt's *Relation*, see below, pp. 368–76.
[5] The *Marmaduke* had entered the Amazon in July 1631 and would have almost certainly returned to England before May 1632. Thomas Cliborne had encountered two survivors of North fort at Flushing in or about October 1631. Williamson, *English colonies*, 1923, p. 138, felt that Day's dismissal of 'the danger from the Portuguese . . . seems to verge upon fraudulence. . . .' Day was justified in arguing that a well-supplied and defended garrison could have driven out the small Portuguese garrisons in Maranhão and Pará and won back the allegiance of the local Indians. Such an undertaking would, however, have required support from the crown as well as considerable private backing, neither of which was forthcoming. Day was certainly guilty of ignoring the increasing difficulty of finding allies among the Tupi, now cowed into submission by the brutal Portuguese *entradas* and unwilling to risk joining with incoming northern Europeans who had insufficient forces to drive out the Portuguese.
[6] See below, p. 376.

Berkshire and his associates must have found these arguments difficult to sustain when their own ship the *Barcke Andevor* returned later in 1632 with further accounts of the Portuguese destruction of Clovell and Hixon's outpost. Berkshire may have been too disheartened by the news to continue or had simply run out of capital. In any event, he sold off the *Barcke Andevor*[1] and apparently surrendered his interest in the projected company to Lord Goring.[2] The latter sent a supply ship out to the Amazon later in the year. Goring's men anchored somewhere near Sapno in early 1633 and, as was usual, sent men ashore to get information from the Indians on the conditions upriver. The reception they got illustrated the changed circumstances in the Amazon. Eight men were captured by the natives.[3] The English assumed that they had all been killed although one Portuguese source states that four of them were taken to São Luis to be interrogated.[4] The rest of the ship's company, hearing that the Cumahu garrison had met the same end as that of North Fort, chose the better part of valour and departed for the West Indies without investigating further.

Perhaps the most striking thing about the history of the efforts of the select group of English peers, English and Irish gentlemen and lesser merchants who promoted trade and settlement on the Amazon is their determination. Their projects between 1628 and 1633 had met with almost unrelieved misfortune and yet they remained convinced that the Amazon was a viable area for colonization. If they could muster sufficient forces to remove the small Portuguese garrisons at Belém and Gurupá, the Indian tribes would come back to their allegiance and the vegetable and mineral riches of a river would be theirs to exploit. In the next ten years these tangible opportunities for profit were enhanced by the revival of the pipedream which had first attracted Sebastian Cabot and the

---

[1] There is no record of when the *Barcke Andevor* and the other patache which had sailed with her to the Amazon returned to England, although they appear to have left the Amazon about February 1632. Day certainly finished *A PUBLICATION OF GUIANA'S PLANTATION* before they arrived. The *Barcke Andevor* had been sold off to Samuel Shielde of Redruth and was said to be employed on a voyage to Norway by early 1633, see below, pp. 363–4.

[2] Sir George Goring (1585–1663), created Baron Goring 1628, earl of Norwich 1644. L. Stone, *Crisis of the aristocracy*, 1965, p. 428, describes him as the 'greatest customs entrepreneur' of the early Stuart peerage. See also T. K. Rabb, *Enterprise & empire* (Cambridge, Mass., 1967), p. 301; *DNB*, 1908, pp. 248–51.

[3] See below, pp. 386–7.

[4] Pereira de Berredo, 1749, p. 270.

duke of Northumberland to the river in the mid-sixteenth century; the prospect of using the Amazon as a highway to the gold of Peru.

This 'Amazon fever' is clearly demonstrated by the actions of Roger North and some of the Guiana Company membership in 1634 and 1635. The corporation was moribund but it was not yet dead. Its finances were in chronic disarray, with much of the original joint stock still owing and over half of the extra £1,000 promised by fifteen new members enrolled since 1627 still to be paid into the company's coffers.[1] To add to Sir Henry Spelman's difficulties, William Bampfield complained to the king in 1634 that the Guiana Company had not made good his losses when he was forced to abandon his intended voyage on the *Exchange* in 1628.[2]

Bampfield's decision to sue for his money may have been prompted by signs that Roger North had renewed hopes of sending colonists out to the Amazon. Some of the Irish captured at Tauregue were now reappearing in England and the United Provinces. William Gayner was in England by 1633.[3] Bernard O'Brien turned up in 1635.[4] North sent Gayner over to Zeeland to try to collect the value of £1,000 in goods which had belonged to the Amazon Company planters massacred by the Portuguese in 1625.[5] North doubtless hoped to use the money for his new venture in which he intended to make use of Gayner's experience.

---

[1] See below, pp. 389–92. [2] See below, pp. 387–8.
[3] See below, p. 394. [4] See below, pp. 425–9.
[5] See below, p. 394.

THE IRISH PETITION THE SPANISH CROWN
FOR A LICENCE TO SETTLE THE AMAZON,
1631–6

To North's fury, Gayner preferred to enter the service of the Dutch. The latter were preparing an enterprise for Guiana in 1634 but it was directed to the Cayenne, not to the Amazon as North assumed and Bernard O'Brien alleged. The Dutch also had colonies in the Essequibo and Berbice.[1] Gayner actually went out in the expedition which established an outpost on Trinidad in 1636, and was captured by the Spaniards almost immediately.[2] Bernard O'Brien, also approached by the Guiana Company, similarly made good his escape to Spain where he attempted to get permission to return to the Amazon under Spanish licence.

O'Brien's actions indicate that Irishmen who had spent any time on the Amazon were, undeterred by their long periods of captivity at the hands of the Portuguese, equally anxious to return there. They were, however, after their experience at Tauregue in 1629, convinced that their best chance of doing so now lay in entering the service of the Spanish crown. By the mid-1630s the Dutch were turning their attention away from the Amazon to Brazil, the rivers further north on the Guiana coast and the West Indies. With no confidence in the efficiency of the English Guiana venturers, the Irish preferred to turn to Spain. They could claim kinship as fellow

[1] For David Pietersz de Vries' shortlived colony on the Cayenne, founded September 1634, see his *Korte historiael ende journaels aenteyckeninge van verscheyden voyagiens in de vier deelen des wereldts-ronde, als Europa, Africa, Asia ende America gedaen* (Horn, 1665), ed. H. T. Colenbrander (The Hague, 1911), pp. 187–225. De Vries attributed the collapse of the plantation to 'the disorders of some English and seamen who were among them'. See also Ghoslinga, 1971, ch. 11.
[2] 'Relaçíon de lo sucedido en la Isla Trinidad siendo Governador y Capitan General destas Provincias de el Dorado Don Diego López de Escobar', B.L., Add. MS 36,324, ff. 31 et seqq.

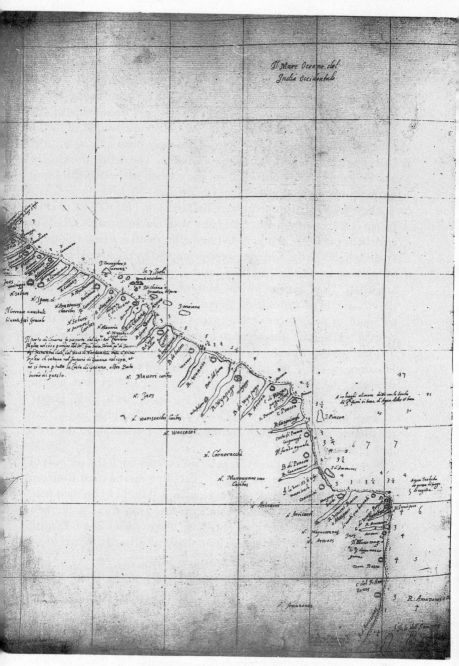

Fig. X. Robert Dudley's MS Chart of the Guiana Coastline, 1636
(Bayerische Staatsbibliothek, Munich, Icon. 139f. 526v.)

111

catholics. The distinguished record of their exiled compatriots in both Spain and the Netherlands was clear evidence of the special relationship between the Irish and the Spanish monarchy and their devotion to its interests. The Irish had expert knowledge of the Amazon, were skilled in the Indian languages and well liked by the tribes of the river. The Portuguese had only been able to win the latter's allegiance by unjustifiable brutality. The Irish, working in partnership with the missionaries, were much more likely to bring the heathen to the acceptance of Christianity.

These kinds of arguments were first tried on Philip IV in 1631 by Jaspar Chillan, the Irish merchant resident in Spain.[1] Chillan's efforts to persuade the king to allow him to take a new colony of Irish catholics to the Amazon were prompted by the arrival in Spain of more of those who had been taken captive at Tauregue in 1625 and 1629. The Capuchins in the Maranhão had once more taken up their cause. Friar António de Merciana and an Irish priest travelled to Spain to join forces with Jaspar Chillan in pleading for their release.[2] The Irish also seem to have sent a petition to the earl of Tyrone asking him to despatch priests and Irish troops from Flanders to come to their aid.[3] Although Tyrone ignored their requests, the Viceroy of Portugal did send orders that all the Tauregue settlers should be sent to Spain with their goods. According to O'Brien, the Governor of Maranhão and Pará released some of the Dutch and English but refused to let the Irish go.[4]

Eighteen of them, however, escaped by boat from the outpost of Caeté sometime in 1629 or 1630.[5] Travelling up the coast fourteen went ashore on Trinidad, only to be stranded there when their boat was swept on to Margarita by the current. They then made their way to Surinam where there may have already been some English refugees from the Amazon.[6] The Irish afterwards joined their

---

[1] See above, p. 72. [2] See below, pp. 407–10, 414–5.
[3] See below, p. 407. [4] See below, p. 415.
[5] Ibid.
[6] Ibid. The earliest reference to the existence of an English colony on the Surinam is contained in the deposition made by Sir Henry Colt after he was captured by the Spaniards at Trinidad in 1633. Colt testified that 'On the coast of the mainland, some six degrees north of the Equator in *Charama* were living some fifty-six English coming from Amazon whence they were thrown out by the Portuguese', see 'Relaçíon de lo que hizo Don Juan de Ulate Gobernador de Margarita, para despoblar a los enemigos ingleses que estaban en la Punta de la

compatriots now settling in increasing numbers in St Christophers. Of those who had been carried to Margarita, three (possibly five) made their way to Spain. They arrived at the Spanish court to find Jaspar Chillan in the midst of negotiations with the Spanish government for an Irish colony on the Amazon. Chillan gives the names of three of them as 'Joan Joanssen, Ricardo Molrran, Juan Alein', and he was most anxious to secure their services before they offered them to the Dutch. Because he could not get a speedy acceptance of his project from the Spanish ministers, he was unable to detain them. They made their way to Zeeland and subsequently went out to the Dutch settlement on the river Essequibo.[1]

Chillan was equally unlucky in his dealings with the Spanish government. Although its initial response was favourable the *Consejo de Indias*, knowing the history of Irish settlement in the Amazon, was unwilling to grant a licence. Its members were particularly concerned by Chillan's admission that he would have to rely on English and Dutch mariners to take his colonists out to the Amazon, and that he intended to seek the protection of Charles I against harassment by Dutch or English shipping. The Council was of the opinion that the Irish would bring heretics into the river and deliver control of it to the English.[2]

Bernard O'Brien fared no better when he arrived in Spain in December 1635.[3] He appears to have inveigled himself into the affections of a Spanish widow and with her support shipped himself from Maranhão in November 1634. He brought with him the son of one of the leading Indian chiefs of the region. O'Brien was to need all his luck on the voyage home. He was captured by Dutch privateers in the Indies. Carried off to Holland he was haled up before the Zeeland Chamber of the West India Company to explain why he had surrendered Tauregue. He claimed that only the desire of the Dutch to make use of him in a new project to the Amazon and Maranhão saved his life. He slipped away with his Indian servant

---

Galera de la isla Trinidad', A.G.I., Audiencia de Santo Domingo 180. David Pietersz de Vries entered the Surinam in October 1634 encountering sixty English under one 'Capiteyn Marreschal', *Korte historiael*, 1911, p. 206, Cornelio de Morg, a Dutchman captured at Tobago in 1637, informed the Spanish authorities on Trinidad that there were 'in Surinama, English; in Supunama Irish'. See above, p. 110, n. 2

[1] See below, pp. 411–2, 415.   [2] See below, pp. 401–4, 413–4.
[3] See below, pp. 414–31.

over the border to the Spanish Netherlands where he contacted the earls of Tyrconnel and Tyrone and tried to get passage for Spain. Unable to do so he went over to Dublin instead and thence to London. His activities there brought the unwelcome attention of the Guiana Company adventurers, who investigated his activities and had his movements closely watched. Feeling that the battle for control of the Amazon was already lost and having no more desire to serve the English than the Dutch, he approached the Spanish Ambassador who spirited him out of the country. Arriving at Bilbao in December he proceeded to tell his adventures to the Spanish Government in hopes of persuading them that the Irish were uniquely fitted to administer the Amazon region. The Spaniards seem to have trusted him no more than they did Jaspar Chillan. Nothing appears to have come of his memorial. He may have ended up in the Spanish Netherlands. There are two listings for a Bernardo O'Brien serving as ensign in the Irish regiments there in 1647 and 1653.[1]

Although O'Brien's memorial is self-serving, and his status and role in the Irish ventures to the Amazon probably less than he claimed, his account does contain much information which is confirmed by other sources. While his report of the plans of the Amazon projectors in England in 1635 is doubtless exaggerated, he was correct in his statement that North and his associates were trying to resuscitate the Guiana Company at that time. O'Brien had contact with the Treasurer, Sir Henry Spelman, and is quite specific that William Howard, a son of the earl of Arundel, planned to go out to the river.[2]

---

[1] B. Jennings, *Wild geese in Spanish Flanders, 1582–1700* (Dublin, 1964), pp. 375, 396.

[2] See below, p. 426.

LAST ENGLISH AND IRISH EFFORTS TO RETURN TO THE AMAZON, 1638–46: APPROACHES TO THE RESTORED PORTUGUESE MONARCHY

Any reconstruction of what the Guiana Company intended to do can only be tentative since the evidence is very slight. O'Brien may have confused William Howard, later Viscount Stafford, with Thomas Howard, earl of Berkshire and son of the earl of Suffolk. Lord Goring may still have been willing to invest in an Amazon colony in 1635. It seems unlikely, however, that any of the promoters who had been involved in such projects in the last decade would have had the capital to plan a major venture. O'Brien's claims that they commissioned him to raise one hundred and fifty Irish soldiers, planned to send out four hundred men and women, and intended to reinforce them in subsequent years with Irish settled in the Leeward Islands, is hard to swallow.[1] Such an enterprise may have been in the air. Some former Amazon planters and traders were to try to get a similar project off the ground between 1638 and 1642. The Guiana Company itself, however, seems to have been unable to fulfil its patent and support any more colonizing initiatives to Guiana. It had no holdings left in the Amazon. Robert Harcourt had died in the Wiapoco in 1631. Some of the people he had taken to the Wiapoco may have lasted on the river until about 1637, supplied by Dutch and English traders. The Guiana Company could do nothing for them, or for any of the other English and Irish in isolated factories and plantations scattered along the Guiana coast.[2]

The failure of the Guiana Company clearly frustrated those who saw the golden opportunities offered by the Amazon being lost for

---

[1] See below, pp. 426–7.
[2] See Lorimer, 'English trade and exploration', 1973, pp. 371–2.

want of initiative. The merchant George Griffith, despite having suffered 'greate losse by sending men into the greate River of the Amazons and planting on the Coaste of Guiana' was, in 1638, still anxious to see the business go forward.[1] Griffith was not listed as a member of the Guiana Company but he could have invested in any of the ventures sent out after 1628.[2] He was particularly concerned that the Dutch conquests in Brazil would give them a monopoly of sugar, which the English normally acquired in Portugal. He argued that the Amazon was the only place left where the English could produce their own supplies of the commodity. He and 'many woorthy men' were willing to undertake this on the condition that 'in your Majestys Cittie of London, they may have the ordering of the Businesse'. The 'ould Company doth nothing therin'. His petition was referred to the Commissioners of Foreign Plantations but there is no record of their response.

It is possible, however, that Griffith and his associates did send an expedition to the Amazon to reconnoitre the situation and attempt to initiate a new colony there. A document only recently brought to light in the Portuguese archives makes it possible to reinterpret the significance of what had previously appeared to be two unrelated pieces of evidence of continuing English interest in the river at the turn of the 1640s. One is the undated prospectus for a plantation near the river Tapajós, written by William Clovell and Thomas Tyndall.[3] The other is a similarly undated petition to Charles I to take into his protection 'the Adventurers unto the river of the *Amazones* or *Guiana* in *America* and theire plantacion there', previously believed to have been presented about 1631 by 'Captain Duppa'.[4]

The links between these documents are suggested by a letter written to João IV of Portugal in October 1642 by his ambassador in England, António de Sousa de Macedo.[5] The latter informed his master that he had recently been approached by an elderly man named 'Jaymes Dupay', who had formerly been a professional seaman but now made his considerable wealth by investing in shipping. This was obviously the James Duppa who had outfitted

---

[1] See below, pp. 432–3.   [2] See below, pp. 390–2.
[3] See below, pp. 433–5.
[4] See below, pp. 439–40. Attributed as 1629 in *CSP Col.*, *1574–1660*, p. 101. Williamson, *English colonies*, 1923, pp. 129–30, placed it two or three years later.
[5] See below, pp. 440–5.

ships to the Amazon over a decade ago.[1] Duppa told Sousa de Macedo that he had recently sent a ship to explore the Amazon. It had returned 'a year and a half ago', indicating that it had gone out sometime about 1638. Its captain had taken it as far upriver as the confluence of the 'Talpia', from the description of it, clearly the Tapajós.[2] He had returned with news of rich mines in the vicinity and of the possibilities of raiding Peru, which he could illustrate with an excellent map. The venturers had then approached the king, through the earl of Pembroke and earl of Northumberland, for a licence to take out men to fortify the Tapajós, open the mines and attack Peru. They had, it appears, suggested that as many as two thousand men might be necessary to accomplish this. The king, not unnaturally considering his circumstances in 1640, had refused to take any interest in the project. Duppa was considering going to the Dutch but had been induced by a mutual acquaintance to lay the matter before the Portuguese Ambassador.

It seems not unreasonable to suggest that Duppa was one of the associates of the London merchant George Griffith and that they had sent William Clovell and Thomas Tyndall to the Amazon some time about 1638 to reconnoitre the Tapajós. Clovell, the former Governor of North Fort, must have been freed by or escaped from the Portuguese in the mid-1630s.[3] Tyndall, an expert pilot, had spent a long period in Spanish service although there is no indication where or when he was taken prisoner.[4] Men like Clovell knew the Amazon and the Maranhão first hand and were intimately acquainted with the strength of the Portuguese garrisons there. Clovell would have known, as the Dutchman Gideon Morris de Jonghe reported to the Dutch West India Company, that there was a potential fifth column of some one hundred English and Irish captives there, who had worked in the sugar mills and helped search for mines.[5] Clovell and Tyndall, or whomever Duppa sent out to the Amazon in or about 1638, would have heard from the Indians of Pedro Teixeira's recent expedition upriver from Pará

[1] See above, pp. 98, n. 2, 101, ns. 2, 3.
[2] See below, p. 440. The date of the expedition is also suggested by the fact that P. Cristóval de Acuña appears to have picked up news of it when he reached the Tapajós in late 1639, see below, p. 437, n. 1.
[3] Bernard O'Brien, Richard Jones and possibly Roger Fry and William Gayner returned from the Maranhão and the Pará about the same time.
[4] See below, p. 435, n. 6.
[5] 'Relatórios e cartas', *RIHGB*, LVIII (1895), 241, 242, 244, 249.

to Quito.[1] The prospectus written by Clovell and Tyndall contains information about the mines in the vicinity of the Tapajós very similar to that acquired from the Indians of the region by the Spanish Jesuit Cristóval de Acuña when he travelled back down to the Atlantic with Teixeira in 1639.[2] Acuña in turn picked up news of an English expedition which had reached the Tapajós sometime previously. While the prospect of approaching Peru from the rear was an added incentive to settle the Amazon, as a major act of war against the heartland of the Spanish Indies it could not be accomplished without a major commitment of capital or even contemplated without royal approval. Moreover the Portuguese garrison in the lower Amazon had been strengthened somewhat. Since 1633 the state of Maranhão and Grão Pará had been divided into hereditary captaincies. Bento Maciel Parente had been appointed governor in 1636 and granted the captaincy of Cabo do Norte in the following year. By 1639 his son had established Fort Destierro south of the Paru, on the site of Adrianzoon Ita's old colony.[3] The Portuguese could be expelled, as the Dutch demonstrated in the Maranhão in 1641–4, but only if the English Crown was prepared to maintain a substantial force in the Amazon. Duppa's undated petition to Charles I requiring the crown to commit three thousand men and invest £48,000 over four years would seem to be the result.[4]

It is not surprising that Charles I, bankrupt and at odds with parliament, showed no disposition to take up Duppa's generous offer. What is interesting is the response of Duppa and his partners. Convinced of the fortunes to be made in the Amazon and of the river's strategic significance they, like the Irish planters, were prepared to go to foreign powers for support. Sousa de Macedo, fearing they would go to the Dutch who had taken the Maranhão only a year earlier,[5] was prepared to string them along. He was fully aware that João IV had only just established a precarious truce with the Dutch but was equally determined to expel them from Brazil if he could do so short of outright war. The return of English heretics to the Amazon was no more welcome, but the English were allies

---

[1] M. Jiménez de la Espada, *Viaje del Capitán Pedro Texeira aquas arriva del rio de las Amazonas, 1638–9* (Madrid, 1889), *passim.*
[2] See below, pp. 437–8.   [3] Kiemen, 1973, p. 44.   [4] See below, pp. 439–40.
[5] C. R. Boxer, *The Dutch in Brazil* (Oxford, 1957), pp. 108, 137, 146, 159, 160, 161.

and it was important to avoid outright offence. Sousa de Macedo held out to Duppa prospects of either a joint Portuguese-English venture or of taking interested English venturers into Portuguese service. The latter arrangement seemed the most likely since the turmoils in England meant that neither the parliamentary leaders nor the king had the leisure to become involved. The enthusiasm of some of Duppa's associates convinced the Portuguese resident that the English would take the Amazon for themselves if given the opportunity. Sousa de Macedo seems to have played a masterly hand over the next two years holding the would-be English venturers at bay.[1] As the letter of João IV to his representative in France indicates, the possibility of such a project was still exercising the Portuguese.[2] On the 28th September 1645 Sousa de Macedo

[1] Sousa de Macedo's letters from England are preserved in the B[ibliotheca] P[ública de] É[vora], Códice CVI/2–7. In a letter of 7th July 1644 (ibid., ff. 300, 300v), he notes that he was instructed by João IV to do everything possible to prevent the English from developing their Amazon project. Duppa's plan had come to nothing because one of the principals in it had been forced to go into exile. Sousa de Macedo does not specify which. I am very grateful to Dr David Hebb for allowing me to see his copies of the letters of Sousa de Macedo preserved at Évora, and for his advice on other matters concerning English naval history during this period. For a list of Sousa de Macedo's correspondence, see J. H. da Cunha Rivara, *Catalogo dos manuscritos da Bibliotheca Pública Eborense* (Lisbon, 1871), III, pp. 320–3.

[2] See below, pp. 445–6. Duppa's proposal seems to have been the last English effort to organize a venture to the Amazon in the first half of the seventeenth century. Sousa de Macedo remained alert to the possibility of such projects and fired off memorials to the committees of the Long Parliament in July and August 1644, protesting against rumoured new enterprises to the Amazon. These turned out to be false alarms. The rumoured expedition of 1644 was actually that directed to Trinidad under the licence of the earl of Warwick, see B. P. É., Códice CVI/2–7, ff. 302v, 304, 305, 341; V. T. Harlow, ed. *Colonizing expeditions to the West Indies and Guiana, 1623–67* (London, 1924), pp. lxiv–v, 128–9. For the history of Sousa de Macedo's embassy in England, see E. Prestage, 'O Dr António de Sousa de Macedo, Residente de Portugal em Londres', *Boletím da 2da class da Academía das Sciencias de Lisboa*, X(19   ), ????; *The diplomatic relations of Portugal with France, England and Holland from 1640 to 1668* (Watford, 1925), pp. 104–8. Prestage, 'O Dr António de Sousa', somewhat exaggerates the degree to which Sousa de Macedo was preoccupied by a possible revival of English Amazon ventures. Apart from the letter printed below, pp. 440–5 Sousa de Macedo did not mention the matter again until two years later in his letters of 18th February and 7th, 14th, 22nd, 28th July and 25th August 1644. João IV did, however, order an inquiry into the mineral resources of the Amazon. Ignaçio do Rego Barreto, Francisco de Souza Coutinho and Felipe de Mattos all submitted reports. February–August 1645. They knew of no gold mines on the Amazon beyond the 'rio do ouro' discovered by Teixeira in 1637; B.L., Add MS 37,042, ff. 30–2v, 39–41v.

complained 'I am always facing jealousies about Grão Pará, because I know that these people love it very much.'[1]

He appears to have been successful in his endeavours. There is no record of any other English expedition to settle the Amazon in this period. Portuguese documents indicate that English ships occasionally called in at Cabo do Norte to fish for manatee in the 1650s,[2] but there is no evidence of any more English efforts to colonize it in this period. When the 'Grand Design' against the Spanish Indies was launched by Cromwell the thrust of colonization shifted northwards to the already established plantations in Surinam and the West Indies.

The old Irish planters may have had better luck than James Duppa and his partners. Sousa de Macedo's correspondence indicates that he was also aware that Irishmen still had hopes of being allowed to settle on the Amazon. He was referring here to the proposal made by one Captain Peter Sweetman to transfer four hundred Irish from St Christophers to live as naturalized Portuguese under the jurisdiction of the authorities of Belém.[3]

Captain Peter Sweetman seems to have been an Irish gentleman and entrepreneur who had made money in trade to the West Indies plantations. He had, he informed João IV, carried out at his expense, a large body of Irish settlers to St Christophers. The rebellion in Ireland in 1641 had adversely affected the Irish on St Christophers. The heretic English planters had begun to oppress the Irish catholics harshly. The only solution was to remove them to the protection of a catholic monarch. The choice of João IV for this role was probably dictated by the presence of former Amazon planters among the Irish who wished to return to the river.[4]

The documentation on Sweetman's appeal to the Portuguese king is incomplete, but there is some material additional to that

[1] 28th September 1645, B. P. É., Códice CVI/2–7, f. 397v.
[2] See also A. Biet, 'Voyage de la France equinoxiale en l'isle de Cayenne, enterpris par les François en l'année MDCLII', 1652, B.L., MS Sloane 1019, f. 44.
[3] See below, pp. 446–8. On 18th February 1644 Sousa de Macedo reported that he had heard from Portugal that João IV was about to grant a licence to Irish from St Christophers to remove to the Amazon. He strongly disapproved of such an action, noting the attachment of the Irish to Spain and predicting that, if they were allowed to settle there, they would soon become more numerous and powerful than the Portuguese planters (B. P. É., Códice CVI/2–7, f. 200v).
[4] See below, p. 415.

published by Aubrey Gwynn which substantially changes the accepted version of its outcome.[1] Sweetman appears to have presented two proposals to João IV before September 1643.[2] Neither of them survive, but they seem to have been successful. On the 2nd September 1643 João IV issued Sweetman with a grant of settlement and naturalization.[3] For some unexplained reason this was not put into effect, possibly because of objections from the donatories that the territory of the state was already spoken for. Sweetman then appears to have come back with a third petition, printed below,[4] which suggested that his compatriots could usefully be settled on the grasslands of the island of Marajó, opposite Belém. The response of João IV seems to have been to direct his ministers to draw up another grant either in late 1643 or January or February of 1644. Excerpts from the undated, unfinished rough draft of this grant were published by Aubrey Gwynn. It provides the king with the alternatives of settling the Irish on Marajó or unspecified territory near Belém. There is, however, a final draft of this grant in the registers of the Chancelaria preserved in the Torre de Tombo in Lisbon. On the 4th March 1644 João IV granted Sweetman the initial right to take up to one hundred and thirty Irish from St Christophers to Pará, to become naturalized Portuguese.[5] They were not, however, to be given the option of settling on Marajó island. Half of them were to be installed in or near Belém itself, half up country in a new town to be founded for the purpose. Even though João IV was willing to give the Irish full rights of citizenship, he was not willing to let them establish themselves in a body at the outer edge of the Amazon delta within easy contact of any foreign shipping coming for Pará or the mouth of the Amazon.

As it was the Conselho Ultramarinho deplored the king's decision. In consultas of the 7th and 14th May they pointed out the dangers of allowing foreigners anywhere near such a strategically significant river as the Amazon.[6] The king of Spain had never permitted it. The Irish would unsettle the natives, and bring in heretics. The Irish, they reminded him, were the vassals of the king

[1] Gwynn, 'Irish in the West Indies', 1932, pp. 196–203.
[2] See below, p. 446.   [3] See below, p. 451.
[4] See below, pp. 446–8.
[5] A[rchivo da] T[orre do] T[ombo], Lisbon, Chancelaria de João IV, livro 1, ff. 196–9v.
[6] See below, pp. 448–51.

of England and were particularly devoted to the king of Spain. Their whole past history spoke against them. They had collaborated with the English, the Dutch and the Spaniards, as the circumstances warranted, in order to maintain a foothold in the river. The inhabitants of Belém were bitterly opposed to the notion of accepting them.

It has always been assumed that these strong representations from the Overseas Council put an end to the Sweetman's hopes. This does not, however, seem to be the case. On the 17th June the king attached a postilla or rider to his former grant, indicating that it was to be particularly understood that only Irish were to be allowed to go with Sweetman.[1] He clearly did not see the catholic Irish as a threat to the security of his overseas territories. It does seem probable that Sweetman did not take up his grant but there is every possibility that some Irish went to Belém. The same register in the Torre de Tombo contains an identical grant made on the 16th August 1646 to an Irish captain named William 'Brun' or 'Brum' to remove the one hundred and thirty Irish catholics from St Christophers to Pará.[2] The Portuguese archives may yet yield up evidence that some Irish planters were allowed to settle permanently on the Amazon.

[1] See below, p. 459.
[2] A.T.T., Chancelaria de João IV, livro 1, ff. 398–401.

CONCLUSION

If some of the Irish from St Christophers did settle on the Amazon as naturalized subjects of the Portuguese crown, their very success in achieving their goal only underlines the fact that there were to be no more independent Irish projects to colonize the river. If João IV did allow them to go, it was because, in spite of the cautions of his advisors, he felt that the Amazon was now firmly under Portuguese control and that the risks of admitting a few catholic Irish were minimal. Certainly any fears that the Dutch or English might come to their support were diminishing. Driven out of the Maranhão in 1644, the tide was turning against the Dutch in Brazil. English interest in Guiana had moved northwards to the Surinam, to be developed in the 1650s as an adjunct of the Barbados plantation. The focus of colonial rivalry had shifted to the Caribbean.

The mid-1640s then, marked the end of a century of English interest in the Amazon and almost fifty years of determined English and Irish effort to maintain trade and settlement there. In looking back over the history of these enterprises, the first and most striking thing about them is their continuity and tenacity, reflecting the fact that the Amazon ventures were always potentially instantly profitable, unlike the colonies in North America. Amazonia was not an impracticable land of El Dorado. It offered realistic and lucrative returns in tobacco, dyes and timber and the possibility of sugar cultivation. It was also a healthy environment for northern Europeans as long as they kept active and maintained a good diet. It is also clear that the loss of the river to the Portuguese was not inevitable. If the Portuguese planters won the struggle for the lower Amazon, it was because of the military and diplomatic initiatives of their crown in their defence at the turn of the 1620s. The collapse of the Amazon Company in 1620, engineered by the Spanish ambassador in England, robbed the English projectors of necessary capital and support just as the Spanish crown was moving to reinforce the Maranhão and Pará settlements. These problems were compounded by the readjustments in the traffic with Zeeland merchants at this time, occasioned by the creation of the Dutch West India Company in 1621. This was particularly problematic for the Irish who had come to rely on the Dutch as their suppliers. It was in the early 1620s that the Portuguese forced the tribes of the lower Amazon into submission. While the latter were still eager to find European allies against the Portuguese, they had to be assured of effective military aid. The reprisals taken by the Portuguese were too terrible to make the support of small groups like Roger Fry's colony worth the risk. Once the Portuguese gained the edge in the Amazon, which they had by 1625, only a heavy infusion of capital and royal support for war against Spanish subjects could have won it back for the English. Neither was forthcoming. Charles I was not anxious for a prolonged war with Spain. The failures of the 1620s had given the Amazon a bad name. The English tobacco trade shifted to the new plantations in the Caribbean, some founded by former Amazon planters. The Irish Amazon projectors, whose initiatives had been less ambitious factory settlements supported by the Dutch, read this turn of events more accurately than their English counterparts and tried to launch any further Amazon projects under the licence of the Spanish and subsequently Portuguese crown.

Finally in comparing the English and Irish efforts, it is hard to escape the conclusion that the Irish were, on the whole, more efficient in their approach to exploiting Amazonia than the English. The English, it is true, took the financial risks, launching ambitious chartered companies in 1619, 1627 and 1632. The Irish, more concerned for profit than monopoly, developed small-scale factory plantations based on Indian labour, and traded with the Dutch or the English as the circumstances warranted. They developed an expert knowledge of the river and the languages of the tribes they worked with. For the Irish, at least until the 1630s, the Amazon had the particular attraction of being an uncontrolled frontier where their small ventures could operate as independent entities without interference from any controlling English interest. The major problem for the English projectors seems to have been a failure to adjust their perceptions of the Amazon after 1625. Robert Harcourt's propaganda for the Guiana Company of 1627 was largely based on his experience of the Wiapoco a decade earlier, and his assessment of the strength of the Portuguese was outdated before the new edition of his *Relation* was published in 1626. John Day cribbed his prospectus for the Earl of Berkshire's venture from Harcourt, and from Purchas's accounts of Charles Leigh's Wiapoco colony of 1604–6. There seems to have been an inverse relationship between the pretensions of these two groups of Amazon projectors and their knowledge of the prevailing circumstances on the river. Ambitious as Duppa's plan for the Tapajós colony of 1628–42 was, it at least had the virtue of recognizing that if the English still wanted to settle on the river they had only two options. They could send a major expeditionary force or, do as the more practical Irish had already decided to do, throw in their lot with the Portuguese.

EARLIEST ENGLISH EXPLORATIONS OF THE AMAZON, 1550–1608

1. SEBASTIAN CABOT TO CHARLES V, 15TH NOVEMBER 1553[1]

Sacred, Imperial, Catholic Majesty. –

When I was almost ready to come to kiss your Majesty's hands and give account of the business which Francisco de Urista related to your Majesty on my behalf,[2] quotidian fevers[3] struck me which so affect me that I am not able to set forth, because I am very weakened and I am certain that I should die before I completed the journey. Considering this and also because at my age, if the infirmity presses upon me, I fear that I may die, before that I would like to declare to your Majesty the secret which I possess. Since I cannot do it in person, for the reasons which I have stated, and because harm might follow from further delay, I have resolved to convey it to your Majesty in writing and to send it to you by the said Francisco de Urista. It is that when the ambassador of France, *Bodofin* [Boisdauphin], was here, he and the duke of *Notarbelan* [Northumberland], likewise, asked me many times what kind of

---

[1] A.G.S., Estado, Correspondencia de Inglaterra, bundle 808. The translation from the Spanish is made from the printed version in M. Fernandez de Navarrete, ed., *Colección de documentos inéditos para la história de España* (Madrid, 1843), III, 512–14, with reference to an earlier translation in R. Tyler, ed., *CSP Span., 1553*, pp. 361–2. Although the original bears the date 1554, probably due to an error by the copyist, an accompanying letter to the emperor from his ambassador Simon Renard, dated 15th November 1553 (ibid., p. 360), makes it clear that Cabot's letter was written on the same day.

[2] Renard's covering letter assigned 'A Spaniard, named Francisco' as the bearer of the letter and the two charts which Cabot wished to convey to Charles V. Cabot, as the omitted portion of his letter indicates, expected Urista both to introduce the business of the letter and explain the maps to the emperor.

[3] A fever or ague of which the paroxysms return every day.

country Peru was, what troops your Majesty maintained there and if it was as rich as was reported. I told him that there were many good Spanish troops there, very well equipped with everything needfull in weapons and horses, and that it was country abounding with mines of gold and silver. I make known to your Majesty that I ascertained from both of them that they wished to raise an expedition for the river Amazon, and this expedition was to be made ready in France, in which were to go four thousand soldiers, besides the mariners. They were to take with them twelve pinnaces,[1] to build a fort at the mouth of the said river Amazon, go upriver with the said pinnaces and destroy and kill all the Spaniards and usurp the territory. Considering that they could very easily, using the said river, catch the Spaniards unawares and scattered throughout the country, they could succeed with their evil intent, which would do your Majesty a very great disservice. In view of which let your Majesty quickly order such dispositions to be made in this as may please you, because this which I write to your Majesty is very certain and the truth. As I have ascertained and learned, the said *Bodofin* carried with him two thousand pounds when he departed from hence, which the aforementioned duke gave him for the said purpose and to initiate the expedition. . . .[2] I beseech your Majesty to accept my goodwill and the desire which I have and always will have, through the grace of God and his most sacred mother, to serve your Majesty. The which may assure you that, were it not for my indisposition, I would rather come to kiss your hands and make the report about all that I say here in person, than send it in writing. God keep etc. From *Londres* [London], the 15th of November 1553.

2. EXTRACT FROM *THE DISCOVERIE OF THE LARGE AND BEWTIFULL EMPIRE OF GUIANA*, BY SIR WALTER RALEGH 1596[3]

How all these rivers crosse and encounter, how the countrie lieth and is bordred, the passage of *Cemenes*, and of *Berreo*[4] mine owne

[1] A small sailing ship of up to about thirty tons equipped with oars for manoeuvrability. Clearly the intention was to take vessels of shallow draught for the passage up the Amazon.

[2] See above, p. 6.

[3] *The discoverie*, 1928, pp. 25–7.

[4] Ralegh refers here to Gonzalo Jiménez de Quesada and Antonio de Berrio.

discoverie, and the way that I entred, with all the rest of the nations and rivers, your Lordship shall receive in a large Chart or Map,[1] which I have not yet finished, and which I shall most humbly pray your Lordship[2] to secret, and not to suffer it to passe your own hands; for by a draught thereof all may bee prevented by other nations. For I know it is this very yeere sought by the French, although by the way that they now take, I feare it not much. It was also told me ere I departed England, that Villiers the Admirall[3] was in preparation for the planting of *Amazones*, to which river the French have made divers voiages, and returned much gold and other rarities. I spake with a captaine of a French ship that came from thence, his ship riding in *Falmouth*, the same yeere that my ships came first from *Virginia*.[4]

There was another this yeere in *Helford* that also came from thence, and had been 14 moneths at an ancor in *Amazones*, which were both very rich.[5] Although as I am perswaded, *Guiana* cannot be entred that way, yet no doubt the trade of gold from thence passeth by branches of rivers into the river of *Amazones*, and so it doth on every hand farre from the countrey it selfe. ... And upon the river of *Amazones* Thevet writeth that the people weare *Croissants* of gold, for of that form the *Guianians* most commonly make them: So as from *Dominica* to *Amazones* which is above 250 leagues, all the chiefe Indians in al parts weare of those plates of *Guiana*. Undoubtedly those that trade *Amazones* returne much gold, which

---

In 1568 Jiménez de Quesada, founder of Santa Fe de Bogotá, was granted the conquest of a tract of land between the rivers Pauto and Papameme, thought to be tributaries of the upper Meta and Amazon. He spent three years, 1569–72, searching for El Dorado in the Venezuelan llanos. After his death, in 1579, Antonio de Berrio inherited the conquest through his marriage to Don Gonzalo's niece. See above, p. 10, n. 2.

[1] See above, p. 12, n. 1.

[2] Ralegh is addressing Sir Charles Howard, baron of Effingham, Lord High Admiral, to whom he had dedicated the volume along with Sir Robert Cecil.

[3] Villars-Brancas, formerly governor of Rouen, appointed to the post of Admiral by Henri IV in late 1594.

[4] 1584. The reference to ships returning from 'Virginia' alludes to the survey commanded by Philip Amadas and Arthur Barlowe, which sailed in April and returned in September of the same year. See 'The voyage of Philip Amadas and Arthur Barlowe to Virginia, at the charge, and direction of Sir Walter Ralegh An. 1584', in D. B. Quinn, *Roanoke voyages* (1955), I, 91–116.

[5] 1595. Ralegh had completed *The discoverie* by November 1595. See above, pp. 15–16, n. 1.

(as is aforesaid) commeth by trade from *Guiana*,[1] by some branch of a river that falleth from the countrey into *Amazones*, and either it is by the river which passeth by the nations called *Tisnados*, or by *Carepuna*.[2] I made inquirie amongst the most ancient and best traveled of the *Orenoqueponi*,[3] and I had knowledge of all the rivers between *Orenoque* and *Amazones*, and was very desirous to understand the truth of those warlike women, bicause of some it is beleeved, of others not:[4] And though I digresse from my purpose, yet I will set downe what hath been delivered me for truth of those women, and I spake with a *Casique* or Lord of people that told me he had been in the river, and beyond it also.[5] The nations of these women are on the south side of the river in the Provinces of *Topago*,[6]

[1] Carib, Arawak and Warrau warriors on the Guiana coast highly valued half-moon, crescent (*croissant*) or spread-eagle shaped ear, nose, lip and pectoral pendants made of a gold-copper alloy. They referred to them as 'caracoli', 'caricuris' or 'Calcari'. They appear to have been disseminated by complex patterns of trade and warfare from gold-working tribes of the upper Caroni. Thevet described the use of bone or shell crescent-shaped ornaments among the Tupinamba. The tribes of the lower Amazon possessed a few gold pendants, acquired by trade with the tribes settled to the east of the inner tributary Jurua. See *HSAI*, 1948, III & IV, *passim*; Andre Thevet, *La cosmographie universelle* (1575), bk. XXI, ch. 10.

[2] Antonio de Sedeño, governor of Trinidad, had trekked from the mouth of the Orinoco deep into the Venezuelan llanos in the 1530s searching for the wealthy Indian civilizations said to lie near the river Meta. He died in 1538 on the *Tisnados* river. Antonio de Herrera's account of Orellana's voyage down the Amazon, in his *Historia general de los hechos de los castellanos en las islas y tierra firme del mar oceano* (Madrid, 1601–15), Decade VI, bk. 9, states that the expedition heard of a powerful chief named '*Caripuna*, who had great quantities of silver'. His territories appear to have lain somewhere near present Óbidos, since it was at this point that the Spaniards noticed the ebb and flow of the tide. The tides sweep up the Amazon as far as Óbidos.

[3] Ralegh's term for the tribes inhabiting the south bank and hinterland of the Orinoco between the confluence of the Caroni and the head of the delta, see *The discoverie*, 1928, p. 51.

[4] To defend himself against those who took his account of Amazons 'for a vain and unprobable report', Ralegh later devoted a section of his *Historie of the world* (1614), bk. IV, ch. 2, sect. 15, to a survey of the classical authorities on the subject, as well as recent accounts of sightings.

[5] Ralegh's informant was likely speaking the truth. John Ley remarked ('Ley his pedigree', Wilts Record Office, 366/1, f. 18v), 'Thes Indians that Inhabit on the Rivers nere the sea are greate traveilers, coastinge the Contrie in their canowes and observinge the risinge and setting of the principall starrs. . . .'

[6] The account of Orellana's expedition in Gonzalo Fernandez de Oviedo y Valdes' *Historia general y natural de las Indias*, bk. XLIX, ch. 4 (in Toribio Medina, *Carvajal*, 1934, App., pp. 399–400), gives *Topayo* as the name of a powerful overlord, vassal to Conori, queen of the Amazons. Conori's realm stretched between the Amazon and the river Plate.

and their chiefest strengths and retraicts are in the Ilands scituate on the south side of the entrance, some 60 leagues within the mouth of the said river. The memories of the like women are very ancient as well in *Africa* as in *Asia*: In *Africa* those that had *Medusa* for *Queene*: others in *Scithia* neere the rivers of *Tanais* and *Thermadon*: we find also that *Lampedo* and *Marthesia* were *Queens* of the *Amazones*: in many histories they are verified to have been, and in divers ages and Provinces: But they which are not far from *Guiana* do accompanie with men but once in a yeere, and for the time of one moneth, which I gather by their relation to be in Aprill. At that time all the Kings of the borders assemble, and the Queenes of the *Amazones*, and after the Queens have chosen, the rest cast lots for their *Valentines*. This one moneth, they feast, daunce, and drinke of their wines in abundance, and the Moone being done, they all depart to their owne Provinces. If they conceive, and be delivered of a sonne, they returne him to the father, if of a daughter they nourish it, and reteine it, and as many as have daughters send unto the begetters a Present, all being desirous to increase their owne sex and kinde, but that the (sic) cut of the right dug of the brest I do not finde to be true. It was farther told me, that if in the wars they tooke any prisoners that they used to accompany with those also at what time soever, but in the end for certaine they put them to death: for they are said to be very cruell and bloodthirsty, especially to such as offer to invade their territories.[1] These *Amazones* have likewise great store of these plates of golde, which they recover by exchange chiefly for a kinde of greene stones, which the Spaniards call *Piedras Hijadas*, and we use for spleene stones, and for disease of the

---

[1] *Thermodon* in Asia Minor was the site of the Amazon capital of Themiscyra where Hercules captured the sacred girdle of the Amazon Queen. According to Herodotus, some of the Amazons captured at the battle of Thermodon escaped into Scythia, and joining with Scythian hunters crossed the *Tanais* or river Don. *Lampedo*/Lampedona and *Marthesia*/Marfisa appear as queens of the Amazons in the twelfth century *Historia ecclesiastica* of Ordericus Vitalis, in the fourteenth century *De claris mulieribus* of Giovanni Boccaccio, and in the popular early sixteenth-century work *Orlando furioso* (1516), translated into English by Sir John Harington in 1591. Medieval and Renaissance writers repeated the ancient myths about random mating and the suppression of one breast. Ralegh's rejection of the notion of breast mutilation was doubtless influenced by his reading in Francisco López de Gomara's *Historia general de las Indias*. López de Gómara contemptuously dismissed the idea. See Toribio Medina, *Carvajal*, 1934, p. 26. Wettan Kleinbaum, *The war against the Amazons*, 1983, p. 16, states that the notion of breast mutilation first appeared in Hellenistic or Roman literature, Hellenic artistic traditions only showing Amazons with one breast bared.

stone we also esteeme them:[1] of these I saw divers in *Guiana*, and commonly every King or *Casique* hath one, which their wives for the most part weare, and they esteeme them as great jewels.

3. JOHN LEY'S EXPLORATION OF THE LOWER AMAZON, 1598[2]

[f. 16] I being made Captaine by the Earle of Comberland of the Ship called the *Alcydo* [*Alcedo*] the whole fleete dep*a*rted from Plymouth uppon fridaie the xth of march Anno d*o*mini *1597*[3] And after that we had expected the Coract outward bound for the East Indians, uppon the Coast of Spaine, a certain space, yt was thought good to goe to the Southward of the Canaries, And their to lie for theire comynge sometyme w*hi*ch beinge p*er*formed the iiiith of maye my Lo*rd* set saile for the West Indyes And I betooke me for my frigatt, to pas on my intended jorney.[4] The ixth we fell with the Ilands, of Cape de Verd, At three of the clock we were with the Eastermost pointes of Cape St Iago, directinge our Coast Southwest westerlie: the xxxth daie the water changed cullor[5] and therefore we sounded and had xx fatham, The first of June we had sight of the Easterlie Cape, and being betwene the two breach we were faine to duble it out againe; And beareinge westward we founde the best of the Channell and discried two smale Ilandes;[6] That Eveninge beinge the second of June we came to an Ancor: under the westermost of them there was a Canow, with Indians a fishinge. They sheweinge great feare came to o*r* Ship side: On this Iland dwelleth noe bodie: But for the great store of fish w*hi*ch is about yt we named yt fishers Iland; The Indians all thereaboutes in great nomber resort thither to fish; Out of this Iland the sea hath worne a very smale Iland with a Tuff of trees on yt, by this we the third daie of Julie[7] came to an Ancor fasteninge a halser a shore here we built our Shallop, duringe w*hi*ch time the Indians came in greate companies, to us, to the number of CCC[8] at one time, provided to

---

[1] Jade, nephrite or silicate of sodium and aluminium, believed to be efficacious in treatment of kidney disease. *Piedra de ijada* means literally stone of the colic.

[2] Extracted from 'Ley his pedigree', *c.* 1609 (Wilts Record Office, 366/1, ff. 16–21v). Marginal notations are placed in [ ] at the place where they occur. See above, p. 20, ns. 2, 3.

[3] 20th March 1598 (N.S.).   [4] See above, p. 23.

[5] See above, p. 17, n. 1.   [6] See the discussion above pp. 23–5.

[7] June. See pp. 23–5.   [8] Three hundred.

have set on my men, buildinge my shallop,[1] but my Ship rideinge
soe nere put them from there purpose: Our shallop beinge
finished, we departed from thence, to two other Ilands, a Leage of:
The indians resorted unto us, and for bugles[2] and trifles brought us
some victualls and Spleene stones.[3]

[f.16v] From this place haveinge a good Channell we went up the
River of Amazone in all about fower score leages with our Ship and
left her nere Indians howses for her better relief heere and in divers
more places, they build there howses about two fatham from the
ground uppon bodies of trees Cut of to that purpose[4] And make
bred of a kinde of fruite; I went up thether with my Shallop, but
then the Indians thereabutes wold not abide us, wherefor my men
were discoraged, speciallie becaus our victualls were well spent, and
fell to be short, a strange wildernes of Ilandes openinge on either
part, wherefore we hastened to retorne to our ship which being
done we presentlie set saile,[5] the winde ever for the most part
blowing up the river, we both night and daie, as the Tyde served,
turned downe, soe that uppon the last of June, we came to the two
Ilands, that we rode at goeinge up: here we staied till the third of
July, and dureinge that time, I went to divers places were Indians
dwelt, to provide ourselves of fresh victualls:[There are in som of thes
howses five hundred people liveinge] while I was awaie fower of my
men, with my smale boate, roade to a greate howse neere them, but
the Inhabitants came marchinge towardes, three and thre in a ranck
And a leader before them with a longe pole, in his hande, the rest
haveinge their bowes and arrowes readie to shoote: my men seeing
that retorned in all hast yet other Indians not a leage of Entreated
or men well, and sought to avoid all suspicon of evill dealinge, for

---

[1] Ley here uses shallop to mean a boat, propelled by oars or sail, for use in
shallow waters.

[2] Tube-shaped glass beads.   [3] See above, p. 132, n. 2

[4] Large communal houses were typical of many culture groups of the South
American tropical forest. Tupinamba long-houses could be up to 500 feet long,
with a rectangular floor and intricate arched or vaulted roofs thatched with palm
leaves. They could accommodate anything from 100–200 occupants. Pile-
building was usual in the seasonally flooded Amazonian várzea. See R. H. Lowie,
'The tropical forests: An introduction', in HSAI, 1948, III, 16–17; A Métraux,
'The Tupinamba', in ibid., 103–5.

[5] If Ley did sail upriver by the north channel for more than 80 leagues or 280
statute miles, he may have reached the confluence of the Xingu and the Canal do
Gurupá. The river at this point would certainly match his description of 'a
strange wilderness of ilandes'.

when the Indians doe come provided with weapons their is noe trust in them, the third daie we endevowred to Cros the river and a head we made an Iland under the which we went to an Ancor all night, but we founde showldes that we were glad to retorne whence we came, In theis partes we had most tirrible tempests of windes, raine lightninge and Thunder, One Eveninge I shewed my Indian a black Cloude comminge threatninge a cruell storme, And sodenlie he said 'naughtie Indian make naughtie weather', And made signes howe they did cut the throate of a man, and utter altogeather certaine wordes as he he, Chy Chy, I am compelled to be short or els I wold write more touchinge this matter,[1] from hence we turned to fishers Iland, and their the next daie we hoysed saile, to cros the River, that we might recover the wester Cape,[2] which being performed we had a violent tempast; a spout fell downe, within a quarter of a mile of us, which the Indians much feare, for it overturneth the Canowes, and ingageth a good Ship yf her sailes be abroade, we beinge nowe within twentie leages of my Indian Countrie, we directed our course thither.[3] The river is called Caw, There we sojourned five daies, my Indyan[4] and a man of myne, all this while laye a shore, and beinge

[1] John Ley's recollections of his two Guiana voyages contain unique ethnographical material on 'The Indians observacon of the stars', and 'The manners and Customes of the people' ('Ley his pedigree', ff. 18v–19). Since his observations were generalized and not specific to the Amazon tribes he encountered, I have not included them here. I hope to publish the entire manuscript subsequently. Ley appears to have had most contact with the Iaos of the river Caux. All the tropical forest tribes had complex mythological systems comprising legends of their origins and culture heroes, deities, demons and animistic spirits. André Thevet made an extensive record of Tupinamba beliefs insofar as he was able to comprehend them. See *La cosmographie universelle* (1575), bk. 21, chs. 4, 5, 6, 7, 8, 11, 12, 14, 15.

[2] See above, p. 22.

[3] Ley gives no indication of his starting point of measurement here. It cannot have been Cabo do Norte. The distance from the latter cape to the estuary of the Caux is over 260 statute miles, which would clearly exclude Ley's estimate of 60 miles, unless his memory or his scribe was at fault. The figure could also have been wrongly transcribed in the preparation of the 'pedigree' from John Ley's original papers.

[4] Both Keymis and Berry had taken Indians from Caux to England. Keymis's guide, 'William of Cawo', returned to Guiana as guide and interpreter for Leonard Berry's expedition in 1597. Berry carried back 'Leonard of Cawe', who remained in Ralegh's household for three or four years before returning to Guiana. Robert Harcourt found him living near the river Conawini in 1609. Ralegh tried to contact him on his own return to the coast in November 1617. John Ley could have picked up his own guide in 1597, or availed himself of the services of William or Leonard of Caux. See Keymis, *Of the second voyage*, in

readie to departe they repaired to the Ship. Then we visited all the rivers which we had ben in the yere before, And so directed our course to St Vincent, from thence to an Iland, nere nevis, where we tooke in wood and water, and founde two extreame hot springes, which did boyle a peece of salt beef in a quarter of an houre, And from thence we directed our course for England, where we Aryved about Alhallowtide. . . .[1]

[f. 17v] Strannge shapes and manners of men

Taparawacur: are people toward the Eastermost part of the River of Amazon, they have great store of greene stones, which we call spleene stones, Their nether lip is verie great hangeinge downe soe lowe as their Chynn: which they desier to force bigger and to turn downewardes: they smoth them and work them downewardes, with thes greene stones:[2] They drink blud and bring up their Children therewith,[3] even from their first birth: and drawe themelves ther mothers brests to the intent they maie be eased of their milk. . . .

[f.18] The women called the Amazones are soe called because they live after the Custome, and manner of the women in Asia, in Auncient time, Although indeed impplie, for first to the intent they might not be hindred in ther shooteinge, they cut of their left papp, And therefore were called Amazons As havinge but one pape, But theis doe not soe for they draw their bowes, puttinge their Arrowe betwene the forefinger and the Thumb, looseinge the Arrowe far from the bodie, soe that their brest is no impeachment to their shooteinge. They except of their neighbours companie two moones in the yeare for procreacon sake, banquetinge and takinge their pleasure dureinge that time, but soe soone as the moone is readie to change the men must be gone: yf it come to pas anie have issue, yf it be a male, the father shall have it given some present to the mother:

Principal navigations (1903–5), X, 457–8; Masham, 'The 3. voyage', ibid., XI, 8, 11; Harris, *Relation*, 1928, p. 80; Sir Walter Ralegh's journal of his last voyage to Guiana, 1617–18 (B.L., MS Cotton B VIII, 153) printed in R. H. Schomburgk's edition of *The discoverie* (London, 1848), App., p. 197.

[1] All Saints day.

[2] André Thevet recorded the use of labrets of a highly polished and valued green stone among Tupinamba warriors of Rio de Janeiro. They were said to have been acquired by trade from the vicinity of Rio Grande do Norte. See *La cosmographie universelle* (1575), bk, XXI, f. 931, bk. XXII, f. 955. As noted above, the jade or nephrite from which the ornaments were commonly made was highly valued by Europeans for treatment of kidney problems.

[3] Probably an allusion to the Tupinamba practice of ritual cannibalism.

yf it be female the mother keepeth it, yt is said they have much gold brought by their neighbours, but none groweinge in their Countrie: they are sterne and Cruell people, and yet of a meane and little Stature, with black and longe heare hangeinge downe behinde from their heades, for belowe their wastes, The Indians speake much of the healthes of those women and strannge manner of provision they have for victualls.

Of thes women of late the river hath taken his name, they Inhabit in two Ilandes, uppon the river: farther I leave to speake of them, untill I shall have better experience of the truth. . . .[1]

[f.19v] Certaine observacons collected in the first and second voioages concerninge the habitation of the severall nations. . . .

[f.20] The Arowa dwell upon both sides of the great River Amasono and in a great Iland and two little Ilandes,[2] they are all Red They have greate and verie longe howses They make drinck of the Juice of Certaine wood, and also bread of the same, and have little or no Cassala. . . .

[f.20v] A discripcon of the severall Rivers and the people Inhabiting uppon them. . . .

[f.21v] Next to them are the Arowa, they dwell uppon both sides of the River Amazona in the Ilands of Crowacurri, warracayew, and Attowa they also dwell in a River called wayapowpa which falleth into Amazona, They make their bodies and faces Red all over,[3] they make bread of a great Tree called Anarola and drink of the Juice thereof, which they doe by poundeinge, and seetheinge, and have little Cassala,[4] they doe not eate men, and are but of smale stature.

---

[1] Ley had little to add to Ralegh's comments here. His remarks on the Amazons and those written by William Davies below illustrate how the traditional stories were adopted and steadily augmented in successive travel accounts.

[2] See above, pp. 24, 25, n. 1.

[3] The Arua, like the Tupinamba and many of the tribes of Amazonia and the Guianas, painted their bodies with vegetable dyes, most commonly using the red pulp of the berry of the Urucu/Annotto or *Bixa Orellana*, and the black dye from the unripe fruit of the genipapa or *Genipa americana*. See Lévi-Strauss, 'Use of wild plants', in *HSAI*, 1963, VI, 477–9.

[4] Presumably one of the many palms which provide edible fruits, oils and sap as well as fibres for manufacture. The Muriche palm (*Mauritia flexuosa*) provides starch for bread, sap for wine, fruits for a beverage resembling a punch, as well as fibre, leaves and wood for manufactures. See Lévi-Strauss, 'Use of wild plants', *HSAI*, 1963, VI, 469. The root of the cassava or Manioc (*Manihot utilissima*), in its sweet (non-poisonous) and bitter varieties is a staple foodstuff in South and

4. CHARLES LEIGH'S VOYAGE OUT TO THE WIAPOCO 1604[1]

The one and twentieth of March 1604.[2] Captaine Charles Leigh in the *Olive Plant*, a proper Barke of some fiftie Tunnes accompanied with six and fortie men and boyes, departed from Wolwich with intention to discover and inhabit some part of the Countrie of Guiana, where he had beene in a former voyage,[3] they stayed in the Downes untill the eight and twentieth of the said moneth, and passing thence they touched in the Ile of Mogador[4] on the coast of Barbarie in the moneth of Aprill, where we stayed about some five dayes, and watered on the mayne land in despite of the rebell Moores, which would have had money for our watering. Thence with prosperous winde coasting the Iles of Cape Verde, we passed over to the West Indies, and upon the tenth of May comming in change of water, which shewed thicke and white, by the next day we were in fresh water,[5] and the next day following about five in the morning wee saw two Ilands in the mouth of the River of Amazones, making account that we were fortie leagues up the River, and came to an anchor in three fathoms under them, which wee found low land covered with high Trees. Then the Captaine with some eight of the best men of the ship went toward the shoare, and finding many Indians comming toward them they returned aboard, and found the ship almost aground, but sounding the Bay brought their ship into the Channell which they found very narrow.[6]

---

central America. The bitter variety produces a flour or *farinha* high in starch content after the prussic acid found in the root has been expelled by grating, soaking and squeezing the pulp. See Sauer, 'Cultivated plants', HSAI, 1963, VI, 507–8.

[1] Extracted from 'Captaine Charles Leigh his voyage to Guiana and plantation there', in *Purchas his pilgrimes* (1625), IV, bk. 6, (1905–7), XVI, ch. 12, 309–10.

[2] (N.S.).　　　　　　　　　[3] See above, p. 26, n. 1.

[4] Mogador.

[5] See above, p. 17, n. 1. The outpouring of the Amazon into the Atlantic constitutes approximately 15% of all the fresh water passed into the world's oceans. The Amazon contribution alone lowers the salinity of the sea in a measurable degree over an area estimated to exceed at times over 2.5 million square kilometres. See O'Reilly Sternberg, *The Amazon*, 1975, p. 1.

[6] Since Leigh does not indicate his starting point of measurement or give any latitude it is impossible to estimate where he was. If he was calculating from Cabo do Norte then a passage of 40 leagues upriver would have taken him, according

Within awhile after foure Indians in a small Canoa shewed themselves unto us, to whom we sent our Boat with some of our commodities, as Hatchets, Knives, Glasses, Beades, they had nothing but Maiz and small blue-headed Parrots, for which we gave them some of our triffles. Not long after another Canoa comming out, our Boat clapt betweene them and the shoare to take some of them, to learne the state of the River by them, but they freed themselves all save one youth, which was brought aboard, which next day escaped leaping into the Sea twelve leagues as we judged from land. Thus we tooke our leave of the River of Amazones, and having uncertaine shoaldings all the way in our way, about ten a clocke in the night wee strooke upon a sand before we could let fall our anchor, where wee beat off a piece of our false keele, before wee could get off. Being gotten off, we came to an anchor in foure fathom and a halfe water, and rode there untill the next morning, where wee descryed the land sixe leagues from us with the entrance of a River.

5. THE TWO VOYAGES OF JOHN LEGAT TO THE AMAZON, 1604 AND 1606[1]

Before my departure from Sivill [Seville], I should have remembred, that about Whitsontide last there were brought into the Prison of the Contraction[2] there, two young men brought out of the West Indies, in one of the Kings Gallions, which were of Captaine

---

to later English and Dutch surveys, to the vicinity of the Ilha do Pará and the confluence of the river Anauíra-pucu. If, as the document reads, the two islands noted were the first sighted, then it is unlikely, given the great number of islands in the estuary, that Leigh penetrated any further upriver than the islands of Bailique, Jáburu or Curua which subdivide the entrance to the Canal do Norte. This assumes that Leigh had made for the Cabo do Norte and the west bank. The channel between the west bank and the aforementioned islands is narrow with a depth ranging from 4 to 7 fathoms. See *South American pilot*, 1945, pt. I, p. 75.

[1] Extract from 'The voyage of Master Henrie Challons, intended for the North plantation of Virginia, 1606. Taken by the way, and ill used by Spaniards: written by John Stoneman Pilot', in *Purchas his pilgrimes* (1625), IV, bk. 10, 1836–7, (1905–7), XIX, 295–6. Stoneman was carried prisoner to Seville with Captain Challons and other members of the company.

[2] *Casa de la contratacion* or House of Trade, Seville, the regulatory body for Spanish trade in the New World.

John Legats company of Plimmouth, which departed out of England, about the latter end of July 1606. bound for the River of Amazons, as hee told me before his going forth, where hee had beene two yeeres before.[1] And comming on the Coast of Brasill[2] as those young men (the name of one of them is William Adams borne in Plumpton neere Plimmouth) reported unto mee whether falling to the leeward of the River of Amazons, or deceived by his Master they knew not. And not being able to recover the said River, were constrayned to refresh in the West Indies, in which time there fell a great disorder betweene the said Captaine Legat and his company, So as one of his company in a broyle within themselves aboard there ship, slue the said Captaine Legat, whether in his owne private quarrel or with the consent of the rest of the Company, they could not tell mee. But this is the more to bee suspected for that he alwayes in former voyages dealt very straitly with his company. After his death his company comming to the Ile of Pinos,[3] on the South-side of Cuba, to refresh themselves, being eighteene persons were circumvented by the trecherie of the Spaniards, and were there betrayed, and taken Prisoners.

6. CAPTAIN THORNTON'S EXPEDITION TO THE AMAZON ON BEHALF OF THE GRAND DUKE OF TUSCANY, 1608

a.   William Davies' account[4]

[Ch. I] I Departed out of England the 28. of Januarie 1597.[5] in the good ship named the *Francis* of Saltash of of (sic) Cornwell [Cornwall], Master Tyball Geare, Owner, and William Lewellyn,

[1] I have interpreted this to mean two years previously although it could conceivably mean twice before. I have not yet been able to uncover any further biographical details on Legat. Clearly he was well known in the English seafaring community of the south-west. Purchas made the following marginal notes about him – 'Cap. John Legat of Plimmouth. Mutine. Cap. Legat slaine by his mutinous crew, which knew not when they had done to bring home their ship, and so stumbled on Spanish Justicers. – I have heard him much commended for a proper and expert Sea-man'.

[2] Presumably Stoneman means the Guiana coast here since a landfall in Brazil would not have taken Legat to the leeward of the Amazon.

[3] Isla de Pinos.

[4] Extracted from *A true relation of the travailes and most miserable captivitie of William Davies, barber-surgion of London, under the duke of Florence.* 1614. Marginal notations are placed in [ ] at the place where they occur.

[5] 7th January 1598 (N.S.).

Master of her, being laden with Fish, and Herings, and such like commodities, then bound for the Strayts and to arrive at Civita de Vecchia to the will and pleasure of God: where we arrived the first day of March insuing. . . .[1]

[Ch. III] Now leave [we] Tunys in the same Ship that I came out of England in, named the *Francis* of Saltash, being bound to Syo within the Arches of Archipelago,[2] and fraighted with Turkish goods by Turkes, and some Turks aboord with us, for wee traded as well with the Turke as the Christian: but we had not sailed above foure leagues out of our Port in the night season, but that we were most fiercely set upon by sixe of the Duke of Florence his Gallies [(]who being in continuall warre with the Turke, tooke us as a Turkish prize) which spit fire like divels, to our great discomfort, but at length couraging of our selves in Gods mercies, we continued fight with them, to the losse of many a mans life of each side, but all in vaine for us, for they were fortie for one of us, and our Sip (sic) torne downe to the water with their Ordinance, our mayne Mast, and missen Mast, shot by the boord, the one end of the Mast with all the sayles lying in the Sea, the other end aboord: thus were we taken, and stript every man starke naked, and then were we distributed, some into one Gallie, and some into another, where we had as many Irons knocked upon us, and more, than then we were able to beare. Our Ship presently sent to Ligorne, [Livorno] being mended as well as they could, but we in the Gallies, continued a moneth before we came thither, to the losse of many of our lives: but at length comming thither, as many of us as were left alive were thus intertained. We were all shaven both head and beard, and every man had given him a red coate, and a red cap, telling of us that the Duke had made us all Slaves, to our great woe and griefe: Where I continued eight yeeres and ten moneths in this slaverie, as in the next discoverie shall be truly spoken of.

[Ch. IV] . . : But at length God of his great goodnesse and mercy, delivered me (according to my hope) in this manner. The great Duke fitted a ship, a Tartane[3] and a Frigot, being very well appointed and victualled, disposing of them into the West Indies, and chiefely for the River of the Amazons, appointing Captaine Robert Thornton,[4] an Englishman to be chiefe Commaunder of the

---

[1] 11th March 1598 (N.S.).　　　　　　　　[2] Sámos?
[3] Lateen-sailed, single-masted vessel used in the Mediterranean.
[4] See above, p. 31, n. 2.

Ship, the Tartane and the Frigot: so likewise was every other Officer appointed by the Duke himselfe; insomuch as speaking of the placing of a Phisition, a Surgion, and a Surgions mate, Captaine Thornton standing by, said, your Highnesse may doe well to deliver a poore Englishman that hath continued a great while in your Gallies: hee is well experimented in Phisicke, and Surgery, by reason of his long practise both by Sea an[d] Land: he is hardned to the Sea, and able to discharge the place better then the three before mentioned: for in the Gallies he doth your Highnes but the labour of one slave: whereupon the Duke demaunded my name. Captaine Thornton answered, and said, William Davies: whereto the Duke replied, I have often beene spoken to for that fellow, whose liberty now I give upon thy good report, Thornton, but yet I doubt his usage hath beene so hard in my Countrey, that as soone as hee is out of chaynes, he will give me the slip and not goe the voyage into the Indies with thee. But if he can give five hundred Crownes securitie to goe the voyage, hee shall be released presently out of chaynes: neyther shall hee want any thing that is needfull for the voyage, for the good of all the Company, or for his owne bodie, and this let him understand as soone as may be: which newes came within two dayes unto me, to my great rejoycing [&] comfort. ... And within a short time after Captaine Thorneton came from Florence to Ligorne, where I was, who then tolde mee the Dukes disposition to the full, and upon what securitie I should be delivered: which securitie I did sodainely procure by an English Marchant, whose name was Maister William Mellyn, of Bristow [Bristol], who passed his Band (sic) for five hundred Crownes to the Duke, for the performance of the voyage by mee: Whereupon I was sodainely released out of chaynes, to my great rejoycing, giving God thankes for his blessings. Then was I presently well apparrelled by Captaine Thorneton, and this Marchant, wanting nothing whereof I was destitute:. . . . By this time all things were prepared and made readie for the performance of our pretended Voyage, now being bound to serve in the good Ship called the *Santa Lucia*, with a Frigot, and a Tartane, well victualled, and well manned, and chiefely bound to the River of Amazones, with other severall Rivers, the which the Duke would have inhabited, hoping for great store of gaine of Gold, but the Countries did affoord no such thing, as hereafter shall be spoken of. Upon this Voyage we were foureteene moneths, making little gaine, or benefit for the Duke, for there was nothing to be gained.[1]

[Ch.VI] The Description and discovery of the River of *Amazons*. [Distant from England 1600 leagues.]

THe River of the Amazons lieth in the highest part of the West Indies, beyond the Equinoctiall line; to fall with this River fortie leagues from Land you shall have eight, sixe, and seaven fadome water, and you shall see the Sea change to a ruddie colour, the water shall grow fresh, by these signes you may run in boldly your course,[2] and comming neere the Rivers mouth, the depth of your water shall increase, then you shall make discovery of the trees before the land, by reason the land is very low, and not higher in one place then another three foote, being at a spring tide almost all overflowne, God knowes how many hundred leagues.[3] It flowes much water there with a very forcible tide. In this River I continued ten weekes, seeing the fashion of the people and the countrey there: This Countrey is altogether full of woods, with all sorts of wilde beasts, as Lions, Beares, Wolves, Leopards, Baboones, strange Bores, Apes, Monkies, Martyns, Sanguins, Marmosets, with divers other strange beasts:[4] also these woods are full of wilde-fowle of all sorts, and Parats more plentifull then Pigeons in England,[5] and as good meat, for I have often eaten of them. Also this Countrey is very full of Rivers, having a King over every River. In this place is continuall tempests as lightning, thunder, and rayne, and so extreame, that it continues most commonly sixteene or eighteene houres in foure and twentie.[6] There are many standing waters in

---

[1] Thornton sailed in September 1608 returning in late June of 1609.

[2] See above, pp. 17, n. 1, 137, n. 5.

[3] The navigational instructions in *The South American pilot*, 1945, pt. I, indicate that Cabo do Norte, the west bank and the islands of the north channel are uniformly low. Vast areas of the flood plain are inundated seasonally.

[4] Although Davies' list of Amazonian fauna is imprecise he was rightly impressed by its amazing variety. The jaguar, ocelot, spectacled bear, maned fox, bush dog, most of the didelphid opossums, many species of monkeys, marmosets, sloths, armadillos, peccaries, tapirs, agoutis, capybaras, guinea pigs are found there. See R. M. Gilmore, 'Fauna and ethnozoology of South America', in *HSAI*, 1963, VI, 360; B. J. Meggers, *Amazonia: Man and culture in a counterfeit paradise* (Chicago, 1971), *passim*.

[5] 89 families of birds, representing at least 2,700 species inhabit Amazonia. Parrots were highly prized by the Indians for their feathers.

[6] Thornton's party arrived in the river at the end of the distinct dry season on the lower Amazon, lasting through July to September. The rains of the remainder of the year are heaviest between December and May. Precipitation

this Countrey, which be full of Aligators, Guianes, with many other severall water Serpents, and great store of fresh fish, of strange fashions.[1] This Countrey is full of Muskitas, which is a small Flie, which much offends a stranger comming newly into the Countrey. The manner, fashion, and nature of the people is this: They are altogether naked, both men and women, having not so much as one threed about them to cover any part of their nakednesse, the man taketh a round Cane as big as a penny candle, and two inches in length, through the which he puls the fore-skin of his yard, tying the skin with a peece of the rinde of a tree about the bignesse of a small packe threed, then making of it fast about his middle, he continueth thus till he have occasion to use him.[2] In each eare he weareth a Reed or Cane, which he bores through it, about the bignesse of a Swans quill, and in length halfe an inch, and the like through the midst of the lower lip: also at the bridge of the nose he hangs in a Reed a small glasse Bead or Button, which hanging directly afore his mouth, flies too and fro still as he speaks, wherein he takes great pride and pleasure. He weares his hayre long, being rounded below to the nether part of his eare, and cut short, or rather as I judged pluckt bald on the crowne like a Frier.[3] But their women use no fashion at all to set forth themselves, but starke naked as they were borne, with haire long of their heads, also their breasts hang very low, by reason they are never laced or braced up:

---

exceeds 100 inches annually. About 20% of rainfall occurs in heavy downpours lasting some one to two hours, accompanied by violent electrical storms. See Meggers, *Amazonia*, 1971, pp. 8–12.

[1] The Amazon and its tributaries teem with a staggering variety of fishes. Over 1,500 kinds have been noted. The common crocodilians of Guiana-Brazil are technically known as caymans. 5 species exist. 4 species of true crocodiles are found on the Caribbean coast of Guiana. Water-boas (anacondas) can range from 11–37 feet in length. See Gilmore, 'Fauna and ethnozoology', *HSAI*, 1963, VI, 405–7; M. Golding, *The fishes and the forest* (Berkeley, 1980), *passim*.

[2] Davies is describing a straw or reed penis-sheath, a common element of warrior attire among the tribes of the tropical forest.

[3] Thevet described how Tupinamba males plucked and shaved hair from their body, beard, eyebrows and the front of their head, achieving a style similar to a monk's tonsure. They informed him that depilation increased their strength and endurance. The partial shaving of their heads and the removal of their beards also made it harder for enemies to seize them in battle. See *La cosmographie universelle* (1575), bk. 21, ch. 10. Reed, bone and shell labrets, ear and nose-plugs were commonly worn by the warriors of the tribes of the lower Amazon. The addition here of a glass bead or button is evidence of the dissemination of European trade goods.

they do use to annoynt their bodies, both men and women, with a kinde of red earth, because the Muskitas or Flies shal not offend them.[1] These people are very ingenious, craftie, and treacherous, very light of foote, and good Bowemen, whose like I have never seene, for they doe ordinarily kill their own foode, as Beasts, Fowle, and Fish, the manner of their Bow and Arrowes is this. The Bow is about two yards in length, the Arrow seaven foot. His Bowe is made of Brazill wood very curious, his string of the rinde of a Tree, lying close to the Bow, without any bent, his Arrow made of a Reed, and the head of it is a fish bone, hee kils a beast in this manner: standing behinde a Tree, hee takes his marke at the beast, and wounding him, he followes him like a Bloud-hound till he fall, oftentimes seconding his shoote: then for any fowle be he neverso little, he never misses him: as for the first, he walkes by the waterside, and when he hath spied a fish in the water, he presently strikes him with his Arrow, and sodainely throwing downe his Bow, he leaps into the water, swimming to his Arrow which he draws a-land with the fish fastned to it,[2] then having each kild his owne food, as well flesh, and fowle, as fish, they meet together, to the number of fiftie or sixtie in a company, then make a fire after this fashion: They take two stickes of wood, rubbing one hard against another, till such time as they be fired, then making of a great fire every man is his owne Cooke to broyle that which he hath gotten, and thus they feede without Bread or Salt, or any kinde of drinke but Water and Tobacco,[3] neither doe they know what it meanes: In these Countries we could finde neither Gold nor Silver Oare, but great store of Hennes.[4] For I have bought a

[1] See the discussion of the use of Urucu above, p. 136, n. 3. Whether Urucu, mixed with animal and vegetable oil and smeared over the entire body, served a primarily aesthetic purpose or was intended as a protection against mosquitoes has been a subject of some debate.

[2] Since stone is rare in the lower Amazon, arrowheads were usually made of cane, bone or shell. For a more recent study of the archery skills of Brazilian Indians, see E. G. Heath and V. Chiara, *Brazilian Indian archery* (Manchester, 1977).

[3] Aboriginal to most, but not all, of the tribes of the South American tropical forest in the sixteenth and seventeenth century, and used largely for magico-religious and therapeutic purposes. The Tupinamba, however, seem also to have smoked tobacco purely for pleasure. See Métraux, 'The Tupinamba', *HSAI*, 1949, III, 115–33.

[4] Davies is probably referring here to the semi-domesticated birds found in Indian villages. Some species of ducks, curassows (family *Cracidae*) and Chachalacas (*Penelope, ortalis*) were kept for food and as pets. Parrots were kept for their feathers.

couple for a Jewes Harpe, when they would refuse ten shillings in money. This Countrey is full of delicious fruit, as Pynes, Plantins, Guaves, and Potato rootes,[1] of which fruits and rootes I would have bought a mans burthen for a glasse Button or Bead. The manner of their lodging is this: they have a kinde of net made of the rinde of a Tree which they call Haemac,[2] being three fadome in length, and two in breadth, and gathered at both ends at length, then fastning eyther end to a Tree, to the full length about a yard and a halfe from the ground, when he hath desire to sleepe, he creepes unto it. The King of every River is knowne by this manner. He weares upon his head a Crowne of Parats feathers, or severall colours, having eyther about his middle, or about his necke, a chaine of Lyons teeth or clawes, or of some other strange beast, having a woodden sword in his hand,[3] and hereby is he knowne to be the King: Oftentimes one King warres against another in their Canowes,[4] which are Boates cut out of a whole Tree, and sometimes taking one another the Conquerers eates the Captives.[5] By this time ten weeks were spent, and being homewards bound, but not the same way that we came, for we sayled unto the River before the winde, because it blowes there continually one way, which forces all ships that come thither to returne by a contrary way.

[Ch. XII] The Description of Morria.

[Distant from England 1620. leagues]

MOrria is a small low Iland, lying in the River of Amazones, the highest part of the West Indies.[6] This Iland is altogether inhabited

---

[1] Pineapples (*Ananas sativus*); Plantains (*Musacae*); Guava (*Psidicun guayaba*); sweet potatoes (*Ipomea batatas*) or yams (*Dioscorea. sp.*).

[2] The hammock. The cordage for the net was manufactured variously from palm fibres, *bromeliaceae*, and cotton.

[3] Feather ornaments in the form of headdresses, necklaces, armbands, anklets and cloaks were highly valued among the tropical forest tribes, and worn during their most significant ceremonials. The Tupinamba preserved these objects in bamboo tube containers. Chiefs and leading warriors had long necklaces of round and square shell and wooden beads, and animal teeth. See Lowie, 'The tropical forests', in *HSAI*, 1948, III, 19–20; Métraux, 'The Tupinamba', in ibid., pp. 105–9.

[4] Both dugout and bark canoes were used among the tribes of Amazonia and the Guianas. The dugouts were sea-going crafts. Bark canoes and balsa rafts were used in shallow waters.

[5] Ritual cannibalism was practised by Arawak, Carib and Tupinamba tribes of Amazonia and the Guianas.

[6] The *Isola dell Amazonas*, one of three drawn in parallel sequence across the equator in Dudley's manuscript chart (see fig. 5) may be William Davies' Morria.

by women, having no Mankinde amongst them: they goe altogether naked, using Bow and Arrowes for the killing of their owne foode: the hayre of their heads is long, and their Brests hang low: and whereas many here in England doe imagine that they have the right Brest seared, or cut off, it is no such matter as now, what hath beene in time past I know not: for this of mine owne knowledge, I have seene fortie, fiftie, or threescore of them together, each of them bearing Bow and Arrowes in their hands, going along by the Sea side; and when they espyed a Fish, they shoote at it, and strike it, and so throwing downe their Bowes, they leap into the water after their Arrowes, and bring the Fish aland, fastned to the Arrow: and so in all other things, as well the dressing of their meate, as their lodging and customes, they resemble and imitate the Indians of the River of Amazons, as you heard before in that discourse. But some of these Women doe use to beare their Children upon their backs, in this manner: They take a peece of the rinde of a Tree, and with the one end thereof they fasten the Childes hammes, and about the arme-pits and shoulders with the other, and so hang him on their backs like a Tinkers Budget, and cast up the brest to him over the shoulder. . . . There is one thing more to be wondred at, that I have also seene, that is to say, very good Oysters and Muskles growing upon trees, for I have eaten my part of many an hundred of them. And for your better understanding how they grow, you shall know that the Trees stand neere the Sea side, and at every full tyde the bowes hang into the Sea a fadome, or a fadome and a halfe, so that when the tyde goeth out, they are found hanging in great clusters upon the branches, like Barnacles to the side of a ship, and at the comming in of the tyde, they receive their moysture.[1]

b.   Robert Dudley's recollections of Thornton's voyage, 1647[2]

[p. 47] . . . In the which river Amazones entered Captain Robert

---

The three islands lie one degree, or a mariner's 20 leagues, from the *C. de R. Amazones*. The latter cape appears to represent the point, guarded by the islands of Bailique and Faustino, where the hitherto south-trending west bank of the estuary turns sharply away from the Atlantic to run south-west inland. As such it would be a logical place from which to measure distance upriver.

[1] The mangrove oyster. Ralegh noted them on Trinidad, Robert Harcourt on the Wiapoco. See *The discoverie*, 1928, p. 12; Harris, *A relation*, 1928, p. 97.

[2] Translation. Extracted from 'Dell'America, e dichiarazione della Carta decimaquarta', in Robert Dudley's *Dell'Arcano del Mare* (Florence, 1646–7), III, 47–8.

Thornton, an Englishman, sent to those parts by order and at the expense of the most serene Grand Duke Ferdinand I, his master.

The said Captain went out, and returned prosperously, and though he had never been in these parts before, nor yet in the West Indies in any wise, nevertheless, by means of the charts and instructions made by the author's own hand,[1] he, by the grace of God, completed the voyage without loss, except one man who died of sickness; and he surveyed the coast of Guiana more exactly than had ever before been done; and he also discovered the good port of Chiana [Cayenne],[p. 48] which is a secure and royal harbour, not very well known by Christians previously;[2] and from whence he brought five or six Indians to present to their highnesses in Florence, the which he did; the which were of those Caribs, who eat human flesh: These died afterwards in Florence, most of them from small-pox, which to them was more virulent than the plague itself, because in their country they have no knowledge of such a disease: Only one of them survived, who afterwards served his serene excellency the Cardinal de Medici[3] at court for several years, and learned to speak the Italian language quite well.

These Indians from Chiana often talked to the author and others of the fertility and riches of the kingdom of Guiana, and how they had been in the famous city of Monoa [Manoa] the metropolis of the kingdom, where the ruler resides who is called the emperor because he has many kingdoms under his dominion; and that this city is rich in gold and situated next to a great lake, and is eight days journey from the port of Chiana; the Indians make the journey very swiftly on foot, covering commonly 50 miles a day, and sometimes more.[4] The Indians said, moreover, that, near Chiana (which is hilly country), there was a very rich mine of silver, which they called Perota, there was also some base gold, named by them Calcari, of which they made certain images and half-moons, for ornaments.[5] This the above-mentioned Captain Thornton confirmed, and besides asserted that the spiders of that country spun

[1] See above, pp. 31, 32, n. 1, 33–4.
[2] Laurence Keymis had described the excellence of the anchorage off the Wia and Cayenne as early as 1596. The Cayenne was a common resort of English, Dutch and French traders thereafter. See Keymis, *Of the second voyage*, 1903–5, X, 458–9, and the accounts of A. Cabeliau and John Mocquet cited above pp. 27, n. 2, 29, n. 1.
[3] Presumably Carlo, cardinal de' Medici (1595–1666), brother of Cosimo II, grand duke of Tuscany.   [4] See above, pp. 17–18.   [5] See above, p. 130, n. 1.

silk, and that there was much dye wood [legno verzino] to be found, and wild sugar cane, white pepper, *legno pardo*, *pitta*,[1] balsam, cotton, and many other kinds of merchandise for abundant commerce if it were well planted by Christians. He said the climate was very healthy, and the entrance to the harbour easy to fortify and to command the port; with other particulars about the country already printed by the author in 1637,[2] to which for brevity we refer the reader. Moreover, the said Captain reported that when he had surveyed the river Amazones, or Orilliano, in the entrance he found a bore, as it is called in English, and Macarea in Portuguese; which is a dreadful tide,[3] and perilous in the days of the new and full moon, noted here in the said chart by the author in the words 'Beware of a bore at six hours and a quarter';[4] and with these few words of warning, the Captain saved his vessel and the subjects of his highness, by the grace of God. As the Captain testified to his highness, without the warning inscribed in that chart he would have known nothing of such peril, for there are few of these bores in the world; and he would have been lost if he had not been advised of the peril in advance, and had not warped the vessel with cables into a safer position, so as to receive the bore on the prow; and thus the vessel did not founder but escaped the danger.

From this example can be seen how important were the warnings inscribed on the author's charts, which through the exposing of hazards not usually noted in other charts, were able with three words to save the vessel and the company on divers occasions.

From the said river Amazones the said Capitano Thornton coasted Guiana and the island of Trinidada or the Trinity, and had great satisfaction in the accuracy and perfection of the author's chart. . . . He commenced the voyage from Livorno in the month of September in the year 1608, or thereabouts, and returned to the same port of Livorno at the end of June following in 1609. or thereabouts.

---

[1] *Ligno pardo* – speckled wood? *Pita*, hemp fibre of any of the bromeliaceous plants, mainly *Bromelia fastuosa* and *serra*.

[2] Dudley published a map of Guiana and the Orinoco delta in Florence in 1637.

[3] The Amazon tidal bore or pororoca, which roars some 200 miles upstream at the spring tides.

[4] See fig. X.

THE FIRST ENGLISH AND IRISH SETTLEMENTS ON THE AMAZON, 1611–20

1. JOHN SMITH.

A briefe discourse of divers voyages made unto the goodly Countrey of
Guiana, *and the great River of the* Amazons;
relating also the present Plantation there.[1]

There are above thirtie faire rivers that fall into the Sea, betweene the River of *Amazons* and *Oranoca* [Orinoco], which are some nine degrees asunder.

In the yeare 1605. Captaine Ley, brother to that noble Knight Sir Oliver Ley, with divers others, planted himselfe in the River Weapoco [Wiapoco], wherein I should have beene a partie; but hee dyed, and there lyes buried: and the supply miscarrying, the rest escaped as they could[2]

Sir Thomas Roe, well knowen to be a most noble Gentleman, before he went Lord Ambassadour to the Great *Magoll*, or the Great *Turke*,[3] spent a yeare or two upon this Coast, and about the River of the *Amazones*; wherein he most imployed Captaine Matthew Morton, an expert Sea-man in the discoverie of this famous River: a Gentleman that was the first shot and mortally supposed wounded to death with me in *Virginia*, yet since hath beene twice with command in the *East Indies*.[4] Also Captaine

---

[1] John Smith, *True travels* (1630), ch. 24, ed. P. Barbour, *The works of Captain John Smith* (Chapel Hill and London, 1986), III, 224–5.

[2] See above, pp. 26, 137–8. Sir Oliph Leigh was brother to the Charles Leigh who attempted to settle the Wiapoco in 1604. For the history of that settlement, see *Williamson, The English colonies*, 1923, ch. 2.

[3] See above, p. 37, n. 2. Roe went as ambassador to the Ottoman Porte in September 1621.

[4] See above, p. 41, n. 1 and below, pp. 196, 197, n. 2.

William White,[1] and divers others worthy and industrious Gentlemen, both before and since, hath spent much time and charge to
discover it more perfitly; but nothing more effected for a Plantation, till it was undertaken by Captaine Robert Harcote, 1609.

This worthy Gentleman, after he had by Commission made a
discoverie to his minde, left his brother Michael Harcote, with some
fiftie or sixtie men in the River *Weapoco*, and so presently returned
to *England*, where he obtained by the favour of Prince Henrie, a
large Patent for all that Coast called *Guiana*, together with the
famous River of *Amazones*, to him and his heires: but so many
troubles here surprized him, though he did his best to supply them,
he was not able; only some few hee sent over as passengers with
certaine *Dutch-men*, but to small purpose.[2]

2. SIR JULIUS CAESAR'S NOTES
ON ENGLISH ACTIVITIES IN GUIANA, 1609–19[3]

15 Mart*es* 1618.	The busines of Guiana.
Northward.	Capt*ain* Harcot hath bene in the river Wiapoco,
Callian.	Whereabouts hee hath planted by h*im*self &
Maravinni.	others on this side of the line equinoctiall: the
Sherana.	River Amazones being on the other side of the
Conawin.[4]	*said* line. Rio de Vins*ent*e nere the river
	Wiapoco. the River of Amazones nere Orellana,

[1] See below, pp. 188–9, 238–9. Smith clearly knew White personally. The
implication of his comment, coming as it does after his remarks on Morton, may
be that White had also been involved in enterprises to Virginia. A labourer of
that name was one of the original planters in Jamestown, see Barbour, *Jamestown
voyages*, 1969, I, xxviii, 128, 145–50, II, 383. A William White was also listed as a
new adventurer in the third patent of the Virginia company in 1621, see
Kingsbury, 1906, I, 534. For a list of all references to men by that name in
Virginia, 1606–24, see P. W. Filby and M. K. Meyer, eds., *Passenger and
immigration lists index* (Detroit, 1981), III, 2248. William White's Dartmouth
associates for the *Laurell* voyages, routinely traded to Newfoundland, see below,
p. 188, ns. 3, 4. A William White sailed master of the *Katheren* of 'Waxforde'
[Wexford] bound for the same carrying 'Bay salt' from Dartmouth in 1624,
P.R.O., E190 Dartmouth, 945/6. White's involvement in the Amazon ventures
would appear to have developed through the Dartmouth connection. He may
have been trading with Purcell's men in 1618, see above, p. 50.

[2] *Ibid.*

[3] B.L., Lansdowne MS 160, f. 109.

[4] Caesar refers to the rivers Cayenne, Maroni or Marowijne, Surinam and
Cuyuni here.

River of the   et Aguada, not far from the River of Domingo.
Arabara.   La Trinidad in the degree 10. Northward from
River of   the equinoctiall. All in the Region of Peru in
Arapoco.[1]   the Province of Tisnada.[2] Mathewe Moreton
planted people in June anno *1611*. in the River of
the Amazones at Sir Roes charge about 6. yeres since. Thomas King
was then there also under the charge of Roe. The patent is from the
River of the Amazones northward to the River of Desiqueba 300.
leagues. – miles 900. [bee] the River of Oronoque about the line
equinoctiall or within the space of the 10. degrees northward.
About the Island of Trinidad is the River of Orenoque.[3]

3. EXTRACT FROM THE COMMONPLACE BOOK
OF SIR STEPHEN POWLE, 24th FEBRUARY/6th MARCH 1610[4]

Guiana, 13 February 1609 being Tuesday Sir Thomas Roe oure
commander for the discovery of Guiana: and Sir George Brooke[5]

---

[1] Probably the river Arowari and the *Arrapoco* said by Robert Harcourt to be
the 'westermost branch of the River of *Amazones* that falleth into the Sea',
Relation, 1613, p. 79. Robert Dudley's MS map of Guiana fig. X shows the river
Iwaripoca entering the north bank of the Amazon between the Arowari and the
cabo di Vincent Pincon. See above, p. 32.

[2] Caesar's notes are virtually unintelligible. He was clearly trying to draw a
distinction between the Wiapoco, Harcourt's area of interest, and the Amazon
plantations, see below, pp. 190–1. His jottings read as if he was not absolutely
certain whether the Amazon and Orinoco were distinct rivers. He may well have
been re-reading the excerpts from Acosta's *Historia natural* printed in vol. III of
the *Principal navigations* (1600), 698–9, see above, pp. 18, 19, n. 1. He seems to
have believed the Orellana to have been another river near the Amazon. It is
hard to know what he meant by the 'River of Domingo', supposedly not far from
either of them. It could result from a mistaken reading of Ralegh's comment
about the distribution of gold artefacts from 'Dominica to Amazones' in *The
discoverie*, see above, p. 129. The river or Bay of Vincente Pincon is generally
shown on contemporary maps entering the Atlantic just above Cabo do Norte.
The river was held to mark the northern boundary between Portuguese Brazil
and the Spanish Indies and as such had no fixed location until the Portuguese
pushed definitively up to the Wiapoco in the 1630s, see below, p. 314, n. 3. For
the province of Tisnados and Aguada see above, p. 130, n. 2.

[3] See above, pp. 41, 45, 46.

[4] Bodleian, Tanner MS 168, f. 2. On Sir Stephen Powle, Clerk of the
Chancery, see D. B. Quinn, 'Notes by a pious colonial investor, 1608–10', *William
and Mary Quarterly*, XVI (1959), 551–5.

[5] Powle refers here to Sir John Brooke. Brooke set sail with Roe but was forced
to abandon the voyage and transfer himself to an English ship bound for Spain
because of acute seasickness. He informed the earl of Salisbury of his actions in a

(as I heare since) departed for Dartmouth where oure 2 shippes and provision for two pinnesses more bestowed in them lay at roade for his comminge: parteners: The Earle of Sowthampton [–]oo^{li},[1] Sir Walter Rawley 600^{li}, Sir Thomas Roe him sealfe with his parteners 1100^{li}:[2] and my sealf 20^{li}: which viage god blesse: the 2 shippes departed from Dartmouth the 24 of February 1609.

4. EDMUND HOWES' ACCOUNT
OF SIR THOMAS ROE'S VOYAGE, 1610–11[3]

The fore-named worthy young Knight, and right valiant Gentleman, in the yeare.1609. [1610] at his, and his friends charge, builded a Ship, and a Pinace, for the discovery of Guyana, hee set sayle from Plimmouth the 24. of February and in the end of Aprill, fell with the great River of the Amazons, which is under the Equinoctiall line, and is in breadth at the entrance thereof, 100. and 50. miles fresh water, and full of Islands, which River hee first discovered, and entred with his Shippe 200. miles, and then with Boates 100. more, and made divers journeyes into the maine among the Indians being well inhabited, and full of good commodities, though not so plenteous as it might be, by reason the natives provide no more then for their necessity, from thence he came along the coast into divers Rivers, and entred the Country by Indian Boates, and went over the Chatoracts and hills, passed over thirty two falles in the River of Wia Poco, from whence hee descended, having with great labour and perill, spent 13. moneths in this discovery, viz. from the river of Amozenes (sic), to the river of Oronoque, at the end whereof, not

---

letter from Portugal, dated the last day of March 1610 (P.R.O., SP 14/53 f. 54). M. F. Strachan suggests that Salisbury may have intended Brooke to act as a watchdog on Roe to ensure that the expedition did not overstep the careful guidelines he had set down.

[1] Quinn, 'Notes by a pious', 1959, p. 554 and Harlow, Colonizing expeditions, 1925, p. lxx, both read Southampton's contribution as £800. Williamson, The English colonies, 1923, p. 50, felt that this reading is questionable since the first digit of the figure is obscured by a blot. I similarly found the figure impossible to decipher with any certainty. For the other overseas investments of Henry Wriothesley, earl of Southampton, see Rabb, Enterprise and empire, 1967, p. 409, and below, p. 204, n. 2.

[2] See above, p. 38.

[3] Edmund Howes' continuation of The annales: or generall chronicle of England, begun first by maister John Stow (1631), p. 1022.

finding all the West Indies to be full of Gold, as some suppose, hee returned by Trenydado, and the Westerne Islands, and arrived at the Wight, in July, one thousand six hundred and eleven: and thus much in honour of his forwardnesse, paines, and industry. I thought fit to mention, though not in his proper place,[1] lest vertue should bee forgotten, and others reape the honour of his labours, since which time hee hath sent thither to make farther discoveries, and maintained 20. men in the River of Amozones, for the good of his Countrey, who are yet remaining there, and supplied.

5. LETTER OF SIR THOMAS ROE TO THE EARL OF SALISBURY, PORT OF SPAIN, TRINIDAD, 28TH FEBRUARY/10TH MARCH 1611[2]

Right Honorable.

If I should trouble your Lordship with a lardge relation of my poore discoveryes, they would be as paynfull to you, as they have beene to mee: I have left them now behind me, and I will doe so here too, least they offend your patience more, then they have benefitted mee.

Your Honor shall fynd nothing new or strange here, though it come from the newest and strangest land, for it beres no other fruict but my respect and service to your Lordship, for which interruption I must also aske perdon; when I shall come home I hope to give your Lordship account that I have not beene idle, and I will not become so, by strange reports of this place, when I shall answer for yt at your Lordships commandement. Yet I may with a humble bouldness presume to say I have seene more of this coast rivers and inland from the Great River of the Amazones under the line to Orenoque in 8 degrees,[3] then any Englishman now alive, and of this I hope to give a reason: I am now past the Wild Coast[4] and arrived at Port d'espagne in the Island of Trinidad, where are 15 sayle of ships freighting smoke,[5] English French Dutch: of thes parts if your Honor will give me leave to relate the little newes and my opinion I will venture them

---

[1] The entry for Roe's expedition was made for the year 1615 (N.S.) and follows upon a report of Roe's departure for India.

[2] P.R.O., CO 1/1, no. 25.

[3] 8°30′ N. – 10° N.

[4] The Dutch name for the coastline between the Amazon and the Orinoco in the early seventeenth century.

[5] Tobacco.

both: The Spaniards here are equally proud, insolent, yet needy and weake: theyr force is reputation, and theyr safety opinion: yet dare they use us whose hands are bound with any contumely and treachery: for me I will resist and prevent both these, and for that end doe rather stay with some English, then for any trade; I hope your Noble disposition will not take it ill that we defend ourselves and the Honour of our Nation: I will not exceed your Honorable caution your Lordship gave me, nor stoope to so wretched an enemy (for so he is here) nor syncke under the injuryes I am able to repulse. I have had some question with them on land, but it is ended with quiett, concerning the Trade of our Contrymen, whom they used woorse than Moores.

All seamen here bless your Lordship, and wish that the state would not be offended if they made themselves recompence, and have gotten a rumor, or made one, of Lettres of Mark, because Mr Hall's prise hath beene admitted: if the example were sure, we could second yt, but we dare not handle fyre, nor cannot take fast hould of ayre.[1]

All the Spanish newes here is of the kynges purpose to plant Orenoque and it is a matter of great consequence, for the River runs into the hart of the mayne and hath much wealth upon it. The Justice of the kyng is dayly expected to come downe, and to be received at Saint Thomas the Plantation of Ferd: Bereo in Orenoque;[2] who is received into the king's protection and hath received his grace. Theyr comes dayly from the mayne men cattell and horse which are to be employed in this woorke, in fortefying the place, raysing a new Cytty, and in pursuing the Conquest of Guiana, which hath long slept, and is now by new and more direct intelligence opened to him: but it will vanish, and be turned all to smoke, for the Governor is lazy, and unapt for labor, and hath more skill in planting Tobacco and selling it, then in erecting Colonyes, or marching of armyes: But the river and Towne is infinite ritch and weake, and may easely be taken away, and as easely held: There is in these parts a Spaniard proscribed, for well treating some English

[1] The losses of the London merchant Richard Hall at the hands of the Spaniards and the reaction of the English government to his grievances are discussed in Lorimer, 'The English contraband tobacco trade', 1978, pp. 144–6.

[2] Fernando de Berrio, governor and captain-general of the province of 'Trinidad y Guayana'. The Orinoco settlement of San Tome de la Guyana lay on the south bank of the river, three miles east of the confluence of the Caroni. See above, p. 40.

fallen into his power; his name is Don Juan de Gambo: he, with divers Spaniards his followers, are fled into the mayne as open enemyes to the kyngs proceedings: I have gotten knowledge by Indyans where he is, and have sent my shallop to seeke him, if I can to speake with him: I know if myselfe may confer with him, which I will adventure for, he may offer good service to your Lordship, for he is a great souldier for thes parts, and knowes all the secretts, passages, strengths, advantages and weaknesses of this land, and all the mayne to the bottom of the bay: and I am sure he knows of mynes undiscovered to the kings officers, and unable for him and his company to overcome. If he fayle me, yet I hope it will not be ill received of me, if I bring one with me home that may doe almost as much, if there be use of him; he is borne a Venetian, but bred in the New Kyngdome of Granada, a priest here, but a souldier there, one that pretends change in his conscience, I cannot see his hart, but I know his professions, and abilityes here: I will present him to your Lordship, if he be not prevented, for he is also one that must runne away when I give the word.

I am now sorry for this presumption but your Lordship gives leave to all, and I account myselfe tyed by many favors to your particular service: if I may presume to add one more at my humble sute, that your Honor will favor me in my last and first request, in advancing my desire to serve the Prince though your Lordships knowledge of me had but late beginning and meaner deservings yet you shall ever fynd that your Lordship shall command the life of

Your Honors unworthy servant

THOMAS ROE

February 28th: Port d'espaigne in the Island of Trinidad: 1610. To the right Honorable the Earle of Salisbury Lord High Treasurer of England.

6. ENTRIES IN THE OVERSEAS BOOK OF THE CONTROLLER OF CUSTOMS AND SUBSIDIES FOR PORTSMOUTH, 1614[1]

Inwardes. The xviith of January i613
In the Lions Clawe of London burthen seventy toonnes Richard H[. . .]er Master from the Islandes of Spayne.

---

[1] P.R.O., E190 Portsmouth, 820/1.

For the Lord Embassadoure of Spaine and for Marchantes strangers unknowne, one thouzand three hundred Fortie and one endes of Brasil woodd al*ias* Fernando Buck wood[1] cont*aining* seaventy and five hundred wayght net valor.

Twenty Nine[Onne] Chestes of white powder sugers cont eleven thousand and three hundred weight net valor.

Fortie and one Chestes of muscavado sugers[2] cont eleven thouzand and three hundred weight net valor.

Fortie and one Chestes of sugers called panneales[3] cont sixteene thouzand & fower hundred waight net valor.

Outwardes   The xxvii[th] of June 1614
In the Lions Clawe of London burthen ffowerscore tonnes Mathew Morton m*aste*r for the Amazons
For S*ir* Thomas R[oe] [Ind] knight thirty dozen of Axis and hatchetts valor————   subs*idy*—v[s]
[two] greate grosse of glasse beades
         valor xxx[s]   subs*idy*—i[s] vi[d]
[...............] of Butchers knives
         valor v[li]   subs*idy*—v[s]4

7. ACCOUNT OF THE NAVIGATION, SETTLEMENT AND TRAFFICK WHICH THE IRISH AND ENGLISH HAVE CARRIED OUT IN THE RIVER AMAZON, AND THE PRESENT SITUATION IN THE RIVER. 1621[5]

Captain Felipe Porcel [Philip Purcell], Irishman, says that it will be twelve years since he went from the port of Dartmua [Dartmouth] in England to San Thome de Guiana[6] in the river Orenoco [Orinoco] with other Englishmen, carrying goods to trade in Trinidad and the river Orenoco for tobacco, and there this captain

---

[1] See above, p. 58.
[2] Moist, dark-coloured, unrefined sugar left after evaporation from cane juice and the draining off of the molasses.
[3] Panele, pannul, panial, pannel; brown unpurified sugar.
[4] This entry is very faded and some parts of it are impossible to read with any accuracy.
[5] Translation. A.G.S., Estado 7031, lib. 374, ff. 162–3v. This report was sent to Spain by the ambassador Don Diego Sarmiento de Acuña, conde de Gondomar. See above, pp. 65–7 and below, pp. 169, n. 3, 223, 233.
[6] See above, p. 154, n. 2.

and many English in other ships, who at that time used to do business in those parts, trafficked with the Governor Berrio.[1]

This captain Felipe Porcel having been in Trinidad for two months and having found out about the river of the Amazons, returned to England and he with other partners chartered a Dutch ship and went to that place.[2] They discovered that the river of the Amazons is entered on the right-hand to the south-west and at its entrance from this coast to that of Brazil is fifty leagues wide, more or less. Coasting this river of the Amazons on the right-hand side,[3] they found the land to be so swampy, so unhealthy, and so densely wooded that they were obliged to go ninety leagues upriver before they discovered the bank of another river, like the Tamises [Thames] of Londres [London], which also rises with the sea at its high and low tides. They went eighteen leagues up this river and, finding good country, disembarked and began to trade with the Indians, who are brownish black, uncivilized pagans who go naked with no covering whatsoever. They gave the Indians glass beads and other things teaching them how to produce large quantities of tobacco, because the Indians only knew how to do it according to their own uncouth fashion, and not with the perfection with which it is produced in San Thome and in the manner in which this Captain Porcel saw it done in the Orenoco.[4] Thus, from the year 1609 in which he made this first discovery he has been out and back twice more. The last time he took with him fourteen Irishmen who have trafficked with the Indians until the past year, 1620, when Captain North arrived there and disembarked nearby one hundred of the English which he took out with him, the which he [Purcell] believes, because they are new to the country and have not been relieved with provisions or any other thing since they arrived, will be all dead, or the major part of them.[5]

The Dutch have settled in the same great river, thirty leagues further up, which comes to one hundred and twenty leagues from

---

[1] Ibid.

[2] See above, pp. 44–5; 50–1.

[3] Clearly Purcell is describing the course upstream here, and thus means the north bank of the river.

[4] See above, pp. 40, 43–5. For the best contemporary description of the method of 'seasoning' or curing tobacco, see Joannes Neander, *Tabacologia* (Bremen, 1622); T.C., *An advice how to plant tobacco in England*, 1615.

[5] See below, pp. 236–42.

the beginning of the river mouth, going up on the same right-hand side.[1]

He does not know whether they have made any fortification or defence worth consideration up to the present, but, nevertheless it seems to him very necessary that your Catholic Majesty should, without delay, order a well-furnished ship to be sent to reconnoitre and uproot the people of whatever nation it may find there, which at the present time, it seems to him, will be easy to do.[2] Dated in Londres 20th of June 1621

8. DUTCH REPORTS OF THOMAS KING'S ACTIVITIES ON THE AMAZON, 1615[3]

Pedro Luis [Pieter Lodewycx], a captain of the fleet, resident of Vlosingas [Flushing], has turned up at la Haya [the Hague] Holland with his son Juan Pedro Alas [Jan Pieterse],[4] both back from the West Indies from the bank of the Viapoco [Wiapoco] where they have built two houses and gathered tobacco.[5] The said Pedro has sailed up the river of the Amazons for about one hundred leagues and on returning brought back much profit in red dye,[6] tobacco and various spices. He learned from the inhabitants there that further on in that country there are many inhabitants and nations and much greater profit for traders, the which has prompted them to return to the

[1] Purcell's estimate of the location of the Dutch settlement, 360 miles upriver, would suggest that he was referring to Adriaenszoon Ita's colony, see above, pp. 53–6. North appears to have planted his men on what was then called the river Okiari at 0°40′ S., possibly the present Ajuraxy or the Cajari. See above, p. 70 and below, pp. 237, 261.

[2] For the Spanish response, see below, pp. 233–6.

[3] Translation. 'Avisos tocantes a la India Occidental en 3 de Abril 1615', B.L., Add. MS 36,320, ff. 202–4v. A report of the duke of Lerma to the *Consejo de Indias*, transcripted from the original in the A.G.I.

[4] Pieter Lodewycx and his son Jan Pietersz. Edmundson, 'The Dutch on the Amazon and Negro', *EHR*, 1903, pp. 644–5, states 'Juan Pedro' is Lerma's translation of the name of Lodewycx's son Jan Pietersz. 'Alas' was the name of Lerma's informant at the Hague, a Portuguese in Spanish pay.

[5] See above, pp. 52–3. An earlier despatch included in a letter of the duke of Lerma, 5th July 1614, appears to record Lodewycx's departure for the Wiapoco and Amazon survey. He reported that the Zeelanders 'have cast their eye on the river Oreliana and already have sent a caravel from Flushing to go up the said river as far as possible and to make the acquaintance of its inhabitants, because they believe the said river to have its origin in the mountains of Peru, and that it is navigable to the kingdom of Cuzco', B.L., Add. MS 36,320, f. 80v.

[6] See above, pp. 57–8.

Viapoco with several ships both to supply the new settlement which they have made there and to go further up the said river of the Amazons to seek traffick. For this he has confirmed a company with the Burgo-master of Wearingas [Flushing] Juan de Moor [Jan de Moor], (and) two members of the Admiralty, the one named Angelo Lemnes and the other Herr van Lodestyn, through whom (he has) the consent of the Estates of Holland to establish the said colony and settlement.[1] This is notwithstanding the great and widespread settlement which the said Estates intend to make in those parts of America in the event that the war will not resume which many hope and hold to be certain, and thus the whole body (of those involved in) maritime trade and commerce is pressing the said Estates to provide some notable assistance so that they may find out about and reconnoitre all the length and breadth of the said river of the Amazons whence the said Estates will take great profit in the future in the course of time. . . .[2]

Moreover the said son of the Captain relates that the French have built an impregnable fort called Marani at two degrees near the line in which they have twenty four bronze pieces and some of iron, and they assert that it was made by order of the king of France and every day many French vessels resort there.[3]

Likewise (he relates) that one Tomas Rey [Thomas King][4] has placed a notable fort in the mouth of the river of the Amazons from whence he makes great and profitable returns so that when the trade and commerce there begins to be managed with some good order the gain which must result will, in the course of time, be of greater benefit and consideration than that from the East Indies.

---

[1] Jan de Moor had invested in trade to the Wild Coast since the 1590s. Everard Van Lodensteyn, burgomaster of Delft and Admiral Michiel Geleynsse both served on the Admiralty board of Zeeland, see Edmundson, 'The Dutch on the Amazon and Negro', *EHR*, 1903, p. 646; Ghoslinga, 1971, chs. 3 and 4.

[2] See above, p. 51.

[3] See above, p. 56, n. 3.

[4] The Spanish rendition of the name is 'Tomas Rey'. While this could conceivably refer to Thomas Roe, as Williamson, *English colonies*, 1923, pp. 58–9, believed, it is much more likely to be an allusion to Thomas King. A Spaniard is unlikely to have transliterated the name Roe as 'Rey', whilst the latter word is a straightforward translation of the well-known word for king.

9. GEORGE PERCY'S ACCOUNT OF CAPTAIN BUDD'S VOYAGES TO THE AMAZON, 1612–15[1]

Right Hon*ourable*/.[2]

Havinge had so certaine a triall that my fitts here in England are more often, more longe, & more greevous, then I have felt them in other partes neerer the lyne; I am veriy desirus, so it may be w*ith* your *Lordshi*pps goodwill & furtherance to embrace an occasion offered for those parts where I may finde moste ease: It is to goe w*ith* Captain Bud[3] for the river, of Amazons to w*hich* place he hath made repaire these three yeers, rather to make up his commod[it]ie, then that his men w*hich* he left to trade there any way needed releefe, the savadges so well affect them and store them w*ith* all necessaries. If your honor will doe me that bountifull favor, as to furnish me w*ith* the som w*hich* I should have at Michellmass next, you shall not only make me for this voyadge but also, I remaininge there two yeers w*ith* that w*hich* shall rest behinde, supply me for the payment of my debts w*ith* money before hand, whereas otherwise I shall not be able to keepe my selfe oute of trouble, unless I will runn into an exstreme distress of want. Wherefore if your *Lordshi*pp shall of your accustomed goodnes preserve me out of theise dangers, as also favor the helth and better estate of bodie, by grauntinge me my request I shall all wayes upon greter reason, as I have ever deservedly remayned/

Your Honors moste bounden Brother.

George Percy.

10. ROBERT HARCOURT'S ACCOUNT OF THE EXPEDITION TO THE RIVER ARROWARI MADE BY HIS BROTHER BEFORE 1612[4]

[p. 42] . . . I tooke possession of the land, by turfe and twig, in the behalfe of our Soveraigne Lord King JAMES: I tooke the said

[1] Percy Papers, X (1611–17), f. 220, also printed in Shirley, 1949, p. 242. The letter is undated. A note in a later hand places it in 1615.

[2] Henry Percy, ninth earl of Northumberland, imprisoned in the Tower for alleged complicity in the Gunpowder Plot, a great friend of Sir Walter Ralegh.

[3] See above, p. 47.

[4] Harcourt, *Relation*, 1613, pp. 42–5, 1626, pp. 55–9, Harris, *Relation*, 1928, pp. 110–14.

posession (sic) of a part, in name of the whole continent of *Guiana*, lying betwixt the rivers of *Amazones* and *Orenoque*, not being actually possessed, and inhabited by any other Christian Prince or State; wherewith the Indians seemed to be well content and pleased.

[The like possession taken at Arraway] In like manner my Brother Capt*ain* Michael Harecourt, and Capt*ain* Harvey,[1] (whom I left as his associate, and hee esteemed as an inward friend,) in a notable journey, which (to their great honour) they performed, to discover the River of *Arraway* [Arrowari], and the Country bordering upon it, (neere adjoining to the river of *Amazones*) did take the like possession of the land there, to his Majesties use.

The dangers and great difficulties which they in that attempt incountred, were memorabe (sic), and such, as hardly any of our Nation in such small Canoes (being onely some-what longer, but not so broad as our *Thames* wherries, and flat bottomed,) ever overcame the like. First the number of their owne attendants besides themselves, was onely one man, and a boy: Their troope of Indians 60. persons. Their journey by Sea unto the River of *Arraway* was neere 100. Leagues:[2] wherein (by the way) they met with many dreadful plunges, by reason of a high going sea, which breaketh upon the flats and shoales; especially, at the next great cape to the North of *Arraway*, (sic) which, in respect of the danger they passed there, they named [p. 43] *Point Perilous*.[3] Then their discovery up the river, was 50. leagues more:[4] where they found a Nation of Indians, which never had seene white men, or Christians before, and could not be drawne to any familiar commerce, or conversation, no not so much as with our Indians, because they were strangers to them, and of another Nation. The discovery of this river is of great importance, and speciall note, affording an entrance more behovefull for the searching and discovery of the inland parts of *Guiana*, then any other river yet knowne upon the Coast; for trending Westward up into the land, it discovereth all the

---

[1] Edward Harvey, see above, p. 39.

[2] As Harris notes, *Relation*, 1928, p. 111, n. 3, this estimate was relatively accurate, the actual distance being some 278 miles by the coast.

[3] See fig. VI.

[4] *Ibid.* The chart is marked by a cross and the initials C: M.H. and C: E.H. approximately 52½ leagues up the Arrowari.

Countries and Nations to the Southward of *Arricary, Cooshebery, Morrownia,* and *Norrack,* which I have mentioned before.[1]

[A great argument of plenty in the Countrey.] Many weekes they spent in this adventure, still taking up their lodgings in the woods at night. Provision of meate they wanted not, for Fish were ever plenty, and at hand: and the woods yeelded eyther Deere, Tigers,[2] or Foule: their greatest want was of bread and drinke, which onely defect did hinder (at that time) the accomplishment of that discovery. For when the Indians perceived their bread to bee neere spent, and their drinke to bee corrupted, they could not bee perswaded to proceede, having no meanes to supply their wants amongst the Arrawaries, the Indians of that river, who would not freely trade with them upon this first acquaintance, but alwaies stood upon their guard, on the other side of the river, where they inhabited: yet they desiring to obtaine some of our English commodities, and make triall of our Indians friendshippe, afforded some small trade for their [p. 44] present releefe during their aboade in that river: So that of force they were constrained to breake off their discovery, and hasten homeward. . . .

[p. 45] This, and much more could my Brother have truely avouched, if hee had lived; but (since his returne into England)[3] it hath pleased God, who gave him life, and preserved him from many dangers, to take him to his mercy. But the other, Captaine *Harvey,* surviveth, whose life hath ever suted with a generous and worthy spirit, professing Armes, and following the warres: who also is generally well knowne, to be a Gentleman, both honest, and of spotlesse reputation; hee will averre and justifie for truth, what heere is mentioned. But I will now returne from whence I have digressed.

[1] Harcourt is referring here to what he called the 'Signiories' and 'Provinces', or territorial divisions of the tribes between the Arrowari and the Wiapoco, *Relation,* 1613, pp. 14–18, 1626, pp. 17–22, Harris, *Relation,* 1928, pp. 19–21, 79–80, 82–3.

[2] Harcourt is probably referring to the jaguar 'tigre' (*Felis,* or *Panthera, onca*) or the striped and spotted ocelot 'tigrillo' (*Felis,* or *Leopardus, pardalis*).

[3] Michael Harcourt and Edward Harvey returned to England in 1612.

11. [EDWARD] FISHER'S VOYAGE TO THE AMAZON, 1613[1]

The governor and colony languishinge in this distresses (sic), the one of hunger, the other discontent, behold a frigate makes to the shore, the which being discovered to be manned with English is wellcomed and pilated into the harbour, and (in a good houre) found to be chiefly laden with Spanish meale: her commandour was named Daniell Elfrye, who servinge under one Fisher,[2] that was sent out upon a discovery into the river of the Amazones; as they went, this Spanish frigate comeinge in their waye their catchinge fingers layd fast hold on her, and this Elfrye (being in good trust with Fisher) was putt into her as master, who takeinge his opportunities, requited him so well as sone after he gave him the slyp and then shaped his course hether; wher he arrived so luckely, as by haveinge his meale shared among the hungry colony much content for the present is recovered, by the governour, and many that wer in very hard distresse fedd and releved. The newe guests restinge here and takeinge their partes of it, untill not long after they were shyped away for England.

12. PIETER ADRIAENSZOON ITA'S ANGLO–DUTCH COLONY, 1616–23[3]

In the yeare i6i6 one Peeter Adriansen[4] in the Golden Cock of Vlusinge [Flushing] sayled for the Amazones and haveing been as high as the Entrance of the strait, they feard they might be in a wrong Chanel, returnd Back again, and between the River Coropatube, & the River Ginipape on a peninsula by a Little River on one side, and an Arme of the Amazones on the other side they built a fort,[5] many of

[1] Extracted from B.L., MS Sloane 750, transcribed in J. H. Lefroy, ed., *The historye of the Bermudaes* (London, 1882), p. 33. Lefroy suggested that John Smith was the author of this MS. E. Arber, *Captain John Smith* (Edinburgh, 1910), II, 624, considers that Governor Tucker of Bermuda is a more likely candidate.

[2] See above, p. 50.

[3] John Scott, 'The Historical and Geographical Description of the great River of the Amazones', Bodleian, Rawlinson MS, A175, ff. 370–1.

[4] See above, pp. 53, 56.

[5] *Ibid.* Earlier in the manuscript, f. 358v., Scott describes the 'Bosphore, or strange narrownesse of the Amazones' where its waters 'reduce themselves by a swich violence, to the necessety of passing in one only channell, so streight that it is not three Quarters of an English Mile in Breadth but of an unspeakable Depth'. The straight lay, according to his calculation, forty leagues upstream from the

these people were English, that (f. 370v) then Inhabited in Vlusing, and at Ramakins, towns then in the hands of the English.[1] they were one hundred and thirtie Men and fourteen of them Carryed thier (sic) famelies to plant with them, they had Bread, Pease, Beefe, and porke, Bakon, otmeal, vinegar, and twentie Hogsheads of Brandy, a store for one whole yeare, besides thier ship, Provisions, they had a fair Corispondance with a nation of Indians thier Nieghbours, Calld Supanes,[2] The Ship haveing stayd thier four months, till thier ffort was finished, and some Huts built, without as well, as within the ffort, the Indians assisted them in Planting Tobacco and Annotta a red Dye, a Bastard scarlet;[3] Things in this Condition, the ship leaves them sayling for Zeeland but returns the yeare following, with recruites of all things necessary, but Bread and meal was not at all now wanting, they loaded the shipp with Tobacco, Anotta and Specklewood,[4] the loading was sould for sixtie Thowsand pounds sterling mony. These were the Two ffirst voyages of the Admiral De Ruyter, the first in the tenth, and the second in the twefth (sic) yeare of his Age A D. *1618*,[5] as I have had it from his own Mouth, as also that the Losse of that Hopeful Colony was, thier Engageing themselves in the Quarels of the Indians assisting the Supanes, against another Nation. Caled the (f. 371) percotes, who were in Aliance with the Portoguezes, this occasioned these Indians, to give them great disturbance, they accompaning the Portogueze in ther vessels to attack them soe that though they Could not make them-selves master, of thier ffort, and Plantation: (The Supanes

---

Tapajós. The Óbidos narrows are approximately 2,500 metres wide, see O'Reilly Sternberg, 1975, p. 3. Scott, ibid., locates Adriaenszoon Ita's fort thus, 'ffifftie ffour Leagues below the East Banke of this River [Coropatube], was a fort built on a peninsula, by some Holdanders in the yeare 1616 ... from which ffort sayling on the North side of the of the River six Leagues you will come to the River Ginipape. . . .'

[1] See above, p. 53.

[2] Hemming, *Red gold*, 1978, p. 580, n. 223, feels Scott may have mistaken the name of the tribe which befriended Adriaenszoon Ita's settlers, pointing out that the prevalence of villages named Sapno, Sapanapoko, Sapanow and Sipinipoia on the river bank and islands near Cabo do Norte indicate that the 'Supanes' lived in that area.

[3] See above, p. 136, n. 3.

[4] Speckled or Letterwood (*Brosium Aublettii*), distinguishable by its black markings resembling hieroglyphics.

[5] Michiel Adriaenszoon de Ruyter, possibly the younger brother of Pieter Adriaenszoon Ita.

thier neighbour, in great Bodies assisting them) yet several of the English, and Dutch, being kild, and wounded; two ships comeing in the year *1623*. they all Imbarked with what they had, Back for Zeeland;[1] bringing with them very Considerable Riches, having by Trade with the Indians, acquierd great store of Amber Greace, and other Things of value, besides thier Tobacco which was also at a high price at Least twentie shillings per pound and thier Anotta at twelve shillings per pound. Thus Ended this hopeful Colonie, who parted with thier Nieghbours the Supanes Indians, with great troble; havein six years togeather. Lived in perfect friendship; and had al along from thier first Landing injoyed thier health. This ship is no sooner arivd at Vlushing, but nine of the English, with thier Effects, take shipping for London, where by thier Report, & the Demonstration they brought with them of the grouth trade and produce of the Country of the Amazones, and how few they had buryed in six years, put divers people upon the wing from London: – and in her ninetie six men, and fortie women, and Children but they were never heard of, so that its supposed, they founderd in the sea.[2]

13. A REPORT ON THE RIVER AMAZON BY MANOEL DE SOUSA D'EÇA, 1615[3]

A log-book of the river of the Amazons given by Manuel de Sosa Dessa to the Lord Vice-Roy[4]

Whoever wishes to go for the river of the Amazons will make for land at two degrees north bearing, the which land is totally flat with high, dense, impenetrable forest and uniformly tall trees. There is no sandy beach, everything is black silt. Next, from this altitude he will

---

[1] See above, pp. 78–9 and below, pp. 245, 251–3, 257, 259.

[2] See below, pp. 268, 271–2.

[3] Translation. 'Derrota del Rio de las Amazonas, dada por el Capitan Manuel de Sosa Dessa al Senor Virrey', A.G.I., Patronato Real, leg. 272, ramo 5, printed in A[nnaes da] B[ibliotheca] N[acional do] R[io de] J[aneiro], XXVI (1904), pp. 277–9.

[4] Manoel de Sousa d'Eça served as captain in the expedition led by Jerónimo de Albuquerque against the French colony in the Maranhão, October 1614. When the opposed forces reached a stalemate Sousa d'Eça was sent to carry notice of the one year truce to Portugal. Travelling via Puerto Rico he reported first to the viceroy, the archbishop primate of Lisbon, and then to Madrid. See above, p. 56 and below, pp. 174–5. For the career of Manoel de Sousa d'Eça see F. A. de Varnhagen, *História geral do Brasil* (Rio de Janeiro, 1926–36), II, 208–10.

head inland southwards in sight of land, holding off three leagues for safety on account of the shoals, and will go by a channel of seven and eight fathoms. At one degree, still to the north, he will sight the point of the first island,[1] which will be nine leagues long and three wide, and if he should find bottom of two or three fathoms at two degrees from the line let him not be afraid and head towards the east, and presently he will fall into the channel. Sighting the island he may head for the west [side] which is very high, and he will anchor at the cape of the said island where he will see an opening which is greater than the other side, and let him be warned that he can only enter it at flood tide and be advised that the waters flow to the west and he should carry good anchor cables, otherwise he will not be able to resist the current which is excessively violent. He will anchor until he may go with the tide. This river is very little less than fifty leagues wide at the mouth and can only be navigated with the tides. The territory is excellent for sugar cultivation, low lying varzeas of *massapé*,[2] without any hills, covered with many large groves of trees. There is great abundance of all kinds of game and great quantities of fish of all types in the river.

The foreigners who go there load tobacco, grain or wheat, good timber and much earth in casks.[3] The company of a stolen caravel loaded with sugar which the English carried off at the said river, gave me this information, whose master is named Antonio Rodriguez Borges, citizen of Buarcos,[4] Manuel Fernandes a Biscayan, his brother-in-law, Matheo Duarte, all residents of Buarque, and Domingo de Mendoza, a passenger, who all came in my company from the Indies and at present are in this city of Lisboa.[5] It will be very important to block this port to the foreigners, for the good of the whole coast of Brazil to the south which extends to this same river, as well as for all the ports of the Castilian Indies straight up the coast to the north, which are very close to it, because if the said foreigners make themselves very strong they will be able, being in the middle, to inflict great damage on both coasts.

[1] Sousa d'Eça is clearly describing the route used by the Dutch and English into the north channel, making for Cabo do Norte at 1°40′ N. and bearing south for the Island of Bailique whose northernmost point lies 1°5′ N.
[2] Black, fertile clayey soil found in north-eastern Brazil, especially suitable for growing sugar.
[3] See above, p. 42.
[4] This may be a mistranscription of Luarca on the Bay of Biscay.
[5] See below, pp. 174–5. The English appear to have disembarked the company of the prize at Puerto Rico.

And also because this river extends to Piru [Peru] and is believed to be totally navigable, which may be a matter of three hundred and some leagues according to those who have already navigated it, the enemy will be able to go on conquering and settling it and reach Piru and harm us all, which may be prevented in these early stages at very little cost and there will be no lack of someone to serve your Majesty in the conquest, he being provided with what is needful.

And also the silver which comes from Piru will be able to be brought out by this river at much less cost than is done at present, because the river is totally navigable. And also, if this place is not occupied the French, who have withdrawn from the Marañón,[1] of necessity will retire to it having no other place from there to the Indies, and thus the conquest of the Marañón will be of no effect because there are only fifty leagues between one place and the other directly up the coast.

Captain Manuel de Sousa Dessa.

Translated from Portuguese into Castilian by me Thomas Gracian Dantisco, holder of the office from the Secretary Diego Gracian my father, and by order and particular decree of the king our Lord, translator of his writings, Councils and Tribunals. In Madrid on the sixth day of the month of July of the year 1615.

14. SUMMARY BY THE MARQUES DE MONTESCLAROS OF
THE HISTORY OF THE PORTUGUESE CONQUEST OF
MARANHÃO AND PARÁ 1613–16,
PRESENTED TO THE *CONSEJO DE ESTADO*, SEPTEMBER 1621[2]

It is understood from some of the ministers of the *Consejo de Portugal* and from Gaspar de Sossa [Sosa] that in the year 1613, Gaspar de Sossa being governor of the state of Brazil, information was received by report of friendly Indians yonder that to the north on certain islands within the mouth of the river Marañón [Maranhão] there were white men who had forts and a settlement, and it appearing to Gaspar de Sossa that it was proper to bring to light the truth of this matter, he sent a ship to reconnoitre and he learned that the settlement [belonged to] Frenchmen who had four

---

[1] Sousa d'Eça is anticipating the surrender of the French in the Maranhão. The relief expedition of Alexandre de Moura did not leave Recife for the Maranhão until October 1615. The French surrendered on 4th November 1615.

[2] Translation. A.G.S., Estado 2515, no. 69. See above, p. 56, n. 3.

forts with artillery and some ships and great traffick with the Indians. Gaspar de Sossa wrote of this to the *Consejo de Portugal* at this court, from which orders were sent to him to gather an armada and send it under an experienced captain to the Marañón to dislodge the French.

Gaspar de Sossa sent Geronimo de Albuquerque on this action with eight ships and three hundred Portuguese in them and a large number of Indian allies.

Geronimo de Albuquerque arrived at the Marañón in October 1614.[1] He disembarked on the mainland in sight of the forts of the Frenchmen, who with Mos de la Rabardière [Monsieur de la Ravardière] their captain and a large number of Indians opposed them. On giving battle the French were routed with the death and loss of some of their number, the rest retreated to a thicket from whence they sought a truce.[2] They agreed that two Portuguese and two Frenchmen should go to Spain and to France to give notice to their sovereigns of what had occurred and, according to what instructions they should be given, the one or the other of them would quit the territory, and for this period they made truces, the Portuguese remaining on the mainland and the French on the islands where they had their forts.

This intelligence reached Spain in 1615. It appearing to the *Consejo de Portugal* that there was no question which of the two nations ought to remain, it was necessary to throw the French out of the Marañón. They ordered Gaspar de Sossa to prepare immediately in Brazil an armada greater than the first and to go with it in person to the Marañón or send a very reliable captain, to try by peaceful and friendly means to persuade the French that they should leave the post, but if it should not suffice to make war on them until they threw them out of those parts. Gaspar de Sossa gathered the second armada and named Alexandro de Mora [Alexandre de Moura] for its captain. He arrived at the Marañón in November 1615 and finding the French distressed and short of supplies from France he besieged them and obliged them to

---

[1] 26th October 1614 (N.S.).

[2] The French were protected by their forts and had control of the sea approaches. They suffered considerable losses when they unwisely left their forts and crossed the bay to attack Albuquerque's forces at Guaxenduba, but still had the strategic advantage over the Portuguese hence the decision to make a truce.

surrender themselves without attempting other means, contenting himself that they should be given passage and embarcation to France, as was done without any other compensation. The Portuguese remained with the four forts and the artillery and munitions and supplies which were in them and dismantling two forts they remained with the other two.

In order that this conquest might go forward it seemed fit to the *Consejo de Portugal* to separate it from the government of Brazil and thus your Majesty named Dom Diogo de Carcamo as governor of the Marañón, who because of his ill-health and great age did not go there and of late Vicente de Breto de Menesses is nominated.[1] Through conversation with the French and their Indian allies in the Marañón it was learned that they were intending to return and occuppy the mouth of the other river which is one hundred and fifty leagues further north called the Gran Pará by the natives, which is the Amazon. A captain with men and armaments was sent from the Marañón to make a fort in the mouth of the said river, as was done, and it has endured since the year 1616,[2] and although Frenchmen were not discovered there, the said Captain was informed that on the other side of the river there were foreigners with two forts and established traffick with the Indians, and according to the aforementioned report from England it appears that these have to be the English which Captain North carried out and the Dutch said to have settled thirty leagues further upriver.[3]

[1] The decision to create a distinct state of Maranhão and Grão Pará was made in or about October 1619, when Dom Diego de Carcamo was nominated governor-general. The state did not officially come into being until 13th June 1621. The move to separate the northern reaches of the coastline from the jurisdiction of Bahia was prompted by the fact that it was easier for advice and supply vessels to travel back and forwards between the new settlements and Lisbon than to sail down the coast of Brazil. Neither Carcamo nor Menesses took up the office. Francisco Coelho de Carvalho was appointed in September 1623, Kiemen, 1973, 25–7.

[2] See above, p. 167, and below, pp. 170–4.

[3] Montesclaros is confusing information about the two Dutch forts, picked up in 1616, with more current information on the settlements of the English and Dutch. An earlier section of his report summarizes the content of Purcell's account forwarded by Gondomar 20th June 1621.

15. ANDRES PEREIRA, 1616

Account of what there is in the great and famous river of the Amazons, newly discovered.[1]

In the first place after the *capitão-mor* Alexandro de Mora [Alexandre de Moura] completed in the Maranhão the matters which pertained [*to the service of the King in casting out the enemy which he did*],[2] the land being quiet and the forts manned as seemed necessary, he set about to have made this new discovery of the great and famous river of the Amazons [*and also to find out what there was in Cabo do Norte*],[3] according to the instructions which he carried from the governor-general of Brazil Gaspar de Souza. Thus he sent 150 men in three companies in three boats with Francisco Caldeira de Castelbranco as *capitão-mor*.[4] We departed on this [*journey*][5] last Christmas day on which began this year 1616, running always along the coast, dropping anchor every night, the pilot António Vizente Cochado taking sightings of the shore and constant soundings, making logbooks of which he will give a good account being the one sent by the said *capitão-mor* Alexandro de mora as *piloto-mor* of this discovery, and he is at this court.[6]

Arriving at this great river, [*having gone some 150 leagues up the coast*],[7] which is 120 leagues wide, [*carrying fresh water 60 leagues out to*

---

[1] Translation. The Portuguese version of this document 'Relação do que ha no grande rio das Amazonas novamente descuberto', printed in *Annaes da Biblioteca e Archivo Público do Pará*, I (Pará, 1902), 5–8, has been compared with a manuscript copy of the contemporary Spanish translation in the B[iblioteca] N[acional], Madrid (B.N. Madrid, MS 20271[12]) which reads differently in some sections. The edges of the Spanish manuscript are damaged creating incomplete sentences. My translation combines the two versions with the differences indicated by italics and footnoted accordingly. For the career of Andres Pereira Themudo, the author, see Barata, *A jornada*, 1916, pp. 213–20.

[2] See above, p. 56, n. 3. B.N. Madrid, MS 20271[12] reads 'the matters which pertained to that conquest, which he did by order of your Majesty'.

[3] Omitted in B.N. Madrid, MS 20271[12].

[4] The instructions given to Francisco Caldeira de Castelbranco, 22nd December 1615, are printed in *ABNRJ*, XXVI (1904), pp. 239–42. On the career of Castelbranco, see Barata, *A jornada*, 1916; Kiemen, 1973, pp. 17–21; 'Memória dos capitães', B.A., 54/XI/27, no. 17, f. 3.

[5] 'New conquest' in B.N. Madrid, MS 20271[12].

[6] See below, pp. 248–54.

[7] Omitted in B.N. Madrid, MS 20271[12]. Pereira is probably reckoning as far as the easternmost cape of the Amazon here. The distance between the bay of Maranhão and the estuary of the Pará is approximately 400 miles.

sea. At that time]¹ it had a very violent current, it being winter.² The armada entered through a narrow arm near the east cape named Sapanara [Saparara] and not trusting ourselves to the greater expanse of the river we kept always amongst the islands, travelling upriver and speaking with the Indians of those parts, who easily and with good will accepted our friendship saying that we were truly valiant men for what we had done to the French and the greater part of the nations on that coast which were our enemies.

[*Throughout those parts the banks showed themselves to be richly wooded and the islands in their abundance filled with much game.*]³ We reached the site where we made the fort for the king our master, which is 35 leagues upriver to the south [*on a point of the mainland on the east bank*],⁴ it seeming to the *capitão-mor* to be a good site. As he was working on it he learned from a Frenchman who had fled there from [*those*]⁵ in the Maranhão that there was a Fleming in some Indian villages further up river, whom others had left there to learn the language and draw the Indians into trade and also that he was awaiting one of his brothers in order to settle in that part where our fort now is, [*from whence three Flemish ships had departed a few days since*],⁶ as the said Fleming confessed subsequently.

The *capitão-mor* Francisco Caldeira sent for this Fleming from whom we got a true account of the Dutch and Flemish enemies in Cabo do Norte about whom we [*already*]⁷ had a good deal of news. There were some 250 to 300 men split between two wooden forts and they had two sugar mills and loaded ships with sugar and other things which the land offers.⁸ Furthermore we learned from some Indians who came from very far upriver to see us Portuguese and to

¹ Omitted in B.N. Madrid, MS 20271¹².
² The rains on the lower Amazon are at their heaviest between December and June.
³ B.N. Madrid, MS 20271¹² reads 'Through all those islands on the one side and the other the lands appear extremely fertile with abundance of woods, full of much game of diverse types, and great quantity of Brazil wood.'
⁴ Omitted in Portuguese version.
⁵ 'the Frenchmen', B.N. Madrid, MS 20271¹².
⁶ The bottom of the folio of B.N. Madrid, MS 20271¹² is torn off. It is possible that this phrase was written on the missing portion.
⁷ Omitted in the Portuguese version.
⁸ Probably a reference to the two forts on the Xingu. See above, pp. 52–3, 158–9, 169. Hemming, *Red gold*, 1978, p. 580, hazards that Materou may have been on the site of present Porto de Moz, and Gormoaru at Veiros. Like Dudley, however, he reverses the order of the forts placing Orange upstream from Nassau, see above, p. 52, n. 5.

become our allies that at the foot of some mountains 150 leagues from our fort were 15 vessels and many people, women amongst them, making a fort which it appears was already effected.[1] The Indians said that these mountains are barren of trees and some of the more experienced men say that these are the mountains of Peru shown on many charts and that there is gold and other metals in them.

The *capitão-mor* was wishful to advise your Majesty that he got two pearls [*the which a French captain who was there says were*][2] given to him by an Indian who said he had found them while eating oysters, and that there are quantities of the same some 70 leagues upriver on the bottom of a creek. These two pearls came to the hands of the lord marques d'Alemquer. They are somewhat spoiled, having been roasted[3] in the aforementioned manner and the shell of the oysters in which they grow is very fine mother of pearl.

Two [*pearls of great value*][4] were also found in this river before we arrived in it, the which, [*a French captain who was there as interpreter told us were stolen by an Englishman from the Frenchman who had them and there is a lawsuit in England over them and they are valued at a great many cruzados*].[5] Cabo do Norte is the other promontory of the river on the West side, it is 3 degrees north of the equator.[6] [*The river appears suitable for a great many things being of the aforementioned breadth, the banks very fertile with a great variety of timber like that of Brazil and better since the trees are remarkably tall, amongst which is a brazilwood [pau] which the Indians call cotiara[7] which is very beautifully formed and graceful to look at. There are in this river, in all parts of it, extremely great numbers of Indians, of different nations, the greater part of them very good-looking without beards. The men wear their hair long like*

[1] See above, pp. 53, 56.

[2] Omitted from B.N. Madrid, MS 20271[12].

[3] The oyster shells had been roasted in the fire to open them.

[4] B.N. Madrid, MS 20271[12]. The Portuguese version reads 'two stones of great size'.

[5] B.N. Madrid, MS 20271[12] reads 'which a Frenchman had, and an Englishman stole them from him, about which there is now a lawsuit in England and they are valued at many thousand cruzados. This is learned from a French captain who served as interpreter there and he is called Monsieur de Vaos'. The interpreter was Ravardière's lieutenant, le Sieur de Vaux, who had first gone out to the Maranhão with Riffault in 1594. See above, p. 16, and Abbeville, *Histoire de la mission des Pères Capucins*, 1963, pp. i–xv.

[6] Pereira's estimate is 1°20' out.

[7] Estácio de Sylveira called it 'cotiara' or 'painted wood', the present Brazilian name for *angelim-coco*, possibly the tree which Sylveira referred to.

women and, from very close, resemble them],[1] whence perhaps was born the tale about the Amazons because there is no other reason to support this belief. The great part of the Indians are like those of Brazil somewhat differing in language. The goods which these people sell to the Dutch[2] are cotton, oroco [urucu], which is a dye like a berry,[3] some kind of pita,[4] and this cotiara tree, [*together with other kinds of wood which are not lacking*],[5] tobacco. They say there are beavers, and [*this French captain who served us as interpreter*][6] said that the Indians had given him a very fine skin of one.[7]

As to the entrances and exits of this river, its depth and all the rest necessary for a fleet to enter and depart from it, the pilot António Vizente has made his rutters in due form, of which he will give account it being his craft.

[*The capitão-mor Francisco Caldeira de Castello branco needing to send this advise to your Majesty, after we had made the fort in which he remains with the said troops, despatched us, Andres Pereira and Antonio da Fonseca, each being a captain of the infantry of his company in that garrison, it appearing to him he would certify it thus. Because in the course of the voyage there were quarrels between them, Antonio da Fonseca remained behind in the island of Terceira, not wishing to complete their journey, in compliance with which they came in a ship which they had embarked in at Santo Domingo, it being very safe. He quit it to remain [behind] with some papers which he had in his possession, it being required that he should embark himself because it was important that the King be advised, and not wishing to give the papers to the said Andres Pereyra, who came himself in the said ship*</i>

---

[1] The passage in B.N. Madrid, MS 20271[12] reads, 'All this river from one side to the other is full of islands inhabited by Indians, the greater part of them (the islands) very [ ] of game, fruits, excellent woods, the foodstuffs which the Indians use, which is manioc flour, corn and other things. There are countless Indians of different tribes. Those called Tapuyas who are very far up in the interior of the river, wear their hair long, and are not bearded and cover their genitals, they are handsome men and to look at their face appear like women. . . .'

[2] 'Flemings' in B.N. Madrid, MS 20271[12].

[3] See above, p. 136, n. 3.

[4] See above, p. 148, n. 1.

[5] B.N. Madrid, MS 20271[12] reads, 'cotiara which is a consummate wood in the form which nature gives it, tobacco'.

[6] B.N. Madrid, MS 20271[12], 'the captain monsieur de Vaos says'.

[7] It is hard to know what De Vaux was referring to here. He could have meant the river otter (*Lutra*) found in the Amazon. The giant river otter, 'Ariranha' (*Pteroneura brasiliensis*) can reach 6½ feet in length and its skin is believed by some to be impervious to water and therefore valuable for clothing, Gilmore, 'Fauna and ethnozoology', *HSAI*, 1963, VI, 365.

bringing with him the pilot necessary for entering this river, and this sample [the pearls] *which he delivered to the lord marques d'Alemquer, viceroy of Portugal, by which means it was sent to him from the capitão-mor Francisco Caldeira.*

This is the truth and what there is in this famous river without having the papers which remained in the hands of the other captain anything worth more consideration, but for a petition for supply for those people and let your Majesty provide in this whatever may be to your service.][1]

Captain Andre Pereyra.

16. MANOEL DE SOUSA D'EÇA

Concerning the affairs of Grão Pará [1618/19][2]

Your Majesty is sending me to Grão Pará for three years to serve as Captain and whatever else your Majesty may think fit.[3] In order that, in that time, I may work to understand everything about this river and leave nothing to be discovered it is meet that your Majesty should take order to grant that which I state below.

What ought to be achieved first is the discovery of the river Corupá [Gurupá] where there are a great many Indians and, so they say, white men, but no Portuguese up to now; and the discovery of the Cabo do Norte, which is not very far from the river Corupá,[4] where English and Dutchmen go every year to trade for tobacco and some dyes such as Orocu and Cariuru[5] and some woods. There can be no doubt about this. I have already given some reports in writing to your Majesty by the viceroy, the archbishop primate, I having come here with the first report of the events of

---

[1] Omitted from B.N. Madrid, MS 20271[12].

[2] Translation. B.L., Add. MS 20,846, ff. 43–4, printed in *ABNRJ*, XXVI (1904), pp. 345 *et seqq.*

[3] The document is undated but must have been written in either 1618 or 1619. According to Friar António da Merciana (see below, p. 185), Sousa d'Eça sailed for Portugal 23rd October 1617. Sousa d'Eça's useage of the title Grão Pará may indicate that he was writing in mid to late 1619, about the time the decision to create the state of Maranhão and Grão Pará was taken.

[4] Sousa d'Eça doubtless means the present Canal do Gurupá, which provided the fastest route from Belém to the Dutch settlements on the Xingu. The forts established by Adriaenszoon Ita and King lay even farther up the mainstream. His information about the whereabouts of the foreign settlements seems still very inexact.

[5] Presumably Carayuru, a pigment from the leaves of *Bignonia chica*.

the Maranhão by way of the Indies where there was a Portuguese caravel which the English had stolen coming from Brazil, and had taken it within the Cabo do Norte of the river Amazon, about which the Indians also give us news. From there it [the caravel] was taken to Porto Riquo [Puerto Rico] where I had arrived, and from them I had this for certain, and how they had found a Dutch ship within the same river, but they had no proper fort, only some factories with men in them to make them a cargo for when they return which is every year. These people neighbour us and it is not good and is the reason why the Indians of that district do not wish to come to trade with us at our fort, because as well as the bad things which they [the English and Dutch] tell them about us (and it may be with good cause), they give them what they want more freely and treat them better and with greater honesty,[1] which is what they desire, even though they neither trust nor understand what good faith is. And secondly, according to what I learned from the French, the latter [these foreigners] extend their trade to the Indians of the river Corupá and must be the Whitemen said to be there. It is necessary to put a stop to this before they increase and I undertake to do it, your Majesty having taken effective order to grant what I request below.

To effect this undertaking I need two or three decked boats [like those Moorish ones][2] and should it be necessary for me to go in one of them to Pará I will do it. These boats are useful for running along all those islands and coastline and to make all the necessary discoveries, which cannot be done properly with canoes because there are many very large bays. It happens many times that when canoes are in the middle of them the winds start to blow and the sea to rise and the canoes and men are lost and the design is abandoned. The boats are better for going to treat for peace with the Indians for, although they may be many of them and they may want to betray us, they will never be able to harm the boats with their canoes. The weapons, ammunition and provisions travel dry in the boats, which cannot be done with canoes.

Here at this court is a cleric by name of Domingos Roiz, who will

---

[1] For the whole question of Portuguese Indian policy in the Amazon region, see Kiemen, 1973, *passim.*; Hemming, *Red gold*, 1978, chs. 9–11.

[2] The phrase reads *'como d'estes de alfama'. Alfama* means a congregation of Moors, or Moorish.

do there and for your Majesty great service in those parts of Pará because, besides being a preacher and very well lettered, he knows the language of those Indians perfectly and is greatly accepted by them. It is he, a religious of the Society of Jesus, who, I being present, made peace with the Aimoré[1] in the captaincy of Ilheos [Ilheus], Porto Seguro and Spirito Santo who made war upon us for sixty years, and with the Guaitacazes[2] neighbouring Rio de Janeiro, Indians whom nobody could subdue up to that point. And since what most needs to be procured for the increase of our holy Faith and of the royal Treasury and the good of the region is universal peace with all the Indians and their conversion which is the principal objective of your Majesty, it is fit to send him in my company.

Belchior Rangel is also here, a good soldier who has served your Majesty in Rio de Janeiro, and Maranhão, being amongst the first to go there in some armadas from this kingdom, and in the caravels in which I travelled with despatches last year, by command of the lord marquis, viceroy,[3] and besides being an experienced soldier he is perfect in the language of the Indians, a very necessary qualification for those whom we employ to assist in the service of your Majesty thereabouts. The position of *sargento-mor* is vacant because the person whom your Majesty had provided comes prisoner by way of the Indies for the affair of Francisco Caldeira.[4] Your Majesty, being so pleased, could appoint the said Belchior Rangel who will be very effective in those parts, during the detention of the other.

For the expulsion of the enemy from Cabo do Norte and further discoveries, one hundred and fifty soldiers are necessary.

[1] Hemming, *Red gold*, 1978, pp. 93–96, 100–1, states that Aimoré, a Tupi word meaning 'evil person', 'thief', or 'killer' was the Portuguese name for the Gê-speaking Tapuia of the hinterland of the captaincies of Ilheus and Porto Seguro. They terrorized that coastline for the second half of the sixteenth century making secure settlement impossible.

[2] Not identified.

[3] The count of Salinas, marquis de Alenquer, appointed viceroy in 1617.

[4] The meaning of this sentence is ambiguous and could again be a clue to the date of the letter. 'Caso' can mean *affair, case, matter* or *instance*. The sentence could mean that the former *sargento-mor*, sergeant-major was being sent back prisoner at the *instance* of Caldeira de Castelbranco, or in the *case* of Caldeira de Castelbranco. The first reading would suggest that Sousa d'Eça assumed the latter still to be governor of Belém. The second reading might suggest that the arrest had followed upon his deposition in 1618 (see below, p. 187). Caldeira de Castelbranco was sent back to Portugal in fetters in 1619. The second reading would put Sousa d'Eça's letter in 1619.

Two hundred Biscayan arquebuses[1] those of *Flanders* burst like glass.

Two dozen flint[lock] shotguns which serve in all weather, whether it may rain or not, for whatever assault or night ambush, in which the Indians are already so skilled, that it is said they prefer to fight us by night than by day, because at night we do not see them and they, seeing our matches alight shoot at them and kill us, and it is well said, for there are few soldiers who know how to cover their match well when it is necessary.[2]

Cases of arquebus and shotgun ball.

Powder, match and lead, as much as possible, which is the staple of every day.

A well-stocked pharmacy.

A surgeon.

A blacksmith, a locksmith, a caulker, an officer of the river-works, two sawyers and a weaver.

Pay for the soldiers and trade goods and linen.

Five hundred fathoms of fishing net.

All the aforesaid things are given to the soldiers in pay, and thus your Majesty will lose nothing but rather gain a hundred percent in everything.

A caravel to carry breeding stock from Cabó Verde for the increase of the territory.

A constable and two gunners and two pieces upwards of eighteen pounds, the others there are cast iron, or three to four pounds. The constable who was there is dead.

Some chambers for the Falcons[3] which are there which are without them.

A thousand cruzados seperately disbursed in trade goods and some clothing for gifts, which is the most effective way to make

[1] Or Harequebus, the early type of portable gun varying in size from a small cannon to a musket, supported on a tripod, trestle or forked 'rest' for use in the field.

[2] Flint-lock guns were fired by a flint, screwed to the cock, which when struck against the hammer produced sparks and ignited the priming in the pan. Matchlocks operated by means of a slow match, cord or wick which had to be kept alight and used to ignite the powder.

[3] A cannon of culverin type, using 2½ to 3 lb. shot, with a bore of about 2¾ inches. The chamber is the part of the gun in which the charge is placed, in this case a separate mug-shaped container; H. L. Blackmore, *The armouries in the Tower of London* (London, 1976), I, 223, 229.

universal peace and subdue this residue of the Tupinambas,[1] which is very important because in addition to being very able Indians, not to pacify them will be sufficient to unsettle the other Indians turning them away from friendship with us with evil results, and the conquest will always be disturbed in this respect, they being an example in themselves of how badly the Portuguese treat those who were the first to receive them in their territories and serve them in both peace and war.

This is what is necessary for your Majesty's service. . . .

Manoel de Sousa deca. n.d.

17. SIMÃO ESTÁCIO DA SYLVEIRA: PLANS FOR THE EXPEDITION TO PARÁ. 21ST SEPTEMBER 1618[1]

Firstly we must carry to the north the exaltation and propagation of our holy Catholic Faith and the conversion of the Indians settled in the region in the spirit of charity and disinterest, because this is the title and escutcheon of the foundation and institution of this realm in the words that our lord Jesus Christ said to the King Dom Alfonso Henrique on the fields of Ourique when he invested him with this crown, the title and mandate to carry his holy name to foreign peoples, saying that he had prepared and chosen the king's vassals for his labourers in remote lands, and other words which mean the same thing.[3] Thus God creating this Portuguese nation on the shores of the ocean from such small beginnings, expanding and

[1] The Tupi-speaking Tupinamba were in the process of migrating out of the Paraguay basin to settle on the central Brazilian coastline when the Portuguese arrived at the beginning of the sixteenth century. The Portuguese drove them steadily northward. One group moved into the Maranhão region after the Portuguese conquest of Pernambuco in the mid-sixteenth century. They had welcomed the arrival of the French as a protection against the Portuguese, Hemming, *Red gold*, 1978, pp. 24, 51–68, 85, 198–216.

[2] Translation. 'Intentos da jornada do Pará' printed in *ABNRJ*, XXVI (1904), 361–6. For the career of Simão Estácio da Sylveira, see D. Damasceno, 'Simão Estácio, capitão de navio, procurador das coisas do Maranhão', pp. 97–102. Estácio da Sylveira presented this document as part of his preparations to go out to the Maranhão and Grão Pará with Jorge de Lemos de Betancor of the Azores, who planned to settle Azorean families there. Estácio da Sylveira sailed as commander in the flagship of the fleet which brought 400 Azoreans to São Luis in April 1619. See above, p. 56, n. 3.

[3] The battle of Ouric or Ourique, 25th July 1139, in which, Prince Afonso Henriques defeated the Moorish governor of Santárem and assumed the title of King of Portugal.

favouring them until they expelled from this land and all of Spain the perfidious Mahometans, and then they passed on to Africa where they took from them many cities, and later they departed to pursue the enterprise, conquest, navigation and commerce of Ethiopia, Arabia, Persia, India and Brazil so that they were settled.

This can well be seen in the discovery of the East that has so flourished by this design. The most serene Prince Dom Henrique sent the first Portuguese there, who arrived at Cabo Verde in the year 1420, after whom João Goncalves and Tristão Vas reached India,[1] at the which discoveries the most excellent Pontiffs added, with their apostolic blessing, all the previous discoveries of the Canaries, until, in the time of King Dom João II, Christóvão Colon discovered the land of the new world, found before by the great Americo Vespusio.[2] The Spanish Pope, Alexandre determined the dispute over this between Portugal and Castile with the line which runs from Pole to Pole four hundred and seventy leagues to the west of the islands of Cabo Verde that demarcates by the meridian between Brazil and the Indies. The which stretches from the Rio da Prata [River Plate] to this new river and the new discovery of Pará, accordingly the which demarcation, favouring us, extends from some territory of the Cabo do Norte, all the mouth of the river, which is one hundred and twenty leagues, and its islands to six and two thirds degrees South. From there cutting directly north–south through the sertão the line exits by the mouth of the Rio da Prata with all its estuary and some small territory of Cabo Branco.[3]

And with this demarcation the province of Brazil, belonging to

[1] Dinis Dias reached Cape Verde in 1441. Tristão Vaz Teixeira reached Madeira in 1419.

[2] Amerigo Vespucci.

[3] The northern boundary between Brazil and the Spanish Indies as created by the meridian drawn through the Atlantic 370 leagues West of the Cape Verde islands in the Treaty of Tordesillas, 1494, remained a matter of dispute between the two crowns throughout the sixteenth century. The issue was not made any easier by the frequent confusion of the Maranhão and the Amazon. It was resolved by default after the establishment of Belém in 1616, when the Spanish crown allowed its Portuguese subjects to infiltrate the lower Amazon, although it was not yet willing to cede Cabo do Norte officially to the Portuguese. The *Consejo de Indias* still claimed the Maranhão as the proper location of the northern limit of Brazil in 1621. The mouth of the Amazon and the coastline between Cabo do Norte and the Rio de Vicente Pinzón passed to Portugal in 1637 with the creation of the captaincy of Cabo do Norte. See Lorimer, 'English trade and exploration', 1973, ch. 1.

the crown of Portugal, was divided from the West Indies, belonging to the crown of Castile.

This river Pará which we call the river Amazon has two sources one the rio de Orelhana from whence it took its name, this Francisco de Orelhana being the first to disembogue into the North Sea, and it begins in Quito in the mountains of the New Kingdom of Granada behind the city of Santa Fée and runs for more than ninety leagues with many great windings to the east. The other which is called Maranhão, named after the Spanish captain who discovered its source, which is a little to the north of Mount Potosí, and it is born in the mountains of Peru in the province of Cusco [Cuzco] and running more than seven hundred leagues to the northeast with fewer meanders it joins the Orelhana more than four hundred leagues before entering the sea. Both form a new archipelago between Brasil and Cumaná; whose islands belong to the crown of Portugal.[1]

The land on the margins of this river is a valley of more than three hundred leagues in breadth of very great abundance, and fertility, treed, with many rivers and settlements up to the territory called Coca, where it is mountainous, and then follows Cumaco, which the Spaniards call the land of cinnamon because of certain aromatic trees there as well as large Laurels that give good clusters of fruit like seed pods. It is the best cinnamon. The country is rough but abundant and rich. Goncalo Picarro [Pizarro] discovered it with two hundred Spaniards when, with Orelhana, he followed the river downstream. He found a cataract that he estimated to be more than two hundred *stadia*[2] high, whose fall made so much noise that it could be heard more than six leagues away, and exploring the river he saw it enter a region where it all runs together into a very narrow cleft, permeating and running with great furor and roaring and in some places it is covered over.[3]

---

[1] Estácio da Sylveira's claims are as excessive as they are muddled here. It is not clear how he derived the existence of the archipelago. He appears to be confusing the Orellana with the Orinoco and, at the same time, trying to describe the Orellana and Maranhão as separate coastal effluents of a single mainstream. Ralegh and Thevet had believed this to be the case, see above, p. 15. If this was Estácio da Sylveira's intention he failed to make it clear. His account turns the old view upon its head, giving the river two distinct sources in the interior instead of two discrete branches entering the Atlantic.

[2] A *stadium* is a measure of length approximately 220 metres.

[3] Estácio da Sylveira's account here seems to have been taken from Garcilaso de la Vega's *Commentarios reales de los Incas*, pt. II, bk. 3, published in 1617. For the translation of the relevant extracts, see C. R. Markham, ed., *Expeditions into the valley of the Amazons, 1539, 1540, 1639* (London, 1859), pp. 6–9.

The mouth of the river is 1° South of the Equator.[1] On the coast there are two summers and two winters each year and two springs that nearly run into one another, and everything that our people sowed grew with great abundance.[2] There are many and very good melons, cucumbers,[3] vegetables, broad beans and green beans[4] are very plentiful and good which grow all year round, and some manioc in the district of the city of Belém. It is hoped that the land will produce wheat, wine, rice and, all the more because of its fecundity, great sugar plantations, and great breeding of livestock, especially on the islands and flats, from the sheep of Peru, where they are used for cartage and carry a man four to six leagues easily.[5]

Its navigation is the easiest in all Brazil, the channel excellent and capacious as well as the many others through which the river spills into the sea. Its mouth has sweet water for more than forty leagues into the ocean.

According to what our people have discovered about the fertility, abundance and salubriousness of the land, it seems it upholds the reputation which the Amazon has in contradiction to the erroneous opinions of the ancients who called it the sole land of the Sun and held it to be an uninhabitable zone.[6] Inasmuch as there were no Amazons at all and the territory is very close to the equinoctial, it is very temperate, fresh and healthy as our people have seen, being two hundred men, newly arrived, passing many months in the sun and open air, eating the fruits and drinking the waters without anyone falling sick, and the fevers disappear by bathing in the waters. The earth promises great riches, and because it has a hot,

---

[1] Incorrect, if he means the Amazon here. The Pará enters the Atlantic between 0°45′ S. and 0°30′ S.

[2] See above, p. 142, n. 6. On the lower Amazon the distinctly dry season occurs between July and September. Belém receives 90–100″ annual precipitation.

[3] Cucumber (*Cucumis sativis*), native to S. Asia, is the literal translation of this word. 'Pepino' is also the common name for the *solanum muricatum*, or 'melon pear'. The best tasting varieties are said to be somewhat like a cucumber. It is, however, a plant of more temperate climates, Sauer, '*Cultivated plants*', *HSAI*, 1963, VI, 520.

[4] For the various kinds of beans native to the lower Amazon, see ibid., pp. 498–504. Estácio da Sylveira's 'broad bean' may be the jack bean (*canavalia ensiformis*) or the lima bean (*phaseolus lunatus*).

[5] Presumably he means the llama (*Lama glama glama*) here which was used as a pack, though not as a riding, animal by the Inca.

[6] For a good discussion of the perceptions of classical geographers about the nature of the torrid zone, see E. H. Warmington, *Greek geography* (London, 1934), *passim*; H. E. Tozer, *A history of ancient geography* (New York, 1971), *passim*.

oriental constellation where the sun rises above the sea, there must be much copper in it, which is already being discovered, and gold and other metals, emeralds, crystal, [*pedras de levar*] and other precious stones, saltpetre and other minerals and pearls in the river, of which we have already seen and made good beginnings.[1]

There are turtles in the river with good meat. Very good oil is made from their eggs.[2] There is a great variety of fish, some very large and all of them good, flatfish and manatees,[3] whose hide is useful. There is a great quantity and diversity of wild-pigs; some are killed when they cross the arms of the river in herds.[4] There are many hinds,[5] tapirs,[6] *pacas* like hares,[7] *gibatos* and *coatis* larger than them,[8] *aperca* like rabbits,[9] fine apes and monkeys, many ducks, hens, little chickens, wild hens, turtle doves, pigeons, *mutums* like turkeys, *jacus*, *aracuas*[10] like hens, many toucans in [flocks] like thrushes, finches and herons and many other birds and parrots for eating and beautiful feathers.

There is an infinity of fruits: pineapples, yams,[11] cashews like *macaris*, *mangobas*[12] with others to make wine and vinegar from, nuts like almonds in flavor which last when dried, palm nuts from which to make an infinite amount of oil,[13] thousands of beautiful trees of

[1] *Ibid.*

[2] The river turtle (*Podocnemis expansa*). The females lay their eggs on the sandbars of the lower Amazon during low water in November. To render them into oil the eggs were crushed, allowed to stand in the sun for some hours, and the ensuing oil was then skimmed off, Gilmore, 'Fauna and ethnozoology', *HSAI*, 1963, VI, 400–2.

[3] Soles (gen. *pleuronectiformes*). Although a marine fish they are found in the low-lying waters of the Amazon basin, Golding, *The fishes and the forest*, 1980, p. 38. The manatee (*Trichechus inunguis*) or 'peixe-boi' was significant for its flesh, hide and fat, Gilmore, 'Fauna and ethnozoology', *HSAI*, 1963, VI, p. 381.

[4] Peccaries (*Tayassu tajacu* and *T. pecari*).

[5] Deer. The small brocket deer (*Mazama*), is found in the region as is the Pampa deer (*Ozotoceros bezoarcticus*).

[6] *Tapirus americanus*.

[7] The *paca* (*Cuniculus paca*) is a highly desirable food animal because of its white meat.

[8] Presumably he means the *coati* (*Nasua rufa* or *N. narica*), a tropical carnivore related to the racoon. I cannot identify the other animal with any certainty.

[9] Possibly the *agouti* (*Dasyprocta*).

[10] Mutums (*Cracidae, Crax, Mitu*), are large, almost turkey-sized, flocking, jungle birds. *Jacus* and *aracuas* are guans (*Penelope, ortalis*) flocking grouse-like birds.

[11] Ordinary yams (*Dioscorea alata, cayenensis* and *batatas*) are native to the Old World introduced into Brazil with the African slave trade. Estácio da Sylveira probably means the sweet potato (*Ipomea batatus*) here.

[12] *Hancornia speciosa*.

[13] Oil can be extracted from several palm fruits by a crushing and boiling process.

great usefulness and infinite great timbers. There is *pao de reo, cotiara*, which is to say *pao pintado*, both are like chestnuts, *pao amarello, pao santo, pao do Brasil, angelim, paos de rosa, pao vermelho, pao preto* like [   ], and other infinite kinds of trees[1] which reach to the heavens, beneath which there is no undergrowth. From these woods yellow, vermilion and orange dye is made, and very good varnish, pitch, resin and mastic in great quantity. There is much cotton, pita, ordinary clay, oyster shell lime and another kind of green clay which is very costly, and everything which is not very close-by is found with great ease by the rivers which are all navigable.

The natives of this region are spirited, ingenious and somewhat more polished than the others in Brazil, very easy and tractable, who desire to procure our friendship and give us their children to instruct, and we should use all justice and charity to edify them and conquer their souls, because in it is counted all the virtues, and one conquers more through charity than through arms as the scripture says. The same must prevail in the judicial distribution of rewards to the well-deserving in the conquest and the partition of the land, for the benefit of which it is necessary to study the cultivation and the experience of the climate of the territory.

As to the rest of the particulars I hope with the favour of God to be of worth in the foundation of the new post, in the selection of the site, which should be: inclined to the east and the north on the bank of the river; with good anchorage in sight of the cliff; defensible; washed by the breezes, not very difficult with the service of a good climate which may be known by the valor and disposition of the natives where there are many old people; close to good water with a fall to move the mill and for other uses; situated with all the streets of good width running north, with the noble squares, workshops,

---

[1] It is impossible to judge whether Estácio da Sylveira has any definite species in mind when he lists these trees. 'Pao de reo' may be the *pau de rainha* – Pará porcupine wood (*Centrolobium Paraense*); cotiara – *angelim-coco*; pao amarello – Brazilian box or stinkwood (*Euxylophora Paraensis*); *pao santo-lignumvitae* (*Guajacum sanctum*); angelim – (*Andira sp.*); paos de rosa – possibly Ceará rosewood (*Dalbergia Caerensis*) or Jacaranda do Pará (*Dalbergia spruceana*); *pao vermelho* – possibly a *cedrela vermelha* (*C. macrocarpa*) or Brazil redwood (*Brosium paraense*) or (*Caesalpina brasiliensis*) from which a red dye is extracted; *pao preto* now refers to E. Indian rosewood (*Dalbergia latifolia*), probably a species of rosewood is meant here.

architecture and fortifications of all for the comfort, endurance and nobility of the city.[1]

The residents in which, at the very beginning, can take great advantage of the timbers, and thus discover the region. Where there are greater ones will be better both for their employment and foundation and also to send as cargo home, for the which I will provide saws or sawyers, and will instruct them in the practice of agriculture in conformity with the new climate and the nature of the atmosphere, and show them ways to form the groves of trees to open up arable lands and irrigate where it may be necessary, and to improve them with the plants and seeds needed. All will work together with more abundance and less toil. For many years I have been a teacher of agriculture helping my country by what I wrote. With the knowledge of this region, its fruits and drugs, I hope to end by inculcating into this realm all the things which there are in the round world which may be of use to it.

I will instruct them to look for mines, to recognize and open them, to forge the metals, and make saltpetre and gunpowder. And I will instruct the natives in the cultivation of everything, and of good flax and hemp, and in working iron which has already been done in the Maranhão and other parts of Brazil and new discoveries. I hope it may be easy to build ships for the service of that state and of this kingdom. . . .

I hope to cross the river in the first vessels to discover it towards the west and along the opposite bank upstream, observing the islands and sandbanks and the Indians, describing everything and revealing how it is made. Having found the passages and subdued the Indians, I hope to open by this river a great port to the riches of Peru, by which they may descend to Spain without the great travails and immense costs with which they are conveyed in the South sea from Lima to Portobello, and from thence by land to Habana and the North sea from whence it comes in the *flotas* of New Spain. This trade is already beginning from Rio da Prata, whose source some Spaniards have revealed to us. . . . Lisboa, 21 September, 1618.

[1] Presumably Estácio da Sylveira is talking about the laying out of a proper settlement or municipality of Belém, which was to be developed under the shelter of the original blockhouse, Fort of the Manger, sited on a bluff five to ten metres high. There is no mention of a second Portuguese settlement in the Amazon, before S. António do Gurupá was founded in 1623. See above, pp. 78–9, and below, p. 241.

18. EXTRACT FROM FRIAR ANTÓNIO DA MERCIANA'S ACCOUNT OF RECENT EVENTS IN PARÁ, 27TH NOVEMBER 1618[1]

Your Majesty's captains saw fit for the state of this conquest to ask me to be the one to advise of what was happening in it, and although, because of the status of my person, I have not dealt with such matters, nevertheless I must do it as follows, and it seems to me fitting for the service of God and your Majesty that you should profit by this from what time has shown me and the information that the particular captains gave to me.

The relief which Captain Andre Pereira brought to this conquest by your Majesty's grace arrived on the 27th last October and with him a ship in which the governor of Brazil sent aid from which payments were made, the Captain Andre Pereira attending to these in conformity with the provision which he brought from your Majesty. He will give account of the manner in which they were made in which he maintained very good procedures.

Last January the governor sent another ship with relief,[2] and having set out from Maranhão it could not continue its voyage, lacking cables which are very necessary between that conquest and this one in order to anchor every night, and the seas running too high it returned to Maranhão where it discharged the aid which was consumed in that conquest.

At the time which the Captain Manoel de Sossa dessa [Manoel de Sousa d'Eça] left this conquest, which was on the 23rd of October 1617,[3] it remained at war with a tribe of nheenouaibas[4] by order of the *capitão-mor* Francisco Caldeira de Castel Branco of which he was to have advised your Majesty. The issue was afterwards very hotly

---

[1] Translation. Letter from Fr António da Merciana to Philip III, 27th November 1618, A.H.U., Pará 728, Papéis Avulsos. Merciana was one of the four Franciscans who arrived in Belém 28th July 1617, the first missionaries in the captaincy.

[2] Presumably Merciana means January and October 1618, commenting on the failure of the first supply from Brazil in January after the safe arrival of the second in October. In the final, unprinted portion of the letter he mentions again that the second supply arrived shortly after the deposition of Francisco Caldeira de Castelbranco.

[3] See above, pp. 174–5.

[4] Nheengaiba. A Tupi word used by the Portuguese to refer collectively to the incomprehensible languages of the many tribes of Carib, Aruak and other stock inhabiting the Ilha de Marajó; Hemming, *Red gold*, 1978, pp. 328–9.

contested for about thirty days, they being Indians who live in stilted, raised dwellings, like two-storey houses. They are routed with the death of almost a thousand, 360 captives and the death of one whiteman and the rest, which would be in all 80, badly wounded.

The soldiers, having withdrawn to this fort on the 21st of last December, news reached it in the middle of the following February that the Tupinamba Indians, who were the most friendly, had revolted and with them were risen the rest, there remaining with us only a poor village of Tapuyas¹ neighbouring this fort and the Apirapes² who were more than one hundred leagues from it, which one of my companions going to their village brought to our alliance, finding them well-nigh ruined by the injuries which had been done to them.

The rebellion began in Caeté, killing two whites who were trading there by order of the said *capitão-mor* Francisco Caldeira, and from thence it came spreading to this Grão Pará where they killed many of our people under cover of peace, and it was very easy for them because of the great assurance in which they were living and because of the good number of people who were trading in the sertão³ by order of the said *capitão-mor*.

These Indians had good reason to rebel because of the continual injuries which were done to them, and the enslavement of them had not been stopped here, and also because of the little order which prevailed in the beginning when it was possible to put a stop to these molestations, they took against us. In continuous assaults they have stolen the slaves of this fort. All the inhabitants of it have their weapons in their hands by night and day, the enemy hindering the bringing in of *farinha*⁴ so that we have all endured great travails and hunger. And what is felt more, they have no hope of succour since the *capitão-mor* Francisco Caldeira did not advise your Majesty, having the means to do so, being the way by which we may be relieved and not in the peril and hazard in which this fort remains with continuous enemy assaults, lack of munitions and so much

---

¹ Tapuia – 'people of strange tongue', was the name used by the Tupi to refer to the non-Tupi speaking peoples, ibid., p. 24.
² Merciana probably means the Tapirapé on the Pacajá river, ibid., pp. 327–8, 497.
³ Hinterland, back country or remote interior.
⁴ Manioc meal.

famine that the soldiers have consumed their hammocks and sleep on the ground.

All these trials and more I suffered in this settlement only regretting not to have employed them in other time in the service of your Majesty which was the least matter, inasmuch as the said *capitão-mor* Francisco Caldeira, forgetful of the respect which is owed to God and through him to his ministers and holy places, the injury being irreparable, ordered the parapet of the fort levelled and used pieces of artillery to pound the house in which these poor brothers live. Without having any reason more than that of which your Majesty was informed, requiring me violently to drag from the house some soldiers which they told me he wished to order killed without them having done anything in disservice of God or your Majesty nor injury to a third party. This populace arrested him, and hold him prisoner and of their proceedings which they told me I sent articles to your Majesty about which may it be disposed as seems fitting to your royal service and the good of your vassals....[1]

19. EXTRACT FROM A GAZETTE LETTER FROM GEORGE, LORD CAREW TO SIR THOMAS ROE, ENTRY FOR MARCH 1617[2]

Some foure or fyve of your men, lefte in the River of Amazons, are richelye retourned in a Holland shippe, the rest of your men remayne there, those which are come home are ryche, and (as I heare) they meane to retourne,[3] it is sayed, that these five brought with them so muche Tobacco, as they have sold it in the Low Countries, where the (sic) first arrived, and in England for 2300[li], and allso itt is reported, that they brought some Ingotts of gold, but to what valew I know nott:

[1] After Francisco Caldeira de Castelbranco was overthrown there were to be six more changes of government by popular election before May 1620. Bento Maciel Parente and Jerónimo Fragoso de Albuquerque were sent to restore order in March 1619. Bento Maciel Parente took office as *capitão-mor* 18th June 1621, governing until October 1626; Kiemen, 1973, pp. 21–2. The rest of Merciana's letter details the needs of the settlement, much of it a repetition of Manoel de Sousa d'Eça's requests printed above.

[2] P.R.O., SP 14/95, f. 45.

[3] There is no indication as to who these men were. Philip Purcell said he had made three return voyages to the Amazon between 1609 and 1621, the last return probably being with Roger North in 1621. Thomas King was back in England by 1618, see above, pp. 151, 157.

20. WILLIAM WHITE'S VOYAGES
FROM DARTMOUTH TO THE AMAZON, 1618[1]

	Valor	/ Custu et Subs
Le Laurell de Dartmouth on*us*		
xxx doll*is* Willmus White[2]		
mag*istro* exivit Amazones fluvium		
ver*sus* x°die ffebruarii		
Nicholas Roope de dartmouth[3]	v^l o^s o^d	o^l v^s o^d
ind*ividuus* et comp*ania* pro uno		
Cheste Cont*inens* quinquaginta		
duo dozen Knives.		
eode*m* pro uno Cheste Conts	i^l v^s x^d	o^l i^s iiii^d
Et duo dozen smale spades	o^l vi^s viii^d	o^l o^s iiii^d
eode pro uno Cheste Conts		
duo mille et sex Centu*m*	v^l o^s o^d	o^l v^s o^d
Cristall beades		
Et quinquaginta quatuor	o^l v^s o^d	o^l o^s iii^d
mille glass beades		
Et quatuor dozen Sicers	o^l v^s o^d	o^l o^s iii^d
Et uno grosse Jues Trumpetts	o^l v^s o^d	o^l o^s iii^d
Et uno grosse Thimbles	o^l v^s o^d	o^l o^s iii^d
Et duo dozen bilhookes	o^l vi^s viii^d	o^l o^s iiii^d

WHITE'S RETURN, 21ST OCTOBER 1618

Le Laurell de Dartmouth *on*		
xxx *doll* Will*mus* White m*gro*		
intravit ex Amazonies eode		
die.		
Willmo Boggan[4] de dartmth ind	xxx^l o^s o^d	i^l x^s o^d
et Comp*a* pro Centu octaginta		
quinq endes Speckled wood[5]		
Conts Cxlv^c w*ay*ght		

---

[1] Dartmouth, Overseas book of the Customer, Christmas 1617–18, P.R.O., E190 Dartmouth, 944/2, ff. 5, 18, 36.

[2] See above, p. 150, n. 1.

[3] Nicholas Roope/Roupe, merchant, owner of considerable property in Warfleet, was a leading trader to Newfoundland and Portugal. See P.R.O., E122 46/50, E190 Dartmouth, 941/7, 942/12, 943/4 *passim.*; P. Russell, *Dartmouth. A history of the port and town* (Toronto, 1950), pp. 105–6.

[4] William Boggan was also involved in trading to Newfoundland and Bordeaux 1618 and 1624.   [5] See above, p. 164, n. 4.

eode pro quadraginta septe ends Red wood[1] [aps] xxx^{c}wht	iii^l o^s o^d	o^l iii^s o^d
eode pro viginti tres ends fusticke wood[2] Conts iii^{c}wht et tres quarters	i^l o^s o^d	o^l i^s o^d
eode p quinq barrels Conts decem Centu wht Annotto[3]	L^l o^s o^d	[ii]^l x^s o^d

WHITE'S SECOND DEPARTURE, 22ND DECEMBER 1618

Le Laurell de Dartmouth *on*
xxx *doll* Will*mus* White *mgro*
exivit Amazones vers*us*
xxii° die decemb

Nicholas Roope de dartmouth ind et Compa pro ducentu Axes	vii^l x^s o^d	o^l vii^s vi^d
eode pro sexaginta longe knives	i^l o^s o^d	o^l i^s o^d
eode pro quatuor Centu dozen Canisarie[4] knives	v^l o^s o^d	o^l v^s o^d
eode pro duo grose Course knives	o^l x^s o^d	o^l o^s vi^d
eode pro quadraginta spaddes	o^l x^s o^d	o^l o^s vi^d
eode pro duo dozen Mattockes et Addesses[5]	o^l x^s o^d	o^l o^s vi^d
eode pro quadraginta tres lib wht glasse beades	ii^l o^s o^d	o^l ii^s o^d

---

[1] See above, p. 58.   [2] *Ibid.*   [3] See above, p. 136, n. 3.
[4] Commissary?   [5] Adzes.

THE FORMATION AND COLLAPSE OF
THE AMAZON COMPANY, 1619–21

I. THE FORMATION OF THE AMAZON COMPANY

1. ROGER NORTH DISPUTES ROBERT HARCOURT'S CLAIM
TO THE AMAZON BEFORE THE PRIVY COUNCIL,
1619

a.   7th/17th March 1619[1]

Upon Complaint made by Roger North[2] esqu*ier* on the behalf of himself, and divers Noblemen, and gent*lemen* of quallity, That whereas it pleased his Ma*jes*tie by *Lette*res Pattents bearing date the *28* of August in the eleventh yeare of his Ma*jesti*es Raigne to graunt unto Capt*en* Harecourt that parte of Guiana, or Continent of America that Lyeth betweene the River of the Amazones, and the River Desequebe [Essequibo] contayning 300 Leagues upon the Sea Coast, and inwarde into the Lande *w*ithout Lymitta*cio*n; The said Capten Harecourt hath not hitherto proceeded in any Planta*cio*n there according to the intent of that graunt[3] but *w*ithall hath refused reasonable and honest Condi*cio*ns offerred unto him from

---

[1] P.R.O., PC 2/30, f. 124.

[2] See above, p. 60, n. 4.

[3] See above, p. 50, n. 1. Harcourt's colony on the Wiapoco numbered about 30 men in 1613 when he acquired his patent. He may have sent vessels to the river in 1613 and 1616. In 1617 his associate, Captain Edward Harvey was reported to have sailed for the river with 70 men. His ship appeared in Zeeland in December 1617 and was arrested at the suit of the Venetian ambassador on suspicion that it was bound for Naples. It was freed and Harvey departed for Guiana. It is not recorded whether he actually settled men on the river. There were still two English factors resident on the Wiapoco in 1623, but there is no evidence as to who had left them there. It does appear, however, that, despite a shortage of capital, Harcourt had tried to maintain some kind of settlement on the Wiapoco after 1613. See Williamson, *English colonies*, 1923, pp. 41–51; Lorimer, 'English trade and exploration', 1973, pp. 359–62.

the peticioners for the Plantacion thereof to the greate preuidice of his Majesties Service in those parts. It is this day ordered that the Lord Archbishop of Canterbury, Lord Stewarde of his Majesties houshold, the Earle of Arundell, the Lord Digbie, Master. Comptroller of his Majesties houshold, and Master. Chancellor of the Exchequer or any fowre of them, calling both parties before them, shall upon hearing of the Cause settle such a Course therein as shalbe most expedient for his Majesties Service.

b.   14th/24th March 1619[1]
                    Sir Edwarde Coke[2]
The busines concerning the Plantacion of the Country lying upon the River of the Amazons in the West Indies being this day heard at the Boarde. It was thought fitt that before any small resolucion were taken therein the patent formerly graunted to Capten Harecourt should be perused and looked unto. And accordingly it is orderred that Sir Julius Caesar[3] knight Master of the Rolles, and Sir Edwarde Coke knight calling Capten Harcourt and Capten North before them, doe take the said Pattent into their consideracion and upon mature advice, and deliberacion, as well of the performance of his Majesties intent therein expressed as of the state and validity of that Graunt, do certifie their opinions to the Boarde, that such further order may be taken therein as shalbe expedient for the advauncement and performance of that undertaking.

c.   16th/26th March 1619[4]
Upon retorne of the report from the Master of the Roles, and Sir Edward Coke concerninge the Plantacion of that parte of Guiana lyinge upon the River of the Amazons in the West Indies. It was orderred that the Patent formerly graunted to Captain Harecourt should bee called in, and Commissions of discovery graunted to him, and Captain North to bee drawen up by the advise, and direccion of the Master of the Rolles and Sir Edward Coke, And upon their proceedings, and discoveries upon those Commissions further order may be taken as shalbe found requisite.

[1] P.R.O., PC 2/30, f. 131.
[2] The celebrated judge and exponent of the Common Law, restored to the Privy Council in 1617 after being sequestred in the previous year; *DNB*, 1908, pp. 685–700; P. W. Hasler, *The house of commons, 1558–1603*, 1981, I. 622–5.
[3] The notes which Caesar compiled from these enquiries are printed above, pp. 150–1.   [4] P.R.O., PC 2/30, f. 133.

2. THE ISSUE OF THE PATENT AND PREPARATIONS FOR THE FIRST VOYAGE

a.   The preamble for subscription to the Amazon Company, with the signatures of the original thirteen adventurers.

6th/16th April 1619[1]

Whereas that goodly Countrye aboute the River of Amazones (limmitted to the Northward by the River of Wyapoco [Oyapock] and Southerly, soe farr as is not inhabited by anie Christian Prince, or State)[2] is by sundry Voiages which of late yeares have ben made thether by diverse, (who to theire great profittes, have found trade, and trafficke in those partes) very well discovered to bee fitt, and not only for healthfull habitacion, but also aboundinge with many rich Commodities, as riche dyes, medicinable drugges, sweete gummes, Cotton Woole, sugar Caines, Choice Tobacco, precious Woods, Nuttmegg trees, and other spices, usefull plantes, and pleazant fruites,[3] which the soile naturally bringeth forth: And

---

[1] B.L., Harley MS 1583, f. 81. The manuscript version of *The preamble* is undated. I have assumed that it dates from, or shortly after, 6/16th April 1619. It was drawn up after the Privy Council took order for the issuing of a commission of discovery, 16/26th March. The underwriters appear to have met on 6/16th April to set down their adventures and agree on the date of first payment. A printed version, with no signatures attached, is to be found in the Coke MSS, formerly preserved at Melbourne Hall but now acquired by the British Library; *HMC, Twelfth Report*, App., pt. I, 107. Sir Thomas Locke wrote to Sir Dudley Carleton on 30th April/10th May 1619 that 'There is a great project in hand for an adventure & plantation upon the river of the Amazones neere Guaiana, & a Companie to be erected whereof Captain North the Lord Norths brother is to be Governor the Earle of Arundell Earl of Warwick and others of great estate are Adventurers, the first voiage they venture a 3ᵈ parte of the whole they underwrite for' (P.R.O., SP 14/108, no. 85).

[2] Clearly the decision to make the Wiapoco the dividing line between North's and Harcourt's 'Commissions of discovery' had already been made. See above, p. 61, n. 6.

[3] See above, pp. 57–9, 182–3. Harcourt, *Relation*, 1626, pp. 43–4, Harris, *Relation*, 1928, p. 155, stated 'this Cotton wooll which (truly is) the finest of all other . . . groweth upon trees, and every Indian house hath commonly store of those trees already about it . . . and if we either set the Seede, or cut some of the branches . . . into small stickes . . . & pricke them into the ground, they will speedily growe up, and beare Cotton with in the space of two yeares. . . .' Sauer, 'Cultivated plants', *HSAI*, 1963, VI, 533–8, lists the *Gossypium hirsutum* and *G. barbadense* as aboriginal to the coastline of the Guianas and north-east Brazil. Sugar-cane cultivation, native to the Caribbean, was introduced to Brazil by the Portuguese. The *massapé* of the Amazon flood plain was especially suitable for sugar culture. The Brazilian nutmeg, *Cryptocarya moschata*, had been found on the lower Amazon, see below, pp. 263, n. 1, 279, 285.

likewise yelding apparant probabilities of rich Mines, and Minner-
alls of sundrye sortes. Nowe upon certaine Informacion of the state
of the said Countrye by men of integritie, prudence, and experience, who have in theire owne persons visited those partes, and are
from thence lately retourned; As also by Letteres from some
Englishe, and other his Majesties subjectes who have for theis sixe,
or seaven yeares inhabited and continewed resident there) the same
beinge well examined, and considered of, both by his Majestie and
his honourable privy Councell, and by diverse other Noblemen, and
gentlemen of qualitie, They have out of an earnest desire of
propagateinge religion, and Christianitye amonnge those barbor-
ous nations, and for the advancemente of the honnor of our
Country resolved with united hartes, and handes of as many of the
nobilitye, and Gentry of this Kingdome, as they shall find affected
and willinge to ingage themselves in soe noble and publique a
worke, forthwith to attempte, and by Gods blessinge to prosecute,
and to effecte, a trade and plantacion, in the said Countrye: ffor
whiche purpose it hath pleased his Majestie allreadye to give order
for Letteres Pattentes to bee drawne whereby all the said Adventurers maye bee united into one bodye, with many large and ample
priviledges that maye give encouragemente, to the cheerefull
proceedinge in soe worthye a worke. But because, a busines of this
ymportannce cannot without greate costes be either sett out for the
present, or maineteined for the future, which beinge borne by many
wilbee the more effectuallie undergone. It is therefore desired that
every man accordinge to his rancke, abilitye, or good affection, to
this intended trade, and plantacion, will sett downe to his name,
such somme, as yt shall please him to adventure, in which Course it
is thoughte good that noe man bee admitted under the somme of
50^l. The same stocke to be ymploied in two, three, or more yeares as
shalbe thought fitt by the said Company, the same subscription both
for names, and sommes to bee made betweene the daye of the date
hereof, and the fifte of Maye next, for the last payemente, And to
be limmitted for former payemente as the Committees of the
Company shall appoint, and the necessitie of the Voiage requires,
intimatinge thereby that what Noblemen, or Gentlemen shall within
the same space underwrite as aforesaid, they shalbe admitted free
of the said Company, and have free voice, in the carriage of the said
bussines, as in other Companies is used, and to that end shall have a
proportionable gaine, and profitt by the retorne accordinge to

theire severall adventures in stocke, and are likewise desired after theire said underwritinge, they would repaire upon Thursdaye in everye weeke att two of the Clocke in the afternoone att Arrandell Howse in the Strond, then and there to advise with the rest of the said Adventurers towchinge the mannaginge of this presente bussines.

It was agreed upon by the Adventurers the sixth of Aprill that every man shall make his firste paiement the eighteenth of the same Moneth.

Lenox threi hundreth pound[1]

RO. Warwicke – two hundred pounds[2]

T[o] Arundell three hundred poundes[3]

Ed: Cecyll one hunderd pound[4]

RI: Dorset three hundred poundes.[5]

W. Hervy. one hundred pownd[6]

Clanricard twoe hundred pounds.[7]

JO: Danvers one hundred pound[8]

Tho. Cheek one hundreth pounds[9]

---

[1] Each man appended his signature and his promised subscription. For Ludovic Stuart, second duke of Lennox, see above, p. 65, n. 2.

[2] Robert Rich (1587–1658), succeeded as second earl of Warwick 24th March 1619, puritan, investor in the Bermuda Co. 1615, Africa Co. 1618, New England 1620, Providence Island Co. 1630; Rabb, 1967, p. 365; *DNB* (1909), pp. 1014–19.

[3] Thomas Howard (1585–1646), fourteenth earl of Arundel, not to be confused with Thomas, Lord Arundell (1560–1639). Arundel invested in the Virginia Co. 1620, the North-West Passage 1612, New England 1620; Rabb, 1967, p. 319; K. Sharpe, 'The earl of Arundel, his circle and the opposition to the duke of Buckingham, 1618–28', in *Faction and Parliament*, 1978, pp. 209–44.

[4] Sir Edward Cecil (1572–1638), son of Thomas, earl of Exeter, created Viscount Wimbledon 1625, investor in the Virginia Co. 1609, North-West Passage 1612; Rabb, 1967, p. 262.

[5] Richard Sackville (1589–1624), third earl of Dorset, investor in the Virginia Co. 1609; Rabb, 1967, p. 370.

[6] Sir William Harvey, knighted 1608, investor in the East India Co. 1618, appointed Receiver for the Amazon Co.; see below, p. 215, n. 3 and Rabb, 1967, p. 309.

[7] Richard Burke (d. 1635), earl of Clanrickarde, Irish peer, Lord Lieutenant of the town and county of Galway, created Viscount St Albans, investor in the Virginia Co. 1612; Rabb, 1967, p. 250.

[8] Sir John Danvers (d. 1655), of Chelsea and West Lavington, knighted 1609, investor in the Virginia Co. 1610, Bermuda 1620; *Trans. of the Bristol and Gloucestershire Record Soc.*, XVII (1892–3), 303; Rabb, 1967, p. 277.

[9] Sir Thomas Cheke (d. 1659), of Pirgo in Essex, knighted 1603, linked to the Rich family by his second marriage to Essex Rich, sister of Mountjoy Blount later earl of Newport. Cheke invested in the Virginia Co. 1612, Bermuda 1620; Rabb, 1967, p. 264; R. E. Ruigh, *The parliament of 1624* (Cambridge, Mass., 1971), p. 67.

Na: Riche one hundred pounds[1]
Du: North two hundred pownds[2]
Roger Northe. three hundred pounds.[3]
George Hay one hundreth pounds[4]

b.   The Privy Council to Sir Thomas Coventry,
              18th/28th April 1619[5]

A Lettere to Sir Thomas Coventree knight his Majesties Sollicitor
generall. forasmuch as our very good Lords the Lord Duke of
Lenox, and the Earle of Arundell, and Roger North esquier have
found out and discovered meanes by Shipping, and are very
desirous to undertake Journeys by Shipping unto the River of the
Amazons in America, and into the Countries lying there abouts
(being inhabited with Heathen and savage people, that have no
knowledg of any Christean Religion for the salvacion of their
Soules, and that are not under the Government of any Christian
Prince, or State). Aswell for the conversion of them to the Christian
ffaith, and for a further discovery in to those Countries. As for
settling a Trade and Traficke with them for some Comodities and
Marchandises which are found necessary for the Subjects of our
Kingdomes and Domynions Wee haveing had Consideracion
hereof by his Majesties direction, hold it very necessary for the
furtherance of this intended worke. That the said Lords and such
others as they shall sufferr to be Adventurers with them be
incorporated as is usuall in Like cases. And therefore wee pray and
require yow to prepare a Bill ready for his Highnes Signiture to that
purpose, whereby they may have as large power, and priviledges
for carrying over of, Shipps, Men, Municion, and Armour, and
doeing of other things necessary for their Voyages, and settling of
their Company or otherwise as hath ben graunted to any others
heretofore upon like Undertakings and Discoveries with such
further priviledges as yow shall thinke fitt And that the places
where they shall have their Plantacion or use their Trade and

---

[1] Sir Nathaniel Rich (1585–1636), grandson of illegitimate descent of Richard,
first Baron Rich, knighted 1617, puritan, investor in the Virginia Co. 1619, New
England 1620, Bermuda 1615, Providence Island Co. 1630; Rabb, 1967, p. 365;
DNB (1909), p. 1005.
[2] See above, p. 60, n. 4.   [3] Ibid.
[4] A Sir George Hay is recorded as receiving a grant of the customs of smalt in
February 1619; CSP Dom., 1619–23 (1859), p. 12.
[5] P.R.O., PC 2/30, f. 158.

trafficke shall extend from the River of Wyapoco to five degrees of Southerly Latitude, from any parte or Brannch of the River of of (sic) Amazons otherwise called Oreliana and for Longitude into the Lande to be Lymitted from Sea to Sea ffor which this shalbe your warrant.

And so etc.

c.   The Privy Council to Sir Thomas Coventry,
                    13th/23th June 1619[1]
                A Lettere to Master Sollicitor

Whereas his Majestie hath ben graciously pleased at the humble Suite of divers of the Nobillity and other principall gentlemen to give way to a Plantacion upon the River of the Amazones in the West Indies: To which purpose there is a Commission of Priviledge to be graunted, and prepared ready for his Majesties royall Signiture. These shalbe to pray and require yow to prepare and make readie the said graunt, with as many Priviledges, and Immunities, as are contayned in a Graunt formerly made to Captain Harecourt of some of those parts, Saveing only, that in this Graunt now in hand, there be noe tyme given by way of favor to exempt the Comodities brought from thence from Custome dutie: But that they pay Custome for all such Comodities as shalbe brought from thence: His Majestie being gratiously pleased to forbeare the Imposicions due upon the same ffor which this shalbe unto yow sufficient warrant.[2]

And so etc.

d.   Mathew Morton plans to return to the Amazon.
        Mathew Morton to William Moreton of Moreton Esquire.
                    4th/14th February 1619[3]

... I have past my worde to my Lord of Arundell & my Lord North his brother to goe to plant men in the river of Amazones & I doubt not but by that meanes to gaine a computent meanes to live uppon./ it will be the later end of may before wee shall depart from England.

───────────

[1] P.R.O., PC 2/30, f. 218.

[2] In the discussion in the Grand Committee of the House of Commons, April 1621 (see below, pp. 219–21), it was assumed that the Amazon adventurers had been freed from customs and impositions. The tenor of the discussion in the Privy Council, July–October 1621, suggests that the MPs were misinformed rather than that James I changed his mind before the patent was issued.

[3] B.L., Add. MS 33,935, f. 23.

Mathew Morton to William Moreton of Moreton Esquire.
15th/25th May 1619[1]

Sir:

Concerninge your sone John[2] I doe not fynd it anyway fitting hee should goe to sea unless he goe in som good fashion for there is never a gentleman that goeth this voyage but hee doth adventure 50[l] at the least & unless hee doe put in so much adventure hee must goe as a laborer./ whereas yow desyer to knowe our desynes & our adventureres & the nomber of men wee carry yow shall understand that wee goe to make a plantation in the river of the Amazones wee leave there 100 men this yeare & wee meane to plant sugar canes & to ereckt ingenies for makinge suger my Lord North his brother staeth as governer in the contrey.[3] I stay in a pines for discovinge the river & the coast but every man to be at liberty to com home the next supply. my Lord of Arrundell: the Duc of Linex: my Lorde of Dorset: my Lord of Warwick: my Lord North & dyveres others are adventureres & have a pattent from the kinge for this plantation, it will bee the last of June before wee depart England.

II. THE SPANISH DIPLOMATIC COUNTER-OFFENSIVE AND THE COLLAPSE OF THE COMPANY

1. THE SPANISH AMBASSADOR, GONDOMAR, MOUNTS HIS ATTACK UPON THE AMAZON COMPANY, 1620

a. Extract from a letter from John Chamberlain to Sir Dudley Carleton, 26th February/7th March 1620[4]

... we expect still the Spanish ambassador, but I know not how yt is after such a manner as the boyes use to play at, he comes and

---

[1] B.L., Add. MS 33,935, f. 27.

[2] Two of William Moreton's sons, William and John, were considering going out to the Amazon with their kinsman Mathew. When the latter decided to sail for the East Indies instead, William Moreton the younger sailed with him. For the correspondence concerning this business, see B.L., Add. MSS 33,935, ff. 29, 31, 32, 34, 38, 40–1.

[3] From this it would appear that Roger North's original intention was to stay on the river as governor of the plantation. After Gondomar's assault upon his enterprise he probably felt himself to be of more use to the colonists in England, defending their interests.

[4] P.R.O., SP 14/112, f. 6ov.

he comes not, for one weeke we heare he is at Paris, and the next that he is not yet on his way; [onie] yt is thought the Lord Digby attends him with great devotion, and I heare of some crosse language passed twixt him and the Lord North at a table in court, about a journy Sir John North[1] is making to river of Amazones in Guiana which the Lord Digbie argued against, as beeing to the prejudice of the King of Spaine, and that the ambassador at his comming wold hinder yt, to which the Lord North replied that then he wisht he might never come, and with all that he tooke the Lord Digbie for the King of Englands ambassador in Spaine, but yt seemed he is rather the King of Spaines ambassador in England.

b.   Letter from the Spanish agent in London,
       Julian Sanchez de Ulloa, to James I, 29th February[2] 1620
       Sir

I have divers tyme this yeere last past represented unto your Magestie the inconveniences which might ensue of the voyage which Captaine North desireth to make for the West Indies, setting before your magesties eyes the fresh example of Sir Walter Rawleigh not with standing all the assurance given by him here not to have offered anie injury to anie of the king my masters dominions or subjects.[3] neverthelesse I ame informed that the foresayd Captaine prepareth him selfe with greate haste to goe to the foresayd countries, and that he caryeth foure hundreth men and much armor with him. wherefore I humbly request your Magestie he would please to looke carefully to the busines not permitting such a voyage to be made, not douting but if it goe forewarde it will cause greater troble and molestation to your Magestie then that of Rawleigh and it is much to be considered that the men which the foresayd Captaine intendeth to carrie with him are not marchants which goe to trafique and consequently it is plane that comming to sea they will doe theire pleasures not regardeing whether it be in prejudice of the king my master and his vassals or noe, soe it be for theire owne profitt. and though they say they goe not to the

---

[1] Chamberlain confused the two younger North brothers, Roger and John, here. Lord Digby.

[2] P.R.O., SP 94/23, f. 309. Sanchez de Ulloa drafted a letter to George Villiers, Marquis of Buckingham, on the same day, see above, p. 64, n. 3.

[3] For the history of the diplomatic exchanges surrounding Ralegh's last expedition, see Harlow, *Last voyage*, 1932, *passim*.

dominions of the king my master yet I earnestly intreat your Mage*stie* to informe himselfe verie well of the busines and your Mage*stie* will find the contrary. I instantly request your Mage*stie* lett me have an answere with all possible speede, for I must send presently the answere w*hi*ch I ame to receive of your Mage*stie* by this messinger, to the king my master giving relation of that w*hi*ch passeth. God all mighty preserve your Mage*stie* many happy years with such prosperity as I your humble servitor doe sincerly desire London 29 of Feb*ruary* 1620

Julian Sanchez de Ulloa.

c.   Sir George Calvert, Secretary of State,
        to Julian Sanchez de Ulloa, 30th February 1620[1]

Sir:

His Majesty has received your honour's letter of the 29th of February and has ordered me to write this to your honour in response. The voyage which Captain North proposes to make to the West Indies has, in his Majesty's opinion, always fulfilled those requirements of a guarantee not to do any violence or harm to the vassals of the king, your honour's master. Up to the present he has found no cause or motive to hinder it, considering firstly that the gentleman Captain North, who is the principal commander of the fleet which is being prepared for the said voyage, is an individual whose loyalty and integrity has never been in question or doubt. Consequently he cannot cause such suspicion as Don Gualtero Raleigh [Sir Walter Raleigh] did, who, being imprisoned in the Tower, was glad to be able to get out by any means or scheme whatsoever. He was a man, as afterward appeared, without honour or conscience and the object of his voyage without semblance of probability, so that there was no more warranty or guarantee on him than the bond that he gave a the time of his departure. Captain North, on the contrary, has for the object of his undertaking settlement, which is in itself feasible and something which cannot prejudice or offend the king of Spain, being in a place inhabited already not by the said king's vassals but by various Irishmen and people of other nations. In addition to this, that which gives the

[1] Translation. A.G.S., Estado 2600, no. 71. Sanchez de Ulloa despatched a copy of Calvert's letter to Spain. Both men gave the date of the letter as 30th February 1620. The latter year was, however, a leap year which would make the date of the letter 1st March.

king my master greater confidence in the loyalty and good conduct of the said North, is that he is one of those who abandoned Raleigh immediately on understanding that his design could not be justified, being something likely to break the concords between the kings our masters.[1] Besides which, the adventurers and promoters of the said enterprise are noblemen and gentlemen whom his Majesty knows to be well affected to those concords, which has always given his Majesty great confidence that these men will not plot anything untoward.[2]

Notwithstanding all of which, his Majesty has ordered me to signify to your honour that he acknowledges that the preparations which are being made seem to him a little strange. Because of that, as soon as he received your honour's letter, he commanded that no further proceedings should be made touching that voyage until he had more definite information and satisfaction, of such a kind as makes it clear to his Majesty that there is no other purpose in the prosecution of the said voyage, than that which he can justify to the king of Spain on his royal word and reputation.

His Majesty, moreover, ordered me to request that your honour be good enough to let him know if what you represented to his Majesty is only based on suspicion, and if that should be so, he hopes that it will be possible to take such care and provision that there remains no possibility of doing harm, even if the voyage goes forward. But if there is anything which your honour knows, beyond that with which his Majesty is acquainted, which leads your honour firmly to believe that there is other evil design or injury intended against his Majesty of Spain or his vassals, then your honour should freely inform his Majesty so that he can more easily put a stop to it, being very concerned when it is in his power, to remove all those occasions which may lead to anything unworthy of the friendship and good correspondence existing between his Majesty and the king your honour's master. With this

[1] Harlow, *Last voyage*, 1932, pp. 56, 84, 86, 97, 257–9.
[2] Sanchez de Ulloa would have known this to be untrue. Gondomar was equally aware that the Amazon venture was supported by those ministers and courtiers anxious to break the peace with Spain, see below, pp. 204–8. James I's disingenuous claim indicates that the Amazon Co. had become a pawn in the complex diplomatic chess game of which the king was such a master. Ralegh's last expedition had suffered a similar fate, see Lorimer, 'Ralegh's Guiana gold mine', 1982, pp. 77–95; Adams, 'Foreign policy and parliaments', 1978, *passim*.

I close, wishing your honour all good health and happiness, and resting from the court in Royston on the 20/30 of February 1620.

Your honour's most loyal friend to command
George Calvert.

d. A letter from Sir George Calvert
to Julian Sanchez de Ulloa enclosing North's answer to
Spanish accusations about his intentions,
10th/20th March 1620[1] Sir:

His Majesty, according to the command which he gave me to write to your honour, has suspended Captain North's going forward, ordering him that in the meantime he should answer to what was alleged against his voyage to satisfy his Majesty. The which he has done. His Majesty was pleased to command me to send it [the reply] to your honour, in order that you may see that there is no other but good and honourable intention. Thus leaving your honour to the blessed protection of God, I remain always.

Your honour's most loyal friend to command,
Jorge Calvart.

Whitehall on the 20th of March 1620.

The humble instance or answer of Rogero [Roger] North to the suspension which his Majesty ordered placed on his departure, occasioned by the objections of the Spanish Agent.

To the case which was made of Don Gualtero Raleigh, against which might be weighed your Majesty's good intentions towards the king of Spain, I answer that the origin and process of Raleigh's venture is very different to this one, inasmuch as his design was known only to himself, and on him alone depended its progress and accomplishment, the action and exploit being solely his. He had

[1] Translation. A.G.S., Estado 2600, no. 73. Julian Sanchez de Ulloa sent another letter to Philip III, 12th March 1620, summarizing his actions in the matter to that point (A.G.S., Estado 2600, no. 68). After Ulloa received Calvert's letter of 30th February/1st March he had an audience with James I and thanked him for his intervention. The king had commanded Roger North to answer in writing the charges against him. The date of Calvert's letter, 20th March, does not make sense since that would mean that he wrote it eight days after Ulloa said he had received it. The most likely explanation is that either the clerk who copied Calvert's letter, or the Spanish translator, added the ten days to make up for the discrepancy between the Julian and Gregorian calendars not realizing that Calvert had already made that correction.

many ships and men equipped for war, all of which could easily cause misgivings to the Spanish ambassador. In addition to this, the warranty that he gave came from none other than the same people who accompanied him on his voyage. The nature of this enterprise, on the contrary, is nothing other than to form a company, and that from the most distinguished people, the state having first made a close and strict examination of the justice of your Majesty's title to that country, without causing any harm or annoyance particularly

Here it may be noted that these men have never heard of any Spanish ship being in those parts

to the king of Spain. Concerning which, the grant which your Majesty authorized to Captain Harcourt seven years ago, and the various countrymen of ours who frequent and sojourn on that coast, give clear testimony and can bear witness to the Agent of the grounds of my petition to your Majesty. The foundation of this undertaking was only to oppose the Flemings, who are newly occuppied in usurping and availing themselves of the interests of our countrymen, who have for eight years been living near that river, which is seven or eight hundred leagues from any Spanish settlement.[1] Finally as to the allegation that I am making great haste and taking four hundred men and many weapons with me, I

say that such has been our haste that we have paid freight charges for one rented vessel for more than ten months, so that, if your Majesty should not be pleased to dispense with your orders concerning me, the company's capital together with my own, I having charge of the outlay, will not meet our daily expenses, being almost ready to make sail. As to the four hundred[2] men and the many weapons for them, although, the Agent says, they are considered to look more ready to rob his masters vassals than to do the business of merchants, in spite of this, they are men who have experience of the country, druggists, dyers, smiths, house-carpenters, sawyers, and I pay more money to this type of people than to others. I am transporting a blacksmith's forge with everything belonging to it, and a good quantity of other fitting

[1] North's assertion that there was no Spanish settlement anywhere near the Amazon was literally true. The nearest was that of S. Tome de la Guayana on the Orinoco. He carefully avoided the fact that Philip III's Portuguese subjects were settled on the river Pará.

[2] North does not indicate how many men he intended to take out. It is unlikely, however, that he had ever planned to take more than the one hundred or so that he eventually sailed with.

goods which are particularly useful for the said river. Moreover, those [men] I most value are some merchants and merchants factors, all of which shows our purpose to be that which we outwardly profess. All our proceeding, being already examined by your Majesty, gives credence and obvious testimony to our sincerity. I acknowledge that there are some ten gentlemen, friends of mine, who wish to adventure their fortunes with me, but they are men who carry no stain of dishonour, either in their own country or abroad.[1] I can give the same account of the rest, as of the seamen and others, and I have always rejected those who have been pirates. Therefore [I] humbly [beg] that your Majesty be pleased to consider how much the objections of the said agent are in error to have procured the stay of so good and just an undertaking, totally disheartening the most forward and well-disposed adventurers, shaking the resolution and final preparations of the people who are going with me, and finally ruining me and many other poor men, of whom there are many waiting and preparing themselves for that voyage, they being truly loyal and faithful vassals of your Majesty. May your Majesty, having been disposed to consider this favourably, be pleased to grant me free and full licence to go forward with the design I have proposed, in order to encourage others to such honourable exploits, and to recover the losses which, by the contrary, I and others will have to suffer. I will always hold it my duty to pray for your Majesty and your long and prosperous reign.

e.   The count of Gondomar to Philip III, 30th May 1620[2]
Sir:
In a letter of the first of April I told your Majesty of how I had found here Captain Norte [North] already embarked with three ships[3] and four hundred men in them to go to conquer and settle the river Amazon in the Castilian Indies, and of the strenuous

[1] See below, pp. 236–40.
[2] Translation. A.G.S., Estado 2601, ff. 16–20. Gondomar's report was received in Spain 16th June. The *Consejo de Estado* forwarded it to Philip III with the recommendation that 'even if North will not now be able to do anything in the foresaid river it will be a good idea to reconnoitre it since it is understood that there are some French and Irish there and that, dealing with it as is convenient, it would not be difficult to destroy the East Indies Company'. Philip III approved Gondomar's actions and referred to the *Consejo de Portugal* 'the part about the River Amazon and East Indies Company which concerns that crown. . . .'
[3] North prepared only two vessels, the *William and Thomas* and a pinnace, see below, pp. 224–7, 276

effort that I had made so that his departure might be suspended until I had been heard, and that the king had remitted the matter to the Council and ordered him detained for twenty days. This was very difficult, because it seemed to everybody here [to be] a point already debated and settled and satisfied to your Majesty, because of the great costs that were occasioned the captain in the delay, and because his suit is highly favoured, the greater part of the Council being interested in it.

I knew that this king had given a commission under the Great Seal for this conquest and settlement, a copy of which I send here to your Majesty. In virtue of it, Captain Norte and Baron Norte his brother and those of his family, which is very powerful here, favoured by the marquis of Boquingham [Buckingham], the duke of Linox [Lennox], the earl of Arandel [Arundell], the marquis of Amilton [Hamilton], the earl of Pembruc [Pembroke], the Archbishop of Cantuaria [Canterbury], the Lord Chancellor, and the earl of Suptanton [Southampton], who are the foremost personages of this kingdom, had formed a company like that for the East Indies. They had appointed the earl of Guaric [Warwick] as President of it, together with all its officers and agents for war and government, exchange and treasury.[1] There were already more than two

---

[1] In the course of this long report Gondomar identifies several privy councillors and courtiers as investors in the Amazon Co. The following do not figure in any of the surviving English documentation on the company's membership but, as the record of their overseas investments shows, they may well have belonged to it: *Sir William Herbert* (1580–1630), third earl of Pembroke, Lord Chamberlain, a puritan and prominent member of the anti-Spanish faction, second President of the Guiana Co. of 1627, investor in the East India Co. 1611, Virginia Co. 1612, North West Passage 1612, Africa Co. 1618, New England 1620, Bermuda 1620; *Sir George Villiers* (1592–1628), marquis of Buckingham, Lord High Admiral, first President of the Guiana Co. 1627, investor in New England 1620; *Sir John Villiers* (1591–1658), brother of the above, Viscount Purbeck, investor in the East India Co. 1617; *Sir James Hamilton* (1589–1625), second marquis, created earl of Cambridge 1619, privy councillor, investor in Bermuda 1615, New England 1620, Virginia Co. 1622; *George Abbot* (1562–1633), Archbishop of Canterbury, fierce anti-catholic with puritan proclivities, patron of Samuel Purchas and author of the geographical treatise *A brief description of the whole world*, 1599, investor in the Virginia Co. and the North West Passage 1612; *Henry Wriothesley* (1573–1624), third earl of Southampton, appointed to the Privy Council 1619, a leader of the anti-Spanish faction, investor in Gosnold's venture 1602, Weymouth's venture 1605, Harcourt's Wiapoco colony 1609, the Virginia and East India Cos. 1609, Hudson's venture 1610, Bermuda and the North West Passage 1612, New England 1620. The membership of Sir Francis Bacon (1561–1626), Lord Verulam, is confirmed in the preamble to the Guiana Co.'s patent 1627, see below, p. 289. Seven of the

hundred individuals in this company, amongst whom were Councillors, noblemen and merchants, who had already staked more than
eighty thousand ducats and were continuing to contribute all the rest
that should be necessary.[1] Thus this business seemed to me to be of
the greatest importance, notwithstanding that the duke of Linox, the
marquis of Amilton and other Councillors came to speak with me,
and to request with the greatest arguments that I should proceed in
this *blanda la mano*.[2] [They argued] it was not offensive to your
Majesty or your vassals or territories, but merely a pagan wilderness
where Dutch and Irish and Frenchmen had begun to settle and
conquer and were at present, and thus it was a grievous matter that I
wanted only to stop the English, trying to embarass me by all possible
means.

I replied to them all that the river Amazon was your Majesty's
territory and belonged to you by virtue of discovery, demarcation
and possession, and that I did not think that the king of England had
a better title to Scotland or Ireland than your Majesty had to the river
Amazon. It was thus the same thing to wish to go to settle there as in
Portugal or Galicia, and if other nations were attempting it, then
your Majesty would order that they be punished, as he had done
before. I said that I wished that this should not happen to the
English, and that I should be a poor man, a poor gentleman and a
poor ambassador if I did not prevent this by making strong representations to avoid it. Time would show their error to those who worked
to the contrary, for they were counselling the king of England to
make war on your Majesty, so that he would find out that I was more
his friend than they were. With this I made more haste to request an
audience with the Council, which they accorded me, the king being
here, for Tuesday the 14th of April at nine in the morning.[3]

---

thirty-four members of the Privy Council of 1620 seem to have belonged to the
Amazon Co. See the appropriate vols. of the *DNB* (1908–9); Rabb, 1967, pp. 233,
238, 305, 313, 394, 395, 409; Adams, 'Foreign policy and the parliaments', 1978,
passim.
  [1] Gondomar's estimate of the total membership and capital of the company was
grossly inflated, see above, p. 62.
  [2] 'With a gentle hand', quietly.
  [3] The Privy Council record of this meeting (P.R.O., PC 2/30, f. 469) is much less
dramatic than Gondomar's, but in agreement on essentials. The Council commended the 'great discretion and moderation' with which Gondomar had hand-
led the matter, but required him to 'take notice that it was not a trafficke new
begunne & erected, but upheld and contynued by this voyage'. They asked him to
put his objections in writing.

I went at that hour and found the Council full, with none of those who were here or in the environs of this city missing. Ready outside were the earl of Guaric President of the company, Baron Norte, brother of the Captain, Viscount Purbeque [Purbeck] brother of the marquis of Buckingham, and many others of the company. They wanted Norte to go, the company to continue, and to maintain the frequent and endless debate between those of the company and myself, going about this with great skill, until the whole Council came out to receive me with great courtesy. After we sat down I requested that we might be private and they so ordered it.

I told them that I was handling the business of an upright man, and that since those who were there were also, and such eminent personages, I had no doubt of the happy outcome. It only concerned me to represent the matter to them because, for the rest, I had a master who, however large his property, God had given him the wherewithal to defend it. But the attempt to require him to abandon it, by one who was so much his good brother and friend as the king of Great Britain, was a thing which could not seem right either to God or to the gentiles. I dreaded, through such misfortune, that there might be cause for a Spaniard to kill an Englishman, as for an Englishman to kill a Spaniard, and that I expected the same of the spirit and goodness of the Council, they being acquainted with truth and equity. That even if they had invested much more money than that which I understood some had in this company, they were better off to lose it than to lose the peace without cause. I was not challenging the judgement of anyone, rather I had very great confidence in those who had most desired to engage in this company, because I knew their good intentions and greatness of mind and love for their king, in looking out for his advantage and honour.

I argued very clearly and manifestly your Majesty's rights, and that, as they knew, what was called the river Amazon had neither water nor land in it but belonged to your Majesty. I concluded [by saying] that I myself was count of a very small estate, but that, notwithstanding, I had in it uninhabited land, and that it was not right that they should go from England to settle it for me, as neither would it be if in Spain commissions should be given to come to settle the vacant places which they had in their estates. That if they saw that it was not reasonable that this should be done here, then it should not be done there either. That my position was this without need to more or to quarrel with anybody, other than to send presently, within one hour, a dispatch to your Majesty giving you an account of their answer.

The duke of Linox and others answered me with outward show of much respect, but with artfulness, malice and ignorance, that even your Majesty would not want all the world to be his. I cut short the discussion as sharply as seemed necessary there.

They spoke amongst themselves, the Archbishop of Cantuaria on one side and the Chancellor on the other. Having different opinions, Baron Digbi, with the leave of the Council, told me that those lords wished to deliberate on the matter a little in order that your Majesty might be better served. Because of this, they begged me to be willing to remain there in my seat in the same council chamber and that they would enter another room within to discuss it, my manner encouraging them to treat me with this familiarity. I told him that not only was I resolved but that I would not in any way permit that the Council should leave its place. They rising to insist no, I rose and all the Council accompanied me, insisting that I should remain, to one of the king's galleries, where I told them that I would wait and that they should go back.

Within half an hour they came back again for me to conduct me to the council chamber. Being seated, the chancellor made a great eulogy in praise of my good intention to preserve the peace and my moderation in conducting the negotiations, using only the force of reason. On the part of his king and the Council, I would find the same correspondence. In proof of this, having considered the gravity and great importance of the affair, they had resolved that Norte should not depart and his embargo should continue until it had been looked into and considered, as was convenient. No decision would be made without informing me. With this I rose and, one by one, they all, very graciously, came to speak with me. The marquis of Amilton, who is the nearest kinsman of this king to the Scottish crown, told me heartily that he had very good money already invested in this company, and that I was ruining him, but that he consoled himself that in the end it was moving with the help of Hercules.

They came out accompanying me to the council antechamber at the head of the staircase, which was all full of people waiting for the outcome of the affair.

They [the Council] gave account presently to the king of my

audience and of what had passed each speaking according to his humour and inclination. I heard that the earl of Pembruc, Lord Chamberlain, notwithstanding that he was interested in this company and a puritan and an avowed enemy of Spain, spoke on this matter very well, saying that the points which I had made had not been answered. The king himself told me this, reflecting on these bad qualities in the earl, and that thus it was a wonder that he should have been overcome. He said that although he had never seen an enterprise so supported, he would endeavour to undo it; that Norte should not go. I spoke with the king on this subject as seemed to me fitting.

Two days afterwards Sir George Calvert, Secretary of State, came to tell me that he had received an order from the king and Council to embargo Captain Norte and his voyage until he should be ordered otherwise, and to inform me that this had been done, so that I might advise your Majesty. This caused great disturbance amongst Norte's kinsmen and supporters and the backers of his voyage, seeing him [already] embarked with his people for so many days and [now] embargoed.

I warned the marquis of Boguingan, [Lord High] admiral of all this telling him that unless these people and ships were not promptly disembarked and some curb put upon the backers, some disorder could be feared, and that Norte might flee to his own and the king's great discredit. He assured me that there was nothing to be worried about, but he has so many concerns and affairs that more than eight days passed, after I gave him this warning, without him sending to confiscate the sails of the ships.[1] When they went Norte had already put to sea with his ship and a pinnace which accompanied him. They tell me that there were less than two hundred men going in both, because, with the stay of the other ship and the embargo, many did not want to go.

As soon as I knew this I advised the king, and everybody assured me that they had never seen him so aroused. He was in Granuche [Greenwich] and he gathered together his Council there shortly afterwards, and it is certain that he spoke to them very strongly. He told them that they had robbed him of his honour, committing and binding him in a trap from which he had not found an exit. That [King] David had killed men and afterwards written psalms

[1] See above, p. 66, n. 2, and below, p. 277.

confessing his sins but that his [James I's] sins were different because he had [already] written books in his own defence, and afterwards they had made him kill men and commit iniquities and wickedness, which would remain an affront to his memory and posterity. The reason for this was his bad ministers. He did not know how to apologize to your Majesty, nor would he have the face to see me. Certainly God had wished to punish him, making him the unhappiest king in the world. [He ordered] that they should look into and inform him about what remedy could be had. He addressed very harsh words to the duke of Linox so that he went down on his knees twice, begging him very humbly that, if he had erred in anything, he [the king] should pardon him, and saying that he had favoured Norte until the embargo but not afterwards, nor [had he] known anything of his departure.

They all talked at length and variously on the case, but the conclusion was that the two Secretaries of State should come to acquaint me and to assure me of the innocence of the king and the [Lord High] Admiral in the accident, and that the whole fault lay in oversight and carelessness. They concluded [by telling me] that the king was placing his authority in my hands, so that I might dispose the punishments and remedies, and all would be carried out as I ordered. Until this had been done to my satisfaction, the king had not the heart to see me, but that afterwards he would be very glad that I should see him. In order not to put me to the inconvenience, in my poor health, of going to look for him at Granuche where he was, he himself could come to London.

I was in such a state that I said to the secretaries that I did not know what to say to them, nor what to answer them. On the matter of Waltero Rale, of the Palatinate, the league with the Dutch,[1] the departure of this Captain Norte, certainly in everything the deeds were so different to the words that, I being English at heart, these things, more than my ills, had made me wish not to return here, and that each day events were demonstrating to me that I had been right. I said what concerned me now was to undeceive your Majesty, to tell you the truth and to request permission to return. For the rest, I must not meddle or give council or advice to so wise and

---

[1] Gondomar refers here to the bid for Bohemia by Frederick, Elector Palatine, James I's son-in-law, and to the ongoing discussion for the merger of the English and Dutch East India Cos. Their respective fleets were already operating jointly in the East Indies.

prudent a king who had such good councillors, demonstrating to the secretaries with temperance and modesty my just and deep sorrow.

They urged that I should give them permission to discuss the proposed remedies with me because the king trusted my opinion greatly. They told me that it was impossible that Norte would go to the river Amazon now, because he had consumed many of his supplies and had not embarked others. A proclamation would shortly be made against him, declaring him a traitor and those who might assist and help him. The commission would be torn up and the company dissolved. It was understood that Norte had not passed Ireland. This king had already sent a galleon of his navy in search of him, and on bringing him back here, he [the king] would order his head cut off, like Waltero Rale's. The king had already sent orders by post to Ireland that he should be arrested, and the same general order to all the ports of his realm where he might come in.[1] This was as much as they had discovered they could do. I should see, if I found or wished for more, that it would be carried out immediately.

I appreciated, as seemed to me just, this demonstration and courtesy, and told them that they should do that which they were telling me immediately and anything else which might seem necessary, for the honour of this king and so that it might be seen that he was acting with truth and sincerity.

The king sent to me after this, Baron Digby, Viscount Fenton, the earl of Cale [Kelly] and others, to signify to me his regret and what good fortune this event had been, because of the great advantage we must draw from it. Baron Digby extolled this to me as a miracle in which God had visibly taken a hand.

On the morning of Monday the 25th of this month the king sent from Granuche to tell me that he would be coming here to his palace at Witaal [Whitehall] at three in the afternoon, and that it would please him much to see me, if I found myself well enough to have an audience. He came and I went. Coming to speak to him, when he had sat down, he told me, with great oaths, that he was ashamed to look me in the face, because he was an upright man and yet there were many reasons why he should be thought the opposite. He hoped and believed of me that I knew his sincerity, but

[1] See below, pp. 213–6.

the [number of] others, guided by the wrongdoing of his ministers, was so great that he did not know how I would be able to reassure your Majesty nor he the world.

He took upon himself the fault in such a way, it seemed to me, that no attorney or your Majesty will succeed in doing it to him more rigorously nor with the details with which he did it, because they aggrieved him more.

He continued excusing himself on each charge with skilled precision, making evident to me, at every step, many particulars by which they had deceived him, and the conclusion of each one was as follows.

On the matter of Bohemia he showed himself absolutely blameless, which was well proved by his continuing not to declare either his son-in-law or his grandchild king, nor to give them a man or a ducat, as he would not give it to them. This affair of Norte had opened his eyes so that he could see how true was that which I had said to him many times, that his real enemies had entangled him insensibly in things against your Majesty from which afterwards he might have no escape. This affair was of this character. If there had been another here, who might have wished to appear loyal and energetic to his king, he might have already sent dispatches telling him that he should not trust the king of England, because he spoke very well but acted very ill. But it was also certain that I was serving your Majesty better than he who might do this other, because in this affair much had been gained and your Majesty would remain the peaceful lord of America, the suit won by adverse judgement against England, and confirmed with the blood of Waltero Rale and Norte. Queen Isabel [Elizabeth I] did not act thus with Drake, neither did she wish to return the money he stole, despite being at good peace with your Majesty and having here a resident Spanish ambassador. But this would not happen in the time of the count of Gondomar, and that his knowing of my affliction in this affair had pierced his heart. He told me three or four times that he beseeched me to have pity on him, and to console him and help him to take remedies. The proclamation was already made, and all of the papers of Baron Norte had been seized, to see if there was anything in them about helping or favouring his brother.[1] He was planning it in such a way that Captain Norte could not escape. He said he

---

[1] See below, p. 216.

hoped that now they would not deceive him any more, and that I was seeing how different things were here to what I had found them, because he was directing them, in order to give complete satisfaction to your Majesty.

I said to him that I was appreciative of the justice of what he was saying to me, and that I hoped that he was satisfied that it merited him my respect and goodwill towards his service. He had spoken to me on these things with such particular and complete information on each one, that I had nothing to add, *en el hecho ni en el derecho*,[1] more than that I believed what he had told me, and that it gratified me, because the evidence of understanding and good will leapt to the eyes. I said that I entreated him, since he was doing me so much favour, that he should consider very carefully the evidence and the discussion that he was surrounded by enemies who wanted to get him into necessity and tribulation, getting him into war with your Majesty, and that this was the most important point because, otherwise, this thing or that might be sufficient, and one day they would set fire to my house and to his.

He told me that I would see from that day forward what a different world it was. That I might assure your Majesty, and give it in his name, his word and mine, that during his lifetime, he would never give a commission or assistance for trade, conquest or settlement in the West Indies.[2] That neither the king of France, who was your Majesty's brother, nor any other prince or republic would do such a thing. Formerly the Dutch were constantly urging the English to unite with them in the navigation of the West Indies, and he thought that those of this company, which he was now disbanding, must have been going with this object. But that he had killed and overthrown all that, and that I could claim this as a great service done for your Majesty, since it was certain that [without] me he had not prevented it.

Because it is good that your Majesty may have a written authentic record of these matters, and he have one himself, I asked this king for one of what he would do. With Waltero Rale it forced him afterwards to fulfil it, overcoming great difficulties. I requested him presently, that for my protection, he might do me the favour of ordering the marquis of Boquingan to write me a document telling me that which he was saying to me. He told me, most certainly, and

---

[1] Absolutely, at all.   [2] See above, p. 66, n. 5.

thus he [Buckingham] wrote it to me, and I send it here, the original and translation, to your Majesty, which your Majesty will order to be preserved.[1]

It does not appear that Captain Norte can now do any harm although they may not catch him, for even if he should resolve to turn pirate, since he will not be able to get any help from here, it is certain that he will come to grief and ruin himself. But still I think it fit that, without loss of time, your Majesty should order that the river Amazon be reconnoitred. They assure me that it is certain that there are some Dutch and Irishmen there, and it could be that Norte might arrive, and then it would be easy to dislodge them and punish them severely and thus avoid another incident like that which we have seen here. I will not guarantee that he will not be able to return within a few months, but, for now, it seems that we have done well and gained much as the king said to me, and it is the truth. May God guard the Catholic person of your Majesty as christianity has need, in Londres [London] on the 30th of May, 1620.

I do not think it impossible to break the league and company for the East Indies, between the English and the Dutch, dealing with it as is convenient.

2. MEASURES TAKEN BY THE PRIVY COUNCIL AGAINST THE AMAZON COMPANY AFTER NORTH'S UNAUTHORIZED DEPARTURE

a.   The Privy Council, 7th/17th May 1620[2]

Whereas Captaine Roger North is lately gonn out from the Port of Plimouth [Plymouth] in a Shipp bound for the River of the Amazons in the West Indies, contrary to his Majesties expresse pleasure, and Comaundement signifyed unto him by a Secretarie of State. And that it is thought fitt and requisite, that the Comission formerly graunted forth Concerninge the voyage and Plantacion in the Country upon the foresaid River bee called in. It is this day ordred that Sir Clement Edmonds knight Clerke of the Councell attendant, doe forthwith repare to the Earle of Warwick, in whose custodie, it is conceaved, the said Comission is nowe remayneinge, and doe pray and require his Lordship in his Majesties name, to

---

[1] Ibid.   [2] P.R.O., PC 2/30, f. 488.

deliver the same unto him, which hee is to bringe to their Lordships to bee disposed of as his Majestie shall please to direct.

b. The Privy Council to the marquis of Buckingham,
7th/17th May 1620[1]

A Lettere to the Lord Marquis Buckingham Lord Heigh Admirall of England. Whereas Captain Roger North is of late gonn out from the Port of Plimouth in a Shipp bound for the River of the Amazons in the West Indies contrarie to his Majesties expresse pleasure and Commaundement delivered unto him by a Secretarie of State: And that it is held very requisite and expedient, that all wayes and meanes bee used for the stay and recallinge of the said Captaine and his Companie. This shalbe to pray your Lordship to take speciall order that all Shippes hereafter outward bound may have direccion and Commaundement. That if they meete with the said Captaine North and his Companie, they apprehend and take him, and his Shipp (if they bee able) and to bringe him backe into this Kingdome to anesweare his said Contempt. Or otherwise if they shall not finde themselves of sufficient streingth to bringe him in, that then they commaund him in his Majesties name and upon his Allegeance to deliver up unto them the Comission hee hath for the said voyage to the River of the Amazons, and to commaund him to desist from anie further prosecucion of the same, byt ymediately to retorne to Englannde: And lastly that noe Shipp doe assist him or convay unto him either victuall, or anie other provision, as they will annsweare the contrary Hereof wee pray your Lordship to have speciall care. And soe. . . .

c. Letters from the Privy Council to some of North's supporters.
16th/26th May 1620[2]

Letteres of the tenor following directed to the persons under named. Whereas his Majestie taketh notice that you have ben a favorer and Assistant unto Capten North now in his Voyage to the River of the Amazons, aswell by yeilding unto him of many Supplies, as by exchainging his Moneys, keepeing of his Accompts and otherwise: And that wee hold it expedient seriously to admonish you not to medle any further in that busines for the future. These shalbe to will and require you, and in his Majesties

---

[1] Ibid. [2] P.R.O., PC 2/30, f. 495.

name straitly to charge and Commaund you upon your duty, and allegiance not to ayde or assist or by any waies or meanes directly or indirectly to furnish the said Capten or his Companie with any Supplie of Money Victuall or any other provision what soever as you will answere the Contrary at your uttermost perrill. And soe etc.

Sir Edward Seimour knight

Master Tuck

Robert Bateman

Jenninges of Plymouth marchant

Bagg Comptroller of the Porte of Plymouth[1]

d.   The Privy Council, 23rd May/2nd June 1620[2]

This day the Governour and Companie of Noblemen, and Gentlemen of the Cittie of London: Adventurers in and aboute the River of the Amazons videlizet the Earle of Rutlands, the Earle of Dorsett, the Earle of Warwick, the Lord Pagett, the Lord Peetre, Sir Thomas Somersett, Sir Edward Cecill, Sir Thomas Cheek, Sir William Harvie, Sir John Danvers, Sir William Cavendish, Sir Marmaduke Dorrell, Sir Francis Lovett, Sir Francis Kinnaston, Sir Peregrine Bartie knighte and others, presentinge themselves to the Boarde, made Surrender of their Charter.[3] And delivered alsoe a

---

[1] It is not clear whether these men also had adventures in the voyage, in addition to being involved in the outfitting of it. A 'Master Tuck' sent trade goods to the Amazon in the *Sea-Nymph* 1629, see below, p. 321, n. 1. *Robert Bateman*, a prominent London merchant, invested in the East India Co. 1599, Levant Co. 1605, Spanish Co. 1606, Virginia Co. 1609, French Co. 1611, North West Passage 1612, New River Co. 1619. Sir *Edward Seymour* Bart. (1580–1659), of Bury Castle, Bury Pomeroy Co. Devon, knighted 1603, succeeded to the baronetcy 1613, investor in New England 1620, East India Co. 1625; Rabb, 1967, pp. 243, 374; G. E. Cokayne, *Complete baronetage* (Exeter, 1900), I, 34.

[2] P.R.O., PC 2/30, f. 505.

[3] Of the fifteen company members named as having surrendered the patent only six were of the original subscribers. It was stated in the Grand Committee of the House of Commons, April 1621 (see below, p. 221), that ten people had surrendered the grant representing only one-fifth of the total membership. Of the nine new members listed here *Sir Francis Manners* (1578–1632), sixth earl of Rutland, was also an investor in the East India Co. The household accounts of the Manners family, July 1618–19 (*HMC, Duke of Rutland, Belvoir* (1905), IV, 516), record that he ventured £200 fully paid in three installments. *Sir William Pagett* (1572–1629), West Drayton Co. Middlesex, fourth lord, invested in the East India Co. 1611, Virginia Co. and Bermuda 1612. *Sir William Petre* (1575–1637), of Ingatestone Co. Essex, second lord, knighted 1603, succeeded to the baronetcy 1613, a Catholic. *Sir Thomas Somerset* (c. 1579–1649), of Troy nr. Monmouth and Badminton Co. Gloucs, was the son of Edward, fourth earl of Worcester, knighted 1605. *Sir William Cavendish* (1593–1676), was created

Lettere of Attorney unto Sir Clement Edmonds knight Clerke of the Councell attendannt to acknowledge the said Surrender which was accordingly acknowledged before the Lord Chancellor And withall the said Governour, and Companie humbly prayed, That whereas they had humbly submitted themselves to his Majesties gracious pleasure and Commaunde in surrendringe their said Charter: their Councell might attend his Majesties Councel Learned, for the draweinge up of an Act of Councell whereby they may bee freed from anie dainger of anie precedent Acts donn by them by virtue of their said Charter, before the Surrendour of the same. which was thought fitt, and ordred accordingly.

e.   The Privy Council to the Warden of the Fleet Prison,
26th May/5th June 1620[1]

A warrant to the Warden of the Fleete signifyinge his Majesties pleasure for the enlargement of the Lord North, and requireinge him to sett his Lordship at libertie accordingly.

III. THE REACTION TO NORTH'S RETURN

a.   The Privy Council, 6th/16th January 1621[2]

A warrant to Hugh Peachie one of the messingers of his his Majesties Chamber to bringe Captaine Roger North before their LLordships to annsweare.

A warrant to committ Captaine Roger North to the Tower of London.

Viscount Mansfield 1620, earl in 1628, marquis 1643 and finally duke of Newcastle. *Sir Marmaduke Dorrell*, of Fulmere, Bucks., knighted 1603, appointed with Sir Allen Apsley 'Surveyors generall of his Majesty's maryne victualls' 1612, was an investor in the Virginia Co. 1610 and East India Co. 1618. *Sir Francis Kynaston*, was knighted 1619, and in parliament in 1621. *Sir Peregrine Bertie* (d. 1639), Knight of the Bath 1610, was a brother of Robert, twelfth Lord Willoughby de Eresby, and an investor in the Virginia Co. 1612. See Rabb, 1967, pp. 246, 262, 277, 327, 352, 357; Hasler, 1981, III, 211, 416; W. A. Shaw, *Knights of England* (London, 1906), 2 vols., *passim*. and the appropriate vols. of the *DNB*.

[1] P.R.O., PC 2/30, f. 505.
[2] P.R.O., PC 2/30, f. 661. Sir Henry Marten, judge of the High Court of the Admiralty, informed Thomas Aleburie, secretary to the Lord High Admiral, 27th December 1620/6th January 1621, that he had 'taken verie sufficient Caution for Captain Northe his Shippe and goods that they shallbe broughte aboute hither soe soone as Conveniently may be' (Bodleian, Clarendon MS, III, no. 176).

b.   The marquis of Buckingham to the count of Gondomar,
6th/16th January 1621[1]
My very honourable Lord

As soone as I heard of the arryvall of Captain North, I caused his person to be arrested, which for the present was as much as could be, hee being a gentleman of a noble house, and very weake and sickly, by reason of travayle. But now that he is in some state of better health, His Majestie hath given command to send him prisoner to the Tower. His shippe and lading of tabaco (which my officer had stayed in the West Cuntry, with one other lately arrested att falmouth, (being a Spanish Bottome, laden with Canarie wines (as I am informed) and taken by Dutch men) is to come about forth with (according to Speciale order which I have given to that purpose) to this Port of London. Hereby your Lordship, may wele preove, how really his Majestie doth intend to have correspondence with his Majestie of Spayne for the happy preservation of peace and amitie God ever keep your Lordship – from the Court 6 January 1620.

c.   The count of Gondomar to Philip III, 17th January 1621[2]

Captain Norte arrived at the port of Artamua [Dartmouth] with the ship in which he departed this kingdom. I learned of it presently and spoke to this king and to the marquis of Bocquingan about it. Thus it was at once ordered that they should arrest him and embargo the ship, as has been done, and even though the Captain returns sick, the king has told me that he will have him put in the Tower as a traitor, and will have him brought to justice as your Majesty will command.

That which I have heard up to now about his voyage is that he went to the River Amazon, as I told your Majesty. He found there some Irishmen and Englishmen who have been in that country for more than twelve years and, in company with the Indians, sow and cultivate tobacco, some of which he has brought back in this ship, and some of the Irishmen whom he found there, leaving yonder some of the English whom he carried out. He and those who return with him swear that they have not committed a hostile act against any vassal of your Majesty, nor against anybody, and I have said,

---

[1] A.G.S., Estado 7031, lib. 374, f. 31. Buckingham's letter and the following reports from Gondomar are extracted from the letter book of the count of Gondomar preserved in Simancas.
[2] Translation, ibid., ff. 27–8.

and I maintain, that it is a hostile act, and a great one, to have settled men in your Majesty's territory, breaking this king's order and the embargo that he should not make this voyage.

Even though this king shows regret for this and offers me remedy and punishment for it, as he demonstrated in cancelling the patent and dissolving the company, I have always told your Majesty that I do not hold this for a secure thing. Thus I beseeched your Majesty that you should give orders to send out and destroy this ship and the few men who went in it, because, for here, the important remedy is the lesson learned with the loss. Your Majesty will give orders for that which is most fitting to be looked into. May God keep your Majesty.

London 17th January 1621.

The marquis of Boquingan, a little while ago, wrote to me on this the letter which I send here to your Majesty, the original and translation, in which it appears that the king is making all effort that he can right now.

d. The count of Gondomar to Philip III, 16th February 162[1][1]

. . . as likewise has been a very good example the imprisonment of Captain Norte, who is in the Tower here, his goods and the ship in which he went to the river Amazon embargoed, as I have advised your Majesty in a letter of the 17th of January. Notwithstanding which, Baron Norte, his brother, and the duke of Linox and many others are making great entreaties to me that I should intercede with the king to pardon him, since he has not done harm or offence to any vassal of your Majesty, nor to anybody. Those who are interceding for him say that they will hang themselves if it should be found to the contrary, and that he left here without permission, desperate, and that he returned when his provisions were exhausted. They try to justify this intercession with that everything that could be claimed for the service of your Majesty has been achieved already, that is the destruction of the company which was formed for the river Amazon, and the tearing to pieces of the patent which the king had given to them for it. I only declared to

[1] Translation. Ibid., ff. 57v–8. This entry begins with an account of the arrest of a 30-ton Spanish ship at Dartmouth, brought in by one Quin and said to have been taken by 'Thomas Alveri' off Galicia, under Dutch letters of marque. Gondomar had requested that the pirates be hanged.

them that this was your Majesty's territory, and thus they will not go there any more nor set their eyes upon it.

And, with these conditions protecting the pardon, it seems to me, in the end, that in this way the matter will be more secure and forgotten than by bloodshed. I have understood that the king wishes that I be of this opinion because he, Norte, is of a very highly connected and powerful family here. Let your Majesty be pleased to command me that which you may hold to be the most fitting for your service. It also seems to me fitting that your Majesty should be pleased to order the reconnaissance of this river Amazon, because they tell me, on good authority, that there are, at present, some Irishmen there and that they are resolved to go from Holland to make a settlement.

And the English thieves' dens in Virginia and Bermuda constitute a matter which requires a very considered and effective remedy. May God keep the catholic person of your Majesty as christianity has need.

London, 16 February 1620 [1621].

e.   The Privy Council to the Lieutenant of the Tower,
              28th February/10th March 1621[1]

A lettere to the Lieutennannt of the Tower requireinge him to enlarge and sett at libertie the person of Captain Roger North heretofore comitted prisonner to his charge.

f.   Proceedings in Parliament on the affairs
              of the Amazon Company, April 1621

Tuesday afternoon, 10th/20th April 1621. Grand Committee.[2]

A Peticion was preferred on the behalf of one hundred Gentlemen and others left by Captain North in the River of Amazons That they might either be releieved or fetched awaye.

Friday morning, 13th/23rd April 1621. Grand Committee.

A Peticion was delivered by Captain North That by virtue of his

[1] P.R.O., PC 2/30, f. 685.
[2] The House of Commons was adjourned 27th March–17th April 1621. The extracts are taken from John Pym's diary published in *House of Commons debates, 1621* (New Haven and London, 1935), eds. W. Notestein, F. H. Relf and H. Simpson, IV, 219, 223–5. Another account of this discussion is to be found in Nicholas, *Proceedings and debates*, 1766, I, 249–51.

Majesties Letters Pattents he undertooke a Vioadge (sic) and plantacion in the River of the Amazons, And haveing contracted with divers Adventurers and Parteners in his absence the Pattent was delivered and at his comming home the goods which he browght seized uppon Complaynt of the Spanish Ambassadour; Soe that by this meanes and the Adventures not performinge their Convenants, Hee is dissabled either to releive or fetch awaye one hundred men which he left behind for that Planatation (sic)

The state of this Cause was further opened by Sir Thomas Roe. The River had been discovered thirteen yeares past by himselfe. This voiadge was long in preparacion, never interrupted till they were at Plymouth. The parties interested summoned to the Counsell Table, yet it was not thowght fitt to heare them against the spanish Ambassador but were urged to renounce their Pattent. The Tobacco in Question was made by Sir Thomas Roes men, and Captain North was to have a 5th parte for the transportinge. A suite was offered by him in the Admiraltie But was stayed by the Spanish Ambassador claymeinge the Tobacco as groweing uppon his Maisters soyle.[1]

Three things being in Question (1) The Title, (2) The Persons, (3) The Goods, It was propownded to leave the first and to thinke of some Provision for the other twoe.

On the other side was alleadged[2] That without determineing of the first we cannot judge of the other twoe. If they were Intrudours or Invadours, they have noe right to the Tobaccoe, for the Interest of the soile carryeth with it all that growes upon the soyle. It was necessarye for encouradgement of other Plantacions to cleare this Title of the Spaniards, for if it be graunted uppon the devision of the Pope Alexander the 6th, Then are those in Virginia and the Summer Ilands in the same Case.

On the other Part.[3] Wee must first consider whether we can

---

[1] Nicholas's account of Sir Thomas Roe's speech is slightly different. Roe asserted that it had cost North and the adventurers £3,000 to equip their voyage. He described North's indecision after the Privy Council meeting of 14th April. He declared that, no matter what the Spanish ambassador might allege to the contrary, 'the Truth is Sir *Thomas Rowe* and his Servants were the first that inhabited and planted in those Parts of *America* which is called the Country of the Amazons'.

[2] According to Nicholas this was Sir Edwin Sandys speaking.

[3] Notestein et al., 1935, IV, 224, n. 4, suggest that Sir Humphrey May was speaking here.

summon the Spanish Ambassador For without heareing him noe Judgment can bee given. And it wilbe likewise good to knowe the Kinges pleasure For if he disclayme his right wee are at an end.

For Replye:[1] A President was urged of a Judgment in the Kinges Bench betwixt one Pounters and the Kinge of Spaine for some Brazill wood,[2] which was claimed as growing uppon that part of the Continent which belonged to the Kinge of Spaine. Both parties joyned issue And the Kinge of Spaine called openly in the Courte, not appeareinge was Nonsuited 12° *Regis*.

If the Kinge showld disclayme,[3] it is to bee considered whether the interest of the Subject bee thereby extinguished For by the Lawe of Nations any bodye may make use of a desolate Countrie whereof noe bodye is in Possession.

For the Goods, twoe things were thowght fitt to be commended to the Howse. That the stop of the suite offerd in the Admiralls Courte showld be removed, it being against the libertye of a Subject to be barred in his legall proceedings. That because Tobacco was subject to spoyle It might bee delivered uppon bayle to answere the vallue, with some provision for the Kinges Custome. To which Poynt was propownded That, by the Pattent, Custome and Impost was discharged But, that Pattent being surrendered, there is demanded 2 *per librum*, which charge will discouradge any man for bayleinge it. But for the helpe of that, it was offered to the Consideration of the Committee, This surrender beeing made but by ten, whereas fifty were in the Graunte, whether the Act of those ten showld bind the rest.

For the Persons, That the Adventueres should either be Commanded to send for them awaye or to supply them accordinge to their Contract.

Tuesday afternoon, 17th/27th April 1621. Grand Committee.[4]

Sir Edward Sackfield. On Forward, and speakes of a Petition of Mr. Roger North's to the Parliament, that the goods may be sold, and when the right owner is knowen. Next, that the gentlemen who

---

[1] Henry Rolle is speaking here, ibid., p. 225, n. 5.

[2] The case in question, brought by the Spanish ambassador against John Pountys for importing Brazil wood from 'a desert place in the partes of America where none but Savadge people and Man eaters do inhabite . . .', is to be found in P.R.O., HCA 24/77, nos. 271, 288, 295.

[3] Sir Edwin Sandys speaking.

[4] Notestein et al., 1935, III, 3. The notes of Sir Thomas Barrington.

are behind may have somm means of releife ther or to be sent for home, and for this to petition the King thought fitt by the Committee. This Mr. North was inforced unto because the Mariners wives called and petitioned for wages, and yet his meanes seazed on.

g.　　　The Privy Council to the Lieutenant of the Tower,
21st April/1st May 1621[1]

A lettere to the lieutenant of the Tower to receive into his charge and keepeing the person of Capten Roger North to remayne prisoner there upon Command from his Majestie untill further order.

h.　　　The count of Gondomar to Philip IV, 2nd May 1621[2]
Sire:

Fulfilling that which your Majesty was pleased to order to be written to me in a letter of the 29th of March about Captain Norte, I have gone back to speak to this king on this business, and he shows himself to be very constant in not permitting that settlement and company to go forward. Thus Captain Norte is imprisoned for the crime he committed in having gone there, and everything he brought back embargoed, which was tobacco belonging to some Irishmen who were there a long time and returned with him. So his voyage and goods have been lost, and that which those who had assisted him had invested.

In Parliament it was proposed that the discovery and settlement of that part of the river Amazon belonged to this crown, and that on the representations of the Spanish ambassador the king had broken the patent and dissolved the company. Thus it was certain that, if this should be permitted, the ambassador would claim that the king should revoke the patents of the rest of the ancient companies that there were in London, and that thus Parliament ought to attend to the remedy of it. The king tells me that he will set about punishing such great effrontery, since it is principally his concern, and he has given order to Norte's guards that they should not permit anyone to speak with him.

London, 2 May 1621.

---

[1] P.R.O., PC 2/31, f. 30.
[2] Translation. A.G.S., Estado 7031, lib. 374, f. 94.

i.   The count of Gondomar to Philip IV, 20th June 1621[1]

In a letter of the 2nd of May I told your Majesty about what Captain Norte had attempted in Parliament, seeking that his patent might be returned to him and that the company might be re-formed for the conquest and settlement of the river Amazon, notwithstanding that the king had dissolved and cancelled it.

And even though I subsequently received the letter which your Majesty was pleased to order to be written to me on the 17th of April, telling me that it would be well to make the approach to this king that I had suggested, that he should pardon this Captain Norte, it has not seemed to me convenient to do it in view of his obstinacy, without he himself first, in writing, acknowledges his fault and that country to be your Majesty's territory, and obligates himself not to go or to send relief or assistance there himself, or through intermediaries, promising it as a gentleman and giving sureties for it. It seems to me that unless he does this it is as well to seek that they should hang him, or that he should die in the harsh prison in which he now is, because I think it less inconvenient that Baron Norte, his brother, and his relatives, who are many and powerful here, and those of Waltero Rale should complain about me as they do than, by forwarding his pardon, to consent that he should go to conquer your Majesty's Indies.

That which had occurred in this [business] of the Amazon and its present condition, your Majesty will order to be studied through the account which goes with this letter, which is a thing of great importance, and it is very necessary it be attended to[2]
London 20 June 1621.

j.   The Privy Council to the Lieutenant of the Tower,
18th/28th July 1621[3]

A Lettere to the Lieutenant of the Tower whereas his Majestie is graciously pleased to give order, that Capten Roger North now Prisoner under your charge in the Tower be inlarged and sett at liberty upon Caution to be taken by the Judg of the Admiralty, that he shall not hereafter any way prosecute his voyage and Adventure to the River of the Amazons Which Caution is already taken

[1] Ibid., f. 160.
[2] Gondomar refers here to the information given to him by Philip Purcell printed above, pp. 156–8.
[3] P.R.O., PC 2/31, f. 100.

accordingly. These shalbe to will and require yow to sett Cap*ten* North at Liberty ffor w*hic*h this shalbe *your* warrant dated etc.

IV. THE FINANCIAL DIFFICULTIES OF THE DEFUNCT AMAZON COMPANY

1. PROCEEDINGS BY ROGER NORTH IN THE ADMIRALTY COURT AGAINST THE OWNERS OF *THE WILLIAM AND THOMAS*[1]

Imprimis v*idelize*t that in the monethes of November December, Januarie, ffebruarie and March Anno D*om*ini iuxta computac*ion*em Eccl*es*ie Anglicane 1619 and allsoe in the monethes of March, Aprill, Maye, June, July, August, September, Oct*ober*, Novem*ber* & December Anno D*om*ini 1620 iam curren and in all some or one of the yeares and monethes aforesaid the foresaid Thomas Johnson, William Cock and Mathewe Cavell were and at this present are Owners and proprietaries of the foresaid shipp the William and Thomas or of the most and greatest p*ar*t thereof And that they the said Johnson, Cock and Cavell or most or one of them in the yeares and monethes aforesaid and in all some, or one of them had the free disposition and letting out to freight of the foresaid shippe called the William and Thomas and of her tackle and ffurniture; hoc que fuit et est verum et manifestum:

Et ponit con   divisim et de quolibet.

2   Item that in the yeares and monethes aforesaid and in all some or one of them the said Rogeri North had treatie and conference w*i*th the said Johnson, Cock and Cavell or w*i*th all some, or one of them for and concerning the hiring and freighting hence of the foresaid shipp the William and Thomas for a voyadge by her to or towards the River of Amazones in the West Indies & backe for

---

[1] P.R.O., HCA 24/79, pt. I, no. 8. Roger North and his associates used a particular procedure of the High Court of Admiralty, a *negocium examinacionis testum in perpetuam rei memoriam*, to establish their claim to damages against Thomas Johnson, William Cock and Mathew Cavell, part-owners of the *William and Thomas*. Such a statement of the matter, later termed a protest, was used as a means of recording evidence in case action should be taken at a later date when necessary witnesses were no longer available.

London in which voyadge the said Roger North was to goe Capten or cheefe Comannder: Et ponit up supra.

3   Item that in the yeares and monethes aforesaid or in some or one of them they the said Johnson Cock and Cavell or some or one of them did lett to freight and hier the foresaid shipp called the William and Thomas unto the said Roger North for a voyadge by her to be made to the River of Amazones & backe to London as aforesaid. And that they the said Johnson Cock and Cavell or some or one of them did convenaunt, promise and contract to and with the said Roger North supra alto Mare en infra Jurisdictionem Admiraltis Anglie that the foresaid shipp at the tyme of the hiring and freighting thereof as aforesaid was strong and stanche and then as and shoulbe sufficiently tackled and apparelled with boate, masts, sayles, sayleyards anchors Cables, Roapes, Cords, Canvas and other Artillerie needfull and necessarie for such a shipp and such a voyadge as aforesaid. Et ponit ut supra.

4   Item that in the yeares and monethes aforesaid and in some or one of them the said shipp did begin and undertake her foresaid and intended voyadge from the River of Thames in this Kingdome of England to or towards the foresaid River of Amazones And that the said Roger North before the departure of the said shipp from the River of Thames aforesaid did acquaint the said Cock, Johnson and Cavell or some or one of them with the tyme of his then intended departure from the River of Thames aforesaid on or towards the voyadge aforesaid And that the said Roger North and many some or one more of the officers Commanders and marriners of the foresaid shipp the William and Thomas before the departure thereof from or out of the River of Thames in or on the voyadge aforesaid did acquaint the said Johnson Cock and Cavell or some or one of them with many defects, faults and insufficiencies in the provision of the sayles & Ropes and in the Guners and Carpenters provision, and did oftentimes or at least once before their departure on the voyadge aforsaid require and intreate the said Johnson, Cock and Cavell or one of them to repaire and supplie the severall defects and want of provisions aforesaid Et ponit ut supra.

5   Item that notwithstanding the severall importunities, requests and desires of the foresaid Roger North and his Company marriners officers aforesaid the said Johnson, Cock and Cavell or some or one of them did refuse or at least neglect to supplie and repaire the defects and wants of provision aforesaid And said or

affirmed that they would allowe noe more or used words to the like effect. Et ponit ut supra.

6   Item that the said foresaid shipp by reason of the defects and wants of necessarie provision as aforesaid during all or most of the voyadge aforesaid could not or was able to beare any fitting sayle for such a shipp but was many times during the voyadge aforesaid forced to lye a hull in the sea or to take in some or more part of her sailes although the wynde and weather were but easie or at least not much tempestuous: Et ponit ut supra.

7   Item that in the yeares and monethes aforesaid and in all some, or one of them the foresaid shipp was destitute of or at least not sufficiently furnished with Okam, pitche, Tarr and other necessaries fitting or sufficient for the stopping of seames or chinks which were occasioned in the said shipp during the foresaid voyadge by sunne or weather. And that thereby the rayne and water did many times during the voyadge aforesaid enter into and offend the Cabins and other parts of the said shipp And thereby did much prejudice to the health and ease of the Marriners and company of the shipp aforesaid. Et ponit ut supra.

8   Item that by reason of the defects and insufficiency of the foresaid shipp and her furniture in the voyadge aforesaid the said shipp was longer in the performeing and ending of the voyadge aforesaid then otherwise she would have byne yf in case shee had bine strong, stanche and well and sufficiently furnished and fitted with Canvas, sayles Ropes Okam pitche, Tarre Twyne needles and other provision fitt and requisite for such a shipp and such a voyadge as aforesaid according to the agreement aforesaid by the space of xx^tie weeks: ponit tamen de quolibet alio numero

9   Item that by reason of defect and insufficiency of the foresaid shipp and her provision and furniture as aforesaid she the said shipp was forced and necessarily constrained to put into Spaine[1] to the greate prejudice charge and danger of the said Roger North and his company, whereas otherwise yf in case the foresaid shipp had bine well and sufficiently repaired and supplied with the provisions and furniture wherein shee was defective aforesaid, she the said shipp had returned by all probabilitie from the said River of Amazons to the coast of England without touchinge in Spaine. Et ponit ut supra.

---

[1] There is no further evidence as to where.

10   Item that at the retorne of the said shipp from the River of Amazons into the Channell or coast of England the wynde and weather was verie favorable and calme and such as by which the said shipp might in all probabilitie have steared and comen directly into the River of Thames All which notwithstanding the said shipp by reason of the defect of sayles, Ropes and other provision as aforesaid in faire weather was forced to linger in the Channell aforesaid by the space of three daies and nights and at last inforced to put into Dartmouth to the greate protraction of the said voyadge and damadge of the said Roger North and companye: ponit tamen de quolibet alio tempis Et ponit ut supra.

11   Item that the foresaid defects and wants of provision were not occasioned or happenned by any extraordinarie stresse or Tempests of weather but merely by the slender and not sufficient provision of the shipp aforesaid, ffor in verie trueth the foresaid shipp dureing the whole voyadge (especiallye untill after her defects & insufficiencies aforesaid) did not meete with or had any extraordinarie tempestuous or unusuall sea weather. hoc que fuit et est verum etc. Et ponit ut supra.

12   Item that the said Roger North and company by reason of the defects and wants of the provision of the said shipp as aforesaid and by reason of his touchinge in Spaine, her lingeringe at Sea and putting into Dartmouth as aforesaid hath sufferred damadge in freight Mens wages & victualls, losse in sale of Commodities and other detriments occasioned as aforesaid in the said voyadge to the some of iii C$^{\underline{libras}}$ legalis et ponit tamen etc. Item quod premissa sunt vera etc.

2. THE SUIT OF THE CREW OF THE *WILLIAM AND THOMAS* AGAINST ROGER NORTH 1621[1]

Schedula de qua fit mentio in primo decreto
Inprimis due unto Mathew Kevill for his service

[1] P.R.O., HCA 24/79, pt. II, no. 89. In early 1621 the crew of the *William and Thomas* arrested the tobacco and goods brought back from the Amazon in the High Court of Admiralty and brought suit against Roger North for non-payment of their wages. After four defaults on North's part, the claimants commenced the pleading by issuing an *articulus ex primo decreto*. The article was accompanied by a bill of costs and a schedule specifying the names and wages of the crew, printed here.

in the said shipp for tenne monethes & a halfe
within the tyme aforesaid at v^{li} per moneth is — Lii^{li} x^s

Item due unto Nicholas Norber for his wages due
in the said shipp for tenne monethes & a halfe
within the tyme aforesaid at five pounds per
moneth — Lii^{li} x^s

Item due unto Allan Colley for his wages for
tenne monethes and a halfe within the tyme
aforesaid at xlv^s per monethe is — xxiii^{li} xii^s vi^d

Item due unto William Burnard for his service in
the said shipp the said voyage for tenne
monethes and a halfe at thirty within the tyme
aforesaid at 30^s per moneth — xv^{li} xv^s

Item due unto Thomas ffoxly for his service in
the said shipp and voyage for ten monethes & a
halfe within the tyme aforesaid at twenty eighte
shillings per moneth — xiiii^{li} xiiii^s

Item due to Henry Slater for the like tyme &
voyage at xxv^s per moneth is — xiii^{li} ii^s vi^d

Item due to Jeffery Hopkins for the same tyme &
voyage at xxx^s per moneth is — xv^{li} xv^s

Item due unto Thomas Cooke for the same tyme
& voyage at xxiii^s per moneth is — xii^{li} i^s vi^d

Item due unto Nichoolas Northcott for his
service in the said shipp the said voyage for tenne
monethes & a halfe within the tyme aforesaid at
xxiii^s per moneth is — xii^{li} i^s vi^d

Item due unto Richard Dixon for his service in
the said ship & voyage the lyke tyme at xxiii^s per
moneth is — xii^{li} i^s vi^d

Item due unto Matthew Atkinson for the same
voyage & the like tyme at twenty three shillings
per moneth is   xii^{li} i^s vi^d

Item due unto Ezechiell Gregory for himselfe
and John Walden his servant the same voyage
and tyme at iii^{li} per moneth   xxx^{li} xi^s vi^d

Item due unto John Last for the like tyme &
voyage aforesaid at xix^s per moneth   ix^{li} ix^s vi^d

Item due to William hugo for eight monethes
and twenty one dayes & voyage at nineteene
shillings per moneth is   [   ]

Item due to Thomas Miller and Roger Morris for
tenne monethes & a halfe within the tyme
aforesaid the said voyage at xxxvi^s per moneth is   xviii^{li} xviii^s

Item due to James Spaice for the like tyme and
voyage at xxiii^s per moneth   xii^{li} i^s vi^d

Item due to William Cocke[1] for the like tyme &
voyage at xviii^s per moneth   ix^{li} ix^s

Item due to Edward Gowers for the like tyme &
voyage at xviii^s per moneth   ix^{li} ix^s

Item due to William Cury for the like tyme &
voyage at xviii^s per moneth   ix^{li} ix^s

Item due to George Pewsey for the like tyme &
voyage at xv^s per moneth   vii^{li} xvii^s vi^d

Item due to John Gournet for the like tyme &
voyage at xv^s per moneth   vii^{li} xvii^s vi^d
                              Somm total   CClix^{li} ix^s vi^d

---

[1] Possibly the son of William Cock, one of the part-owners.

3. PROCEEDINGS IN THE PRIVY COUNCIL CONCERNING THE CUSTOMS AND IMPOSITION OWING ON THE TOBACCO IMPORTED BY NORTH AND THE IRISH PLANTERS

a.   The Privy Council, 18th/28th July 1621[1]

Uppon a peticion exhibited to his Majestie by the Irish interessed in the Tobaccoe Lately brought from the River of the Amazons, and referred to the Lord Heigh Treasurer of England, and now brought to be orderred by the Boarde, concerning an Imposicion of 6[d] upon the pound demaunded by the ffarmors of Tobaccoe for Importacion. Their LLordships haveing had consideracion thereof, doe see noe cause, wherefore any thing should be demaunded for any the Tobaccoe soe imported by way of Imposicion,[2] And doe therefore order, that the Lord Heigh Treasurer of England doe give present order to discharge the Tobaccoe out of the Custome House brought from the River of Amazons upon payment of his Majesties Custome for the same.

b.   The Privy Council, 27th July/6th August 1621[3]

The busines concerning the Tobaccoe, and other goods brought from the River of the Amazons formerly orderred by this Boarde, was this day brought againe to their LLordships at the instance of the ffarmors of the Imposte upon Tobaccoe. And upon full hearing and debate thereof, and consideracion of the Allegacons there made It is now finally orderred with consent of all parties. That the Lord Heigh Treasurer of England doe give order for the delivery aswell of the said Tobaccoe, as the other goods brought from the River of the Amazons, paying besides the duties of Custome to his Majestie threepence upon the pound by way of Impost And likewise to make defalcacon of the other three pence upon the pound unto

---

[1] P.R.O., PC 2/31, f. 102.

[2] Imported tobacco, excepting that from Virginia and Bermuda, was charged 1/– per lb. imposition, 6d per lb. additional duty and 6d custom, 2/– per lb. in total. Virginia and Bermuda tobacco was charged 6d per lb. custom. See C. A. MacInnes, *The early English tobacco trade* (London, 1926), ch. 3; A. Rive, 'The consumption of tobacco since 1760', *Economic Journal*, supp. I–IV (1926–9), 58; N. Williams, 'England's tobacco trade in the reign of Charles I', *The Virginia Magazine of History and Biography*, LXV (1957), 404–5.

[3] P.R.O. PC 2/31, f. 109.

the ffarmors of the Impost.[1] And withall to provide that what shalbe wanting of the Assignement made over to the Lord Digbie out of those Imposts be otherwise supplied. And lastly it is orderred that such of the Irish or others as have Interrest in this Tobaccoe or other goods shall not take any advantage against Captaine North, or any other of the Late Adventurers to the Amazons for not performance of Articles formerly agreed on or uppon any other pretences concerning theis retournes from thence.

c.   Petition of the late undertakers for the
                  importation of tobacco, 1623[1][2]

Captain North and some Irishmen had imported Tobacco from the River of the Amazon, contrary to their contract with His Majesty. At the Council it was agreed that they, the undertakers, should receive 3^d per pound i.e. on 28,000 lbs. Ask a warrant.

d.   Roger North to Sir Albert Moreton,
          a clerk of the Privy Council, 15th/25th September 1621[3]
        Sir Albert,

I have bene at the Custome house, since you acquainted me that it was the Lords pleasure that I should give notice of the summe my Tobacco would amount unto, in particular, and I find it will amount unto 7000. waight, according to the last waight thereof apearing by their bills & myne which at 9^d upon the pound will be 262^l 10^s which being discharged I shall still have other charges for houseroome, waying, portrage & carriage, to defray my selfe, whereof you may please to make mention at the board, as you shall thinke fitt & convenient, And so I shall rest to be commanded by you, as dated this 15th September, 1621.

                                        Your servant R: North

---

[1] £500 was reserved out of the £8,000 rent of the tobacco farm 'for defalcacions of certayne Tobacco brought in by the Irishe men from the Amazones', 4th January 1622, *HMC, Sixth Report*, p. ???.

[2] MSS of the Earl de la War, *HMC, Fourth Report*, App., pt. I, 283.

[3] P.R.O., SP 14/122, f. 123.

e.   The Privy Council to the farmers of customs and
          imposition on tobacco, 19th/29th october 1621.[1]

A Letter to the farmors of the Custome and Impost upon
Tobacco. Wee conceived that our Late directions of the .26.th of
September last for the discharge and deliverie of that parcell of
Tobacco brought by Captaine Roger North from the River of
Amazones would have both freed this board from any further
trouble, and him from further charge concerning that busines. But
forasmuch as wee are informed by his humble peticion that
although yow the customers have yeelded to the remitting of 3[d]
upon the pound being one halfe of the Custome, yet yow insist
upon satisfaction of the other halfe As in like manner yow the
farmors of the Impost refuse to dispence with the other three pence
upon the pound due for your parts, although the Tobacco be now
found and soe certified to us to be of verie little value. Upon
consideration whereof as also of former directions from his Majestie
and this Board, and of the Patent granted to the Adventurers for
thos parts, which though it be recalled, yet in divers good respects it
was intended they should injoy the benefitt thereof for this yeare in
the point of exemption from the payment of Impost. Wee have
thought good hereby to lett yow know that wee doe accordingly
expect yow should presently discharge and deliver unto the said
Captaine North the Tobacco belonging to his share & not exceeding
7000. waight or thereabouts without custome or Impost to be paid
or without any defalcation to be accounted unto his Majestie for the
same.

---

[1] P.R.O., PC 2/31, f. 166. The Privy Council's final decision on this matter
reflected two further discussions, 24th September/4th October and 26th
September/6th October (P.R.O., PC 2/31, ff. 144–5, 148). North had petitioned
that his tobacco was so worthless it was hardly worth the 'nyne pence in the
pound' demanded by the farmers of customs and impositions. The Privy Council
had ordered the tobacco to be inspected and, finding it 'soe badd, as it is now of
verie smale value', ordered it released free of all charges.

THE ABANDONED ENGLISH AND IRISH COLONISTS, 1620–5: FIRST STRUGGLES WITH THE PORTUGUESE

1. A REPORT OF THE CONSEJO DE ESTADO TO PHILIP IV ON MEASURES TO RECONNOITRE THE AMAZON AND CLEAR IT OF FOREIGN INTERLOPERS, 28TH SEPTEMBER 1621[1]

Sire:

In a *consulta* which the Council made on the 24th of August of this year, representations were made to your Majesty about what the conde de Gondomar had written on the navigation, settlement and trade which Irish, Dutch and Englishmen have made in the river Amazon, and that in order to dislodge them from the foothold that they have taken, it was fit that your Majesty should be pleased to command that a well-provided ship might be sent out to reconnoitre those coasts and put to flight whatever people there might be on them.[2] And the Council was of the opinion, in the *consulta*, that this matter might be considered in the Councils of Portugal and the Indies, and by that the tribunal where it appertains, or by both parties, the preparation and dispatch of this ship may be forwarded with so much brevity and vigour as to bring it to effect. To the which your Majesty was pleased to reply, that the marques de Montesclaros should discuss this matter with Gaspar de Sosa, the former Governor of Brasil,[3] and that that which might result from this conference should be considered in the Council, in order that it might give its opinion of everything.

And in fulfilling that which your Majesty ordered, the marques

---

[1] Translation. A.G.S., Estado 2515, no. 68.
[2] See above, pp. 156–8, 223.
[3] Gaspar de Sousa, Governor of Brazil 1612–17.

de Montesclaros[1] has informed himself from the said Gaspar de Sosa on everything that has occurred in this matter from its beginning, and its present condition, and it is he who is referred to in the enclosed document, the substance of which is abridged here.[2] The Irish continue that commerce, although with few forces; the English have not taken much root because they are newly arrived in that country; the Dutch, it is not known if they may have made any fortifications or defences worth consideration; the French were expelled by *armadas* sent for this [purpose] from Brasil, although they are intending to return to occupy the mouth of the other river which they call the Gran Pará, as is all set forth more clearly and distinctly in the said account.[3] And considering it, it seems to the marques de Montesclaros, that it is of the greatest importance to settle, at intervals, all the coast which runs from Brasil to San Thome de Guyana and Bocas del Drago,[4] in all the river mouths. In all those which should be of such width that the artillery may not reach from one side to the other, both sides might be fortified. Thus will be denied to the northern nations the ports which they might be able to find there for making *armadas* against the West Indies, as well as the havens which, in whatsoever anchorage of those rivers, would be given to the pirates to obstruct the trading ships of Cumaná, Cartagena and Santo Domingo, and even to hinder your

[1] Juan de Mendoza y Manrique, marques de Montesclaros.
[2] The reference here is to A.G.S., Estado 2515, no. 68, a report written by Montesclaros 'on the state of the conquests of the rivers Marañón and Amazon', based on Gondomar's reports and on consultations with Gaspar de Sousa. The latter's communications with the council are to be found in B.L., Egerton MS 1131, ff. 36-8.
[3] Even after the expulsion of the French from the Maranhão the Portuguese authorities continued to fear that they would attempt to return there under the leadership of the sieur de la Ravardière. The latter was held prisoner in Portugal until 1619 and detained there after being released until 1620. James I had ordered Sir Francis Cottington to intervene on his behalf in 1619, possibly indicating that the English Amazon venturers hoped to avail themselves of his services. After la Ravardière left Portugal, Spanish agents continued to watch him closely. He visited England in 1621 to thank James I for his support and to discover the condition of the Amazon Co. In 1622 and 1623 he was rumoured to be negotiating with the Dutch West India Co. La Ravardière's main objective appears to have been to induce the Iberian monarchy to compensate him for the surrender of the French garrison in the Maranhão in 1615. There is an extensive correspondence about him in A.G.S., Estado K1431, K1432, K1438, K1439, K1479.
[4] S. Tome de la Guayana on the south bank of the Orinoco, three miles east of the confluence of the Caroni. Bocas del drago, the dangerous strait between Punta Peñas, Venezuela and the north-westernmost point of Trinidad.

Majesty's *Armadas* and *Flotas*. Besides which all along the coast there is opportunity to make expeditions inland into the provinces of which there are rumours and of whose riches great exaggerations have always been made, and although they have been attempted by many parties up to now they have had no result, perhaps for the lack of this convenience [of forts at the river mouths]. By the demarcation of Pope Alexandro the sixth, in the division of the world between the two crowns of Castile and Portugal, all the land and sea which lies 180 degrees from the river Marañón to the West belongs to the crown of Castile and ought to be so conquered and settled.[1] Notwithstanding, considering the present state of your Majesty's forces in the West Indies, and the difficulty and cost even if it will be possible to form an *armada* and raise Spanish settlers in the provinces neighbouring this coast, and considering that the Portuguese have this action already well advanced, and can continue it better with the nearness of Brasil, it seems to him that the design should be pursued from yonder. Inasmuch as they already have a fort and settlement on the river Amazon, which is that which we call Orellana and the Indians of the country Gran Pará, and that the news of settlements of English and Dutchmen is on the other bank of the river, it would be possible from the fort, with one or two flat-bottomed boats and experienced individuals, passing along the other side, to coast up the river making use of the tides which enter one hundred and ninety leagues up it.[2] Then it would be impossible to conceal from them what there is yonder because, besides the fact that the foreigners who might have arrived there would not be able to have gone further up the river than the point to which the tide would help them, because of the difficulty of the powerful currents, it is certain that on the actual banks of the river, much before the settlements, cultivated clearings and other signs may be encountered which will warn them that there are foreigners. Having discovered the truth, they will be able to cross the river and return by the shore of the former (south) side and, with the going out of the tide and the favourable current, in a little time they will arrive at the fort from whence they departed, informed of everything that there is on both banks. Then it will be

---

[1] See above, p. 179, n. 3.
[2] The influence of the tide is felt some 500 miles upstream, to the neighbourhood of Óbidos.

possible to come to a decision and provide what is needful to dislodge those who might be there. Since, in order to execute this with greater ease and to make the proper directions for the purpose, ministers of both crowns are necessary, it seems to him that your Majesty could order that they should consult together for it. Then everything will come to the desired conclusion and with the speed which stimulates the military actions of such distant provinces.

The Council having seen that which is offered by the marques de Montesclaros, concurs entirely with his opinion.

Your Majesty will order in this that by which you might be most served, in Madrid, 28th September 1621.

2. JOHN SMITH'S ACCOUNT OF NORTH'S AMAZON COLONY, 1620–5[1]

Thus this businesse lay dead for divers yeeres, till Sir Walter Rauleigh, accompanied with many valiant Souldiers and brave Gentleman, went his last voyage to *Guiana*, amongst the which was Captaine Roger North, brother to the Right Honourable the Lord Dudley North, who upon this voyage having stayed and seene divers Rivers upon this Coast, tooke such a liking to those Countreyes: having had before this voyage more perfect and particular information of the excellencie of the great River of the *Amazones* above any of the rest, by certaine *Englishmen* returned so rich from thence in good commodities, they would not go with Sir Walter Rauleigh in search of gold;[2] that after his returne for England, he endevoured by his best abilities to interest his Countrey and state in those faire Regions, which by the way of Letters Patents unto divers Noblemen and Gentlemen of qualitie, erected into a company and perpetuitie for trade and plantation, not knowing of the Interest of Captain Harcote.[3]

Whereupon accompanied with 120. Gentleman and others, with

---

[1] Extract from Captain John Smith, *True Travels*, 1630, ch. 24, Barbour, 1986. III, 225–8.

[2] On the return of some of Roe's men to England see George, Lord Carew's letter to Sir Thomas Roe, March 1617 above, p. 187. We have only Smith's word for it that Ralegh approached some of the returning Amazon planters but it would have been sensible of him to have done so.

[3] Hardly likely.

a ship, a pinnace, and two shallops, to remaine in the Countrey, hee set saile from *Plimouth* the last of April 1620;[1] and within seven weekes after hee arrives well in the *Amazones*, only with the losse of one old man: some hundred leagues they ran up the River to settle his men,[2] where the sight of the Countrey and people so contented them, that never men thought themselves more happie. Some *English* and *Irish* that had lived there some eight yeeres, only supplyed by the Dutch; he reduced to his company and to leave the *Dutch*.

Having made a good voyage, to the value of more than the charge, he returned to *England* with divers good commodities, besides Tobacco.

So it may well be conceived, that if this action had not beene thus crossed, the Generalitie of *England* had by this time beene wonne and encouraged therein. But the time ws not yet come, that God would have this great businesse effected, by reason of the great power the Lord Gundamore, Ambassadour for the King of *Spaine*, had in *England*, to crosse and ruine those proceedings: and so unfortunate Captaine North was in this businesse, hee was twice committed prisoner to the Tower, and the goods detained till they were spoiled; who beyond all others was by much the greatest Adventurer and Loser.

Notwithstanding all this, those that he left in the Amazons would not abandon the Countrey. Captaine Thomas Painton, a worthy Gentleman, his Lieutenant being dead; Captaine Charles Parker, brother to the Right Honourable the Lord Morley, lived there six yeares after;[3] Master John Christmas, five yeares; so well, they would

---

[1] The estimates of the number of men that North took out with him vary from 100–120, see above, p. 219, and below, pp. 241, 284. Smith's information on the Amazon ventures was very accurate, as witnessed by his knowledge of North's departure date, see above, pp. 213–14.

[2] For the probable location of North's settlement see above, pp. 70, n. 2, 158, n. 2.

[3] Captain Charles Parker had sailed with Ralegh in his last expedition, see Harlow, *Last voyage*, 1932, pp. 59, 60, 80, 82, 84, 231, 237, 238, 309, 323, 329, 330. Vasconselhos' statement about the fate of Parker is ambiguous, as is that of António Vicente Cochado. Williamson, *English colonies*, 1923, p. 102 and Hemming, *Red gold*, 1978, p. 583, assume that the company aboard Adriaenszoon Ita's ship was massacred, relying on the assertions of the eighteenth-century historian Pereira de Berredo, 1749, pp. 218–19. John Smith reported that Parker lived on the Amazon for six years, giving no indication that he died there. Pieter Adriaenszoon Ita was to have his revenge in various naval engagements against Spanish and Portuguese shipping in the next decade.

not returne although they might, with divers other Gentlemen of qualitie and others: all thus destitute of any supplyes from *England*. But all authoritie being dissolved, want of government did more wrong their proceedings, than all other crosses whatsoever. Some releefe they had sometime from the Dutch; who knowing their estates, gave what they pleased and tooke what they list.

Two brothers, Gentlemen, Thomas and William Hixon, who stayed three yeares there, are now gone to stay in the *Amazons*, in the ships lately sent thither.[1]

The businesse thus remaining in this sort, three private men left of that Company, named Master Thomas Warriner, John Rhodes, and Robert Bims, having lived there about two years, came for *England*: and to be free from the disorders that did grow in the *Amazons* for want of Government amongst their Countrey-men, and to be quiet amongst themselves, made meanes to set themselves out for St. *Christophers*; their whole number being but fifteene persons, that payed for their passage in a ship going for *Virginia*: where they remained a yeare before they were supplyed, and then that was but foure or five men. . . .[2]

This great River lieth under the Line, the two chiefe head lands North and South, are about three degrees asunder,[3] the mouth of it is so full of many great and small Iles, it is an easie matter for an unexperienced Pilot to lose his way. It is held one of the greatest rivers in *America*, and as most men thinke, in the world: and commeth downe with such a fresh, it maketh the Sea fresh and more than thirtie miles from the shore.[4]

Captaine North having seated his men about an hundred leagues in the Maine, sent Captaine William White, with thirtie Gentlemen and others, in a pinace of thirtie tun, to discover further: which they did some two hundred leagues, where they found the River to divide it selfe in two parts,[5] till then all full of Ilands, and a

[1] See below, pp. 340, 351–3.
[2] For the history of Thomas Warner's settlement on St Christopher's, see Harlow, *Colonizing expeditions*, 1925, pp. xv–xxviii, 1–17 and *A history of Barbados* (Oxford, 1926); J. A. Williamson, *The Caribee islands under the proprietary patents* (London, 1926); Andrews, *The Spanish Caribbean*, 1978, pp. 243–5.
[3] Calculating from Cabo do Norte to Cabo Saparara, approximately 2° apart in latitude.
[4] See above, pp. 17, n. 1, 137, n. 5.
[5] See above, p. 70, n. 4. We do not know which measurement of a league Smith was using here. By the English standard of three miles, his estimate of the distance travelled would suggest they reached the confluence of the river Negro.

Countrey most healthfull, pleasant and fruitfull; for they found food enough and all returned safe and in good health.

In this discoverie, they say many Townes well inhabited some with three hundred people, some with five, six, or seven hundred; and of some they understood to be of so many thousands, most differing verie much, especially in their languages: whereof they suppose by those *Indians* they understand, are many hundreds more, unfrequented till then by any Christian; most of them starke naked, both men, women and children, but they saw not any such giant-like woman[1] as the Rivers name importeth.

3. ROBERT HARCOURT'S ACCOUNT OF THE ACTIVITIES OF NORTH'S MEN ON THE RIVER AMAZON, 1620-3[2]

[p. 5] But of late, such hath beene generally found the goodnes of that Country, in & about the said river of the *Amazones*, and the gentle disposition of the people inhabiting the same, that many of our Countrymen (who since that time have lived there, some sixe, some seaven, and some eight yeares space, and more) have taken so good a liking, and so great affection to those parts, that they desire nothing more to raise their Fortunes, then to be imployed under the favour, and protection of their owne Country having hitherto subsisted without any succour or reliefe from it.

[A Pinnace of 30. Tun sailed 300. leagues up the river of *Amazones*]

And farther, I have beene certainely informed of these particulars: That (about 5. yeares since) a Pinnace of about 30. Tunne, called the *Reliefe*, with about 28. persons, Gentlemen and others

---

If, as Harcourt states (see below, p. 240), they still felt the influence of the tide at the farthest point of their journey, they are not likely to have gone much past Óbidos, some 500 miles upriver. According to the *South American pilot*, 1864, I, 276, some perceptible tidal movement could be noted every ten hours as far as 600 miles upstream but the influence of the tide ceased to be felt about 500 miles from the mouth.

[1] Amazon.

[2] Passages added to the 1626 edn. of Harcourt's *Relation*, pp. 5–8, Harris, *Relation*, 1928, pp. 70, 144–7. Harcourt interpolated this material after his statement that he had decided to defer the discovery of the Amazon in 1609. The marginal annotations are placed in [ ].

(being of the Company which that Noble Captaine Roger North left in the said river of the *Amazones*) did in pursuite of his directions for discovery, saile 300. leagues up in the same;[1] These men were all the while in good health: Fared well by such provisions as they daily met with by the way: And they saw many great inhabited places, hearing a fame of others farre surpassing them. And also (at last) they met with such a frequent report amongst the Indians, of certaine Lands, or Ilands, [A warlike Nation of women in the river of *Amazones* who admit no men to dwell among them] not farre from them, inhabited by *Women* only, that hath left a beleefe in all the Company, of the truth and certainty thereof.[2] The fame of these *Women* was, that by their use & practise in the warres, they are fearfull and terrible to their enemies and neighbours; And they admit (at certaine months & seasons) the societie of men: with other manners, and ceremonies, not yet perfectly knowne unto any Christians.

Their farther proceeding up the said river, was neither hindered by any suffering, unwillingnes, nor wearinesse in such a pleasant discovery, delighting them daily with rare variety of objects, and encounters: But was meerely caused by divisions among themselves; ensuing upon the stopping and anihilating the whole businesse in *England*, whereof they had advertisement, by *Proclamations* delivered unto them.[3]

It may seeme to these parts of *Europe* to be a thing incredible which these men certainely affirme, by [p. 7] this discovery; Namely, that they found a swelling and abating of the water (according to the course of Tides) by estimation about two or three foote, even at the furthest of their journey, being (as aforesaid) about 300. leagues from the entrance they made into the said river.[4] [The Count of Gondomar] And here I thinke it fit to give notice of the dealing of a *Spanish Ambassadour* (whilest he resided in *England*) against these men, after he had procured them to bee altogether abandoned by their owne Country, by his false suggestions, and violent importunity: For not content and satisfied to have wrought a

---

[1] Clearly an allusion to White's expedition. Neither Smith nor Harcourt provide very probable estimates of the extent of White's reconnaissance upriver, see above, p. 238, n. 5.
[2] See below, p. 264, n. 7.
[3] See above, p. 71.
[4] See above, p. 238, n. 5.

suspension of all proceedings upon the Patent of the *Amazones*, so well and happily begunne, and setled here in *England* he was still troubled at the leaving of a hundred persons in those parts, (though as aforesaid, destitute of all their expected, and promised supplies,) and underhand made a dispatch into *Spaine*, to procure a Force to supplant and ruine them; whereupon 3 ships were sent from *Spaine*, that had their directions and commission to fall with *Brasill*, & to take in there a competent force to effect the same; [An attempt made by the *Spaniards* to ruine the *English*.] which ships with 300. *Portugals* and *Spaniards*, accompanied with about 1500.[1] of their Indians in their *Periagos[2] [*Great Indian Boates.] came into the river in the pursuite of this designe, but being constrained to stop many Tides, and to pass many narrow channels, before they could come to our Country-men, they were so closely watched by them and their Indians, that many of their said enemies were slaine by ambush in the way, every bancke and bushy covert serving our side for a sufficient retrenchment; which advantage was [p. 8] still followed upon the enemie after their landing: but by reason of the want of government, and that the small number of ours were dispersed, and some would not, and others could not conveniently meete together, way (at last) was given unto the enemie, by running up farther into the Country and the inland parts, (where they might remaine secure against a farre greater force) so that the enemie not daring any farther attempt (through want of experience in the Country, & the enmitie of our Indians,) after they had done some spoile about the houses, were forced to withdraw themselves into their ships, and to depart the river, leaving some of their men thereabouts, then to beginne that *actuall possession*, which the Count of Gondomar had two yeares before bouldly affirmed to be in being on the behalfe of his Master,[3] when hee obtained the *Suspense* of the

---

[1] Harcourt's estimate of the forces at the disposal of Luis Aranha da Vasconselhos and Bento Maciel Parente was inflated, see above, p. 77 and below, pp. 244, 245. Harcourt was anxious to prove that the Portuguese represented no serious threat to English settlement in the Amazon. Kiemen, 1973, p. 23 and Hemming, *Red gold*, 1978, p. 226, accept the assertion of V. do Salvador in *História do Brasil* (Sao Paulo, 1931), p. 500, that Aranha de Vasconselhos took 1,000 Indians with him. Cochado's estimate, coming from an eyewitness, is far more realistic.

[2] Piragua.

[3] Harcourt refers here to the founding of the Portuguese garrison of São António in the Canal do Gurupá at Mariocay. He ignores the fact that the Portuguese had been in Pará since early 1616.

forementioned Patent of the *Amazones*, and of all the proceedings thereupon; which act of his, may (perhaps) be esteemed in the number of his greatest practises amongst us.

[The Dutchmen slaughtered by the Spaniards.] The mischiefe intended unto our Country men, was bitterly, at the same time, effected upon divers Dutchmen, to the losse of their lives, because they were more loosely seated, and more openly exposed unto the enemie upon the borders, or ilands of the maine river.[1]

[The Spaniards chased away by the English.] The men left there by the *Spaniards*, were afterward chased quite away by the *English* going aboard the next Dutch ships that came into the river.[2]

4. EXTRACTS FROM A *CONSULTA* FROM THE *CONSEJO DE PORTUGAL* ABOUT NEW INFORMATION RECEIVED ON FOREIGN SETTLERS IN THE AMAZON, 1ST SEPTEMBER 1623[3]

Consejo de Portugal – Benito Maciel Parente,[4] who is captain of the fort on the Pará situated in the mouth of the river Amazon, gives notice of having rebuilt it on a suitable site, and that he had left off finishing the work for lack of the materials which he had requested, reminding that whoever should go to succeed him must take them out. He also gives notice that he has discovered some rivers and ports, and that, from the confession of two Flemings whom he had in his hands, it was understood that the foreigners had settled in two places called Cuimena and Comorno,[5] having in each one twelve soldiers and four pieces of artillery. In addition to which, in the mouth of the river on the north shore, they have a settlement with one hundred and fifty Flemings, Flushingers, Irish and English, although they did not know if they had artillery. It was affirmed that last May they were expecting one hundred and twenty large ships which were to go to settle on that coast, from which they

---

[1] The Dutch forts of Orange and Nassau on the Xingu, see below, pp. 244–54.

[2] Pieter Jansz of Flushing destroyed São António do Gurupá later in 1623, B.L., MS Sloane 179B, f. 8.

[3] Translation. B.L., Add. MS 36,321, ff. 252–4v.

[4] See above, pp. 57, n. 4, 187, n. 1.

[5] Presumably the Portuguese version of the Indian names for the sites of forts Orange and Nassau on the Xingu. See also Cochado's map fig. 3 and below, p. 249, n. 1. The Dutch version of these Indian names was *Materu* for fort Orange and *Gormoarou* for fort Nassau, see above, p. 52, n. 5.

make great profit.[1] Benito Maciel says that, wishing to expel the foreigners from yonder, he forbore to attempt it for lack of men and boats which he requested repeatedly from the governor of Brazil. Further he says that favour ought not to be shown to an Indian of the Marañón called Don Luis de Sosa, who is now present in Lisboa with hope of returning to those parts. . . .

The *Consejo* is of the opinion that, the suspicion having been confirmed that foreigners were fortifying themselves in the mouth of the river Amazon on the north shore to which discovery went Luis Araña de Vasconselos who has not returned, it is very important to discuss the remedy with the greatest dispatch, before delay and neglect make it more difficult. Your Majesty ought to order that, the governor of the Marañón being delayed again, the captain of the Pará[2] should go immediately without waiting for him and take with him the Indian Don Luis de Sosa, with orders that unless he finds him guilty he should free him. For that which is being undertaken it is very important to have the natives of the country as allies, and this man is a person of consequence amongst them. The expulsion of the foreigners should be entrusted to Benito Maciel, giving him the things that he requests, and ordering that the captain of the Pará and the governors of the Marañón and Brazil aid and assist him. But, because it could be that the enemy may be found so well established that this action may not be sufficient to dislodge him; and because the Treasury of the crown of Portugal is so consumed and with so many demands for the aid and provision of the Indies and the defence of the sea that it will not be able to support more expenditure; and since the matter equally concerns the crown of Castile because of the proximity of the West Indies in which region the lands that the enemy is occupying presently fall; and because of the harm which he will be able to do from there to the passage of the *flotas*; the *Consejo* recommends to

[1] It is not clear what this refers to. The Dutch West India Co. was sufficiently mobilized by 1623/4 to keep three or four fleets operating simultaneously in American and African waters, besides the large numbers of vessels which sailed for the salt pans at Araya. The Dutch took Bahia in 1624. Possibly Maciel Parente's prisoners had heard of preparations for that expedition.

[2] The Council refers here to Manoel de Sousa d'Eça, *capitão-mor* designate of Pará. The governor-general designate of the new state of Maranhão and Grão Pará was Diogo de Carcamo. He proved to be so dilatory in his preparations to take up his new post that he was replaced by Francisco Coelho de Carvalho 23rd September 1623; Kiemen, 1973, pp. 26–7.

your Majesty that he ought presently to order to be discussed in the
Junta de Guerra de Indias how so grave a matter will be supported, so
that it may be disposed of in due time and in the assured execution
may be won the good success which is so important.

5. ACCOUNTS OF THE PORTUGUESE ATTACK ON THE FOREIGN SETTLEMENTS IN THE XINGU AND THE NORTH CHANNEL, JUNE–SEPTEMBER 1623

a.   A report from Luis Aranha de Vasconcelos to Philip IV
on his reconnaissance of the Amazon, June–September 1623,
30th April 1625[1]

Complying with that which your Majesty sends to inquire of me in
a letter of the 18th of April 1625, I report that I went to make the
discovery of the river Amazon and Cabo do Norte by a directive
made in Aranjues on the 4 of May of 1622 by the Secretary
Francisco de Lusena, and signed by your Majesty. In virtue of it,
and of a letter of your Majesty and of other documents, I was given,
in this city of Lisboa, a caravel, seamen, twelve soldiers and certain
provisions, and six thousand reales *ajuda de custo* for my outfitting,
and eighty thousand reales in trade goods, in axes, scythes, knives,
glass beads, combs, fish hooks and other trifles. Making a voyage
from here to Pernãobuquo [Pernambuco], in order to pick up and
take in my company the pilot António Visente[2] who was serving in
that port as *patrão*, the governor, Matias dalbuquerque [Mathias de
Albuquerque], gave me, by virtue of a letter from your Majesty, a
launch and some soldiers, seamen, provisions and supplies for war
and navigation, and had me paid two hundred thousand reales,
which your Majesty did me the favour to order to be given to me
there as *ajuda de custo*[3] for my outfitting above the two hundred (?)
which I received in this city. Continuing the journey I went to call at
the Maranhão and Pará, where I also took on some soldiers and a
brigantine and six canoe complements of friendly Indians, with

---

[1] Translation. A.H.U., Pará, Papéis avulsos, 1625, printed in *ABNRJ*, XXVI
(1904), 391–4. This report was submitted 30th April 1625.

[2] António Vicente Cochado, see below, p. 248, n. 1.

[3] Real, réis (pl.), a small Portuguese copper coin, abolished in the sixteenth
century, but its multiples were still retained to use as a money of account. It
would be worth approximately an eighth of an English penny in the seventeenth
century. The phrase *ajuda de custo* means contribution towards expenses.

whom I began the discovery.[1] In the course of it I made peace with and reconciled to obedience to your Majesty a great number of heathen, and persuaded them to accompany me with their canoes and weapons.[2] With them I subdued and took two forts from the Dutch, which were situated in that great river, the one called Matieru[3] and the other Nasau, capturing them completely and myself taking possession of artillery, arms munitions and slaves from Angola which they contained. I also sank a ship with the loss of many men, in which were six English gentlemen, one of them called Captain Parqua [Parker], brother of one of the king of England's councillors, who had sacked the island of Trinidad in those parts and killed its governor.[4] Moreover I had two battles with a great number of hostile heathen, who sallied forth to make war on me in support of the Dutch and English, in which I killed very many. All of which is well known, and is fully and clearly demonstrated in the relations, *autos*, certificates and documents which are in Madrid in the hands of Master Francisco de Lusena where your Majesty commanded me, by the said directive, to go personally to give account of the outcome of the said voyage, in the which and in the discovery I spent two and a half years. The eighty thousand reales which were given to me in this city in trade goods, I spent amongst the Indians. Since the services which I did, assisted by them, are so innumerable that it seems that they overshadow part of the deeds of the ancient heroes, I gave them a further four thousand cruzados[5] of my own, part of which I took out from my estate to make use of and part from that which fell to my lot of the booty that I won. This not sufficing for everything, and in order to show them that your Majesty's vassals are the true white children of the Sun and of the Tupana (as is to say God),[6] whom they must obey

---

[1] Aranha de Vasconselhos glosses over the fact that the unruly behaviour of his men offended the *capitão-mor* of São Luis do Maranhão, António Moniz de Barreiros, see above, p. 77, n. 3.

[2] With the help of the Capuchin, Cristóvão de São José whom he also fails to mention.

[3] Orange.

[4] See above, p. 237, n. 3. Bento Maciel Parente also claimed the credit for destroying Adriaenszoon Ita's ship, see below, p. 257, n. 1.

[5] A Portuguese coin equal in value to 400 réis, approximately worth 4/– English in the early seventeenth century.

[6] Tupan was the demon of thunder and lightning in Tupinamba mythology. The missionaries adopted the name for their Christian God; Métraux, 'The Tupinamba', *HSAI*, 1963, III, 128; Hemming, *Red gold*, 1978, pp. 56, 58.

and respect not the Dutch and the English, I gave them all the clothing and shirts that I had and the cloths, napkins and dishes of my table, being left to eat with their calabashes without anything with which to serve myself. I won by this and other deeds such reknown amongst them, that they worship me like an idol, the which is well known and witnessed in the documents which are in the hands of Master Francisco de Lusena. The artillery, weapons and munitions which I took in the forts from the enemy, together with the fifth of the slaves and more booty, I surrendered in the captaincy of Pará, and I encharged everything by receipt to the *almoxarife*,[1] Francisco Madr[ei]ra, as is evidenced by the certificate attached to the rest of the aforementioned documents. It is very important that, with great speed, your Majesty should order the completion of the conquest of the English who held out against me in the great river, who will number 250 to 300,[2] before they have time to augment themselves further, to win over to themselves all the heathen, and to so fortify themselves that much capital may be necessary to dispossess them afterwards. Besides, with the known robberies which, as a result of having that haven, they make on the coast of Gine [Guinea], Brazil and the Indies, and with the profits which they draw from the country in tobacco, urucu[3] and carajuru[4] which are dyes, as well as corn and cotton, hemp,[5] valuable woods and other things with which, as is manifested by the confession of the Dutch, they will load twelve to fifteen ships each year, they make themselves powerful and the customs continue to increase. Your Majesty will command that which may please him, I only advising that, in order for this action to have effect and for a fort to be built on that north shore, your Majesty ought to entrust the preparation particularly to the governor of Brazil, giving him sufficient jurisdiction for that, and to choose and furnish for the conquest the infantry captains and the rest of the necessary officers and to name

---

[1] *Almojarife*. The customs officer who collected the *almojarifazqo*, an *ad valorem* duty.

[2] Aranha de Vasconselhos inflated these numbers as much as he did his own achievements. With the loss of forts Orange and Nassau and the departure of Adriaenszoon Ita's colonists, the combined number of English and Irish colonists cannot have been more than 150, if that many, before the arrival of Oudaen and Philip Purcell with their party swelled their numbers.

[3] Annotto, *Bixa orellana*.

[4] A funnel vine, *Arrabidea chica*. Its leaves yield a red pigment.

[5] Probably a reference to *pita* hemp fibre, see above, p. 148, n. 1.

their stipends in conformity with the rest in that government. And may your Majesty command that at least six thousand cruzados of trade goods may be given and entrusted to me in this city, in order that I may constrain the heathen to accompany me with their canoes and weapons and persuade the very many that the English have on their side to turn to us. Moreover, these Indians have to be the sappers by whom the entrenchments and diggings have to be made together with all the labour of the fort, such as cutting and bringing the necessary woods and materials, and it seems that they are not, nor can be, given supplies or wages other than worthless trifles, shirts and iron tools for which they obligate themselves. Also your Majesty ought to consider, for your service, that you might send me to direct and organize that which there is to do, and appoint me *capitão-mor* of that conquest, and let the stipends which I may earn in it be paid to me in money in the captaincy of Pernãobuquo, and let a letter be given to me by which your Majesty may inform the governor of Maranhão of the purpose for which I am going, and order him that he should assist me with particular care in everything possible. Today the 30th of April 1625.[1]

Some of the Dutch which I captured in the two forts of Maturu and Nasau I left prisoners in Pará, where they are today so that your Majesty may order that which may please you, and I brought four of them in my company, two from one fort and two from the other, witnesses also of the ship which I sank. Twelve leagues from this coast, to my misfortune and their luck, they escaped, we being captured by two Turkish ships and one of their nation which were all acting in consort. In whose power I remained for twenty four days, and at the end of them, I and four men of my company, escaped miraculously in a launch. The rest of those who came in the caravel are still captives in the *alcaçar* of Sale.

[1] In the following year, June 1626, Aranha de Vasconselhos submitted a memorial offering to return to the Amazon to reconnoitre upriver to discover 'the mines of emeralds, gold and silver which there are on the border of the said great river' and to investigate whether the silver of Potosí could be transported that way down to the Atlantic. (A.G.I., Charcas 260, no. 13). Simão Estácio da Sylveira presented a memorial in Spanish on the same subject 15th June 1626 (B.L., Add. MS 13,977, ff. 485–6).

b.   The report which António Vicente Cochado makes of the
discovery of the river Amazon and Cabo do Norte, which he went to
make by order of your Majesty, June–September 1623[1]

In the end of March 1623 I departed from Parnambuco by
command of Matias de Albuquerque, *capitão-mor* of Pernambuco,
under an order from your Majesty, in a caravel of sixty tons, in the
company of Luis Aranha its captain and twelve soldiers besides.

We arrived at Pará on the 20th of the month of May of the said
year, where we remained equipping ourselves with everything
necessary for the boat and launch which we carried from Pernambuco, and where we left behind the caravel, it being thus more
convenient.

We departed from the said Pará for the discovery on the 11th of
June 1623 with the said boat and launch and forty canoes, of which
the *capitão-mor* of Pará gave us part and the rest we acquired in the
course of the journey, together with the necessary Indians and
soldiers which we brought from Maranhão, and with the Father
brother Cristóvão,[2] a Capuchin, by whose order the rest of the
canoes were assembled because of the obedience which the heathen
show towards him. In them we took four hundred bowmen.

We camped at Aranhanbanha[3] on St. Anthony's day, the 13th of
the said June. The Father said mass. He gave a talk to the heathen

[1] Translation. From the transcript printed in Guedes, *Brasil-costa norte*, 1968,
pp. 37–9. António Vicente Cochado served as a pilot under Alexandre de Moura
in the conquest of Maranhão and surveyed and recorded Francisco Caldeira de
Castelbranco route to the Pará in 1616. Subsequently he made two voyages as
chief pilot of supply vessels bound out for the new garrison at Belém and three as
pilot of the *armada da costa* of Brazil. He was serving in Pernambuco as 'patrão e
juiz dos calafates' in 1623 when Aranha de Vasconselhos recruited him for the
Amazon expedition. His map of the Amazon delta, made after the latter survey,
'descrição dos rios do Pará, Corupá e Amazonas, descoberto e sondado de
mandado de S.M. por António Vicente, patrão de Pernambuco', is printed below,
fig. VIII; see Frazão de Vasconcelos, *Pilotos das navegações Portuguesas dos seculos
XVI e XVII* (Lisbon, 1942), pp. 16–18; 'Trabalhos dos Portugueses no Amazonas
no século XVII', *Boletim Géral do Ultramar*, XXXII (1957), 78–86; 'Contribução dos
Portugueses para o conhecimento do Amazonas no seculo XVII', *Boletim Geral das
Colonias* (1950), 49–68; Guedes, op. cit., pp. 37–46; 'Accois navais', 1975.
[2] Father brother Cristóvão São José, O.F.M. It was his preaching which won
Indian support for the expedition. On his mission in Maranhão and Grão Pará,
see Kiemen, 1973, pp. 18, 23, 42–3; A. César Ferreira Reis, 'The Franciscans and
the opening of the Amazon region', *The Americas*, XI (1955), 173–93.
[3] Not identified, but most probably an aldeia in the area of Cametá where the
Portuguese generally raised the Indian warriors for their *entradas* in the 1620s, see
below, pp. 308, 316.

telling them where we were going and who we were. He said that we were sent by the lord of those lands, by the great king who is your Majesty; that this conquest was his and not the Dutchmen's nor the Englishmen's; that your Majesty was making war on them with much more right, they coming to our conquests together with many other arguments which the Capuchin Father knew how to tell them in their tongue, and through others which he knew. They answered him with due thanks, showing the good will for your Majesty's service which they have held for a long time. Presently their gifts of trade goods which your Majesty sent were given to them, such as axes, scythes, mirrors and shirts, and other things of this kind which they most value yonder. They are a tameable people, well disposed, lovers of truth, who keep their word. Some of them are christians baptized by the Fathers.

We continued sailing with boat, launch and the said canoes, and we arrived at Maturus,[1] which is the first Dutch fort. Before reaching it, our scouts, who went in front, had a skirmish with many savages who were in ambush. Putting themselves in their canoes, ours sank one of theirs. The rest fled, it being night-time. Only the people of the said canoe were killed by our Indians, and of ours, three or four were wounded. We arrived at Maturus, where we were by daybreak of the 16th of the said month of June; right below the fort, so that they had no opportunity to warn their savages or the other fort, because we had taken their landing stages. We sent a canoe to the fort at daybreak with a white flag: the message was that they should vacate the territories, which were the king of Spain's and not conde Mauricio's. They replied that they should be granted their lives, the which was promised them on the part of your Majesty. They came to embark themselves. The weapons which they were carrying, which were arquebuses, swords and pistols, were taken from them and we put them under the hatches,

---

[1] Fort Orange. See above, p. 52, n. 5. Orange was downstream of Nassau as Cochado clearly indicates and as demonstrated by his map, fig. VIII. The confluence and lower reaches of the Xingu are depicted, according to the prevailing conventions of Portuguese cartography, as a series of roughly rectangular islands. The 'fortalesa de mecuros de Olandeses quemada' (Orange), lies near the river mouth on the right bank. The 'fortalesa do Olandeses quemada' (Nassau) lies upriver. Cochado's map would appear to place the latter on the left bank rather than upstream of Orange on the right. The most likely explanation here is that Cochado used the convention of islands to represent the imperfectly surveyed creeks and channels of the right bank.

separating them with good sentries. The captain went to take possession of the fort and the keys of it were handed over to him with all the contents, which were Blacks from Angola and Indians and trade goods of all kinds, cotton, tobacco, artillery. The Dutch numbered 14. Presently it was ordered that the fort should be demolished and burned, as was done, burning also the coat-of-arms of Conde Mauricio which was displayed there.[1]

We left that same day, at night, for the fort of Naçau which was 12 leagues from there. On the way our canoes met up with five from the fort to which we were going. They taking to flight, our canoes gave them chase and overtook two of them which they sank killing all those who were in them, about fifty Indians, leaving only a boy to inform us where the canoes were going and what was happening in the fort. Of our heathens they killed two chiefs. They pierced two whites with arrows, and wounded some blacks. Having questioned the boy who survived about where the canoes were going, he replied that they were going to find out what the pieces of artillery were which they had heard the other day discharged at fort Maturus and that he thought that they were from ships from Holland which were expected at the fort.

This day, during the night, we dug in close to the fort, with the launch and our canoes, with our trenches and scouts, so that if anyone should come out of the fort we might capture them to inform ourselves on what was happening. But nobody left, they were so faint-hearted. The two vessels and forty canoes that we brought caused great fear. With the coming of daylight, Thursday the 17th of the said month, a canoe went ashore with a white flag and with a message that they should at once vacate your Majesty's territories; if they did not we would put them to fire and slaughter. With this, and since they knew that we were carrying their countrymen from the other fort, they begged for their lives. One came aboard with the message, and going back with the reply all came to embark themselves, leaving the weapons behind. Securing

[1] Cochado says that the Dutch in fort Orange put up little resistance. A late seventeenth-century Franciscan source asserts that fort 'Moturu' was defended by 30 Dutch and English. They were tricked into surrender when the Portuguese dressed their Indian allies in shirts to make it appear as if there were a large number of Portuguese in the attacking force; 'Relação sumaria do que obrou a Provincia de Santo Antonio por seus filhos em servico de ambas Magestades', 1696 (Biblioteca e Arquivo Público do Pará, MS Códice 1086), printed in Ferreira Reis, 'The Franciscans', 1955, pp. 185–93.

them like the rest, the captain and notary went to take possession of the fort, and the keys were handed over to him. The contents were gathered together, which were Blacks from Angola, many iron tools, Indians and other things, artillery including one *peça de boca* and one very large and other small stone-guns,[1] and a lot of victuals for the soldiers, namely *farinha*,[2] domesticated pigs which they raised, many doves, dried sea-cow and other provisions. The fort was demolished and burned as we did at the other, Maturus. It was stronger and held twice as many men as the other. We were here until the 19th of the said month of June.

On this day we left for our fort at Pará, for we found ourselves more than 90 leagues from it with the vessels loaded with the Dutch and Blacks and heathen, who would number in all one hundred and thirty individuals. We were also worried about the boat which was old, and the savages that we took with us, who were displeased to have gone so far.

We had news that the English had two fortified outposts in this area, where they produced their tobacco.

Pursuing our journey towards the fort, we met the *capitão-mor*, Bento Maciel, 20 leagues from it, who was coming to our assistance, understanding us to be in danger. The *capitão-mor* remained here and we went to Pará, to unload what we were carrying, to place the Dutchmen in custody, and to put the caravel in order for us to go finish making the discovery on the outerside of the delta.

Having put this into execution, we left Pará in the said caravel on the 15th of August 1623. We took the same boat and caravel, the canoes remaining, on the order of the *capitão-mor* at the said meeting place. We had handed over what we were carrying to your Majesty's *almoxarife*, for which the captain brings quittance, the Dutchmen remaining there, bringing with us four.

We made the said discovery on the outside of all the islands, as is shown in the map, entering through dangerous parts previously unknown. We met the *capitão-mor* on the 22nd of the said month of August, who had attacked the English before we arrived and

---

[1] 'Peça de boca' may mean a muzzle-loading gun. A stone-gun was a gun with a separate firing chamber, shooting stone rather than iron shot, Blackmore, 1976, I, 245.
[2] Manioc meal.

captured two in one of the outposts.[1] The rest had fled to where the Irish were.[2] They boarded a ship of one hundred tons which they had there, of which was captain one Parca [Parker], the brother of one of the king of England's councillors, with the intention to attack us by sea, and by land with savages at the mouth of the river where the first outpost had fled.

The *capitão-mor* being on this island with the rest of the said canoes, we met him the next day with the said boat and caravel

---

[1] There is no real evidence of where Maciel Parente struck before Vasconselhos rejoined him. If he rounded the southern tip of the Ilha Grande de Gurupá he could have turned against any one of the cluster of foreign settlements in that area. He may have made a feint against Adriaenszoon Ita's colony near the Paru before turning down towards the Okiari and Tauregue. John Scott says the Anglo–Dutch colony was attacked, but not taken, in 1623, see above, p. 164–5. After Maciel Parente returned to Portugal he appears to have had three maps of the Maranhão and Grão Pará produced, to be presented to Philip IV to illustrate memorials outlining his services and declaring his opinion on the appropriate administration of the state. The maps, known as the *Anonymous atlas of Maranhão*, produced *c.* 1629, are printed in Cortesão and Texeira de Mota, Lisbon, 1960, V, plates 600, A, B, D, see also Guedes, *Brasil-costa norte*, 1968, pp. 44–5. '*MARANHÃO TABÔA TERCERA*', fig. IX, depicts the Amazon delta in a crude, rectangular form and the difficulties of interpreting it are increased by the fact that the Equator was ruled north to south. Two rivers, the '*GRANDE PARÁ*' (clearly the present Tocantins) and '*AMAZONAS*' are shown flowing into what should be the N.W. and S.W. corners of a rectangular inland lake, named '*LAGO DORADO*'. A '*PROVINCIA DOS TAPUYOSSUS*' is marked lying to what should be the north and a '*Provincia dos Tocantins*' on its south-east margin. The territory between the east shore of the lake and the Atlantic is depicted as a series of largely rectangular islands, of varying sizes, bounded on the S. by the '*Rio Pará*' and on the N. by the '*GRAN CANAL DAS AMAZONAS*'. The information on foreign settlement in the map represents the sum of Maciel Parente's information on the subject when he left the river in 1626. Orienting the map correctly it is possible to find the Portuguese fort of São António in the Gurupá, '*Forte nosso derrubado*', founded and destroyed in 1623. Two forts are marked near the mouth of the '*Braço do Parnayba*', the Indian name for the Xingu; see Markham, *Valley of the Amazons*, 1859, pp. 129–30. One, in the Canal do Gurupá E. of the confluence of the Xingu, '*Forte que tomamos aos Olandezes derrubado*', is almost certainly Oudaen and Purcell's fort at Mandiutuba, destroyed in 1625. The '*Forte que tomamos aos olandezes derrubado*' marked on the left margin of the Xingu close to the confluence, must be Orange. Various '*CAZAS FORTES*', belonging to the English and Irish, are marked on the north bank of the Amazon in the '*PROVINCIAS DOS TUCUIUS*' or Sertão do Tocujós. Maciel Parente probably hit some of these in 1623. The '*FORTE QUE TOMAMOS aos olandazes derrubado*', marked 70 Portuguese leagues upriver from Cabo do Norte is not meant to be Adriaenszoon Ita's colony, since the Genipape or Paru is clearly marked farther upriver. Maciel Parente must have meant the English plantations on the Okiari where Oudaen and Philip Purcell made their last stand in 1625.

[2] Presumably the Tauregue.

which we took. The English arrived close by to where we were without having sight of us, it being almost night.

With the consent of all, the said ship was attacked. It was carrying eighty men betwixt the English and the Irish. We fell upon them in the dawn watch splitting their rudder and grappling with all vessels. It was resolved to set fire to it as was done, from which escaped one 18 year-old boy. It cost us four soldiers and many savages who were caught by the fire. The ship sank to the bottom without anything emerging from it, except some things which came out through the hatch.[1]

The *capitão-mor* remained here and we proceeded to finish making the discovery, coming close to the port of Capanoa,[2] which is the port where they go to anchor and furnish themselves with necessities. Two launches sallied forth against us, so that we were obliged to continue our departure further off between very many shoals and to go to Cabo do Norte, where we proceeded to finish making the discovery as is shown in the map which I present to your Majesty.[3]

Taking information from the Dutch and the English, they said that the Dutch had been living there for eighteen years and the English and Irish for fourteen.[4] They said that they were waiting for three ships with settlers in order to go exploring and fortifying, that Captain Parca was disposing everything, and that it was this man who laid waste Trinidade when he put ashore there. Taking details from these Dutch and English about the trade and commerce that they had there and with what they loaded their ships, they said that every year they drew from the two forts and outposts of the English and Irish more than eight hundred thousand pounds of tobacco, which brought in very much money in

[1] Forrest's journal see below, p. 261, states that Adriaenszoon Ita's ship ran aground off the Okiari.

[2] Sapno.

[3] The first sheet of Cochado's map, fig. VIII, marks the soundings of his journey from Belém to Gurupá and back, then from Belém round the Atlantic coast of the Ilha do Marajó and through the dangerous passages into the north channel. It is quite clear from the map that when Vasconselhos reached Sapno on his return downriver, he was forced to turn sharply, picking his way out to the N. Atlantic through the hazardous shoals between the islands of Caviana and Marajó. The two parts of Cochado's map are printed in Cortesão and Teixeira da Mota, 1960, V, plate 599. See also Guedes, *Brasil-costa norte*, 1968, pp. 45–7.

[4] This would put the first Dutch settlement on the river as early as 1605. There is no other corroborative evidence for this, see above, p. 27, n. 3.

their country, and much red dye which serves in place of [grain], and much cotton, and they had just finished loading oricotiara wood,[1] and another kind of wood which they say yields them two dyes, which not being able to remember I do not give the name of it. Those who did not complete loading there went to Cabo do Norte, that had, they say, much there. All the savages remain peaceful. They give good hopes of there being mines.

The enemies who frequent the coast of Mina,[2] Cabo Verde and Brazil go to the port of Çapanoa to repair and grease their ships, refresh the crews, and furnish themselves with victuals like cassava, manioc meal, wild pigs, deer, sea-cow and many other fish which there are in the country. They do the same at Cabo do Norte, and from here go to the Indies where they do much harm and nothing escapes them. By the map your Majesty will see the depth of the rivers and their shoals, and where they [the enemy] were situated, and the port of Çapanoa and the Cabo do Norte.[3]

Because of the very great harm which may result in the event that they should fortify themselves there where they were, it is of importance to your Majesty, for the security of those ports and discoveries, that they should be ordered to build a fort where the fort of Nação was, which in other language is called Pernaiba, and in the port of Çapanoa and at Cabo do Norte. In this manner your Majesty avoids the great damage which they do in the Indies, and the great amount which it may cost to cast them out, once they have fortified themselves. May your Majesty dispose of everything as it may seem to you. Speed is what matters most.

c.   Extract from a memorial by Bento Maciel Parente describing his service in Gran Pará, in particular his assaults on the Dutch and English settlements in 1623[4]

Having arrived at Gran Pará,[5] after sorting out the affairs of that

[1] See above, pp. 172, n. 7, 183, n. 1.

[2] Corruption of the name of the fort of São Jorge da Mina founded on the Gold Coast, West Africa in 1482.

[3] See Cochado's map, fig. VIII. Opposite '*Cepanoa*' Cochado made a notation to the effect that this was the '*Porto donde dão fundo os navios que trat[am]com os gentios*'.

[4] Translation. B[iblioteca] N[ational do] R[io de] J[aneiro], Códice Pernambuco, cota I, 1–2-no. 35, ff. 26v–27v, printed in Guedes, *Brasil-costa norte*, 1968, pp. 31–2. This memorial was presented in Spanish.

[5] Bento Maciel Parente was sent up to Pará to restore order in 1619 as '*capitão da guerra aos Indios rebeldes*'. He became *capitão-mor* of Pará in June 1621.

post, and crushing the insurrections which resulted from the late disturbances, he dealt with its fortification. And by his good offices he directed the Indians to build there for your Majesty a fort with [pressed earth walls] with 90 fathoms of rampart on the land side, 7 spans thick and 17 spans high, with three balvartes and [petriles], all of concrete with their sentry posts, gun aprons [reparos], company of guards, gabions, quarters, strong gates, magazines, and outside it another storage warehouse: he had them build three churches, administrative buildings, and many others for the soldiers and settlers. To all of which the estate of the captain and his Indians contributed a great deal, so that, all this work worth many ducats,[1] did not cost the royal Treasury four hundred.

The fort being built, he pacified many different tribes of Indians, as well as those who had rebelled as others who never been subjugated, and conquered others with the force of arms, and to secure himself from their habitual rebellions he persuaded them to move and to come to live near to the said fort under the protection of his weapons, where he had them instructed in the faith, and civilized, engaging them in cultivation of the fields.[2] And in order to keep the communication with the Marañón secure, he ordered a road to be opened from the said Pará as far as the Marañón fifty leagues inland from the sea, in which there are one hundred and ten leagues, and in the middle he had a village established for the relief of the travellers,[3] by the which road the trade was opened up and the rounding up of the Indians which may be enslaved according to the royal laws. Because many of these were redeemed who had been imprisoned by their enemies in order to be eaten by them, the territory became populated and fruitful,[4] the famines and privations which there were before ceased, and by this good means the deficiency of the twenty thousand ducats of supplies a year which your Majesty was wont to send and which were not

[1] Spanish. Formerly a gold coin, it was by the seventeenth century a unit of account worth 375 maravedís.

[2] See above, p. 57, n. 1.

[3] Shown on the second map 'MARANHÃO TABOÃ SEGUNDA' of the *Anonymous Atlas of Maranhão*, c. 1629, in Cortesão and Texeira da Mota, 1960, plate 600B, running from the north-east Margin of 'Lagoa Maracu', the source of one of an unnamed tributary of the river Pindaré to 'Rio Guama', tributary of the river Capary on which Belém was sited. The village at the half-way point is clearly marked.

[4] Maciel Parente is glossing over what had been truly terrible reprisals against the neighbouring Indian tribes, see above, p. 57, n. 1.

enough was not felt. In the time that the said captain governed it was not more than 8 [thousand] cruzados, and the royal revenues of these new conquests brought in more than five thousand cruzados, not yielding before more than five hundred, and each day they increase and already it has two sugar mills and other important expectations and profits.

While the *capitão-mor* continued to conquer and discover these lands and rivers with constant wars with various Indians, his engagements and battles demanding a very long history, he had information that on the other side of the river, which is nearly one hundred leagues across, there were Dutch and English, who were trading tobaccos, cottons, pepper, ginger and other drugs and dyes, and from there they were furnishing their ships with which they went to rob the Indies. Laying his ambushes for them he caught two, one of which he sent to Lisboa, and, in his letter of the 20th of April 1625, he offered himself to your Majesty to make that conquest and to throw the enemies out of it. Although your Majesty by your royal *cédula*,[1] which is attached here, accepted this offer with the promise to send him help with men, arms, munitions, vessels and provisions, and that you would do him favour according to what should result from it, he was neither given the authority that he asked to make *encomiendas*[2] from the Indians for those who should assist him, as is done in the Indies, nor any other thing before the regular supplies failed because of the capture of Bahia.[3] For all that, the said *capitão-mor* worked at it very much and with great valour and obstinacy, having many different engagements and battles by water and by land with many different tribes of very warlike Indians, some of whom fought with poisoned arrows, and

[1] Bento Maciel Parente's chronology becomes very confusing here. After routing the Dutch from the Xingu in 1623 he received further news of continued foreign settlement in the north channel and the Canal do Gurupá. He thus wrote to Philip IV, 20th April 1625, offering his services to drive them out. A royal *cédula* of 8th August 1626, granting him permission to do so, arrived after he had already despatched Pedro Teixeira, Pedro da Costa Favela and Jerónimo de Albuquerque against the intruders in May 1625. Maciel Parente did not accompany this expedition. His description of his battle against a ship 'Whilst attacking a Dutch fort', refers back to his attack on Adriaenszoon Ita's vessel in 1623.

[2] Philip IV consistently refused Maciel Parente's suggestion that the Spanish system of organizing Indian labour and tribute, *encomienda*, should be applied to Portuguese Brazil.

[3] 1624.

all instructed and assisted by the said Dutch and English. These latter came between them to more than four hundred, of whom he took and killed more than two hundred, taking from them and their Indian allies three forts with artillery, vessels, slaves, other baggage and trade goods.[1] All this was put in the royal Treasury and amounted to many thousand ducats, with which was made up the deficiency of the supplies which did not come. Whilst attacking a Dutch fort, and one of their ships coming to help them with much artillery and eighty men, the said *capitão-mor* went to meet it with nine canoes. Five being wrecked and the other three fled, he along with five men and some Indians lashed himself to the prow of the ship and fought them with arquebuse and arrows for the space of four hours so valiantly that when a relief boat and other canoes reached him, the Dutch set themselves afire. The *capitão-mor* ordered those who were swimming in the water to be killed. In the conflict four Portuguese died and some Indians. Continuing the war against their Indian allies, he conquered twelve provinces of them, namely the Guajaijaras, Tupinambas, Tocantines, Nhuanas, Aruans, Mapuazes, Pacajares, Curupas, Mariguis, Quanis, Tapuyusus, Iacares, Vguapes, Anduras and Pirapes,[2] who occupied the

---

[1] He could be referring here to the two Dutch forts on the Xingu taken by Vasconselhos in 1623 and to the third outpost said to have been destroyed by Maciel Parente before Vasconselhos' party caught up with him again. Alternatively he might be describing the destruction of Oudaen and Purcell's fort at Mandiutuba and of the plantations on the Okiari and Tauregue in 1625. The fact that he immediately goes on to describe his battle with Adriaenszoon Ita's ship would suggest that he is describing the events of 1623.

[2] Maciel Parente pinpointed the territories of these tribes on the three maps in the *Anonymous Atlas of Maranhão, c.* 1629; see Cortesão and Texeira, 1960, V, plates 600 A, B, D and below, fig. IX. The '*PROVINCIA DOS GUAJAJARAS*' is marked in Maranhão up the river Pindaré; that of the *TUPINAMBAS* up the coast, lying inland between the rivers Tucy and Guararopy (Gurupi); the '*PROVINCIA DOS TACANTINS*' is shown E. of the '*Braço do Pará*' (Tocantins); the Nhuanas are probably the '*NHEENGHAIBA*' marked as living W. of the Ilha Marajó. The '*PROVINCIA E ILHAS DARUANS*' appears to be the present Ilha Caviana. The Mapuazes are sited on small islands just W. of those occupied by the Nheenghaiba. Maciel Parente locates the Pacajares and Mapuazes between what he calls the '*Brazo do Pacajar*' and '*Braço do Parnayba*', clearly meant to be somewhere in the territory between the rivers Pacajá and Xingu. The Uguape and Anduras are placed between his '*Braço do Pará*' or Tocantins and the Pacajá, and the Pirapes between the same closer to '*LAGO DORADO*'. The Iacares are located on the island between the Xingu and the south margin of his '*GRAN CANAL DAS AMAZONAS*', the Ilha Grande do Gurupá. The '*TAPUYOSSUS*' reside on what should be the north margin of the latter. The '*MORIGUIZ*' inhabit the north shore of the Amazon close to Cabo do Norte. See also Maciel Parente's references to the territories of these tribes, pp. 316–17.

territories from the Marañón to the river Vicente Pincón,[1] in which there are more than two hundred and thirty leagues of coastline, and many others inland, and more than two thousand towns with infinite people, without counting others which he was not able to visit. All are under obedience to your Majesty, through the supplicant's great valour and the spilling of his blood, who suffered many wounds and some injuries. The encounters and wars which he had with them demand a very long account, which he carried out with the very greatest profits, much more than he offered in the said letter without the assistance which he requested for it, and was commanded to be given to him by your Majesty's aforementioned *cédula*. Because of all which he is confident that your Majesty's royal generosity will be pleased to honour him and order him to be attended to, making use of his person in important posts, esteeming his person and honouring him for his valour, prudence and good fortune with which he hopes to do even greater services for your Majesty, as will be seen in the other separate document which he submits.

Bento Maciel Parente

6. REPORT OF A VISIT TO THE ENGLISH AND IRISH SETTLEMENTS BETWEEN 22ND OCTOBER AND 4TH DECEMBER 1623, BY WALLOON SETTLERS BROUGHT OUT TO THE RIVER BY THE DUTCH WEST INDIA COMPANY[2]

On Monday the 16th[3] the wind South East and afterwards East South East – our course West South West, in order to enter the River

Amazons. At noon we reached 1 degree 35 minutes. At this time we caught sight of a ship which was coming the same way. Having joined it, we found it was Pieter Jansz of Flixingues [Flushing], who left Pleimouth[4] before us. We went on together, our course to the West a quarter South. In the evening we again saw the North star.

[1] The river Wiapoco.

[2] 'Journal du voyage faict par les pères des familles envoyés par Messieurs les Directeurs de la Compagnée des Indes occidentales pour visiter la coste de Gujane', B.L., MS Sloane 179B. The translation here is that made by R. W. Forest, ed. *A Walloon family in America* (Boston, 1914), II, 191–235.

[3] October.

[4] The *Pigeon* and Pieter Jansz's vessel, the *Mackerel*, had been driven into Plymouth by bad weather at the outset of their respective voyages, B.L., MS Sloane 179B, ff. 2, 2v.

On Tuesday the 17th the wind East a quarter South – our course West a quarter South. At noon we were but 1 degree 5 minutes North of the Line.

On Wednesday the 18th the same wind and the same course. At noon we were but 47 minutes. We now steered South West a quarter South.

On Thursday the 19th the wind East – our course as before. At noon we were North 35 minutes. We now noticed the water show pale and found the bottom at 23 fathoms, which made us run West. At 3 o'clock we sounded and found ten fathoms, sandy bottom; in the evening we found 8 fathoms, which made us run West a quarter North; at midnight we put to the North West to reach the Cap de Nord and two hours afterwards we anchored in 7 fathoms, sandy bottom.

On Friday the 20th at 6 o'clock in the morning we weighed anchor – the wind East – running North West. At noon we were in latitude 1 degree 53 minutes North. Two hours afterwards we saw the Cap de Nord to the West North West of us, land low and overflowed. It was 50 days since we had left Pleimouth. We made for the side which projects into the Amazon, and trends South South West, coasting all the time in 8, 7, or 5 fathoms of water. Very soon we saw the first island, towards which we ran and keeping to the right of it anchored about the middle.

On Saturday the 21st we weighed anchor, coasting along the island, so near that one could easily throw a stone upon it, which we did, also passing by the others but not so near, until having come to the right of the River of   we crossed towards the island of Sapno, making for the village.[1] This village has three long houses built on high piles on the edge of the river. The Maraons[2] Indians told us that the Spaniards were up the river and that they had taken a Dutch ship near Sapanopoke,[3] which set us pursuing them, after having obtained some fresh provisions; but Pieter Janss grounded himself on a sand-bank to the East of the village about two musket shots off, which forced us to anchor.

On Sunday Pieter Janss sent his pinnace towards Sapanopoke. At high tide we weighed anchor but Pieter Janss ran aground again.

---

[1] The village and island of that name off the present Canal do Gurijuba.
[2] Arua, see above, p. 25, n. 1.
[3] Ihla do Pará, opposite the river Anauíra-pucu, see above, p. 75, n. 1.

On Monday we weighed anchor again, seeing that Pieter Janss was making us waste time on purpose to give his pinnace an opportunity to trade with the English and the Irish. We ran South East towards a little island between Sapno and Quariane, not coasting near Sapno by reason of the sand-bank which comes from the point of Wetalj.[1] From there we ran South South West towards the island of Arouen,[2] but Pieter Janss ran his boat on a sand-bank which comes from the north point of the island of Arouen. We passed lower down in a strong current of 2 fathoms of water, and came to anchor half-way down the said island before a village.

On Tuesday the 24th Pieter Janss came to find us. At high tide we weighed anchor, coasting along the shore of the island, but when we wished to pass from the extremity of that island to the mainland Pieter Janss ran aground again, and we returned to coast along the islands, anchoring West a quarter South of Cocqs Island.[3]

On Wednesday the 25th we were anchored to the East a quarter North of Rooden hoec.[4]

On Thursday the 26th we ran towards the said Rooden hoec, running West a quarter South, passing between two sand-banks; but on approaching the land we saw some rocks at the distance of a musket shot from the said Roden houc, which kept us more in the offing. We passed between the mainland and the island of Tapelraka by a channel 300 paces wide and 4 and 5 fathoms deep.[5] The island of Tapelraka and the mainland are raised above the level of the water more than 15 feet. At the outlet of the channel we saw a high island at the mouth of a beautiful and deep river, where we anchored, thinking that this was Sapanopoko.

On Friday we came out of the said river, running towards the North point of Sapanopoko, but we grounded on a sand-bank near two little islands which are between the islands of Sapanapoko and

[1] Laet (1633), bk. 17, 631, (1640), bk. 17, 591, described Wetalj as a point of land on the north bank of the Amazon extending eastward into the river. The island of 'Quariana' lay one league farther E. Hessel Gerritsz's illustrative chart places Point 'Waetali' approximately 83″ N.

[2] Caviana, see above, pp. 24–5.

[3] See above, p. 74. Laet (1633), bk. 17, 632, (1640), bk. 17, 571, describes this as a long island in the middle of the channel off Roohoeck, or Red Cliff.

[4] Red Cliff, modern Point Macapá, so named because of the bluff of *terra firme* which dominates the river bank.

[5] Laet (1633), bk. 17, 632, (1640), bk. 17, 571, gives the name 'Appelrack' to both an island and the deep channel which divided it from the north shore, lying one and one half leagues W. of Roohoeck, Macapá.

Tapelraka, where we lay high and dry. At high tide we barely managed to float off, and ran towards the village of Sapanapoko, coasting all the time along the island on a good bottom. There we anchored. We found that Pieter Janss, whom we had left aground, had already assembled the English and Irish. They assured us that Pieter Arianss[1] of Flixegue had been attacked by a large Spanish ship which had 8 bronze cannon and 120 matchlocks and that, after fighting for a day and a night, having only 32 men and two small pieces of cannon and seeing he could not save himself from being run aground on a sand-bank at the mouth of the Okiari he had set fire to his ship.[2]

On Saturday we got our pinnace ready.

On Monday [Sunday] the 29th we weighed anchor to go to the Okiari river, where the English were living. We passed the equinoctial line, which crosses a little island between the village of Sapanapoko and Caillepoko.[3]

On Tuesday [Wednesday] the 1st of November we arrived near Pieter Janss anchored in Tauregne river, (sic) where the Irish live.[4]

On Thursday we were anchored before Okiari river 40 minutes to the South of the line, between the same and an island opposite. The same day we were taken to see Tilletille, an English settlement six leagues within the said river and one league inland. We found it an agreeable place, being an open country studded with little groves and some small lakes, but the place is for the most part arid.

On Saturday the 4th we arrived at our ship.

On Sunday the 5th we were taken to Ouarmeonaka among the English settlements, five leagues higher than the other and on the same river. This also was an agreeable site. In both places the English had many fields for planting Tobacco.

On Tuesday the 7th having returned to the ship, the Master asked us if these places pleased us, to which we replied No! – not for establishing families there, because the Spaniard,[5] being already settled at Pará, from which place he could come and go as he liked with the help of the tides in the river Amazons, if he knew there

[1] Pieter Adriaenszoon Ita.
[2] See above, p. 78.
[3] Laet (1633), bk. 17, 632, (1640), bk. 17, p. 571, places 'Callepoke' on the right-hand bank of the river passing upstream. Hessel Gerritsz's map marks it as a village or settlement just above the Equator.
[4] See above, pp. 45–6.   [5] Portuguese.

were families there, would not fail to visit them to their death; so that it was thought better to go along the coast to look for some river to which the enemy, if he came there from Pará or Maragnon [Maranhão], could not return without going to the Essores [Azores] to pick up the wind, and could not bring any Indians.

On Thursday the 9th of December [November] we left Okiary to return to Sapanapoko.

On Saturday the 11th we arrived at Sapanapoko.

On Friday the 17th the Master, seeing that he could neither leave us nor induce us to stay with the English, delivered to the English 150 lbs. of Coucaul,[1] 150 axes, and a barrel of powder containing 100 lbs. After having made a compact with them in the name of the Company[2] he gave them a feast, and as he ordered that the cannon be fired and hurried the gunner to do it, the cannon ball cut the mast of our pinnace and wounded three people. This led to a quarrel between the Master and the sailor who brought him the news on shore where they were drinking, which grew so violent that the Master was twice wounded with a knife. Finally, when they were getting him, weak with wine and loss of blood, to the ship, he fell into the water and was all but drowned.

On Saturday the 18th the mast of the pinnace was mended.

On Sunday the 19th the English left, our pinnace conveying them and their belongings.

On Sunday the 26th we set sail from Sapanapoko and came to anchor at Tapelraka.

On Monday the 27th we came to anchor before Roden houc and landed with many prayers. We found a very beautiful country covered with meadows, where there was very good land. We found much fruit called Gujaves,[3] which are of the size of a small orange with very good flavour. Walking about the country we found a cemetery full of earthen pots of different shapes and designs and in them bones of the dead.[4]

---

[1] Not identified.

[2] Dutch West India Co.

[3] Probably the Guava, *Psidium guajava* which has orange-coloured fruits. The Genipa also has an edible, orange-like fruit.

[4] Urn burial sites are common on the Ilhas do Marajó and Caviana, some of those on Caviana having been found to contain European glass beads, knives, axes and brass bells indicating that the practice was still continuing in the early seventeenth century. The Arua, who inhabited the two latter islands and part of the north bank in this period, practiced urn burial. Funerary urns have also been

On Tuesday the 28th we crossed from the mainland towards the islands, where we ran aground between Cocqs Island and the other islands.

On Wednesday the 29th we anchored near Arouen island.

On Thursday the last day of November we anchored opposite the village of Arouen.

On Friday 1st December we came opposite Sapno and thence to Nutte Muscade[1] Island.

On Saturday we came to anchor near the last-named island.

On Sunday the 3rd we anchored about the middle of it.

On Monday we anchored three leagues from Cap du Nord.

On Tuesday the 5th we anchored three leagues out at sea above the cape.

7. BERNARD O'BRIEN'S ACCOUNT
OF IRISH ACTIVITIES IN THE AMAZON, 1621–4[2]

Sire:

Captain general Don Bernardo Obrien del Corpio [Carpio][3] says, that his father Sir Cornelio Obrien being, in Ireland, a noble gentleman of the house of the conde de Tomonia [Thomond] one of the most ancient and illustrious of that country, and lord of three estates in which he used to hold three castles, was taken by the English in the year of 1621 and accused of following the catholic party in the wars of that kingdom and of being in the service of the Spanish Crown, and they confiscated his inheritance and goods.[4]

At this time the supplicant, being 17 years of age, was in England, in London, where he as also with an English gentleman called Sir Henrique Ro [Henry Roe],[5] who had been a partner of Sir

---

discovered on a small tributary of the river Maraca which enters the north bank of the Amazon almost at the Equator, just upstream from where Forest was walking. See Meggers, 'The Archaeology of the Amazon basin', *HSAI*, 1963, III, 149–60; with C. Evans, 'Archaeological investigations', 1957.

[1] Nutmeg Island. See above, p. 192, n. 3, below, pp. 279, 285.

[2] Translation. A.G.I., Seccion 5, Indiferente General, legajo 1872, first published in the original Spanish by T. G. Mathews in *Caribbean Studies*, X (1970), 89–106.

[3] See below, p. 302, n. 3.

[4] See above, p. 74, n. 1.

[5] Presumably Sir Thomas Roe, see above, p. 73, n. 2.

Francisco Draque [Francis Drake] and Sir Valterio Ralyo (Walter Ralegh] in their voyages. To whom certain nobles and commoners of England, with a commission from King James,[1] gave a ship of 200 tons with artillery and provisions to follow up the discoveries of Sir Francisco and Sir Valterio, and to make a foothold and settlement in the great river of the Amazon, of the which country information and great report was held of being rich and very profitable and it had not been settled before by white men. Sir Henrique Ro departed in this vessel in the aforementioned year of 1621 with 124[2] persons and the supplicant went amongst them, without discussing it with his relatives or friends, because of the desire he had to see countries and strange things.

They arrived at the margin of the river Amazon, and, sailing up it about 10 leagues, came to the village and plantation of Indians named Sipinipoca.[3] They established good relations with them, explaining themselves at first by signs until they came to understand the language, which they themselves [the Indians] call Arrua. They went about 60 leagues further up the river to a place which formerly the natives called Pataví, and ever since Cocodivae.[4] Here Sir Henrique disembarked 16 persons, 12 Irish, and 4 English who were servants to the Irish, all of them catholics, leaving them to the supplicant as captain, and ordering him to maintain the friendship of the Indians and sustain himself there until he sent him help from England or Ireland. For this he delivered to him a large amount of beads, bracelets, knives, mirrors, boys' whistles, combs, axes and other different small things. The said Sir Francisco (sic)[5] returning in the ship did not send them help in three years.

In the meantime the supplicant, who had soon learned the language of the Indians, even though he was winning their friendship, built, notwithstanding, for his own safety and that of the other 15 christians a wooden and earthen fort, surrounding it with

---

[1] Clearly a reference to the Amazon Co.

[2] O'Brien most probably sailed with Roger North in 1620, see above, pp. 72–4.

[3] Sapno.

[4] See above, p. 74.

[5] O'Brien must mean Sir 'Francisco Draque' here, whom he refers to earlier. The most charitable explanation that might be offered is that he had, after sixteen years, forgotten the exact names of the organizers of his first expedition to the Amazon. To my mind a more likely one is that he was anxious to conceal from Philip IV that he had first willingly gone out to the river with Roger North under the auspices of the English Amazon Co.

a ditch, and for its defence he had 40 muskets with powder and munitions and other weapons. The Indians there followed many different chiefs, whom they called *bateros*,[1] and they have continual quarrels and wars amongst themselves. Their weapons are wooden swords,[2] stone axes which have a handle of heavy wood two cubits long,[3] bows and cane arrows with tips of stone, or of bone or very hard wood,[4] wooden spears longer than the height of a man, tipped at the top like the arrows and some of them poisoned,[5] and large wooden four-cornered targets.[6] The supplicant, going out sometimes to help the Indians of his plantation and district, gained the victory for them with muskets and strategy, and by this won them to his side, and obliged them to cultivate tobacco and cotton for him, and to give him the food and drink of that country.

Amongst the Irish were 4 good scholars and latinists who resolved to bring the knowledge of God to the Indians, who had no religion nor did they worship anything as a god or idol. The christians persuaded more than two thousand of them that there was a God, paradise with relief from care, and a hell with torments after life.

After the supplicant had been there a year he went, with four others of the Irishmen carrying five muskets and trade goods, about seven hundred leagues up the Amazon by water and by land,[7] taking always about fifty armed Indians as guides, helpers and interpreters from one village to another, and four canoes. They reached country where they saw no men but many women, which

---

[1] Not identified.

[2] O'Brien appears to be alluding to the paddle-like, hardwood war club used by the Tupinamba. Métraux, 'The Tupinamba', *HSAI*, 1963, III, 119, describes it as consisting 'of two parts: a long rounded handle and a flattened, round or oval blade with sharp edges'. Some Caribs used a wooden, dagger-shaped club; J. Gillin, 'Tribes of the Guianas', ibid., p. 852.

[3] Métraux states that 'Tupinamba stone axes were hafted with a withy bent double around their butts and held fast with a bast', ibid., 109.

[4] See above, p. 144, n. 2.

[5] A thrusting spear.

[6] Lowie, 'The tropical forests', *HSAI*, 1963, III, 34, states that shields vary greatly in make and shape amongst the South American forest tribes, but are most commonly circular and covered with Tapir hide. Oblong shields of lightwood were recorded amongst the Caribs of Cayenne in the early historic period.

[7] O'Brien may have made the initial part of this journey with William White. Harcourt, see above, p. 240, states that White's party picked up rumours about Amazons.

the Indians call *Cuna Atenare*, which means masculine women, to the christians – Amazons. These have very small right breasts like men, [treated] by arts so that they do not grow, in order to shoot arrows, and the left breasts are as large as other women's. They are armed like the Indians. Their queen, who is called *Cuna muchu*,[1] which means great woman or lady, was at that time on an island in the river. The supplicant sent to her in his canoe an Indian woman as an ambassadress, and she carried for her a mirror and a Dutch linen shirt as a gift and sample of the merchandise he was carrying, and orders that she should say that he had not gone to harm her; rather if it would please her that she should look at what he was sending to her, and if she was pleased, that he might go and speak with her; that she should send him hostages. She sent him three of the most distinguished of her women and asked him to go and speak with her. He did so. She asked him if it was he who had sent the gift. He said yes. She asked him what he wanted. He replied peace and permission to pass through her kingdom and to trade in it. She replied that it was granted to him and gave three of her slaves in exchange for trade goods. He had her dressed in the Dutch linen shirt, of which she was very proud, and at the end of a week, when he took his leave promising to return, she and her subjects signified that they were grieved by his departure.

The supplicant went up river to a country where there were Indians so fierce that in no way would they meet him nor did they wish to speak with him. Therefore he went back down the same river again and, presently, by another river which departs from it and runs through the country called Harauaca, where there are crystalline and other glittering stones which the Indians value greatly as good for treatment of melancholy and troubles of the spleen. They descended by the river to the coast, where the river is called Serenan, from there (from the North) they came back by land to the mouth of the Amazon, and from there they returned to their fort at Cocodivae.[2]

At this time a ship from Holland arrived at the river Amazon,

---

[1] Hemming states that this is the Inca term for 'Great Lady'; *Red gold*, 1978, p. 225.

[2] See above, pp. 74–5. Robert Harcourt reported 'Topases' with 'as good a lustre as any Diamond', in the so-called 'Signiory of Coosheberry' (Cassipore), north of the river Connawini near Mount Cowob or Canopi; *Relation*, 1613, p. 15, 1626, p. 19, Harris, *Relation*, 1928, pp. 80–1, 157.

whose captain was named Abstan.[1] They sent to ask the supplicant that he might think it good that they should settle nearby, and that he might give them an interpreter to trade with the Indians, and they would establish good relations with him and agreements according to his liking. He answered them that he had four thousand warlike Indians in his alliance thereabouts, and would have more if it should be necessary. With them he was not only intending to keep the river but also to extend into more territory, and that thus the Dutch should depart. They went from there to the river Coropá,[2] near the conquest of Gran Pará, where they began their settlement help coming to them from Holland and sending there tobacco and cotton.

After the supplicant had been there for three years making different journeys by land, rivers and islands, there arrived at the mouth of the river Amazon another ship, and he, thinking that it was the relief that was come, went aboard and found that it was a Dutch warship and that it was accompanied by a pinnace. The supplicant, entrusting the authority that he held to another Irishman called Don Philippe Porzel [Philip Purcell],[3] agreed with the captain of the Dutchmen that he should carry him to the Old World with tobacco and cotton he possessed. The Dutchman, very willing because of the shortage of tobacco that there was in Holland and Ireland at that time, accepted him. Having departed from the river Amazon, they doubled Cabo de Norte and reached the river of Canoa,[4] which is in two and a half degrees of [latitude]. From there they passed to the river Dulce,[5] which is in three degrees, and to the South of Serenam in 6:[6] From here to the Gulf of Paria in 7 degrees,[7] from there to the rivers Orinoco and Guiana in 7 degrees[8] and further to the Island of Trinidad in 8,[9] by the eastern cape to

---

[1] Nicholas Oudaen, see above, pp. 79–80.

[2] The Canal do Gurupá. The Dutch and Irish settlement under Nicholas Oudaen and Philip Purcell, Mandiutuba, lay close to the mouth of the Xingu not far from the river Maxipana.

[3] See above, p. 43, n. 4.

[4] Cunany or Connawini 2°55′ N.(?).

[5] O'Brien may mean the Wiapoco, 3°54′ N. here.

[6] Surinam. O'Brien's latitude is approximately correct.

[7] The Gulf of Paria between eastern Venezuela and the west coast of Trinidad, lies between 10° N. and 10°50′ N.

[8] The Orinoco delta stretches between 8°30′ N. and 10° N.

[9] Trinidad lies between 10° N. and 11° N. O'Brien incorrectly places the Gulf of Paria south of Trinidad.

the Island of Tabago, from there to Cumaná in nine and a half degrees,[1] to the Tortuga (which is mainland not an island),[2] to the Island of Margarita in 11 degrees,[3] here to the coast of Caracas, to the Island of Corosao, to the Island of Buenos Ayres in 11½ Degrees.[4] They sighted Española in 18 degrees.[5] They went to the coast of the Island of Cuba: from there to the Islands of S. Christoval, Monserrate, San Martín, Antigua, Guadalupe, Santa Catholina, Nieves, Barbados and Vermuda: they came by the Islands of the Azores in 39 degrees,[6] from there to Flores and Corva:[7] finally they reached Zeeland. In all this time the Dutch were surveying the capes, rivers, shorelines and harbours, and they took 8 Portuguese ships laden with sugar and other cargo, and they gave account of all of this to the Council of Zeeland.[8]

The supplicant sold his tobacco and cotton for 16,000 *escudos*,[9] worth ten silver *reales*, and took part of the money and a letter to collect more in London, England and Dublin, Ireland. In London he gave account of his exploits and settlement to the English lords,[10] and they requested him to return with the relief which they were sending to the Amazon.[11] He told them that he could not at that time because he had news that his father was imprisoned in Ireland, accused of the crime of treason. They gave him letters from the king of England to the viceroy of Ireland, that he should release his father freely and send the supplicant back again shortly to England. With the letters his father was released, giving securities, to appear when they called him, and the supplicant paying the four thousand *escudos* for his expenses in prison, but they did not return his three castles, nor more than a sixth of his lands,[12] and in claiming the rest the supplicant delayed until the supply ship departed.

---

[1] The correct latitude should be 10°29′ N.
[2] It is hard to know what would have led O'Brien to believe this.
[3] Approximately correct.   [4] Bonaire 12° N.
[5] Correct. It lies between 18° N. and 20° N.
[6] 38° N.   [7] Part of the Azores group.
[8] The Zeeland Chamber of the Dutch West India Co.
[9] Standard Spanish gold coin, valued at 440 maravedís from 1609 on. The Spanish silver *real* equalled 34 maravedís.
[10] Presumably the former Amazon Co.
[11] See above, p. 79, n. 3.
[12] There is no trace of this anywhere in the surviving State Papers Domestic or Irish for these years. For a discussion of O'Brien's possible parentage, if indeed he was as well-connected as he claimed, see above, p. 74, n. 1.

8. A DUTCH EXPEDITION TO THE WIAPOCO
CONTACTS SURVIVORS FROM THE AMAZON COLONIES
DESTROYED BY THE PORTUGUESE IN 1625[1]

Up to the present we have given account of what our fleets and ships which were sent out last year have done; we now pass on to write of those which started out this year of 1627. We will begin with the three ships which the Zeeland Chamber outfitted; the which are, the *Ter Vere*, of 90 lasts, equipped with 14 culverins and 6 stone-throwers,[2] manned by 73 seamen, having as admiral and captain Hendrick Jacobsz Lucifer, a brave naval hero; the *Leeuwinne*, of 100 lasts, equipped with 14 culverins and 6 stone-throwers, having 69 seamen, the master, and vice-admiral Jan Pietersz; and the *Vlieghenden Draeck* of 45 lasts, equipped with 8 culverin and 6 stone-throwers, 42 men , the master Galeyn van Stapels.[3] These left from before Vlissinghen [Flushing] on the 22nd of January of this current year of 1627 and had such good speed that, having sailed by the Canary Islands and along the coast of Africa, they sighted the low land of the North Forland of the famous river Amazon on the 3rd of March. They had much rain and wind since it was the depth of winter there.[4] The next day they held along the coast N.N.W. in heavy thunder and rain, so that sometimes they saw the land, and sometimes again not. On the 5th they dropped anchor in 4 fathoms of water, about 2 miles from Comaribo.[5] They sailed the next day to the river Wiapoco, where they had orders to land some colonists.

On the 7th they dropped anchor before Caribote[6] in 3 fathoms of water, and with low water grounded. Since the Indians who lived about that place did not come on board, two shallops were sent to

---

[1] Translation. Johannes de Laet, *Iaerlyck verhael van der verrichtinghen der geoctroyeerde West-Indische Compagnie in derthien boecken* (1644), pt. I, bk. 4, from the edn. of pt. I, bks. 4–7 by S. P. L'Honore Naber (The Hague, 1932), 16–8.

[2] See above, p. 251, n. 2.

[3] Lucifer and Van Stapels had taken out Oudaen and Purcell's colonists to the Amazon in 1624, see above, p. 80, n. 1.

[4] See above, p. 142, n. 6.

[5] Harcourt, *Relation*, 1613, p. 41, 1626, p. 55, Harris, *Relation*, 1928, p. 110, refers to 'Gomeribo' as 'the uttermost point of land to the northward in the bay of Wiapoco'.

[6] Caripo. According to Harcourt, *Relation*, 1613, pp. 6–7, 1626, p. 10, Harris, *Relation*, 1928, p. 71, this was an Indian village 'scituate upon the east side of the hil in the mouth of Wiapoco'.

Comaribo to fetch some of the same on board. Thus the next day they brought two who would lead them to the other inhabitants. Going up river once more in the shallops, they came to a place called Wacogenive by the inhabitants. There only two small houses were found. They well perceived that the savages, taken by surprise, ran away at the arrival of our people, but they could not resolve the reason why. The next day they inspected the site and they found the same very suitable for the people they had to set down here. Thus on the 10th they began to unload the goods of the same and brought them ashore. The Savages, who were afraid, took to flight. They understood the proper cause first on the 13th from a Black, who came to them and told them that christians had come from the river Amazon in a ship and two shallops, and they had held out here for a month. They then distributing themselves amongst four sites thereafter, the Savages had overrun them unexpectedly and killed them all, except for three, one of whom was in Comaribo and the other two higher up the river Wiapoco. Our people having understood this, held three savages and a woman which were on board fast and sent to Camaribo for the Dutchman, threatening to kill the imprisoned savages if they did not bring him to them. The next day the same was brought on board, but they got few answers from him because he had almost forgotten his mother tongue, a strange thing. Thus the other two were sent for, who first came aboard on the 17th.

Then one, named Jan Hendricksz, told them the whole occasion of this slaughter. That about eighteen months ago the Spaniards or Portuguese came in large numbers and suddenly fell upon the colony in the river Amazon which was left there under the command of Captain Oudaen. The latter, after he had for half a day defended valiantly against the enemy, had repaired to his ship with the loss of seven or eight men, and sailed with same to the creek where the English entertained them with some food for exchange. The captain having landed with eleven or twelve men amongst the English, the enemy entered in the same creek with their canoes and overcame and put to death the English and the Dutch.[1] The Lieutenant Pieter de Bruyne hearing this the next day, fled with the ship and the forty-six men that were yet remaining to the river Wiapoco, and settled himself there, hoping that they were

[1] See above, pp. 80–1, 84.

safe. But after they had been there two or three days, the Sergeant Matruyt shot the lieutenant, and the people scattered themselves into four places. The Savages in the meantime, having determined amongst themselves to rid 'them of these guests, came to them under the pretence of friendship with their drink which they call Pernau,[1] and having made the people wholly drunk, fell upon them with a great shout, and with hatchets and broad knives grievously put them to death. These three aforementioned alone they spared. Although this atrocious deed rightly required a great punishment, nevertheless because the company purposed to place and hold a colony here,[2] they found it adviseable to bear with the inhabitants of that region, who showed great sorrow over this deed, promising the Netherlanders to be loyal henceforward and to hurt them no more.

9. STATEMENT BY GEORGE EVELING [1627][3]

[f. 111] That understandinge of a great Trade that some volenteers of our Countryes made in the West India (which traffique they maynetayned by the commerce they had with the ffluisshingers) I about fower years since[4] sent a Servant of my owne caled Thomas ffanninge, willinge him to lett mee understand the certaynetye thearof: the which accordinglye hee did with conforma-

---

[1] Harcourt, *Relation*, 1613, p. 28, 1626, p. 36, Harris, *Relation*, 1928, p. 94, describes a 'kinde of drinke of cassavi, called Parranow, very good and strong much like unto our best beere in England. . .'.

[2] Jan van Ryen settled on the river with 36 colonists under the Zeeland Chamber of the Dutch West India Co. All but four or five of his men were wiped out by the Indians.

[3] P.R.O., CO 1/5, ff. 111–2v. Undated. George Eveling Esq. became a member of the Guiana Co. after 1627. Although his statement is undated it was most likely composed in the summer or autumn of 1627. There are two indicators as to its date. It was obviously written in response to a complaint from the Guiana Co. that Eveling had infringed their patent, conferred 19th May 1627. Eveling had negotiated with Abraham van Pere of Flushing about joining with him in the settlement of the river Berbice. Van Pere put the proposal for his Berbice colony before the Dutch West India Co. in March 1627 and sailed for the river in July. It would appear that Roger North and the Guiana Co. had acted quickly to block Eveling's activities. His statement does not suggest that he did manage to send colonists with van Pere, but it does read as if it was written after the latter had departed. Williamson, *English colonies*, 1923, p. 103, dated this statement *c.* 1623.

[4] 1623 or 1624. Fanning was probably sent out in a Dutch ship, see above, p. 79.

cion of all what I had heard, and desired to bee supplyed onlye with twentye menn by whose strength hee shewed mee mannifest reasons hee could mayntayne as good a trade as annye of the other ffactoryes (whoe some of them had returned above fourtye thowsand powndes in one year uppon lesse then three hundred powndes Cargasone) wheare uppon I not onlye labored to send him the sayd 20 menn but strove all I could to have gathered strength sufficient to have transported 60 – or 100 – menn, but after I had with great labour and exspense proved all the gentrye, and marchants of my acquayntance and could not possible perswade them to joyne to sett fourth Shippinge into those partes to reduce that beneficiall trade heither I resolved by meanes of the ffluissingers to transport such menn as I was able of my selfe to sett fourth (which wear twentye /and that God prosperinge us I might in time have meanes to reduce the sayd comerce to our owne Countryes. But when I came to fflushinge I thear heard as I had doone here that the Portugalls had surprised all our Countryemenn and the Dutch [f. 111v] in soe much that the west India Companye thear would send noe more Shippinge to the Amasones untill they had certayne newse of the proceedinge of thear people and ours theare: to which intent they had (imediatlye uppon that ill newse) sent three shipps departinge by monnthes distances the first settinge sayle in October last:[1] whose returne they daylye expected. But to other ports of the same coast they had three Shipps and twoe Pinnaces designed: Soe I seeinge smale hope of the Amasones without a powerfull Navye to regayne it I resolved to joyne with one of the west India Governors called Abraham van Pere and that wee should settle a trafique at river of Berbeeces the Dutch to have the one side of the River and the English the other, beeinge confident by this meanes to make apeere unto our State the great proffitt and Honnor that might bee gayned in settlinge a trade in those parts which I cannot conceive to bee inferior to Peru or Mexico.

It is trew that while I was solicitinge this buissnes I found Captayne Roger North and Captayne Leake[2] uppon the same

---

[1] Most probably October 1626. It is noteworthy that Lucifer's fleet, which took out Jan van Ryen's colonists to the Wiapoco made no attempt to enter the Amazon in March 1627, probably indicating that they knew that there were no Dutch settlers left on the river.

[2] Captain Simon Leake, listed in the Guiana Co. patent, see below, p. 294, n. 4.

buissnes, and haveinge often conferred with them I sawe noe possibillitye of proceedinge.

I have doone all things soe cleere that I never did annye thinge private but alltogether publique and had I intended annye waye sinisterlye I was not ignorant of the wayes how to have performed it and could have saved a great part of the charge that I have byne at, meerelye to bennifitt our Countrye –

[f. 112] The Comodityes which are staple comodityes are

Sugers and Tabacco

Cotton woll

Annotto dye

India fflex[1]

Hunnye

weax[2]

[G]auacum[3]

Speckled wood[4]

and divers sortes of other woods for diers and potthicaryes use as all soe severall herbes and plantes which are excellent druggs abound-ance of *Corns* Almondes[5] much better then those of Spayne allsoe ginger[6] in aboundance allsoe thear is the [T]unall[7] trees which bear the Cuchinillia and the [herbe] that maketh the Annill[8] with divers other Comodityes. Allsoe our Cattle beeinge carried theather by reason of the continuall Summer increase much from which great proffitt will bee drawne.

---

[1] See below, p. 279, n. 2. This allusion to flax, or 'silke grasse' as Harcourt calls it below, presumably refers to the hemp fibre of any of the bromeliaceous plants, see above, p. 148, n. 1.

[2] Harcourt, *Relation*, 1613, pp. 28–9, 1626, p. 36, Harris, *Relation*, 1928, p. 95, comments on the 'great store of hony in the Country . . . being taken out of trees and buries in the earth. . . . The hony and the waxe, are also good commodities for merchandise'.

[3] Presumably the resin *guaiacum* of the lignum vitae, *Guajacum officinale* and holywood lignum vitae, *G. sanctum*.

[4] See above, p. 164, n. 4.

[5] It is difficult to know which of the many kinds of nuts available in the Amazonian forest Eveling is referring to. He may mean the nut of the *Pequi* or *Piqui*, 'Almendras del Brasil', *Caryocar brasiliensis*.

[6] Lawrence Keymis, 'Of the second voyage', 1596, in *Principal navigations* (1600), III, 675, (1903–5), X, 458, speaks of the 'Wiapassa' root with a flavour like that of ginger.

[7] See above, p. 246, n. 4.

[8] The berries of the *Genipa americana*, the *Anil-trepador* and the *Anil-assi* all produce a blue, indigo-like dye.

allsoe great quantitye of the trew balsome[1] that groweth in Egipt
Allsoe gold and Silver with divers pretious stones are heere found
DOCKET: *Master* Yveling concerning his voyage to the West
Indies. Amazons

---

[1] See below, p. 279, n. 4.

TEXT V

THE CREATION OF THE GUIANA COMPANY,
1626–7

1. JOHN SMITH'S ACCOUNT[1]

Thus this Ile,[2] by this small beginning, having no interruption by their owne Countrey, hath now got the start of the Continent and maine Land of *Guiana*, which hath beene layd apart and let alone untill that Captaine *North*, ever watching his best opportunitie and advantage of time in the state, hath now againe pursued and set on foot his former designe. Captaine *Harcote* being now willing to surrender his grant, and to joyne with Captaine *North* in passing a new Patent, and to erect a company for trade and plantation in the *Amazons*, and all the Coast and Countrey of Guiana for ever.

Whereupon they have sent this present yeare in Januarie [1629],[3] and since 1628. foure ships with neere two hundred persons; [of] the first ship with 112. men, not one miscarried; the rest went since, [and are] not yet heard of, and [they] are preparing another with their best expedition:[4] and since Januarie [1629] is gone from *Holland*, 100. *English* and *Irish*, conducted by the old Planters.[5]

---

[1] Extract from Captain John Smith, *True travels*, 1630. Ch. 24, Barbour, 1986, III, 227.

[2] St Christopher's. See above, p. 238, n. 2.

[3] *True travels*, published in 1630, was entered in the Stationers' Register 29th August 1629, see Arber, *A transcript*, 1877, IV, 184.

[4] Smith's tally would include Harcourt's company of 112 which went out to the Wiapoco, a second vessel sent out in January 1629 and the two which carried out William Clovell, Thomas Hixon and their party in the summer. The vessel 'preparing with their best expedition' prior to August 1629 was probably Taylor's *Amazon* which sailed with the *Sea-Nymph* in the late summer. Smith's account would seem to have been finished well before preparations began for the despatch of the *Exchange*.

[5] See below, pp. 301–4.

2. A SUMMARY RELATION CONCERNING THE PATTENT FOR THE RIVER OF AMAZONES, & THE COUNTRIE & COAST ADJOYNING. [1625][1]

Some 5 yeares since I informed King Jeames by Peticion of his right unto those parts, requiring his Majesties Letters Pattents for the encouragement of such as should advannce the same: it was refferred unto the Counsail Table, where after full information, of his Majesties just and lawfull title, & also of the particulars of the countrie itselfe, & that the said parts were not in the present & actuall possession of the King of Spaine: their Lordshipps satisfied the King therein & procured his graunt of Letters Pattents with great immunities to such as should engage themselfes therin: Divers orders were made by the Counsail herein as being for his Majesties speciall service.[2]

Wherupon the busines went on with a great affection & cheerefullnes of the Nobilitie & Gentrie, & the Pattent past the Great Seale: & a ship & a Pinnace, the men & all the provisions being in a faire way & readines, the Spanish Agents (who had before still laboured in opposition) did now urge it to the King by Letter[3] in the highest nature, with all forging divers suggestions against me, which procured a commaund unto me in his Majesties name signified by my Lord Marshall, that I should suspend the voiage & not proceede therein till further order.[4]

At this time was I out my private estate upon the undertaking, & divers Gentlemen & other my freinds provided & depending upon my going, hereupon I repaired to the Duke of Richemond[5] who bad me not despaire, & he gott me a coppie of the Agents Letter, he delivered the King my aunswere, & returnd me word that his Majestie was satisfied on my behalfe, & had given order to Secretary Calvert that my aunswere should be put into Spanish, & sent unto

---

[1] P.R.O., CO 1/4, ff. 7–8v. Docketed 'Captain North's relation of his patent concerning the river of Amazons.' North's 'some five years since' could put this document as early as 1624 since the Amazon Co. was granted its patent in 1619. It is more likely that it was presented later in 1625, since Charles I's warrant for the issue of a patent predated the moves to publish a second edition of Harcourt's *Relation* in February 1626 and North's prospectus and *Preamble for subscription* printed March 1626.

[2] See above, pp. 190–6.   [3] See above, pp. 198–9.   [4] See above, pp. 199–201.

[5] Then Ludovic Stuart, second duke of Lennox, created earl of Richmond 1613 and duke of the same 1623.

the Agents:[1] in the meane time the Count of Gondomar came over, (who also had before his arrivall used his best meanes to hinder this proceeding) & spared neither solicitation not importunitie to stop the voiage insomuch as he came to the Counsail Table for this only busines, & did there bouldly & confidently affirme, that his Master had the actuall & present possession of these countries, but he would not heare our witnesses to the contrary.[2]

Hereupon it followed that whilst I petitioned for a free leave, I could obtaine no manner of aunswere, neverthelesse the Ship & Pinnace & all the Mariners & Landmen, were suffered to go about to Plimmouth, & I gott my Commission & agreements from the commpagnie dispatched: I continued suing at the court, whilst the compagnie at Plimmouth were in despaire of my comming & ready to disperse themselves, which forced me downe: in the meane time I desired my freinds to lett me know, how it would be taken: I staied by the way & at Plymouth some three weekes after my going from London, till I receaved Letters that all was well & that the world expected I should goe without bidding etc.

When Gondamare had knowledge that I was at sea, nothing would pacifie him but a proclamation against me for my returne, & a stop of further proceedings by the compagnie, wherein notwithstanding the busines was not disclaimed, but onely suspended for a time: & after my returne he could not gett the Goods by any Law from me.[3]

3. CHARLES I TO THE ATTORNEY GENERAL, [JAN./FEB.] 1626[4]

Warrant for Captain Northe patent for the Amazons

Whereas Roger North, and Robert Harcourt Esquires have founde out and discovered meanes by shippinge (and are desirous) to take Journeyes unto the River of the Amazons in America, aswell for the conversion of the people inhabitinge thereabouts to the Christian faith as for the enlarginge of his Majesties domynions, and setling of trade, and trafique for diverse comodities of his Majesties kingdoms with those Nations; Consideracion haveinge bene taken of the importance, and consequence of soe good a worke his Majesties

---

[1] See above, pp. 201–3.   [2] See above, pp. 203–8.   [4] See above, pp. 213–14.
[4] P.R.O., CO 1/4, ff. 17–18v. Undated. The reasons for placing it early in 1626 are discussed above. See above, pp. 85, n. 4, 276, n. 1.

pleasure is that you prepare a Bill fitt for his Signature contayninge a graunte of incorporacion to the said Roger North & Robert Harcourt and such others as they shall suffer to be incorporated with them, whereby they may have as large powers, and priviledges for carryinge over of shipps, men, amunicion and armour, and doeinge of other thinges necessarie for their voyages, and settleinge of their Company as have bene heretofore graunted to any others uppon the like undertakings, with such further priviledges as you shall thinke fitt. And that the places where they shall have their plantacion, and use their trafique shall extend upon the Continent of America from the River dissequebe[1] Southward unto the River Amazons, and from thence further Southward five degrees in latitude from any parte or branch of the said River of Amazons, and extendinge from East to West throughout the Continent from Sea, to Sea, and all Islands, and Terrytories within Twenty myles adjacent,[2] And alsoe that they shalbe free from impost for any goods by them or any of them, to be imported or exported in that service: And for soe doinge this shalbe your warrante from the Courte at Whitehall this.

4. INDUCEMENTS TO JOIN THE NEW COMPANY INCLUDED BY ROBERT HARCOURT IN THE NEW EDITION OF HIS *RELATION OF A VOYAGE TO GUIANA*, 1626[3]

[p. 80] A RECAPITULATION, OF THE COMMODITIES OF the Country: Together with an addition of the nature of the Returnes to be expected.[4]

NOw I will more at large explaine some materiall points, of the *Commodities*, and proffit of the Country: Togeather with the nature of the *Returnes* to be expected from thence, which being well and truely understood, may fully satisfie and resolve all unpartially

---

[1] Essequibo.   [2] See above, p. 85.

[3] Harcourt, *Relation*, 1626, pp. 80–3, Harris, *Relation*, 1928, pp. 159–61, see above, p. 276, n. 1. Harcourt's marginal annotations are placed in [ ] at the beginning of the paragraph they refer to.

[4] In the second edition Harcourt eliminated the material pertinent to investment in his earlier Wiapoco colony, namely his synopsis describing the suitability of Guiana for plantation and his statement of the terms of adventure, *Relation*, 1613, pp. 64–71, Harris, *Relation*, 1928, pp. 133–40, replacing it with the following 'Recapitulation'.

affected Persons, that the mony this way adventured, is upon sure grownds, and according to good Judgement.

[First of the Commodities] First, of the *Commodities*, which have rather presented themselves unto our view, than bene found out & discovered by any curious search, or Industry; They are as followeth:[1] *Sugar-canes, Cotton-woolls, Silke grasse,*[2] *Dyes in graine,*[3] *Sweete Gummes, Ambers, Balsamums,*[4] *Oyles,*[5] *Hony, Wax,*[6] some *Spices. Drugges and Simples,*[7] rich *Woods,*[8] *Feathers, Tobacco, Cristall, Jasper, Porphery, Saphyres, Topases, Spleen-stones,*[9] *Mineralls,* and plenty of wilde *Nuttmeggs,*[10] with the *Mace.*

[Secondly of the Returnes to be expected and the nature of

---

[1] All of these commodities were discussed in the 1613 edition of the *Relation*, with the exception of sapphires and nutmegs, see above, pp. 192, 263, 279.

[2] See above, p. 273, n. 1.

[3] Earlier in the *Relation*, 1613, pp. 32–3, 1626, p. 44, Harris, *Relation*, 1928, pp. 100–1 Harcourt lists Annotto, 'another berry that dyeth blew', see above, p. 273, n. 8, and unspecified woods which yield yellow, red and purple dyes. See above, pp. 57–8.

[4] Earlier Harcourt expands 'The sweet gummes of inestimable value & strange operation in Phisick & Chirurgery, are innumerable; there is yellow Amber, Gumma-Lemnia, Colliman, or Carriman, Barratta, and many more which I omit.' Ambergris is an aromatic resin specific for certain complaints; Gum elemi, *Protium heptaphyllum, P. guianense,* a white-greenish resin. 'Colliman, or Carriman', copaiba, *Copaifera officinalis,* a black, pitch-like resin, Harcourt said to be good for the cold, giddiness, back pain and gout. 'Barratta' or Balata, *Manilkara bidentata,* was excellent in the 'cure of greene wounds'. See Harcourt, *Relation,* 1613, p. 33, 1626, pp. 44–5; Harris, *Relation,* 1928, pp. 101–2.

[5] Presumably palm oil from the innumerable species in lower Amazonia.

[6] See above, p. 273, n. 2.

[7] Harcourt, *Relation,* 1613, pp. 34–5, 1626, pp. 46–7, Harris, *Relation,* 1928, pp. 102–4. By simples Harcourt means herbal medicines. In the 1613 edition he listed 'Spiknard, Cassia-Fistula, Sene; and the earth yeeldeth Bole-Armoniacke, and Terra Lemnia. ... a little greene Apple by the Indians called in their language the sleeping Apple; which in operation is so violent, that one little bit thereof doth cause a man to sleep to death: the least drop of the juce of it, will purge in a vehement and excessive manner. ... a Berry ... very excellent against the bloody-fluxe, by the Indians it is called *Kellette*. The juice of the leafe called uppee, cureth the wounds of the poisoned arrowes. The juice of the leafe called Icari, is good against the head-ache.' For the identification of the 'sleeping Apple', see Harris, op. cit., p. 103, n. 2. 'Bole-Armoniacke' and 'Terra Lemnia' were valued for their styptic and astringent qualities.

[8] Harcourt noted a 'red speckled wood', *Brosium aublettii* in the 1613 edition, p. 36, 'another hard black wood like ebony', and 'another heavy red wood, but not speckled', in the 1626 edition, p. 48, Harris, *Relation,* 1928, pp. 104–5.

[9] Spleenstones, see above p. 132, n. 1. Also said to refer to Calculi or concretions found in the stomach of some ruminant animals, particularly the manatee, *Trichechus inunguis.*

[10] See above, pp. 192, n. 3, 263, n. 1.

graine, rich *Woods, Tobacco,* &c.) We may certainly, and in present, make a *Returne* to recompence a good and reasonable Charge, even of the First voyage in transporting of men to establish the *Colonie* in those parts: which will arise, par-[p. 81] tly by trading with the Indians, and partly by dealing with our owne Countrymen there allready seated.[1]

[The second voyage] The second voyage in conveying over more men, we shall, in the Returne thereof, add to the aforesaid helps and advantages, a further proffit drawen from the *Colonie,* *consisting aswell of such as have bene* anciently there abyding, [*As may appeare by an agreement under their hands, made with Capt. North. Anno 1620.[2]] as of those there settled the first Voyage: who will be both willing, and well able to yeald and afforde the Company here in England, a *Third parte* of all the gaine, proffit, and Commodities, which they shall rayse and under gett in the Country.

[The Third Voyage;] The *Third* Voyage (still sending out more Supplyes) the Returne will bee augmented, according to the number of men and in the Country, as aforesaid, and also according to the advantage of tyme: by improving, preparing, and getting some other of the forementioned *Commodities,* which will yeald a sensible and certaine increase after a yeare, two or three: as in the *Cotton Woolls,* and *Sugar-canes,* &c. whereof more at Large, Page 41. 42. 43.[3] wherby may be conceived and concluded a Multiplying of benefitt: the Charge of the Supplyes, and setting out, remayning still the same.

[By transportation of Com*mo*dities to the Colonie] Unto this I add, as a note of noe small waight and Consideration: That forasmuch as concerneth the *Colonie,* they will bee so farre from becoming chargeable unto the adventurers and Company in England, that they will be able to afforde and yeald them a certaine gaine, for such things as shall be requisite for their use: as all manner of *Cloathing, Apparaile,* &c. And what els they shall desire, for plenty, or

---

[1] Harcourt obviously was not aware that the Portuguese had wiped out the English and Irish colonies in 1625.

[2] This would appear to be a reference to Roger North's agreement to bring back the tobacco produced by Philip Purcell's Irish colonists in return for a percentage for the Amazon Co., see above, p. 220.

[3] Reference to the 1626 edition.

superfluitie: as *Aquavitae, Wines,* &c. For it is known by the experience [p. 82] of many yeares, that the *Dutchmen* have gayned by them at least *Centum per Centum,* in all Commodities they Carried unto them; any abatement whereof by the way and meanes of their owne Country, will be very gratefull and acceptable unto them: and also proffitable to the Adventurers, and Company in *England.*

[Objection.] And because it is often objected, that the *Spaniards* when they please, may subvert and ruine our Plantation.

[Answeare.] I Answere: That the feare thereof most neerely concerneth the *Colonie* there abyding: who may, and can subsist, with reasonable care and providence, against any attempt that shall be made upon them: some testimony whereof may appeare in the former Relation, by a few dispersed men, being altogeather without Governement. *Page* 7. 8.[1] As also by the voyage of Sir *Walter Raleigh,* which was set out at a great expence, and being of thirteene saile of ships great and small, they could hardly spare and furnish so many men, as were sufficient to take the towne of Saint *Thome* in the west Indies: but by their Resolution and suddainnes on the one side; and the former securitie and present amazement of the Spaniards on the other side, having made themselves masters of the same, they were neverthelesse altogether unable either to gaine and possesse the Country, or to supplant and roote out the Spaniards, & after a months space, their provisions being spent, they were forced to quit the Countrie. And of more late experience, the Dutchmen having taken the Towne of *Todos los Santos*[2] in *Brasill,* could not for all that, get any further interest or possession of the Country by reason of the firmenesse [p. 83] of the Country people unto the *Portugalls.* And for asmuch as concerneth the Adventurers, & Company in *England*: They have farre greater advantage of the Spaniards, and many more wayes and meanes to endamage them, and secure themselves, or to recover any losse, or detriment they shall sustaine by their meanes. Neither can the Spaniard (although he were free from all other cares, incombrances, and imployments) ever assure himselfe to supplant, or Roote us out of those Countryes, whilest the

---

[1] Reference to the 1626 edition. The material Harcourt alludes to is printed above, pp. 240–2.

[2] Bahia, taken by the Dutch in 1624 and surrendered again 30th April 1625.

Natives remayne so adverse irreconciliable unto them, and so firme and Constant unto us.[1]

5. ROGER NORTH'S PROSPECTUS FOR THE GUIANA COMPANY, ISSUED CIRCA MARCH 1626.[2]

[f. 11] Breefe notes of the River Amazones, and of the coaste of Guiana, contayned in the new grant from his most excellent Majestie, unto a Corporation.[3]

[1 *Of the River of Amazones and*] THe[4] River of *Amazones* (considering the length and breadth thereof, with the mayne Channels,[5] and the number of By-rivers and Branches[6] falling into them,) is truly judged the fairest of[7] the world, although[8] the greater part, by reason of the vast Extent, hath never been passed through by any Christian, much lesse hath the Inland[9] Countries adjoyning been discovered. The wind serves constantly to sayle up the River, with the floud, and we are sure to turne it downe againe with the streame.[10]

---

[1] Harcourt's arguments for the security of the English and Irish settlements in the Amazon would be undermined as soon as the news of the Portuguese attacks upon them in the previous year became known. The Portuguese at Belém, like those at Bahia had shown that they had a firm foothold in the river and the support of the natives, even if it was obtained by brutal methods. Those who followed Harcourt's logic might reasonably argue that it was hopeless to try to dislodge the Portuguese.

[2] Three identical copies of the printed version of this prospectus exist in the P.R.O., CO 1/4, ff. 11–12, 13–14, 15–16. The transcription here is made from ff. 11–12. It was printed by Thomas Purfoot 1626. It can be dated more narrowly by reference to the slightly variant rough draft of the same (P.R.O., CO 1/4., ff. 9–10v), which was sent to the Duke of Buckingham 16th March 1626. It is written in the same secretary's hand as that of the 'Summary relation'. The differences between the draft and the printed version are noted. The marginal notations are placed in [ ] at the beginning of the paragraph they refer to.

[3] P.R.O., CO 1/4, f. 9, is entitled 'Breif noates of the busines of the Amazones.'

[4] 'This', P.R.O., CO 1/4, f. 9.   [5] 'Braunches', P.R.O., CO 1/4, f. 9.

[6] 'and Braunches', omitted P.R.O., CO 1/4, f. 9.   [7] 'in', P.R.O., CO 1/4, f. 9.

[8] 'not withstanding', P.R.O., CO 1/4, f. 9.

[9] 'Inland & continent', P.R.O., CO 1/4, f. 9.

[10] 'The winde & Tide serve to saile up the river, & we never faile to turne it downe with the streame', P.R.O., CO 1/4, f. 9. Between July and December the winds blow continually from the E., making this the best season for ascending the Amazon when dependent on sail. Between January and June, the season of heaviest rains, calms predominate interrupted by heavy squalls from the N.E. round by the W. to S.W. Navigation upriver at this time is slow and difficult against the force of the stream and current; *South American pilot*, 1864, I, 287.

[*Of the seate thereof.*] It is seated[1] in the middest and most marchandable quarters of the Earth, being[2] in the way of the East *Indies*, and in the heart of *America*[3]: In our course outward, we have it fairely at our choyse, to take by,[4] or to leave the *Canaries, Barbary, Affrica*, and *Brasill*: And homeward,[5] we may conveniently fall with the Coast of *Guiana, Trinidado*, or any of the Savage Islands,[6] or we may upon liking passe into the west *Indies*, and visite *Virginia*, the *Bermudas, Newfound land*, or the *Terceras*. Our passage from *Plimouth* outward, is commonly of Seaven weekes: and homeward of Eight or Nine weekes.[7]

[2 *Of the Country, and *of the people*[8]] Concerning so much of the Country as we have discovered: The temper of the Ayre, with the infinite variety of Nature (in the fruits of the Earth, and for Beasts, Foule and Fish,) is there as excellent and admirable as in any part of the world.* It is inhabited by many Nations of different languages, who had rather admit of any Christians to live amongst them, then by[9] the *Spaniards* or *Portugalls*.

[3 *Of the English there abiding, and*] There was transported thither, Six yeares since a Hundred persons, Gentlemen and others, who found that some of his Ma*j*esties Subjects, had lived safely amongst the Indians divers yeares before their comming: Many of these men are at this time remaining dispersed without governement amongst the Indians, raunging about a spatious Country, and have learned the Languages of seuerall Nations, by meanes whereof, they may make use of many thousands of the Indians against any Invaders; These Indians also house them, worke for them, bring them victualls and commodities, (which advantages, no other Country in the *West Indies* can intirely afford;) their payment is in

---

[1] 'This river is conveniently seated', P.R.O., CO 1/4, f. 9.

[2] 'in the middest of the richest & most marchandable, quarters of the earth, lying', P.R.O., CO 1/4, f. 9.

[3] 'West Indies', P.R.O., CO 1/4, f. 9.

[4] 'by', omitted P.R.O., CO 1/4, f. 9.

[5] 'in our way homeward', P.R.O., CO 1/4, f. 9.

[6] 'fall with divers goodly rivers upon the coaste of Guiana, & with any of the Savage Ilands, (in either of which parts, the English have friendshipp & commerce with the Indians,)', P.R.O., CO 1/4, f. 9.

[7] 'or nine,' omitted P.R.O., CO 1/4, f. 9.

[8] 'Of the Countrie with the poeple (sic) &c.', P.R.O., CO 1/4, f. 9.

[9] 'by' omitted P.R.O., CO 1/4, f. 9.

glasse beads, Iron worke, or some such other like contemptible stuffe.[1]

[*How they are supplied, and have subsisted against the Portugalles.*] They are supplyed by the *Dutchmen*, who are lately setled upon the same River neere unto them,[2] for a Plantation under the west Indian Company in *Holland*, who doe earnestly solicite our Countrymen,[3] to depend and hold of them, the Country they possesse. They have subsisted, with the onely ayd of the Indians[4] against a great attempt of the *Portugalls* to supplant and ruine them, which at the same time, was effected upon the *Dutchmen*; And this exployt,[5] about Foure yeares since,[6] was wrought and procured by the Count of *Gondomer*,[7] whilest he resided in *England*.

[4 *Of the Coast of Guiana, and *How advantagious in the returne from the Amazones*] The Coast of *Guiana* contayneth many goodly Rivers, and harbours, and is well peopled, where the *English* are more desired then any Nation whatsoever. As of the *Amazones*, so of the continent

---

[1] P.R.O., CO 1/4, ff. 9, 10 reads 'I left there 6 yeares since 100. Gentlemen & others, divers of them ar still remayning about the same parts, wher I disposed of them, although their supplies from England have bene stopped: they live dispersed amongst the Indians without governement, & have raunged about a large countrie, & can speake the Languages of severall nations, by meanes wherof, they may make use of many thousands of the Indians, who ar rewarded with glasse beades, & Iron worke, or some such like contemptible stuffe, [f. 10] for the which, they howse them, worke for them, bring them victualls, and commodities: which ar advantages, that no other countrie in the West Indies doth affoord.'

[2] 'in other parts of the river', P.R.O., CO 1/4, f. 10.

[3] 'who earnestly solicite the English', P.R.O., CO 1/4, f. 10.

[4] 'And our countriemen have subsisted with the aide of the Indians, without any from the Dutch', P.R.O., CO 1/4, f. 10.

[5] 'intended to supplant & ruine them, (as at the same time befell the Dutchmen) which exploit was', P.R.O., CO 1/4, f. 10.

[6] North alludes to the destruction of forts Orange and Nassau on the Xingu in 1623.

[7] The paragraph of the rough draft ends here. The remainder of P.R.O., CO 1/4 f. 10 reads: '4ly of the course intended in the said business. The chiefe course in present to be intended is by his Majesties favour, to renue & establish our formerly suspended Pattent, (wherby the Adventurors, were incorporated under the name of the Governour & compagnie of Noblemen & Gentlemen of the cittie of London Adventurors etc.) & to insert therinto, the names of such of the first Adventurors & others, as will agree & subscribe unto some reasonable articles to be propounded unto them: which once effected this great busines, will be perpetuated without any burthen & charge unto his Majestie, unto whom the glory & advantage therof, will principally redound, by the enlarging of his dominions, & the good of his Subjects.'

of *Guiana*, the greater part, and the riches thereof, hath never been discovered by any Christian, *The shipping returning from the *Amazones* may with a constant wind, and the currant of the Sea,[1] securely fall with any part of this coast either to leave men in the sayd Rivers, or to trade with the Indians, and to take in, the commodities raysed and gotten by their owne men, against the time of their arryvall.

[5 *Of the Commodities.*] The profit and commodities these Countries either doe or may afford, hath never beene sufficiently searched into: yet there hath been found *Sugar Canes, Cotten Wooll, Dyes in grayne, rich woods, Drugges, Oyles, Gummes, Waxe, some Spices, Tobacco, Silke grasse, Cristall, Saphires, Topases, Spleen stones*, and divers *Mineralls*,[2] which were never tried, and some peeces of Mettall have beene found worne by the Indians which were mixed with a third part Gold; There are whole Islands of wild *Nutmeg*-trees, bearing a perfect little Nutmeg with the Mace; And we may well expect as great Riches from hence, as the *Portugalls* from Brasill.

Conclusion. The surest and easiest meanes of interessing his Majestie and his Subjects in the West Indies, is by settling these and such like parts, where by the friendship of the Natives, and the goodnesse of the Country, we may be secured against an enemie, and subsist without burthen and charge unto our *Country*; And likewise our Shipping repayring to the Indies,[3] may be refreshed and relieved; In the defect whereof, did (as I conceive) maynely consist the error of former times.

6. CONDITIONS FOR SUBSCRIPTION TO THE GUIANA COMPANY, PRINTED MARCH 1626[4]

The Coppie of the Preamble, for the Subscriptions, intimating the conditions of Adventure.

WHereas His most excellent Majestie, upon the humble suite of Roger North Esquier, hath been pleased to direct a warrant to his

[1] See above, p. 17.
[2] North presents a slightly edited version of the list in Harcourt's 'Recapitulation', printed above pp. 278–82.
[3] Presumably North means ships returning from the East Indies here.
[4] P.R.O., SP 16/24, no. 20. *The Preamble* was also printed by Thomas Purfoot.

Atturney Generall, for the preparing a Bill ready for his Majesties Signature, contayning a Graunt of a Corporation, to the sayd Roger North, and unto Robert Harcourt Esquier, and such others as they shall nominate, to bee incorporated with them, and such extents of Lands, and all the powers, immunities, and priviledges as are contayned in Two severall Graunts or in either of them: the one bearing date the 28. of *August* 1613. unto the said R. Harcoutt (sic) and his heires: the other bearing date the First day of *September*, 1619. unto a Corporation (by the name of Govenour (sic) and Company of Noblemen and Gentlemen of the Citty of *London* Adventurers, &c.) The sayd R. Harcourt being now willing for a publique good, and upon very reasonable termes, to make surrender of his foresaid Graunt; WEE who have hereunto subscribed, in consideration that Wee shall be nominated by the sayd Roger North, and Robert Harcourt, and our names put as part of the Corporation, and as Grauntees in the sayd Patent, doe severallie promise and engage ourselves to them, the sayd R. North, and R. Harcourt, to adventure thereupon, the severall Summes of Money here, underwrighten respectively with our names, meaning that such onely, who shall by this (or the like) writing expresse their adventures, bee inserted into the new Letters Patents, which being past the great Seale, Wee promise respectively to send immediately, into the hand of some one of us, that shall be chosen Treasurer of the Company, the third part of our Adventures respectively, towards the first voiage with all speede to be set out; and the residue we also promise respectively to pay in afterwards, at such severall times as the new Governour and Company shall order for the same. AND further, wee are willing and doe give our consents, that the sayd R. North, and R. Harcourt, shall have and receive from the new Govenour and Company (soone after the passing the sayd Patents under the great Seale) at the least as good, ample, and availeable, Commissions, Covenants, and agreements, on their behalfes, for all the extent that is to bee graunted in the sayd new Patent, as was before ratefyed unto the sayd Roger North under the hands and seale of the former Governour and Company, ordayned by the sayd Patent made *Anno.* 1619.[1] as aforesaid. AND all clauses, which solely doe or can, in the sayd Covenants and agreements

---

[1] There appears to be no surviving record of the agreement made between the Amazon Co. and Roger North in 1619.

formerly made, concerne the said R. North, We intend shall be interpreted according to equitie and good conscience, and the true intent and meaning of them, on the behalfe of him the said R. North. AND we give our consents, that the said R. North shall bee payd out of our first thirds, the moneyes by him expended, about the present settling of our new Graunt. AND also we are willing and doe give our consents, that the sayd R. Harcourt, in consideration of his right surrendered, (whereby the extent of the other graunt made 1619. is greatly enlarged,) shall bee allowed and accounted to have an Adventure, in the Common or joynt stocke, according as the new Governour and Company, shall hereafter in reason determine and proportion the same.

DOCKET: received 3rd April 1626

7. ROGER NORTH'S PETITION FOR THE GRANT OF TWO PRIZE SHIPS TO BE USED BY THE GUIANA COMPANY, 1627[1]

To the Kings most Excellent Majestie
The humble peticion of Roger North Esquire
Humbly shewing,

That your, petitioner according to his dutie, and by your Majesties royall favour & permission doth daylie labor in a worke that concearneth the publique good of the kingdome, and alsoe reflecteth in a most especiall manner upon the honnor & proffitt of your Majestie by the *enlarging of your dominions upon the river of Amazons, & countrie of Guiana*, & the encrease of the Customes & other duties payble to your Majestie./

Now forasmuch as it is ordered by the Lords of the Councell, that divers reprisall shippes that are, or shall be taken, may be disposed of by way of adventure *upon thirds*: And for that your Majestie hath of late bene pleased to bestowe the St Anne by way of adventure upon the Adventurors for Guiney, who doe not soe really intend to interest your Majestie in the Countrie by way of plantacion as is intended by the Adventerors for those parts of the West Indies. And alsoe for that your petitioner can procure soe many men to goe unto

---

[1] P.R.O., SP 16/54, ff. 52–4. North's petition is undated but the docket was written 11/21st February 1627.

the foresaid parts as he shall have meanes by shipping to transporte./

His most humble *suite* is . That your Majestie (for the better effecting & strengthning of a worke soe greately ymporting your highnes service) will be graciouslie pleased to graunt your pet*itioner* *one or two of such shipps as now are, or hereafter shall be fitt for this ymployment,* and to referr the direccions and appointment thereof to the *Lord Admirall,* under such Condicions as his Grace shall thinke reasonable/.

And your pet*itioner* shall ever pray &c.

DOCKET: At the Courte at Whitehall 11° Febru*ary* 1626 His Ma*jes*ty approving well of the peticioners services and endeavours, Is graciously pleased to Referr the Consideracion of this Peticion to the Lord Duke of Buckingham his grace to take such order in this the Peticioners humble suite as to his grace shall seeme good/. Mountagu[1]

8. EXTRACT FROM THE PATENT OF THE GUIANA COMPANY ISSUED 19/29 MAY 1627[2]

Charles by the grace of god king of England Scotland ffrance and Ireland & defender of the faith &c To all to whome these presents shall come greeting. Whereas divers & sundrie of our faithfull and loving Subjects in the time of the raigne of our late royall father of blessed memorie deceased and att other tymes being stirred and moved with a desire to enlarge our Dominions and to increase the trade and traffique of their native countrye have in severall voyages by Sea not onlie adventured unto and landed in parte of the continent of America in and about the river of Amazons and in and uppon the Coaste and Country of Guyana the same not then being in the actuall possession or occupacion of anie Christian Prince or State. And alsoe have taken possession to the use of our said father and us of some [mem. 23] part of the said Continent and with the consent of the natives of that Countrie and Territory have in that part of the continent aforesaid beene risident by the space of divers

---

[1] Henry Montagu, earl of Manchester, Lord President of the Privy Council.
[2] P.R.O., C66/244, membranes 22–31. Signed by Charles I 19/29th May it passed the seals 2/12th June 1627. I have omitted repetitive passages of legal terminology common to such charters, summarizing the content where necessary.

yeares. And whereas our late royall father by his Letters Patent under his greate Seale of England bearing date the eight and twentith day of August in the eleaventh yeare of his said late majesties Raigne of England ffrance and Ireland for the consideracions therein mencioned did give and graunte unto Robert Harecourt Esquire and John Ravenson Esquire deceased and Sir Thomas Challoner[1] knight alsoe deceased and the heires of the said Robert Harecourt not onlie divers Territories Countries and land mencioned in the said Letters Patent but alsoe sondry powers priviledges authorities and other thing in the said Letters Patent conteyned minding and intending thereby the benefitt and good of his Subjet (sic) the encrease of trade enlarging his Dominions and the propagacion of the Christian fayth in the aforesaid Continent. And whereas alsoe uppon the humble suite of Roger North Esquire on the behalfe of himselfe and of divers Noblemen & gentlemen of quallitie our late Royall father in performance and further advanncement of soe excellent a worke was graciouslie pleased by his highnes Letters Patent under the greate Seale of England bearing date on or about the firste daie of September in the seaventeenth yeare of his said late majesties Raigne of England to give graunte and confirme for him and hieres (sic) and Successors unto his late majesties then right trustie and right welbeloved councellor ffrancis Lord Verulam then Lord Chancellor[2] of England and the saide Roger North and others therein declared Thatt they should be one body pollitique and corporate of themselves in deede and name by the name of Governor and Companie of Noblemen and Gentlemen of the Cittie of London Adventurers for a plantacion in or about the River of Amazons. And them by that name one bodie Corporate and pollitique did by the said Letters Patent make create ordeyne constitute appointe and confirme with divers powers priviledges and Authorities in the said Letters Patent conteyned as by the said Letters Patent maie more att large appeare. And whereas since as well the said Roger North as Robert Harecourt on the behalfe of themselves and divers Noblemen and Gentlemen their frends desirous to become Adventurers with them have humbly besought us for the better strength and support in this soe good a worke to extend our grace and favour unto them therein and both the said

[1] See above, p. 50, n. 1.   [2] See above, p. 204, n. 1.

recited Letters Patent being now surrendred into our hand[3] to be Cancelled have humbly desired that by new Letters Patent we would vouchsafe to incorporate them the said Roger North and Robert Harecourt and such others as they should nominate into a bodie pollitique and Corporate in deede and name with such other as large priviledges Extent and immunities as in either of the said Letters Pattent are conteyned or as shalbe necessarie for them to have or as have uppon the like discoveries or undertaking beene graunted to others. We therefore taking into our Princelie consideracion our funccion royall and power as well Ecclesiasticall as Civill and contynuing the lyke purpose and intencion of our royall father for a plantacion in the said Continent aswell for the propagacion of the Christian Religion and reclayming the people of those parts to civillitie and humanity as also for the enlarging of our Dominions and the encrease of trade and traffique within our Realmes And likewise holding it not onlie a dishonor but also doubting itt maie prove dangerous to our nacion to omitt any good occasion or give waie to any stranger for supplantacion in that continent. And hoping that the good agreement of the said Roger North and Robert Harecourt having bine both undertakers of one and the same designe maie happilie produce effects answerable to the Expectacion heretofore had of the same and greatlie affectinge the effectuall pursuite and happie Successe of the said enterprise and of their endeavour to settle a plantacion and trade in that parte of the continent aforesaid And much commending their good and worthy desires therein. Wee doe hereby first declare that wee have and doe for us our Heires and Successors take into our actuall and reall Dominion possession and proteccion all the Territories land and Dominions as well aforesaide as hereafter in these presents mencioned as parcell and members annexed to the Imperiall Crowne of this Realme of England and for the better and further encouragement of the said Roger North and Robert Harecourt and for and in performance and accomplishinge of soe excellent a worke of our especiall grace certaine knowledge and meere mocion we doe by these presents for us our Heires and Successors give graunte and confirme unto our right trustie and right welbeloved Cousens and Councellors George Duke of Buckingham our Highe Admirall of

---

[1] The Amazon Co.'s patent had been cancelled in 1620. Presumably this is a reference to Harcourt's patent.

England William Earle of Pembrooke Lord Steward of our household[1] Phillippe Earle of Mountgomery Lord Chamberlaine of our household[2] James Earle of Carlile[3] Henry Earle of Holland[4] And to our right trustie and right welbeloved Cousens Anne Countese Dowager of Dorsett[5] and Edmund Earle of Mulgrave[6] and to our right trustie and welbeloved Cosen and Councellor Edward Viscount Killutagh[7] one of our Principall Secretaries of State And to our right trustie and right welbeloved Cousens William Viscount Mansfeild[8] and Henry Viscount Rochford[9] And to our trustie and right welbeloved Oliver Lord St John of Bletsoe[10] Mildmay Lord le Despenser[11] Henrie Lord Ley[12] And to our right trustie and welbeloved and the right reverend fathers in god George Lord Bishoppe of London[13] and Thomas Lord Byshoppe

[1] See above, p. 204, n. 1.

[2] Philip Herbert (1584–1650), created earl of Montgomery 1605, succeeded his brother as fourth earl of Pembroke 1630, investor in the Virginia Co. 1609, East India Co. 1611, North-West Passage 1612 and privateering 1625; Rabb, 1967, p. 312.

[3] James Hay (1580–1636), created earl of Carlisle 1622, investor in the Virginia Co. 1612, New England 1623, privateering 1625; Rabb, 1967, p. 31.

[4] Henry Rich (1590–1648), created earl of Holland 1623, investor in the Virginia Co. 1612, Bermuda 1620 and the Providence Island Co. 1630. His brother, Robert, second earl of Warwick and his cousin, Nathaniel Rich had invested in the Amazon Co. *DNB* (1909), pp. 997–1000; Rabb, 1967, p. 365.

[5] Relict of Richard Sackville, third earl of Dorset, one of the original subscribers to the Amazon Co.; Rabb, 1967, p. 370.

[6] Edmund Sheffield (1565–1646), created earl of Mulgrave 1626, investor in the Virginia Co. 1609, New England 1620; Rabb, 1967, p. 375.

[7] Sir Edward Conway (d. 1631), appointed a principal Secretary of State 1623, created Viscount Killultagh of Killultagh Co. Antrim and Viscount Conway of Conway castle, Caernaervon 1627, investor in the Virginia Co. (1609); *DNB* (1908), pp. 975–6; Rabb, 1967, p. 269.

[8] See above, p. 215, n. 3. Present at the surrender of the Amazon Co. patent.

[9] Henry Carey (1580–1666), succeeded as fourth Lord Hunsdon 1617, subsequently created Viscount Rochford and earl of Dover 1628; *DNB* (1908), p. 982.

[10] Sir Oliver St John (1603–42), eldest son of the fourth Baron St John of Bletsoe who was created earl of Bolingbroke 1624. The son was known by the courtesy title of Lord St John after his father's elevation. He was also an investor in the Virginia Co. 1622, *DNB* (1909), p. 604.

[11] Sir Mildmay Fane (1602–66), Lord Le Despenser, son of Thomas Fane created earl of Westmorland 1624, succeeded to his father's earldom 1629.

[12] Henry Lord Ley (1595–1638), succeeded as second earl of Marlborough 1629. His father James Ley, first earl, was the brother and biographer of John Ley, the first Englishman known to have entered the Amazon; see above, p. 20 and *DNB* (1909), p. 1085.

[13] George Mountaine, bishop of London 20th July 1621–19th February 1628.

of Coventry and Lichfeild[1] And to our right trustie and welbeloved Dudley Lord North[2] Henry Lord Gray of [G]rooby[3] and Horace Lord Vere of Tilbury[4] and to our trustie and welbeloved Sir Thomas ffinch[5] knight and Baronett Sir Robert Naunton master of our Court of Wards[6] Sir Dudley North[7] knight of the Bathe Sir Cristofer Nevill[8] knight of the bath Captaine Roger North Esquire Sir John Hobarte[9] knight and Baronett Sir ffrancis Wortley[10] knight and Baronett Sir John Mounson[11] [mem. 24] knight of the Bath Sir Allen Apsley[12] leitenant of the Tower Sir James Ouchterlony[13] knight Sir Henrie Spillman[14] knight Sir Samuell Saltonstall[15] knight

[1] Thomas Morton, bishop of Coventry and Lichfield 6th March 1619–2nd July 1632.

[2] See above, p. 60, n. 4. Founder member of the Amazon Co.

[3] Sir Henry Grey (c. 1598–1673), second Lord Grey of Groby, created earl of Stamford 1628.

[4] Sir Horace Vere (1565–1635), brother-in-law of Robert Harcourt, created Lord Vere of Tilbury 1625, investor in the Virginia Co. 1609; Rabb, 1967, p. 394; DNB (1909), pp. 235–9.

[5] Sir Thomas Finch (c. 1575–1639), of Eastwell Co. Kent, knighted 1609, succeeded to the baronetcy c. 1618–20, styled Viscount Maidstone after July 1628, succeeded to the earldom of Winchelsea 1634; Cokayne, Complete baronetage, 1900, I, 36; Rabb, 1967, p. 291.

[6] Sir Robert Naunton (1563–1635), of Alderton Co. Suffolk, knighted 1615, appointed Master of Requests 1616, a principal Secretary of State 1618–23, Master of the Court of Wards 1623–35; DNB (1909), pp. 126–9.

[7] Sir Dudley North (1602–77), Knight of the Bath 1616, eldest son of Dudley third Baron North, succeeded as fourth baron 1666.

[8] Sir Christopher Neville (d. 1649), Knight of the Bath 1626, second son of Edward, eighth Lord Abergavenny, see below, pp. 321–45.

[9] Sir John Hobart (1593–1647), of Blickling Co. Norfolk, knighted 1611, succeeded to the baronetcy 1625, investor in the East India Co. 1627; Cokayne, Complete baronetage, 1900, I, pp. 12–13.

[10] Sir Francis Wortley (c. 1592–1652), of Wortley Co. Yorks., knighted 1611, created baronet 1611, investor in the Virginia Co. 1610 and the East India Co. 1629; Cokayne Complete baronetage, 1900, I, 48; Rabb, 1967, p. 408.

[11] Sir John Monson (1599–1683), of South Carlton Co. Lincs. and Broxbourne Herts., Knight of the Bath 1627, succeeded to the baronetcy 1641; Cokayne, Complete baronetage, 1900, I, 39; Rabb, 1967, p. 343.

[12] Sir Allen Apsley (d. 1630), knighted 1605, investor in the Africa Co. 1618, New England 1620; see above, p. 215, n. 3, and Rabb, 1967, p. 235.

[13] Knighted 1603.

[14] Sir Henry Spelman (1564–1641) of Congham Norfolk, knighted 1604, sheriff of Norfolk 1605, author of Icenia or a topographical description of Norfolk c. 1641, investor in New England 1623, subsequently Treasurer of the Guiana Co.; Rabb, 1967, p. 380; Norfolk Archaeology, XXIV (1932), 66–8.

[15] Sir Samuel Saltonstall, son of Sir Richard Saltonstall Lord Mayor of London, collector of customs, investor in the Spanish Co. 1605, Virginia Co. 1612; Rabb, 1967, p. 371.

Sir Henrie Mildmaie of Mouldsham[1] knight Sir Alexander Temple knight[2] Sir Oliver Cheyne[3] knight Sir Edward Peyto[4] knight Sir Roger North[5] knight Sir Charles Cavendish[6] knight Sir Arthure Gorge[7] knight Sir John Washington[8] knight Doctor Henrie King[9] Doctor of Divinitie Captaine Robert Harecourt Esquire Carew Ralegh[10] Esquire William Trumbull[11] Esquire Clarke of the Concell Henry Seckford[12] Esquire Raphe Whitfeild[13] Esquire Edward

[1] Sir Henry Mildmay of Waltham Co. Essex, brother and heir of Sir Thomas Mildmay Bart. of Moulsham Essex who died February 1626; W. C. Metcalfe, *The visitation of Essex* (London, 1878), pp. 251, 453.

[2] Sir Alexander Temple (d. 1629), younger brother of Sir Thomas Temple Bart. of Stowe, Co. Buck., knighted 1604, commander of Upnor castle Kent, buried Rochester cathedral; *Archaeologia Cantiana*, XI (1877), 1–9.

[3] Sir Oliver Cheyney, possibly of the East Sussex branch of the family of that name. A Sir Oliver Cheyney sold off property in the neighbourhood of Crall Sussex before 1624. Cheyney sailed to the Wiapoco with Robert Harcourt in 1628 as deputy governor; *Sussex Archaeological Soc.*, LXV (1924), pp. 47–51.

[4] Presumably Sir Edward Peyto of Chesterton Co. Warwick, knighted 1611, as opposed to Sir Edward Peyton of Iselham Co. Cambridge, also knighted 1611 but succeeded to the baronetcy 1616; Cokayne *Complete baronetage*, 1900, I, 15, n. b.

[5] Presumably an error by the clerk and intended to read Sir John North (d. 1638), brother of Dudley third Lord North and of Roger North, Knight of the Bath 1616, associated with Neville and Mildmay in financing the despatch of Clovell's colony to the Amazon in 1629 and of the *Amazon* and *Sea-Nymph* to supply them shortly afterward.

[6] Sir Charles Cavendish, knighted 1619, brother of Sir William Cavendish, see above, p. 215, n. 3.

[7] Sir Arthur Gorges (d. 1661), knighted 1621, eldest son of Sir Arthur Gorges the poet, translator and courtier who died 1625; Hasler, *House of commons, 1558–1603*, 1981, p. 206; *DNB* (1908), p. 241.

[8] Probably Sir John Washington (d. 1668), of Thrapston Co. Northants, knighted 1624; *The Genealogists Magazine*, I (1925), 81–4; W. C. Metcalfe, *The visitations of Northamptonshire, 1564 and 1618–19* (London, 1887), p. 152.

[9] Dr Henry King (1592–1669), appointed canon of Christ Church Oxford 1624, Dean of Rochester 1639, bishop of Chichester 1642; *DNB* (1909), pp. 133–4.

[10] Carew Ralegh (1605–66), second son of Sir Walter Ralegh, investor in the Virginia Co.; *DNB* (1909), p. 648.

[11] William Trumbull (d. 1635), of Craven Co. York., resident ambassador in Brussels 1609–25, appointed to an ordinary clerkship of the Privy Council 1614, granted Easthampstead Park Co. Berks. 1628, investor in the East India Co. and Levant Co. 1618; *DNB* (1909), pp. 1191–2.

[12] Presumably Henry Seckford Esq. of Seckford Hall in Woodbridge, Co. Suffolk. His daughter, Sarah, married John second son of Dudley Lord North (see above, p. 60, n. 4); W. C. Metcalfe, *Visitations of Suffolk, 1561, 1577, 1612* (Exeter, 1882), p. 64; A. Campling, *The history of the family of Drury* (London, 1937), p. 22.

[13] A Ralph Whitfield Esq. was returned to parliament in 1624 for Clitheroe Co. Lancs., created King's Serjeant-at-Law 1634 and knighted 1635; Ruigh, *The parliament of 1624*, 1971, p. 419; J. H. Baker, *The order of the Serjeants-at-Law* (London, 1984), p. 544.

Johnson[1] Esquire Hugh Maie[2] Esquire John Ingleby[3] Esquire
Captaine Simon Leeke[4] Esquire Simon Rowse[5] Esquire Edward
Palavicin[6] Esq*uire* ffrancis Burnett[7] Esquire Captayne William
Saker[8] Esquire Daniell Gookin[9] and William Martyn[10] gentleman
and to all such other our loving Subjects as shalbe admitted into the
said Company in manner and forme hereafter mencioned. That
they shall be one bodie pollitique and Corporate of themselves in
deed fact and name by the name of Governor and Company of
Noblemen and gentlemen of England for the plantacion of Guyana.
...[11] And that itt shall and maie be lawfull to and for the said
Governor and company and their Successors to use and have a
com*m*on Seale for all causes and bussines. ...[12] And we have
further by our more especiall grace certaine knowledge and meere
mocion absolutelie given and graunted and by these p*r*esents for us
our Heires and Successors doe absolutelie give graunte and
confirme unto the said Governor and Company of Noblemen and
gentlemen of England for the plantacion of Guyana their Successors and Assignes all those Lands Countries and Territories in the

[1] Possibly Edward Johnson, captain of a merchant ship impressed into the
king's service 1625. An Edward Johnson also invested in the East India Co. 1622;
see *CSP Dom., 1625–6* (1858), p. 268; Rabb, 1967, p. 324.

[2] In all probability the Gentleman of the Privy Chamber of that name, granted
the office of Receiver General of Middlesex, Essex and Herts; *CSP Dom., 1623–5*
(1859), pp. 287, 308, 375, 427; *1625–6*, p. 567.

[3] Not identified.

[4] Presumably the professional soldier who, having served in the Low
Countries and under the king of Denmark, petitioned for a company in the
forces bound for the United Provinces 1624 and appears to have been granted a
command; *CSP Dom., 1623–5*, p. 288; *1627–8*, p. 188.

[5] Not identified.

[6] An Edward Palavicino invested in the Virginia Co. 1620, otherwise not
identified; Rabb, 1967, p. 352.

[7] Not identified.   [8] Not identified.

[9] Daniel Gookin was an English planter who held an estate at Carrigaline, Co.
Cork. He transported 40 men from Ireland to Newport News, Virginia in 1622
and established the trade in Irish cattle to the colony; F. W. Gookin, *Daniel
Gookin, 1612–87* (Chicago, 1912), pp. 32–47; A. Gwynn, 'Early Irish emigration
to the West Indies (1612–43)', *Irish Quarterly*, XVIII (1929), 386–8; N. Canny,
'The permissive frontier: the problem of social control in English settlements in
Ireland and Virginia 1550–1650', *Westward Enterprise* p. 26; M. MacCartney-
Murrough, *The Munster plantation. English migration to southern Ireland, 1583–1641*
(Oxford, 1986), pp. 210–2.

[10] Not identified.

[11] With perpetual succession, full rights to hold and dispose of property and
to plead and be impleaded, answer and be answered before the law.

[12] To be altered as necessary from time to time.

Continent of America lying betweene the River of Amazons and the River of Desequebe and all Ilands Lands and Territories beinge within twentie leagues thereunto adjacent. And also all Lands Countries and Territories lyinge from the River of Wiapoco Southwarde to the River of Amazons and from thence further Southwards five degrees of latitude from any parte or braunche of the said River of Amazons and extending from Easte to West throughout the Continent from Sea to Sea which heretofore hath bine gayned or possessed by anie Subiects of us or anie of our Progenitors to the use of our deere Sister of Famous memorie Queene Elizabeth or our said deere father or us or to our Heires and Successors or which they shall hereafter Subdue or otherwise gayne either by conquest or by consent of the natives and Inhabitants of those partes And which were not att the time of the said graunte or Letters Patents made unto the said Robert Harecourt or others lawfullie inhabited and in the actuall and lawfull possession and occupacion of some other Christian Prince or State now in Amitie with us And all and singular soiles and grounds . . .[1] together with all Prerogatives Jurisdiccions Royalties priviledges ffranchises and pre-eminences within or betweene the uttmost bounds or limitts aforesaid . . .[2] which shalbe by the said Governer and Company and their Successors . . .[3] conquered or gayned or which they shall enjoy hold or possesse with the Consent of the Natives respectivelie or which by anie other lawfull waies or meanes they can gett obteyne or acquire or which they shall find voide or destitute of Inhabitants with full power and Authoritie to treate order direct and dispose of all the said Inhabitants and people resident or being [mem. 25] in the said Countries within the bounds or limitts aforesaid and of all other persons whatsoever that now doe or which shall at anie time hereafter reside or inhabite within the said Regions or Countries . . .[4] in as large and ample manner to all intents construccions and purposes as wee by our Letters Patents maie or can graunte or as wee or anie of our Progenitors or Predecessors have heretofore graunted to any Adventurer or Adventurers Undertaker or Undertaker of anie discoveries plantacion or traffique of in or into anie forraigne

[1] With mines, waters, fishing and hunting rights etc.
[2] Not possessed or inhabited as aforesaid.
[3] Officers and agents etc.
[4] To establish a christian government.

partes. . . . To be holden of us . . . in free and common Socage . . .
yeildinge and paieing therefore to us our heires and Successors
onlie the fifte parte of all Oare of gold and silver. . . .[1] And for the
better orderinge and governing of the said Company we will . . .
there shalbe one of the said Company to be elected . . . governor of
the said Company and one other to be his Deputy. . . . We have
ordeyned . . . the said George Duke of Buckingham to be the firste
and presente Governor . . . And wee doe hereby . . . give and
graunte unto the said Governor and Companie . . . that it shall and
maie be lawfull . . . in and uppon the firste Mundaie in the moneth
of December yeerelie to assemble themselves and meete together in
any place or places convenient in our Cittie of London or elce where
. . . to chose and nominate one of the said Company to be governor
of the same Company and another to be his Deputie both which
Offices shall continue and remaine for the space of one whole yeare
. . . to assemble themselves in anie Place or places convenient att
anie tyme or times within threescore daies after the date of theise
presents and in and uppon the firste mundaie in the moneth of
December yeerelie for ever hereafter . . .[2] [mem. 26] to elect . . . a
certaine number . . . to be . . . our Councell for Guyana. . . . And wee
doe further give . . . full power and authoritie for ever hereafter to
assemble themselves . . . everie yeare uppon the last Wendsdaie of
everie terme. . . . And to hold . . . one generall courte of Assemblie
. . . to ordeyne and establishe a forme and frame of pollicie and
government . . . and further to order and appointe what matters or
things shalbe determined heard done or ordered in ordinarie Court
for the said companie . . . to be assembled with the assent of anie two
of our said Councell of Guyana . . . to make and ordeyne all . . .
casuall or particular matters or occurrances of lesser weight and
consequence. . . .[3] [mem. 28] the said Governor and Company or
the greater parte of them assembled with such respective assent as
aforesaid shall thinke fitt and appointe in any such voyage into the
said continent of America extending as aforesaid And to comerce

---

[1] The company is granted treasure trove, goods and chattels and jurisdiction
over felons, waifs and strays and wreck.

[2] Provisions for administration of corporate oaths and for the replacement of
the governor and deputy governor in the event of their death etc.

[3] The company is granted admiralty rights, the power to divide their territory
into appropriate administrative units and to erect fortresses, towns and villages
with the necessary officers and justices. They may set vessels to sea with the
necessary armaments.

trade and have intelligence with the people of those part and within the the said limitt (that are possessors of the same albeit they be infidell and for ever hereafter to have use and enjoye the whole entire and onlie trade li*be*rtie use and priviledge of trade and traffique. . . .' [mem. 30] And for that wee are crediblie informed that in such and the like enterprises and voyages greate losses and hinderances have happened by the malicious and disorderlie carriage of those which are or maie be shipped and imployed in the said voyadges because none of them have bine sufficentlie authorised to punishe the Offendors according to their demeritts for reformacion whereof the said Governor and Company have bine humble Suitors That such Generalls Captaines and Com*m*manders as shalbe imployed by them in any of their voyadges or shall have com*m*aunde of the collony or collonyes in the Territories aforesaid or in the passages by Sea to and from the saide Territories might have power and authoritie to use and exercise marciall lawe uppon sich mutinous and disordered p*e*rsons as shall happen to be amongst them. . . .²

9. ACCOUNT OF THE AFFAIRS OF THE NEW GUIANA COMPANY, PUBLISHED TO ENCOURAGE INVESTMENT, JUNE 1627³

A breefe Relation of the present state of the busines of *Guiana* Concerning the proceding therein.

The King by his Letters Patents which past the great Seale the 2.

' The company is granted the right to transport colonists to its territories and resist intruders by force of arms, although this does not constitute a warrant to commit hostile acts against subjects of a friendly power. It is freed of taxes, imposts and impositions on imports and exports for ten years and subsidies and customs for seven. Re-exported goods are free of duty, provided they are taken out of the realm within thirteen months of their importation. English and foreign traders must seek a licence of the company to traffick within its territories. Licences are to be given only with the consent of the General Court. The fine for admission after the issue of the patent is set at £20 for twenty-one years, to be reduced thereafter to £6.13.9d. All born within Guiana are to be full subjects of the English Crown.

² The company is to provide regular supplies. All outward bound passengers must take the oath of allegiance to the crown before departure. The patent may be renewed and amended.

³ Two printed copies of this survive in the P.R.O., CO 1/4, ff. 73, 75. The version printed here is CO 1/4, f. 75, which has one handwritten notation, not found in the other copy marked in [ ]. The *Breefe Relation* was printed by E. Allde.

June, and beares date the 19. May in this third yeare of his Raigne, erected the Adventurers into a Corporation, by the name of *The Governor* and *Company of Noblemen and Gentlemen* of England *for the Plantation of* Guiana.

I. The Aduenturers, be the Duke of Buckingham appointed in the Letters Patents, to the present Governour.

5. Earles	21	Baronets, Knights, and men of that rancke.
1. Countesse.	1.	Doctor of Divinitie.
3. Viscountes.	14.	Esquires.
6. Barons,	2.	Gentlemen.
2. Bishops.		

In all 56.[1] whereof 24. have subscribed to adventure 100. pound a peece, some 150. pound: none under 50. pound, nor any may, and the payments are to be made at severall times, and portions.

To this *Corporation* and all that are or shall be admitted into it, the king hath graunted the spatious Regions of *Guiana*, with the Royall River of *Amazons*, and Parts about it.

He hath also graunted as ample priviledges and immunities as formerly have beene usuall, with some additions, [& a clause of confirmation, upon passing in Parliament.]

Generall Courts to be holden but foure times in the yeare, vi*delizet*. the last Wednesday of every Terme: In them only are the *Forme of Governement, Lawes, Generall Orders*, and *things of greatest consequence* to be debated, and enacted: and the times are certaine, that all may take notice of them.

Ordinary Courts are to be holden as the Generall Courts shall appoint, and to deale only in such matters of lesser consequence, as they shall commit unto them.

The first *Election* of the *Counsell* and *Officers*, is to be within 60. dayes after the Date of the Patent: From henceforth the Governor and they, are yearely eligible and removable upon the first Munday of December. The Counsell is stiled by the Letters Patents, *His Majesties Counsaile for Guiana*

No *Generall Court* can be holden without foure at leaste of the *Counsell*: no *Ordinarie* without two. All have equalitie of voyce, and the greatest part prevaileth.

According to the premises there have beene two *Courts* or meetings of the Adventurers in *Grayes-In* Hall.

---

[1] Two more than listed in the patent, see below, pp. 390–1.

The first, 8° Junii, where the Letters Patents were published, and Captaine Roger North (brother to the Lord North) received for *Deputy Governour*, being hereto constituted by a Letter of Deputation under the Dukes hand and Seale. Then were chosen to be of the *Counsell* all the Lords Adventurers, with divers of the Company then present, and likest to attend the meetings.

The second, was 13. Junii where Sir Henry Spelman was by generall consent chosen *Treasurer*, and required by order of the court to call in presently the first third part of every mans mony subscribed. (And insomuch as the whole proceeding now resteth hereupon; it is desired that all the Adventurers would accordingly send it to him at his Lodging in *Barbican*.) A course being setled for the safe keeping and issuing out thereof. Then also was prescribed the manner of summoning and holding *Ordinarie Courts*, and what they should deale in till the next *Generall Court*.

Some other necessary matters were likewise ordered and provided for.

And although by the Patent the Company may take 20. pound of every man that shall now be admitted into their *Corporation*; yet insomuch as many that would have joyned formerly in the Patent, could not come to underwrite their Adventures, it is agreed that all that come in before the next *Generall Court* shall be discharged of that fine, and charged no otherwise then the Patentees themselves.

Now it hath beene thought requisite to give notice unto the Lords and other the Adventurers that were absent, aswell of the premises which concerne the establishment of this undertaking, and the proceeding therein: as also of an intendment to augment and encrease the first underwritten stocke, to the end that if they please, they may acquaint and bring in such of their friends and acquaintance, as shall be willing to joyne with them in a worke no lesse profitable then honorable: the advancement whereof will be more throughly intended and Perfected (God *wi*lling) the last Wednesday in Michaelmas Terme next ensuing the Date hereof. June the 20./ 1627.

THE 'OLD' IRISH PLANTERS GO OUT TO THE AMAZON FOR THE DUTCH WEST INDIA COMPANY, 1629

1. PASSPORTS FOR TWO OF THE 'OLD' IRISH PLANTERS TO TRAVEL INTO HOLLAND[1]

10 Sept*ember* 1628.

A Passe for James Purcell to goe into Holland. Another for Mathew More to goe thither also.

2. O'BRIEN'S ACCOUNT OF HIS RETURN TO THE AMAZON IN EARLY 1629[2]

Then the supplicant, wanting to travel, went through Denmark, Muscovy, Poland, Germany, Italy and reached Portugal from whence he returned to Zeeland to collect a debt. Whilst he was there he was approached by the Council of Zeeland and they brought him two Irishmen who had come from the river Amazon and whom the Council of Zeeland was sending back again with two ships and a company of Irish, English, French and Dutch soldiers. And when the Council found that the supplicant had been the leader of the Irish and had governed them well and was esteemed by the Indians, they made him captain general, merchant, pilot, and interpreter of the two ships,

---

[1] P.R.O., PC 2/38, f. 453. Mathew More was one of the three Irishmen freed by Manoel de Sousa d'Eça in 1627, see below, p. 306, n. 1. In a letter of 24th November 1629, Francisco Coelho de Carvalho said that Tauregue was commanded in 1629 by 'Gomez procel and the other Mortoni Mor of the three to which Manoel de Souza d'Eça gave licence to leave Pará for their lands'; see 'Consulta do Conselho sobre informações prestadas por Francisco Coelho de Carvalho', Studart, 1904–21, IV, 38. Presumably O'Brien's 'Don Matthias Omallon' was the same man, see below, p. 302.

[2] See above, p. 263, n. 2.

providing him with goods which the Indians liked to the value of 18,000 escudos,[1] on condition that three times this amount was returned in Indian goods, and this debt being paid, all the rest which he and the company should earn was their own; and they should go out and return following whatever religion they chose. And it promised them reinforcements of Irishmen every year, and more merchandise to be sold on the same condition.

The supplicant departed from Zeeland on the 24th of January 1629.[2] He arrived with the two ships, one of which had 18 pieces of bronze and iron artillery and the other 6, at the river Amazon in April of the same year. After shooting off the artillery the Indians came aboard and recognizing the supplicant, they and all those of the region accepted his authority.

The supplicant went 60 leagues up the river with the two ships and asking the Indians about those he had left behind, they told him that other whites had arrived to make war on them and both sides had suffered losses, and those of the Irish left alive departed freely with the others taking with them many Indians who also went voluntarily.[3]

The supplicant established a fort in a place called Foherégo,[4] fortifying it with a piece of artillery and 4 stone mortars,[5] leaving there part of his men and at the head of them the two Irish men whom he had met in Zeeland returned from the Amazon (the one was called Master Matthias Omallon [Matthew More?] and the other Master Diego Porcel [James Purcell]. He himself went into the interior with 42 soldiers to treat with the Indians and pacify them, for they were making war on one another. Having travelled some 40 leagues, it being then June, news came to him from the fort that enemies had come, killed the Indians, burned their dwellings and established another fort near the forces of the supplicant without having said who they were, why they came or asking who was there already. The supplicant returned to the help of his people with the 42 whites and 10,000 Indians, and before reaching the fort he encountered the enemy, with some 200 whites and 7,000 Indian warriors.[6] Having fought, with losses on both sides, the supplicant

[1] See above, p. 268, n. 9.   [2] Confirmed by John Smith, see above, p. 275.
[3] A reference to the surrender of Tauregue in 1625.   [4] Tauregue.
[5] See above, p. 251, n. 1.
[6] Figueira states (see below, p. 307), that Pedro da Costa had about 40 White soldiers and 800 Indians. Francisco Coelho de Carvalho's letter, 24th November 1629, estimated the initial assault force at 'one hundred men in twenty canoes, with three hundred Indians', in 'Consulta do Conselho', Studart, 1904–21, IV, 37.

was wounded by two bullets and an arrow, and his Indians fled, giving him up for dead. Notwithstanding he and the 42 whites continued the struggle and overcoming his adversaries held the victory. He captured some of the hostile Indians and two whites. He discovered that they were Portuguese and they told him that the leader of the attackers was a Portuguese mulatto called Pedro de Costa,[1] sent by order of the governor of Marañón to drive out foreigners. He released the two Portuguese and the Indians charging them that they should tell Pedro de Costa, that he and the Irish he commanded were catholics and did not intend to make war on the king of Spain, rather they would willingly serve his Majesty. No answer was sent to him, Pedro de Acosta leaving in the night with his expedition.[2] The Portuguese, seeing that the supplicant was called Bernardo and that he won a victory with 42 whites after his Indians fled and that he released the prisoners, called him Bernardo del Carpio[3] and this became his name in the Indies.

The following September[4] a Portuguese, Pedro Texeira, came by order of the same governor of Marañón with more than 300 whites and 15,000 Indians against this supplicant.[5] He made a surprise attack on the fort by night and beseiged the garrison. The news reached the supplicant who was 16 leagues inland with 16 whites and he came to the relief of the fort with them and more than 30,000 Indians. Pedro Texeira lifted the siege retiring to his canoes at the landing stage, where he had built a barricade for his defence.

[1] O'Brien correctly identifies the leader of this expedition. Hemming, *Red gold*, 1978, 584, thought O'Brien had misidentified him as Pedro da Silva. Coelho de Carvalho, 'Consulta do Conselho', Studart, 1904–21, IV, 37, reported that the defenders killed two Portuguese soldiers, wounded others as well as many of their Indian allies and forced them to retreat to Gurupá.

[2] Doubtless invented after the fact. Since the whole object of his memorial was to win the patronage of the Spanish crown, O'Brien would have been foolish to belabour the unpalatable fact that he had gone out to the river in the service of its Dutch foes in 1629.

[3] O'Brien's nickname was a Portuguese 'in-joke'. Doubtless amused by his tall tales about his prowess and adventures they dubbed him Bernardo del Carpio, after the mythical Spanish hero of thirteenth century *chansons de geste*, who was said to have killed Roland at the battle of Roncevaux. See R. Baker, *The knight and chivalry* (London, 1970), p. 55.

[4] Figueira, p. 309, and Francisco Coelho de Carvalho, 'Consulta do Conselho', Studart, 1904–21, IV, 38, both agree that the second Portuguese assault began 28th September.

[5] Figueira states that Teixeira had only half that number of White soldiers and 1,600 Indians.

At this point, three ships arrived in the Amazon, two English[1] and one from Zeeland. The latter brought reinforcements for the supplicant. The two English ships carried orders from England to notify the supplicant that he and the rest of the Irish would be held as traitors to the king of England if they did not obey the commander of the two ships.[2] This commander who knew from the boat which the supplicant always kept in the river[3] that the supplicant was at war with the Portuguese, and concealing the order which he carried for him, offered him help in a friendly manner and advised of the arrival of the Zeeland ship with supplies for him. At the same time 2,000 Indians called Angaynas,[4] who used to be allied with the Portuguese, came to his support. They are the bravest of those peoples. At the same time an Irishman, who came with the 400 men in the two English ships, wrote to the supplicant secretly in his own language about the orders which the English commander carried for him.

The supplicant called the Irish to a council, it seeming to him that if they joined with the 400 English[5] and the reinforcements from Zeeland, the Irish and Catholics would lose command to the heretics and the Indians would be heretics not Catholics. He sent three Irishmen and a mulatto to communicate to Pedro Texeira that he would prefer to serve the king of Spain than heretics, and would do so and surrender the fort, if he gave him good terms in the name of your Majesty and of the governor general of the Marañón and Gran Pará.[6] He and his captains and officials present, soldiers as well as civilians, and Friar Luys de la Assumpción[7] his chaplain, swore on a missal by the holy evangelists, kneeling before a crucifix, that the Irish and other foreigners with them should have the freedom of their lives, slaves, free Indian servants and goods: that they might freely trade with the said Portuguese: that they would give them lands and Indians to cultivate tobacco and they

[1] William Clovell and Thomas Hixon's party, see below, p. 339.

[2] Doubtless true. Clovell and Hixon were later to accuse James Purcell's party of treacherously surrendering to the Portuguese, *ibid.*

[3] The Irish leaders had probably sent a boat down to Sapno to look for the expected supply ship.

[4] Nheenghaibas(?). See above, p. 185, n. 4.

[5] An exaggeration. Clovell took out about 100 men.

[6] Figueira's account which, given O'Brien's objective in writing his memorial is likely to be more reliable, states that the Irish leaders approached the Portuguese furtively without the initial consent of their garrison.

[7] Luis de Assunção, O.F.M.; Kiemen, 1973, pp. 42, 61–5.

would have possession of all the fruits and profits of such lands: that when your Majesty and the king of England should make peace, they would give them passports, transport and provisions for those who wished to come to Spain with their goods, and those who wished to remain might do so on the conditions referred to: and these terms they wrote down and signed in Portuguese and Irish.

The supplicant surrendered the fort to the Portuguese and went with them.

3. FATHER LUIS FIGUEIRA'S ACCOUNT OF THE ASSAULT ON TAUREGUE, 1629

Account of various events, both of peace and of war, which took place in Maranhão and Grão Pará, against the Dutch rebels, English and French and other nations.' 1631.[1]

By the care with which a man plants a garden and digs a ditch and fences it to defend it from damage by the weather and wild animals so that they cannot gnaw with their teeth, trample with their feet or root with their snouts; and as this man charges a gardener to protect it, so we understand how much he values it and how he hopes to savour the sweetness of the fruit of his trees.

In a similar way we can to some degree declare and know how much God values this new church in Maranhão as his garden, and how he wishes the trees of the holy Faith and christian virtues to grow and fructify, whose sweet fruit he intends to gather. When this divine gardener began planting there is much to consider and take care of, building in the midst of it not only one tower as in the vineyard of Israel, as says the prophet Isaías [Isaiah] ch. 5,[2] but three very strong towers that will guard his garden, which are the three mendicant religious orders, that is to say that of our lady of Carmo [Carmel], and that of the Capuchins, and the Company of Jesus, the which in the beginning were brought here almost before

---

[1] Translation. Real Academia de la História, Madrid, Papeles de Jesuitas, t. 109, ff. 71–2, printed in M. Jiménez de la Espada, *Viaje del Capitán Pedro Texeira*, 1889, pp. 122–31. For biographical details on P. Luis Figueira's missions to Brazil, from his first visit to Ceará in 1607 to his death by shipwreck off Marajó island in 1643, see S. Leite, *Luiz Figueira. A sua vida heróica e sua obra literária* (Lisbon, 1940); Kiemen, 1973, 1–55.

[2] Isaiah ch. 5, verses 1–2.

there were settlers. And in addition to these three forces, which are the leading ones, this garden is also defended by the arms of our most Catholic king, Philip III of Portugal,[1] who through the endeavours of his Portuguese soldiers either captures or puts to flight the Dutch, English and French heretics.

And since the victories and fortunate achievements in Maranhão and Pará were many in these past years, in the time of Jerónimo de Albuquerque the first conquistador, who killed two hundred Frenchmen who went out to meet him intending to prevent him entering the large island of Maranhão, and afterwards with the arrival of Alexandre de Moura the rest of the French, another two hundred, abandoned the fort of S. Felipe [St. Philip], handing over themselves, the weapons and the fort to the Portuguese;[2] and afterwards in the time of Captain Bento Maciel [Parente], who at various times took the Dutchmen who were growing tobacco and had factories; and on one occasion with two canoes and six or seven Portuguese attacked a ship, and grappling on to the helm so tightly with such vigour that he obliged its company to set fire to it and burn it.[3] From the which achievements we can gather that the souls of the Portuguese are still strong; when God for his just reasons does not wish to punish them as was the case in Bahia[4] and Pernãobuco,[5] as is evident, for the grave sins they committed against his divine majesty. But in this our Maranhão and Grão Pará up to now he has helped and favoured, demonstrating that he wishes to plant his holy Faith. Especially, besides the past events, this is seen now in the achievements of our first governor Francisco Coelho de Carvalho,[6] which were as follows.

In the year 1626, at the end of August, the first governor Francisco Coelho de Carvalho arrived at this new government of Maranhão, and was received with great applause by the conquest, the which applause has not diminished until today and without doubt he will be taken leave off with good wishes because of the good success of his government. He brought in his company the *capitão-mor* of Pará, Manoel de Souza dessá,[7] whom, in a few days, he sent to the fort that the king had commended him, succeeding the *capitão-mor* Bento Maciel Parente, who for more than four years had governed

[1] Philip IV of Spain. [2] 1614–15. See above, pp. 167–9.
[3] 1623. See above, p. 257. [4] Briefly lost to the Dutch 1624–5.
[5] Taken by the Dutch in 1630. [6] Appointed 23rd September 1623.
[7] See above, p. 165, n. 4.

with great approval, augmenting the conquest, scourging and killing and capturing the pirates who had arrived there, demonstrating on various occasions his valour and good government, as a result of which there were in that captaincy many prisoners, Dutch and other nations who came with them to raise tobacco and trade with the Indians on the north bank of the river Amazon.

Amongst the prisoners there was one called Diogo Porse [James Purcell], Dutch by birth, who tried to get a licence to travel to his country; and for this he had recourse to a certain religious who was residing there, by whose means with importunities he got a licence from the new captain, Manoel de Saá (whom his capture had cost nothing) to go via the Antilles in the company of the same religious. And he finally embarked with him, taking with him under the same licence another two of his companions from the prisoners.[1]

They having left Pará, their departure came to the notice of the governor, who presently showed his displeasure at this. And going to visit the captaincy of Pará a few months later, he despatched from there requests to the governors of those islands that they should take the aforesaid foreigners who had taken off without his order against his Majesty's instructions. (Of which the Captain Manuel de Sousa de Saá, who issued the licence, and the religious who interceded knew nothing.) And with this despatch and the requests travelled the Captain Bento Maciel Parente, whose prisoners they had been. He departed from Pará in June 1627. He arrived at those islands, found the foreigners, presented his requests, had them taken; but being about to hang them the same religious who had carried them off came out on their behalf sponsoring them, and again, at the expense of Captain Bento Maciel had them freed, embarked them with him, carried them to Spain and from there sent them to their country. From whence in a short time they returned to fortify themselves, some merchants[2] giving them a ship,

---

[1] Figueira refers here to the Franciscan António da Merciana. The latter procured licences for James Purcell, whom Figueira mistakenly identifies as Dutch, Mathew More and a third man, who must have been 'Estevão Corse', to depart from Pará. The certificate from Merciana, verifying that 'Corse' surrendered freely to Pedro Teixeira in 1625, is printed below, pp. 409–10. It came into the hands of Jaspar Chillan when he approached the Spanish authorities on behalf of Purcell, More and 'Corse' on their arrival in Spain in 1627. He attached it to a memorial presented to Philip IV in 1632 as evidence of the good will of the Irish towards the king's subjects, see below, pp. 406–10.

[2] The Zeeland Chamber of the Dutch West India Co.

arms and merchandise which would amount (as they said) to sixty thousand cruzados,[1] so that they could grow tobacco. And later they would send them more people and capital, (because tobacco is of such importance to them). They came in April 1628 [1629],[2] to the river Amazon, to a place called the Tucujú,[3] where they fortified themselves making a wooden fort with an earthwork twenty palms high and another fifteen wide, a stockade twelve palms high and fifteen wide, with its parapet on top four palms high and another four wide, and all the fort squared off. It had four stone mortars, and one large piece of artillery. There they summoned the Indians, who grew them the smoke and trafficked with them, and because there were already older planters who had been there they knew the language very well.[4]

At the beginning of the year 1629 the captain of Pará Manoel de Sousa de Saá had notice of their settlement. He sent there Captain Pero da Costa [Pedro da Costa] (who is a very good soldier, born in Pernambuco, and with much experience in that conquest of Pará against both Indians and foreigners), giving him thirty or forty Portuguese soldiers and 800 Indian bowmen in forty canoes. Pero da Costa arrived at the enemy settlement, made an earthwork in front of the fort within arquebus range, and installed himself in it with his people. He then had notice that there were seven or eight Dutch in a certain plantation. He sent twenty Portuguese with some Indian bowmen to capture them. Arriving they found fourty eight enemies.[5] But our men did not retreat because of this but confronted them courageously, and the conflict lasted for two hours on a plain, in the which two Portuguese were killed and others wounded. And on the enemy's part another two killed and also others wounded, and unfortunately the Indians who were with the Portuguese, seeing the Indians who accompanied the Dutch, threw

[1] A coin equal in value to 400 réis. See above, p. 244, n. 3.

[2] Williamson, *English colonies*, 1923, p. 113, confused James Purcell's colony, sent out in 1629, with Harcourt's party sent out by the Guiana Co. in 1628 and diverted to the Wiapoco. Part of the reason for this confusion is that he accepted Figueira's date of April 1628 for the arrival of Purcell's party. All the other English, Spanish and Portuguese sources make it quite clear that Purcell arrived in the Amazon in April 1629.

[3] Sertão do Tocujós.

[4] The Irish became quite expert in the Indian languages, see below, p. 360.

[5] This may be a reference to the battle in which O'Brien claims he commanded 42 other Whites against a party of Portuguese. James Purcell may have given O'Brien charge of an inland factory or plantation.

themselves upon them and pursued them making a great slaughter, thus abandoning the Portuguese who were left fighting the Dutch with such uneven numbers, having few Indians to help them. And the one and the other fought until they were exhausted on both parts and drew off. And our men finding themselves without ammunition, or [shot] retreated to the earthwork where Captain Pedro da Costa was with the rest of the men.

And finding themselves short of munitions and the enemy well fortified, they took counsel to vacate the post in which with more courage than consideration they had placed themselves and thus retreated to Curupá[1] four or five days away, from whence they advised the governor Francisco Coelho de Carvalho, who was in the Maranhão, of what had happened. The governor regretted the events and the withdrawal, and with all speed equipped canoes with soldiers and Indians from Maranhão. He sent a warrant to Pero Texeira[2] as *capitão-mor* of the expedition, giving him a *regimento*[3] and instructions that he should try to prevent the enemy from trading and trafficking with the Indians, surrounding them and cutting them off from the relief which they might be expecting, which was a form of siege because the enemies could not last very long without Indians. And as to the rest he should do what the circumstances permitted.

Having received the advise and the orders of the governor, Pero Texeira departed with all possible speed from Pará with the Indians which came to him. He went to Camutá[4] which is on the way, to prepare *farinha* and recruit some more friendly Indians. And with

[1] The Portuguese fort of Saõ António do Gurupá, rebuilt in 1625.
[2] For details of the military career of Pedro Teixeira, see Jiménez de la Espada, 1889, *passim*; Mello Cardoso Barata, *A jornada*, 1916, pp. 21–3; Calmon, *História do Brasil*, 1941, II, 105; Kiemen, 1973, pp. 24, 42, 54.
[3] Standing orders.
[4] Camutá or Cametá, the area bordering the river Pará between the Tocantins and the Jacunda. Bento Maciel Parente defines it below, p. 316, as a series of islands. It is depicted thus in the third map of the *Anonymous Atlas of Maranhão, c.* 1629, see fig. IX. Cametá also appears to have been the name of an *aldea* or Indian village. Cristóval de Acuña passed by it in 1639, remarking that 'in times past, it was very famous in these conquests, as much for the number of its inhabitants, as for being the place where they usually collected their vessels, when they were about to make an inroad. But now there are left neither people, all having removed to other lands, nor provisions, there being no one to cultivate the ground, nor anything besides the ancient site and a few natives', in Markham, *Valley of the Amazons*, 1859, pp. 131–2.

this he met with Pero da Costa in the Corupá[1] where they made an enumeration of all the men and found themselves with 120 Portuguese soldiers, effective men, few in number but very resolute in spirit, and they had with them 1600 Indian bowmen. All of which embarked themselves in 98 canoes in search of the enemy, with their scouts ahead in lighter canoes.

When Pero Teixeira arrived half a league from the Dutch fort on the 28th of September, he ordered the canoes to be brought ashore, made his earthwork and trench of earth and wood, and on the following day marched to within sight of the enemy fort, the which he encircled with a large earthwork in which he placed the men and thus had them surrounded by the following day, there being many exchanges of arquebus shots without any harm to our side. And because there were many houses built of dry palm leaves in the fort, our men tried to set them afire with burning arrows. And undoubtedly they would have had effect had not an Indian hit and set alight a house which was outside the fort, which served as a warning to the enemy that they should dismantle the palm houses.

Our captain seeing that this was not effective retreated to his trench intending to busy himself assaulting the enemy, and they also came out to reconnoitre our forces several times and in these sallies we had various encounters in which our men always came off best, because they killed twelve of their men, and many Indians, and they did no more damage to us than to kill three Indians whom they came upon wandering about. And one Portuguese soldier was wounded in the chest by a ball that did him no more harm than graze the skin, and for some days he bled from the mouth and nose. Another Indian took a ball in the belly and in the same manner it fell to his feet without doing him any harm. In the which it was well seen that heaven was defending us and the enemy was amazed when they were told later that their arquebus shots did us no harm. After five or six encounters of this kind (in one of which we killed one of their leading Indians, who was their sole recourse, because at his orders provisions were brought them from the villages), the enemy came to be in a miserable state, but still in good heart since they were expecting relief any day.

It being the 17th October, four men appeared with a white flag who came in search of our trench. Our men responded with

[1] Gurupá.

another white flag and Captain Aires de Sousa went to meet them with some soldiers, to whom they immediately surrendered their weapons, and went with him to present themselves to Captain Pero Teixeira. They made the customary ceremony of blindfolding them and on removing [the blindfolds] they questioned them. Three of them were Scots,[1] one of them a gentleman with spurs on his boots as is the custom in his country, another a very good scholar,[2] a third[3] was a mulatto from the household of the conde de Santa Cruz, whom they had taken at the Cabo Verde carrying him off with them.

These three foreigners declared that they had been deceived, and that they did not conceive we were Portuguese nor that they were at war with catholics nor did they wish it. And as to the rest, that they were so short of supplies that they understood they would surrender on whatever terms. This served to inspire our men, and they tightened their grip upon the enemy and there was much exchange of fire between them, from which our men received no harm. Finally those who had come over to us began to talk to them from the earthwork where they were with our men fighting against their fellows.[4] Those in the fort responded to them and this practice was continued, the combat now ceasing, and what resulted from the practice was that the following day they sat down to settle peace and the manner of the surrender.

On the following day letters were written, hostages exchanged and the captains met each other; and finally it was agreed that the Dutch[5] would give up their weapons and munitions, but they could keep their goods to trade to the Portuguese and, once [their nation] was at peace with the king, they would be given passage to their countries and this would be put into effect in three days.

The three days having passed they asked for another three, giving as reason that some of their companions were absent. This

---

[1] Figueira presumably means Irish here.

[2] O'Brien also states that three Irish and a mulatto conducted the negotiations. He may well have been one of the party, although one would have expected him to have admitted it if he was. The Portuguese and the English believed James Purcell to be the commander of the garrison.

[3] Figueira must mean the fourth here.

[4] Compare this to O'Brien's version of events.

[5] It is nowhere stated how many of the mixed group of planters were Dutch. Gedeon Morris de Jonghe was captured at Tauregue in 1629, see 'Relatórios e cartas', *RIHGB*, LVIII (1895), 237–319, and above, p. 106.

second term having passed they asked for more. It was a subterfuge to delay until the expected relief arrived, which became known the same day when an Indian fell into our hands who was carrying a roll of arquebus match and some letters from two ships which were downstream in the river Pará, and now had notice of the situation at the fort and told them in the letters to delay the Portuguese by peace or by war, that they would soon be with them to help them.[1] Knowing this our captain insisted that they should immediately effect what they had agreed to, and if not it would be done by the severity of war. With this resolution they surrendered the same day with everything they had. The fort was abandoned and set on fire and razed and the following day our captain, Pero Teixeira embarked with some of his men and the prisoners divided amongst them, and left for Curupá, leaving many of us there.

Two or three days after our captain departed, there arrived at the said place two ships, and a patache,[2] and another two or three launches, which came to relieve their beseiged fellows. They shot off a great deal of artillery in vain and tried to put some men ashore, but our men, from the ambushes that they made, received them in such a way as to kill four of them and with this made them retreat again. And setting sail again they turned back whence they came. These it is affirmed were Englishmen in the company of Captain North, who soon thereafter found a site and built another fort, not very far away,[3] of which afterwards our men had news. And now the same Captain Pero Teixeira has turned [against them] by order of the governor with the same instructions that he was given for the Dutch, we hope with divine favour for the same success.[4]

On this occasion some Indians distinguished themselves, showing great valour in the skirmishes; amongst whom was one called Caraguatajuba, a Potiguar[5] of the Rio Grande, who, going into an attack and seeing in the river three canoes of Indians allied to the

---

[1] O'Brien said that the Dutch West India Co.'s relief vessel and the two ships carrying William Clovell and the English colonists arrived at the same time, and that the English did establish communications with him.

[2] A small auxiliary vessel.

[3] For the location of North fort or 'Pattecue', see above, pp. 93–4.

[4] See below, pp. 355–61.

[5] Hemming, *Red gold*, 1978, p. 71, describes the Potiguar as 'the most powerful and populous of all the Tupi tribes', fierce warriors, inhabiting the coastline between Rio Grande and the Maranhão.

Dutch, he took a sword in his mouth and plunged in swimming and went from one to the other swamping them, and they coming ashore suffocating he killed many of them. In another encounter with the Dutch this same Indian saw one of them, of good appearance, and assailed him to bring him back to us alive. And without doubt he would have brought him back had not four or five other Dutchmen appeared who prevented him with knive thrusts, from which he defended himself with a *rodella*[1] and with his hands and, despite knife wounds, he got under some trees and branches and escaped from them. Others did other noble deeds, with none dying but the three which we spoke of earlier, and the two Portuguese soldiers in that first encounter. And in all this time the Indians made a remarkable force for the Captain who left them to scale the fort which they ventured to enter, showing themselves to be impatient of the delay of the fighting and wanting to come to blows with the enemies. For all their work they have not received a single reward in the name of the king.

Once all our men had regrouped at Curupá with Captain Pero Teixeira, the prisoners (who were a little less then eighty) were sent to Camutá to the sertão close to our settlement, and the city of Belém do Pará, where the governor afterwards sent the greater part of them to Maranhão, others remaining in Pará itself, and others in Caneté [Caeté] a new captaincy halfway between Maranhão and Pará, so that dispersed like this there would be no possibility of evil deeds, because there were already many of their countrymen taken on previous occasions.

By this and by the many other past achievements we may understand that God our lord favours these conquests, and wishes to establish our holy Faith in them, even though there is an insufficiency of labourers and ministers of the gospel to care for the Indians. The which business, like everything else depends upon your Majesty favouring this affair assigning some alms to those who occupy themselves in it. And it is evident that to get rid of the foreign traders in those parts your Majesty has no better means than using the religious to civilize the Indians so that then they will not receive them to make tobacco. And even though it is not possible to have religious there without force of arms, it is more important to have the religious than the armaments, because in the

---

[1] See above, p. 264, n. 2.

end force of arms will not make the foreigners leave off making tobacco if the Indians give them entry and manage their tobacco plantations for them, the which they could not do without this help from the Indians. This touches upon the good, temporal advantage and quiet of your Majesty's vassals, the which is witnessed by the events in the state of Brazil where in Rio Grande and Paraiba only the Indian villages in the charge of the religious have not rebelled; and the rest have thrown in their lot with the Dutch. As to the spiritual good and conversion of the Indians, it is obvious that it depends solely and totally on the religious who dedicate their lives to this for the good of souls and the honour of God, suffering insupportable travails, without pretending nor taking for themselves any temporal benefit, rather lacking everything in their convents. I do not know if these lords of the Councils consider this, who are so stingy of your Majesty's Treasury for this universal good and liberal in other matters which are as nothing compared to these. Good proof of the great travails they endure, is the religious of Sancto António [St Antony] in the Maranhão, who not able to bear them being so overwhelmed, relinquished this past year their administration of the Indian villages, even though these religious were so zealous and were put into the villages by a special warrant of your Majesty. Thus surrendering them to the governor they withdrew to their convent,[1] leaving the villages absolutely abandoned as they are, [the Indians] dying each day without confession and without baptism, crying out for it every day, to the great regret of those who know and can do nothing to remedy it.

4. BENTO MACIEL PARENTE'S ASSESSMENT OF THE NEEDS OF THE STATE OF MARANHÃO AND GRÃO PARÁ, 1630[2]

In order to preserve and increase the conquest and territories of the Marañón and the natives in them which the *capitão-mor* Benito

---

[1] In March 1624 administration of the Indian villages of Maranhão and Grão Pará had been removed from secular captains and transferred to the Franciscans under their *Custos* or major superior, Fr. Cristóvão de Lisboa. Shortage of funds and steady opposition from the lay authorities obliged the friars to abandon any extended work in the villages of the sertão after 1630; Kiemen, 1973, ch. 2.

[2] Translation. The original is in Spanish. B.N.R.J., Códice Pernambuco, cota

Pariente [Bento Maciel Parente] pacified, the following things are necessary and useful. 1630.

The territories of that conquest should be divided into captaincies,[1] giving them to persons of wealth and responsibility so that in his jurisdiction each one may attempt to settle, fortify and supply the territory, reserving to the royal crown the captaincies of the Marañón and that of the river Amazon, which are the most important of that state: because the Marañón is already settled and the river Amazon conquered: they are the chiefest ports of that state, many things may be hoped for from each one of them, and because of the great navigability of the rivers, particularly of the Amazon or true Marañón which penetrates America and through which a doorway may be opened to the riches of Piru [Peru] and to all the rest which they may be to discover and conquer in that new world. Also in these places there is plenty of timber and other things for shipbuilding as in Abana [Havana].

The government of the Marañón, beginning in the captaincy of Ceará and terminating at the river of Vicente Pincón has three hundred and eighty leagues of coastline from three degrees south of the Equator to three degrees north, the coast running west one quarter northwest.[2]

From Paraoasu the captaincy of Marañón with its islands may begin and finish at Point Tapuitapera, between which is more than fifty leagues of coastline and this captaincy may be divided at the mouth of the river Mearin [Mearim] and at the Pynate [Pindaré]

I, 1–2–no. 35, ff. 28–9, printed in Guedes, *Brasil-costa norte*, 1968, pp. 33–4. Marginal annotations are placed in [ ] at the place where they appear. The rivers, place-names and tribes referred to by Maciel Parente are clearly marked on the three maps of the *Anonymous Atlas of Maranhão, c.* 1629. For the commentary on Pará see fig. IX.

[1] Territories awarded to hereditary proprietors or 'donatorios'. Brazil was originally divided into fourteen.

[2] Actually the captaincy of Cabo do Norte, subsequently granted to Bento Maciel Parente, extended to the river Wiapoco or, as the Portuguese called it, the river Vicente Pincón, at 4°22′ N.; A. G. Ferreira Reis, *Limites e demarcações na Amazonia Brasileira. A fronteira colonial com a Guiana Francesa* (Rio de Janeiro, 1947), *passim*. Parente suggests that the southernmost captaincy, Ceará should run from the river Iguatibi to the river Mondohytuba. The present fort of Ceará has twenty-five soldiers and two pieces of artillery in it. The next captaincy, Iurucoaquara would extend up the coast fifty leagues to the Paroasu. There were no Portuguese there.

further on. In it is All Saint's Island with the city of San Luys [São Luis] in which there must be five hundred men counting soldiers and settlers, with three convents of Capuchins, Carmelites and Jesuits. On the mainland, in the river Itapicoru are two sugar mills and others may be established. The land supports good cotton, tobacco and ranching and contains much good timber and is fruitful in sustenance, about which the Captain Simão Estácio [da Sylveira] made a report which has been printed.

[The free city of San Luis has a small fort which contains 17 pieces of artillery and 80 soldiers. On the bar it has a wooden redoubt with 8 pieces and 30 soldiers. The city and island holds 300 settlers and 100 soldiers. Moreover on the mainland there is a wooden fort, 4 leagues from the sea with 30 soldiers and 2 pieces of artillery. Bento Maciel built it to control the Indians when he settled the mainland.] . . .[2]

From the captaincy of Cayté follows the captaincy of Pará, which will begin at the said river Acotyperu and cut up from Point Separara by the mouth of the river Pará upriver and along the first branch of this river from the east as far as the first fall of the river and province of the Tocantines, which is one hundred and fifty leagues distant from the sea or a little less. The which captaincy has thirty leagues of coastline up to Point Separara and then widens upriver so that it comes to be as big as the others as will be seen on the map. The land will provide some sugar although it is not as fruitful of provisions as those which lie inland. It has much timber and necessaries for shipbuilding. In this captaincy is the city of Belén [Belém] with the fort called Presépio [the Manger] which the *capitão-mor* Benito Maciel Pariente had constructed of mud [bricks] with strong gateways and three bastions with earthworks and more fortifications in the modern fashion, all of which is worth many thousand ducats and cost the royal Treasury less than four hundred. [The free city of Belen has 150 men, the greater part of them [enlisted],. . . . The fort is sheer cliff on the west side and on

---

[1] The captaincy of Cumá is next extending from the Itapuytapera to the river Pindohytuba, some forty leagues of coastline with two good ports at Cumá and the island of San Juan. The captaincy of Cayté runs from Pindohytuba to the river Acotyperu. The governor Francisco Coelho de Carvallo had established sixty settlers from Pará and Marañón there, on the river Oatacapubic. A notation in the margin indicates that there are presently forty settlers in the village without any fortification. They produce sugar, cotton and tobacco which has to be carried to Belém in boats because nothing of greater draft than a patache or caravel can cross the bar of the river.

the east has mud walls 7 feet thick and in the centre of the rampart is a bastion and another to the north and another to the south. If it might have 150 settlers it is sufficient to have in addition, 100 soldiers, which comes to 250 in all. It is necessary to widen the rampart which is already underway and to finish the ditch so that the river surrounds it.]

From Point Separara, which is on the Equator on the east side of the river, running northwest to Cabo del Norte is the mouth of the river Amazon, the true Marañón, and it is eighty leagues of sweet water, and within this archipelago are many islands populated by many natives, the which islands may be divided into four captaincies.

The first will be the Island de las Juanes[1] and islands of the Aruans, Mapuas, Inhengahybas of Parijó, land suitable for ranching, rice and some sugar and tobacco although it is unhealthy being just below the Equator.

The second may be made from the island which is between the arm of the Pará[2] and that of the Pacajá, which is twenty leagues wide and forty long and comprehends the provinces of the Anduras and the Uguape and Pitapez Indians, together with all the small islands of the Camutá which neighbour it, country good for ranching, cotton, sugar, containing much timber and natives.

The third may be made on the island falling between the arm of the Pacajá and that of the Parnahyba,[3] which will be twenty leagues wide and forty five long within which are the provinces of the Pacajares, Goanapus, Caraguatas and Iuruhunas, very unhealthy country. It yields good cotton, tobaccos and food stuffs, and will provide some sugar and ranching.

The fourth may be made in the island between the arm Parnhyba and the main channel of the Amazon[4] with the distinct islands in the main channel and on the north side, which will be twelve leagues wide and forty long. It contains the province of the Iacares and other natives, by whom it is thickly populated, fertile country with much timber and will yield good cottons, tobaccos, rice and some sugar.

From the other side of the river at Cabo del Norte the coast runs

---

[1] Marajó. Intended to include the present islands of Marajó and Caviana, see fig. IV.
[2] The Tocantins. [3] The Xingu.
[4] The Ilha Grande de Gurupá.

east to the river Vicente Pincón, three degrees north of the line. It will be a matter of forty leagues between the main channel and the boundary between Portugal and Castile.[1] Here another captaincy can be made. It is a country of hills, prairies and small lakes, good for ranching, it yields good tobacco and cotton. It might be extended upriver to the mouth of the river Amazon and the province of Tapuyosus[2] comprehending also the provinces of the Tocuyus and Mariguins about two hundred leagues upriver.

Besides these captaincies others may be demarcated between the river Amazon and Gran Pará, beyond the province of the Tocantines, the river being very navigable and the land fertile. It is understood it will support wheat and vines and things from Spain, as in the new kingdom of Granada, which neighbours it and is in the same altitude, and also there are many mines hereabouts as in New Granada and perhaps richer.

It is particularly necessary to place people there immediately, up to three hundred married men, and to found a city with them on the other side of the river Amazon on the arm of the river Ginipapo,[3] to hearten the settlers and the subject Indians and to prevent them from turning to trade with the Dutch and the Dutch from returning there, as they have intended after being thrown out. With these settlers may go friars of all the orders to instruct in the *encomiendas*[4] and with them your Majesty might send vestments and the necessaries for administering the masses and divine offices. Some of the female wards under royal protection may marry the new *encomenderos* and also with that wealth some timber may be carried to Spain for the building of large ships and in the future they may be built over there as in Abana. . . .[5]

---

[1] See above, p. 179, n. 3.

[2] Tapajós.

[3] Paru. After Maciel Parente was appointed governor of Maranhão and Grão Pará, his son founded the fort of Destierro near present Almeirim. The fort was in place by 1639, see below, p. 436.

[4] The Spanish system of assigning Indian labour and tribute in the New World.

[5] Parente goes on to suggest that an encomienda system should be established with one-third of the profits going to the crown to support fortifications. The river offers an alternative route for shipping the silver of Potosí to the Atlantic. Settlers should be carried out from the Terceras by the contractor Jorge de Lemos Betancor and others.

TEXT VII

THE DIFFICULTIES OF THE GUIANA COMPANY'S
NEW COLONY, 1628–31

1. THE DESPATCH OF THE FIRST COLONISTS 1628.
ACCOUNTS OF HARCOURT'S DIVERSION OF THEM
TO THE RIVER WIAPOCO.

a. 17/27 SEPT. 1630.

Voluntary Deposition of lewes Jackson of the Citye of London merchant.[1]

who sayth that in the moneth of November 1628 hee tooke shipping of Gravesend in a shipp of london called the little Hopewell bound for the Amazones, but the Companye of the said shipp landed at wyapoko in the parts of America in ffebruarye following where hee remained by the space of fifteene moneths or thereabouts, and then hee came from thence to the Barbados, where hee stayed about tenn weeks space, and from thence hee came in a shipp called the Black George to the said towne of Southampton on Munday last being the xiiith of this instant September, And hee further sayth that during his abode at wyapoko aforesaid one Thomas Duppe the servant of Robert hayman[2] heretofore of Exeter in the Countye of Devon gent (whom this deponent knew very well) and one Cornelius Conquest[3] of london gent, told this deponent that the sayd Robert hayman was dead, and that hee died so farr from the English plantations where his place of abode was, that they had neither spade nor shovell to digge his grave, but made a shift to digge a hole to burye him in by

---

[1] Corporation of Southampton, 'Book of Examinations, Informations and Depositions, 1622–44', printed in R. C. Anderson, ed., *Examinations and Depositions, 1622–44* (Southampton, 1931), II, 65–6.

[2] See above, p. 88, n.2.

[3] Listed by Sir Henry Spelman in 1634 as admitted to the Guiana Co. after the issue of the patent, for a venture of £50, see below, p. 391.

the waters syde with a Cassada Iron,[1] And that the men marchandize and provision which hee had at his death came to the hands of one Edward Ellman of the Citye of Exeter merchant who was his partner,[2] And hee further sayth that the said Ellman dyed shortly after at wyapoko aforesaid And by that meanes the said men merchandize and provision came into the hands of william knevett of london ffishmonger.[3]

b. 23 SEPT./3 OCT. 1630.
Voluntary Deposition of Jonathan Selman of Ludlowe in the Countye of Salop gent.[4]

who deposeth and sayeth that in November 1628 this Deponent and Robert Hayman sometyme of the Citye of Bristoll gent with many others to the number of 100 persons at the least, tooke shipping at Gravesend in a shipp of london called the little hopewell bound for the Amazones, but they landed at wyapoko in the parts of America on the xviith day of ffebruarye then next following or thereabouts; And that they sayled from thence about the xxvith of March last, or thereabouts, and arrived at the Barbados about the second of Aprill last, and remained there about two moneths space, And shortly after, Thomas Nevynson Esquire, Lewes Jackson marchant, and this deponent (being all of the Companye that then Came out of the said voyage from wyapoko)[5] returned amongst others that were then at the Barbados from the Barbados aforesaid and from St Christophers Island as passengers for England in a

---

[1] Cassava iron. Presumably an iron tool used for digging up and chopping the tuberous roots of the plant of that name, see above, p. 136, n. 4.

[2] Ellman is not mentioned by name in Hayman's will (see above, p. 8, n. 2), but was probably one of the 'divers' others with whom Hayman entered into partnership before his departure for Guiana.

[3] It is not clear whether Knevett was another partner or merely came into possession of the goods through claims to the late Ellman's estate, see Selman's statement below.

[4] Anderson, 1931, II, 67–9.

[5] Jackson and Selman sailed as far as Barbados with John Ellinger in the *Guiana* (see below, p. 331, n. 1). Anthony Ison testified before the High Court of Admiralty, 23rd June/3rd July 1631, that Robert Harcourt gave licence to Master Thomas Nevison, his two servants Jonathan Selman and Ralph Miller, to Lewes Jackson and 'one Ayleworth & Herman to departe from the Wiapoco with the sayd John Ellinger' (P.R.O., HCA 13/49, f. 404v). The two licences granted by Harcourt on 12/22nd March 1629, one to Nevison and his two men, the other to Jackson, Thomas Aileworth and Martin Heardman, are to be found in P.R.O., HCA 30/865, no. 7, schedules 1, 2.

shipp called the blacke George And the said Thomas Nevynson and this deponent landed at Plimouth on the xxviiith day of August last past or thereabouts; And hee further sayth that hee became acquainted with the said Robert Hayman at the begynning of the said voyage, And that during theire stay at wyapoko aforesaid, the said Robert hayman about the moneth of October last past and a servant of his called Thomas Duppe with Axes, bills Cassada Irons, strong waters and diverse other Commodityes went upp the river from his plantation called by the name of the wast (sic) towne unto the Narrack (being a people of that Countrey distant from his said plantation about twentye dayes journey)[1] in a Canoo of one Captaine loader chief Captaine of the Charibes in and neare wyapoko aforesaid, And this deponent saith that about the same tyme hee with *master* Cornelius Conquest and one George Manwaring went from theire plantation which belonged to Sir Oliver Cheney knight being within a stones cast of the said Robert haymans house, with such Commodityes, as the said Robert hayman carried with him, and that they went upp the same river in another Canoo to the Narrack aforesaid and did there traffique with them likewise; And hee further saith that in November last past the said Robert hayman having ended his traffique at the Narrack aforesaid departed thence with his said servant in his Canoo, purposing to return to his said plantation, and about xii houres after his departure, this deponent, the said Cornelius Conquest and George Manwaring departed likewyse from the said Narrack in theire Canoo and followed the said Robert hayman with as much speed as they could; And hee further saith that by the way they overtooke the Canoo wherein the said Robert hayman was Carried and that the said Robert hayman was dead about fyve or six houres before they came to him And that the said Thomas duppe the said Robert haymans servant then told this deponent that the said Robert hayman dyed in the said Canoo of a burning fever and of a fluxe,[2] which this deponent verely beleveth to be true: And hee further saith that hee this deponent did then and there see the said Robert hayman dead, and did also see the said Thomas duppe with 3 or 4 of the Indians that rowed in the said Canoo wherein the said

---

[1] Robert Harcourt, *Relation*, 1613, p. 17, 1626, p. 21, Harris, *Relation*, 1928, p. 83, places the 'Norrak' or Nourague Caribs inland up the Wiapoco on the margins of the tributary Arwy or Yaroupi.

[2] Dysentery.

Hayman was Carried, digge his grave close by the waters side, with paddles and Cassada irons and did see them burye him there And after his death one Edward hellman his partner possessed himself of his goods and servants, and the said hellman dying about Christmas then following one William Knevett of london ffishmonger possessed himself of hellmans whole estate.

Jonathan Selman.

2. THE TROUBLESOME VOYAGE
OF THE *AMAZON* AND *SEA-NYMPH*, 1629–30.[1]

a. Deposition of Sir Francis Neville Knight, of Chichester, Sussex, 28th June/8th July 1630[2]

within the tyme articulate the articulate Sir Christopher Nevill Sir John North Sir Henry Mildmay Master John Lucas & Company were & still are for ought hee knoweth owners of the articulate shippe the Amazons & her tackle & furniture & they within the tyme aforesaid victualled & sett her out from this porte of London to the river of Amazons & soe into the West Indies for a mann of warr,[3] & to returne for England & appointed this examinate Captaine. . . .

---

[1] Three different cases arising out of the voyage of the *Amazon* and *Sea-Nymph* were heard before the High Court of Admiralty between June 1630 and December 1632. Sir Christopher Neville, Sir John North, Sir Henry Mildmay, John Lucas and associates sued John Taylor, master of the *Amazon*, and John Ellinger, master of the *Sea-Nymph*, separately for misappropriation and wilful damage to their ships and goods. John Ellinger countersued for the wages of the crew of the *Sea-Nymph*. The calendar of the three suits can be pursued through the Acts of the court (P.R.O., HCA 3/30, ff. 274v *passim*; 3/33, ff. 215v–68v *passim*; 3/34 ff. 11v–172v *passim*). The allegations and depositions of witnesses in the three suits are to be found in HCA 24/87, nos. 82, 102, 116, 188; 24/88, nos. 5, 234, 235; 13/49, ff. 52v–66v, 230, 245–9, 308–11v, 404v–5, 411–12, 418–20v; 13/107; 30/865, no. 7, schedules 1–7.

[2] P.R.O., HCA 13/49, ff. 65v–6v, testimony in the case of Neville and associates against Michael Taylor. Sir Francis Neville gives the clearest statement of the ownership of the *Amazon*.

[3] Sir Francis Neville received a warrant for letters of marque from the Lords Commissioners of the Admiralty 3rd March 1629 (P.R.O., SP 16/130). The Trinity House certificates for 11th and 29th March 1629 indicate that both the *Amazon*(90) and the *Sea-Nymph*(50) were prizes awarded to Neville and his associates for their use.

b.   Deposition of Samuel Lockram, Mariner of Wapping,
11th/21st June 1630[1]

[f. 53] ... That within the tyme ar*ticula*te Sir Christopher Nevell
Sir John North Sir Henry Mildmay John Lucas & Company were &
still are Owners of the ar*ticula*te shipp the Amazons & her tackle &
furniture and victualled & sett her out from London on a voyage
for the river of Amazons & backe to London, and appointed
ffrannces Nevill Capt*aine* of her and Michaell Tayler M*aste*r of her,
& the said Tayler tooke uppon him to bee M*aste*r of her for that
voyage but was very disorderly and often druncke before shee gott
cleere of the coast of England outwards bounde & was sometymes
distemperd[2] & outwards bounde, the said shippe by contrary
windes was driven into Dartmouth, & afterwards putt into Plim-
*m*outh to take in her Purser & victualls, the Purser beeing sent
thither by the Capt*aine* from Dartmouth to provide victualls,
afterwardes by contrary windes shee was driven into ffalmouth, &
at all those severall places the said Tayler wente a shoare and was
sometymes druncke & lay some nights a shoare from the said
shippe, sometymes neglectinge the busines of the shippe and at
Dartmouth the Capt*aine* said hee had sent for the said Tayler to
come a board and hee did not come but the shippe putt from thence
without him but hee came a board her before shee was cleered of
the range, yet hee saieth that shee stayde some tyme for him the
said Tayler & the winds came contrary soe that shee could not gett
out to sea as otherwise she might have donn, but yf shee had gott
out the winde would have brought her in againe, & at Plimouth the
said Tayler without the Captaines order, as the Capt*aine* said, did
shipp and take in a mann into the said shippe who went the voyage
& eat of the shipps victualls, & whilste the said shipp road at
ffalmouth the winde came faire to proceed on her intended voyage
to the Amazons & then the said Tayler was a shoare at Perin
drinkinge & neglectinge the care of the shippe & voyage & Capt*aine*
Nevill sent his Purser a shoare to require Taylor to come aboarde

[1] P.R.O., HCA 13/49, ff. 52v–4, testimony in the case of Neville and associates
against Taylor. On Lockram, see below, p. 363.
[2] Lucas Browne, 11/21st June 1630 and John Cullens 12/22nd June 1630 had
a more tolerant view of Taylor's potations. Cullens agreed with Browne that
'many tymes in the voyage hee would bee drinckeinge but never so druncke but
that hee was able to directe the business of the shippe' (P.R.O., HCA 13/49, ff.
54–6v).

which hee did not presently doe but some words passinge betweene them, beat the Purser & broke his head,[1] [f. 53v] & the Boatswaine Trumpetter & others of the company of the said shippe beeing then alsoe a shoare at Perin in Company with the said Taylor, did not come aboard untill Taylor came & soe the said shippe was inforced to stay & lost the opportunity of that faire winde & the Company of the other shipps that then sett saile from thence,[2] which was a hindrance to the voyage And this hee affirmeth uppon his oath to be true who was one of the Masters Mates of the said shipp the voyage aforesaide,. . . .

That commeinge into the mouth of the river of Amazons and the boate goeinge before & soundinge founde that there was but fower fathom water, which the Captaine perceaveinge, commaunded Taylor to bringe her to an anchor which Taylor refused to doe,[3] but contrary to the Captaines commannd carried the shipp still on & within a quarter of an houre after she strooke uppon the sands & came a grounde, and was in very great daunger of castinge away & the Sea Nimphe her Viceadmirall followeing her was there cast away, but soe soone as the Amazons was a grounde before, soe soone as shee came into shoale water the Amazons putt out two lights which was aggreed to bee donn by the said shipps to give notice one to the other when either of them should come into daunger, And this hee affirmeth uppon his oath to bee true. . . .

That the articulate Michaell Taylor since they came home from the voyage articulate did tell this examinate that the Owners did knowe that hee the said Tailor had sould away from the said shippe a quoile of roapes & a barrell of tarr, & the barrell of tarr hee thincketh coste here about 28 or thirty shillings. . . .[4]

---

[1] William Vines, the purser of the *Amazon*, testified 15/25th June 1630 that 'the said Taylor drewe his sworde uppon this examinate & fought with him & strooke upp the Captaines heeles & threatened him & at that tyme fower of the passingers for sooke the voyage seeinge (as this examinate conceiveth the ill carriage of the said Tailor. . . .' (P.R.O., HCA 13/49, f. 59v).

[2] Vines testified (ibid., ff. 59–60) that Neville lost the opportunity to sail with English ships bound for St Christophers, as well as with three Dutch men of war, and 'was no longer in performeinge her outwards voyage to the Amazons then otherwise shee would have been by the space of a moneth'. This would suggest that the two vessels should have sailed with Clovell's party.

[3] Taylor's action is accounted for by him 'beeing then in drincke', according to Vines (ibid., f. 60).

[4] John Cullens testified that Taylor embezzled these before he left England (P.R.O., HCA 13/49, f. 57).

[f. 54] That in the ryver of Amazons the said Taylor did Trucke and doe away in trade divers hatchetts, axes Knives & scissers fitt for the trade of that Countrye, which were the goods of the articulate Sir Christopher Nevill & Company & therwith did gett & obtaine some Monkies, Parratts & such thinges which hee afterwards sould at the Barbathoes for Tobacco which hee brought to the Cowes & there lefte And this hee affirmeth uppon his oath to bee true. . . .

That returneinge from the voyage articulate the said Taylor with the said shipp putt into the Cowes & there tooke out of her three tonns & one hundred & a half of lead which belonged to the said Sir Christopher Nevill & Company & sould the same for eight pounds eighteene shillings a hundred. . . .[1]

That in the ryver of Amazons, by the order & direccion of the said Captaine Nevell, two ffallcons were putt out of the shipp the Amazons to be carried a shoare to the fforte in a boate, & the boate with the same sancke by the shipps side. . . .

c.   Extracts from the Deposition of John Barnes, Mariner of
        Ratcliffe, Middlesex, 11th/21st June 1630.[2]

[f. 55v] hee saieth That entringe into the mouth of the river of Amazons one Matthew Murrell one of the quarter Masters of the said shipp standinge in her chaines[3] and soundinge, founde that there was but fower fathom and a quarter water, and then the Captaine willed the Master to come to an anchor untill the next morneinge & hee tolde him hee woulde yf hee founde any lesse water and soe wente on, and hee at the lead still sounded fower fathom & a quarter untill the shippe strucke uppon the grounde, & when they founde her strike the Master asked the said Murrell what depth, & hee still saide fower fathom & a quarter & then another of her Company went to the ledd & founde not two fathom water in the place where Murrell reported fower fathom & a quarter, & by that meanes the said shipp the Amazons was in great daunger of castinge away, & the articulate shipp the Sea Nimphe followeinge

---

[1] Lucas Browne claimed that he did so to procure victuals for the company (P.R.O., HCA 13/49, f. 55).
[2] P.R.O., HCA 13/49, ff. 55–6, testimony in the case of Neville and associates against Taylor.
[3] Strong plates of iron bolted to the ship's sides and used to secure the shrouds.

the Amazons was caste away, but the Amazons soe soone as she strooke putt out a lighte to give notice to the [f. 56] Sea Nimphe of the daunger that shee was in accordinge to aggreement betwixte them, & since their comeinge home the said Taylor hath in this examinates heareinge confessed that he did convey out of the said shipp a barrell of tarr & a quoile of roape, which were the goods of the said Sir Christopher Nevill and Company, & in her returne homewards the said shippe the Amazons putt into the Cowes, & there the said Taylor tooke out of her three tonns one hundred & a half of the lead, which hee sould for nyne pounds a tonn to buy victualls (as hee the said Taylor said) for the shipps company & the remainder beeinge eleaven pounds tenn shillings hee said hee delivered to the Purser, & the Purser in this examinates heareinge hath confessed the receite thereof, and hee saieth, That in the river of Amazons against the fforte, the said Taylor caused two peeces of Ordnannce called ffallcons[1] to bee putt out of the said shipp into her boate to bee carried to the fforte, the Captaine haveinge promised to them in the ffort two peeces of ordnannce out of his shippe, & layde those gunns uppon two Capstenn barrs[2] crosse the boate & this examinate & others of the Company of the said shippe perswadinge him to stowe those Ordenannce downe lower in the boates holde, & tellinge him that they did thincke that the boate would not carry them as they lay, hee the said Taylor, said that hee would warrant that the boate would carry them as they lay, & this examinate tellinge him that hee had seene ordnannce stowed before, Taylor called this examinate foole & Asse but soe soone as the gunns were in her the boate overturned by the shipps side & those gunns were loste one of them weigheinge a thousand & the other eleaven hundred weight & the same were the goods of the said Sir Christopher Nevill & Company, and coste here in England but thirteene shillings a hundred, . . .

d.   Deposition of John Ellinger,
          22nd December 1630/1st January 1631[3]
. . . the foresaid Sir Christofer Nevill and Company aforesaid or any of them in the monethes of November, December, January,

---

[1] See above, p. 177, n. 3.
[2] Removable bars or rods from the ship's capstan.
[3] P.R.O., HCA 24/87, no. 102. Ellinger's testimony in response to the suit brought against him by Sir Christopher Neville and his associates.

ffebruarii and March, in Anno domini i628 or in any of the monethes in Anno domini i629: or in the monethes of March, Aprill, May, June, July, August, September or October in this present yeare i630, or in any of the said yeares, or monethes aforesaid did lade, or cause to be laden abord the said shipp the Sea Nimphe any Beades, knives, or other Commodities to be trans-ported to the River of Amazones aforesaid to be delivered the partners, ffactors or Assignes, of the said Sir Christopher Nevill, and his Company aforesaid, ... the goods and merchandizes mencioned, and contayned in the Schedule here unto annexed ... were, all, and singuler the goods, wares and merchandizes which were laden, or putt abord the said shipp, the Sea Nimphe by the said Sir Christofer Nevill, and his company aforesaid. ...

Item that, all, and singuler the goods, wares and merchandizes, mencioned in the foresaid Schedule hereunto annexed, were truely and really delivered, to William Clovell, Governor and Thomas Hixon Deputie Governor of the said Sir Christofer Nevill, and Company aforesaid,[1] in the River of Amazones by the said Ellinger the times, and places mencioned in the said Schedule hereunto annexed. ...

Item that the said William Clovell, in all some, or one of the yeares, and monethes mencioned in the first Article of this Allegacion, and especially att the time of the delivery of the said goods in the Amazones aforesaid, and att the time of the subscript of the note or Schedule aforesaid by the said Clovell, and Hixon as aforesaid[2] was, and att this present is Governor, and factor of, and to the said Sir Christofer Nevill, and Company in the River, and parts of Amazones aforesaid, And that the said Thomas Hixon dueringe all some or most of the time aforesaid, was and att this present is deputie Governor, and ffactor, for, and to the Company aforesaid. ...

Item that in the yeares, and monethes aforesaid when the said shipp the Sea Nimphe in the voyage aforesaid, did sayle, and proceede to the Amazones aforesaid there was another shipp called the Amazones, in Company, and Consort shipp with the said shipp

---

[1] Oliver Havers, 31st December/10th January 1631 and Anthony Ison, 7/17th January 1631 also stated that William Clovell and Thomas Hixon were 'the reputed Governours and factors for the sayd Sir Christofer Nevill and companye' (P.R.O., HCA 13/49, ff. 217v, 245).

[2] See below, p. 338–40.

the Sea Nimphe, And that the said shipp the Amazones, was, and went Admirall in the said voyage, to the said shipp the Sea Nimphe and the said shipp the Sea Nimph in the voyage aforesaid was, and went Viceadmirall to the said shipp the Amazones. . . .

Item that the said Ellinger, and Company of the said shipp the Sea Nimphe or some of them before the departure of the said shipps the Amazones and Sea Nimphe out of this kingedome of England aswell by Charter partie, and other Covenaunts, and directions, agreed uppon, and given in Charge to the said Ellinger by the said Sir Christofer Nevill, and his Company, was bound, and enjoyned to attend uppon and not to parte Company with the said shipp the Amazones, without expresse commaund, and consent of the Captayne of the shipp the Amazones aforesaid, or by extremitie of wynd and weather. . . .

Item that the said twoe shipps, the Amazones and the Sea Nimph dueringe all the time of theire outwards voyage from England to the River of Amazones aforesaid did keepe Company, and consort togeather. . . .

Item . . . att or about the time that the said twoe shipps the Amazones, and the Sea Nimphe did enter into the mouth of the River of Amazones aforesaid, it was agreed uppon concluded and resolved by and betwixte the Captaine, and the Company of the shipp the Amazones aforesaid And the said Ellenger, and Company of the Sea Nimphe aforesaid, That the said shipp the Amazones, should sayle before, and leade in pursuite of the voyage upp the River of Amazones aforesaid, And that the said shipp the Sea Nimph should followe, . . .

Item . . . it was further concluded and agreed uppon, . . . That if any danger either by the Sea or from the Lande should befall or happen to either of the said shipps . . . that then, and in such Case, the Captaine or other Commannder of such of either of the said shipps as should be in danger as aforesaid should shoote of a peece of greate Ordinance or ells to sett upp twoe lights, one above the other in a conspicuous place of the said shipp soe in danger of purpose to forewarne and prevent the other of the said shipps from that or the like danger. . . .

Item that the Shipps the Amazones, and the Sea Nimph . . . did begine to enter into and proceed in the River of Amazones aboute the hower of sixe of the Clocke in the afternoone. . . .

Item that when the said twoe shipps came first to the mouth of the River of Amazones aforesaid the said Ellenger was unwillinge to have entered into, and proceed in the said River that night but did desire to have forborne untill the next morneinge of purpose to have taken the day before him for his more securitie, And that the said Ellenger did then and there acquainte the Captayne and Company of the said shipp the Amazones with the foresaid desires. . . .

Item that the said Captaine, and Company of the shipp the Amazones aforesaid contrarie to the desire, and Resolucion of the said Ellenger att or about the hower of sixe of the Clocke aforesaid did by all possible hast, and speed sayle, and proceed with the said shipp the Amazones upp the River of Amazones aforesaid And did alsoe commannd, and will the said Ellenger, and his Company to followe him in the same Course with the said shipp the Sea Nimphe which the said Ellenger did accordingely. . . .

Item that within the space of 2:3:4:5: or att least 6 howers after the entrance of the said twoe shipps into the River of Amazones aforesaid the foresaid shipp the Amazones came or was on ground, and there stucke fast whereby much water videlizet to the value of 10:9:8:7:6:5:4:3: or att least twoe foote water did come into, and remayne in the said shipp the Amazones aforesaid whereby the said shipp the Amazones was in greate danger, of perishinge and sinckeinge, and soe much was well seene and perceaved by the Captaine and Company thereof. . . .

Item that notwithstanding the agreement, and Resolucions, hadd, and made betwixt the Captayne and Company of the shipp the Amazones aforesaid and the said Ellenger, and his Company of the Sea Nimphe as aforesaid, And notwithstandinge the Eminent danger that the said shipp the Amazones was in as aforesaid yet neverthelesse neither the Captayne or any of the Company of the Shipp the Amazones aforesaid did shoote of a greate peece of Ordinance, or sett upp twoe lights the one above the other or give any other signe or note to the said Ellenger, and his Company of the Sea Nimphe of the greate danger the shipp the Amazones was then in, or of the shallowenes of the River in that place, or of any other inconveniencie or danger. . . .

Item that the said Ellenger, and his Company beinge ignorant of the danger that then the shipp the Amazones was in (accordinge to the comannd and direction given him by the Captayne of the Amazones aforesaid) did followe, and attend the said shipp the

Amazones up the River of Amazones in prosecution of the voyage aforesaid. . . .

Item that shortly after the shipp the Amazones aforesaid was on ground as aforesaid the foresaid shipp the Sea Nimphe in her ordinary, and commannded Course aforesaid in followeinge and attendinge the said shipp the Amazones did alsoe come or touch uppon the ground, and thereby and not by any [supind] negligence wilfulnes or want of skill, or Art, or industrie or indeavour of the said Ellenger, and his Company was cast away or perished. . . .

Item that the said shipp the Sea Nimphe att such time as she came or was on ground as aforesaid was not yare[1] but evill, and difficult steeridge. . . .

Item that the said Ellenger dueringe all the time of the outwards voyage, aforesaid, and especially at such time as he entered into the mouth of the River of Amazones aforesaid, and untill the time of the Comeinge on ground of the said shipps the Amazones and the Sea Nimphe aforesaid, and untill the time of the perishinge, and castinge away of the said shipp the Sea Nimphe did use, and exercise all possible meanes, paines, and dilligence, care and endeavor that a discrete, and expert mariner could use for the preservation of the said shipp the Sea Nimphe and her ladinge. . . .

Item . . . the boate, or Pinace seized and taken by the said Ellenger, and Company in theire outwards voyage aforesaid . . . was . . . repayred, furnished, and fitted by the said Ellenger, and his Company, and intended, destined and appointed, to proceede in the said River of Amazones, and there to take in such ladinge as the said Sir Christofer Nevill, and his Company aforesaid, or his or theire ffactors or assignes did or would lade abord the said boate or Pinnace . . . yet in truth, . . . the said Ellenger, and Company presently or shortly after the comeinge on ground and casteinge away of the shipp call (sic) the Sea Nimphe aforesaid did withall possible meanes, endeavor, Art, and industrie that then could be used, and that Cuntry then did or could afford repayre, build fitt, and provide the said boate or Pinnace[2] soe by them taken in theire outwards voyage aforesaid for the best imployment, benifitt, and Advantage, of the said Sir Christofer Nevill, and his Company. . . .

Item that soe soone as the said Ellenger and his Company, had

---

[1] Yare, answering readily to the helm.
[2] Renamed the *Guiana*.

329

repayred built, and fitted the said boate or Pinnace fitt to brooke the Sea he the said Ellenger, and his Company accordinge to the directions of the ffactors, and Assignes of the said Sir Christofer Nevill, and his Company aforesayd did sayle and steere the said boate, or pinnace soe repayred as aforesaid to the Way of Pocowe,[1] in the said Cuntry of the Amazones And there therewith did safely arrive. . . .

Item that the said Ellenger, and his Company after theire arrivall with theire said boate or Pinnace in the Way of Pocowe aforesaide did intimate, and insinuate unto the the ffactors and Assignes of the said Sir Christofer Nevill, and his company aforesaid, or to their Agents ffactors, or Assignes that the said Ellenger and his Company were ready, and did attend with the said boate or Pinnace soe by them repayred, and fitted, to receave take aboard, and to transporte to this Kingedome of England all such goods wares, and merchandizes as any of the Agents, ffactors, or Assignes, of the said Sir Christofer Nevill, and his Company did or would lade, or putt abord the said boate or Pinnace, And that the said Ellenger, and his Company aforesaid did stay, and remayne in the said Way of Pocowe aforesaid after such theire arrivall there, and after significacion, and intimacion made as aforesaid by the space of 8:7:6:5:4:3: or att least twoe weekes with full purpose, intent, and resolucion to take abord the said boate or Pinnace all such goods wares, and merchandizes. . . .

Item that after the said Ellinger, and his company of the Pinnace aforesaid wayted, and attened (sic) in the way of Pocowe aforesaid. . . . The Governors, ffactors and Agents of the Company of Sir Christofer Nevill aforesaid and his Company or some of them did cleare, quite, and discharge the said Ellenger, and his company and the boate or Pinnace aforesaid from any further attendance or expectacion to receave any goods or ladinge in the Way of Pocowe. . . .[2]

Item that shortly after the discharge or release att and from the way of Pocowe . . . the foresaid Ellenger, and Company did with all possible speed, and conveniencie shape theire Course with the said

[1] Wiapoco.
[2] Anthony Ison stated, 7/17th January 1631, that Robert Harcourt 'tould the sayd ellinger and companye that most of his companye were starved for want of merchandizes to trucke or trade for victualls'. (P.R.O., HCA 13/49, f. 245).

boate or Pinnace, repayred or built aforesaid for this Kingedome of England. . . .

Item that before the said Ellinger, and his Company had sayled, and brought the said boate or Pinnace in the Course aforesaid soe farr, or to the hight of St. Christofers Ilands,[1] three, or att least twoe of the mayne timbers, and divers others of the planckes and parts of the said boate or Pinnace were broken And a greate parte of her Ridgeinge, Tacklinge, and furniture soe wasted, and spoyled, and her victuals were soe farr spent and consumed that in all probabillitie she neither then could, or would any longer brooke the Sea, or att least wise was nott able in all probabillitie to hould out, and safely sayle to this Kingedome of England. . . .

Item that the Company of the said Ellinger in the boate, or Pinnace aforesaid or some of them . . . did unterly (sic) refuse to venture theire lives, and to sayle in the said boate or pinnace directly to this Kingdome of England. . . .

Item that the Company of the said boate or Pinnace notwith-standinge the manifold intreaties and perswations, of the said Ellenger did utterly refuse to sayle the said boate or Pinnace for England but did force or att least overule the said Ellenger to beare upp and carrie her to the Islands of St *Christ*ofers. . . .

Item that shortly after the arrivall, of the said boate or Pinnace in the Islands of St *Christ*ofers aforesaid the said Ellenger did againe attempt to perswade his Company to helpe bringe or sayle the said boate, or Pinnace to the Kingedome of England but they utterly refused soe to doe, whereuppon he the said Ellenger beinge altogeather utterly [un]provided of Marriners to bringe or conduct the said boate or Pinnace to England, And haveinge spent all or most part of his victualls, and beinge utterly disabled to revictuall or furnish his said boate, or Pinnace in the said Islands of St *Christ*ofers or in any other place neere thereto adjacent uppon necessitie, and for noe other Cause or reason, was forced and Compelled, to abondan, and leave or ells to sell, and dispose of the said boate or Pinnace in the said Islands of St *Christ*ofers, And that thereuppon,

---

[1] The *Guiana* had previously called at Barbados where Thomas Nevison, Lewes Jackson, Jonathan Selman and the other passengers taken aboard at the Wiapoco went ashore, refusing to risk themselves in her any further. Anthony Hough, a sea captain at Barbados at that time, testified 12/22nd January 1631, that she was 'a very scurvye patched weake vessell'. (P.R.O., HCA 13/49, ff. 230, 246).

and for noe other reason he the said Ellinger did sell or barter away the said boate or Pinnace for the some or value of 700[li]: weight of Tobacco, and noe more, att the rate of 4[s]: per pound legalis monete Anglie. . . .

Item that the foresaid boate or Pinnace att the time of the sayle or truckeinge thereof away att the Iland of St *Christ*ofers aforesaid was not there worth to be sould above the some or vallue of 700[li]: weight of Tobacco att the rate of 4[s] per pound as aforesaid. . . .

Item that shortly after the sale or truckeinge away of boate or Pinnace aforesaid the marriners, and company of the boate or Pinnace aforesaid did cause, and procure the said Ellenger to be arrested, or convented before the Governor, or other Officers of the Iland of St *Christ*ofers aforesaid for theire wages in the forepast voyage, And that the said Ellenger after such arrest, and convention did to his uttermost labor, and endeavor to reserve the heareinge of the busines, untill theire reture (sic) into this kingedome of England. . . .

Item that notwithstandinge all the labors, and endeavors mentioned in the next precedent article the foresaid Governor, or other Officers of the Islands of St *Christ*ofers aforesaid did force, and compell the said Ellenger to pay and satisfie, unto the Marriners of the boate or Pinnace for their wages in the foresaid voyage not onely the foresaid some or vallue of 700[l] weight of Tobacco for which the said Boate or Pinnace was sould but alsoe the quantitie or vallue of 300[li]: weight more of Tobacco out of the private Estate of the said Ellenger in satisfactione of theire wages aforesaid.[1]

e.   Further deposition by John Ellinger,
              26th January/5th February 1631[2]
    . . . Item that in all or one of the yeares, and monethes aforesaid, and especially on or aboute the twenty fifth day of Aprill in Anno

---

[1] Ellinger submitted two affidavits to the court in his defence. One, signed by Jonas Colbache secretary to Sir Thomas Warner, Governor of St Christophers, affirms that Ellinger sold the pinnace, and her ordnance to Warner and gave the proceeds of 700 lbs of tobacco to the crew in lieu of ten months wages. The second, signed by members of the company of the *Charity* of Bristol in which Ellinger took passage home, confirms Ellinger's version of the events at St Christophers (P.R.O., HCA 30/865, no. 7, schedules 5, 7).

[2] P.R.O., HCA 24/87, no. 116. Ellinger's libel against Sir Christopher Neville and associates.

domini 1629:[1] aforesaid the foresaid, Sir Christofer Nevill, Sir John North Sir Henry Mildmaye, John Lucas, and Company or some of them ... did covenant, contract and promise, to and with the said John Ellenger to pay and satisffie to the said John Ellenger his Executors, or Assignes six pounds of lawfull money of England for every moneth that the said Ellenger should serve, or be imployed in the voyage, or voyages aforesaid. ...

Item that in all some, or one of the yeares, and monethes aforesaid the foresaid Sir Christopher Nevill, Sir John North, Sir Henry Mildmaye, and John Lucas, or some, or one of them or some or other of their deputies, and Assignes ... did contract, covenant and agree to and with the said John Ellenger well, and truely to pay, and satisfie to all the marriners, and Company of the said shipp or Pinnace called the Sea Nimphe to be hired and appointed by the said John Ellenger all such wages, pay and Composition, as the said John Ellenger should contract for, promise, or compound to pay to the marriners, and Company the said Pinnace called the Sea Nimphe for theire severall imployments, and wages in the said Pinnace the voyage, or voyages aforesaid And that the said Sir Christofer Nevill, and Company aforesaid and all some or one of them within the time aforesaid did alsoe contract covenant promise and agree to and with the said John Ellenger cleerely to acquite, and discharge, the said Ellenger against all person or persons, whatsoever, of, for, and concerneinge, all such wages made, and agreed uppon betwixt the said Ellenger and Company for, and concerneinge the voyage and voyages aforesaid. ...

Item ... that ... the foresaid Sir Christofer Nevill, and Company ... did further ... agree to and with the said John Ellenger, and all the marriners and Company ... should ... be paid halfe of the said monethly wages aforesaid from and after the foresaid 25th day of Aprill Anno domini 1629 aforesaid untill the foresaid Pinnace should fall downe or come to the porte of Gravsend [Gravesend] in her outwards voyage aforesaid, And that from the time of her falleinge downe, or comeinge of the said Pinnace to Gravsend in her outwards voyage they the said Sir Christofer Nevill, and Company would pay and satisfied unto the said Ellenger the some of 6[l]: per moneth, and to his Company all such wages as the said

[1] Further evidence that the ship was being outfitted at the same time as those which took out William Clovell and the North fort colonists.

Ellenger should agree, or compound for dueringe the voyage or voyages aforesaid. . . .

Item that the said Ellenger . . . did hold contract with all, covenant, and compound withall, and singuler the severall persons mentioned in the schedule annexed to the allegation for their severall wages. . . .

Item that the said Ellenger did serve, and continue master in the said Pinnace called the Sea Nimph from the 25th: of Aprill Anno domini i628:[1] untill the 22th day of March in Anno domini . . . i629: and did proceede in the said voyage, And that all, and singuler the persons or mariners mencioned in the said Schedule did serve, and were imployed in the said Pinnace called the Sea Nimph in the performance of the said voyage dueringe all the time mentioned in the said Schedule. . . .

f.   Extracts from a further deposition by John Ellinger,
10th/20th May 1631[2]

. . . that before such time as the said Ellinger did proceede, or departe from this porte of London in the voyage where the pretended damage is questioned in this Cause, it was contracted . . . betweene the foresaid Sir Christofer Nevill, and his Company, . . . And the said Ellinger . . . that he the said Ellinger should carrye, outwards Adventure, and trade with him the voyage aforesaid, for the proper accompt of the said Ellinger, any goods, or merchandizes whatsoever nott exceedinge the vallue of tenn pounds of lawfull money of England. . . .

Item . . . the said Ellinger, any time or any porte dueringe the voyage in question, did trade . . . for his owne proper accompt . . . yet in truth he the said Ellinger in such his trade did nott make use of trucke, or barter any of the goods, or merchandizes of the said Sir Christofer Nevill, and Company, but onely by and with such goods and merchandizes as the said Ellinger did carrye outwards, from England. . . .

Item that the Companye of the shipp called the Sea Nimphe . . . att the time of her arrivall in the Amazones the voyage in question, were in greate want, and much distressed for want of victualls. . . .

---

[1] 1629.
[2] P.R.O., HCA 24/88, no. 5, response of John Ellinger to the allegations of Neville and associates.

Item . . . any of the goods, or merchandizes which were laden in the said shipp by the said Sir Christofer Nevill and Companye . . . were delivered to the said Ellinger and by him disposed of . . . in the Amazones . . . yet such goods . . . as came . . . to the hands . . . of the said Ellinger the voyage aforesaid in the Amazones aforesaid . . . were soe delivered to the said Ellinger by the deputyes, ffactors, or Assignes of the said Sir: Christofer Nevill, and his Companye And that the said goods, and merchandizes soe delivered to the said Ellinger, in the Amazones as aforesaid were but onelye one Chest of Turrenavyes,[1] and halfe a dozen of knives, and one pound of beads, and noe more. . . . And that the said Ellinger . . . did buye . . . victualls, which he the said Ellinger was forced to distribute . . . to the Company of the shipp the Sea Nimphe. . . .

Item . . . the said Ellinger after the said shipp the Sea Nimphe was in danger to perishe did land out of the said shipp and safely deliver on shoare, all such goods, and merchandizes as had bine formerly laden by the said Sir Christofer Nevill . . . entirelye, and without diminucon and did not reserve, or keepe, any parte thereof for the use of him the said Ellinger. . . .

Item that the said Sir Christofer Nevill, and his Companye did send many passengers in the said shipp the Sea Nimphe in her outwards voyage to the Amazones, and that those passengers, after that the goods, and merchandizes were landed and putt on shoare by the said Ellinger as aforesaid did breake open divers, or some of the Chests of the said merchants goods, and did ripp the said shipps sayles, and make themselves clothes thereof, and did committ divers other outrages contrarye to the Will and power to refuse of the said Ellinger. . . .[2]

Item that att the time of the beinge of the said shipp att Wayapoco the voyage in question the Indians did slaye 60:50:40: or att least 30 Dutch men and did likewise resolve, and practice to put to death, and committ divers insolencies uppon the English then there, and that there uppon the said Ellinger by and with the

[1] Not identified.
[2] Robert Barker, 13/23rd March 1631, testified that the day after the *Sea-Nymph* came aground John Ellinger said to him 'come lett us goe downe into holde & helpe ourselves to make ourselves a voyage, or used wordes to that effecte & this examinate denied to consente there unto but that nighte or the nexte day Ellinger & some others of the said shipps company with him wente downe into her hould & broke open some chests of goods belongeinge to the said Sir Christopher Nevill & company. . . .' (P.R.O., HCA 13/49, f. 308v).

Command directions, and approbation, of the Governor and Councell of the English in those parts, did enter into fight with the said Indians ... yett he did nott in that fight take prisoners, and detayne above the number of five Indians, And that the Governor, and Councell aforesaid shortly after that fight did give, and bestowe the said five Indian Prisoners unto, or uppon the said Ellinger for his said service. ...[1]

Item ... the said Ellinger did leave an Indian[2] in the Iland of St *Christ*ophers aforesaid which was brought abord the said Pinnace in the Amazones the voyage aforesaid ... yet the said Indian was there soe left in respect there was noe provision of victuall for his passage to England, and alsoe in respect the Carpenter, and boatswayne of the said Pinnace did not, or would suffer or permitt the said Ellinger to procure, any passage for the Indian for England in respect, as the said Carpenter then affirmed that the Indian did belonge unto him, and that the said Carpenter and boatswayne (when the said Ellinger offered, or endeavored to procure the said Indian passage for England) or one of them offered to stabb the said Ellinger, and gave him such other affronts that he was justly putt in feare of his life. ...

3. DOCUMENTS SUBMITTED BY ELLINGER TO SUPPORT HIS VERSION OF EVENTS

a. Schedule of the wage claims of the crew of the *Sea-Nymph*[3]

Inprimis Oliver Haver[4] from the 22th of Maye i629: to the 22th of March followeinge att 3:[li] per moneth cometh to

	l	s	d
	30—	0—0	

[1] Jan van Ryen's colony (see above, p. 271, n. 2) had been massacred by Caribs shortly after their arrival on the Wiapoco in 1627. Harcourt and his company found that the Indians of the river were no longer willing to tolerate European settlers. Various witnesses reported that Sir Oliver Cheyney had been engaged in hostilities with the Yaios neighbouring the English plantations. Ellinger sold the five Indian slaves given to him by Harcourt in Barbados (P.R.O., HCA 13/49, ff. 246v, 309–10v).

[2] Anthony Ison, 7/17th January 1631 and Robert Barker testified, 13/23rd March 1631, that this Indian was from the Amazon and had come onboard voluntarily to make the trip to England (P.R.O., HCA 13/49, ff. 246v, 309).

[3] P.R.O., HCA 24/87, no. 116, annexed schedule.

[4] Oliver Havers had been associated in the voyage of the *Lions Clawe*, 1609–11, see above, p. 38, n. 3.

	l	s	d
Item Thomas Yates Gunner for the like time att xxxvi: [ˢ] per moneth cometh to	18–	0–0	
Item Robert Barker for the like time att xxxviˢ per moneth cometh to	18–	0–0	
Item William Smalebone[1] for the like time att xxxviˢ: per moneth cometh to	18–	0–0	
Item Thomas Sp[rou]dens for the same time att xxiiiiˢ per moneth cometh to	xii–	0–0	
Item John Cuttler for the like time att xxviˢ per moneth cometh to	13–	0–0	
Item Robert Morley at lvˢ per moneth for the like time cometh to	27–	0–0	
Item Silvester Brickingeshawe for the like time att xxxviˢ: per moneth cometh to	18–	0–0	
Item Anthony Ison for the like time att xxiiiiˢ per moneth cometh to	12–	0–0	
Item Gabriell Odgar for the like time att xxiiˢ: per moneth cometh to	11–	0–0	
Item William Leves att xxiiˢ per moneth for the like time cometh to	11–	0	
Item James Wood att xviii:ˢ per moneth for the like time cometh to	9–	0–0	
Item Thomas Gardner for the like time att xxˢ: per moneth cometh to	10–	0–0	
Item John Wood for the like time at xxiiˢ per moneth cometh to	11–	0–0	
Item William Robertson for the like time att xviiiˢ per moneth cometh to	9–	0–0	
Item Richard Kendall for the like time att xxˢ per moneth cometh to	10–	0–0	
Item Robert Huggins att xxiiˢ per moneth for the like time cometh to	11–	0–0	
Item John Cranfeild for foure moneth att 3:ˡⁱ per moneth cometh to	12–	0–0	
Item John Cooke for foure monethes att xxiiˢ per moneth cometh to	4–	0–0	

---

[1] William Smallbone advised Roger Fry in the purchase of the *Barcke Andevor* in 1631, see below, p. 363.

	l	s	d
Item James Blaseby for sixe moneths att xii^s per monethe cometh to	3	12	0

Item James Blaseby for sixe moneths att xii^s per
monethe cometh to   3–12–0
Item Thomas Nipkine for 9 monethes att xxii^s per
moneth cometh to   9–18–0
Item John Croaker for 9 monethes att xvi^s per moneth
cometh to   7– 4–0
Item Erasmus Huffield for the same time att xxxvi^s per
moneth cometh to   18– 0–0
Item Thomas Dodd for the like time att xxiiii^s per
moneth cometh to   12– 0–0

b.   Receipt for goods delivered to William Clovell and
             Thomas Hixon at North fort on the Amazon, 1629[1]
             1629   this 14th of november

Received from the Sea Nymph

9 . Chests of Companyes trade.
1 . Chest with Ammunicion.
1 . box of Terrenaries
1 . halfe hogshead of oyle
1 . halfe hogshead otmeale[2]
1 . halfe Barrell of Iron trade
2 . Barrells of Peese[3]
3 . halfe Barrells of flover (sic)[4]
2 . Barrells of Clothes
1 . halfe barrell of shooes
1 . halfe Barrell of grocerii
1 . Barrell with Seyne[5] lynes & twyne
1 . Roundlett of Aquavita
1 . firkin of sugar
1 . pigge of lead[6]
1 . barrell of powder
1 . Roundlett[7] of small shot
11. Shovells
11. Spades

---

[1] P.R.O., HCA 24/87, no. 102 annexed schedule.
[2] Oatmeal.   [3] Peas.   [4] Flour.
[5] Seine or fishing lines.
[6] Oblong mass of lead as run from the furnace.
[7] A barrel or cask.

3 . grindstones
6 . belts for swords
1 . halfe barrell of match.

Noe ye that wee have receaved All these goods abovenamed from aboard the Sea Nymph/

And Noe ye also that there were Twentie eight men delivered ashore in the River of the Amazones which came in the Sea Nymph/

In Testimony whereof we have hereunto subscribed our names

William Clovell   Thomas Hixon.

c.   Letter from the Governor and Council
              of the same plantation, 1629[1]

Whereas wee the Governors and Counsell of Guiana for the English Plantacon have (at our intreaties) obteigned and had of Captaine ffrancis Nevill Esquier Michaell Tailor Master of the good Shippe called the Amazones and John Ellenger late Master of the good shippe called the Sea nymphe this Amunition followinge (videlizet) Two ffalcons one Murderer[2] two Chambers two Ladles two spunges – xxiiii round shott two Sows[3] of lead weighinge about 200 weight and two Carriags[4] all things thereunto belonginge for our better safeguard and defence and for the better Mannageinge and strengtheninge of our forte where wee are to abide and remayne: All which we have receaved and had at the hands of the said Master John Ellenger out of the said Shippe called the Sea Nymphe for all which wee thinke our selves verie much beholden into them not doubtinge but that you will allow of the same in regard of our extraordinarie want thereof ffirst for that the Portugalls of themselves are verie stronge, and have burnt and consumed all the Indyan Townes for (at least) 100: leagues upp the River,[5] And allso for that the Irish who came with Captaine Pursell and was settled here,[6] did at our comeinge yeild upp themselves and all theyr Armes into the Portingalls hands, and did Trecherouslie betray divers English, who were with them in theyr Plantation and slew them, And for that we haveinge A shalloppe would be in verie great danger to passe anyway in the River and retourn safe

---

[1] P.R.O., HCA 30/865, no. 7, schedule 6.
[2] A mortar shooting small shot or 'murthering shot', intended to scour the decks of personnel; Blackmore, 1976, p. 236.
[3] Pigs.   [4] Gun carriages.   [5] See above, pp. 300–17.
[6] This should not be taken to mean literally on the same site.

againe/: without which said Ammunition we were by no means able to subsist and defend ourselves in our forte, but with great danger of all our lives, and the utter Ruyn and overthrow of our plantacion, And this we thought good to give under our hands not doubtinge but yow will give the owners good satisfaccion for the same, for the discharg of the Captaine and the said Company/ In Testimony whereof we have hereunto subscribed our names/

Francis Nevill   Thomas Hixon
                    William Cloville
James Croft[1]   Edward Blenerhayset.[2]
Henry Mandcitt[3]
Gabriell Ellys[4]
Thomas Godbold[5]
Ruben Serle[6]

d.   Letters from Robert Harcourt to John Ellinger,
                    March 1630[7]

Knowe all men by these presents that I Robert Harcourt Governour of the English Plantation in the River of Wiapoco in Guiana, have given & granted unto Captaine John Ellenger five Indians of the Yaio nation which I had taken Prisoners. videlizet:[8] two men, two women, & one Boy; to have & to holde them as his owne, to dispose of them, at his will & pleasure, in wittnes whereof I have hereunto sett my hand & seale the xiiith day of March 1629 [23 March 1630]

                    Robert Harcourt
Thomas Nevinson[9]
Lewis Jackson[10]
Sealed & delivered in the presence of.

---

[1] Presumably a member of the council.
[2] See above, p. 89, n. 2.
[3] Presumably the Henry Mandit gent., listed by Sir Henry Spelman as having come into the Guiana Co. subsequent to the issue of the charter, see below, p. 391.
[4] Gentleman. Listed by Sir Henry Spelman as entering the Guiana Co. subsequent to the issue of the charter, see below, p. 391.
[5] Not otherwise known.
[6] Not otherwise known. Presumably both Serle and Godbold were members of the Council.
[7] P.R.O., HCA 30/865, no. 7, schedules 1, 4. The two letters bear Harcourt's signature.
[8] See above, p. 336, n. 1.   [9] See above, p. 319, n. 5.
[10] See above, pp. 318–19.

Good Captaine: to give you full Content as you have well deserved, I have sent you a deede of gifte, & a warrant included for the great Shallop; as also a bill of my hand to the Company in England, to satisfie you for the Trade I have received of you, of which I make noe doubte; I have alsoe written to Sir Christopher Nevill in your behalfe, to allowe of what you have done for us, & to move the Company for your satisfaction for the same.[1] I have likewise Commended you to the Company in my particular letter to them; as also to the Treasurer of the Company Sir Henry Spellman my especiall frend, & I sent those my letters to them,[2] & others, unto Sir Oliver Cheyney to be delivered to you.

Good Captaine, yf you will doe me the Curtesie to send me a pinte of oyle, a quarte of vinegar, a pound or two of Cheese, & a quarte of Aquavite, yf you can possibly spare them, I shall rest highly beholding to you; & I pray you forgett me not for as much salte as you can spare; & if ever you returne into this Country, I will requite your Curtesie (God willing) & so with my best salutings to you I Committ you to God & rest

Your assured frend

This 19th of March 1629 [29 March 1630]   Robert Harcourt

4. THE ALLEGATIONS OF SIR CHRISTOPHER NEVILLE AND ASSOCIATES AGAINST ELLINGER

a.   Extracts from the libel entered in the High Court
of Admiralty by Neville, Mildmay, North, Lucas and company,
22nd November/2nd December 1630[3]

... That in the yeares and monethes aforesaide or some or one of them the saide Sir Christopher Nevill knight, Sir John Northe and Sir Henry Mildemay knights John Lucas Esquier and Companie aforesaide did lade ... Beades, knives, and other comodities fitte for the trucke and trade of the River Countrie of Amazones to the value of five hundred pounds. . . .

Item That the said John Ellinger willfullye or careleslye & by his

---

[1] Harcourt obviously regards Sir Christopher Neville's syndicate and the Guiana Co. of which some of them were members and under whose licence they operated, as separate entities.
[2] Not found.
[3] P.R.O., HCA 24/87, no. 82.

faulte did caste awaye the said shippe the Sea nimphe & her tackle & furniture & theerby the said Sir Christofer Nevill his partners aforesaid did sustaine dammage by losse of the said shippe & her tackle & furniture to the value of 700^{li} lawfull money of Englande. . . .

Item That the said goods wares and merchandices before specefied . . . were not by him delivred at the Amazones to the factors & Assignes of the said Christofer Nevill & companye or at the leaste a greate parte of them but disposed of by the said John Ellinger at his pleasure & theerby the said Sir Christofer Nevill & partners aforesaid have received & sustained damage to the value of iii C^{li} lawfull monye of Englande. . . .

Item That after the losse & castinge awaye of the said shippe the Sea nimphe in the Cuntrye of Amazones aforesaid the said Sir Christofer Nevill & his partners aforesaid or theire factors or Assignes at theire costs & chargs did builde & furnishe an other pinace & delivered her to the charge & conducte of the said Ellinger . . . to saile her for theire use to WayaPoco & theere to take in goods for the said Sir Christofer Nevill and companie & carrie them to theire use in the said pinnace to Engelande. . . .

Item That the said John Ellinger did not saile the said pinace . . . accordinge to the directions aforesaid but solde & disposed of her & her tackle & furniture at his pleasure. . . .

Item That the said pinace & her tackle & furniture at the time of the sellinge & disposeinge theerof were worthe the summe of 300^{li} . . . and the said Sir Christofer Nevill and companie by the injurious sale & disposeinge theerof by the said John Ellinger have sustained damiage in theire affaires dependeinge upon the imploimentt of the said pinace to the value of 500^{li}. . . .

Item . . . the saied John Ellinger did trucke & doe awaie for his owne benefitte and vantage the said pinace builte & provided in the Weste Indies as aforesaid & divers knives & other comodities fitte for the trade of that Cuntrye . . . & therwith did gette provide to his owne use 4 hoghedds or other vessells of Anatte & 2000^{li} weight of tabaccoe. . . .

Item That the said John Ellinger did bringe the said Anatte & tabaccoe to Bristoll & theere lefte the same in the Custodie . . . of one Master Derricke Popleye. . . .

Item the said John Ellinger beinge arrived heere at London & questioned by the said Sir Christofer Nevill & companie for sellinge

& disposeinge of theire said pinace & undue disposeinge of theire goods aforesaid did write a letter to the said derricke Popleye of the tenor of the said scedule heerto annexed. . . .

Item That the Anatte & tabaccoe aforesaid were worthe the sume of iii C^{li}. . . .

b.   Further allegations made against Ellinger,
11th/21st March 1631[1]

. . . Item that after the casteinge away of the Seanimph by the sayd Ellenger as aforesayd in the river of Amazones theere was theere a Pinnace builte . . . called the Gwayana and comitted to the Charge of the said Ellinger with direction that he theerewith should waite and attend upon an other shippe called the Amazones belonginge to the sayd Sir Christopher Nevill and Company. . . .

Item that the sayd Ellinger puttinge to sea with the sayd Pinnace the Guiana out of the river of Amazones did not accordinge to his direction followe the sayd shippe the Amazones, but for his owne Endes and purposes left the Companye of the Amazones and wente with the sayd Pinnace to Wayapoco. . . .[2]

Item that the sayd Ellinger beinge comen to WayaPoco did theere committ dyvers outrages by killinge dyvers Indians that were belonginge to the Plantation theere belonginge to the sayd Sir Christopher Nevill and Company or at least correspondents and ffreindes to the sayd English Planters and seized upon divers Chests and other things belonginge to the sayd English Planters and tooke out of them and disposed to his owne use gunnes and other Comodityes and damnifyed the sayd Sir Christopher Nevill and Company English Planters at Wayapoco aforesayd by his sayd outrages misbehaviours and unjust dealinge to the valewe of 2000^{li}. . . .[3]

Item that the sayd Pinnace the Gwyana soulde at St Christophers or some other of the sayde Islands by the sayd Ellinger, at the tyme of her selling and disposeinge away by the sayd Ellinger was stronge stanch and sufficiently provided and able in all respects to have beene brought for England had not the sayd Ellinger injuriously

[1] P.R.O., HCA 24/87, no. 88.
[2] William Smallbone, 13/23rd March 1631, testified that the *Amazon* and the *Guiana* left the river Amazon together but were parted by foul weather (P.R.O., HCA 13/49, ff. 309v–10v).
[3] Contradicted by p. 336, n. 1 and by Harcourt's letters pp. 340–1.

and unjustly without any just grounde or cause sowlde her for his owne Advantages. . . .

Item that the sayd Ellinger hath dyvers and sundry tymes or at least once acknowledged and confessed that he did gett and gayne in the sayd voyage wheerein he cast away the Seanimph and disposed the sayd Sir Christophers Nevills goodes and solde theyr Pinnace called the Gwyana[1] ar*ticula*te aforesayd the summe of 4000[li] lawfull money of England. . . .

c.   Letter from John Ellinger to Derek Popley,
          merchant of Bristol, 4th/14th July 1630[2]

Sir

My service alwayes unto you remembred &c alsoe given you many thanks for your kindnes unto me shewed, soe yt is that noe soner I came to London but that Sir Christopher Nevill, and the rest of the owners, that ymployed me unto the Amazones, caused me to be arrested upon an accion ten thousand pounds, and hath cast me into prison, yet I Doubte not, but that god will Rayse me frends to bayle me, uppon there accion, Sir nowe yt is my Earnest Desyer that you wilbe pleased to shew me that favoure, that yf Sir Christopher Nevill, Sir Henry Myldmay Sir John North, knights or Master John Lucas or any other for them, shall happen to come into your parts to make any Enquirie of me, that you will soe Deale for me, with Captaine Stanffast,[3] that yf he be questyned about the pinnas I sould in St Christophers, he would enforme them, that she had two of her Reebes broken, And that she was not able to goe to sea without Danger of all her mens Lifes, And for the two ffats of Dyinge stuffe Called Anotta and the two ffatts of Tobaca I Lefte with you, I Doe also Desyer you to kepe close that yt may not be knowne, And yf you cane convenenly make sale of the Anotta I pray doe yt is worth her in London vi[s] per pound at the feirst hand and for the tobaca Sell yt as you may Kepe the monnyes in your hands, ffor I purpose as sone as I have my libertie to visite you and make you parte of ammends for all Curtizes thus in hast I leave you

---

[1] *Guiana.*
[2] P.R.O., HCA 24/87, no. 82, annexed schedule.
[3] The captain of the *Charity* of Bristol. Popley secured the required affidavit preserved in P.R.O., HCA 30/865, no. 7, schedule 7.

with your good beedfellow[1] unto the protecion of thallmightie and will remayne

> Yours ev[er] at your service to be Commanded
> John Ellenger

July the 4th
1630

To his most Resptictave good ffrend master Derek popley Marchaunt in Bristill these –

5. TROUBLES PRECEDING THE VOYAGE OF THE *EXCHANGE*, SENT OUT WITH ORDERS TO REMOVE HARCOURT'S SETTLERS TO THE AMAZON, JANUARY 1630

[f. 1] 'A happie Shipwrack or the losse of a late intended voyage by Sea recovered by a Briefe of this experience', by Richard Thornton.[2] . . . Most noble Lord

The benefitt of nature, & a happie educacion hath made mee not more prone to reseolve then willing to knowe my owne resolucon, as holding that man unfitt for anie designe, whoe is not able to give a reason for his accions. . . . Whereupon I make bold to present unto your Lordship the causes of my undertaking & desistinge from this voyage, lately intended for Guiana, at the directions of an honorable Companie, whereof your Lordship being Governor maye well expect a just & faythfull accompt of my proceedings, that soe by my returne I maie neither prejudice the generall good of that most hopefull plantation, nor give your Lordship & the world anie occasion to thinke mee of their number, whoe upon like designes are esteemed . . . waveringe mynded men unstable in all theire wayes. [f. 1v] When I resolved upon this voyage, Religion had taught mee in the first place to respect the

---

[1] Bed fellow, wife.
[2] Bodleian, Ashmolean MS 749, no. II. A substantial portion of the manuscript was printed in Harlow, *Colonizing expeditions*, 1925, pp. 148–74. Harlow's transcription has, however, some grave errors in it which are noted below. Thornton addressed his memorial to the Governor of the Guiana Co., William Herbert third earl of Pembroke, see above, p. 204, n. 1. Hoping for a preferment, Thornton demonstrated his scholarship by interlarding his account with tedious Latin aphorisms, which I have edited out here. Thornton's work is, nevertheless, very valuable in that it preserves copies of some of the otherwise lost court records of the Guiana Co.

glorie of God, by propagatinge his Gospell accordinge to the duties of my callinge, wherein that I might not bee thought impatient of ancient constitutions, & ambitious of innovation, or shewe anie appearance of a babling vagabond, & schismaticall, wherewith manie in these daies are possessed, & like heards of Swyne runne headlong into the Sea, but (in a due remembrance from whence wee came) really preserve the doctrine & discipline of the Church of England, lest anie should hereafter complayne of us ..., I moved the Company to send a large Bible, a Common prayer booke of Articles the booke of Homilyes, & a Communion Cupp.... All which were accordingly provided, & by mee carried on Shipboard....

In the next place I intended the temporall happines of the plantation & of that above others, because of your Lordships governement, to whome the utmost of my power shall ever bee devoted in an humble acknowledgement of all dutie for manie noble favours heretofore receyved, the freedome whereof commannds my thankfullnes.... And therefore in testimony of my sincere affeccion to this buisines I procured 160.^{li} to bee adventured in the joynt stocke, whereof 100^{li} is passed under my hande, & alreadie payd in, by vertue whereof I am a member of the Company, & maie justlie enquire after such proceedings & spend my Judgement accordinglie....[1]

In the third place I confesse from the generall good of that State I did particulerly reflect upon myselfe ... [f. 2] & ayme to repaire some fortunes which had formerly been lost by my too much confidence in the Judgement & honestie of those whoe prosequute lawe suits....[2] [f. 2v] I resolved to goe this voyage, & eyther to sitt at ffortunes Table, or to gather up the Crummes in a forraigne Countrey....

[f. 3] Lastly, that I undertooke this voyage at this tyme was cheiflie because of the presence & Companie of a newe Governour[3] appoynted for those parts, by whose meanes together with the providence of the Company ... I might well presume to bee freed

---

[1] Thornton was not mentioned in Sir Henry Spelman's list of arrearages owing to the company by those who came in after the issue of the patent, presumably he paid his subscription in full.

[2] Thornton devotes some considerable space to complaints against unspecified prelates who had deprived him of his livelihood.

[3] William Bampfield.

from all extraordinarie care in temporall affaires, & both in that Countrey, & the passage thither to bee accommodated withall things answereable to my place & callinge, the duties whereof were my cheifest meditation.

Upon these motyves not without great charge I prepared myselfe, & went on Shipboard neere Gravesend upon Saturdaye being the 14th November. 1629. On Munday our newe Governour takeinge the occasion to reade his Commission there fell out a difference betwixt him, & the Captayne of the Shipp about the bounds of theire severall authorities.... Wherein howe I behaved myselfe, there was a Certificate sent to London about the same time under the hands of divers wittnesses ... but they twoe goeing to London, the difference was there accorded & wee enjoyed at least in appearance some benefitt of their agreement, till about the 9th of December; ... the fire of contention beinge onelie smothered not altogether quenched, the flame brake out most violently betwixt our Governour & the Seaman (sic), the chiefe cause at first beinge ... the fallinge out of Servants on shoare, which being variouslie reported on Shipboard, & beleeved according to each mans fancie made soe great a noyse in effect, that scarce any could bee heard [f. 3v]....

Nowe all the passengers were inraged with revenge, or greife, now joyfull, ... the Captayne of the shipp will once againe for London, a happie motion to divide those bodies, whose hearts did soe ill agree. And seeing reason outfaced by passion, whereby my part was acted, I thought it best to goe on Shoare the same time to refresh myselfe, but cheiflie to escape the great danger of a furious mutenie....

Upon the 16th daye[1] of december followeing, the Captaine of the Shipp returned from London with divers members of the Companie whoe came purposely as ffarre as the downes to mediate an agreement, but all in vaine .... the Seamen are resolute not to goe at all in our Governours companie .... whereupon our Governour perswaded himselfe to leave the voyage.

Nowe it fell out that I was intreated as a member of the Companie & one of the Councell for those parts, there beinge noe other in the Shipp of that quality to keepe the writinge sent from the Company,

[1] These tumults occurred between 14/24th November and 16/26th December 1629.

& to take some oversight of the goods and passengers. The windes then likely to bee faire ... I presently yeilded, & returned againe to the Shipp on ffriday being the 18th of December following.[1]

Our newe Governour haveing thus left us, I began to read the writings, & a little to examyne the buisines, wherein I was ingaged .... that soe I might bee able to give satisfaction both to my selfe and others.

[f. 4] The mayne buisines of the Companie at this tyme I found to bee the remoovall of a Colony from the Ryver of Wiapoco to the Ryver of Amazones, both graunted under the same patent, & scituated neerest together, & then the change of a Governour. ...

To remoove the Colonie, or to lessen it in that place stands with the present resolutions of the Court,[2] whose proceedings are farre beyond my censure, & yet ... I could bee loath to assist the execucon of those designes (whereunto I am not bounde) whereof I cannot apprehend the reason. Indeed it is fitt authoritie should bee observed.... And happilie the Amazones is more honorable for a capitall plantation then Wiapoco, & *ceteris paribus*[3] will afford more profitt. But that a Colonie (allreadie setled above a yeare though contrary to directions) in a place necessary to bee inhabited by the English, (otherwise why should part of them bee permitted to staie there at the Governours discretion), haveing cleered, & planted the ground, made provision for victualls & convenient habitations, acquainted with the Indians, & noe question by their assistance gotten a perfect discoverie of those parts, should nowe bee remooved 200. leagues[4] into Amazones, destitute perhapps of such conveniences for the present, & whereunto passengers maye be daylie sent hereafter, to make that the cheife & principall Colonie, stands not meethinkes with any conclusion of profitt or safetie, answereable to the losses & dangers which must be susteyned.

[f. 4v] .... this course will bee a punishment not more inflicted upon those in Wiapoco, then upon the whole Companie, who in this case are likely to suffer as much by their owne directions, as Captaine Harcourts offence.

---

[1] 18/28th December 1629.

[2] The decision seems to have been taken by the Governor and Council in the Ordinary Court of the Guiana Co., see below, p. 353, n. 1.

[3] 'Other things being equal.'

[4] The distance from Cape Orange to Cabo do Norte is approximately 190 miles. Even allowing for the journey upstream to Pattecue or North Fort about the Equator, Thornton's estimate of the distance involved is still inflated.

1. ffor first howe can they bee remooved 600 myles by water without danger of their lyves in that part of their passage by Sea in Shallopps. . . .

2. If all of them bee remooved to the Amazones, then wee loose their labours heeretofore spent in plantinge, in makinge sugar workes, in fortifications, & the like. . . . And if the greater part of them bee onely removed, the remaynder, beinge not much above 50 in nomber, wilbee in as great danger to bee destroyed by the natyves, as those 60 Dutchman[1] whoe not long since lost their lyves in the same place. . . .

3. . . . when they in Wiapoco shall fynde the effect of this order, the Copy whereof is here inserted.

'Octo: 16. It is ordered that such provisions as are sent to any of the colony at Wiapoco shalbee kept at the Amazones till they come thether for them, or as they shalbee disposed unto them, accordinge to such orders & instructions as are now sent by the Companie in the good Shipp called the Exchange.

And when by vertue of this order, they shall see that noe provisions eyther publicke or private are sent to supplie their wants, which noe question wilbee great by that time, haveing beene arrived in those [f. 5] partes ever since the 17th of ffebruary 1628. . . .[2]

When likewise they shall heare that noe provisions at all must bee sent to anie of them, till there bee some intelligence of their affaires returned to the Governour in the Amazones, and that hee give leave for part of them to abide at Wiapoco, which cannott bee dispatched without great expence of tyme . . . . either they will generally concurre against the rules of authority nowe prescreibed (notwithstandeinge their covenante to the contrarie) & rather trafficke with the fflemmings whoe use those parts & can speedilie supplie their wants, than send their comodities home into England, especially in this Shipp called the *Exchange*, which will not staye in the River with them above tenne daies, & must not bringe them anie supplyes at all, but only directions for better conformitie . . . . and this distast will breed some bitter factions . . . & the rather because

---

[1] See above, p. 336, n. 1. The ships which took Harcourt's colony out probably brought back this news, although it could equally well have been picked up by any ship's company trading in the West Indies. Four of van Ryen's colony survived. Two escaped to St Vincent and two to Tobago. They were picked up in 1628, see Ghoslinga, 1971, p. 413.

[2] 17/27th 1629, see above, p. 318.

some of them, & those of the best rancke, are alreadie much displeased & very ill affected towards some amongst us, whoe beare the greatest swaye in these affayres. And wee knowe ... the remembrance of former unkindnes will easily stirre up an apprehension of present injuries, & make them more apt by these proceedings to suspect (what I wish maie not bee found) an affectation [f. 5v] of private honour & personall revenge, then to conforme themselves to authoritie, especially as the case will then stand with the present state of that government[1] And nowe by the waie lett mee appeale to all the world, if that order were so charitable, as it might have been, which will not suffer anie provision to bee sent to those, whoe (notwithstandinge) must come to the Amazones, & yet they cannott well come thither without some provision. . . . Had there beene sent them with all expedition at least their owne private possessions of strong waters, very requisite in those hott Countries, & other necessaries to supplie their wants for the present till they could dispose of their affaires, & in case they remove to comfort & releeve them by the waie, the proceedings had beene more according to the rules of charitie . . . . especially when by such extremities all in the Colony must suffer for that which is taken & soe reputed to bee but the offence of one.[2]

[f. 6] The other mayne buisines at this tyme is to change a Governour.[3] To remoove a Colony was difficult in itselfe, & by withholding supplies made lesse possible; but nowe the Commission must bee taken awaie from Captaine Harcourt whoe alone had most of these large Territories graunted by Patent to him & his heires forever, & afterwards resigned them to bee animated by this noble Societie. But going to Wiapoco whenn hee was directed to the Amazones, hee hath offended the Companie... Hee alone must bee deprived of authoritie in those partes, and returne into England, though it be declared under the hande of the Councell, that hee was the last whoe gave consent to that enterprize. . . . For my part I make noe other conclusion but only this, that eyther Captaine Harcourt was very powerfull with the rest or the rest very

---

[1] An oblique reference to the deputy governor of the company, Roger North.
[2] Robert Harcourt.
[3] Harlow's transcription reverses the order of the MS folios at this point, printing extracts from the material on ff. 7, 7v before that on ff. 6, 6v. This does very considerable disservice to the logic of Thornton's argument as a comparison of the two versions quickly demonstrates.

willing to goe to Wiapoco. And then it must needs followe, that either they will bee very loath to part with Captaine Harcourt whome they soemuch observed before, or very obstinate to bee withdrawne from that place, which they themselves soe much desired. . . . And yet the punishment is greater, because the nowe intended Governour[1] hath desisted from the voyage, an accident which fell out upon the English shoare & might well have brought backe againe the present buisines & affaire of that governement to a further consideration . . . [f. 6v] the presence of a newe Governour had beene best to take awaie the authoritie of the old, that soe it might be thought, the change is made not soe much out of displeasure to the one, as favour to the other, unles it were certeyne that his power & favour with the rest were as easily cutt of as his authority, otherwise wee cannot thincke that Captaine Harcourt seated in the height of ffortunes long expected with much patience, and greater expence, should nowe descend without a noyse, before himselfe bee heard, & not bee obstinate to withstand an inferiour tytle of governement (for soe it will prove) raised by his ruines, (and perhapps amongst those under his owne command whoe had never beene chosen for desert, but the necessity of the times; But notwithstandinge the next Governor's Commission must go on, & the buisines must bee prosequuted, as though hee had dyed by the waie. Indeede had hee dyed by the waie, there had beene noe possibilitie of better directions . . . . & now goeing forward, it must arrive in Guiana without a head, (& soe it might then bee taken in another sence, for it was not the Companie, but a private member whoe at first gave that direction). There this newe Commission was to bee published, first to declare Captaine Harcourts authority void, without which there could bee noe further proceedings, (which likewise made void the Commission for Master Clovill & Master Hixson if anie such were found there[2] . . . And then to establish a Councell in the Amazones whose directions they in Wiapoco were to followe. Nowe the government must bee transfferred by waie of election amongst ourselves upon a president, the electors all of the Councell, of which nomber those in the Wiapoco (though offenders) were to continue if they came to Amazones. . . . In the meane

---

[1] William Bampfield.
[2] The ships which took out William Clovell and Thomas Hixon had not returned by October 1629. The Guiana Co. did not, therefore, know whether they too had decided to throw in their lot with Harcourt in the Wiapoco.

while if the election were made before they came, they might take exceptions, & perhapps study to be revenged on them, whoe made soemuch expedition.

. . . And if the election were not made before they came, there seemed to bee a bodie without a governement. . . . [f. 7] And in case some man of quallitie were chosen to hold the government till they came from Wiapoco, yet after their cominge, if the same president beinge the first that ever was chosen, were not contynued in his place, hee might take it ill; if hee were, they might take it worse. . . .

But heere is not all . . . it was not then knowne, neyther could it bee presumed, that Master Clovill & Master Hixson with their Companie were arrived in the Amazones. Whereupon manie of the passengers tooke notice that haveing lost a Governour by the waie, & perhapps fyndinge none there, they had not one amongst themselves capable of that place, none being capable but one of the Councell, & there being none of the Councell, but myselfe uncapable by reason of my callinge . . . . though some were troubled, others perhapps were joyefull with a supposed libertie of doeigne (sic) what they list[1] in those partes.

And nowe the difficulty of the buisines being inlarged, the uncerteynetie of governement made the proceedings seeme desperate, which beinge murmured abroad by our long stayinge in the Downes, I founde my selfe by many private passages[2] . . . either accused of weakenes in not consideringe, or suspected for some notorious offender in goeinge forward this voyage. . . .

Whereupon . . . I beganne to recollect my selfe, & on the xith of January followinge,[3] I referred the summe of these exceptions in a private letter to the consideration of a worthy member the Treasurer for the Company[4] [f. 7v] (one whome since I understand was never willinge to have the Colony removed, but offered to tender his reasons in writinge to the contrary). I made knowne likewise my owne resolution to returne. . . .[5] And that perhapps I would bring back the writings of the Companie intimatinge their pleasure, hopeing as I then expressed to gyve as a good reason for their returne, as my owne, & with asmuch satisfaction as any that did oppose it. . . . The case as it then stood had never beene publickly discussed before the Companie, for meethought it

---

[1] Wished.
[3] 11/21st January 1630.
[2] Conversations with others.
[4] Sir Henry Spelman. [5] To London.

seemed strange, that the grave resolutions of the Court,[1] signed with your Lordshipps hand, should be conveyed after such a meane & uncerteyne manner, & that to an end, promisinge soe much difficulty & soe little advantage. Surely as the Case stood, ... it seemed better & more honorable to take some other course for the present.

This private letter it seemes was reade to the Companie,[2] whoe by reason of other particulers concerninge our wants were pleased in a publicke letter to returne some satisfaction. But one of the Companie (remembringe that before my departure from London I dislyked the inaequalitie of some proceedings about servants, & nowe fyndinge my Judgement differinge from his owne, ... conveyed this letter privately to the Captaine of the Shipp, notwithstandinge it was directed to mee by name, that thereby he might reade it openly without giveinge mee anie notice of it before, or the keepinge of it after, the copy whereof I have procured since my cominge to London, & heere sett downe.

Wee the Governour & Companie of Noblemen & Gentlemen of England for the plantation of Guiana have receyved a letter from Master Thornton, And doe desire that hee proceede accordinge to the directions given to him by Captaine North & Master Blenerhasset.[3] Wee have intreated Captaine North to write[4] to Captaine Smith to renewe the outward bound store of Aqua vitae, which our passengers have spent. For other wants of our Companie wee knowe none in particuler, Captaine Duppa[5] beinge bounde by charterparts (sic) to provyde for our Companie all necessary victualls, & which hee hath nowe upon Master Thornton's letter taken order for. And if it shall happen that upon the landinge in the Amazones of our men nowe sent, you shall fynd neither Sir Oliver Chyney, nor Master William Clovell, nor Master Thomas Hixson, nor others (other than Captaine Harcourt) formerly authorised for governement, wee doe hereby authorise you nowe sent (which shall arrive there) to choose one of yourselves to bee President, & govern accordinge to our former

---

[1] The patent of the Guiana Co. provided that matters of consequence, such as the removal of the Wiapoco colony, should be brought before the full membership in the General Court of the corporation. Thornton infers that this procedure had not been followed.

[2] He probably means the governing council of the Ordinary Court here.

[3] Edward Blenerhasset was in the Amazon in November 1629. This must be Henry Blennerhasset, listed by Sir Henry Spelman as one of the adventurers who came in after the issue of the patent, see above, p. 340, and below, p. 391.

[4] Roger North.   [5] James Duppa, see above, p. 98, n. 2 and below, pp. 440–5.

directions for governement, untill such tyme as Sir Oliver [f. 8] Chyney, Master William Clovell or Master Thomas Hixson, or some other formerly appointed by us for governement, Provyded that it shalbee in our power to revoke our authoritie hereby, given at our pleasure. Given under the Seale of one of the members of our Companie which wee nowe use for our Common Seale this 12 of January 1629.[1]

To Master Richard Thornton Clerke & all other of our men nowe transported in the good shipp called the *Exchange* bound for the Amazones.

Thus the mayne buisines in poynt of governement being made more certeyne upon occasion of my exceptions, & seeinge my other objections answered by Silence, & that I was intreated by publicke directions to proceede, answereable to those private directions which I had formerly received, I became inclynable to goe forward the voyage. . . .

But by the manner of conveyinge this letter, I have an evident Argument of Jealousie, . . . And accordingly I first tooke my just exceptions, and then desired to bee satisfied in some particulers wherein (contrary I presume to the will of the Company) I found my selfe too much sleighted, & for that purpose made bold to returne this Answere. . . .[2]

. . . [f. 10] And nowe the daie of expectation was come, beinge Saturday the 23th of January, the first daie of the eleventh weeke since my goeinge on Shipboard. But I founde noe Answere of my letter at all, . . . for which imediately I prepared my selfe, & went to Canterbury the same night. . . .

[f. 10v] On Tuesday followeinge I came to London, where I understood the noble intendemente of the Companie were very willinge to satisfie my expectation, but at that time they wanted leasure to meete . . . or with I rather beleeve his sollicitation, whoe

---

[1] 12/24th January 1630.

[2] Thornton includes here a copy of a letter which he sent to the company in London complaining that both they and his fellow passengers had failed to pay proper respect to his quality and calling. He refused to continue in the voyage unless some special provision was made for him. He was particularly concerned that all passengers were condemned to the same common seaman's diet and that they were obliged to spend their own money to procure better victuals ashore. He set the return of the next carrier as the deadline for an answer from the company.

could hinder it.[1] And nowe fyndinge from manie free expressions of respect & sorrowe that I was noe better accomodated, & hearinge that a gentleman of speciall rancke was desirous to goe the voyage at this tyme, better Companie then I left on Shipboard . . . . I was once more perswaded to goe the voyage. . . . The wyndes are turned fayre, & there is newes come that the shippes are gone awaie, whereby I became disingaged. . . .[2]

6. ACCOUNTS OF THE LOSS OF THE *HOPEWELL* IN 1630 AND OF THE PORTUGUESE ATTACK ON NORTH FORT, 1631

a. Deposition by Edward Glover, haberdasher of the parish of St Katherine Creechurch, London, 12th/22nd January 1632[3]

. . . [f. 547v] the shipp the Hopewell of London where of John Hall was Captayne (as he hath bene informed by some who said they were of the sayd shipps company) arryved at the Amazones in the monethe of August or September Anno domini 1630 last past where the sayd shipp and all her companye except eleaven were cast away seaven wherof were saved by swyminge & the other fower by a pinnace belonginge to the sayd shipp which came up to them and that as he was informed by those which were saved the sayd shipp was cast away neere Sephanoa[4] about five or six leagues within the mouth of the sayd river where cominge to an anchor her anchor brake or came to her agayne, it beinge then full sea in that place and

---

[1] Thornton appears to have a particular grievance against Roger North. He writes elsewhere that it is unfair that gentlemen adventurers in purse only should be able to engross the profits of the labour of large numbers of indentured servants in the colony. He refers obliquely to 'one member (notwithstanding his residence in London, or his experimentall knowledge of the busines, or his authority amongst the Colonyes).' Later he expresses his resentment of North directly, asking the company to explain 'the favour lately graunted to Captaine Norths Servants in as large a proportion as to any that paye their thirds; (being supplyed with trade out of the common Cargazone at the charge of the Company) should have the same favour, priviledge, & advantage as those Servants who are supplyed with trade out of a private Cargazone at the charge of perticuler men'.

[2] Thornton subsequently presented six motions to the Guiana Co. which he includes in his memorial. He was concerned to show that it would be more equitable if all indentured servants were bound to the service of the company so that all adventurers could benefit equally by their labour.

[3] P.R.O., HCA 13/49, ff. 547v–548. Edward Glover was resident at North fort in 1630. Glover testifies on behalf of 'Captain Duppa'.

[4] Sapno.

by that meanes the sayd shipp drove to the side of a bancke in the sayd river where she was oversett, and cast away as aforesayd, and those eleaven men which were saved came up in the sayd pinnace at a plantacon called North ffort, where this examinate then lived and related unto him the premisses, and that he sawe noe shallopp or other vessel belonginge to the sayd shipp the Hopewell but the foresayd pinnace which was about the burthen of ten or twelve tonnes.

. . . the sayd pinnace was seized uppon by the Portugalls and five or sixe of the sayd eleaven men which were saved as aforesayd dyed at North ffort aforesayd and all the rest (excepte one which was sent to Stephanoa to provide victualls for the sayd ffort and is since as he hath heard come into Holland in a shipp which came to the Amazones)[1] were cutt off with most of those which lived at the sayd fort, by the Portugalls, and that this examinate and some fewe others beinge persued by the Portugalls escaped in Canoos and afterwards lived with the Indians in the Amazones by the space of about five or sixe moneths.

. . . he was tould by those which were saved as aforesayd that aswell the sayd shipp [f. 548] the Hopewell as alsoe all and singuler the goods wares and merchandizes caryed in her to the Amazones were in the sayd moneth of August or September 1630 aforsayd utterlye lost and cast away in the River of Amazones and noe part therof saved, and that he doth neither knowe beleive or ever heard that any part of the sayd shipp or goods were saved, or recovered, and he farther sayeth that those which were saved when they came up to the ffort aforesayd were very bare in apparrell and as they sayd escaped onlye with their lyves which he beleiveth to be true for that the pinnace wherin they came had noe goods abord her.

. . . he neither knoweth or ever heard that, . . . Captayne William Moulsworth[2] was in the sayd shipp the Hopewell when she was cast awaye nor, what became of him, but beleiveth that if he were in the sayd shipp when she was cast away, he was likewise cast away for that he was none of the eleaven which were saved and came up in the pinnace to North's fort aforesayd.

[1] See below.
[2] Not identified.

b.   Deposition of Thomas Cliborne, mariner of Wapping,
4th/14th October 1633[1]

. . . [f. 435v] aboute two yeares since hee was at fflushinge in zealand and there hee spake with two English menn that came thither in a shippe that came from St. Christophers, one of which menn was called James Wall, but the name of the other of them hee knoweth not and hee saieth that the said Wall tolde him that hee was one of the company of the shippe called the Hopewell whereof John Halle was Captaine when shee was cast away, & the other mann said that he was a Planter within the river of the Amazones & the said Wall tolde this examinate that hee was shipped for the West Indies in a shippe called the Sea Rutter & hee lefte them both at fflushinge, but what is since become of them hee knoweth not.

. . . the said Wall and the other party aforesaid did relate to this examinate that the said shippe the *Hopewell* was cast away about three leagues within the river of the Amazones neere to a place called Arrowarra[2] to [f. 436] his best remembrance and they tolde this examinate that there beeing little winde the boate of the said shippe Hopewell was toweing her upp the river, and that for wante of lettinge fall of an anchor the said shippe drove up a sande and oversett, & that all her company excepte seaven that saved themselves in her boats & uppon the wracke, were drowned. . . .

c.   Deposition of Henry Clovell Esq., West [Lain]nngfield, Essex,
18th/28th October 1633[3]

. . . [f. 447] he verilye beleiveth that the shipp the Hopewell of London (wherof John Hall was Captayne) was cast away in the river of Amazones, for that betweene Michaelmas and Christmas in Anno 1630. there came up ten or eleaven men to North's fort al*ias* Pattacue in the Amazones, where this dep*onent*s brother was chiefe Governor[4] who related unto this deponent & his brother that they

---

[1] P.R.O., HCA 13/50, ff. 435v–6. Cliborne's testimony is docketed 'Cap*tain* Duppa:/Thomas Cliborne of Wappinge Marriner aged 28 yeares or thereabouts sworne before the wor*shipfu*ll doctor Merricke Surrogate to the ri*ght* wor*shipfu*ll Sir Henry Marten K*nigh*t Judge of his Ma*jes*ties highe Courte of the Admi*ral*ty and examined uppon certeine Interrogatories ministred on the behalf of Peter Jones & others. . . .'

[2] The confluence of the river Arrowari.

[3] P.R.O., HCA 13/50, ff. 447–8. Docketed 'Pro Petro Jones et al.' Brother of William Clovell.

[4] The phrase 'and this dep*onent* one of the Councell' is crossed out.

were of the companye of the sayd shipp the Hopewell, which as they
sayd was cast away within sighte of Cape North and he alsoe beleiveth
that it was betwixte the Islands and Cape North,[1] because the sayd
eleven or some of them did affirme that the Pilott of the sayd shipp
tould the master a little before she was cast away that there laye Cape
North, and the master sayd noe, but that Cape North laye more to the
Southward and soe bearinge up Southwardly towards the Islands the
sayd shipp was runn uppon the shoales and presently the tyde
arisinge with great force tooke her uppon the broade side and soe
oversett her, and by that meanes the sayd shipp & goods and all her
company were cast awaye (excepte the sayd ten or eleaven who as
they sayd escaped some of them uppon lasts[2] of the sayd shipp and
some of them in the pinnace,). . . .

. . . the names of some of those which came up to Norths fort alias
Pattacue as is before deposed, were one called ould Bryan one of the
quarter masters (as he nowe remembreth) John Browne another of
the quartermasters, Peter Terry Gunners mate, and one Rugman,
that (as it was said) belonged to the gun roome of the said shipp the
Hopewell and one James Wall but the names of the rest he
remembreth not. . . .

. . . at the tyme aforesayd hee was not of Captayn Hixons Counsell
one of the Governors of the English plantacion at the Amazones,
(who had injuriously chosen a Counsell for himselfe, this deponents
brother the chiefe governor beinge sicke and those which were
saved out of the sayd shipp the Hopewell as aforesayd were (as he
hath heard) examined before the Governor of the said plantacion
but this deponent was not present when they were examined but
afterward he spake with them and then they toulde him as much in
effecte as he hath before deposed and further he cannott depose.

. . . [f. 447v] uppon the examination of the men aforesayd the
sayd Captayne Hixon went downe in the sayd pinnace which came
up as aforesayd to Norths forte, to the place where the sayd shipp
the Hopewell was cast awaye in hope to save her ordenance and
some of her goods, and for feare of foule weather the sayd pinnace
returned to Norths forte agayne.

---

[1] 'river of Amazons betwixte the Islands and the said Cape', crossed out. In his
answer to the second interrogatory Clovell stated that he believed the ship was
wrecked 'ten miles thereabouts within the freshwater'. This information was
crossed out.
[2] Cargo.

... he sawe the sayd John Browne one of those which was saved as aforesayd weare a newe Canvas suite which (as he sayd) he tooke out of a hamp¹ or cheste which was driven on shoare after the sayd shipp was cast awaye, & was the Chirurgeon or the Chirurgeons mates suite (as he remembreth) of the sayd shipp, and that the sayd Browne likewise sayd that after he came on shoare he drancke some sacke or stronge waters which were likewise driven on shoare from the sayd shipp, And he alsoe sayeth that he sawe an Indyan weare a Satten doublett made after the English fashion which he supposeth came likewise out of the sayd wracke because he never sawe any other man weare the sayd doublett uppon the plantacion. . . .

. . . the Indians at the Amazones did reporte of a shipp cast away about the tyme before mencioned. . . .

. . . some of those which escaped out of the sayd shipp the Hopewell dyed in the Indyes of fluxes & other sicknesses and all the rest excepte the foresayd James Wall (who was amongst the heathens and afterwards (as he hath heard) escaped in a Holland shipp) were killd by the Spaniards² at the assaulte made by them uppon the English at Norths ffort in ffebruarye in Anno *1630* [1631] And further he cannott depose otherwise then he hath before deposed.

d.   Deposition of Roger Glover, merchant of St Anne, Blackfriars, London, 18th/28th 1633³

. . . [f. 447v] he verily beleiveth that the interrogate shipp the Hopewell (wherof John Hall was Captayne) was cast away within the mouth of the river of Amazones within sighte of the lande of Amazones betweene Michaelmas and Christmas in the yeare of 1630 ffor that in the moneth of Jullye 1631 this deponent cominge thither in the shipp the Marmaduke of London (wherof John Barker was master) was tould by some Indians there Inhabitinge (as it was interpreted by some which this deponent caryed with him which understood the Indians language) that an English shipp was lately cast away within the mouth of the river of Amazones, and pointed to the place, and afterwards goeinge up higher into the river mett with divers English which had lived in that Country some certayne tyme, who made a relation to him under their hands and

---

¹ Hamper.   ² Portuguese.
³ P.R.O., HCA 13/50, ff. 447v–8. Brother of Edward Glover.

seales the first of August 1631 (amongst other things) verbatim as
followeth videlizet That about [f. 448] six weeks after Michaelmas
last the Hopewell Captayne Hall was cast awaye within sighte of
Cape North, where Captayne Hall the shipp men and goods did all
perish excepte eleaven seamen who escaped in the pinnace, and
came to North fforte, and were there likewise taken with the rest,
and the names of those which made the sayd relation are Henry
Clovell, Edward Glover John Holmes Robert Lloyd, Robert Leake[1]
and Raphe Hutchinson and that by conference with those men this
deponent under stood that the sayd shipp cominge aground at lowe
water, when the tyde came in was oversett by a stronnge violent tyde
which they called a boare, and soe cast awaye.[2]

e.   Deposition by John Barker, mariner of Ratcliffe, Middlesex,
18th/28th October 1633[3]

. . . [f. 477] in the moneth of Julye in anno 1631 this deponent
arrivinge into the river of Amazones in the shipp the Marmaduke
of London (wherof this deponent was master) there came certayne
Indians abord the sayd shipp who did relate unto him & his
company (by the interpretation of an Irishman abord the sayd shipp
who did well understand and speake the language of the Indians)
that there was a shipp cast away in the entrye of the river of the
Amazones betweene Arawarry & the North Cape,[4] within sighte of
the lande, and afterwards this examinate and company goeinge
further up the river of the Amazones they mett with five or six
Englishmen (who had lived uppon that continent a certayne tyme.)
who told this deponent & company that they had understood by
eleaven of the [f. 477v] company of the sayd shipp the Hopewell
(that came up to the[5] fforte and were afterwards slayne at the
assaulte made by the Portugalls, uppon the English inhabitinge in
the sayd forte). . . .

. . . he sayeth that he hath heard that all the company of the
Hopewell which escaped) were taken at the forte by the Portugalls,

---

[1] Possibly a relation of Captain Simon Leake one of the original patentees of
the Guiana Co., see pp. 272, 294, n. 4, 391.

[2] See above, p. 148, n. 3. Roger Glover estimated that the *Hopewell* was cast
away about twenty miles upriver.

[3] P.R.O., HCA 13/50, f. 477v.

[4] He estimated that the shipwreck occurred some sixteen miles upriver.

[5] 'Norths' is crossed out.

excepte one that was lefte at Corians Island[1] and afterwards by a dutchman caryed into Holland.

f.   Deposition by Thomas Harman, mariner of Ratcliffe,
                Middlesex, 18th/28th October 1633[2]

. . . in the moneth of december last past was twelve moneths videlizet in anno 1631 this deponent arrivinge at the Amazons in the shipp the Amitye of London wherof he was then master)[3] was there tould by the Indians that Captayne Hall his shipp and company were all cast awaye (as this deponent did understand by their signes which they made) within Cape North in the entrance of the river of the Amazones. . . .

. . . whilest this deponent and company were in the river of Amazones the tyme aforesayd he sent two of his men with some Indians to gett provision for his shipp, and those men at theire returne tould this deponent that they had seene in the Indians houses neere the North Cape certayne chests a payre of breeches of skarlett, and two Chamber potts which as they understoode by the signes made to them by the sayd Indians were driven on shoare neere the sayd North Cape out of the sayd Captayn Halls shipp. . . .

---

[1] Quariane or Quariana, see above, p. 260, n. 1.
[2] P.R.O., HCA 13/50, f. 477. Docketed 'Pro Petro Jones et al'.
[3] See above, p. 101, n. 2.

THE LAST ENGLISH SETTLEMENTS
ON THE AMAZON, 1630–3

1. CAPTAIN QUAYLE IS COMMISSIONED TO EXPLORE
THE AMAZON, 19TH/29TH MARCH 1630

Capt*aine* Quayle: *Carolus* Rex:[1]

Charles by the grace of God king &c To all *christ*ian people &c.
Whereas we are gratiously pleased to take into our Princly
conside-rac*i*on the worth and demiritts[2] of the bearer hereof
Capt*aine* Rich*ard* Quayle and having alwayes found him to be our
Loyall and faithfull sub*ject* in and upon all occasions he hath bene
imployed in, in (sic) our service,[3] and knowing his iudment (sic) and
experience in maritime affaires are worthy of our approbac*i*on
encouragm*ent*, It is therefore our will and gratious pleasure to
imploy him in our good shippe called the seahorse to range the
Riv*er* of the Amazones and all other the Coasts and Rivers of
aMerica soe farre forth as God shall pr*o*tecte him, his direcc*i*on shall
guide him, and his pr*o*vision store shall supporte him;[4] And we doe
therefore require all our neighbouring princes Allies and ffriends,
and doe will and require all our loving sub*ject*s That at what tyme
soev*er* the, said Captain R*ichard* Quayle shall happen by sea or by
land to give them or any of them a friendlye meetinge, that they &
ev*ery* of them in the due tender of us, our Crowne and dignity, doe
afford and offer him the s*ai*d Captaine Quayle and all others that
are or shalbe under his Command all good respectes and such faire
quarter as is befitting his peace and imployment, and as the man
that we are thus gratiously pleased to intrust in affaires of this

[1] P.R.O., SP 12/237, f. 98.
[2] Demerits, meaning merits or deserts.
[3] See above, p. 102, n. 3.
[4] See above, p. 102, n. 6.

nature, And we doe further require our neighbouring princes
Allies and friends & doe will & require all our loving subjects in and
upon all occasions of distresse & disasterous fortune betyding &
befalling the said Captaine Quayle to be ayding & assisting to their
and every of their powers & abillities unto the said Captayne Quayle
& all others that are or shalbe under his command, He & they
behaving themselves honestly and soberly towards our said neighbouring princes Allies & friends & our said loving subjects, And this
to be donne as you and every of you will answere the Contrarie upon
paine of our highe indignacion and displeasure
Given ut supra dat 19th day Martii 1629.[1]

2. THE EARL OF BERKSHIRE'S PLANTATION, 1631–2

a. Deposition of John Day gentleman of Windsor, Berks,
20th February/2nd March 1633[2]

. . . aboute May last was twelve monethes – Captaine Roger ffrye,
Samuel Lockram and William Smallbones[3] were sent over to
Dunckercke to buy a shippe there for the use of the righte
honorable the Earle of Barckshire and others his partners whereof
hee the examinate is one, and aboute that tyme the foresayd
Captaine ffry did buy a certaine shippe there beinge fflemishe
builte and of the burthen of about eight score tonnes[4] of one
Captaine Outeily (as hee this examinate, was tolde) and afterwards
brought the said shippe over to this porte of London, and that hee
this examinate and the said ffry by bill of exchange did pay to one
ffranncis Syon a dutch marchant the sume of twoe hundred and
odd pounds for the same; and that after she was soe brought at
Dunkercke and brought into the River of Thames shee was called
by him this examinate and the said ffry by the name of the Barcke
Andevor,[5] and since that sold by him this examinate with the
consent and approbacon of the Earle of Barkshire to one Samuel
Sheilde of Rederiffe[6] marriner for the sume of twoe hundred and

---

[1] At Whitehall.
[2] P.R.O., HCA 13/49, f. 612.
[3] See above, pp. 322–4, 337.
[4] 160 tons burthen.
[5] Fry and Day named the vessel the *Barcke Andevor* or Andover, after their
patron the earl of Berkshire, Viscount Andover.
[6] Redruth, Cornwall.

sixty poundes, and that since shee was soe sold by this examinate to the sayd Sheilde, as hee hath heard and beleeveth divers Englishe men subjects to the Kinge of England have parte, and interest in the said shippe with the said Sheilde, and that shee the said shippe is nowe bound out uppon a voyage for Norway as the said Sheild hath confessed to this examinate. And this he saieth by vertue of his oath.

b.   Privy Council warrant to the earl of Berkshire,
                     22nd July 1631[1]

Whereas our very good Lorde the Erle of Barkshire having bestowed great costes in making a Plantation in the Southerne Continent of America and shall have necessary use for diverse pieces of Ordinance, both for the fournishing of such Ships as his Lordship shall have occasion to send thither. As also for the better strengthening and fortifying of the saide Plantation against the invasion of an Enimy, and doth therefore desire he may buy for his money ffifty pieces of these severall sortes, vizt fowre Culverin, fower demi Culverin,[2] twelve Saker,[3] Twelve Minion[4] tenne ffaulcon,[5] foure Saker-Cutts, and foure Minion Cuts.[6] These are therefore to signify unto all such persons whom it may concerne, that they are not to interrupt or hinder the said Erle either from buying, putting on Shipboarde, or from transporting any such Ordinance, not exceeding the number nor several sortes before specifyed in this our Warrant, provided also that good security be given that they shall not be otherwyse employed then for the saide Ships and Plantation And this shalbe their warrant.

---

[1] *CPC Colonial, 1613–8* (1908), pp. 166–7.

[2] Blackmore, 1976, pp. 224–7, describes the culverin as a cannon long in proportion to its bore, the brass version weighing between 20 and 49 cwt., the iron between 23 and 63 cwt., with a shot of 15–20 lbs. The demi-culverin ranged between 29 and 32 cwt. by the mid 1630s with an average round shot of 9 lb.

[3] A gun of the culverin type, the brass versions weighing between 12 and 22 cwt. and the iron between 12 and 26 cwt. in the 1630s, with a round shot of 5–6 lbs.; *ibid.*, pp. 240–1.

[4] One of the smaller guns of the culverin type, brass versions weighing between 8 and 14 cwt., iron between 12 and 17 cwt., with a round shot of 3–4 lb.; *ibid.*, pp. 234–5.

[5] See above, p. 177.

[6] Presumably cut down versions of the saker and minion.

C.   Roger Fry undertakes to make astronomical observations
from the Equator[1]
John Bainbridge, Professor of Astronomy at Oxford, to Roger Fry,
1631.[2]

John Bainbridge:
To his loving friend Master Roger Frye esquire

I have sent you here enclosed a breif but significant declaration of
my opinion concerning the observations to bee made in Guaiana;
and also a note of some [particulars] which are [   ] to bee
elsewhere. If Sir Thomas Roe[3] will by his bountye enccurage you
and reward your payns, I doubt not but you will bee carefull to
make good the [instructiones] which I have given, and to satisfye
bothe his and [my] expectations.

Enclosure; statement by Bainbridge to be presented by Fry to
Sir Thomas Roe in support of his request for patronage

Astronomicall observations beeing the only certain and undoubted
principalls and complements of that excellent Science; It hathe
been muche desired that besides the accurate observations made in
these Northern regions the like mighte be made in other places
more towards the south especially in Alexandria of Ægypt (where
Hipparchus and Ptolemy[4] and other famous Astronomers observed
and some place under the Æquator or nere thereabouts where
besides the discovery of all the Souther stars (which neither here nor
yet at Alexandria can bee seen [many] observations may bee made
of the Sun, Moon and Planetts, which beeing accurately performed,
and collated with the like made in these parts will clear many doubts
in the moste principall poynts of Astronomy and bee of singular use
in Geographye and Navigation all which I will [easillye] demonstrate

[1] Trinity College, Dublin, MS 386/1, ff. 43, 43v. These are the original, rough
drafts of Bainbridge's letters. The hand writing is barely formed in some places
and in others obscured by many erasures. Uncertain transcriptions are enclosed
in [ ].
[2] See above, pp. 104–5.
[3] *Ibid.*
[4] Virtually illegible, If the transcription is accurate then Bainbridge refers to
the Greek astronomers Hipparchus of the second century B.C. and Ptolemy of
the second century A.D. Ptolemy had adopted Hipparchus' system to explain the
variation in the solar eclipses which were sometimes total and sometimes
annular. These anomalies were difficult to accommodate in a universe believed
to be made up of concentric spheres where the distance of each heavenly body
from the earth was assumed to be invariable.

when I shall have the observations, for obteyning thereof a fayr opportunitye is now offered by Master Friey who undertaking a voyage to Guaiana and being (of that I know) most able to accomplish suche a bisiness, hathe received from mee particular instructions therein, and will engage himself the performance thereof, if hee may bee thereunto enccuraged by a kinde and munificent benefactor, whose name shall bee resplendent in these observations; when all other the most pretious jewels that ever were brought from either India shall bee consumed and forgotten.

c.   Extracts from the prospectus for the earl of Berkshire's
   joint-stock company, written and published by John Day, 1632[1]
A PUBLICATION OF GUIANA'S PLANTATION Newly undertaken by the Right Honorable the Earle of BARKSHIRE (Knight of the most Noble Order of the Garter) and Company for that most famous River of the *Amazones* in *America. Wherein is briefly shewed the lawfulnesse of plant*ations in forraine Countries; hope of the natives conversion; nature of the River; qualitie of *the Land, Climate, and people of* GUIANA; with the provisions for mans sustenance, and commodities therin growing for the trade of Merchandise: and manner of the Adventure. *With an Answer to some objections touching feare* of the Enemie.... LONDON Printed by William Jones for Thomas Paine .... 1632.[2]

[p. 1] *To all faithfull, and well affected Christians.*

FOR as much as diverse of this Nation are departed hence into forraine Countries, as well for the propagating of Gods truth (most likely) as their owne private benefite, whereby the word of the Lord might bee fulfilled in those Heathen (through Gods infinite goodnes & mercy).... Neither is it to be doubted, but that there are divers yet remaining, which retaine the like Christian resolution, but [p. 2] want of true knowledge of a plantation (that may proove profitable to the Church of God & them-themselves) causeth such to live heere like plants, which many times prove lesse fruitfull in their

[1] The initials I[J]. D. appear at the end of the prospectus. The author declares his own intention to settle on the Amazon 'with my wife and friends', see below, p. 375. Williamson, *English colonies*, 1923, p. 137, in my opinion, correctly identified the author as the same John Day of Windsor who testified as one of the earl of Berkshire's partners before the High Court of Admiralty, see above, pp. 363–4. Marginal notations are supplied in [ ] as is the pagination of the original text.
[2] See above, p. 106, n. 3.

naturall soile, then when they are removed to places better liking them, for which cause I have thought good at this present, to discover briefly (to all such as are wel affected) the knowledge of a most hopefull plantation newly undertaken by the right honorable the Earle of *Barkeshire* (Knight of the most noble order of the Garter) and company, for that famous river of the *Amazones* in *America*, as by that which followeth may appeare.

But before I proceede further herein, I thinke it not amisse to speake somewhat of the lawfullnesse of plantations in forraine countries, wherby such as make doubt thereof, may be beetter (sic) satisfied herewith.

Now in plantations there are these two principalls to be considered: first, whether it be lawfull to remove from one place or countrey to another, secondly, whether it be lawfull to possesse a countrey already inhabited by others: touching the former . . . . [p. 3] wee may gather, that men may lawfully remoove with their familyes from one place to another, and that for divers causes; as here the Children of the Prophets did, by reason of the straitnesse[1] of the land wherein they dwelt: and it is to be feared that [p. 4] many also among us have as great cause to doe the like, by reason of the daily increasing of all sorts of people, whereby cittyes townes and countries, are so thronged, that men can hardly live well one by another, as appeareth by the generall complaynt of many in these tymes.

. . . [p. 5] It remayneth in the next place, that I shew the lawfulnesse of possessing a countrey already inhabited by others, which is our second question:

True it is, that all men through Adams fall were deprived of the glory of God, and worlds good, until by Christ the use of the creatures was againe restored to all beleevers, therfor the right of that which we possesse, commeth now to us by Christ, for which cause, the heathen have no right to that which they deeme theirs, notwithstanding, the Lord hath beene pleased to suffer such to live on earth with his, and not to be rooted out from the place of their habitations untill the day of harvest, during which time the Land wherein such have lived hath beene called theirs . . . . [p. 6] from whence we may gather, that God permitteth not his to dispossesse a people or nation of their ancient habitatiou (sic) for the enlarging of

[1] Limited amount, scarcity.

their owne borders; neverthelesse, if such shall bee willing that Gods people shall inhabit with them. . . . In such acase (sic) men may doubtlesse possesse a country already inhabited by others: But the inhabitants of *Guiana* are willing that our nation should inhabit that goodly and spatious country with them (as appeareth more fully in Mr. *Harcourts* relation of *Guiana* dedicated to the Kings most excellent Majestie, 1626)[1] Therefore without all question, the plantations there made of late by our nation are lawfull.

Thus having briefely shewed the lawfullnesse of the plantations in forraine Countries, for the better satisfiing of such as make doubt thereof, I come in the next place to speake somewhat of the nature of the river, qualitie of the land, climate, and people of *Guiana*, with the provision for mans sustenance, and commodities therein growing, whereby such as are ignorant of the same, might bee encouraged to adventure for the good of themselves, and of [p. 7] those poore natives, which sit still in darknesse, and in the shadow of death.

[*Harcort*] As touching that great and famous River of the *Amazones* in *America*, it is called for the excellencie thereof, (by *Josepus Acosta*) the Empresse and Queene of all Flouds, and for the large extent of the same, it is called by the others the sweet Sea, supposed to bee the greatest River (not onely of all *India*, but also) of the whole world; it is said to flow from the Mountaines of *Peru*, and runneth with many windings and turnings for the space of 1500 leagues, containing at the mouth thereof neare sixtie leagues in breadth; in it are many Ilands, divers of which are inhabited by the Indians; it doth ebbe and flowe neare three hundred leagues,[2] and hath in it great store of excellent fishes for the use of man: of which more shall bee said hereafter, when wee shall come to speake of the provisions of the country for mans sustenance.

The quality of the land is of divers kindes; as low, middle, and mountainous, (as here with us) it aboundeth in woods in divers sorts, having plaines in some parts thereof, with plentie of grasse, besides pleasant streames of fresh waters, all which are very needfull and fitting for a plantation.[3]

The earth in those parts is of sundry mixtures, as blacke mould,

[1] Day refers here to Harcourt, *Relation*, 1626, pp. 14–15.

[2] Day is paraphrasing Harcourt, *Relation*, 1626, pp. 4–7, in Harris, *Relation*, 1928, pp. 68–9, 145–6.

[3] Paraphrase of Harcourt, *Relation*, 1626, pp. 34–5, in Harris, *Relation*, 1928, pp. 93–4.

clay, rossey,[1] and such like, besides stone for building if occasion serve.

The seasons there differ much from ours, for the dry weather which wee call there summer, beginneth about *August*, and the raines and windes, which we account there winter, begin about *Febru*-[p. 8] *arie*; which latter season is termed by us their winter, by reason of the raines then falling extraordinarie, and not by reason of the coldnesse of the weather; for there are no frostes or snowes, as with us here, but a continuall spring and summer season: for no sooner doe the leaves wither and fall away, but presently it beginnes to spring againe, as here with us some yeares it seemeth the like; for when our autumne proves somewhat warme, then commonly appeareth a second spring, which yet never commeth to perfection, and that by reason of the suns declining from our horizon, and the cold winters present approaching, which causeth alwayes our latter spring to keepe backe, untill the time of our summer season: which is *Guiana* is not so, for there is little difference of heat and cold throughout the yeare, but a most pleasant growing weather, which commonly causeth those parts to bee much more fruitfull then many other parts of the world.

The day and night are there alwaies equall, the Sunne rising at six of the clocke in the morning, and setting at six in the evening or neare thereabout the yeare throughout.[2]

The provisions for diet are many, as first, the roote called Cassavie, of which the *Guianians* make their bread; there is likewise a kinde of great wheat called Maix, it yeeldeth great increase, and maketh excellent meale, or flower for bread: of the aforesaid Cassavie, and this wheat, is made a sort of drinke called Paranaw, much like the best march beare here with us; other sorts also they [p. 9] have, which for brevity sake I omit here to speake of.[3]

There are Deere[4] of divers sorts, wilde Swine,[5] Hares and

[1] Marshy, from *ross* meaning marsh or morass; *OED*, 1910.

[2] From Harcourt, *Relation*, 1626, pp. 28–30, in Harris, *Relation*, 1928, pp. 89–90, 134, 149.

[3] Paraphrase of Harcourt, *Relation* 1626, pp. 35–6, in Harris, *Relation*, 1928, pp. 94–5, 151; see above, pp. 136, 271.

[4] Based on Harcourt, *Relation*, 1626, pp. 37–8, in Harris, *Relation*, 1928, pp. 95–6, 98, 151–3. See above, p. 182, n. 5.

[5] Harcourt described two kinds of wild pig 'the one small, by the Indians called *Pockiero*, which hath the navile in the backe; the other is called *Painqo*, and is as faire and large as any we have in England'. The former is the Peccary, *Tayassu pecari* identifiable by its dorsal gland or 'navile in the backe', see above, p. 182, n. 4. Harcourt's 'Paingo' is a larger species of peccary, probably the *Tayassu Tajacu*. See Harcourt, *Relation*, 1626, p. 37, in Harris, *Relation*, 1928, 95, n. 6

Conies[1] in great plenty, besides which there is a great beast called Maipnry (sic) which in taste is like beefe, and will take salt;[2] there is also another creature which usually commeth into the fresh waters, and feedeth upon the grasse and weedes in the marshes, (and is called by us the sea-Cow) being in tast like beefe, and will also take salt, as the former;[3] of these there are great store in their seasons, they wil serve wel for the victualling of ships homeward bound, as of late hath beene proved.

Of fowles there be divers kindes, namely, wild-duckes, wilde-geese, hennes, herons, cranes, storkes, pheasants, partridges, pigeons, stockdoves, parrats of sundry sorts, besides ravenous fowles, and hawkes, with divers other sorts not knowne in these parts.[4]

The variety of fish is great,[5] as first, mullet,[6] sea-breame,[7] soale,[8], scate,[9] thornebacke,[10] swordfish,[11] seale,[12] a fish like a

---

[1] Rabbits. Harcourt, *Relation*, 1626, p. 37 and Harris, *Relation*, 1928, pp. 95–6. The paca (see above, p. 182, n. 7), resembles a hare as does the *agouti*, *Dasyprocta agouti*. See Estácio da Sylveira's description of the *aperca*, *ibid.*, n. 9.

[2] Maipury or Tapir, see above, *ibid.*, n. 6. Day is using Harcourt's *Relation*, 1626, p. 38 in Harris, *Relation*, 1928, pp. 96, n. 4, 151–2, n. 1.

[3] *Ibid.*, n. 3. Paraphrased from Harcourt, *Relation*, 1626, pp. 39–40 in Harris, *Relation*, 1928, p. 98, ns. 1, 2, and p. 153.

[4] Paraphrase of Harcourt, *Relation*, 1626, pp. 38–9 in Harris, *Relation*, 1928, p. 96, n. 9, and 97, ns. 1, 2. As Harris notes, Harcourt applies English names to the wild fowl of Guiana. Day copied the greater part of them into *A PUBLICATION*.

[5] From Harcourt, *Relation*, 1626, p. 39 in Harris, *Relation*, 1928, pp. 97–8, 152.

[6] Gilmore, 'Fauna and ethnozoology', *HSAI*, 1963, VI, 409, states that mullet, *Mugilidae* are commonly found throughout the coastal, brackish and fresh waters of the Caribbean and South America.

[7] Of the family *Sparidae*, not found in the Amazon according to Golding, *Fishes and the Forest*, 1980, ch. 2.

[8] The marine sole of the family *Soleidae* and order *Pleuronectiformes* has been found in the fresh waters of the lower Amazon; Golding, 1980, p. 38.

[9] Not found in the lower Amazon according to Golding, 1980, ch. 2.

[10] A ray with spines on the back and tail. The fresh-water sting-rays, *Potamotrygon rajiformes* are about 1 metre long, the tail constituting half the total length, with a spine near the centre of the dorsal surface; Gilmore, 'Fauna and ethnozoology', *HSAI*, 1963, VI, 408.

[11] Sawfish, *Pristidae rajiformes* are found in the Amazon, according to Golding, 1980, p. 38.

[12] Gilmore, 'Fauna and ethnozoology', *HSAI*, 1963, VI, 378–9 states that seals mostly herd off the southern coasts of South America. The monk seal *Monarchus tropicalis* is native to Antillea. It is now almost extinct.

sammon, but differing in coulour,[1] shrimpes,[2] lobsters,[3] and oysters,[4] other sorts there are, besides freshwater fish of many kindes, which in these parts of *Europe* are not knowne to us.

The fruites there growing[5] are the Pina,[6] Plantana,[7] Medler,[8] Plumbes and Nuts of divers kindes, beside store of Potatoes,[9] as for the Pina, it exceedeth all other fruites in those parts, being in taste much like ripe straberries (sic) with clarret wine and sugar; the Plantana tasteth like an old pippin,[10] the medlers exceede ours in greatnesse, and the nuts in sweet-[p. 10]nesse.

Having thus briefly touched the severall sorts of provisions necessary for mans sustenance, it remaineth I shew the varietie of commodities[11] therein growing for the trade of Merchandise, which in short time (by Gods assisting our endeavours) may bee brought to returne great profit to the undertakers.

The first commodity of estimation there growing are sugar-canes, whereof in some parts there are store, which by orderly planting and erecting of convenient workes, for boyling and making of sugars, may (through Gods blessing) bee returned yearely great profit to the adventurers, as the plantation of sugarcanes made hertofore in *Barbary* by the *Moores*, and since that in *Brasseile* by the *Portingals* may witnesse.

---

[1] Probably a reference to one of the species of unarmoured catfish in the Amazon. The Dourada 'gilded one', *Brachyplatystoma flavicans* has delicious flesh. This could alternatively be a description of a pirarucu, *Arapaima gigas*, up to three metres long with tasty pink flesh; Gilmore, 'Fauna and ethnozoology', *HSAI*, 1963, VI, 411.

[2] Fresh water shrimp are found in the lower Amazon.

[3] A spiny, clawless lobster, *Panulirus* is native to the Antilles and the east coast of South America.

[4] Many visitors to the Guiana rivers noted the oysters in the mangrove swamps, see above, p. 146, n. 1.

[5] Paraphrase of Harcourt, *Relation*, 1626, p. 40 in Harris, *Relation*, 1928, pp. 98–9.

[6] Pineapple.

[7] Plaintain. Harris, *Relation*, 1928, p. 98, n. 3, feels that Harcourt, Day's source, was describing a banana.

[8] Harris, *Relation*, 1928, p. 98. n. 5 suggests that this fruit is the Sapodilla or *Achras sapotaceae*. Like the Medlar, *Vanqueria*, it is only suitable to eat when it appears to be overripe.

[9] See above, p. 182, n. 11.

[10] A name for various types of apple grown from seed.

[11] The following eight paragraphs are largely paraphrased from Harcourt, *Relation*, 1626, pp. 40–50 in Harris, *Relation*, 1928, pp. 99–105, 153–7.

There is also cotton wooll growing of the finest sort, it is a profitable commodity, for the making of fustians, callicoes and candle-wicke.

There is a naturall hempe, or flax, of great use, it is much like raw silke, and is called of some silke-grasse.[1]

There are likewise many commodities for diers, as namely a red berry called Anotto, which dieth a perfect oringe-tawny in silke, and a yallow in cloath, of which there may bee gotten good store every season;[2] for my selfe with some others setting forth a ship formerly for those parts, (by way of trade) received upon returne, above three thousand waight of the said Anotto, which then bore a good price here, but much better in [p. 11] the neatherlands, other dyes there are (besides hope of Cutcheneale) which at this present I purpose briefly to passe over.

There are likewise found of late, store of Nutmegs growing,[3] with their Mace, some of which I have recevied (sic) upon returne of my foresaid adventure, which noe man (I suppose) but my selfe can shew the like, excepting some gentlemen, which upon request have received some of mee, which no doubt may in short time bee brought to a more fuller perfection, by either cropping the old trees and dreaning the waters from them, or by transplanting the young trees, as by experience is commonly seene, how that nature is much helped by art and industry.

There is likewise, Gumma, Lemina,[4] Barrata, Ginnipepper,[5] long Pepper,[6] Cascia fistula, Tobacco, spleene stones, speckled wood, Hony and wax.[7]

As for mineralls, or mynes of mettals, it is very likely this country

---

[1] See above, pp. 273, n. 1, 279.   [2] See above, p. 136, n. 3.

[3] See above, pp. 192, 263, 279, 285.

[4] Gum elemi, see above, p. 279, n. 4.

[5] Cayenne pepper acquired from the dried and ground seeds and husks of a species of Capsicum, especially *C. annuum* and *C. frutescens*. Described by Harcourt, *Relation*, 1626, p. 46, in Harris, *Relation*, 1928, pp. 155–6 as 'codded Pepper which commonly is called *Guinea* pepper: It is a good Spice for many uses: the Indians make an excellent Sauce therewith, which they ordinarily use with their meate, and we have found it very good and wholesome.'

[6] Prepared from the immature fruit spikes of the allied plants *Piper officinarum* and *P. longum*. Harcourt, *Relation*, 1626, p. 46, in Harris, *Relation*, 1928, p. 156, says 'I have had a good testimony of another sorte of Spice, commonly called Long-pepper, which beareth (amongst the Druggists) a better price then the former [Guinea pepper].'

[7] See above, p. 273, n. 2.

affordeth many, not onely of the basest, but also of the richest, which hereafter may come to bee discovered, if God shall be pleased, which hee grant to his glory, and our good, or that otherwise they may ever lie hid.

Now as touching the nature of these people they are generally held harmelesse, tractable, trusty, and somewhat laborious;[1] in which respect they differ much from all other Americans, and which is better to bee liked in them, there is good hope conceived of their conversion to the Christian faith, ... [p. 12] so have some of these poore ignorant soules desired Captaine *Charles Leigh*, to send into England for some men to teach them to pray [Purchas. p. 1021.];[2] since which, one [Harcourt. p. 9] being converted, and became a Christian, being at the point of death, desired some of our nation then present, to sing a Psalme with him, which being ended, hee told them hee could not live, & did withall acknowledg (sic), that he had been a wicked sinner, but did hope that hee should bee saved by the precious blood of our Saviour Jesus Christ; and moreover, hee desired all of them there present, to beare witnesse that hee died a Christian; yea said hee, a Christian of England.[3]

... [p. 14] As for the temper of the climate[4] it exceedeth not so in heate as some men have thought of it, for though the scituation be in part under the equinoctial, yet it is habitable, as appeareth by the experience of our countrimen, which have lived in those parts, and found it both healthfull, and pleasant; for God in wisdome hath so ordered the heavens in their horizon, as that by meanes of a brieze (or fresh gale of winde) blowing in the day time,[5] it quallifieth the heate, and maketh the climate much more temperate, as with us is often felt the like in heate of summer.

Besides the dewes there falling commonly in the night, addeth much to the cooling of that climate, [p. 15] and which is to bee noted, the continuall absence of the Sunne from the horizon, for

---

[1] Hard working.

[2] The account of this incident is found in 'Captaine Charles Leigh his voyage to Guiana and plantation there', in *Purchas his pilgrimes*, 1625, IV, bk. 6, 1251, and 'Captaine Charles Leigh's Letter to Sir Olave Leigh his Brother', ibid., p. 1253.

[3] Harcourt, *Relation*, 1626, pp. 9–10, in Harris, *Relation*, 1928, p. 147.

[4] The following two paragraphs are constructed from Harcourt, *Relation*, 1626, pp. 30, 34, in Harris, *Relation*, 1928, pp. 89–90.

[5] Day, courtesy of Harcourt, refers to the morning sea breeze which refreshes the coastal area of the Guianas daily, see Harris, *Relation*, 1928, p. 93, n. 1. Strong easterly breezes prevail in the lower Amazon during the dry season.

the space of twelve houres every day, cannot but cause the temper of that clymate to be moderate, there being a perfect mixture of heat and cold, each qualifiing the other in the space of twentie foure hours by an equall division of day and night, as before hath beene shewed.

Their houses are built (most commonly) in length, like our barnes here with us, some of which are so large, as they containe in them above an hundred persons, having therein hanging beds, (in which they lie) called hamackoes, made of cotten woll very artificially,[1] their vessels for use are made some of clay, of which sort some are so great as that they will containe more then one hogshead of water.

They will worke a month or more for an axe of eighteene or twentie pence price; for which they will fell your timber, cleare your ground, plant your sugar canes, Anotto, and Cotten trees, and build your house after their fashion: which in other plantations is not so,[2] for in all other our plantations, the adventurers are enforced to carry men over to doe their worke for them, least otherwise they bee driven to worke themselves, as Virginia, St. Christophers, new England; with others can witnesse.

Besides which, in most former plantations except new England, men have adventured onely upon hope of one commoditie (as namely Tobacco)[3] but here are many more commodities then one, (as [p. 16] hath beene shewed) therefore is this plantation more hopefull then all others: the foundation of which being already laid, may give men better incouragment to become joynt adventurers herein, especially being thereupon presently intressed in the shipping stocke, and profits of the said plantation; for the preservation whereof, wee have not onely sent divers honest and able men (marren and other) but also some peeces of great

[1] Paraphrased from 'The relation of Master John Wilson of Wansteed in Essex, one of the last ten that returned into England from Wiapoco in Guiana 1606', in *Purchas his pilgrimes*, 1625, IV, bk. 6, 1263.

[2] Day's statement is a rather free interpretation of Wilson's account of his experience amongst the Indians of the Wiapoco in the early 1600s. 'At our returne to Wyapoco we gave to the Indians for their paines, and providing of us victuals in our journey an Axe, for which they would have travelled with us two or three moneths time. . . . And for an Axe they found us victuals two moneths time at our houses, as Bread, and Drinke, and Crabbes, and Fish, and all such kinde of flesh as they killed for themselves, for the same price . . .,' ibid.

[3] North American colonies, like Virginia, had experienced great difficulty in establishing a cash crop in their early years. The Guiana ventures were a notable exception. The tropical forests provided instantly profitable returns.

ordnance, with amunition, and other materials very usefull towards building of a fort, for the better securing of our planters persons from the danger of an enemy; having moreover caused a pinnace to bee sent to abide with the Colony in the river, for their better safetie and trade in the country;[1] intending likewise this summer (if God shall bee pleased) to sett out a new supply of more men (as artificers and others) besides women, as also more ordnance, amunition, and other materials, fitting for the defence of the plantation, besides another shipp, greater then the former, to stay and abide there together with the Colony in the river, for their better defence and trade in the country aforesaid: in which supply I also purpose (God willing) to goe with my wife and friends, to inhabit some part of that spacious and goodly countrie.

[*Object.*] But here some may object for feare of the enemy. [*Answ.*] Answer. it is no other then what hath bin usualy vented at the first setting forth of al our plantations for America, as Virginia and others can witnesse; and if there were so great cause to feare (as some have [p. 17] supposed) men would not assuredly have adventured so freely; but this plantation here mentioned is farre from the Spaniards habitation, and therefore lesse cause to be feared.

[*Object.*] But yet it may bee further objected, that though the Spanyard bee somewhat farre distant, yet the Portugals in Brasill (being neare unto it) may prove as ill neighbours as the other. [*Answ.*] Answer, if wee consider the spatiousnes of the country (being supposed to bee more then twenty times greater then this kingdome of England) wee have no such great cause to feare them; for if wee like not their neighbourhood, (there being roome enough, and divers goodly rivers besides in the country) wee may (if we please) goe further out of their reach, where no doubt (through Gods assisting of our indeavours) wee may come to returne as great profit (by meanes of sugar canes and such like commodities growing in those partes) as in the river aforesaid: for to speake truly, it were great weaknesse in any to presume to sit neare an enemy, and have not sufficient strength to oppose him, or having roome enough to go out of his reach, will notwithstanding abide neare him; yet I deny

---

[1] Day refers here to Fry's settlement. According to Jácome Raymundo de Noronha's 'Report' (see below, pp. 379–84), Fry's group went out in the *Barcke Andevor* and two patches, one of the latter remaining in the river with the colonists.

not, but that a Colony may bee able to subsist neare an enemy by meanes of fortification, and especially when they are such as feare God, being provided with amunition, victuall, and all other things needfull for the defence of the same: for to raise a fort for the reliefe of a Colony, and not to victuall it, (as some have carelesly neglected through indiscretion)[1] were to make it (with such) our peoples [p. 18] grave, and not their preservation: and if an hundred of our nation, or thereabout (having neither fort, nor artillery for defence) were able (not long since) by meanes of the natives, to cause about eighteene hundred of the enemy to retrayte, and abandon the river, with losse of many of their lives;[2] how much more then being fortified, and fitted with all things needfull for the defence of the same, may wee bee better able, (through the helpe of the almighty) to repell and beat backe a more potent power.

Now as the raising of forts for the defence of Colonies, and neglect of storing of them with victuall, and other things needfull for the preservation of the same, sheweth the great indiscretion of some sort of people: So in like manner, is their folly as great, who looking after present profit, neglect planting provisions needfull for the preservation of their lives: which wee taking into consideration, have given expresse charge, that first of all they take care to plant provisions needfull for sustentation, whereby they may bee able in short time to subsist themselves, without helpe of the natives, which usually furnish our English plantations with store of provisions for diet, at marvelous low rates; yet notwithstanding wee have sent thither some few cattell for breed, besids other creaturs, which in those parts have not yet beene heard of by us to have beene amongst them.

And if any man shall desire to bee further satisfied concerning the proceed of the said plantation, [p. 19] or shall make doubt of anything, they may please to repaire to the place of meeting (hereafter mentioned) and there receive further satisfaction.

Now as toucheth the manner of the adventure, it is as followeth.

Every one that shall be admitted into the Colony, or company of the Right Honourable the Earle of *Barksheire* for his plantation in

---

[1] Day may have been alluding to the disorders which preceded the collapse of North fort.

[2] Day is relying on Harcourt's account of the Portuguese assault on the foreign colonies in the Amazon in 1623, which at that time left the English and Irish settlements largely unscathed, see above, pp. 241–2.

Guiana, is to be admitted one of these three wayes, that is to say; either in person and purse, or in purse, or in person onely. The first are called personall adventurers, the second, purse adventurers, and the latter are servants to the Collony.

Concerning the former, they are such as not onely adventure their persons, but also their purses; of which sort none may bee admitted under fifty pounds at least, put into the joynt stocke (being a single share) in consideration whereof, every such adventurer is to have for his personal service (over and above the profits of his stocke of adventure) his transportation and diet free, (both in the passage and country,) besides a certaine stipend or yearly allowance (as others) toward the maintenance of his apparrell & bedding, and also aleventh part of a twelfth, of all the profits that shall arise by the industry and labours of the Collony beyond sea; and lastly, a proporton of land over and besides his stocke of adventure of fifty poundes, or more as every one pleaseth to put in, whose respect in the Collony, is held fitting to be measured according to the greatnesse of every mans adventure, worth and qualitie.

[p. 20] As for those which are called purse adventurers, they are such which adventure their monies but not their persons, whose names, and summes adventured, are not onely registred, but also acknowledged by indenture under seale, by Authority from the said Earle, (for their better security, and more assurance of faithfull dealing) to become joynt adventurers with the said Earle and company, for his plantation aforesaid, and that at every returne, (during the terme of five yeares) after the first returne from the plantation, every adventurer, his heyres, executours, administratours or assignes, shall receive the profits of his stocke of adventure, and shal the first returne from the plantation (after five yeares shall be expired) receive out the just residue and remainder of his stocke of adventure, & profits therof, or may if he please, continue the same longer in the joynt stocke then the terme aforesaid, for his further benefit: and shall have moreover, set forth for his use a proportion of lande correspondent to his said stocke of adventure: and to the ende that every adventurer, his heires, executors, adminstrators and assignes may clearely see, that they have the due proportion of the profits of their adventure, it is covenanted in the said indenture, that the heires, executors, administrators & assignes of them shal upon every setting forth & return, see the full summe of all the disbursements, and receits from time to time, paid and received, touching the proceede of the said joynt stocke, and plantation: which in like manner, every adventurer, as well personall, servant, as other, hath the [p. 21] like indenture for their better satisfaction, and more assurance of faithfull dealing, as aforesaid.

Now concerning the latter, which are servants to the collony, they are such, which adventuring onely their persons, are bounde by indenture to serve the said Earle and company in the plantation five yeares, in consideration whereof, the said servantes, (as well wives, maides, as men) are to have their transportation thither free, as also their diet, lodging and apparrell, and all other materialls needfull, provided for them, at the charge of the joynt stock, for the terme aforesaid (apparrelling themselves here for the first yeare) and to receive moreover, (for their beter incouragement) a twelfth part of all the profits that shall arise by their labours and industry, and the women a fifteenth (as of sugars, nutmeggs, mace, cotton wools, Anottoes, honey, wax, tobacco, mineralls, and all other such like commodities, as shall be gotten in the plantation, in manner aforesaid) as also at the end and terme of five yeares, every man servant to have livery, and season of thirty, and some forty acres of land, and women twenty, which said landes are to be set forth for their use, by the governour, or governours, and councell then being.

And to the end that every one may know what profits are due unto them by reason of their service, it shall be free for them to make choyse of any two or three amongst themselves, which shall once in the yeare, or thereabout (upon reasonable request made to the governour, or governours then being) see the accompts, and what is due unto them up-[p. 22] on the foote of the same, for their better satisfaction and avoyding of suspition.

And furthermore all such servants, as shall bee artificers. As Suger-cane, and Vine planters: Sugar bakers, Druggists, Dyers, Lapidaries, Minerallmen, Refiners, Founders, Potashe makers, Barbersurgeons. Ingeners, Gunners, Survayers, Shipwrightes, Mill-wrightes, Carpenters, Joyners, Coopers, Turners, Wheelers, Sawyers, Oare makers, Blacke-smiths, Locke-smiths, Gunn-smiths, Pike-makers, Armorers, Cutlers, Edge-toole-makers, Ropers, sayle-makers, Mariners, Net-makers, Fishermen, Bakers, Butchers, Brewers, Distillers of hot-waters, felt-makers, Spinsters, Weavers,

Taylers, Tanners, Curriers, Tawyers of Furres,[1] Fellmongers,[2] Girdlers, Glovers, Shoomakers, Potters, Masons, Bricke-makers, Bricke-layers, Basket-makers, Thatchers, and such like; are to receive a ninth part of a twelfth (more then others, which are no artificers, of all the profits that shall arise by their labours, and industry) as a recompence of their severall arts for their further incouragement.

And lastly, it shall and may bee free for every servent appertaining to the colony, to put into the joynt stocke such summes of mony, as they shall be able from under fifty pounds to five (as already some have done) the receit of which summes being acknowledged by indenture, shall be as sufficient a warrant for them to receive the just profits of the same, correspondent to their severall stockes of adventure, as to any otherbefore mentioned.

[p. 23] And now to conclude, seeing that workes of this nature require some time for preparation of shipping, and all other things needfull for transportation, and that the summer season is most convenient for the performance of the same: it is therefore thought fitting to give notice to all such, as shal become willing adventurours with the said Earle and company, to bring in their stockes of adventure, (so soone as conveniently they may, and the sooner the better, for the reasons aforesaid) to the place of meeting appointed to be kept (for the receiving in of adventurers, and servants to the company) at the house of Master.Edwards the Kings Pikemaker in Phillip lane neare Cripplegate: London: which first meeting is appointed on thursday the first of March (at two of the clocke in the afternoone) and so to continue every thursday after, untill such time as the joynt stocke, number of adventurers, and servants shall be full. . . .

d.   A Portuguese account of the destruction of *Cumahu*,
Roger Fry's settlement in 1632.
'Report by Jácome Raymondo de Noronha on matters pertaining to the preservation and increase of the state of Maranhão.' 1637.[3]

---

[1] Tawyers worked skins into leather by soaking them in alum and salt.
[2] Dealers in skins and hides.
[3] Translation. B[iblioteca] N[acional], Lisbon, Collecção Pombalina, Códice 647, ff. 111–4, also transcribed in *ABNRJ*, XXVI (1904), 435–41. For discussion in Lisbon of Noronha's report see 'Informações de Jácome Raymundo de Noronha, Provedor da Fazenda do Estado do Maranhão e de João

One thing that is well understood is that the whole defence and strength of the conquest of Maranhão and Pará consists in the native and Indian inhabitants of those great rivers and lakes, because, if they are friends and confederates of the Portuguese, neither the Dutch enemies nor other foreigners will have the power to conquer them and draw them into their friendship: and, on the contrary, should they be against us, they will join whatever nation of northerners might arrive to the total destruction of the Portuguese and all that state, making it impossible for your Majesty to take and reduce them to the condition and obedience in which at present they are. They are all very subdued because they have witnessed that whenever the Portuguese have made war on the foreigners who wanted to live amongst them and make their tobacco plantations, they [the foreigners] were always defeated, and their goods, weapons and fortifications seized, as Captain Pedro Teixeira did in the year 1628[1] at the fort of *Torrego* [Tauregue] which surrendered to him with all the foreigners in it in exchange for their lives, and finally in the year 1631 when the said Jácome Reymundo de Noronha, as *capitão-mor* with the authority of governor, went to the river *Phillipe*[2] which is on the other side of the river Amazon and gave battle taking a fort with four pieces of heavy artillery and *roqueiras* and many weapons, killing 86 and capturing 13 of the foreigners who were in it with the destruction of all their Indian confederates.[3] The rest [of the Indians] were left so terrified that they will never make alliances with the foreigners again nor abandon the protection of your Majesty and given that the preservation and friendship of these natives and Indians is so important, it is advisable that much consideration be given to the most convenient ways and means to keep them pacified and in our friendship. Since they are by nature unstable and untrustworthy, only the people who have had a lot of dealings and experience with them can ascertain the manner of handling them, and as I have spent 16 years in these conquests travelling amongst the said natives in peace and war, I can speak of what I understand of this business

---

Pereira de Caceres, Capitão do forte de Santo António do Gurupá', 1637, in ibid., pp. 413–34. Jácome Raymundo de Noronha, chancellor of the Exchequer of the State of Maranhão and Grão Pará in 1637, had served as interim governor during the lifetime of Fry's colony.

[1] 1629. [2] See above, pp. 93–4.
[3] North fort. *Roqueiras* were presumably rock or stone guns.

and what may be convenient for the service of God and of your Majesty and the general good of these conquests.

Firstly, all the said natives are brought to submission because of the fear and good opinion that they have of the valour and might of the Portuguese, for which reason they do not dare to throw off their obedience. In order not to lose this good opinion that they have of us it is very important that the two forts which we have in this conquest, that of Maranhão and that of Pará, be fortified in such a manner that they cannot be overcome by the Dutch enemies, the which your Majesty may easily do by ordering the continuance, in Maranhão, of the fort which the said Jácome Reymondo ordered built at the mouth of the entrance to the bar and the making of another opposite, with which the enemy will be prevented from entering with any force of ships neither could the mainland be conquered before the two forts were overcome. With the artillery which there is at present in that captaincy, which would be 50 great pieces, these two forts may be adequately furnished. At present, however, this artillery is so poorly maintained that the greater part of it is left on the beaches, unmounted and useless, and if this captaincy of Maranhão had a garrison of 200 men it could be defended against all the power of the enemy with the help of the settlers and their slaves and also the free Indians from the villages, all of which, seeing the good state of the defences, will fight with great spirit. The present state [of the defences] undermines everyone's spirit.

And consequently, your Majesty should order the continuance of the fortification of Pará in the way in which Jácome Reymondo began it, being governor of that Captaincy in the time of the Governor Francisco Coelho de Carvalho, from whom he had a particular mandate to fortify that fortress. The method was to surround all the city with a wide ditch filled with water, a circuit of 700 fathoms. By this fortification, in the judgement of everyone, this city and fortress can be impregnable, having 200 men in the garrison, [and] adding more artillery than what there is at present, which would be thirty pieces. Rounding up within this fortification, at time of war, the Indian chiefs and their wives from nearby villages would prevent them from rebelling and all the Indians will assist with their weapons and supplies. Your Majesty should order that all the remaining force of settlers and weapons which is spread throughout the conquest, that is in Siará [Ceará], Curupá [Gurupá] and Caitté [Caeté] be withdrawn to these two fortresses, because these latter are so short of men and arms that they serve no purpose except to discredit us with the natives who see how easily they may be overrun with the death and capture of the defenders, as happened to the fort of Siará which only had 30 men and was taken by less than 60 Dutch with the loss or imprisonment of all the defenders in the year 1637. They left behind 40 Dutchmen and the natives, when they saw us vanquished, went over to them.[1] May it please your Majesty to restore this fort, not so much because it is a loss but to demonstrate to the natives and Indians, on whom depends all the credit of the conquest, that enemy forces cannot prevail against us, the which may be done easily if your Majesty orders the Governor bound for Maranhão to retake Siará on the way and restore it with the soldiers which he has with him. This will be of great value to preserve the friendship of all the natives of that conquest.

The thing most necessary in those parts to keep the natives quiet, is to have them visited and cared for by the Franciscans of St. Anthony, whom the natives venerate and love as the only remedy for their necessities, because they know the charity with which they treat them and the perils they undergo to defend them in peace as in war, the which they have well witnessed in all the wars which they have fought in that conquest. For the religious of this order were always found there for their relief, as the Father Friar Cosmé and Friar Manoel were in the beginnings and the seizure of Maranhão from the French,[2] as Father Friar António da Merciana and Father Custos Friar Christóvão de Lisboa and Father Friar Christóvão de São José[3] were in the continuation of the wars of Pará; they and all the other religious have always offered themselves for the labours of that conquest and at present Father Friar Agostinho is engaged on the discovery of the great river Amazon which can be navigated to the city of Eqitu [Quito] in Peru.[4] In the last war against the

---

[1] For the Dutch assault on Ceará 1637 and the subsequent history of the Dutch garrison, see Boxer, *The Dutch in Brazil*, 1957, pp. 85, 220–1, 241.

[2] A reference to the two Capuchins who accompanied Jerónimo de Albuquerque in his expedition against the French settlement in the Maranhão 1614.

[3] See above, p. 248 and below, pp. 407, 409–10.

[4] Two Franciscans, Domingo de Brieba and Andres de Toledo, accompanied by six soldiers, descended via the Napo and the Amazon to Belém in 1637. Jácome Raymundo de Noronha despatched Pedro Teixeira to make the journey upriver from Belém to Quito. He set out in October 1637, arriving in Quito in

Dutch in *Torrego* and in the war of river *Phillipe*, where their forts were totally overcome and seized, the Father Friar Luis d'Assumpção[1] was everywhere giving encouragement and consolation to the Portuguese and winning great esteem of the natives. Wherefore may it please your Majesty for the security of those great ports and navigations, to send the said religious from this kingdom in sufficient numbers to assist in such a protracted conquest, and to command that they be esteemed and venerated by the governors and captains and that any crimes committed against them in that conquest will be punished as crimes against the service of God and your Majesty, to give example to all the natives and to increase among them the love and reverence they have for the Friars.

And in order that your Majesty may understand the importance of defending these conquests from your enemies, I will tell what I understand, according to my experience of these parts. Firstly, God forbid, should the enemy take hold of Maranhão and Pará, it will be not only the loss of these two captaincies but, I conceive, all the America is at risk because they will be at the heart of it and masters of the two most admired and important rivers and navigations known to the world, peopled with innumerable civilized natives, with very fertile lands from which more sugar can be taken than up to the present from all other territories that produce it, and with many kinds of wood to build as many boats as may be desired with which they may run along the whole coast to the Indies in 15 days, and going up the rivers they may penetrate to Peru. This they may do if they have friendship and alliance with the natives and Indians of the territory, without which in no way will they be able to settle or set foot in the territory even if all the forces of Holland and the whole world should come. If your Majesty defends the said two captaincies and fortresses, bringing in two companies of 30 soldiers for each one, flying forces with canoes, who will go about the villages continuously with Franciscan Fathers, remaining 15 days in each one to instruct them in Christian doctrine, compelling the chiefs to go each year to make their submission to the governor

---

June 1638. He was accompanied by Friar Agostinho das Chagas, superior of the Franciscan house in Belém; see Jiménez de la Espada, *Viaje*, 1889, *passim*; Markham, *Valley of the Amazons*, 1859, pp. 41–134.

[1] See above, p. 203, n. 7.

and to the *capitão-mor* of Pará to confirm the alliances, they will see our strength. With this they will always be our firm allies and will not admit foreign enemies even when they come with the gifts of iron tools which they greatly like, because of their fear of our forces which, accompanied by the Friars of St. Anthony, were always victorious in those parts, and of being punished with death or captivity if they were friendly with the interlopers, as were those who sided with them before now. With this fear they will always be firm in our alliance and much more so now that they see the route opened again by the great Amazon river to traffick with the Spaniards.[1] With the latter in their rear throughout the interior we can make war on them from both sides, and they will not dare to forsake our alliance and the obedience due to your Majesty.

And these are the most efficient means possible to control the said natives on which depends all the security of that state, without it being necessary for your Majesty to make major war expenditure for the defence of those extended rivers and ports in which large enemy fleets can enter without resistance but cannot remain without being wiped out unless they are supplied by the native Indians. This can be seen by the experience of 40 foreigners who reconnoitred those parts in a patache and settled on land in a fortified site called Camahu, in which all died of hunger and necessity because the Indians of the region did not ally with them, and only 11 remained [debilitated] and sick when they surrendered themselves with their captain, the fort they had built and the patache that they came in to the Portuguese, which was in the year 1632.[2] The said patache and people came with another large ship and two pataches to supply the foreigners who were fortified on the river Phillipe.[3] Receiving news at the port of Sapano [Sapno], which is just within the river Amazon, that they had been wiped out as was previously stated, they turned to depart, seeing that they could not remain amongst the natives who were now hostile to them and their shipping. . . .[4]

[1] See above, p. 382, n. 4.
[2] Noronha is alluding to Fry's settlement here, see above, p. 105, n. 3.
[3] Clovell and Hixon's plantation at North fort.
[4] Fry remained on the river with forty men and one of the pataches. The wording of Noronha's report suggests that some of those who had intended to settle with Fry returned to England in the two remaining ships. The relevant passage in the 'Informaçóes de Jácome Raymundo de Noronha', *ABNRJ*, XXVI (1904), 421 reads that after the capture of North fort 'in the following year after

e.   Letter from Roger Fry to John Bainbridge, 10th May 1633[1]

Worthy Syr I shall count it a great happinese unto me if these may arrive safe at your hand[2] and that they may induce to observe the ☽[3] and ♂[4] and ♀[5] in the meridian I have a curious instrument which I have made here for altitudes of 10 foote semidiameter to trouble your serious thoughts with perticulerizing the storie how I was taken by the portugales with an armie that was 300 fold greater then mine I think it inpertinent but I hope after I have finished my observations to be at libertie to see your Worshipp[6] and bring you my observations the ☉[7] entred into an eclips at this towne[8] Aprill the 8th 1633[9] when the ☉ was 42[10] distant from the zenith and by my calculation the distance of this place from Venece is 59[11] but future observationes will I hope better discover this eclipse did not appere in the middle nor in the end because of the raine that chanced at the time. Master Gelebrand[12] hath a quadrant and I doubt not but he will observe being advertized by your Worshipp the caput ♌[13] cumeth into ♈[14] and [limes boreus][15] will be in ♋,[16] there the lattitude will well be discovered and paralax alsoe of the ☉ & ☽[17] by that which I have

---

the said campaign an English ship and two pataches came which came with relief and people to those who were settled there and learning that they had been wiped out by the Portuguese they turned back and only left one of the two pataches which went to a site called Camahu. But because the Indians had been chastised by the war which had been made on them, they did not dare ally with the foreigners nor bring them victuals so that they remained in need of necessities. At the end of two months after being very weak and twenty-six of the forty men being dead, the rest surrendered themselves to the Portuguese who razed the fort they had made and brought them back prisoners with the said patache which they also surrendered. . . .'

[1] Trinity College, Dublin, MS 382, ff. 105, 105v. Fry was using the Gregorian calendar here.

[2] Fry's observations and calculations were recorded in tables in his notebook (Trinity College, Dublin, MS 433, ff. 16, 16v, 27). Nicholas Tyacke notes that Bainbridge announced Fry's observations in his lectures at Oxford, 'Science and religion', 1978, p. 83. It would appear that Fry sent the notebook back to England with his letter.

[3] Moon.   [4] Mars.   [5] Venus.
[6] See above, p. 106.   [7] Sun.   [8] São Luis, Maranhão.
[9] 29th March 1633 [O.S.].   [10] 42°.   [11] 59° W. by Fry's calculations.
[12] Henry Gellibrand of Trinity College, Oxford, who became Professor of Astronomy at Gresham College, London in 1627, a former student of John Bainbridge; N. Tyacke, 'Science and religion', 1978, pp. 78–9, 88.
[13] Leo.   [14] Aries.   [15] Not identified.   [16] Cancer.   [17] Sun and Moon.

begun I thing sumthing of Tychos[1] asumsions will be altred the altituds may be often taken as by me they shall evrie night whereby the . may be observed in divers places of anomalie and thusse desirin your Worshipp to excuse my bouldnesse with you with my service remembred to your Worshipp and all yours and my respects to Master Gelebrand and Master Graves[2] for whose sake I am sorrie of my misfortune and thuse I commend you to the protection of the almightie and rest at maranham 2:42 south[3] lattitud one the cost of braseele may 10th 1633.

Yours Worships servant
R Fry

I shall be willing to stay heere the longer hoping that you will please to observe

I pray Syr lett your man doo me that favor as to write a word or two to give my father a littell comfort.

Master Thomas fry at Ashly neere Litten[4] and direct the letters to be caried to master powells house apotticari in Taunton in the county of sumerset for he is my brother in law and there is a carier that lieth at the maiden head in Oxford that useth thither

3. LORD GORING'S MEN VISIT THE AMAZON IN 1633
EXTRACT OF A LETTER FROM FRANCIS,
LORD COTTINGTON[5] TO SIR JOHN COKE,[6]
22ND JUNE/2ND JULY 1633[7]

... The ship belonging to my Lord Goring his company for a plantation in the River of Amazons is returned and the men report that eight of their best men being betrayed ashore were killed by the savages, and their boats taken;[8] so as they returned without going so high as their fort,[9] which they conceive is also taken, and the men

---

[1] Tycho Brahe the Danish astronomer who lived from 1546–1601.

[2] John Greaves of Merton College, Oxford, appointed Professor of Geometry at Gresham College, London in 1630, also a former student of John Bainbridge; N. Tyacke, 'Science and religion', 1978, pp. 78–9, 83–9.

[3] Actually 2°30′ S.

[4] Litton Co. Somerset, 6 miles N.E. of Wells.

[5] Created Baron Cottington of Hanworth Co. Middlesex 10th July 1631, member of the Privy Council since 1628, DNB (1908), pp. 1218–21.

[6] Secretary of State 1625–40; DNB (1908), pp. 700–2.

[7] HMC, Twelfth Report, pt. II, Coke MSS, 21–2.

[8] See above, p. 108.   [9] Cumahu.

murdered: for so they heard it reported, and did choose rather to believe it than to go and see. Captain Quayle (my Lord Treasurer's favourite)[1] is dead, but these men of Macapo[2] (my Lord Goring's) say they were aboard that ship at the Barbadoes, where she came infinite rich, and will be here shortly, and that Quayle's company told them my Lord of Denbigh is coming home in the James.[3]

4. EFFORTS TO REVIVE THE GUIANA COMPANY, 1634–5

a.   To the King's most excellent Majestie
       The Humble peticon of Captaine William Bamfeild[4]
                            Sheweth

That your peticoner in the yeare 1629. was by the Guianian Companie elected Governor of the plantacon.[5]

That your peticoner by the earnest perswation of that Companie accepted of that service, and with greate expence of time and monie fitted himselfe for his voiage.

That your peticoner haveinge Commission granted him was advanced soe farr as the Downes stayeinge there 10-weeks for a winde was without cause countermannded by the said Companie with promise of Satisfaccon which yet he hath not received.

That your peticoner by meanes thereof hath expended 800[li] and suffers much losse in his Creditt.

May it therefore please your majesty to referr the Consideracon hereof to the Earles of Bedford[6] and Dover[7] beinge of the said companie or to either of them giveinge them power to call the rest of the companie before them to thend the said companie may make such satisfaccon to your peticoner as theire Lordships or either of them shall thinke fitt.

[1] See above, p. 362.
[2] Macapá. Cumahu lay near Roohoek or Point Macapá. The Portuguese built the fort of São António do Macapá on its ruins in 1688, see 'Memoria dos Capitães', B.A., 54/XI/27, no. 17, f. 11v.
[3] William Feilding, first earl of Denbigh, sailed to India in 1631, *DNB* (1908), p. 1154; *CSP Dom.*, *1629–31*, p. 329.
[4] Bodleian, Tanner MS 114, f. 156.
[5] See above, pp. 346–7.
[6] Francis Russell (1593–1641), succeeded as second Lord Russell of Thornhaugh 1613, as fourth earl of Bedford 1627. Not listed in the patent or arrearage list of the Guiana Co., see above, pp. 290–4 and below, pp. 390–2.
[7] See above, p. 291, n. 9.

DOCKET: At the Court of Greenwich 11th May 1634.[1] his Majestys pleasure is that the Earles of Bedford and Dover shall forthwith take this peticon into serious consideracon and call the Guianian Companie before them as is desired by the peticoner, And if theire Lordships find the Companie have done the peticoner such wrongs as are herein alledged that then they take such course for the peticoners full satisfaccon as they in theire discretions shall think fitt which the companie shall refuse then theire Lordships are to certifie his Majesty thereof that soe his Majesty may take such further course for rightinge the peticoner as in honor and Justice he shall thinke fitt

ffrancis Windebanke[2]

b. Letter from the earls of Bedford and Dover to
Sir Henry Spelman, Treasurer of the Guiana Company,
22nd May/1st June 1634[3]

To our very Good ffreind Sir Henry Spellman Knight Treasorer of the Guiana Company[4]

wheras by a Peticon of Captaine Bampfeild, and a reference from his Majestie of the eleventh of May 1634. his Majestie was pleased to reserve the Consideration of the Peticoners Complaints unto us, whose names are heere subscribed, to Compose or report, the State of the Businesse, betweene the Guiana Company, and Captaine Bampfeild, we haveing had two meetings with divers of the sayd Company, and with the helpe of the Booke of Orders,[5] wee findeinge one thing wanting, for the Cleering and certifyeing of our Judgements, which is the State of the Accompt of the Payers and Subscribers, and what remaynes yet unsatisfied of that, to the Company, and in what speedy way, it is put for the recovery therof, which we conceive you that are the Treasorer of the Company, can best informe us, of the State of the businesse, which we desire you to doe, As allsoe to certifie us, what hath beene paid to Captaine Banpfeild of that some of one hundreth ninety eight

[1] 21st May 1634 [N.S.].
[2] Sir Francis Windebanke, Secretary of State.
[3] Bodleian, Tanner MS 70, f. 16.
[4] See above, p. 292, n. 14.
[5] Not extant.

pounds, tenne shillings and fower pence, wherof he acknowledgeth
the Receipt of sixty five onely.
At Bedford house
22th May 1634   Francis Bedford
                                                       Henry Dover

your Certificate we expect as speedely as may be:– if it please you on
Satturday the 24th of this Instant May

c.   The reply of Sir Henry Spelman, 24th May/3rd June 1634[1]
                    24th May 1633[4]
The humble answer of Sir Henry Spelman to the letteres of the R
Right honorable Francis Earl of Bedford & Henry Earle of Dover.
   May it please your Lordshipps to consider that I am but a servant
of the company of Guiana and that I neyther ought nor am willinge
to doe any thinge of note in their affayres without their privity –
assent & order especially in a businesse prosecuted against them in
soe high a nature as complaint to his Majestie and a reference from
him to your Honours And though it be fitt that your selves beinge
Patentees and of that Company shoulde be acquainted with any
thinge that is under my hand yet your Llordships now standinge as
Iudices dati[2] to heare and consider of the differences & controversie
betweene them & Captaine Banfeilde and that the service required
of me is to serve their Adversaries turne I humbly desire that I may
acquaint them the Company with your pleasure and for mine owne
discharge receive their order & direccion herein att a Court for that
purpose according to all form usage, without which I conceive that
noe particular members can either acte or or (sic) answere any thing
in their behalfe nor (under correccion) doth his Majesties reference
(as I conceive it) implie any other proceedinge or the nature of a
corporacon properly admitt.

[f. 161] Arrerages due to the Company of Guiana from them of that
society undernamed according to their subscriptions[3] vidilizet Of &
from

---

[1] Bodleian, Tanner MS 71, ff. 160–2.
[2] Assigned judges.
[3] For the original patentees listed below as in arrears on their subscriptions,
see above, pp. 291–4.

George Lord duke of Buckingham deceased}
for his 2. laste parts————————————}   88– 0–0

Philip Earl of Mungomery Lord Chamberlyn}
for all his three parts————————————}   100– 0–0

Henry Earl of Holland for his 3 parts——   100– 0–0

Edmund Earl of Mullgrave for his 3 parts   100– 0–0

Edward viscount Killùlcagh alias Lord   100– 0–0
Convay————————————————

Mildmay Lord le dispenser for 2 parts   66–13–4

Henry Lord Ley now Earl of Marlborough   55– 0–0
for all————————————————

George Lord Bishop of London

Henry Lord Grey now Earl of Stanford}
for his 3ᵈ parte————————————}   33– 6–8

Horace Lord Vere of Tilbury for all   100– 0–0

Sir Thomas ffynch viscount Maideston for   40– 0–0
2 parts————————————————

Sir Alan Apesley leiutenant of the Tower}
for 2 parts————————————————}   80– 0–0

Sir James Outherlany his laste parte   33– 6–8

Sir Samuell Saltinston his whole   100– 0–0

Sir Alexander Temple his whole   50– 0–0

Sir Roger North[1] his 2 laste parts   33– 6–8

Sir William Heydon[2] his whole 3 parts   60– 0–0

Sir Arthur George his 2 last parts   33– 6–8

Sir John Massington[3] his whole 3 parts   50– 0–0

Carew Rauleigh Esquier ultra 10[1]   40– 0–0

Captain Simon Harecourt[4] now Knight}
his whole————————————————}   50– 0–0

[f. 161v] William Trumball Esquier Clark of}
your Councell all————————————}   60– 0–0

---

[1] See above, p. 293, n. 5.

[2] Not listed in the patent 19/29th May 1627. Fifty-four members were named in the latter. The discrepancy is accounted for by the addition of Sir William Heydon and Captain Simon Harcourt. See above, p. 298, n. 1, and below, n. 4.

[3] Washington, see above, p. 293, n. 8.

[4] Not listed in the patent. Sir Simon Harcourt (1603–42), eldest son of Robert Harcourt the Guiana projector, professional soldier, serving under his uncle Sir Horace Vere (see above, p. 292, n. 4) in the Low Countries, knighted 1627, later served under the Prince of Orange, appointed Governor of Dublin 1641, DNB (1908), pp. 1205–6.

Henry Seckforde Esquier his 2 last parts	40– 0–0
Edward Johnson Esquier his whole 3 parts	50– 0–0
Hugh Maye Esquier his whole	60– 0–0
John Ingleby Esquier his 3[d] parte	33– 6–8
Captain Simon Leake for the arrerage} of 150[li]————————}	120– 0–0
Edward Palavicini Esquier his whole	50– 0–0
ffrancis Burnell Esquier his 2 last parts	16–13–4
Captain William Saker his whole 3 parts	50– 0–0
Daniell Gookyn gentleman his whole	60– 0–0
William Martyn gentleman his whole 3 parts	100– 0–0

Adventurers comminge in since the Patent obteyned

George Eveling Esquier[1] his last 3[d] part	50– 0–0
Richard Boothby[2] gentleman his laste 3[d] parte	20– 0–0
Cornelius Conquest[3] his last 3[d] parte	16–13–4
Thomas Littleton[4] gentleman his 2 last parts	33– 6–8
Doctor Humfrey Ailworth[5] last 3[d] parte	20– 0–0
John Pinchin Esquier[6] his 2 last parts	40– 0–0
Master Mason[7] his 2 last parts	40– 0–0
Henry Blenerhalsset[8] Esquier his 3[d] parte	33– 6–8
Nathaniel Hobert[9] Esquier his last 3[d] parte	20– 0–0
Henry Mandit[10] gentleman his last 3[d] parte	16–13–4
Gabriell Ellis[11] gentleman his last 3[d] parte	20– 0–0
Edward Blennerhasset[12] his last 2 parts	40– 0–0
Robert Sanderson[13] Clarke of his last} thirde parte————————}	10– 0–0

[1] See above, p. 271, n. 3.

[2] Rabb, 1967, p. 249 lists Richard Boothby as a merchant, trading to France and Spain and an investor in the New Merchant Adventurers 1615, Virginia Co. 1619, and East India Co. 1623.

[3] With Harcourt in the Wiapoco in 1629, see above, p. 318.

[4] Listed by Rabb, 1967, p. 334 as a merchant.

[5] Not identified.

[6] Listed by Rabb, 1967, p. 358 as John 'Pinchon', merchant.

[7] A 'Master Mason' served as secretary to the Duke of Buckingham in the Isle of Rhé expedition 1627, CSP Dom. 1627–8, passim.

[8] See above, p. 353, n. 3.

[9] Possibly related to Sir John Hobart, see above, p. 292, n. 9.

[10] At North fort 1629, see above, p. 340.

[11] See above, p. 340.

[12] At North fort 1629, see above, p. 340.

[13] A man of that name was recommended to the living of St George's, Southwark, December 1627, CSP Dom. 1627–8, p. 462.

Thomas Nevison[1] gentleman his last 3ᵈ parte   20– 0–0
Richard Wagstaff[2] gentleman his last 3ᵈ parte   20– 0–0

d.   Committee for Foreign Plantations, March 1635[3]
March: *1634*   Whitehall
Captain North to have his Patent againe upon condition that he &
his Company submitt to the order of the Comission both for
Ecclesiasticall & civil government, for which there is yet no provision
in the patent:[4] & likewise that they begin theire voyage by
Midsommer next.
A difference in this company concerning moneyes: A subscription
on both sides, but no money paid.[5]
DOCKET: 17 March: 1634 [27 March 1635] forain Plantations.

e.   Letter from the earls of Bedford and Dover to Charles I,
                    6th/16th May 1635[6]
            May it please your most Excellent Majestie
In obedience to your Majesties Commands according to a reference
made to us the 12th: of March Touching Captaine Bampfields
demannds[7] against the Guiana Company, about which we have
often-times mett with them, and have examined all perticulers of
that Busines with them, They haveing since mett as a Company, and
have offered to Captaine Bampfeild the somme of one hundreth
pounds out of certeine Debts in arreare to the Company, besides
what is due to Captaine Bampfeild of a former Somme of one
hundreth ninety & eight pounds, tenne shillings and fower pence,
formerly allowed, by a generall assent of a Committee, chosen to
that purpose. And wee Conceiveing his expence, and charge, with
losse of time, may require a Considerable reparation. Yet he is
content (for preventing your Majesties further trouble) to accept of
Three hundreth pounds, with the somme of one hundreth ninety &
eight pounds tenne shillings and fower pence, There being

---

[1] At Harcourt's colony in the Wiapoco 1629, see above, p. 319, n. 5.
[2] Investor in the East India Co. 1622; Rabb, 1967, p. 395.
[3] P.R.O., CO 1/8, f. 148.
[4] Presumably a reference to the Book of Orders, issued by the Privy Council in
1631, which tightened the control of the crown over all aspects of the work of
local Justices of the Peace and other officers of local government.
[5] This most probably alludes to the Bampfield business.
[6] P.R.O., CO 1/8, ff. 162, 162v, 163v, 165.
[7] See above, p. 387.

deducted, and defaulked, such Moneys as he hath received and given Acquittances for, under his owne hand, which the said Captaine Bampfeild, is a most humble Suiter to your Majestie for the rescuing of his present necessities, May be paid him within Three weekes, after your Majesties Gracious approbation therof. All which wee humbly represent to your Majesties gracious Consideration, with the Answere of the Guiana Company heerunto annexed.

Francis Bedford Henry Dover

[f. 163v] DOCKET Captain Bampfield Guiana Company Guiana 6th May 1635

ENCLOSURE:

[f. 165] To the right Honorable the Earles of Bedford and Dover. The Answeare of the Guiana Companie concerning Captaine Bampfeilds buissines given at a Generall Court held the sixt of May 1635./[1]

May it please your Lordships.

According to your Lordships pleasures wee have againe taken into consideracion the peticion and demannds of Captaine Bampfeild, and upon perusall and examinacion of his pretence and our former Answeare, wee cannot finde any sufficient cause either in equitie or honor to move us to enlarge what by our former Annsweare appeares to have bin allowed unto him, which then at the instance of Noble Persons, was given by way of bounty and not for that the Companie did conceive themselves by right bound to have conferred the same upon him: Which allowance beinge 198^{li}. 10^s. 3^d. wee conceive fitt that Captaine Bampfeild should receive upon the honor of that Consent of any part thereof remaine unpaid upon due Accompt. And further in speciall respect to his Majesties Reference and to the end his Majestie may not further bee troubled by Captaine Bampfeild wee have assigned him 100^{li} out of the first moneys cominge of certaine Arrears of Adventure, which to this purpose are nowe perticulerly assigned and sett over videlizet The Adventure of the Earle of Moulgrave beinge 100^{li}. the Adventure of the Earle of Marleborough being 50^{li}. the Adventure of Sir Simon Harcourt beinge 50^{li} and the Adventure of Hugh May Esquier beinge 60^{li} who have bin lately called upon and served with

[1] 16th May 1635.

an Order from the right hono*rable* his Maj*es*ties Comissioners for Planta*ci*ons for the speedie payment of their said Adventures./

John Collingwood./[1]

5. THE GUIANA COMPANY ATTEMPTS TO PREVENT THE 'OLD' IRISH PLANTERS FROM GOING OUT TO GUIANA WITH THE DUTCH, 1635

a.   Captain Roger North to Sir John Coke,
                     16th/26th December 1633[2]

William Gayner the bearer married to a Dutch woman hath legacies bequeathed to his wife and children, and debts due to him in the same parts he is desirous to pass over with his wife and children, with purpose to return hither. I have had experience of him in the West Indies[3] to which place I am confident he hath a determination to go again in my company.

b.   Reasons to stay W*illia*m Gayner from proceeding to
                        Gwiana.[1634][4]

Reasons for the staye of Will*ia*m Gayner an Irishman & his associates from proceading in their viage out of holland to the river of Amazons and parts thereabout.[5]

The King hath graunted those cuntryes to the Company of Noblemen and Gentlemen of England adventurers for those p*ar*tes[6]

---

[1] Not identified.

[2] *HMC, Twelfth Report*, pt. II, Coke MSS, 39.

[3] It seems most likely that Gayner first went to the Amazon with North in 1620. North's testimony, taken together with that of Richard Jones (see below), suggests that Gayner was sent to sue for the deceased planters' goods because he had knowledge of their dealings with Samuel Lucason and Henry Jacobson Lucifer, Like the other Irish Amazon planters he may well have been out to the river two or three times. His marriage to a Dutch woman may have taken place on the Amazon or subsequent to his return to Holland in a Dutch ship. The timing of his involvement in the affairs of the Guiana Co., 1633–5, suggests that he, like the other Irishmen 'Joan Joanssen', 'Juan Alein', 'Ricardo Molran' and Bernardo O'Brien had only recently returned from the river. He may have gone out with James Purcell and O'Brien in 1629 or have been in captivity in the Maranhão since 1625.

[4] P.R.O., CO 1/8, no. 87, undated. Printed in Gwynn, 'Irish in the West Indies', 1932, p. 183. Clearly from the Guiana Co., probably drafted by Roger North. Jones' statement below suggests that it dates from 1634.

[5] See above, p. 110.

[6] The Guiana Co.

with speciall prohibition that none of his subjectes shall trade thither without their licence.

The Lords of the Counsell have thereuppon stayed some English Gentlemen that were going into holland to make a viage thither from thence.

The saide Gayner being now in holland & in some confederacy with those restrayned Gentlemen prepareth at Flusshing[1] for a viag thither under Comission & assosiation of the Dutch (as is credibly informed) and havinge no knowledg of any other parte about the Amazons then what hath bene possessed by his Majesties Subjectes about XVI yeares is like to bringe the Dutch uppon those partes and thereby quarrell and bloodshed both betwene the Nations & among our selves.

The English ar thereby likely to be driven from their wonted places and to seeke a new plantation among new Indians and uppon new hazarde.

This Gayner is a Romish Catholicque consorted with others of that religion and their intent is to raise unto themselves a plantation there exempte from the English goverment and mayntayned against it by the Dutch.

Gayner lieth at one Cliftons an English Inkeper in fflushn

c.   Deposition of Richard Jones, 11th/21st October 1637[2]

Richard Jones of Drury Lane London gentleman aged 31 yeares or therabouts sworne before the right worthie Sir Henry Marten Knight Judge of his Majestyes highe Courte of the Admiralty, & examined uppon certeine Interrogatories ministred on the behalf of Captain Roger North sayeth & deposeth therto as followeth videlizet:

To the first hee sayeth That hee was told in the River of Amazons by divers Englishe Planters there that they had delivered to Samuel Lucason & Henry Jacobson Lucifer Inhabitants of fflushing who were trading in the said river about yeare 1622 divers goodes & merchantdices to the valewe of one thousand poundes or upwardes to be carried to fflushing & there sould for the best benefitt & advantage of the said English Planters or Captain North

---

[1] Very probably the Guiana Co. was concerned about the preparations of some English to go out to the Cayenne with David Pietersz de Vries in 1634, see above, p. 110, ns. 1, 2.

[2] P.R.O., HCA 3/53, ff. 351v–2.

their Governor. And this hee affirmeth to bee true, who about two or three yeares after went to the said river & there planted.[1]

To the second hee sayeth That the said English Planteres were taken prisoners or killed by the Portugalls[2] before they (as it was said) received anie satisfaction for their monies made of their said goodes.

To the third hee sayeth That about three yeares[3] since this exami*na*te arrived at fflusheinge beeing escaped from the Portugalls[4] & there they founde W*illia*m Gayner an Irish gentleman who had there begane a suite in the name of Capt*ain* Roger North as haveing an interest in the said Planters goodes aforesaid by right to the plantacon where they lived, as by administrac*i*on of their goodes comm*i*tted to him, against the said Samuel Lucason & the widdow of the said Henry Jacobson Lucifer before the Magistrates of fflusheinge, & the said Gayner beeing then to goe againe to the West Indies, this exami*na*te was ymployed by the said Capt*ain* North to prosecute the said suite & did there prosecute the same by the space of two yeares & so [des] untill the same was ended by a diffinitive sentence, And this affirmeth uppon his oath to bee true:

To the 4.th hee sayeth That in the processe of the said suite the said Samuel Lucason & the widdow of the said Henry Jacobson Lucifer by theire owne Account (& pretenses of defalcations & chardges what some beeing deducted & allowed) did acknowledge to remain in their handes for the proceeds & sale of the said English Planters said goodes the sume of one hundred & fifty pounds sterlinge, & were ordered by the Magistrates of fflusheinge to bringe the sume one hundred & fifty poundes into the handes of the quarter M*aste*rs of fflusheinge,[5] And this hee affirmeth uppon his oath to bee true:

To the fifte hee sayeth That the said some of one hundred & fifty poundes beeing brought accordeinge to the order aforesaid into the handes of the quarter Masters of fflusheinge the Bayliffe for the Prince of Orange there made an arreste of the same & in the name of the said Prince obtained sentence againste the sume of two hundred & eighteene poundes flemish of the same & one Gaspar de Maiie one of the Lordes & quarter Masters of fflusheing uppon

---

[1] See above, p. 79.　　　　[2] 1625.　　　　[3] 1634.
[4] See below, p. 415.
[5] A guild official, having charge of the guilds in a quarter or district of the city.

the bench when this examinate moved him for the said money, used these wordes (walke Englisheman – I have the money & I will keepe yt) & yt was said that the said monies were adjudged to the Prince of Orange as Marques of fflusheing & Trevere, for that as yt was said the said English Planters died in the West Indies without heires And this hee affirmeth uppon his oath to bee true.

To the sixte hee sayeth That this examinate by himself & by letter from Sir William Boswell knight his Majestyes Resident at the Haughe [Hague] written to the Magistrates of fflusheinge did oppose the said sentence & did sollicite to have the said monies delivered to the use of the said Captain North, but they the said Magistrates used this examinate harshly & would not suffer his Proctor to speake, but said that they did adjudge the same to the said Prince for the reasons aforesaid And this hee affirmeth uppon his oath to bee true.

THE IRISH PETITION THE SPANISH CROWN
FOR A LICENCE TO SETTLE ON THE AMAZON,
1631–6

1. JASPAR CHILLAN'S ATTEMPT TO ESTABLISH AN IRISH
COLONY ON THE AMAZON UNDER A LICENCE
FROM PHILIP IV, 1631–2[1]

a.   Memorial by Jaspar Chillan presented to Philip IV
prior to 11th August 1631[2]

Gaspar Chillan Irishman – Says that it is six years since he came
from his country to Bilbao following up some important lawsuits
concerning himself and some eminent citizens of London and
which are pending in the royal Chancellery of Valladolid, as can be
seen in the affidavits and sureties which he presents. And thus this
supplicant being resolved to return to his native land and because of
the experiences which I have I desire to serve God and your Majesty
in matters of great importance, being Irish and so well affected to
your Majesty, I offer for the preservation of your royal Treasury,
the following particulars at no cost to your Majesty or your vassals
but only to my own estate and that of my native land. And in order
to judge whether what I propose is useful, advantageous and the
truth and whether I am the suitable person for this your Majesty
may seek information from the Nobles and religious of my country
who reside in this Court, together with the affidavits and sureties
presented.

From the advices and news which the supplicant has received he

[1] The last of the extant series of documents on Chillan's proposal dates from
10th December 1632. Chillan may have pursued the matter further but, as yet,
there is no evidence that he did so.

[2] Translation. A.G.I., Secretaria del Peru, Audiencia de Quito, Estante 77, caj.
3, legajo 18. A Spanish transcription was printed by Gwynn, 'Irish in the West
Indies', 1932, pp. 172–5.

knows it to be a sure thing that the Dutch and other nations are every day settling the river and territory of the Amazon and the coasts of Guyana in your Majesty's West Indies and if no solution is found soon then they will become masters by sea and land which would be of great harm to the holy Catholic Faith. For the one because they will plant their faith among the savages, the other because they will have the fruits and benefits of the region from which they, with their ingenuity will make great wealth to sustain wars against your Majesty.

What the supplicant solicits is that your Majesty may be pleased to give [him] your royal letters patent with authority to send a colony of Irishmen, all catholics, to these territories and that they may, making war in your Majesty's name, fight and throw out the said enemies from that place, the said Irish to remain there to defend it from thenceforward in the said colony.

And so that your Majesty may be satisfied and secure, the supplicant commits himself under oath that he will not allow any other nation but Irish to go on his ships, only five or ten English or Flemings for every hundred, because they are experienced in matters of sea[manship], warfare and manufacture, nor will he allow any commerce or contract except with Spain and Ireland under penalty of losing the authority which your Majesty gives him.

Since it is such a great service to God and the security of your Majesty it is clear that it would be a great shame to lose the opportunity which the supplicant offers, knowing the harm which might result and should it be successful the great benefit which would follow winning souls for heaven and avoiding much robbery. All the peoples may navigate [there] without any fear and in particular those from Brazil, because it is well known to your Majesty that they frequently suffer captivity and loss of their estates principally because those territories are so big without any population and your Majesty cannot settle it with a more loyal and catholic people.

In order to assure the voyage and that it may be put into effect may your Majesty be pleased to write to the king of England in favour of this supplicant so that his ships and those of Holland on their part may not molest them and with this there will be no enemies to impede them by sea.[1]

---

[1] See below, pp. 404–5. Chillan reasoned that, since Charles I of England was at peace with the Dutch, the Irish, as English subjects, would have the special advantage of being able to travel under safe conduct from the English crown in the service of that of Spain.

The supplicant is on the point of departing shortly for his native land and cannot spend or waste his time here neglecting his affairs in his country. The said supplicant begs your Majesty may decide shortly either for or against and that he will receive especial favour in it.

DOCKET: Sire Gaspar Chillan Irishman.

[ANOTHER HAND]: Send to the lord marques de Leganés.[1]

[NOTE IN ANOTHER HAND]:[2] I have seen the memorials which Gaspar Chillan, Irishman, has provided and considered what he proposes and examined the coasts of the River Amazon from the River Paraa [Pará] up to that of the Urino [Orinoco] which is near to the Island of Trinidad. It is uninhabited territory about which there is no more information than that discovered by the ships passing by that part on the way from Brazil to the Indies. I do not find it inconvenient to settle this land with catholics, on the contrary it seems to me that many conveniences may result from it in the service of Our Lord and of his Majesty adjusting the conditions of the warrants to the points which the supplicant proposes in the three memorials[3] which he has presented, and to those points which it would most seem to the Council[4] in its customary prudence to secure its success.

I believe the Irish to be well affected to this Crown and a good relationship can be hoped for with them.

Because these coasts are contiguous to the provinces of Peru I am of the opinion that the *Consejo de Indias* should be advised of this proposal so that it may be seen if its settlement presents any difficulty in those parts and if the harvest of its produce might hinder the sale of that from the Indies and, in this case, what should be done. The Council will resolve that which is most appropriate....

11 August 1631.   [Initials][5]

---

[1] Diego Mexía de Guzmán, marques de Leganés.

[2] Gwynn, 'Irish in the West Indies', 1932, p. 175, assumed this note to have been written by the marqués de Leganés who had been asked to comment on Chillan's memorial.

[3] One of the three may be that printed above and a second that enclosed with the *consulta* of the *Consejo de Estado*, 22nd August 1631, see below, pp. 404–6.

[4] *Consejo de Estado*.

[5] Indecipherable.

b.   A report of the deliberations of the *Consejo de Estado*
    on Chillan's proposal, 22nd August 1631, forwarded for
    consideration to the *Consejo de Indias*, 6th September 1631[1]

DOCKET: My *Consejo de Estado* having seen the proposal of Gaspar
Chillan to settle the River and territories of the Amazon made me
the *consulta*, of which a copy is enclosed signed by the Protonotary,
and I am in agreement with it and thus I remit it to this Council [*de
Indias*] so that it may consider the opinion of the [*Consejo*] *de Estado*.

[Signature]

In Madrid 6 September 1631
    To the conde de la Puebla de[l] Maestro.[2]

Sire –

Gaspar Chillan, Irishman, refers in a memorial which has been
seen in the Council,[3] that it is six years ago that he came from his
country to follow up lawsuits of much importance in the Chancellery of Valladolid and returning now to his native land he wishes to
serve your Majesty in matters profitable to your royal Treasury
without any cost to it or to your vassals. He reports that from the
advices that he has received he knows it to be certain that the Dutch
and other nations are every day settling the river and territories of
the Amazon and coast of Guiana in your Majesty's West Indies and
that unless a solution be found soon they will become masters by sea
and land, to the great damage of the natives of those parts because
they will instruct them in their evil doctrine, and of your Majesty
because of the profits and great wealth which they will extract from
thereabouts to sustain wars against your Majesty. To obviate these
losses the supplicant offers to carry out a colony of Irish Catholics to
those territories, he being given a letters patent of permission for
this and to make war on them in your Majesty's name. They will
expel the enemies of your Majesty which might be there.

He will commit himself under oath not to let pass in his ships
persons of any other nation but Irish, except for, among one
hundred of this nation, five or ten English or Flemings, because

---

[1] Translation. B.L., Add. MS 36,322, ff. 158–162v, printed in Gwynn, 'Irish in
the West Indies', 1932, pp. 179–81.
[2] Lorenzo de Cardenas y Balda, conde de la Puebla del Maestre, Governor of
the *Consejo de Indias* 1628–32.
[3] *Consejo de Estado.*

they are more experienced in matters of seamanship, war and manufacture.

Neither will he allow trade or contract except with Spain and Ireland under penalty of losing the authority which your Majesty might give him.

To assure this business it will be necessary that your Majesty should be pleased to write to the king of England that his ships and those of the Dutch should not molest the supplicant in his voyage.

Another document[1] states as an advantage that by means of this colony those pagan Indians will be brought to the holy Catholic Faith and that the Irish being so well affected to your Majesty's service will not allow any enemy of your crown to enter that coast.

Being at peace with England it will be possible to prevent the Dutch capturing Portuguese ships which leave Brazil, if they carry an affidavit from the leader of the Irish which go out in his colony.

Should your Majesty need people from this nation they may be drawn from the Canary Islands where they are to receive the veteran soldiers from Flanders which your Majesty [was] pleased to send them.[2]

He will try to take the pilots from Holland and England who have knowledge of those parts so as not to allow them to return.

The prosecution will be without cost to your Majesty and as an assurance of this the supplicant will leave behind in these kingdoms one of his brothers[3] with more than twenty four thousand ducats of property.

The removal of the Irish may be expedited with the king of England by representing to him the profits which his vassals will make from this commerce and the supplicant offers to procure them.

Also to obtain letters from the king of England to the effect that the rebel provinces[4] should issue a general order that the supplicant should not be hindered in the prosecution of this project.

The Council studied what is referred to and agreed that the marques de Leganés should hear Gaspar Chillan on all this and

[1] See below, pp. 404–6.

[2] Canary Islands. Presumably Philip IV had made provision for retired Irish veterans from Flanders to settle in the Canaries.

[3] Unnamed. One 'Patrick Chilam Irisheman' exported goods from London to Tredahe, in the *Content* of Milfort, 27th April/7th May 1621, P.R.O., E190, London, 24/1.

[4] United Provinces.

acquire more particular information on that part of the Indies where he wishes to make the colony, and the conveniences and inconveniences which might result from it, and being fully informed render his opinion.

The marques de Leganés heard him and found that the proposal and the means by which he thinks to undertake it are the same as those which have been referred to your Majesty in this consulta, that the territory is very good and fertile without any colony of Spaniards or of any other foreign nation, inhabited only by pagan Indians without any settlement, and by means of a map[1] he demonstrated its location and boundaries and, deferring to the wisdom of the Council the judgement of whether the colony is convenient or not, he said that he noted that if the Irish or whatever other nation were introduced there it was likely that they would trade to the north with the produce of the same region, such as tobacco and other things, and that this could turn aside the traffick of the Indies with these kingdoms.

The Council having heard the marquis de Leganés, considers that what this man proposes in the disposition, has major inconveniences in the execution because he must request a licence from the king of England to go to settle in the dominions of your Majesty and it is nearly obvious that if he should be given it he will go [out] dependent on that king, and that English catholics and heretics will be intermingled with the Irish, and at the least in carrying out a number of people who cannot be got together in secret, the leaders will be heretics appointed by the king of England so that all that colony will be his and its commerce also if there should be any.[2] And the intention to convert those Indians to the Catholic Faith which might be moved [in his favour], not only will it be achieved but it could open the door to false doctrines in those parts and provoke other nations to settle there if they should find the territory convenient and profitable. Thus it would seem to the Council that the proposal should not be admitted, and that one should answer this man with appreciation for his evident zeal and that your

---

[1] There is no indication as to which chart Leganés used.

[2] It is surprising that Chillan failed to anticipate how the Spanish government would react to his proposals to seek a licence and safe conduct from Charles I of England. While it may have seemed to him the only practicable way of getting permission to raise and transport immigrants from Ireland, it merely served to emphasise that the Irish were subject to the English crown.

Majesty will continue looking into what he proposes so as to be able to make a decision, and that in the meantime he should attend to his business without embarking or detaining himself in this. And so that your Majesty might decide what might be to your greater service it could be remitted to the *Consejo de Indias* to give its opinion since it is a matter which concerns it and in which it could have more particular information and reports. Your Majesty will order whatever is to your service.

In Madrid the 22nd August 1631.

His Majesty's response. I have ordered it be remitted to the *Consejo de Indias* as appears.

c.   Enclosure with the *Consulta* despatched by the
        Consejo de Estado to Philip IV, 22nd August 1631[1]
                            Sire

The benefits which your Catholic Majesty will receive from having Irishmen on the River Amazon and coast of Guyana.

– Firstly the great service to God in bringing those savages which are so many thousand souls to the obedience of his holy mother church. – Another is that your Majesty cannot have people more faithful than those said Irish who will do nothing that your Majesty does not command and will not permit any enemy of your Majesty of whatever other nation to enter or settle in those said coasts and territories. – Another is that while there is peace between England, France and Holland the Dutch will not be able to seize the Portuguese from Brasil as they do lying in wait for them on those coasts. Carrying an affidavit from the leader of the Irish who go out in his colony they [the Portuguese from Brazil] will travel without risk. – Another is that should your Majesty have need for the Irish for whatever place they may be drawn from the Canary Islands where they are obliged to refresh and receive the veteran Irish soldiers from Flanders which your Majesty was pleased to give them. From this settlement will be taken the soldiers of the said nation that your Majesty might have need of. – Another is that they will throw out the Dutch or whatever other nation that they find there because they are not yet a significant number. And they will try to carry out [with them] all the pilots which may be found in Holland and England which know those said territories, never

[1] Translation. A.G.S., Estado 2045.

allowing them to return, as well as those they may find yonder so that the enemies may not have anyone who knows the said territory. – Another is that all this will be done without cost to your Majesty and the supplicant will leave as security in these kingdoms his brother with more than twenty four thousand ducats of property and the conde de Tiron [Tyrone] will vouch for him, and all the rest of his countrymen, that he is a man of means and honour and that he will accomplish all the aforesaid.

The arguments with which the king of England may be moved to permit the removal of the Irish.

The first thing is he does not seek more than the commerce in those territories which will be very profitable for his [Charles I's] kingdoms and employ the soldiers and idle people which there are among the Irish, and the king of England will easily agree because of the hopes of the profit from the trade. And they will be all the more pleased that the Irish should remove from Ireland so that the kingdom may be depopulated of its native inhabitants, with the hope of what they will be rid of. As the proverb says, one thief inside the house gives more anxiety than four outside. In order to extract this licence from the king of England, to expedite and solicit it there is no person more eloquent in the English language or with more experience who will know how to handle this undertaking better than the supplicant.

Now if the king of England asks him to take English in the said enterprise he has the reply in hand saying that your Catholic Majesty had only given him a licence for the Irish.

He will extract from the king of England letters for the Dutch by virtue of the peace which he holds with them which give a general order that none of them should molest him being [one of his vassals] so that he may safely undertake this enterprise as is said in the second memorial.[1] Touching the defence and security of each person, the first three or four hundred men do not go to fight but to fortify with forts and to win the affection of the savages and hold them in their service to help them until the second and third supply arrive which will be three or four thousand people with their weapons. With the savages on their side there will be no need for a store of provisions and within two or three years, with God's favour,

---

[1] Further examples of Chillan's infelicitous reasoning, unlikely to convince the Spanish crown that his project was in its best interests.

there will be five or six thousand Irish, religious as well as soldiers.

d.   Memorial and accompanying documents presented by
Jaspar Chillan to Philip IV, 1632[1]

Philip IV to the count de la Puebla del Maestre,
23rd March 1632

Let the enclosed memorial of Gaspar Chillan Irishman be seen in
the *Consejo de Indias* and it will advise me of its opinion of what he
requests in it.

[signature of Philip IV]

In Madrid on 23rd of March 1632.

To the conde de la Puebla del Maestre.

Most Excellent Lord –

Gaspar Chillan, an Irishman – says that in the year of 1622 Sir
Thomas Rodriguez [Thomas Roe], an English pirate, went with five
ships to the river Amazon and coast of Guayana; one of them was
lost, the passengers escaping. Not having sufficient vessels he left all
the Irishmen which he had [with him] ashore, with a promise to
send them help, which he never did.[2] God provided that the Irish
freely won over the savages, and they built a fort for their defence.
A little afterwards Dutch ships came, negotiating with the Irish to
let them settle beside them, offering them great rewards and
moneys. The leader of the Irish entertained the masters and
commanders of the Dutch and detained them as prisoners, until he
had forced them to unload and carry all their pieces of artillery and
powder to the Irish fort.[3] Soon afterwards they left without being
able to win the goodwill of the Irish, because it was contrary to the
service of God and of his Catholic Majesty. The year 1625 Captain

[1] Translation. B.L., Add MS 36,322, ff. 164–8v, printed in Gwynn, 'Irish in
the West Indies', 1932, pp. 175–8.
[2] See above, p. 73. Chillan's garbled account probably reflects a mixture of
ignorance and policy. He knew that the Irish settlers had some connection with
Sir Thomas Roe and that some of them had gone out to the river in the 1620s,
only to be abandoned by their English backers. His tale that the Irish had been
marooned on the river by a shipwreck may have been a deliberate invention to
mask the fact that the Irish had gone out to settle there under the licence of the
English Amazon Co. in 1620.
[3] See above, pp. 79–80. A reference to Nicholas Oudaen and Philip Purcell's
colony. O'Brien similarly tried to convince Philip IV's ministers that the Irish
had not cooperated willingly with the Dutch.

Pedro de Texeira went there with some Portuguese, with pretended orders from your Majesty, accompanied by the Father Brother António de Marciana, Provincial of the Order of St Francis. The 70 Irishmen surrendered their fort and all the country without fighting, as the said Father well knows whose account may be taken in this, together with one of the passports which the said captain gave to one of the Irish who was captured by the Portuguese, which is included with this.[1] After the Irish surrendered themselves, the Portuguese killed 54 of them and carried off the rest captive to Brazil, the country being left without a christian leader. Moreover the Spaniards went four times to conquer the said river, and they never could avail themselves of it, neither the English nor any other nation have won over the savages; only the Irish have been the ones who have held under their alliance twenty two families,[2] which are more than ten thousand individuals. The said Irishmen wrote to the lord conde de Tiron [Tyrone] that he should send them priests and soldiers from Flandes [Flanders] and when the said lord *conde* saw that they did not have a licence from your Majesty, he did not answer them, nor did he send them any men.[3] The said Gaspar Chillan, having communicated to the lord conde de Tiron all the arguments here expressed with the others besides contained in his memorials to the lords of your Majesty's *Consejo de Estado* and *Consejo de Indias* to which he refers, he [Tyrone] had him write to his brother in the kingdom of Ireland that he should attempt to maintain and protect the five Irish who were on the river Amazon until he knew your Majesty's will in this enterprise. The which, once discharged by me, it may be presumed will go to the Dutch or other enemy nations to carry them out to the River Amazon[4] because they

---

[1] 'Estevão Corse', Steven Coursey? See below, pp. 409–10.

[2] Presumably tribes.

[3] Séan O'Neill, succeeded as titular third earl of Tyrone 1616, still recognized as *conde de Tiron* in Spain; brought to the Low Countries at the time of the flight of the earls September 1607; educated in Louvain; appointed in 1625 to the actual command of the Irish regiment in Flanders formerly under his deceased half-brother Henry; made knight commander of the Spanish military order of Calatrava 1632. See Jennings, *Wild geese*, 1964, pp. 4–5; J. J. Silke, 'The Irish abroad, 1534–1691', in T. W. Moody, F. X. Martin and F. J. Byrne, eds., *A new history of Ireland* (Oxford, 1978), III, 605.

[4] Chillan's sentence is rather difficult to follow. Presumably the 'five Irish' referred to had arrived in Spain and planned to leave for England. O'Brien (see below, p. 415) states that two or three Irishmen returned from the Maranhão to the Spanish court but departed to take service with the Dutch when Philip IV

know the language and customs of those savages, whatever people those Irish carry out there are well received by the said savages. If your Majesty does not take order soon he will lose all those territories because the Dutch are settling them and the king of England has given patents and authority to his English vassals to go to settle in the said river Amazon and the coast of Guyana. Since the river is very dangerous at the mouth because of sandbanks and shoals it is not possible to send a heavy fleet or ships of great tonnage and thus the colony will rest more secure for your Majesty or whoever else might have it, and it is more than six hundred leagues by an impassable route from Peru and from the most of the territories which your Catholic Majesty has settled, and it is below the line of the Equator, an impossible climate for Spaniards to inhabit. Supposing all this to be true which it is, it is better to make use of the Irish, as the most faithful friends of Spain which they are, than heretic enemies. Taking into consideration that it will cost your Catholic Majesty nothing nor does it now bring any profit. Although I am going to request a licence from the king of England it is not with any other intention than to preserve the friendship between the both kings and ensure the voyage so that the Dutch and the same English may not molest the Irish, as your vassals, until they are established there. That being so your Majesty may appoint the leaders you wish and besides this the lord conde de Tiron will bind himself that all the people who go there with my passport and order will be most faithful to your Catholic Majesty. It is to be noted that this is of such great service to your Majesty that the Irish will hold themselves ready to receive and maintain your Majesty's army whenever it might occur to him to order his enemies removed from those territories and deprived of all its profits. On the contrary it will not cost your Majesty anything to defend the Irish since they already have the just claim to those savages and territories to which neither the Dutch nor any other can alledge any right. And thus it behoves your Majesty to order that the Irish might return to the settlements and ensure that which they have won and assured to the service of God and of your Catholic Majesty for whose cause they

refused to grant a licence for an Irish colony on the Amazon. The five men Chillan mentions appear to have been living under his protection and he feared to discharge them in case they went to the Dutch. It is reasonable to assume that three of them were 'Joan Joanssen', 'Ricardo Molran' and 'Juan Alein', the men he tried to prevent from leaving Spain in August 1632, see below, pp. 410–12.

will sacrifice a thousand lives, and they will bind all the kingdom of Ireland to hold as mortal enemies those who venture against their claim holding the licence which the said Gaspar Chillan requests of your Catholic Majesty. He suspects that the *Consejo de Indias* has little knowledge of the great losses of the Irish and their loyalty and zeal for your Majesty and the holy Catholic Faith which is the reason why your Majesty can safely entrust them with the said colony. Because of this and because of the common aversion which they [the *Consejo de Indias*] have to foreigners he considers it very difficult to get them to concur to this unless your Majesty makes clear to them the loyalty of the said Irish who have never been found to be false or traiterous to your Majesty, informing them of the benefits which might result to your Majesty in not losing the opportunity offered by the supplicant who will do more with one hundred thousand ducats than your Majesty can do with a million if he executes it soon before the enemy sends more relief to those who are already there. And if the enemy gains the savages and the territories that the Irish had it will cost many more lives and ducats to throw them out of there once they are fortified.

DOCUMENTS ATTACHED TO THE MEMORIAL:[1]

Pedro Teixeira[2] captain of infantry and discoveries for his Majesty in this conquest of Grão Pará I hereby certify, swearing on the Holy Gospels, that Estevão Corse [Steven Coursey?] Irishman [by birth that I know him to have been] one of those who surrendered themselves to me by agreement [in the assault] which I went to make on the foreigners who [invaded] the sertão of Tucujú. And for surety I have given him this certificate made, signed and sealed by me with the signet of my arms in this city of Belém on the 24th of December of the year 1626.

I, Father António de Merceana custodio[3] in this conquest of Pará of the [Custodia] which there is in it, of the order of our angelic father St Francis, certify that the content of the certificate of the Captain Pedro Teixeira is the truth, as verified by me in the said war and sent to negotiate the [passage] of the said foreigners by order of the said Captain, [amongst whom] Estevão Corse [agreed] with the

---

[1] These documents are barely legible in parts and the transcription remains somewhat tentative.
[2] See above, p. 81, ns. 2, 3.   [3] See above, p. 407.

rest to surrender himself [in witness of which] were made documents to record the terms of the said agreement and this I pronounce to be the truth and being requested I give at present made and signed by me in the conquest of Pará on the first of January of the year 1627.

The which I swear happened thus by my word as a priest.

Father António da Merceana.

e.   A synopsis of the advantages of Chillan's proposal, [1632][1]

Sire

The following observations for your Catholic Majesty on the enterprise of Gaspar Chillan or the settlement of Irish on the river Amazon and coast of Guyana. –

– The first, as is contained in his memorials, the service to God and your Majesty by winning souls to the obedience of the holy Catholic Faith and securing your territories with such loyal and faithful people.

– Another is that the Dutch rebels have made a company of fourteen or fifteen of the most powerful and rich [men] which there are in Holland and Zeeland merely to win the ports of the Marinon [Marañón] and Gran Pará[2] where your Majesty has a small force of Portuguese, and other nations which like them seek to win the river Amazon envy them. If there are Irish in the river Amazon nobody will venture to the Marinon, Pará or other part of Braçil as far as Gran Baya [Bahia] neither to all the coast of Guyana.

– Another is that there are already two or three colonies of English near the mouth of the river Amazon on the coast of Guyana at the charge and expense of the Captain Diego Norte [James North],[3]

[1] Translation. B. N., Madrid, MS 4163, f. 58. Undated, but most probably produced in 1632. It was clearly written after Chillan's proposal had been discussed and rejected for the first time by the *Consejo de Indias* in October 1631 and was probably presented as Chillan made his second attempt to that council in May 1632. See below, p. 413.

[2] The Dutch had numerous settlement projects on the coast of Guiana in the 1630s but nothing directed to the Maranhão until 1641. Gedeon Morris de Jonghe played a major role in convincing the Dutch West India Co. of the advantages of conquering the Maranhão after his return to the United Provinces in 1637; 'Relatórios e cartas', *RIHGB*, LVIII (1895), 237–319.

[3] Presumably he means Roger North, although he could conceivably be referring to Sir John North who associated with Sir Christopher Neville in founding the colony at North fort.

their leaders are Master Roberto Genig[1] and the Captain Guillermo Hicson.[2]

– Another is the great harm done by the pirates who rob the islands of Santo Domingo, Trinidad Margarita and all the other islands and ports as far as la Abana [Havana] may be avoided. One or two warships sent from Spain merely with munitions and a warning to the Irish colony will suffice as if it were a full armada from Spain, taking into consideration that there will be no lack of men or provisions and that the Irish will be to the windward and will go with their boats and the savages which they possess to follow the leaders and the command of your Majesty.

– Another is that your Majesty should not lose the opportunity, although some of your *Consejo de Indias* may say what they wish not understanding the envies and designs of the enemy and his confederates, since everything may be known to be true by means of the agents which your Majesty has in England, France and Holland. And may it please God that your Majesty should have the Irish to settle and secure all your remote kingdoms and territories, considering that they are more inclined and affected to Spain than to any other nation of Europe and consequently they cannot go to or make use of any other king or potentate in the world to protect them except your Catholic Majesty. And thus let your Majesty do this favour for them by which they will rest more obliged to attend to your Majesty's service. They will remain forever rather vassals of your Majesty than the king of England, and this is in agreement with that which your *Consejo de Estado* has discussed, which grasps and understands this undertaking better than your *Consejo de Indias*.

f.   Jaspar Chillan to Philip IV, 25th August 1632[3]
Sire,

Gaspar Chillan, Irishman. He says that it is important for the surety of his undertaking for the settlement of the river Amazon and for your Majesty's service that all the justices of these kingdoms be commanded to hold any individual of those named below because the supplicant is trying to prevent them going to the [West

---

[1] Robert Harcourt?

[2] Chillan seems to have confused the names of William Clovell and Thomas Hixon, the governor and deputy-governor of North fort respectively.

[3] Translation. B.L., Add. MS 36,322, ff. 170–171v. A Spanish transcription was printed by Gwynn, 'Irish in the West Indies', 1932, pp. 178–9.

India] Company of Holland where they wish to go to seek its favour, until your Majesty decides about the licence which the supplicant is requesting. It is important that they should not leave and the supplicant is willing to maintain them as he has done up to now. And thus I beg that your Majesty be pleased to send your royal order to this effect so that with it the supplicant, or whoever should have his warrant may have recourse to the ordinary justices. And this must be done soon and with all possible brevity. May he receive favour in it.

Joan Joanssen
Ricardo Molran
Ju[an] Alein.[1] These men are of those who went with Sir Thomas Ro the English pirate to the River Amazon.[2]

DOCKET: In Madrid the 25th of August [1]632. Sire. Gaspar Chillan. [IN ANOTHER HAND] It has already been decided what is appropriate. Let this be looked into. [Two signatures] On the 26th of August 1632.

[IN ANOTHER HAND] The last *consulta* which was made on this dates from 10th October [1]631 and an order which his Majesty sent afterwards on the 23rd March 1632 that the memorial from the said Gaspar Chillan which came with it be looked into and a *consulta* made by the Council.[3] Up to now it has not been done.

g.   Reports to Philip IV on the standing of Chillan's business,
December 1632[4]
Sire – Andres de Roças.[5]

[This accompanies] a copy of the *consulta* made by the *Consejo de Estado* on the 22nd of August [1]632 [1631][6] on the proposal of Gaspar Chillan and he declares he had no other documents. His Majesty sent a copy of this *consulta* with the order of the 6th September [1]631.[7]

I send to your Majesty a copy of the consulta made by the *Consejo de Estado* on Gaspar Chillan's proposal to settle the river and

---

[1] See above, pp. 113, 407, n. 4.
[2] See above, p. 406, n. 2.
[3] See above, pp. 406–10.
[4] Translation. B.L., Add. MS 36,322, ff. 171–3. The Spanish transcription is printed in Gwynn, 'Irish in the West Indies', 1932, pp. 181–2.
[5] Andrés de Rozas, Secretario de Estado de Norte en gobierno.
[6] See above, pp. 401–4.   [7] *Ibid.*

territories of the Amazon and coast of Guiana and there are no other of his papers in this office.

May God protect your Majesty as I desire.

Madrid on the 10th of December 1632.

Andres de Roças.

Master Fernando Ruiz de Contreras.[1]

His Majesty, by a decree of the 11th of November of 1632, was pleased to order that a memorial which Gaspar Chillan presented about the settlement of Irishmen on the river Amazon and the coast of Guiana, together with the other documents which are in the possession of Master Fernando Ruiz de Contreras, should be seen in the *Junta de Guerra de Indias*, meeting together for this in the Junta with Master Inigo de Briçuela, as guardian of the Irish nation,[2] and requesting from Master Secretary Andres de Roças a copy of the *consultas* which had been made on this matter by the *Consejo de Estado* so that with complete knowledge of everything it might consider its opinion. The *Junta de Guerra*, having seen the decree of the former commanded that they should request these copies from the Master Secretary Andres de Roças and assemble all that he had. Master Andres de Roças replied that he possessed no more than one *consulta* and handed over a copy of it, the which *consulta* is the same as that which his Majesty had referred to the Council with the decree.[3] The content of the documents which exist on this matter is as follows. By a decree of the 6th of September of 1631 his Majesty referred to the conde de la Puebla the *consulta* of the *Consejo de Estado* previously mentioned to look into the proposal of Gaspar Chillan. The Council[4] advised his Majesty on the 10th of October of the same year that it was not appropriate to allow Gaspar Chillan's proposal for the reasons contained in the *consulta*[5] which it made, to which his Majesty was pleased to reply 'it is good'.

On the 23rd of May of 1632 – his Majesty referred to the Council[6] another memorial from Gaspar Chillan[7] and ordered that what he requested should be considered.

---

[1] Fernando Ruiz de Contreras, secretary to Philip IV.
[2] Not identified.   [3] See above, pp. 401–4.
[4] *Consejo de Indias*.
[5] This *consulta* by the *Consejo de Indias* does not appear to be extant.
[6] *Consejo de Indias*.
[7] See above, pp. 406–10.

413

All the documents were assembled and studied and another *consulta* was sent to his Majesty on the 2nd of September of 1632[1] the which contained the same as that of the 10th of October of 1631 and his Majesty responded the same as to the other.

This is everything which these documents contain – there are others with them concerning a proposal made by Luis de Arana de Basconcelos[2] but since there is nothing in them touching Gaspar Chillan they are not mentioned in the report.

DOCKET: Report of what the documents concerning the proposal of Gaspar Chillan contain.

2. BERNARD O'BRIEN'S ACCOUNT OF HIS ADVENTURES FROM THE TIME OF HIS SURRENDER TO THE PORTUGUESE IN 1629 TO HIS ARRIVAL IN SPAIN 1636[3]

. . . When they [the Portuguese] arrived at their settlements and garrisons they robbed the supplicant and the rest of his people of their goods and clothes which were worth 14,000 ducats.[4] And they confined some and killed others and maltreated all of them, dividing their goods between the governor general of the Marañón called Francisco Cuello de Caravallo [Coelho de Carvalho], Captain Pedro Texeira, the *oydor* Antonio de Basbaro,[5] the *Proveedor mayor* and others. They forced them to work and to trade for the Portuguese, as they do to this day, without keeping their word or their oaths.

Seeing this, the said Friar Luis de la Assumpción, Friar Christobal de S. Joseph and other religious,[6] petitioned that their goods be returned to the Irish and that the terms made with them and sworn to in the name of your Majesty, be kept. And since they did not achieve this they imposed an interdict and sent Friar António Marciana to Spain to give account to your Majesty and his ministers. There came with him an Irish priest who wrote to Gaspar Chilam (sic) that he should present this case to your Majesty in this court.[7]

[1] Apparently not extant.
[2] Luis Aranha de Vasconselhos. Presumably a reference to his memorial of 1626, see above, p. 247, n. 1.
[3] Translation. See above, p. 263, n. 2.   [4] See above, p. 255, n. 1.
[5] Judge. O'Brien correctly identifies the holder of this office during the period of his captivity.
[6] See above, pp. 248, n. 2, 382.
[7] See above, pp. 112, 406–10; Kiemen, 1973, pp. 42–3.

And although the viceroy of Portugal sent orders that the Irish should be sent to Spain with their goods, the governor of the Marañón, Caravallo, did not do it. On the contrary he gave licences to some Dutch and English to return to their countries, keeping the Irish under the said oppression.

18 of the Irish and others which the governor Caravallo held at Caeté (which is a post between the Marañón and Gran Pará),[1] oppressed by various afflictions, fled in one of the governor's boats. They touched the Island of Trinidad in 11°.[2] 14 of them went ashore to look for food. The boat with the other 4 was carried by the force of the current and wind to the Island of Margarita. The governor of Margarita sent three of them to Spain. Two of them came to court, and when they found that your Majesty was not giving the Irish permission to settle in the Amazon, and that those who had trusted in the governor of the Marañón were not free, they went to Zeeland. From thence they returned with a ship and 100 men to Seguive [Essequibo] where they fortified themselves and reinforcements were prepared for them in Zeeland.[3] The 14 who went ashore on Trinidad established friendship with the Indians there and went over to the mainland in their canoes, and from there to the Serenam [Surinam] river where the English have a settlement.[4] From there some went to S. Cristoval [St. Christophers], others to Monserrate [Montserrat], others to la Barbada [the Barbados] (in which parts the English, Dutch and French have colonies) and in the end they reached England.[5]

When the governor Caravallo found out that the 18 had fled in his boat, he put the rest of the Irish in prison in irons. The supplicant was held in fetters for one year. And in the end they exiled him, sending him and others among the cannibal Cururios Indians,[6] who eat human flesh. Friar Christobal de S. Joseph, *Predicador* for your Majesty and *Custodio*[7] of the province of

---

[1] See above, p. 315, n. 1.
[2] See above, p. 267, n. 9.
[3] See above, pp. 112–3, 411–2.
[4] See above, p. 112, n. 6.
[5] For the history of Irish emigration to the West Indies in the first half of the seventeenth century, see Gwynn, 'Irish in the West Indies', 1932; 'Early Irish emigration to the West Indies', 1929, 377–93; 'Indentured servants and negro slaves in Barbados', *Studies*, XIX (1930), 279–94; 'Cromwell's policy of transportation', ibid., pp. 607–23.
[6] Cururi.   [7] Superior.

Marañón and Gran Pará alluded to the fetters and other matters of government in a sermon. In particular he said that he was not amazed that a serpent should kill a stag since he had heard that in Pernambuco a rabbit had swallowed a ship with all its complement, referring to when Francisco Cuello de Caravallo was governor of Pernambuco a ship belonging to the Catholic vassals of your Majesty arrived, and the next day disappeared. At midnight, following [this sermon], Portuguese soldiers began to throw stones at the monastery in which the *Predicador* lived, awakening the friars, they put two bullets through the window into the head of one of the friars who resembled the *Predicador* and was at the high altar lighting the vigil lamp, leaving him dead.[1]

The supplicant, in his exile, earned the friendship of the cannibals. He learned their language and went more than 200 leagues inland, surveyed the rivers, mountains, drugs and secrets of the Indians and brought an Indian province to his alliance (as well as teaching them a better way of living). Caravallo fearing that he would make war on him with the aid of the Indians, sent a captain to look for him to request him to return to Marañón, making him many offers. Having returned he induced his Indian allies to accept Caravallo's authority. But when Caravallo would not allow the supplicant to govern them they withdrew from submission to Caravallo's jurisdiction.

Moreover the supplicant discovered that the religious and gentlemen of Marañón were disturbed by the abovementioned murder of the friar, by that of Don Manuel de Sosa who died in prison,[2] that of a silversmith who was found hanged, and by the fact that no one could send a letter to Spain or receive one without Caravallo or his brother, your Majesty's secretary in Lisbon, reading it. Also it was questioned whether Caravallo had licence from your Majesty to begin a silver mine which he had developed there, and whether he ought to detain a Dutch servant to whom he gave a licence to return to Holland, being that the French who were the first whites who settled in the Marañón affirm that there are mines of gold, silver and quicksilver

---

[1] On the friction between the friars and the secular authorities, see Kiemen, 1973, pp. 29–47.

[2] Manoel de Sousa d'Eça, see above, p. 165, n. 4. He died shortly after being unjustly incarcerated by Francisco Coelho de Carvalho; Kiemen, 1973, p. 42.

there.[1] In the same manner he saw that the Indians free as well as slave, and the white settlers, rich and poor, were complaining of Caravallo's vexations and regretting that he should have governed them for nine years and they did not know when he would be sent a successor.

In particular the Irish followers of the supplicant suffer grave affliction and so they begged him when he should arrive [at court] to give account to your Majesty. Also to state that, if given permission to return to settle the river Amazon where they used to hold the Indians in their alliance and are acquainted with the territory and the harbours and understand the language, they would serve your Majesty with great loyalty. And four of the highest chiefs of the Indians of the Amazon, whom Caravallo holds captive at present, charged him with the same message and that they and their followers would obey whatever governor your Majesty should send them there, as long as he was not Portuguese because the Portuguese do not observe good relations, but rather rob them and make them slaves. And as a surety for their offer, one of the four handed over to the supplicant his only son whom he brings with him. And they took an oath of him [O'Brien] that he would come and give an account to your Majesty and not offer his service to any other prince until he had done so, as he does by this memorial. Anxious to do so, he departed from Marañón on the 21st of November 1634. He placed his property and that of the other Irish, up to the value of 19,000 *reales de a ocho*,[2] with the help of a Spanish widow called Doña Maria a native of Sevilla, aboard a Brasil frigate, whose captain was Pedro Merino and master Alonso García. These men carried two chests, approximately four spans long by three in height and two in width, full of silver money (if not gold as well), and many other goods which Caravallo sent on board at night to be carried to Caracas where he had a son, and a factor and generally he sent goods.[3] The pilot of the frigate knew very little of that coast and was not willing to be guided by the supplicant, and thus on the

---

[1] Gedeon Morris de Jonghe informed the Dutch West India Co. that several mines had been uncovered and tested in the neighbourhood of Belém and São Luis and that the English prisoners knew their whereabouts; 'Relatórios e cartas', *RIHGB*, LVIII (1895), 242, 244.

[2] A Spanish silver coin, worth 272 maravedís.

[3] In other words Francisco Coelho de Carvalho was illegally salting away capital in Caracas. The Portuguese were legally barred from trade in the Spanish Indies.

28th November 1634 he reached the islands of the Cavezes Vajas[1] and from there the Serenam river in 6° without understanding where he was, although the supplicant, whom the Portuguese did not wish to believe knew because this river flows out of the Amazon and he had navigated it as said before.[2] Anchoring they shot off muskets. A canoe full of fishermen came aboard thinking they were English. The supplicant, talking with them in different languages discovered they were Harauacos [Arawaks] allied to the English, who have a fort and a colony in the Serenam river with 400 fighting men as well as women,[3] and that there were at that time among them some of the Irish and English who had been with the supplicant in the Amazon and had fled in the boat from Caeté as mentioned above.

The Portuguese, finding that the Indians and the supplicant agreed in their accounts followed his advise until he got them out of the river some 20 leagues to sea, where entrusting themselves to the Portuguese pilot they put to sea and ran aground in the Gulf of Paria. Grounded in the middle of some reefs they beseeched God for mercy and the supplicant to take responsibility to get them out of danger and guide them. He did so, guiding them to Margarita where he encountered one of his Irish settlers previously mentioned, who told him that three of his companions had come to Spain as has been said.[4] From there he piloted them to Caracas as the Portuguese wished, and there they unloaded their cargo and that of governor Caravallo and that of the supplicant and that of Doña Maria, the widow from Sevilla. There, many of the Spaniards, creoles and mestizos were sick with boils, infections and other illnesses of which the supplicant, in the matter of two months which he was there, cured more than 40 of them with herbs, drugs and other medicines learned amongst the Indians and in various European countries.

At this time the Indians of Caracas, going ashore on the island of

---

[1] Low heads? Cows' heads? Possibly the Connétables, 4°49' N., or the Remire islands eighteen miles to the westward. The waters near the both these groups of rocky islets are very dangerous to shipping because of shoals and the extreme velocity of the tide and current in that area.

[2] See above, p. 75, n. 2.

[3] See above, p. 112, n. 6. O'Brien greatly exaggerates the number of colonists, doubtless in hopes of advancing his own case to the Spanish crown.

[4] Earlier O'Brien states that only two Irishmen made it to the Spanish court, see above, p. 415.

Corosao [Curaçao] took one of the Dutchmen who were fortified there[1] and carried him to Aguayre. And in his examination made by order of the lieutenant major Gabriel Mendes de Carrasco, the supplicant acted as interpreter and his statement was sent to Spain in the despatch boat of Captain Blanco, February 1635.[2]

The supplicant left Aguayre, the port of Caracas with a licence and 20,000 *reales de a ocho*[3] in money and goods on the 4th of March 1635 in a vessel named the *Buenaventura* of Sevilla, whose captains were called Andres Blasquez de Garnica and Christobal de la Cruz. They went to Havana to come from there with the *flota* to Spain. On the 9th of the same month, between the islands of Buenos Ayres and Española [Hispaniola] they encountered and were captured by three warships from Zeeland, which having left reinforcements on Corosao were returning home laden with Brazil wood. There was with the Dutch an English surgeon who had been under the command of the supplicant in the Amazon and he told them how the supplicant was the general whom the Zeelanders had sent to the Amazon and that they would be very glad to have him in their jurisdiction. They were carried to Cape Tivuron [Tiburon][4] where they picked up English and French who had fled from the Island of Tortuga in three boats, and who told them how the Spaniards, guided by an Irishman, had taken the island from them, killing some and capturing others.[5] Captain Maltman,[6] a great Dutch pirate, arrived at this same Cape with three warships and his seamen told the supplicant that the three Dutch ships were in the harbour of Tortuga and the guns of the Spanish ships began to fire on them when they ran aground amongst the reefs at night. Sending the shallops ashore by night for some pieces of artillery which they had disembarked on the beach to lighten a ship to free it, one or two Spaniards captured three whites and two mulattos

---

[1] Settled by the Dutch.
[2] Not apparently extant.
[3] See above, p. 417, n. 2.
[4] The south-western point of Haiti.
[5] A Spanish force invaded Tortuga in January 1635 massacring the English and French inhabitants. For the history of early settlement there, see A. P. Newton, *Colonizing activities*, 1914; Harlow, *Colonizing expeditions*, 1925, pp. 14, 81; K. O. Kupperman, 'Errand to the Indies: puritan colonization from Providence Island through the Western Design', *WMQ*, XLV (1988), 70–99. Dr Kupperman has produced a new edition of the company's papers which the editor had not seen at time of printing.
[6] David Pietersz de Vries, *Korte historiael*, 1911, pp. 212–13, reports that he met the privateer Pieter Jansz Maertman at Cape Tiburon, 22nd February 1635. Maertman told him of the events at Tortuga.

who had escaped earlier by swimming. After a few days, tying them one to another they threw them into the sea. This Captain Maltman carried 11 Portuguese and Spaniards with him as pilots and interpreters and in three months he took 28 caravels and frigates belonging to Spaniards and Portuguese from different places, as the supplicant has heard the Captain himself and other members of his crew say.

The companies of the six Dutch ships took counsel about what to do with the Spaniards and this supplicant whom they had taken, and it seemed to them that if they threw the Spaniards into the sea leaving the supplicant alive, he would reveal it and if they threw him into the sea with the Spaniards the English surgeon would tell of it. Moreover they would be neglecting the service of their republic by not returning the supplicant to give account of what he had undertaken. Thus the three ships, separating from those of Captain Maltman, put the Spaniards ashore near the Cape of S. Nicolas[1] on Española and they took the supplicant with them. They came to Tortuga, one of the three boat-loads of English and French being with them, the other two went to the Isla de las Vacas.[2]

They were at Tortuga for 15 days taking on potatoes and peas and the supplicant went all over the island and encountered 44 blacks who did not wish to be governed by the English and French who had survived and returned. Some English here told him that, before the Spaniards arrived, their Governor had hanged an Irish priest. They returned to Española to the Vaya de los Limones[3] where they took on the meat of wild cows and pigs and water and they appointed one of the Dutch ships General and Admiral of the prize taken from the Spaniards. They passed the Vermudas at 36°. It being Lent, one of the Dutch informed the supplicant that he was doing wrong not to eat meat with them and the supplicant replied that they were doing worse in eating it. On account of these words there was a quarrel in which the supplicant wounded two of them and received three wounds himself. To avoid more trouble the General moved him from the Vice-Admiral to the Admiral.

Three days out from there they sighted a vessel and the flagship and prize making chase lost sight of the Vice-Admiral, which was a

[1] The north-westernmost point of Haiti.
[2] Isla de Vaca off the south-west coast of Haiti.
[3] Bahia de Manzanillo, north-west Haiti?

better ship. Three days later the Admiral and the prize encountered three Dutch ships coming from Pernambuco carrying Portuguese and they told them what the Dutch had accomplished there. Four days later they met another four Dutch warships coming from Guinea laden with gold and ivory.

Afterwards they met up with 90 Dutch ships, only one of them a warship, which were going to lade fish and salt in the islands.[1] The following day they encountered an English vessel which came from Guinea with a cargo of gold and ivory. They reached the English Channel. The prize went to Zeeland and the Admiral to Holland to the city of Squidam [Scheidam]. Its captain was a catholic and the supplicant begged him not to lay charges against him or say who he was. This he did, surrendering him to the council of the city of Durf saying only that they had found him in a Spanish ship.

The supplicant, examined by the council of Durf, said that he was an Englishman, native of London, whom the Spaniards had captured in the Indies and sent to Spain. When he was asked to enter the service of the Dutch Republic in the Indies he replied that he had first to go to England to see his family. They gave him a passport and 200 reals for the journey. He went to other cities of Holland such as Rotherdama, Delphe [Delft], La Haya [The Hague] where he ran into many Portuguese and Indians from Brazil who are seeking employment in the service of the state of Holland. In La Haya the widowed *Condessa de Palatino*[2] gave him an English passport and 200 reals.

He went to Amsterdama where a man, coming up to this supplicant's Indian boy, asked him who he was. The boy said that he belonged to Bernardo del Carpio. Presently the man came towards the supplicant and embraced him, speaking in Indian and calling him Bernardo del Carpio and saying that it pleased him very much to see him in that country. The supplicant asked him, also in Indian, who he was who called him thus and for what reason. He said that he was Father Moraes of the Company of Jesus who had been *lenqua mayor* of Brazil and *procurador de los Indios*.[3] Since it was Sunday, the

---

[1] On the Dutch salt trade, see Ghoslinga, 1971, ch. 6.

[2] The Princess Elizabeth Stuart, widow of the Elector Palatine, sister of Charles I, a close friend of Sir Thomas Roe.

[3] Protector or guardian of the Indians. This is the former Jesuit Manuel de Moraes. Moraes surrendered to the Dutch at Paraiba in January 1635. For his life history, as eventful as O'Brien's, see 'Proçesso de Manoel de Moraes, sacerdote e theologio ... preso nos carceres da inquisição de Lisboa, 1647', *RIHGB*, LXX (1908), vi–i, 1–165; Boxer, *Dutch in Brazil*, 1957, pp. 58, 267–9.

supplicant asked him if he had said mass that day because, if not, he would like to hear it. He, smiling, said that time was past and he would not say any more masses. The supplicant, realizing that he was a renegade, dissimulated asking what brought him to Holland. He said that in Pernambuco, [because he was] protecting an Indian, Mathias de Albuquerque, governor yonder, called him an Indian and he went to Portugal to seek justice against him from your Majesty's ministers. They did not defend him or protect his honour, neither was he rewarded for his great service or paid the money he was owed and he, to revenge himself for everything, went to Holland, took the religion of the Dutch and guided and conducted them to capture Pernambuco and Paryba [Paraiba]. The Dutch were governed by his opinion on matters which concerned Brazil and he was negotiating to marry the sister of the Dutch governor of Brazil.[1]

Presently the same man went to inform the Council of Amsterdama that the supplicant was in the city and that he was the most important man they might find for Indian matters. The supplicant was arrested by the Council of Amsterdama on the 1st of July 1635 and they told him that Cornelio Joseph, captain of the ship the *Unicornio*[2] which captured him, had reached Zeeland and the Council of Zeeland had advised them that they should send him from wherever they found him and he was accused of having surrendered the fort of the river Amazon to the king of Spain. They brought as witnesses against him the Dutch servant of Caravallo and an English man and his wife which Caravallo had given licence to depart from the Marañón for their countries. He responded that he had not undertaken to make or defend a fort or settlement for the Dutch or Zeelanders or the English, that he was merely under obligation to return three times the goods which the Zeelanders gave to him, and if he had not accomplished this he would do it with the property he held in Ireland. Besides the Zeelanders had not sent him to their own territory but to that of the king of Spain and it seemed just to him to return it to its owner, and, in any case, had he wished to hold on to it the Zeelanders did not

[1] Moraes married twice in the United Provinces. His first wife was the daughter of Arnaldo Vanderhuit, a merchant of Harderwijk in Guelders, and his second Adriana Smetz of Leyden; 'Proçesso de Manoel Moraes', p. vii; Boxer, 1957, p. 268.
[2] Not yet identified.

send relief in time as they promised. With all this he was condemned to death.

In this the priest, Manuel de Moraes, defended him effectively, saying that nothing was gained by his death but by his life and service much could be won employing him again in the conquest of the Marañón, Gran Pará and river Amazon. He was a great pilot, interpreter and well-loved by the Indians. It was not significant that the Spaniards should have deceived him the first time since he was young and of their religion, but that he [Moraes] would go bail that they would not deceive him a second time. He himself would go on the expedition, and Pernambuco and all of Brazil was little in comparison to the new conquest which the two of them would make in the parts referred to. They offered to spare the supplicant's life and whatever favours and honours he might request if he went General of the expedition. He said that he accepted if they gave him what was necessary for the purpose. They asked him what he required. He said to take with him 700 men and 6 warships. They then promised him to send relief each year. They released him and gave him authority to raise men.[1]

While he was raising the men the Father Manuel de Moraes although he had given life to his body wanted to take away that of his soul, harassing him that he should become a heretic and marry a heretic wife, daughter of a councillor of the city of Amsterdama. Also the Jews, which are many in Amsterdam and have a synagogue there, gave him remembrances to their relatives in the Marañón, Gran Pará and those parts, enjoining him to treat them well and defend them.[2]

The supplicant, taking what he could in money and other things, one night put himself aboard a boat bound for Utreque [Utrecht], and from thence he took the stage for Arnam [Arnhem], and from thence to Vysel [Wesel], and from there to Ursoo [Orsoy], other places which are under Dutch jurisdiction, and in order to travel without hindrance he used the passport which they had given him in Durf from the widowed condessa de Palatino, as is said.

[1] For Dutch activities in Cayenne, Essequibo and Berbice 1634–5, see Ghoslinga, 1971, ch. 16.

[2] Presumably O'Brien presented this as further evidence of the spiritual perils to which he had been exposed. On the history of Jewish settlement in Brazil, see A. Wiznitzer, *The records of the earliest Jewish community in the New World* (New York, 1954); 'The number of Jews in Dutch Brazil, 1630–54', *Jewish Social Studies*, XVI (1954), 107–14; Boxer, 1957, pp. 123, 133–4, 227, 241–5.

He travelled to Queysers wear [Kaisers werth] where there is one of your Majesty's garrisons, the governor of which gave him an escort to Disseldorf [Dusseldorf], where the duque de Neoburgo [Newburgh] the younger was.[1] D. Hugo Mahuno[2] and the vice-lieutenant-colonel, both Irish, were in his service; at whose representation, the duke gave him 48 soldiers with colours and standard as an escort to take him to Hinsprig [Hinsbeck], his own city, and a letter in which he ordered the governor there to send him to the duque de Lerma at Stevinsvers [Stevensweert]. Since from there he was in neutral territory, the governor of Hinsprig sent with him 4 soldiers, an Englishman among them, who, having traversed one league, carried him to a wood and robbed him and the Indian boy, taking their clothes down to their shirts and a portion of their passports and documents and, in particular, 400 *reales de a ocho*[3] which he carried in his travel bag and 34 gold buttons, each one of which had cost him two reales, which he had acquired with the money which they had given him in Holland for his expenses and to raise men. Also they stripped him of half a pound of amber which would be worth one hundred *reales de a ocho*.

The supplicant and the Indian boy returned to Hinsprig by night and complained to the Governor, who gave them two old suits of clothes and apprehended the Englishman. He said that he had not found the other three or the goods and that the lieutenant major of the city would protect them because he took a share of the robbery. He gave to the supplicant a letter to the duque de Lerma and governor of Stevinsverd requesting the duke to send him a company of soldiers to the city with which he might bring the lieutenant major and the robbers to justice, and also he sent him with a 40 man escort. The duque de Lerma, though he saw him so ill-treated took no notice of it, even though the conde de Tirconel [Tyrconnell][4] spoke for him. Thus he told him that he should repair to the lord Cardinal Infante[5] and show him the letter which

---

[1] Presumably O'Brien means the elder son of Wolfgang Wilhelm, Duke of Newburgh (1578–1653).

[2] Not identified.   [3] See above, p. 417, n. 2.

[4] Hugh Albert O'Donnell, son of Rory O'Donnell, titular second earl of Tyrconnell, still recognized as *conde de Tirconel* by the Spanish Crown; appointed knight of the Spanish military order of Alcantara 1629, commissioned as colonel of a regiment of Irish infantry in Flanders January 1632; see Jennings, *Wild geese*, 1964, pp. 7–8.

[5] Fernando, Cardinal Infante of Spain, Governor of the Spanish Netherlands 4th November 1634 to 9th November 1641.

he brought from the governor of Hinsprig, giving him a passport to go along with a mounted company bound for Dist [Diest].

Here the supplicant spoke at leisure to the *Secretario de Camara*[1] and the lord Cardinal Infante and related his adventures, and in particular how he had come across the 90 Dutch ships which were going to the islands to the fishery and were not taking more than one warship, and he said that with 4 warships from Dunquerque they would be able to take them. The lord Cardinal Infante sent vessels from Dunquerque which took and burned the Dutch fleet, as afterwards he learned in Dunquerque, and gave the supplicant hopes that he would have his property returned to him. But his highness went to Maytrique [Maastricht] and the supplicant, seeing that his suit went slowly, wrote to the conde de Tirconel that he should attempt to recover the property, and he himself went to Lovayna [Louvain] and from there to Bruxelas [Brussels] where the baron Lord Dermicio Omalle [Dermot O'Mallun],[2] his kinsman, gave him [ ] weapons and money to come to Spain.

Departing from Bruxelas within three leagues he came across the conde de Giron [Tyrone] and his infantry regiment, marching towards the borders of France, and the count sent him with an escort from Mount San Eloy [St Eloi] to Dunquerque where there was plague. Since he did not find passage for Spain, he travelled in an English ship for England and to the port of Dublin. Waiting for a passage to Spain and finding himself without money, he went to London where he had Irish kinsmen and acquaintances. In London he came across the Doctor Cuaresma, former governor of the Island Tomarca [ ], with his wife, children and servants, 29 slaves and much property and he departed England for the Algarbes in an English ship.[3]

Here [in London] his friends and kinsmen advised him to present a memorial to the king of England recounting how three Zeeland ships from the cities of Medilburg [Middleburg] Surrigse [Zeirikzee]

---

[1] D. Martín de Axpe held the office of Secretario de Estado y Guerra in the Spanish army in Flanders 1634–6. This may be an allusion to him.

[2] Presumably Dermot O'Mallun/O'Mallum, created Baron Glean O'Mallun and Courchy of Co. Clare 1622; appointed knight of the Spanish military order of Calatrava 1616; served in the Netherlands as lawyer to the Archdukes Albert and Isabella; in Brussels 1636 when the Cardinal Infante wrote commending him to Philip IV; see Silke, 'The Irish abroad', 1976, pp. 606, 613; Jennings, *Wild geese*, 1964, p. 286.

[3] Not identified.

and Sqidam [Schiedam] had robbed him of 20,000 *reales de a ocho* in money and goods coming from Caracas. He should relate that they had carried him captive to Holland and obliged him to enter the service of the Dutch Republic against his will and petition for the restitution of his goods. He did so. The petition was referred to the admiral of England who ordered that any ships of the three cities which reached England should be embargoed until satisfaction was given to the supplicant for what was owed him by right.[1]

In doing this the supplicant was recognized because there were present in London at that time eight others who had been under his command in the river Amazon.[2] He was taken before the Guiana Company, as the committee of lords and merchants concerned with the conquest of Guiana in the Indies (which is where the Amazon is), is called there. They examined him and he told them what he could. They gave him twenty *escudos* (at ten *reals* each)[3] for maintenance each week and the Treasurer of the company, Don Herrique Spelman [Sir Henry Spelman], paid it punctually to him every Saturday. But they gave orders to the keeper of his inn, as he found out afterwards, to ensure that when he went out his Indian servant should be detained, whom they knew to be the son of one of the most powerful chiefs on the Amazon. When the Indian boy went out they detained him [O'Brien] or one of the household accompanied him, so that neither he nor the boy were out of the house without somebody of the household being with one or the other of them. The Treasurer of the Guiana Company purchased mirrors, axes, knives, bracelets and other goods which he handed over to him to trade with the Indians. The supplicant raised followers and gathered together 200 soldiers, 150 of them Irish and the rest Scots and English. Amongst them went with him Don Guillermo Hovardo [Sir William Howard], second son of the conde de Arandel [earl of Arundel] and a cousin of conde de Norte [Lord North].[4] They agreed that the supplicant was to return to the

---

[1] No such petition survives in the State Papers Domestic or Irish or the Privy Council records in the Public Record Office, and reference to the matter has not yet been discovered in the records of the High Court of Admiralty.

[2] He cannot be referring to William Gayner here since the latter was already in the United Provinces.

[3] See above, p. 268, n. 9.

[4] Sir William Howard (1614–80), fifth son of Thomas earl of Arundel, was created Viscount Stafford in 1640. O'Brien may be confusing him with Thomas Howard, earl of Berkshire, son of Thomas earl of Suffolk, see above, p. 194, n. 3.

Amazon as captain general, guide, chief pilot and chief factor with three ships and 400 men and women, and after three months they would relieve him with another two ships and 300 men and women. He was instructed that if the Dutch should arrive at the Marañón and Gran Pará under Father Manuel de Moraes or whatever other leader, he should absorb those who wanted to come to him. Similarly, if the Portuguese of the Marañón and Gran Pará should ask him for help he was to give it on condition that they and their government of Marañón and Gran Pará acknowledged the king of England. He was to place a garrison in their forts and establish good relations and dealings with them. But if the Portuguese made war on him, he was not to give them quarter, nor to make an agreement with them but to put them to the sword as they did the English in those parts. Moreover they promised the supplicant that if he maintained himself in the Amazon for three years with the supplies that they would send every six months, then at the end of three years they would reinforce him with all the colonists from the Barbadas [Barbados], the Vermudas [Bermudas], San Christoval [St Christophers], Monserrate [Montserrat], Nieves [Nevis], Antigua, St Cathalina [Catalina], and with the supply of 300 men and women, English subjects and six Portuguese, which at that time they were sending to Serenam, and with the rest who were there before, amongst whom were two married Portuguese, and with all they had in the Indies, excepting those in Virginea.

Here may be seen the conditions and agreement which the supplicant was to enjoy for himself and guard in favour of the crown of England, and they were that the supplicant and his sons and heirs were to be captains general of the conquest and return to the Guiana company every two years in goods from the Indies three times that which he might be given from England. All those who might go to the colony of whatever nation, even though they might be pirates or debtors or transported for murders or other criminal acts, they would be free at the end of seven years. In particular the Irish were given liberty of conscience and, since they were papists, they would give them two Irish priests who were imprisoned in the Tower of London, and furthermore licence was given to other priests and friars who might want to go on the expedition and none of the Irish were obliged to swear what they call the oath of supremacy, which the English swear that the king is the head of the faith. But the supplicant, as general of the expedition, must affirm within seven days that he would be loyal all his life to the crown of England, and procure its increase and carry forward the colony with all earnestness, and not surrender ever to the Spaniards or the Portuguese or serve another king, or prince than England.

The supplicant engaged himself with the English for two reasons: the one to see if they would pay him the 20 thousand reals which the Dutch took from him, and the other because since he was to be general and chief pilot of the three ships he intended to bring them into Bilbao or San Sebastián or another port of Spain and relinquish them to the disposition of your Majesty. But when they requested him to be loyal to the crown of England and not to serve any other prince but the king of England he had scruples about swearing what he had no wish to accomplish. Simultaneously, some of his countrymen to whose notice this came, told him that he should not swear it, nor make the conquest for heretics.

And thus the supplicant went to speak to Don Joan de Nicolalde [Juan de Nicolalde], your Majesty's ambassador in England,[1] and gave him an account of all his adventures and proposition and he told him that he would give him his opinion within seven days. In this period Don Joan de Nicolalde informed himself by various means of what the Guiana company was doing. The day arrived that the supplicant was appointed to swear and this day he went, in the morning, to tell Don Joan de Nicolalde that he would have to be either in or out with the English. Presently Don Joan gave him a large packet for your Majesty and a letter for Pedro Ricote, one of your Majesty's merchants in London, ordering him to send him [O'Brien] to Spain with speed and secrecy, and he dressed him in the habit of Santiago so that he would be well received and attended to for your Majesty. By night he got his Indian boy out of the inn for him, saying that he was a vassal of your Majesty and that if he owed anything he would pay it, and he was delivered to him together with a youth from Bilbao to bring his bag in which were the papers and books and, in particular, a description and cosmography, which the supplicant wrote in Irish, of the territor-

---

[1] There are no references to O'Brien's dealings with Nicolalde in the State Papers Spanish in the Public Record Office.

ies referred to and the ports in which he went in the Indies. The supplicant sent the boy from Bilbao ahead to the ship with the bag, while he went to collect the despatches from Pedro Ricote, and he did not see the boy again, but after embarking a Spaniard, a friend of his, told him that he [the boy] had returned to Don Joan de Nicolalde's house.[1] The supplicant, even though he had already changed his clothes, for fear of being arrested did not return for him. Thus embarking himself he came by the river Themes [Thames] to Gravelin [Gravesend?], 7 leagues and from there by stage to Doble [Dover?], where he saw the *récamara*[2] of the conde Palatino who came from Zeeland in two Dutch ships.

Since he did not find embarcation there he went to Dunos [Dunes] where he saw a large ship from Amsterdama in Holland which carried 300 soldiers for the relief of Pernambuco. Also here he came across Don Andres Ruanes, oydor of the Canarias[3] and a friar and a Spanish cleric, and the oydor told him that Don Joan de Nicolalde commissioned him in London that if he ran into him he should bring him to Spain. As he did, embarking him in an English merchant ship which brought him to Bilbao, where the supplicant gave to the corregidor of Bilbao the packet from Don Joan de Nicolalde to send to your Majesty and also a letter for himself. From thence he came to this court on the 21st of the month of December of the past year 1635 and spoke presently to the count duke[4] and Master Antonio Carnero[5] and handed over the letters which Don Joan de Nicolalde gave him. The count duke referred him to the secretary Master Fernando Ruys de Contreras[6] and up to now they have not [attended] to him.

Considering which, since the Dutch and English are in competition as to which of them will be the first to send a colony to the river Amazon and that they are already close by, the English in

[1] O'Brien's 'description and cosmography' has still to be discovered, if indeed he did produce something other than the present memorial. If such a 'cosmography' came into Nicolalde's hands he would most likely have forwarded it to Spain and it may yet be found in the Spanish Archives.

[2] The word means either 'dressing room' or 'breach of a gun'. Presumably he means here the household possessions or effects of the deceased Elector Palatine.

[3] Crown judge of the Canaries.

[4] Gaspar de Guzman, conde duque de Olivares, chief minister of Philip IV, 1622–43.

[5] Antonio Carnero, secretary and confidante of Olivares.

[6] See above, p. 413.

Serenam and the Dutch in Seguive both with hopes to enter the river Amazon, and already one or the other might be in it if they had not waited for the supplicant. They will not lack guides from the Irish, English, Dutch and Portuguese and Spaniards who were there and are with them, and perhaps they will both join to carry out the undertaking. Your Majesty has yonder more territories than people to send to settle them, and the loyalty and devotion of the Irish nation both to the Catholic Faith and to your Majesty's crown is well known. The supplicant is the man most knowledgeable about those parts and holds the affection of more Indians than can be found for this undertaking, and he renounced doing it for the Dutch and English to do it for your Majesty, and he surrendered the fort and colony which he had there into the hands of your Majesty's ministers although capable of keeping them and even taking your Majesty's settlements. This river belongs to the conquests of the crown of Castile. He begs that your Majesty may be pleased to give licence through the *Consejo de Indias* for the supplicant to return there to settle and that they return to him for this the Irish which he had there wherever they may be in the Maranhao or other parts, and that other Irish, Spaniards, Biscayans may go with him as they may freely desire, laymen and clerics, to maintain that territory for your Majesty against the English and Dutch and dispossess them, the one and the other of their settlements which they might have at its borders and parts which the supplicant reached. Or if not, that at the least they may be freed with their property which was taken from the aforementioned Irish who surrendered themselves trusting in the royal word of your Majesty[1] which your ministers gave them, and that he and they may be employed in your Majesty's service where your Majesty offers [. . .][2]

Should the supplicant be employed in the river Amazon it will be more to the service of God, because besides bringing those nations to obedience to your Majesty, also he will draw the blind and the heathen to the knowledge of his divine Majesty and his holy Faith (as they themselves seek), by means of the priests and preachers of the gospels which he would carry out. The which, not

[1] At Tauregue in 1629.
[2] Illegible.

merely not to discourage but to espouse and forward is a thing worthy of the christianity of your Majesty, especially since the English, Dutch and French, who already have settlements near there, are making them heretics.

TEXT X

LAST ENGLISH AND IRISH EFFORTS TO RETURN TO THE AMAZON, 1638–46: APPROACHES TO THE RESTORED PORTUGUESE MONARCHY

1. ENGLISH PLANS TO ESTABLISH A COLONY ON THE TAPAJÓS, 1638–42

a.   To the Kings most Excellent Majesty[1]

The humble petition of George Griffith[2] marchant

Humbly showing, That whereas your said petitioner hath had greate losse by sending men into the greate River of the Amazons and planting on the Coaste of Guiana, by the opposition of the Portugalls and Treachery of the Indian Natives in those parts,[3] & since finding that your Majestys subjects are assuredly like to loose a good trade into Portugall, by reason the Dutch nation are like to gaine the Coast of Brasile & parts adjacent to the Amazons which is the only place now fitt for the planting of sugars, & by that trade with Portugall yowr said subjects had great vent of the Manufactures of this Kingdome as Bayse[4] perpetuanoes,[5] stockings, Newland[6] fish &c & had for returnes Sugars & silver, which said

---

[1] P.R.O., SP 16/363, f. 272.

[2] Rabb, 1967, p. 303 lists a George Griffith, merchant, as an investor in the Levant Co. 1618, the East India Co. in 1624 and involved in privateering in 1625. There is no evidence as to whether this is the same man.

[3] Griffith appears to have invested in one of the former Amazon ventures, although he is not listed anywhere as a member of the Guiana Co. His allusion to the 'Treachery of the Indian Natives', might apply equally to the problems experienced by Harcourt's planters on the Wiapoco or to the sufferings of Fry's men, starved out on the Amazon.

[4] Baize. A woollen fabric, whose manufacture was introduced into England in the sixteenth century by refugees from France and the Netherlands. It was of a finer and lighter texture than the present fabric of that name.

[5] A durable woollen fabric, manufactured in England from the sixteenth century.

[6] Newfoundland.

432

manufactures and Sugars &c beside the imployment of many your poore Subjects in making the said Manufactures, and Navigation yeelded greate sommes yearely unto your Majesty in Customes which is likely totally to be lost if the Dutch gaine Brasill, as they are like to doe, and theire Sugars are like to be found at excessive Rates, which your Peticioner taking into Consideration, hath mooved many woorthy men, who are content to adventure for planting of Sugars in the River of Amazons, soe that in your Majestys Cittie of London, they may have the ordering of the Businesse/

Wherefore, & for that your Majestys Subjects were the first Christians that ever planted in the said greate River of the Amazons,[1] & that the ould Company[2] doth nothing therin, your petitioner being assured that there is noe forraigne designe hopefull at present for the future honnour and benefitt of your Majesty and all your subjects in generall as the well planting of the greate River of the Amazons

It may therefore please your Royall Majestie to take the premisses into your into your Highnesses serious Consideration, and to be gratiously pleased to direct some speedy Course, that woorthy adventurers may be incouraged to underwrite and that the businesse goe on with effect, that your subjects be there planted before the Dutch & other Nations doe it./

And your peticioner &c

Att the Court at Whitehall i6th: Aprill: *1638*
His Majesty is pleased to referre this petition to the Lords Commissioners for forraine Plantations who are to consider thereof and take such order therin, as they shall find fitt for his Majestys service

francis Windebank

b. A short discription of a rich plantation called the Tapoywasooze & the Towyse-yarrowes Countryes lying upon the Coasts of Guiana from the West Indies distant Eastwards 350. Leagues discovered by Captaine William Clovell. and Thomas Tyndall.[1640][3]

---

[1] See above, pp. 27, 51, 253.
[2] The Guiana Co.
[3] P.R.O., CO 1/10, ff. 202–3v. Undated. Williamson, *English colonies*, 1923, pp. 144–5, believed the document dated from about 1640. Sir Arthur Hopton, mentioned below as 'now Lord Ambassador for his Majestie in Spayne', did not take up that office until 1638. Prior to 1638 he served as resident agent.

The said plantacion is distant for the silver Myne 60. leagues,[1] and easie to be possessed and kept, by reason all the Natives of the Countrie are our friends and the discoverers have learnt their language.

This plantacion is 80. leagues from the golden river[2] west southwest up in to the land. The cheefe comodities which are acceptable there in trade, are Axes, knives, bills, -hoes, glasse beades of all colors, combes, ribbans, looking glasses etc.

ffor ffood, there is deare, hare hog, land turtle, water Turtle, abundance of wyld hony, great plentie of ffish both in Creekes and rivers, Indian Corne, pease, beanes,[3] Cussadoe rootes[4] and Potato rootes.[5] Balsome oyle[6] in abundance of sovereigne use for Cures. and divers sorts of fruites wherewith to make other usefull oyles, divers sorts of fruites wholsome for foode and to make wynes or drinke. Abundance of ffowle and henns, ducks and other wyld ffowles.

There is rich Indico[7] for dyers worth 10s. a pound at least and Annatto for grayne colors worth 100li per Tonne at least.[8] ginger, which the said discovers have there planted./[9] there is yellow wood for dyers, rich speckled wood, gummes of great value, great store of phisicall drugs, excellent Tobacco, comparable to the best Verina;[10] great store of Cotton, suger Canes; the plantacion upwards in the Countrie is inriched with gold and silver Mynes, whereof the discoverers have certeyne experience having bene in some of those Mynes.

---

[1] 180 miles. Cristoval de Acuña, see below, p. 438, reported a silver mine on the river Guruputuba approximately the same distance from the Tapajós, 40 Spanish leagues or 160 miles away.

[2] Clovell and Tyndall estimated that the 'golden river' was 240 miles away. It is not clear from their sentence whether it lay up or downstream. Teixeira's expedition picked up news of a gold trade from the inner reaches of the river Jupura, approximately 274 Spanish leagues or 1,096 miles from the Tapajós. It seems unlikely that Clovell or Tyndall would have heard of mines so far inland. They could be describing the gold workings on the Guruputuba 160 miles from the Tapajós; see Acuña below and in Markham, *Valley of the Amazons*, 1859, pp. 101–3.

[3] See above, p. 181, n. 4. [4] See above, p. 136, n. 4.
[5] See above, p. 182, n. 11. [6] See above, p. 279, n. 4.
[7] See above, p. 136, n. 3. [8] *Ibid.*
[9] See above, p. 273, n. 6.

[10] Varinas. Roll tobacco formed of leaf plaited into a thick twist, acquired from the Venezuelan town of the same name and thought to be the best of the tobacco cured by the Spanish method, see above, p. 157, n. 4.

About 1000. Men will settle this plantacion, and that for ten thowsand pounds charge for food & provision for the first yeare onelie;[1] except onelie for edge Tooles & other the foresaid slight comodities to trade with the Natives

This charge will be returned double to the Adventurer within one yeare after the arrivall there. by Cottons, wood for dyers, Annatto, Tobacco, and Gummes./

[f. 202v] The next yeare after, maie be returned into England greate store of gold, silver, Indico and Gynger./

As for Sugar, it must have 3. yeares growth before it will come to perfection./

This Plantacion is distant from the Island called Margaretta[2] 350. leagues, being the neerest plantacion the Spanyard hath there./

But the Portugall hath a plantacion within 160. leagues of the discoverie./ peopled with 150. persons.[3]

The spanyard cannott come neere our sayd plantacion by reason the wynds and currents are alwaies against him[4] and by land it is impassible by reason of the mountaynes and thicknes of the woods besides the Natives are their enymies and our friends./

Thomas Tyndall one of these discoverers – hath gone Master these 24. yeares of shipps both in his Majesties service and for Merchants, and hath bene compelled by reason of his Judgement & experience to be Pilott for the King of Spayne in all parts of the West Indies & in the golden river[5] for manie yeares. and hath certificates under the hand of Sir Arthure Hopton now Lord Ambassador for his Majestie in Spayne importing the sayd Tyndalls abilityes & wrongs suffred by the Spanyards./[6]

[f. 203v] DOCKET: Indian Plantation [   ]

[1] Compare Duppa's estimates below.
[2] The island of Margarita off the eastern coast of Venezuela.
[3] Clovell and Tyndall are probably referring to the settlement of Belém here. Acuña's estimate of the distance from the mouth of the Tapajós to the latter settlement was 180 Spanish leagues, in Markham, *Valley of the Amazons*, 1859, pp. 128–31.
[4] See above, p. 17.
[5] It is difficult to know what this alludes to. Tyndall may mean the river Amazon. Acuña (see below), reported that both the Guruputuba and Paru were rich in gold. Portuguese slaving expeditions raided upstream as far as Tapajós from the mid 1620s on and Clovell or Tyndall may have accompanied some of them.
[6] Hopton's letters from Spain in the 1630s contain various references to English seamen in Spanish service, but Tyndall is not mentioned by name; P.R.O., SP 94/36, 37, 38 *passim*.

c.   Father Cristoval de Acuña's account of his visit to the
Tapajós Region in 1639.[1]

Forty leagues from this narrow part, on the south side, is the
mouth of the great and beautiful river of the Tapajosos, taking the
name from the tribe who live on its banks which are well peopled with
savages, living in a good land full of abundant supplies. These
Tapajosos are a brave race, and are much feared by the surrounding
nations, because they use so strong a poison in their arrows, that if
once blood is drawn, death is sure to follow. For this reason the
Portuguese themselves avoided any intercourse with them for some
time, desiring to draw them into friendly relations.[2] However, they
received us very well, and lodged us together in one of their villages,
containing more than five hundred families, where they never
ceased all day from bartering fowls, ducks, hammocks, fish, flour,
fruit, and other things, with such confidence that women and
children did not avoid us; offering, if we would leave our lands, and
come to settle there, to receive and serve us peacefully all their
lives. . . . The humble offers of these Tapajosos did not satisfy a set of
people so selfish as are those of these conquests, who only undertake
difficult enterprises from a covetous desire to obtain slaves, for which
object the Tapajosos were placed in a convenient position. This was
going on when we arrived at the fort of Destierro,[3] where the people
were assembled for this inhuman work, and though by the best
means I could, I tried, as I could not stop them, at least to induce
them to wait until they had received new orders from the king; and
the *sargente mayor* and chief of all, who was Benito Maciel, son of the
governor,[4] gave me his word that he would not proceed with his
intended work, until he had heard from his father; yet I had scarcely
turned my back, when, with as many troops as he could get, in a
launch with a piece of artillery, and other smaller vessels, he fell upon
the Indians suddenly with harsh war, when they desired peace. They
surrendered, however, with good will, as they had always offered to
do, and submitted to all the Portuguese desired. The latter ordered
them to deliver up all their poisoned arrows, which were the weapons
they most dreaded. The unfortunate Indians obeyed at once; and,

---

[1] Extract from *El nuevo descubrimiento del gran rio de las Amazonas* (Madrid, 1641),
trans. and ed. in Markham, *Valley of the Amazons*, 1859, pp. 124–9.
[2] See above, p. 118.   [3] See below, p. 439, and above, p. 118.
[4] Son of Bento Maciel Parente.

when they were disarmed, the Portuguese collected them together like sheep, in a strong enclosure, with a sufficient guard over them. They then let loose the friendly Indians, each one of them being an unchained devil for mischief, and in a short time they had gutted the village, without leaving a thing in it, and as I was told by an eye-witness, cruelly abused the wives and daughters of the unfortunate captives, before their very eyes. Such acts were committed, that my informer, who is a veteran in these conquests, declared he would have left off buying slaves, and even have given the value of those he possessed, not to have beheld them. . . .

Returning, however, to the subject of the Tapajosos, and to the famous river which bathes the shores of their country; I must relate that it is of such depth, from the mouth to a distance of many leagues, that in times past an English ship of great burden ascended it, those people intending to make a settlement in this province, and to prepare harvests of tobacco. They offered the natives advantageous terms, but the latter suddenly attacked the English and would accept no other than the killing of all the strangers they could get into their hands, and the seizure of their arms, which they retain to this day. They forced them to depart from the land much quicker than they had come, the people who remained in the ship declining another similar encounter, (which would have destroyed them all), by making sail.[1]

---

[1] Edmundson, 'The Dutch in the Amazon and Negro', 1903, 654–6, believed Acuña was listening to an oral tradition of Pieter Adriaenszoon Ita's reconnaissance upriver beyond the Paru in 1616. Williamson, *English colonies*, 1923, pp. 142–6, noted that when the friars Domingo de Brieba and Andrés de Toledo descended the Amazon in 1637 they saw muskets, linen shirts and pistols in the possession of the Indians in that region which they were said to have obtained by the massacre of some Dutch who had tried to settle there; Jiménez de la Espada, *Viaje*, 1889, p. 86. Williamson, however, also notes the comment of the comte de Pagan concerning the river Tapajós in his *Relation . . . de la grande rivière des Amazones* (Paris, 1655), p. 99, to the effect that 'about the year 1630 the English ascended its broad channel with a ship, landed on its banks, and stayed there some time to sow and reap tobacco: but being chased out with loss by the Indians they retired without their harvest.' Williamson tended to the opinion that Acuña's comment referred to a later English venture and that it was linked to Clovell and Tyndall's prospectus for a Tapajós plantation. My own discovery of Sousa de Macedo's letter (see below, pp. 440–5), would appear to confirm this suggesting that the expedition had been relatively recent. Acuña's 'in times past' should not necessarily be interpreted as 'long past'. Clovell and Tyndall may well have commanded the ship despatched by James Duppa to explore upstream to the 'Talpia' [Tapajós] in or about 1638 and Acuña could have heard about their activities on his route downriver.

... At a distance of little more than forty leagues from the mouth of this river of the Tapajosos, is that of Curupatuba, which is on the north side of the Amazons, and gives name to the first settlement or village[1] which the Portuguese hold in peace, and subject to their crown. This river does not appear to be very large, but is rich in treasures, if the natives did not deceive us. They affirm that, after ascending by this river, which they call the Yriquiriqui, for six days, a great quantity of gold is found, which they gather on the shores of a small rivulet, which bathes the skirts of a moderate sized hill, called Yaguaracu. They also say that near this hill there is another place, the name of which is Picuru; whence they have often taken another metal, harder than gold and of a white colour, which is doubtless silver, and of which they formerly made axes and knives, but finding they were of no use, and that they were soon notched, they made no more of them. ...[2]

The river Ginipape,[3] according to report, does not promise less treasure. It falls into the river of Amazons on the north side, sixty leagues below the village of Curupatuba. The Indians say so much of the quantities of gold that might be collected on its banks, that, if all they say is true, this river would leave the most famous in Peru far behind. The territory bathed by this river belongs to the captaincy of Bento Maciel the father, governor of Marañón, a province which is larger than all Spain put together, and there are many notices of mines in it. The greater part of it consists of good soil, fit to produce more fruits and other provisions than any other part of this immense river of the Amazons.

All this territory, on the north side, contains vast provinces of Indians, and, what is of more consequence, it encloses, within its jurisdiction, the famous and extensive land of Tucujù,[4] so much coveted, and so often occupied, though to their own damage, by the Dutch enemies, who, recognizing in it the greatest advantages in the world for enriching its inhabitants, are never able to forget it. It is not only suitable for great harvests of tobacco, capable of sustaining, better than any of the other discoveries, numerous sugar estates, and of producing all kinds of provisions; but it also has excellent plains, which would supply pasture for innumerable flocks and herds.

---

[1] Indian village.
[2] See above, p. 434, n. 2.
[3] Paru.
[4] Sertão de Tocujós.

In this captaincy, six leagues from the mouth of the Ginipape, there is a fort belonging to the Portuguese, which they call 'El Destierro', with a garrison of thirty soldiers and some pieces of artillery, which are useless for defending the river, but merely serve to keep up the authority of the captaincy, and to awe the vanquished Indians. Benito Maciel abandoned this fort, with the consent of the governor of Curupá, which is thirty-six leagues lower down, and where he was established for many years in a very good position; as the ships of the enemy usually come to reconnoitre, in that direction.

d. Inducements to bee propounded to his royall Majestie, to take the proteccion of the Adventurers unto the river of the *Amazones* or *Guiana* in *America* and theire plantacion there.[1640][1]

Inprimis under certaine covenants and articles to bee performed on his majesties part there is much probabilitie and likelihood, for the advannceinge unto his Majestie and his successors ffifty thowsand pounds per annum for xxi^tie yeres[2] To beginne after the first fower yeeres of settlinge the plantacion in the Amazones as aforesaide.

ffor the payment of the rente aforesaide this assistannce and Charge is to bee expected from his Majesty videlizet.

i) His majestie to take the proteccion of his subjects tradeinge into *Guiana* or the river of the Amazones, wherby they may enjoy the benefit of theire labours, accordinge to theire expectacion./

2.) His majestie to send 3000 men att his owne Charge, with a proporcion of meale apparrell for 4 yeeres & in manner followinge videlizet ....}

{The first yeere – 1,000[3]
{The second yeere – 800
{The third yeere – 600
{The fourth yere – 600

3.) His majestie to send ioo peeces of Ordenance, powder, and municion, beeinge Brasse and Iron with feild Carriages[4] to Arme two good & sufficient forts.

---

[1] P.R.O., CO 1/5, ff. 77–8v. Undated. For a discussion of the possible date of this document see above, pp. 116–8.

[2] Clovell and Tyndall argued that the Tapajós plantation would return £20,000 on an investment of £10,000 after only one year.

[3] Clovell and Tyndall suggested that 1,000 men should be sent out in the initial settlement.

[4] Gun carriages.

4.) His Ma*jes*tie to furnish six of the Whelpes,[1] and three shippes yeerely for transporta*ci*on of those men. And for the remaines of the time after thexpira*ci*on of the said fower yeeres for exporta*ci*on and importa*ci*on of such Comodities as the Adventurers shall produce by the industry of theire servants, and assistance of the Country etc.

Whereof two of the said whelpes are to remaine in the River to protect the said Adventurers, and theire Estates.

The Charge of transportinge and furnishinge theis 3000 men, att xvi[^{li}] *per* man, amounteth unto 48000[^{li}]./[2]

Which somme, may bee quallified and lessened by disburseinge the some of i5000[^{li}] ready money.

[f. 78v] DOCKET: River of Amazons Guiana re*ceive*d from Capt*ain* Duppa[3] India Oc*cidental*.

e.   António de Sousa de Macedo[4] to João IV, 2nd October 1642
Paper from Doctor António de Souza de Macedo about the report of certain mines.[5]

In this city lives an Englishman, now elderly, called Jaymes Dupay [James Duppa] who years ago was a pirate, afterwards captain of some of the king of England's ships, and now he is very wealthy and has shares in ships.[6] Because of information which he possessed he conceived of making some profitable undertaking in the river Amazon, and in order to proceed on a firmer basis he despatched men in a ship to discover what it would be possible to attempt. The ship returned a year and a half ago and the captain of it persuaded him that by navigating upriver he will discover mines and beyond this he will disembark not very far from Quito where are the majority of the mines of the king of Castile and he will be able to conquer them, for the which [enterprise] two thousand white men is more than sufficient and eight or ten ships. A good fort has to be built on the river on an island 6 leagues from the place called Talpia [Tapajós] from whence, it being a narrow place,[7] the passage may

---

[1] Six of ten pinnaces constructed as auxiliary war vessels in Charles I's reign, apparently originally so-called because they were designed to attend on H.M.S. *Lion*. For a listing see *CSP Dom.*, *1628–9*, p. 103.

[2] Clovell and Tyndall's estimate amounted to about £10 per man.

[3] See above, p. 98, n. 2.   [4] See above, pp. 116–20.

[5] Translation. B.A., Códice 51/V/17, ff. 121–6.

[6] See above, p. 98, n. 2.

[7] The Óbidos narrows.

be denied to other nations as well as the Castilians who might wish to go that way to relieve their own men. Five hundred men must remain in the fort and for the rest they have to raise Blacks from the same region, enemies of those which live on the route to Quito, and with them they must finish the enterprise. All this he explains by a map which he brought made of where he went.[1] The said Jayme Dupay either, as he says, because of his friendship with the counts of Pembruye [Pembroke] and Nortanborland [Northumberland],[2] or because he does not dare [to attempt] such a project alone, communicated the affair to them so that they might enter into a company. They accepted but, with due respect, petitioned a licence from the king who, possibly because he favours the affairs of the king of Castile and does not wish to give cause for upsets, or for another reason, replied, as they say, that the enterprise was more suitable for a king and he would undertake it once rid of the affairs of Parliament and they would all profit. The said Jayme Dupay and the discoverer[3] waited and, seeing that the increasing disorders of this kingdom delayed the fruit of their labour, having made expenditures, negotiated with a merchant, a friend of his named Richarte Vequemant,[4] that they wished to give the project to the Dutch and enter into partnership with them. Speaking of the voyage they pointed out that Cabo Verde was very suitable for taking on supplies and whatever else might be necessary.

Vequemant, who is our friend and has trade in this kingdom, proposed to him beforehand that, granting that the Portuguese have territories and people in those parts of America and they would be able to be very useful, it would be better to deal with your

---

[1] On first reading this would appear to refer to an English chart made by the unspecified explorer. Sousa de Macedo said it was much more detailed than those presently on the market. No such English chart has yet been discovered. The chart collections at the Public Record Office, however, contain a map of the lower Amazon, clearly based on a Portuguese original (P.R.O., ADM 7/887), which may either indeed be the chart which Duppa and his associates used to illustrate their project, or perhaps more likely, one used by Sousa de Macedo in his protests to the parliamentary leaders in 1644 to illustrate that the Amazon was Portuguese territory.

[2] Philip Herbert, fourth earl of Pembroke and Montgomery, succeeded to the Pembroke title 1630, in the Guiana Co. patent as earl of Montgomery; see above, p. 291, n. 2. Algernon Percy (1602–68), tenth earl of Northumberland, succeeded 1632. Both men sided with Parliament at the outbreak of the Civil war in 1642.

[3] Not Duppa. Very probably William Clovell or Thomas Tyndall, see above, pp. 433–5.

[4] Not identified.

Majesty; the which the English merchants saw very easily because, through envy, they are hostile to the Dutch. Vequemant spoke to me and we met with the aforesaid [men], who showed me the map, much more detailed than those which are sold, but they did not want to give or lend it to me and what we discussed is referred to [here].

I, observing the cost of the present wars[1] to your Majesty's treasury, set in train the negotiation that the choice would remain with your Majesty whether to enter into a company with capital or to take all the undertaking to your account. In the latter case the discoverer is to go as guide on the condition that should the expedition yield no profit he would not be given anything, but having asked that he should be given a third part of whatever might result from the mine, sack of cities or other profits, for the first time only. Because I represented to them that it was too much, they adjusted it to a fourth part to which I, without finalizing anything, did not show myself averse because it occurred to me to beguile them so that they would not deal with the Dutch. However, so as not to be found guilty afterwards by Parliament,[2] as they say, of offering to another nation what they could give to their own, they decided to ask them for a licence to negotiate with your Majesty, speaking with only four of the leading Parliament men in secret[3] so as not to publicize the business. In the full Parliament they responded, according to what the said Jayme Dupay told me, that they would not give them such a licence because the Parliament would undertake that enterprise. The count of Nortanborlart, who was one of the Parliamentarians to whom they spoke, blamed them particularly for wishing to abandon the company which they had offered him, affirming that he and the count of Perbruq had no other matter more in mind and that very shortly, whether Parliament was the victor or defeated by the king, either with the king or Parliament or by themselves, they would put it into effect. Since the business had been communicated to me, either the king or Parliament or they themselves would enter into some form of

---

[1] Portugal was at war with Spain. Although a ten year truce had been concluded with the Dutch in July 1641, hostilities continued in the colonies for another year.

[2] The Long Parliament. Its remaining sitting members were now at war with the king.

[3] Sousa de Macedo very seldom specifies who his parliamentary contacts are in any of his correspondence.

company with your Majesty's Treasury. I, to make sure, waited upon the count as at other times because he is our friend and I found him qualified to speak on this matter. He answered me with some difference between what the other [Duppa] had told me, and what he had communicated to him, – that it was more worthy and suitable for a king than private individuals, that the king and the Parliament were willing to undertake it but the present disorders did not permit it. Finally, in response to some proposals which I made with as much skill as I was capable of in order to learn more, he concluded that he conceived that both of us would be dead before England was pacified enough to deal with this business overseas and because, he feared that the Dutch in the meantime might attempt the enterprise, it would be good for your Majesty to prevent them. He regretted not being able to enter into this because of the affairs of the kingdom and he would tell Dupay that he might deal with your Majesty as he wished and not speak more of this to Parliament. All this I told Dupay presently. I arranged with him that I would write to your Majesty and he would see the reply with all speed.

Following this it is not necessary to negotiate about a company since Dupay alone will not put anything substantial into it, neither do I think it appropriate to do so because, besides other reasons, these people are very selfish and not very punctilious in agreements and it would give rise to conflict. I think, however, that it is appropriate to deal in some manner with this business, not only (it being put into effect in which I see difficulties), for the profit which could result to this crown and harm to that of Castile, but because it will be good to prevent the Dutch seizing it. In this respect, with greater power they may make themselves masters of those parts. Already it could be that they might, with this intention, order the issue of shares to whomever might wish to go for the river Amazon, as I write in the other letter because the latter material is already sealed.[1] According to what another Englishman told me and also a Portuguese merchant named Miguel da Sylva native of the island of San Miguel spoke to me about it who, travels about here and has sailed for those parts, it will be the worst that they might conceive because on the voyage Cabo Verde is near enough for them to

---

[1] Sousa de Macedo's other letter of 2nd October 1642, preserved in B.P.É., Códice CVI/2–7, f. 167 does not contain any reference to this business.

launch any design upon it at any time.[1] If it should not be convenient at present to commit greater capital your Majesty will order consideration that at least a fort might be built at the place indicated[2] so as to dash the hopes of all of them or make other precautions. As for the person of the discoverer, it could be useful for him to go, your Majesty advising me of the share that you may be pleased to give to him, and if he is not necessary he need not be made use of, for which I have already forwarned him telling him that the Portuguese have already made the same discovery as indeed [they go] with the same intention. However, I did not tell him in such a way as to make him lose confidence that your Majesty will make use of him, so that he will not have recourse to the Dutch. May your Majesty be pleased to send me advice on what I should tell him and this by the first ship for this kingdom, France or Holland because I promised him as much, warning that should your Majesty not employ him he will go to the Dutch. Thus it will be fitting to exercise caution in those parts and watch what happens. With this I send to your Majesty a memorial, translated from English, of the charges which these men have estimated, what the fort will cost and the complete enterprise.[3] Having negotiated to this point the said Dupay came to speak to me with Vequemant carrying a letter from one Jorge Martin [George Martin], a very rich man who is captain of one of his ships in the royal fleet chartered by the Parliament.[4] The said Dupay wrote to Jorge Martim, who is anchored fifty leagues from here, about what he was negotiating. He replied to him that he and one of his brothers and other friends will enter with seventy thousand cruzados,[5] which they have ready, and take care of what will be a little less than half of the necessary expenses and, if necessary, they will increase the capital up to, in effect, putting in one thousand men on their part with a half

[1] Sousa de Macedo is suggesting that the Dutch might launch a double-pronged attack, assaulting the Portuguese holdings in West Africa *en route* to the Amazon.

[2] Tapajós.

[3] The title of the memorial 'Huma estimação das despezas de mil homes para se transportarem a hum ryo da America, e se dobrara havendo de ser dous mil' (see above, p. 439, n. 3), was copied by the scribe into the códice immediately following upon Sousa de Macedo's letter, B.A., Códice 51/V/17, f. 126.

[4] A 'Captain Martin', commander of the ship of the same name, served in the parliamentary summer fleet of 1642 and requested money owing to him from the parliamentary Committee for the Navy in January 1643; *CSP Dom., 1641–3* (1887), p. 555.

[5] A Portuguese silver coin, fixed at 400 reis, and worth about 4/– English in the seventeenth century.

more of everything, and that he [Duppa] should tell me that he [Martin] would be in this city about the end of this October when the time of his charter will be completed and would negotiate in detail about the conditions and terms. However, they wish to take to this place a thousand Englishmen. They say that since certain Blacks which have to be dealt with are enemies of the Portuguese and friends of the English this Jorge Martim wishes to go as their captain, which I suspect is so that they may assure their advantage and not trust their capital to the Portuguese. May your Majesty be pleased to send a response with all speed, as I already said, because I replied promising it, and, should it appear that this company is possible to notify me, to save time, of the terms which may be arrived at, and meanwhile, when this man [Martim] arrives I will take details of what pertains. However it will be good, without waiting for him, for your Majesty to send me some pointers about what must be done so that I may write to your Majesty at the first opportunity with some decision, or at the very least with the business more digested. They declare that they have discovered mines[1] of which they brought a sample. . . .

London the second of October 1642.

f.   João IV to the Portuguese ambassador in France,
17th September 1644[2]

Count Admiral my Ambassador.[3]

I the king send you many greetings as he whom I love. By this ship will be delivered to you the books which you sent to request . . . and a bill [of exchange] for two hundred cruzados for you to send them to be bound there in the fashion of the country; I commanded that the precautions to prevent the expedition which those in England intend to make to the river Amazon be put in order in the manner which here seemed convenient; I thank you for the warning and for the solicitude with which you do not lose an opportunity in any matter of my service, even if it may be in those which seem not to be so much to your account.[4]

---

[1] See above, p. 434.

[2] Translation. B.N., Lisbon, Códice 7.162, f. 336. Also printed in P. M. Laranjo Coelho, *Cartas de el Rei D. João IV ao conde da Vidigueira (marques de Niza) embaixador em França* (Lisbon, 1940), I, 166.

[3] Vasco Luis da Gama, conde da Vidigueira, Resident in France 1642–6.

[4] See above, p. 119, n. 2.

Written in Lisboa on the 17th of September of 1644
The king – For the Count Admiral Ambassador in France.

2. PROPOSALS TO TRANSFER IRISH COLONISTS FROM ST CHRISTOPHERS TO THE AMAZON, 164[0]–1646

a. 3rd proposal of Pedro Sotmão [Peter Sweetman] Irishman to settle or conquer the province of Maranhão with 400 Irish people.[1]

Sire

The coast of Maranhão runs to about Cabo do Norte from east to west. In the river Amazon on the eastern side is the city of Belém (in the captaincy of Grão Pará) which has about 300 inhabitants, not including soldiers. Up river is the captaincy of Cametá which is granted to António de Albuquerque Coelho and it is 24 leagues distant from the city of Belém and will have about 20 inhabitants and a royal sugar mill.[2] From the limits of this follows the captaincy of Corupá [Gurupá] which reaches as far as the river called Vicente Añés Pinsón [Vicente Yañéz Pinzón] running along the [river bank] as far as the first falls of the Tapujussus [Tapajós], which is granted to Bento Maciel Parente.[3] In it there is a settlement at the place called Mariocaio[4] in which there is a fort belonging to your Majesty where the inhabitants of the said captaincy live [are present]. The which settlement is 80 leagues distant from the said city of Belém and will have 50 inhabitants not including the soldiers. In sum, from Maranhão to Cabo do Norte will be a distance of 250 leagues and there is no land or any part which your Majesty and your governors have not given to private individuals, the which land is administered by the donatories as also the Indian villages of their districts. In these no other than the donatories may live or those whom they install themselves, whom they can expel from their properties and lands as often as they wish.

As it appears, there is no space left for he, Captain Pedro Suetman, and his people to live among the said settlements because there is no land left at all to cultivate or plant, it all belonging to the donatories and others to whom they have granted it at their will and

---

[1] Translation. B.L., Add. MS 37,042, ff. 17–20, Portuguese transcript printed in Gwynn, 'Irish in the West Indies', 1932, pp. 196–8. See above, pp. 120–2.
[2] See above, p. 316. [3] See above, pp. 118, 316–7.
[4] See above, p. 91.

disposition, as I have said; the which is not good for he Pedro Suetman and his people since they want to hold lands of their own from your Majesty's hand, to cultivate them with more pleasure and care without worry or fear of removal.

Pará. In front of the city of Pará is an island called Ihla das Joanes[1] which will have a circumference of 80 leagues and is eight or ten leagues distant from the city of Pará and which your Majesty has not given to anybody at all. On it, by order of the governors are some settlements and villages of little note because of the negligence and carelessness of the inhabitants. He the captain Pedro Suetman offers to live on this island with his people together with the present Portuguese inhabitants and those who may wish to [inhabit it] from now onwards, the which lands will be divided up among the new inhabitants by the governor, at his judgement and that of Pedro Suetman, according to the means of each one. Where he hopes, with all his people, to serve your Majesty in such a way that over time your Majesty will find yourself to be well pleased and obligated to show him and his people much favour. From its size they will expect that as the settlements increase so also will the returns. Your Majesty will have trustworthy vassals who defending their lives and property [will] resist any invasion of the enemy without it being necessary to withdraw soldiers from the realm, and should the enemy attack the city of Pará it can be relieved from the said island and the island from Pará in a similar case.

He Captain Pedro Suetman reminds your Majesty that the cause is catholic and as such worthy that your Majesty as a catholic prince give it consideration, seeing that he with the rest of his fellow Irishmen, harassed by the English heretics on the island of S. Christovão [St. Christophers], are deserving of your Majesty's protection, to live under you as catholics and vassals of such a catholic prince, not wanting to accept a whole island which the governor of the said island of S. Christovão gave them because they would not live under his orders or have new uncertainties on account of religion.

He Pedro Suetman will be the *capitão-mor* of all his countrymen and of the new settlement in the same manner as the rest of the *capitão-mores*, as is indicated in the document given to Mathias de Albuquerque,[2] which he asks may be looked to. Those who may

[1] Marajó.

[2] Former governor and commander-in-chief of the four north-eastern provinces of Brazil 1629–35.

447

wish to live in Pará or in any other part of the mainland, as seems best to each one, will be under his orders. On the occasions that there are alarms, with his combined forces, he and his men will show their valour and zeal to serve your Majesty. He and his people will enjoy all the privileges, freedoms, exemptions of natives of this realm for which they will be so eager, as he requests in the first paper, that he also asks should be looked into, both [for those who settle] in the said state and those who come from it to this realm as inevitably they will come over the course of time as they grow in responsibilities and wealth.

Finally he the captain declares that his intention and that of his people is solely to live in his religion under shelter and protection as vassals of a Catholic prince such as your Majesty to whose service his nation has a particular devotion, cultivating in peace and quiet the lands which your Majesty will order to be given to them with all faithfulness and loyalty; about which your Majesty can acquire information from respectable persons of his nation who reside at this court.

b.　On the disadvantages of the Irish settling in the Maranhão.[1]

To the *consulta* that was made by this Council[2] to your Majesty on the 4th of this present month of May about holding back the licence which the Irish have to go to settle the state of Maranhão, your Majesty commands in response on the 9th of the said month that at least the causes and disadvantages which exist to obstruct the licence which your Majesty has given them to go to make the said settlement and habitation should be referred to you.

In the first place it is represented to your Majesty that that state promises many benefits and profits to the royal Treasury and to your vassals who might inhabit or trade there, being very fertile in sustenance and fruits of the soil, of tobacco, cotton and there could be much indigo. It is very rich in sugar cane and many sugar mills can be built in it and there are infinite and good timbers for ships, that can be built at little cost, there only lacking iron. All the rest is there and very cheap. And there is in it and in the river Amazon much gold according to information which is held.

It contains the river Amazon by which it is possible to navigate as

---

[1] Translation. B.L., Add. MS 37,042, ff. 35–8v. Portuguese transcript printed in Gwynn, 'Irish in the West Indies', 1932, pp. 201–3.

[2] *Conselho Ultramarinho.*

far as the kingdom of Quito in the Castilian Indies the possessions of which are all of such value that they are envied and desired by all the nations of the north. And I think it good that he not be given the opportunity to set foot in this conquest nor settle in it because with these riches their increase will be such that they will take power and become masters of that state,[1] leaving your Majesty deprived of it and your vassals destitute of this commerce by which they enrich themselves and your Majesty's Treasury is increased.

And the king of Castile during the years that he possessed this kingdom, fearing that this conquest and commerce would be put at risk if the foreigners went to it, ordered that they should not be permitted to inhabit that state, and in fulfillment of this order the governor Francisco Coelho de Carvalho threw out all the Irish and English whom he found in it and Filiciano Coelho took a ship of Englishmen there and among them he found one who carried a patent from the king of England in which he was named as governor of that state of Maranhão.[2]

And that state is so big and totally populated by Indians and the fertility such that it cannot be settled by the conquistadors without the labour of the said Indians. Because they [the Indians] are by nature fickle it is important that they only have information from the one nation which governs them, because if there are settlers from diverse nations each one tries to subdue them to their own advantage. And that nation will prevail which brings together a greater number of Indians, and since these Irish and other nations of the north are more liberal in their customs and proceedings than the other nations and better accommodate themselves to what suits their interest than conscience, they continue by this means winning over more easily the Indians necessary to them, and this being so will continue lords of what they possess.

And let the first example of this be what we saw in the conquest of Brazil in that wherever the foreigners entered neither was there any disturbance nor force which could disturb it, so that when they took Bahia because they had not also drawn in the Indians they could not defend it and shortly lost it.[3]

---

[1] Antonio de Sousa de Macedo expressed the same opinion in his letter of 18th February 1644, B.P.É., Códice CVI/2–7, f. 200v.

[2] The Council is referring to the capture of Roger Fry on 14th July 1632, see above, p. 105.

[3] See above, p. 305, n. 4.

And on the contrary when they entered Pernambuco and had time to communicate and negotiate with the Indians before long they defended and took a major part of the state of Brazil.[1] And thus also the Irish and English who, through the neglect of Castile settled the Island of Santa Catherina of the Castilian Indies, and because they did not take heed at the beginning of the harm which this habitation could later cause, there came such an increase of their traffick and robberies and shipping that the king of Castile sent troops against them and it cost a great deal to overcome and expel them.[2]

And finally it is noted that these Irishmen will be vassals of the king of England and very well affected to Castile whose king is said to be their protector and they pride themselves on being descendants of Spaniards. Should one of these kings wish to conquer this state it cannot be doubted that these [Irish] will go over to their side and their favour or make war on us if they can.

And for these reasons and for the others pointed out to your Majesty in a *consulta* on this same particular of the 7th of May, 1644 that went to your Majesty with a document by witnesses which is remitted[3] and proves what is stated above with more forceful reasons, no further testimonies were taken because those seemed sufficient, granting that all these persons said the same as the information that this Council has. This licence which has been given to the Irishmen is very poorly received by all the population of the city[4] and the foreigners who live in it, and they attribute the concession of it to your Majesty not being informed of the above, and thus it appears fitting that your Majesty should revoke it.

And it is not a consideration that these men have made expenses in respect of it to put the voyage to this settlement in order, since it is accepted that it was given both because your Majesty did not have information of the harm which would follow both to this realm and that conquest in prejudice to your own vassals, things which must be considered and are sufficient in justice and conscience to revoke it; and because it is a conquest of such importance and value, and the manifest danger of losing it with great disturbance of this kingdom and of the commerce which is expected from it for the way of life of your Majesty's vassals was not taken into account

---

[1] See Boxer, *Dutch in Brazil*, 1957, pp. 32–158.
[2] Providence Island; see Newton, *Colonizing activities*, 1914.
[3] Not extant.　　　　　　　　　　　　[4] Belém.

And besides this temporal interest it must be considered that these foreigners are not concerned with spiritual matters and the increase of Christianity. Besides the fact that many of them are heretics, those which are Christians are only concerned with what suits their own interests without taking into account the increase in Christianity, This, being the main objective that your Majesty insists operates in your conquests so as to bring their Indians to belief in our holy Catholic Faith, will be impeded by means of these people and the heretics that live among them in that state, principally because the Indians, having information of their sects and heresies and greater freedoms, will follow them disparaging the doctrine of our holy Catholic Faith.

This account was made by the hand of João Delgado Figueira[1] with the interlineations by the hand of the secretary of this Council. Lixboa, 14th of May 1644.

Made the same day.

Four signatures.

c. Grant and donation of settlement[2] to Pedro Setmão [Sweetman], Irishman and 400 companions in the Grão Pará that his Majesty commanded be solemnized and I made these records 2 September [1]643.[3] This did not have effect and this is rectified by the new petition he made and it was conceded to him and changed for him in the way in which it is marked sic erat in fatis.[4]

Letter of grant, settlement, naturalization in the state of Grão Pará and River Amazon in Maranhão of which his Majesty makes

---

[1] Not identified.
[2] Translation. See above, pp. 120–2. In order to avoid unnecessary repetition, I have combined in the following document the undated, unfinished, rough draft of the grant to Sweetman, presented to João IV for his consideration some time in January or February 1644 (B.L., Add. MS 37,042, ff. 21–8, extracted by Gwynn, 'Irish in the West Indies', 1932, pp. 198–201), with the final draft of the grant made 4th March 1644 and amended with a *postilla* or rider on 17th June 1644 (A.T.T., Lisbon, Chancelaria de João IV, livro 1, ff. 196–9). The rough draft offered João IV the option of settling the Irish on Marajó island or on the mainland near Belém. The king selected the second option and the references to Marajó island were removed in the final draft. I have placed the eliminated material in [ ] square brackets. Another copy of the final grant with the postilla of 17th June 1644 is to be found in A.T.T., Livro dos Regimentos do Conselho Ultramarinho, ff. 37 et seq., printed in *RIHGB*, LXIX (1908), pt. I, 123–30.
[3] See above, p. 121.
[4] Introduction to B.L., Add. MS 37,042, ff. 21–8.

favour to captain Pedro Sultman Irishman by birth, and to the rest of his party resident in the Island of St Christovão.[1]

Don João by the grace of God, king of Portugal and the Algarves, on this side of the sea and on the other in Africa, Lord of Brazil and Gine [Guinea], and conquest, navigation and commerce of Aethiopia, Arabia, Persia and India etc. I make known to all that this my letter of grant, settlement, donation and naturalization given to Pedro Suetmão [and] Irish catholic[s] resident in the Island of S. Christovão. Let them whom it may concern see that on behalf of Pedro Setmão, in his name and of the rest of the Irish of his company and household, inhabitants of the said Island [of St. Christovão], it was proposed to me that they were true catholics, recognizing the holy mother church of Rome and living under its obedience [of the holy fathers] and professing the holy Catholic Faith, and because of their confession have suffered great persecutions and travails. Because of the pressure of war and land they went to settle and live on the said Island of S. Christovão, 170 leagues from the coast of my state of Brazil, the which island is occupied and inhabited by [the English nation and] Irishmen. He Pedro Satmão[2] had carried out at his expense and for his account many farmers and soldiers to settle and break and open the land and the wars between England and his countrymen of Ireland increasing again,[3] the English lords of the said island, being greater in number and strength and of a different confession, persecuted and tyrannized them in such a manner that he the captain and leader of them and many of the said Irishmen, who were 400 and amongst them 50 or 60 married men with their families, desired and determined to depart to go to settle another province in which they could [settle and] profess freely the holy Catholic Faith. The

---

[1] This title is included in B.L., Add. MS 37,042, ff. 21–8 and the copy of the final grant found in A.T.T., Livro dos regimentos do Conselho Ultramarinho, f. 37. The copy of the final grant contained in the A.T.T., Chancelaria de João IV, livro 1, ff. 196–9, begins at the following paragraph. The grant made to 'Guilherme Brun', 16th August 1646 (A.T.T., Chancelaria do João IV, livro 1, ff. 398–401) also begins at the latter point. The grant conceded to 'Brun' is almost identical to that given to Sweetman on 4th March 1644. One minor difference is noted below.

[2] The notary gives several different versions of the spelling of Sweetman's name throughout the grant.

[3] He refers here to the Irish rebellion against the English Crown which began October 1641; see P. J. Corish, 'The rising of 1641 and the Catholic confederacy 1641–5' in Moody et al., New history of Ireland, 1976, III, 289–315.

which gave him their agreement, which is annexed to this letter and grant,[1] with which he had recourse to me, as such a catholic [and merciful] prince, patron and protector of all exiled catholics and especially of the said nation receiving them and giving them within this kingdom convents and monasteries for monks and nuns and seminaries for their nation with great alms and particular compassion [and magnanimity]. Thus he begged me to give them the same favour and protection and because in those my [the wide] provinces [and territories] of Brazil, much is uninhabited for lack of settlers [until the present and without hope of being able to provide them], I should do them the favour, either in the province of Maranhão or [province] of Grão Pará and river Amazon to assign and concede them lands to inhabit and settle [and in particular the island named dos Joanes[2] which is at the entrance and mouth of the said river which will be 80 leagues in circumference, not being granted to any particular captain and having few Portuguese with the Indians of the region so that they could settle] in it, and they would defend it and submit themselves to us as the rest of the vassals [and settlements] and colonies of the said [island and] province, recognizing me as king and natural lord and assisting with their fees and tributes as the other native Portuguese. And having commanded that his request be looked at [with those of my Council][3] after resolving to shelter and admit them and to favour their petition, I ordered that the said form, clauses and conditions with which the said favour, grant and donation should be conceded and solemnized to them, as to the said Captain and those of his company, be adjusted by Doctor Thome Pinheiro da Veiga of my Council, *desembargador do Paço*[4] and *procurador*[5] of the crown, and having seen everything which he showed to me and adjusted according to the further information and opinion of those of my Council, according to the form which the kings my predecessors observed in the territories of the kingdom and the new conquests and gave them to be settled by their grants to their vassals, and which has been observed in the captaincies of Brazil for their

---

[1] Not apparently extant. [2] Marajó.
[3] *Conselho Ultramarinho.*
[4] The *Desembargo de Paço* was the highest court of judicature and its lawyers were the most important political class in Portugal.
[5] Crown official responsible for watching over the financial and other interests of the Crown.

settlement and inhabitation and the honour of deserving vassals. And wishing to give grace and favour to the said Pedro Suetmão and to the said catholic Irishmen in his company and transportation, I think it good and it pleases me of my certain knowledge and royal and absolute power, notwithstanding laws and regiments and prohibitions and acts of the *Cortes*[1] because [up to now] it was forbidden and not permitted to any foreign nation, or from Spain, persons or ships, to enter or inhabit those said parts of Brazil, to concede them [what] as I do to the said Captain and the rest of his company up to 130 of the said 400 inhabitants of the said island for now, that they may enter, settle and inhabit the said captaincy of Pará [my Island of dos Joanes] in the form of this grant and letter of settlement and donation which I concede to them in the following manner.

1st. That the said Pedro Satmão and the said Irishmen of his company who might be catholics (which is the principal reason why I gave him this favour and asylum), so many as may be entering the said [island and] territory with the agent or agents that I ordain for their transportation, may go directly to the port of the city of Belém [thereabouts] where [may be] my governor resides and be given all the welcome for the time necessary until they are assigned to the territories and place of their habitation and settlement where they will be established and recorded in a book for that purpose which is located in the Council of that city, attended by the *capitão-mor* and the *ouvidor-general*[2] of that Province who designate them. By the said act I immediately do and hold as accomplished the favour of naturalizing them and their descendants and take them for native Portuguese, vassals and subjects of this crown and obedient to the Holy Apostolic See, as good and true christians, with all the graces, privileges and freedoms and exemptions that the natives of these kingdoms of Portugal and its dominions now have, as if they were by origin, birth or habitation [as those to whom they were conceded previously were]. And they as such subject vassals, for themselves and their descendants will recognize me as king and lord as the rest of my natural vassals, renouncing any other lord, nature and dominion and as if each one had been born in this kingdom and had made esteem and particular homage and oath of loyalty as by the

[1] Parliament of the three estates, clergy, nobility and commons.
[2] Chief justice or senior crown judge.

signing of the said book it is and was understood to be done by all for all privileges. And thus, on the contrary, they will incur penalties of treason and *lèse-majesté*, divine and human, as the rest of my vassals and subjects under my laws and the jurisdiction the Holy Inquisition and ecclesiastical censure in everything and for everything, married men with their dependants as well as single, whether they might marry in the territory, or with women who go from the realm or any others from their own island or country.

In these circumstances the said captain may take in each of the two voyages that he declared he could take in the year, 60 to 70 of the said Irishmen, the married men of the said 130 of his company, and the rest in the order for which I subsequently may give him permission, procuring that the most possible be married or may marry in the territory. And as soon as they enter in the established manner in the said captaincy and city of Pará, a half little more or less, the which might be the best and the rest at our pleasure and of the said captain, will be received as citizens and inhabitants of the said city and its environs and boundaries and Indian villages where they might best live with all the privileges and freedoms of the rest of the citizens so as to enter into the duties of government in peace and war with all the prerogatives of natural subjects. For the which I think it good that two of the most honorable married men should enter immediately, one as *vereador*,[1] the other as *almotace*,[2] being favoured in everything. For the which the governor and *ouvidor* and person who commands the said transportation with the said captain and two of his company and two more people from the city [and two of the said Irish] may make allotment with liberality of sufficient lands in the said district in the most suitable and most fertile sites which they may assign to them. Which shall be all which they shall be able to cultivate and open up for themselves and to be their own, saving the tithe to God, and as such to come to their heirs and be disposed of as their own as the rest of the natural subjects, allocating them with the said liberality from what at present and in the future may be subdued. For cultivation and for their livestock, farms, barns, without prejudice to the inhabitants of the city, shall be so that they may hold the lands that they may be able to turn to good

[1] Alderman or municipal councillor.
[2] *Almotace[l]*. A market inspector responsible for inspecting and regulating the sale of foodstuffs and maintaining public hygiene.

account as the rest, continuing for all the company of the said their captain as in the ordinances as is affirmed beforehand.

The which captain with the other half, a little more or less, for now will be able to found another settlement and principal town, with his men and others of the region which henceforward may wish to inhabit it, up the river and country in a suitable site of some leagues, which will be called São João.[1] To which we give arms and insignias with the privileges of the other towns of the realm and of the said state. For which the said governor and captain and the aforesaid persons will look into the most suitable site for foundation and defense and communication with the said city of Pará with the least disruption of the Indians of the territory, and with marsh lands and of such fertility that it is able to sustain itself and flourish. And the said governor, in my name, shall elevate it to a town with *pelourinho*,[2] *camara*,[3] jurisdiction and charter and the privileges of Pará or São Luis, and with the said persons assign it the boundaries and district, the leagues and sufficient lands for all the said settlers and those who may wish to live with them, and those to whom I might in the future give permission, with sufficient liberality not only of parks and common grasslands of the town, but for agriculture, planting, mills, cattle pastures, farms, and Indian villages to be distributed amongst the settlers to open up as their own for ever in the form aforesaid, and as the other natural subjects.

And to the said Pedro Sultman, I think it good that he be assigned one square league of land which may be his own, for his use to dispose and make of it and its fruits and revenues as his own possession, to bestow, lease, give or sell as might seem best to him, with the acknowledgement and responsibility for the persons to whom I have made the gift of lands in the said state, within and outside that town, and in all the other parts. To keep, in everything, my laws and ordinances, both criminal and civil, and his government in peace and war with his judges, *vereadores* and *procurador*, *almotaceis*, and notaries and *alcaide*[4] and other officers, as in the rest

---

[1] I have yet to find any record of such a settlement being founded at this time. If a party of Irish did go out to the river with 'Guilherme Brun' they were probably absorbed into the established Portuguese settlements.

[2] Decorative column or pillar marking the public square of a Portuguese municipality.

[3] *Senado de Camara*, a municipal council.

[4] See below, p. 457, n. 5.

of the kingdom and of the said state, making his elections, city ordinances and agreements and order of government.

For the which, this first time, for instruction and creation of officials, I think fit that the person who goes with the said captain, or who might be assisting the said captain in that place, may call the said settlers with the rest which by this act may be found, to come to vote for the officials *a som de campa*[1] and hold elections in the form of the ordinance, the said *julgador*[2] holding the votes and verifying the *pellouros*[3] with the said captain. And for this first election there will be a *juiz dos povoadores*[4] and another of those of the territory so they might be instructed in the laws and government, and a native notary and the other *vereadores*, *almotace* and notary from the settlers and the other officials, and from thenceforward without distinction one from the other, and the names of those elected shall come to the governor to be confirmed in my name, without paying other fees of officeholders.

And the Portuguese and other persons of the territory to whom it may seem good may come to reside in the said town and its Indian villages and the Irish go to live with the natural Portuguese in their settlements without prohibiting election or residence to one or the other, as between the other towns, and the same in the communication, trade and marriages, to acquire domicile without distinction. And likewise they will be able to bring from the realm and the island where they are and from their country by way of this realm, their wives and dependants and those with whom they might contract marriage, and with the permission of the council and governor will be allowed to go, and also married couples and natives of the realm which might wish to go to live and settle with them, with their privileges.

And to the said Pedro de Sultman, I think good to favour that he be and be designated *alcaide-mor*[5] of the said town from his arrival in

---

[1] Literally 'at the sound of the hand bell', presumably meaning the summons of the town crier.

[2] Scrutineer.

[3] The *Pelouro* or *Pauta* was the voting list. The names of the citizens deemed fit to serve in local offices were inscribed on slips of paper rolled into *pelouros* or small wax balls and drawn by lot.

[4] People's tribune or judge. The labourer's representative on the municipal council.

[5] *Alcaide-mor.* Governor or captain in charge of the garrison and defence of a municipality with civil and military jurisdiction.

it, with the rights, prerogatives and privileges which *alcaide-mores* hold by my ordinance, and for it, it is incumbent upon him to do me homage and respect or to the hands of my governor, so that he may confirm for him my letter. And likewise he may be and be designated his own captain and two of his company, wherever he wishes they might be, as captain of the ordinance with his own lieutenant, and of those of Pará [and this] with the *regimento*[1] of the said ordinances; and this for the duration of his life for the present, both the *alcaidaría-mor* and the captaincy, subordinate to the governor and the governor-general of the state and his *ouvidor*, in the manner of other towns and settlements of the province.

And I think it good that for the first five years that he may nominate an *ouvidor* confirmed by the governor, who should be a native Portuguese.

To whom should come the appeals and grievances, which end with him, up to ten thousand reals in cattle in civil matters, and up to four in the penalties; and two years of exile in criminal matters and ten thousand reals in money for those, which will be imposed by him;[2] and he will be nominated by me; and this for the inhabitants in the said town and the period for which they might have contracted domicile in it or committed the offence in it, either native Portuguese or foreigners, and for slaves and servants in which is included vile treachery, up to whipping and exile for two years.[3]

And each and other of the said company will pay in entirety the tithes and *permicias*[4] and other things owed to the church and dioceses as and in the manner which the native Portuguese pay them, with all the responsibility and obligation to the church and prelates and order of the holy canons without exemption in the practice to the contrary, in all and by all as the other native Portuguese.

And for the other royal dues and taxes, they will be exempt for that which they might newly cultivate and open up, and the sugar mills which they might build, and other tillage in the manner and

---

[1] Standing orders.

[2] The grant defines the extent of the crown judge's jurisdiction. More serious cases involving larger sums of money, heavier fines or more serious punishments would be referred elsewhere.

[3] The rough draft (B.L., Add. MS 37,042, ff. 21–8) ends here.

[4] *Premissa* or *primiçias*, first fruits owed to the parish.

for the years which those who construct and break ground by charter of the state are exempt. And I think it good to exempt them further up to nine years, paying the other customs duties in the Island[1] just as in the realm, wherever they might handle their goods and produce of the land and acquisitions and merchandise, for which will be given to them all the favour and vessels and to their shipping all good depatch for the said goods and merchandise and produce; and in the same manner, so that they might handle and bring those goods from the said province their own cargos and forward them to my custom-houses wherever the other native Portuguese send them, paying their duties in the territory and the realm saving those aforesaid in their charter or others which by other provisions I may do him the favour of exempting them.

And they will be obliged to observe in entirety the *regimentos* and prohibitions of the said state of Brazil, not admitting any foreign ship or person of any kind nor of their nation without my express order, nor of Castile or other nation, nor navigating for any save this realm and its islands, in the form of the *regimentos* and ordinances and orders given in this matter without any difference from other vassals and others which might be so employed.[2] And for confirmation of everything I order him to be given this letter of grant and naturalization signed and sealed by me with the pendant seal. Balthezar Gomes made it in Lixboa on the 4th of March the one thousand six hundred and forty fourth year after the birth of our lord Jesus Christ. Balthazar Roiz de Abreu had it inscribed.

The King

Note.

[All the which will be understood as declaration that the aforesaid people that the said Pedro Sultman is to take in his company be all of the Irish nation, without any other persons of another nation, and the governor of Maranhão, as soon as they enter that state, should take from all and from each one in particular the oath of homage and loyalty in the said book provided for in this letter and for this effect] and by this note an entry will be placed in the registers. Lixboa the 17th of June of 1644. The king.

[1] St Christophers.
[2] The material in [ ] in the *postilla* or note added to Sweetman's grant on 17th June 1644 was incorporated into the body of the 16th August 1644 grant made to 'Guilherme Brun' at this point.

459

REFERENCES

I. MANUSCRIPT SOURCES

ARQUIVO NACIONAL DA TORRE DO TOMBO, LISBON
Chancelaria de João IV, livro 1.

ARCHIVO GENERAL DE INDIAS, SEVILLA
Audiencia de Quito. Estante 77, caj. 3, leg. 18.
Audiencia de Santo Domingo. 180.
Charcas. 260.
Indiferente General. Estante 143, caj. 3, leg. 12; 1872.
Patronato Real. 272.

ARCHIVO GENERAL DE SIMANCAS
Estado. K1431; K1423; K1438; K1439; K1479; K1559/59, 61, 63, 67,
    71, 72, 79, 83, 86; 2045; 2515; 2600; 2601; 7031, lib. 374.

ARQUIVO HISTÓRICO ULTRAMARINO, LISBON
Maranhão 828.
Pará 728.

BIBLIOTECA DE AJUDA, LISBON
Codices 51/V/17; 54/XI/27.

BIBLIOTECA NACIONAL, LISBON
Codice 7.162.

BIBLIOTECA NACIONAL, MADRID
MSS 4163; 20271[12].

BIBLIOTECA PÚBLICA DE ÉVORA
Codice CVI/2–7.

BODLEIAN LIBRARY, OXFORD
Ashmolean Manuscripts. 749.
Rawlinson Manuscripts. A175.
Tanner Manuscripts. 70; 71; 114; 168.

BRITISH LIBRARY
Additional Manuscripts. 13,977; 17,940A; 33,935; 36,317; 36,320;
    36,321; 36,324; 37,042.
Cotton Manuscripts. Cotton B VIII.

Harley Manuscripts. 1583.
Lansdowne Manuscripts. 160.
Sloane Manuscripts. 173; 179B; 750; 1019; 1133.

PUBLIC RECORD OFFICE, LONDON
Chancery, Patent Rolls. C66/244, 1986.
Exchequer, Customs Accounts. E122/46/50.
   Port Books. E190/22/5; 24/1; 820/1; 941/7; 942/12; 943/4; 944/2; 945/
      6; 1133/3; 1323/1; 1326/6.
High Court of Admiralty, Oyer and Terminer Examinations. HCA 1/
   44.
High Court of Admiralty, Acts, Instance and Prize. HCA 3/30, 33, 34,
   35, 53.
High Court of Admiralty, Examinations, Instance and Prize. HCA 13/
   41, 49, 50, 107.
High Court of Admiralty, Libels, Instance and Prize. HCA 24/59, 73,
   74, 75, 76, 77, 78, 79, 87, 88, 89, 90.
High Court of Admiralty, Miscellanea. HCA 30/857, 865.
Privy Council Registers. PC2/27, 30, 31, 38.
Prerogative Court of Canterbury, Wills. PCC1, Russell.
State Papers Colonial. CO 1/1, 4, 5, 8, 10.
State Papers Domestic, Mary. SP 11/17.
State Papers Domestic, Elizabeth. SP 12/235, 237.
State Papers Domestic, James I. SP 14/50, 53, 95, 108, 112, 122.
State Papers Domestic, Charles I. SP 16/24, 54, 130, 157, 163, 229, 363.
State Papers Spanish. SP 94/23, 36, 37.
State Papers Tuscany. SP 98/2.

TRINITY COLLEGE, DUBLIN
MSS 382; 386/1; 433.

WILTSHIRE RECORD OFFICE
WRO 366/1.

II. PRINTED PRIMARY AND SECONDARY SOURCES

Adams, S. L. 'Captain Thomas Gainsford, the "Vox Spiritus" and the
   Vox populi', BIHR, xlix, 1976, pp. 141–4.
   'Foreign policy and the Parliaments of 1621 and 1624', in Sharpe, K.,
      ed., Faction and Parliament, London, 1978.
Ainsworth, J. (ed.). The Inchiquin Mss. Dublin, Irish Manuscripts
   Commission, 1961.
Alexander, M. V. Charles I's Lord Treasurer: Sir Richard Weston, earl of
   Portland (1577–1635). London, 1975.
Allison, A. F. English translations from the Spanish and Portuguese to the year
   1700. London, 1974.

Almagía, R. *Commemorazione di Sebastiano Caboto nel IV centenario della morte.* Venice, 1958.

Anderson, R. C. (ed.). *Examination and Depositions, 1622–44 Southampton,* Southampton Record Soc., 1929–31.

Andrews, K. R. (ed.). *English privateering voyages to the West Indies 1588–95.* Cambridge, Hakluyt Soc., second ser., CXI, 1959.
'Caribbean rivalry and the Anglo-Spanish peace of 1604', *History,* LIX, 1974, pp. 234–54.
The Spanish Caribbean: trade and plunder, 1530–1630. London, 1978.
'Beyond the equinoctial: England and South America in the sixteenth century', *Journal of Imperial and Commonwealth History,* X, 1981, pp. 4–24.

Arber, E. (ed.). *A transcript of the registers of the Company of Stationers of London, 1554–1640 A.D.* 5 vols. London, 1875–94.
(ed.). *The Travels and Works of Captain John Smith.* 2 vols. Edinburgh, 1910.

Baker, J. H. *The order of the Serjeants-at-Law.* London, 1984.

Baker, R. *The knight and chivalry.* London, 1970.

Ballesteros y Beretta, A. (ed.). *Correspondencia oficial de don Diego Sarmiento de Acuña, conde de Gondomar.* 4 vols. Madrid, *Documentos inéditos para la historia de España,* 1936–45.

Barata, M. de Mello Cardoso. *A jornada de Francisco Caldeira de Castello Branco. Fundação da cidade de Belém.* Belém, 1916.

Barbour, P. (ed.). *The Jamestown voyages under the first charter.* Cambridge, Hakluyt Soc., second ser., CXXXVI, CXXXVII, 1969.
(ed.). *The works of Captain John Smith.* 3 vols. Chapel Hill and London, 1986.

Beazley, R. *John and Sebastian Cabot.* London, 1898.

Beer, B. L. *Northumberland, The political career of John Dudley, earl of Warwick and duke of Northumberland.* Kent Ohio, 1973.

Bekkers, J. A. F. *Correspondence of John Morris with Johannes de Laet, 1634–49.* Assen, 1970.

Berredo, B. Pereira de. *Annaes históricos do estado do Maranhão.* Lisbon, 1749.

Bindoff, S. T. 'A kingdom at stake', *History Today,* III, 1953, pp. 642–8.

Bingham, W. P. 'James Ley, earl of Marlborough', *The Wiltshire Archaeological and Natural History Magazine,* XXV, no. lxxiii, 1891, pp. 86–99.

Birch, T. *The life of Henry, Prince of Wales.* London, 1760.

Blackmore, H. L. *The armouries in the Tower of London: Ordnance.* London, 1976.

Boxer, C. R. *The Dutch in Brazil.* Oxford, 1957.

Breard, C. & P. *Documents rélatifs a la marine normande et ses armements au XVIe et XVIIe siècles.* Rouen, 1889.

British Admiralty. *The West Indies Pilot.* London, 1955.

British Admiralty. *South American Pilot.* London, 1864.

British Admiralty. *South America Pilot.* London, 1945.

Brown, M. J. *The life of Sir Thomas Roe: 1580–1644.* Ann Arbor, Michigan, 1964.

C., T. *An advice how to plant tobacco in England.* 1615.

Caetano da Silva, J. *L'Oyapoc et l'Amazone: question brésilienne et française.* 2 vols. Paris, 1861.

Calmon, P. *História do Brasil. A formação, 1600–1700.* São Paulo, 1941.

Campling, A. *The history of the family of Drury.* London, 1937.

Canny, N. P. 'The permissive frontier: the problem of social control in English settlements in Ireland and Virginia 1550–1650', in Andrews, K. R., Canny, N. P. and Hair, P. E. H., eds., *The Westward Enterprise*, Liverpool, 1978, pp. 17–44.

Carter, C. H. *The secret diplomacy of the Habsburgs, 1598–1625.* New York, 1964.

Cell, G. T. *Newfoundland discovered, English attempts at colonization, 1610–30.* London, Hakluyt, Soc., second ser., CLX, 1982.

Chapman, W. *The golden dream.* Indianopolis, 1967.

Chytraeus, N. *Variorum in Europa itinerum deliciae.* Herborni in Nassau, 1594.

Clarke, A. *The Old English in Ireland, 1625–42.* London, 1966.

Coelho, P. M. Laranjo. *Cartas de el-Rei D. João IV ao conde da Vidigueira (marques de Niza) embaixador em França.* Lisbon, 1940–2.

Cokayne, G. E. *Complete baronetage.* 5 vols. Exeter, 1900–1906.

Corish, P. J. 'The rising of 1641 and the Catholic confederacy 1641–5' in Moody, T. W., Martin, F. W. and Byrne, F. J., eds., *A new history of Ireland*, III, 1976, pp. 289–316.

Cortesão, A. & Mota, A. Texeira da. *Portugalia monumenta cartographica.* 5 vols. Lisbon, 1960.

D'Abbeville, Claude. *Histoire de la mission des Pères Capucins en l'isle de Maragnan et terres circonvoisins, 1614,* Métraux, A. and Lafaye, J., eds., Graz, 1963.

Davies, W. *A true relation of the travailes and most miserable captivitie of William Davies, barber-surgion of London, under the duke of Florence.* 1614.

Day, J. *A Publication of Guiana's plantation.* 1632.

De Vries, D. P. *Korte historiael ende journaels aenteyckeninge van verscheyden voyagiens in de vier deelen des wereldts-ronde, als Europa, Africa, Asia ende America gedaen, 1665,* Colenbrander, H. T., ed., The Hague, 1911.

Duarte, J. Hygino. 'Relatórios e cartas de Gedeon Morris de Jonge no tempo do dominio Holandez no Brazil', *Revista do Instituto Histórico e Geografico Brasileiro*, LVIII, 1895, pp. 237–319.

Dudley, R. *Dell'Arcano del Mare.* 3 vols. Florence, 1646–7.

Edmundson, G. 'The Dutch in Western Guiana', *EHR*, XVI, 1901, pp. 640–75.

'The Dutch on the Amazon and Negro in the seventeenth century', *EHR*, XVIII, 1903, pp. 642–63.

Edwards, E. (ed.). *The life of Sir Walter Ralegh.* 2 vols. London, 1868.

Edwards, R. Dudley. *Ireland in the age of the Tudors.* London, 1977.

Espada, M. Jiménez de la. *Viaje del Capitán Pedro Texeira aguas arriba del rio de las Amazonas, 1638–9.* Madrid, 1889.

Filby, P. W. & Meyer, M. K. (eds.). *Passenger and immigration lists index.* 3 vols. Detroit, 1981.

Forest, R. W. (ed.). *A Walloon family in America.* 2 vols. Boston, 1914.

Foster, Sir W. (ed.). *The embassy of Sir Thomas Roe to the court of the great Mogul, 1615–19.* London, Hakluyt, Soc., second ser., I, 1899.

Fournier, G. *Hydrographie contenant la theorie et practique de toutes les parties de la navigation.* Paris, 1643.

Gaffarel, P. *Histoire du Brésil Français au seizième siècle.* Paris, 1878.

Gardiner, S. R. (ed.). *Letters relating to the mission of Sir Thomas Roe to Gustavus Adolphus, 1629–30.* Westminster, Camden Society, 1875.

Ghoslinga, Ch. C. *The Dutch in the Caribbean and on the Wild Coast.* Assen, 1971.

Gilbert, J. T. *Calendar of ancient records of Dublin in the possession of the municipal corporation of that city.* Dublin, 1891.

Gillin, J. 'Tribes of the Guianas', *HSAI*, III, 1963, pp. 799–860.

Gilmore, R. M. 'Fauna and ethnozoology of South America', in *HSAI*, VI, 1963, pp. 345–464.

Golding, M. *The fishes and the forest.* Berkeley, 1980.

Gómara, F. López de. *Historia general,* 1552, Menendez-Pelayo, M., ed., Madrid, Biblioteca de autores Españoles, XXII, 1946.

Gookin, F. W. *Daniel Gookin, 1612–87.* Chicago, 1912.

Gosselin, E. H. *Documents authentiques et inédits pour servire a l'histoire de la marine normande et du commerce Rouennais pendant les XVIe et XVIIe siècles.* Rouen, 1876.

Guedes, M. J. *Brasil-costa norte, cartografía Portuguesa vetustissima.* Rio de Janeiro, 1968.

'Acçoes navaís contra os estrangeiros na Amazonia, 1616–33', *Historia naval Brasileira*, I pt. 11, 1975.

Gwynn, A., SJ. 'Early Irish emigration to the West Indies (1612–43)', *Studies*, XVIII, 1929, pp. 376–93, 648–63.

'Documents relating to the Irish in the West Indies', *Analecta Hibernica*, IV, 1932, pp. 139–286.

'An Irish settlement on the Amazon, 1612–1629', *Proceedings of the Royal Irish Academy*, Section C 41, 1932, pp. 1–54.

'Cromwell's policy of transportation', *Studies*, XIX, 1930, pp. 607–23.

'Indentured servants and negro slaves in Barbados', *Studies*, XIX, 1930, pp. 279–94.

Hagen, V. W. von. *The gold of El Dorado: the quest for the golden man.* London, 1978.

Hakluyt, R. *The principall navigations, voiages and discoveries of the English nation.* 1589.

The principal navigations, voyages, traffiques and discoveries of the English nation. 3 vols. 1599–1600.

The Principal Navigations, Voyages, Traffiques and Discoveries of the English Nation. Glasgow, Hakluyt Soc., extra Ser., I–XII, 1903–5.

Harbison, E. H. *Rival ambassadors at the court of Queen Mary.* Oxford, 1940.

Harcourt, R. *A relation of a voyage to Guiana.* 1613, 1626.

Harlow, V. T. (ed.). *Colonizing expeditions to the West Indies and Guiana, 1623–67.* London, Hakluyt Soc., second ser., LVI, 1924.

A history of Barbados. Oxford, 1926.

(ed.). *The discoverie of the large and bewtiful empire of Guiana by Sir Walter Ralegh.* London, 1928.

(ed.) *Ralegh's Last Voyage.* London, 1932.

Harris, C. A. (ed.). *A relation of a voyage to Guiana by Robert Harcourt 1613.* London, Hakluyt Soc., second ser., LX, 1928.

Harrisse, H. *John Cabot, the discoverer of North America, and Sebastian Cabot his son.* London, 1896.

Hasler, P. W. (ed.). *History of parliament. The house of commons, 1558–1603.* 3 vols. London, 1981.

Hearne, T. *A collection of curious discourses written by eminent antiquaries upon several heads in our English antiquities.* London, 1775.

Heath, E. G. & Chiara, V. *Brazilian Indian archery.* Manchester, 1977.

Hemming, J. *Red gold. The conquest of the Brazilian Indians.* London, 1978.

The search for El Dorado. London, 1978.

Herrera, A. de. *Historia general de los hechos de los castellanos en las islas y tierra firme del mar oceano.* Madrid, 1601–15.

Hoak, D. 'Rehabilitating the duke of Northumberland: politics and political control, 1549–53' in Tittler, R. and Loach, J., eds. *The mid-Tudor polity, c. 1540–1560,* Totowa, New Jersey, 1980, pp. 28–51.

Howat, G. D. *Stuart and Cromwellian foreign policy.* London, 1974.

Howe, E. *The annales; or generall chronicle of England, begun first by maister John Stow.* 1631.

Jennings, B. *Wild geese in Spanish Flanders, 1582–1700.* Dublin, Irish Manuscripts Commission, 1964.

Jones, J. R. *Britain and Europe in the seventeenth century.* London, 1966.

Julien, C. A. *Les Français en Amerique durant la premiere moitié du XVIe siècle.* Paris, 1946.

Les voyages des découverte et les premiers établissements. Paris, 1948.

Keymis, L. *A relation of the second voyage to Guiana.* 1596.

Kiemen, M. C. *The Indian policy of Portugal in the Amazon region, 1614–93.* New York, 1973.

Kingsbury, S. M. (ed.). *The records of the Virginia Company of London.* 4 vols. Washington, 1906–35.

Kupperman, K. O. 'Errand to the Indies: puritan colonization from Providence Island through the Western Design', *WMQ,* XLV, 1988, pp. 70–99.

Laet, J. de. *Nieuwe wereldt.* 1630.

Novus orbis. 1633.

L'histoire du nouveau monde. 1640.

Iaerlyck verhael van der verrichtinghen der geotroyeerde West-Indische

Compagnie in derthien boecken, pt. I, bks. 4–7, 1644, L'honore Naber, S. P., ed., The Hague, 1932.

Lee, A. G. *The son of Leicester: The story of Sir Robert Dudley.* London, 1964.

Lefroy, J. H. (ed.). *The historye of the Bermudaes.* London, 1882.

Leite, S. SJ. *Luiz Figueira. A sua vida heróica e sua obra literária.* Lisbon, 1940.

Levi-Strauss, C. 'The use of wild plants in tropical South America', in *HSAI*, VI, 1963, pp. 465–86.

Levillier, R. *El paititi, El Dorado y las Amazonas.* Buenos Aires, 1976.

Lincoln's Inn. *Admissions from A.D. 1420 to A.D. 1893. The records of the Honorable Society of Lincoln's Inn.* London, 1896.

Lorimer, J. 'English trade and exploration in Trinidad and Guiana, 1569–1648', unpublished Ph.D., University of Liverpool, 1973.

'The English contraband tobacco trade in Trinidad and Guiana, 1590–1617', in Andrews, K. R., Canny, N. P. and Hair, P. E. H., eds., *The westward enterprise.* Liverpool, 1978.

'The location of Ralegh's Guiana gold mine', in *Terrae Incognitae*, XIV, 1982, pp. 77–95.

Lowie, R. H. 'The tropical forests: An introduction', in *HSAI*, III, 1948, pp. 1–56.

Lussagnet, S. (ed.). *Le Brésil et les Brésiliens par Andre Thevet.* Paris, 1953.

MacCarthy-Morrogh, M. *The Munster plantation. English migration to southern Ireland, 1583–1641.* Oxford, 1986.

MacInnes, C. A. *The early English tobacco trade.* London, 1926.

Maclean, J. (ed.). *Letters from George Lord Carew to Sir Thomas Roe, ambassador to the court of the great Mogul, 1615–17.* London, Camden Society, 1860.

Markham, Sir C. R. (ed.). *Expeditions into the valley of the Amazons, 1539, 1540, 1639.* London, Hakluyt Soc., first ser., XXIV, 1859.

(trans. and ed.). *History of the Incas by Pedro Sarmiento de Gamboa and the execution of the Inca Tupac Amaru, by Captain Baltasar de Ocampo.* Cambridge, Hakluyt Soc., second ser., XXIIa, 1907.

Marsden, R. G. 'The voyage of the *Barbara* of London to Brazil in 1540', *EHR*, XXIV, 1909, pp. 96–100.

Matthews, T. G. 'Memorial autobiográfico de Bernardo O'Brian (sic)', *Caribbean Studies*, X, 1970, pp. 89–106.

Medina, J. Toribio. *The discovery of the Amazon according to the account of Friar Gaspar de Carvajal and other documents*, trans. from the Spanish by Lee, B. T., ed. Heaton, H. C., New York, 1934.

Meggers, B. J. 'The archaeology of the Amazon basin', in *HSAI*, III, 1963, pp. 149–66.

Amazonia: Man and culture in a counterfeit paradise. Chicago, 1971.

Meggers, B. J. & Evans, C. *Archaeological investigations at the mouth of the Amazon.* Washington, 1957.

'An interpretation of the cultures of Marajó island' in Gross, D. R., ed., *Peoples and cultures of native South America*, New York, 1973, pp. 39–47.

Metcalfe, W. C. *The visitation of Essex*. London, Harleian Soc., 13, 14, 1878.

Visitations of Suffolk, 1561, 1577, 1612. Exeter, 1882.

The visitations of Northamptonshire, 1564 and 1618–9. London, 1887.

Métraux, A. 'The Tupinamba', in *HSAI*, III, 1948, pp. 95–133.

Mollat, M. 'As primeiras relações entre a Franca é o Brasil: dos Verrazani a Villegagnon', *Revista de História*, XXXIV, 1967, pp. 343–58.

Morison, S. E. (ed. and trans.). *Journals and other documents on the life and voyages of Christopher Columbus*. New York, 1963.

Morrin, J. (ed.). *Cal. of the Patent and Close rolls of Chancery in Ireland, Charles I, 1–8*. Dublin, 1863.

Mowat, R. B. 'The mission of Sir Thomas Roe to Vienna, 1641–2', *EHR*, XXV, 1910, pp. 264–75.

Neander, J. *Tabacologia*. Bremen, 1622.

Newton, A. P. *Colonizing activities of the English puritans*. London, 1914.

Nicholas, E. *Proceedings and debates of the House of Commons in 1620 and 1621*. Oxford, 1766.

Nicholl, J. *An houre glasse of Indian newes*. 1607.

Nimuendaju, C. 'The Arua', in *HSAI*, III, 1948, pp. 195–8.

Notestein, W., Relf, F. H. & Simpson, H. (eds.). *House of Commons debates, 1621*. New Haven and London, 1935.

Ojer, P., SJ. *La formación del oriente Venezolano*. Caracas, 1966.

Oltman, R. E. *Reconnaissance investigations of the discharge and water quality of the Amazon river*. Washington, U.S. Geological Survey, circular 552, 1968.

Oppenheim, M. (ed.). *The naval tracts of Sir William Monson*. 5 vols. London, Navy Records Soc., 1902–14.

Oviedo y Valdes, G. F. de. *Historia general y natural de las Indias, islas y Tierra Firme del Mar Oceano*. 4 vols. Madrid, 1851–5.

Perez, D. Ramos. *El mito del Dorado. Su genesis y proceso*. Caracas, 1973.

Perrin, W. G. (ed.). *The autobiography of Phineas Pett*. London, 1918.

Prestage, E. *The diplomatic relations of Portugal with France, England and Holland from 1640 to 1668*. Watford, 1925.

'O Dr. António de Sousa de Macedo, Residente de Portugal em Londres', separate publication of *Boletím da 2da class da Academía das Sciencias de Lisboa*, X, (1916).

Pullen, N. *Travel and voyages into Africa, Asia, and America . . . Performed by Mr. John Mocquet keeper of the cabinet of rarities, to the king of France, in the Thuileries*. London, 1696.

Purchas, S. *Hakluytus posthumus or Purchas his pilgrimes*. 4 vols. 1625.

Hakluytus posthumus or Purchas his pilgrimes. 20 vols. Glasgow, 1905–7.

Quinn, D. B. (ed.). *Roanoke voyages*. London, Hakluyt Soc., second ser., CIV, CV, 1955.

'Notes by a pious colonial investor, 1608–10' in *WMQ*, XVI, 1959, pp. 551–5.

England and the discovery of North America, 1481–1620. London, 1974.

'James I and the beginnings of empire in America', *Journal of Imperial and Commonwealth History*, II, 1974, pp. 135–52.

'Depictions of America', in Wallis, H., ed., *The maps and text of the boke of Idrography presented by Jean Rotz to Henry VIII now in the British Library*. Oxford, Roxburghe Club, 1981, pp. 53–6.

Rabb, T. K. *Enterprise & empire*. Cambridge, Mass., 1967.

Ralegh, Sir W. *The discoverie of the large, rich and bewtifull empire of Guiana*. London, 1596. STC. 20635.

Reis, A. G. Ferreira. *Limites e demarcações na Amazonia Brasileira. A fronteira colonial com a Guiana Françesa*. Rio de Janeiro, 1947.

'The Franciscans and the opening of the Amazon region', *The Americas*, XI, 1955, pp. 173–93.

Rivara, J. H. da Cunha. *Catálogo dos manuscritos da Bibliotheca Pública Éborense*. 4 vols. Lisbon, 1850–71.

Rive, A. 'The consumption of tobacco since 1760', *Economic Journal*, supp. I–IV, 1926–9.

Ruigh, R. E. *The parliament of 1624*. Cambridge, Mass., 1971.

Russell, P. *Dartmouth. A history of the port and town*. Toronto, 1950.

St Hoare, Sir R. C. Bart. *The history of modern Wiltshire – Hundred of Westbury*. 6 vols. London, 1830.

Salvador, V. do. *História do Brasil*. São Paulo, 1931.

Sauer, C. O. 'Cultivated plants of South and Central America', in *HSAI*, VI, 1963, pp. 487–543.

Schlesinger, R., & Sattler, A. P. *André Thevet's America*. McGill, 1986.

Schomburgk, R. H. (ed.). *The discoverie of the large, rich and beautiful empire of Guiana by Sir W. Ralegh, Knt*. London, Hakluyt Soc., first ser., III, 1848.

Sharpe, K. 'The earl of Arundel, his circle and the opposition to the duke of Buckingham, 1618–28', in *Faction and Parliament*, 1978, pp. 209–44.

Shaw, W. *Knights of England*. 2 vols. London, 1906.

Shirley, J. W. 'George Percy at Jamestown, 1607–12', *The Virginia Magazine of History and Biography*, LVII, 1949, pp. 227–43.

Silke, J. J. 'The Irish abroad, 1534–1691', in Moody, T. W., Martin, F. X. and Byrne, F. J., eds., *A new history of Ireland*, III, Oxford, 1978, pp. 587–633.

Skelton, R. A. 'The cartography of the Cabot voyages', in Williamson, J. A., ed., *The Cabot voyages and Bristol discovery under Henry VII*. Cambridge, Hakluyt Soc., second ser., CXX, 1962, pp. 322–4.

'Ralegh as a geographer', *The Virginia Magazine of History and Biography*, LXXI, 1963, pp. 131–49.

'Sebastian Cabot', *DCB*, Ottawa, 1965.

Squibb, G. D. F. (ed.). *Wiltshire visitation pedigrees, 1623*. London, Harleian Soc., 105, 106, 1954.

Sternberg, H. O'Reilly. *The Amazon river of Brazil*. Weisbaden, 1975.

Steward, J. H. (ed.). *Handbook of South American Indians*. 6 vols. Washington, Smithsonian Institution, Bureau of American Ethnology, Bulletin 143, 1946–63.

Stone, L. *The crisis of the aristocracy*. Oxford, 1965.

Strong, R. 'England and Italy; the marriage of Henry Prince of Wales', in *For Veronica Wedgwood These*, ed. Ollard, R., & Tudor-Craig, P., eds., London, 1986, pp. 59–87.

Studart, G. Barão de. *Documentos para a história do Brasil, e especialmente a do Ceará*. 4 vols. Fortaleza, 1904–21.

Taylor, E. G. R. *Tudor Geography*. London, 1930.

Thevet, A. *Les singularitez de la France antarctique*. Paris, 1558.

The new founde worlde or Antarctike. Trans. T. Hackett, London, 1568.

Tozer, H. E. *A history of ancient geography*. New York, 1971.

Tyacke, N. 'Science and religion at Oxford before the Civil War', in Pennington, D. & Thomas, K., eds., *Puritans and revolutionaries*, Oxford, 1978, pp. 73–93.

Tyacke, S. 'English charting of the river Amazon c. 1595–c. 1630', *Imago Mundi*, XXXII, 1980, pp. 73–89.

Varnhagen, F. A. de. *História geral do Brasil*. 2 vols. Rio de Janeiro, 1926–36.

Vasconcelos, F. de. *Pilotos das navegações Portuguesas dos seculos XVI e XVII*. Lisbon, 1942.

'Contribução dos Portugueses para o conhecimento do Amazonas no seculo XVII', *Boletím Géral das Colonias*, 1950, pp. 49–68.

'Trabalhos dos Portugueses no Amazonas no seculo XVII', *Boletím Géral do Ultramar*, XXXII (1957), 75–86.

Vasques, F. *Conquista e colonização do Pará*. Lisbon, 1941.

Viveiros, J. J. *História de comercio do Maranhão, 1612–1895*. 2 vols. São Luis Maranhão, 1954.

Wallis, H. (ed.). *The maps and text of the boke of Idrography presented by Jean Rotz to Henry VIII now in the British Library*. Oxford, Roxburghe Club, 1981.

Warmington, E. H. *Greek geography*. London, 1934.

Wettan Kleinbaum, A. *The war against the Amazons*. New York, 1983.

Wieder, T. *Monumenta cartographica*. 6 vols. The Hague, 1932.

Willes, R. *The history of travayle in the West and East Indies*. 1577.

Williams, N. 'England's tobacco trade in the reign of Charles I', The *Virginia Magazine of History and Biography*, LXV, 1957, pp. 403–49.

Williamson, G. C. *George, third earl of Cumberland*. Cambridge, 1920.

Williamson, J. A. *English colonies in Guiana and on the Amazon 1604–1668*. Oxford, 1923.

The Caribbee islands under the proprietary patents. London, 1926.

Sir John Hawkins, the time and the man. Oxford, 1927.

The Cabot voyages and English exploration in the reign of Henry VII and Henry VIII. London, 1929.

Hawkins and Plymouth. London, 1949.

The Cabot Voyages and Bristol discovery under Henry VIII. Cambridge, Hakluyt Soc., second ser., CXX, 1962.

Williamson, J. W. *The myth of the conqueror. Prince Henry Stuart: A study of 17th century personation*. New York, 1978.

Wire, A. P. 'An Essex worthy: Sir Thomas Roe', *Essex Review*, XX, 1911.

Wiznitzer, A. *The records of the earliest Jewish community in the New World.* New York, 1954.

'The number of Jews in Dutch Brazil, 1630–54', *Jewish Social Studies*, XVI, 1954, pp. 107–14.

Zarate, A. de. *A history of the discovery and conquest of Peru.* Trans. T. Nichols, London, 1581.

INDEX